EFFECTIVE
BUSINESS
COMMUNICATIONS

Second Edition

EFFECTIVE BUSINESS COMMUNICATIONS

HERTA A. MURPHY
Professor Emeritus of Business Administration
University of Washington

CHARLES E. PECK
Late Professor of Business Administration
University of Washington

McGraw-Hill Book Company

New York   St. Louis   San Francisco   Auckland   Düsseldorf   Johannesburg
Kuala Lumpur   London   Mexico   Montreal   New Delhi   Panama
Paris   São Paulo   Singapore   Sydney   Tokyo   Toronto

Library of Congress Cataloging in Publication Data

Murphy, Herta A
    Effective business communications.

    Includes bibliographies and index.
    1. Commercial correspondence. 2. Communication
in management. I. Peck, Charles Edwin, dates.
II. Title.
HF5721.M85 1976   651.7'4   75-25799
ISBN 0-07-044061-1

EFFECTIVE BUSINESS COMMUNICATIONS

    34567890 DODO 79876

This book was set in Press Roman by Allen Wayne Technical Corp.
The editors were William J. Kane and Annette Hall;
the designer was Nicholas Krenitsky;
the production supervisor was Charles Hess.
R. R. Donnelley & Sons Company was printer and binder.

Contents

Preface

This revised edition, like its widely accepted predecessor, emphasizes that the purpose and receiver of every message profoundly affect its organization and content. The book includes substantial additions, updating, and revisions; yet it also retains the unique features of the first edition, in more compact form.

Purpose and Approach

Anyone preparing for or already in a business job that requires effective written and oral communication will find this book useful as both a text and a reference guide. It is designed to help you communicate through messages the receivers can easily understand and to which they will react favorably. Specific, integrated teaching and learning aids are presented in clear conversational style. They aim to develop better understanding of human behavior, psychology, and communication theory, and to acquaint you with typical business communication problems, modern media, basic principles, and organizational plans. Explanations suggest WHAT to do and WHY; illustrations show HOW; checklists provide summary guidelines. End-of-chapter exercises, ranging from simple to complex problem-solving activities, invite you to apply principles by analyzing, comparing, researching, writing, and/or speaking.

This book is written for students in universities and colleges, community and junior colleges, business schools, and special training programs for middle-management or supervisory personnel. Whether you communicate as a business executive, professional person, government employee, organization officer, or an individual consumer, the material is adaptable to your needs. Chapters are composed so you can benefit even if you select only a few, independently of other chapters.

Special Features

The revised edition contains these features, including major changes:

1. A new chapter on the process of communication and miscommunication (expressed concisely in nontechnical terms and illustrated with everyday practical examples)
2. A revised overview chapter introducing four basic organizational plans and two psychological approaches before the later chapter discussions on specific messages
3. An updated and extensively revised chapter on job applications, with new information sources, checklists, résumés, application letters, and examples adaptable for recent college graduates as well as for older job changers
4. A revised chapter on other job application messages, including interviews and 23 examples of follow-ups written by applicants and employers
5. New sections in report chapters—regarding proposals, abstracts, graphic aids, outlines, checklists, documentation; progress reports, conference reports, standardized reports; and new examples of letter, memo, printed form, and other reports
6. New sections on conference leadership, small-group communication, and interpersonal instructions
7. Revised coverage on oral reporting, platform speaking, listening, interviewing, and dictating business messages
8. A new section on mailgrams, telegrams, radiograms, and form messages
9. Seven new checklists, plus the previous 39 popular capsule checklists, thus providing handy summaries for most types of messages (They are to be used only as guidelines and reminders—not as "recipe lists," because each message requires careful planning depending on circumstances and purpose.)
10. Examples of 361 complete business messages plus numerous other paragraph and sentence illustrations (Though examples are based on actual business situations, most names, figures, and products have been changed—to protect anonymity.)
11. Marginal notes that analyze significant parts of many examples showing well-written messages
12. Chapter title-page outlines that preview contents
13. Selected bibliographies within some chapters, for further readings on related topics
14. New motivating material on how effective business communication "pays off"
15. A brief discussion on legal aspects of business communications
16. New sequence of improved and/or updated text material in all chapters

Plan of Organization

This 19-chapter text begins with 6 background-for-communicating chapters, comprising Part 1. They introduce you to the importance, process, planning steps, principles, and media for effective written and oral business communication. Part 2 consists of four chapters, each presenting in depth one of the four major organizational plans—direct request, good news, bad news, and persuasive request. Illustrations and 39 capsule checklists focus on letters and memos. They cover inquiries, claims, references, recommendations, adjustments, credits, orders, favors, sales, announcements, and transmittals. Part 3 includes both oral and written specialized messages. Each chapter discusses one type of message—job applications, follow-ups, collections, goodwill— instead of one plan of organization. You will see how the four plans are adaptable to these message types.

Three substantially revised and expanded chapters on business reports make up Part 4. They discuss the planning steps, research, organization, visual aids, essential parts, and qualities of most-used short and long formal reports. In Part 5 two chapters on nonwritten communication include the group and interpersonal communication areas listed in items 6 and 7 under Special Features. Finally, three appendixes present a brief discussion on legal aspects, mechanics, style, and symbols for checking papers.

Acknowledgments

Many people have earned my heartfelt gratitude for their suggestions and contributions. I am indebted and extend sincere thanks to the executives who have provided hundreds of illustrative materials from business, industry, and professional offices; to my American Business Communication Association colleagues, whose ideas, preferences, research, and writings along with those of other scholars through the years have enriched my knowledge and influenced the scope of this book; and to former students who have brought numerous examples from their employment and organizational experiences.

Since the death of my co-author, Professor Charles E. Peck, in 1972, writing this revision has been my responsibility. Though the present text retains parts of our joint efforts on the first edition, its broader and updated content is the result of welcomed suggestions and ideas from many competent persons, to whom I express sincere gratitude.

Special thanks go to the professors and other teachers across the country who, after using the first edition, returned a questionnaire (unsigned) expressing thoughtful comments and helpful viewpoints. Also I am grateful to three of my University of Washington colleagues—Dr. Mark Clevenger, Dr. Donald Stem, and Leona R. Casteel for their useful specific suggestions; and to L. R. Goldberg, J.D., at Shoreline Community College, Seattle, for reviewing the summary on legal aspects.

To the authors and companies that have given permission to quote from their writing and whose names are mentioned throughout the text in footnotes, I express sincere thanks. Also deserving special mention and appreciation are Professors Loretta L. Mazzaroppi of Louisiana State University and James Bougill of Clinton Community College, Plattsburg, N.Y., who in reviewing my manuscript for this edition offered suggestions that helped broaden its scope.

In appreciation of the thousands of students who have given reliable feedback regarding text content and assignments, I dedicate this revision to all its users who want to improve their oral and written communication ability.

Herta A. Murphy

EFFECTIVE
BUSINESS
COMMUNICATIONS

PART 1

BACKGROUND FOR COMMUNICATING

1 Importance of Effective Communication in Business

You have a highly valued asset if you can communicate well, orally and in writing. Executives of American business, industry, and government have repeatedly expressed their concern regarding the need for better communication. In numerous surveys business executives have ranked ability to communicate first among the personal factors necessary for promotion to and within management—and they have selected business communication as one of the most useful college studies in their work.

This chapter includes answers to the following questions regarding the importance of effective communication in business:

How does effective business communication "pay off"?

What is the volume and cost of written business communication in the United States?

How can you meet the challenge of communicating for business?

How Effective Business Communication "Pays Off"

Effective communication is the "life blood" of every organization and a key to success in your business career as well as in your personal life.

"Life Blood" of the Organization

So important is communication that without it an organization cannot function. Since an organization is a group of people associated for business, political, professional, religious, athletic, or other purposes, its activities require human beings to interact and react; to exchange information, ideas, plans, proposals; to coordinate; to make decisions. Because this book is concerned primarily with effective *business* communication, the discussions and illustrations you will read pertain mainly to business firms. However, you can apply them to other organizations.

Both within and outside the organization, effective business communication "pays off." *Inside* the company, employees can be better motivated and more efficient because of appropriate written and oral communication. *Outside* the company, a communication to customers, inquirers, suppliers, and the public can have a far-reaching effect on the reputation and ultimate success of the company. The right letter, telephone call, or personal conversation can win back a disgruntled customer, create desire for a firm's product or service, negotiate a profitable sale, help an inquirer who is a potential customer, and in general create goodwill. Successful messages eliminate unnecessary additional correspondence, save time and expense, build favorable impressions, and help increase company profits.

Advantages for Your Career

Often your job, status, and professional reputation depend on the success or failure of your written and oral communication. Especially if your career requires mainly mental rather than manual labor, your progress will be strongly influenced by how effectively you communicate your knowledge, proposals, and ideas to others who need or should get them.

Subscribers to *Harvard Business Review* have affirmed that the prime requisite of a promotable executive is "ability to communicate." Notice that it is the top rung of the ladder in Figure 1-1.[1] Members of management spend about 90 percent of their working day communicating—receiving and sending messages.

As a management trainee on a new job, you have opportunities to discuss problems with coworkers and to submit memos, reports, and letters that test your ability to communicate clearly and quickly. A frequent complaint of managers is the inability of college graduates to make themselves heard, read, or understood. Your messages can reveal how well you are doing your job, and they help management to evaluate your fitness for a substantial promotion. For example, imagine that you are one of several highly trained employees in an organization that requires everyone to submit frequent reports to clients or company personnel. If there is an opening for promotion and you each rate about the same except that you alone can write effective reports, then clearly you have the advantage over the others.

Numerous surveys and articles have confirmed the statement that effective communication is essential for success in business. They have included, altogether, responses from thousands of university business graduates and executives across the United States. In answer to the question "What has been the most valuable subject you studied in college?", such titles as Business Communications, Business Letter and Report Writing, and Written and Oral Expression were always listed among the top three. Respondents (including top, middle, and operations managers) have repeatedly asserted that business communication skills influenced their advancement to executive positions.[2]

[1] John Fielden, "What Do You Mean I Can't Write?" *Harvard Business Review*, May–June 1964, pp. 144–145.

[2] The following is a representative list of references: William Arthur Allee, "A Study of the Graduates of the College of Commerce. State University of Iowa, 1921–1951," Ph.D. dissertation, Iowa City, 1951; James C. Bennett, "The Communication Needs of Business Executives," *The ABCA Journal of Business Communication*, Spring 1971, pp. 5–11; William P. Carr, "An Evaluation of Accounting Curriculum Subjects," Loyola University of the South, New Orleans, *Collegiate News and Views*, October 1952, pp. 5–10; William Grogg, "The Importance of Business Writing to the Student—A Businessman's Viewpoint," *The ABCA Bulletin*, June 1972, pp. 1–5; J. M. Hunter, Anthony Koo, and R. F. Voertman, "What Happens to Our Economics Majors," (Michigan State University, East Lansing) *Collegiate News and Views*, March 1954, pp. 11–13; R. R. Kay, "To Manage You Must Communicate," *Iron Age*, July 15, 1965, p. 55; Raymond V. Lesikar, *A Summary of Needs of Education for Small Business Based on a 1959 Survey of Louisiana Businessmen*, Louisiana State University Press, Baton Rouge, 1959; Charles E. Peck, "Survey of Curriculum Opinions of Business Administration," *University of Washington Business Review*, Seattle, 1958; Bill Rainey, "Professors and Executives Appraise Business Communication Education," *The ABCA Journal of Business Communication*, Summer 1972; C. Wilson Randle, "How to Identify Promotable Executives," *Harvard Business Review*, May–June 1956, pp. 122–124; Rollin H. Simonds, "Skills Businessmen Use the Most," *Nation's Business*, November 1960; J. B. Steinbruegee, T. J. Hailstones, and E. E. Roberts, "Personnel Managers Evaluate a College Business Program," (Xavier University, Cincinnati), *Collegiate News and Views*, May 1955, pp. 7–11; Stella Travaek, *An Opinion Report of the College of Business Administration, The University of Texas, 1917–1954*, Bureau of Business Research, University of Texas, Austin, 1954; Clarence E. Vincent, "Personnel Executives Examine the College Graduate," *Collegiate News and Views*, March 1966, pp. 12–16.

Figure 1-1 Requisites for a promotable executive.

A further confirmation of the preference for communication skills is found in the job descriptions listed by companies wishing to employ college graduates. For example, Dr. Francis W. Weeks, Executive Director of the American Business Communication Association,[3] found in a six-year study of job listings at the University of Illinois Coordinating Placement Office that 340 jobs in 30 fields required communication ability.[4] Among the specific descriptions were requirements like these:

Must be able to communicate effectively with all levels of management.

Must have substantial experience/training in oral and written presentations and demonstrate good writing skills.

Will prepare special analyses, research reports, and proposals.

Needs ability to compose effective correspondence.

Must have ability to communicate and "sell" ideas.

Must be able to cultivate and maintain good customer relationships.

Needs skills in gathering, analyzing, and interpreting data and in writing analytical reports.

Advantages in Your Personal Life

Effective communication also helps you to better accomplish certain aims as an individual in society. You will sometimes need to write letters and reports or to present your views orally as committee chairperson, club officer, or private citizen. In these various roles you might communicate with public officials, business firms, suppliers, or club members. Whatever your purposes, you will usually achieve them more effectively when you apply the same skills that help you communicate effectively in business.

Additional benefits that enthusiastic students of business communication have gained are better grades in some of their other business courses that require analytical problem solving and high-quality, well-organized reports.

Volume and Cost of Written Business Communication in the United States

No one knows just how many billions of dollars United States industries spend on communications, but the amount is enormous. Thousands of hours are devoted daily to interviews, conferences, meetings, in addition to the time for planning and writing letters, memos, reports, employee manuals, advertising aids, news articles, and bulletins. The following discussion is intended to give merely an estimate of the volume and costs of *some* phases of *written* communications in American business.

---

[3] The American Business Communication Association, organized in 1935, with its national office at the University of Illinois, Urbana, has members in major colleges and universities as well as businesses across the United States.

[4] Francis W. Weeks, "Communication Competencies Listed in Job Descriptions," *The ABCA Bulletin*, September 1971, pp. 18–37, and December 1974, pp. 22–34.

According to Lou Kriloff, president of Letterpower Institute, if all the letters written in the United States in one day were laid end to end, they would circle the country nine times.[5]

The Postmaster General's office has reported that in a recent year Americans mailed about 90.1 billion pieces of mail; of these about 74 percent—66.7 billion pieces—were *business* mail.[6] Even if only one-third of these business messages were personally dictated and typewritten, that would mean 22.2 billion pieces during the year.

How much does an individually dictated and typewritten letter cost? According to The Dartnell Institute of Business Research, *average* costs climbed from $1.17 in 1953 to $3.41 in 1974.[7] Some cost consultants have asserted—after considering stopwatch timings and misuse of expensive machines—that too many business and government letters cost as much as $15 to $20 each. These estimates include the expenses of:

Total time devoted to the message by the executive who composes and dictates it. (The executive's salary is the chief element in overall message cost.)

Total time of secretary, mail room employees, and file clerks working on correspondence.

Inefficiencies necessitating revisions, lags, idleness of expensive equipment, use of higher-paid employees than desirable for routine tasks.

Fixed charges (heat, rent, light, depreciation).

Material costs (stationery, carbons, postage).

To get a conservative idea of the estimated total annual cost of individually dictated mailed business messages in the United States, we can multiply the 22.2 billion by the $3.41 average. The result is a staggering $75.7 billion in one year. (This amount increases every year as total volume and costs increase.) The figure does not, of course, reveal the cost of *ineffective* letters—those that require additional messages of clarification or that lose a customer because of various faults.

If the $75-billion business correspondence costs were decreased even 10 percent because of improvements in message preparation, American business could devote an estimated $7.5 billion annually to other productive services. The savings could benefit the companies, employees, customers, and perhaps the general public. Many firms and government offices that have communication improvement programs report significant savings.[8]

---

[5] Lou Kriloff, statement in *The ABCA Bulletin*, September 1974, p. 21.

[6] Figures (for 1974) courtesy of E. V. Dorsey, Senior Assistant Postmaster General, Washington, D.C., April 1975. His office has also reported that the total United States mail volume increased an average of 1.3 billion pieces of mail a year from 1970 to 1974.

[7] "Analysis and Staff Report," *Dartnell's Annual Cost of a Business Letter Report*, The Dartnell Corporation, Chicago, January 1975.

[8] Here are two examples: A Hoover commission report to Congress regarding paperwork stated that for every $1,000 the federal government spent on correspondence management, it saved $32,000 in net operating expense. Mutual of New York reported saving an estimated $85,000 a year for ten years by reducing both the number and length of letters written.

The Challenge of Communicating for Business

Because communication plays such a major role in the operation of a firm and in possible promotion for the individual, communicating for business should be a challenge meriting your best efforts. Like any other worthwhile activity, the quality of communication is affected by the individual's attitude and preparation.

Developing the Right Attitude

Some communications are so important to a firm that they can win thousands or even millions of dollars worth of business or goodwill. If you were working on such a message (for a letter, report, speech, or crucial interview), you would probably devote several hours—perhaps days—to your best thoughts, imagination, and planning. But what about the other messages—especially the minor, routine kind that you will be handling daily? They may not be individually worth a million dollars, but each is part of the life blood of your organization. Each is an opportunity to build goodwill—to get a favorable response toward you and your company. Furthermore, such messages might lead to major business transactions. Collectively, the overall effect of thousands of routine messages is far-reaching.

"To the customer, you are the company," is good advice that public relations officials often give to their employees. AT&T's board chairman forcefully expressed this view when he urged all the firm's employees to be responsive to their customer's needs and concerns.[9]

> If you were to sit at my desk and read and answer the mail I get about telephone service, you'd come to realize, if you don't already, how much "little things" mean; how sometimes lifelong impressions of the character of our business are formed on the basis of a single contact with just one employee. Rather significant, I'd say, when you consider that the Bell System employs more than a million men and women. . . .
>
> The key element in all the letters . . . I get is how the customer was treated by an employee of the company. . . . Intermixed with complaints are a goodly number of commendation letters . . . about how an employee treated the customer in a manner so unusually satisfying that the customer felt compelled to write to me about it.

The "personality" of your company is an extension of many individual personalities; you are one of these important personalities.

Doing an honest job enthusiastically and competently helps both the doer and the receiver. Ask yourself if your company's image is a little better because of you. The following discussion is an example of why writing for business should and can be a challenge:[10]

[9]John D. de Butts, "When We Tell Customers, 'We Hear You,' We'd Better Be Listening," *Bell Telephone Magazine*, September-October 1973.
[10]From *Effective Letters*, New York Life Insurance Company, November-December 1962.

Letter writing is a boring job. It's also exciting and invigorating. Sounds like a paradox, doesn't it? But that's just the way two correspondents described their work to us recently. Both of them write letters for the same department of an insurance company. Yet one found his job as dull as last week's newspaper, while the other thought it interesting and challenging. Why such contradictory reactions? Could the identical job be both dull and exciting at the same time? And why? We thought we knew the answer. But to prove it to ourselves and to the correspondents, we tried a little experiment.

We gave each writer the same letter to answer as an exercise. It was a case of a policy owner who had asked what to do about his lost insurance policy.

First, here's the response of the correspondent who said he was bored with his job:

Dear Sir:

With regard to lost policy #23456, we are enclosing a lost policy form. Kindly complete this form and send it to us as soon as possible.

Upon receipt of the above requirement, this company will consider the issuance of a replacement policy.

                         Very truly yours,

Now let's see what the other correspondent wrote:

Dear Mr. Robinson:

Your lost policy can be easily replaced. Please don't let it worry you. I've enclosed a form that will help us replace it for you.

All you need do is fill in the requested information and send it back to us. We'll see to it that you get your policy within 3 days after this form reaches us.

                         Sincerely yours,

The first writer let a routine situation lull him into a routine attitude which made his response mechanical and impersonal. He didn't realize it, but he was boring—himself and his readers—with his own routine-sounding messages.

The second correspondent, on the other hand, had a different outlook. He viewed the routine question as a challenge to make his answer less routine. After all, though lost policy cases were familiar to him, they certainly weren't to the reader. This approach gave him incentive to put more effort into his work. And he had the satisfaction of writing a message that was warm, personal, and not the least bit boring for either the reader or himself.

Moral? While some of the work in business correspondence may not be terribly exciting, it need never be boring. If you catch yourself writing stale, repetitive messages, it may mean that it's time to try a new—and in many cases a more personal—approach. Like any other job, letter writing is only as interesting or as dull as the individual makes it.

Preparing Adequately

Most individuals can learn to communicate effectively for business if they desire to do so and are willing to devote whatever effort is necessary to prepare themselves adequately.

In addition to the right goodwill-building attitude, it is desirable to have the following requisites:

Intelligence and sound judgment in the choice of ideas and facts

Good humor and understanding—even in dealing with the unjustly insulting reader

Integrity, backed up by a sound code of ethics

Reasonable facility with the English language

The effective message for business pays off. If you thoroughly understand the basics of business communication and then diligently apply these basics with a liberal dose of common sense, you will continue to improve your ability to communicate effectively. With that goal in mind, you should find a challenge in every message you prepare.

In the following chapters you will study various typical business communication situations. Your communications will involve thinking, analyzing, solving problems, planning, and organizing messages according to acceptable contemporary procedures and central principles which are the basis for effective business communication. In so doing, you should gain a better understanding of people, learn how to win favorable responses from them, and make friends for your company. The background provided should give you the confidence to tackle almost any task you might face in writing letters, memos, or reports and in communicating orally.

2 The Process of Communication and Miscommunication

Communication is a process of transmitting a message so that the recipient understands it. The communication is considered effective when it achieves the desired reaction or response from the recipient. Simply stated, communication is a two-way process of exchanging ideas or information between human beings.

In actual practice, however, the communication process is not simple. Sometimes quite complex and imperfect, it malfunctions easily and may result in miscommunication. This chapter includes a brief overview of communication factors and basic general principles relative to communication and its problems. The information presented is adapted from various studies in such fields as psychology, sociology, semantics, communications, and human relations.

Factors of Communication

The process of communication consists of four elements or factors:

1. Sender—writer, speaker, encoder
2. Message
3. Medium—letter, memo, report, speech, chart, etc.
4. Receiver—reader, listener, perceiver, decoder

Role of Sender and Receiver

The interrelationship of message sender and receiver profoundly influences communication effectiveness, as is shown later in this chapter and others.

When you send a message, you are the writer or speaker, depending upon whether your communication is written or oral. You are likewise the "encoder"; you try to choose symbols—usually words—that will be meaningful to the recipient.[1] The receiver of your message is your reader or listener. In all cases the receiver is also the perceiver and "decoder." If the receiver incorrectly perceives (decodes) your message, you have miscommunicated.

The Message and Medium

The medium you choose for your message depends somewhat upon the interrelationship of sender and receiver. When you communicate with persons *inside* your organization, the written media are usually memos or reports. To persons *outside* your organization—customers, prospective customers, suppliers, job applicants, and others—your written media may be letters, reports, telegrams, Mailgrams, cablegrams, radiograms, postcards.[2] Oral media to persons both inside and outside your firm include inter-

---

[1] In addition to words (the verbal symbols), you may also communicate, to a lesser extent, with nonverbal symbols—such as facial expressions, handshakes, bodily movements, job status, appearance.

[2] Other media, outside the scope of this book, are: *internal*—employee manuals, bulletins, job descriptions, commendations, policy statements, company magazines, news sheets, posters, and notes in pay envelopes; *external*—brochures, advertisements, annual reports, news releases, circulars, bulletins, sales presentations.

views, telephone conversations, speeches. You can also communicate visually by charts and pictures.

Some General Communication Principles and Problems

Each person's mind is a unique filter. What is already in this mental filter affects the meanings a person places on messages and, to some extent, determines the new ideas the person chooses to accept or reject. Because no two people in the world are alike mentally, physically, or emotionally, the innumerable human differences may cause problems in conveying the intended meanings. Communication difficulties are more likely to occur when the communicators' filters are sharply different.

The message sender's meanings and the receiver's response are affected in numerous ways. Among them are their interpretations of words, their perception of reality, and the influence of their attitudes, opinions, and emotions. The consequences of miscommunication may range from mild or humorous to extremely serious and costly, as revealed in the following examples and suggestions for improvement.

Interpretations of Words

A fundamental general principle of communication is that the symbols the sender uses to communicate messages must have essentially the same meaning in the sender's mind and in the mind of the receiver. If the symbols are misunderstood or misinterpreted, miscommunication results. Another basic truth is that meanings are in people. The knowledge a person already has in mind regarding any given subject affects the meaning placed on words. Different word interpretations are often especially noticeable in "bypassed" instructions and in reactions to denotative and connotative meanings.

Bypassed Instructions. When the message sender and receiver attribute different meanings to the same words or use different words though intending the same meaning, bypassing may occur. Many words have several dictionary definitions; a few have over 100.[3] Moreover, some people have their own unique meanings which are not in a dictionary. Thus, confusion sometimes arises easily, as these incidents illustrate:

1. An office manager handed to a new assistant one letter with the instruction, "Take it to our stockroom and burn it." In the office manager's mind (and in the firm's jargon) the word "burn" meant to make a copy on a company machine which operated by a heat process. As the letter was extremely important, she wanted an extra copy. However, the puzzled new employee, afraid to ask questions, burned the letter with a lighted match and thus destroyed the only existing copy!
2. An equipment supervisor told a new night-duty employee: "You'll have to crack all the valves before you clean the settling tank." The next morning the supervisor found a floor full of smashed castings. "Crack" to the supervisor

---

[3] For example, in one abridged dictionary the little word "run" has 71 meanings as a verb, plus another 35 as a noun and 4 more as an adjective.

meant opening each valve just enough to allow minimum flow. You may be surprised that the supervisor was discharged because of the inadequate instructions that resulted in costly miscommunication.

3. An American motorist driving in England narrowly escaped a car accident because he misinterpreted road signs which used different words than signs in America to convey the same meanings (shown in parentheses): Diversion (Detour); Double Bend (S Curve); Concealed Turning (Blind Corner); End of Prohibition (Danger Zone Passed).

4. A superintendent (Jane) said to Tim, a maintenance worker, "Plant 2 is having trouble with its automatic control. Whatever the trouble is, go out there and get rid of it." The next day, after receiving angry complaints from Plant 2, Jane berated Tim for yanking out completely and discarding the entire control unit and installing a new one, even though Plant 2 had purchased the original unit only five months before. The company had a new, rigid cost-cutting program with rules to repair, rather than replace, all salvageable equipment whenever possible. But Jane had failed to inform Tim of that rule. Thus Tim thought that because the control unit was causing the trouble, that's what he should "get rid of." Jane had wrongly assumed that her instructions were clear, but Tim's meaning was entirely different from Jane's.

To avoid communication errors of bypassing when you give instructions, be sure to ask yourself whether the words and sentence structure you are using will convey the intended meaning for the recipient. Also, when you are the recipient of unclear instructions, before acting on them ask questions to determine the sender's intended meaning.

Reactions to Denotations and Connotations. Almost everyone has at some time been surprised that a remark intended as a compliment or a matter-of-fact statement or a joke was interpreted by the receiver as an insult. Or a statement intended as a good deed was distorted into something evil or self-serving.

Some of these communication problems may occur because words have both denotative and connotative meanings. The denotative meaning is the literal word meaning on which most individuals will probably agree. It informs and it names objects (or people or events) without indicating positive or negative qualities. Such words as *conference, desk, book* convey denotative meanings. In contrast, connotative meanings arouse qualitative judgment and personal reactions. The expression *meeting room* is denotative. *Directors' lounge, executive suite, rickety firetrap, rat-filled joint*—though they each denote a meeting place—also have connotative meanings.

Some words—such as *efficient, gentle, prompt*—usually have only favorable connotations. Others—such as *lazy, coward, delinquent*—usually have only unfavorable connotations. Still other words have favorable connotations in some contexts, but unfavorable meanings in others. Compare, for example, *fat check, fat girl, fat chance; free enterprise* and *free love; sucker* (customer) and *sucker* (candy); *cheap product* and *cheap price.*

The connotative meanings for words and labels are also affected by the communicator's different backgrounds and interests. Words such as *amnesty, unions, generation gap, hippies, fair wages, women's liberation* may arouse mixed feelings and arguments.

Euphemisms such as *maintenance worker* instead of *janitor, slender* instead of *skinny, Salisbury steak* or *hamburger* instead of *choice ground dead steer* have obvious connotative advantages. Furthermore, advertising slogans or labels can help make or break a product's effectiveness. For example:

> One basically sound product—a vibrating mattress, which could have been a great help to sufferers of insomnia and industrial fatigue—failed mainly because the advertisements stressed "Shake yourself to sleep." The connotation of the word "shake" was the deathblow to the marketing effort.

To communicate effectively you need to be aware of the usual connotative meanings of various terms and also to realize that some people may have their own unique meanings because of their experiences and background. Thus, choose your words carefully, considering both their connotations and their denotations to convey the idea you want to express and to achieve the desired results. Whenever possible, choose words with positive (favorable) rather than negative connotations.

Comprehension of Reality

Reality is complex, infinite, and continually changing. Also, for each human being, sensory perceptions are limited and mental filters are unique. Therefore, people perceive reality in many different ways, and their statements about an object, event, or person are necessarily incomplete. They make various kinds of abstractions, inferences, and evaluations.

Abstracting. The process of focusing on some details and omitting others is *abstracting*. In countless instances, abstracting is necessary and desirable—for both written and oral communication. Whether you write a memo, letter, or report, or converse by telephone, you will be limited somewhat by time, expense, space, and/or purpose. You will need to select—honestly—facts that are pertinent to accomplish your purpose and to omit the rest (as you do, for example, in a one-page job application letter about yourself). Also, when preparing a business report you may—after gathering perhaps a "mountain" of data—have to abstract and condense it into a "molehill."[4]

You, as the communicator, must also anticipate the likelihood that others may not be abstracting as you are. Yet—though they select differently from the infinite details in reality—they may have as good points as you have. For example:

> When reporting on an event—a firm's new-store dedication ceremony, a factory explosion and fire, a football game, a traffic accident—no two witnesses give *exactly* the same descriptions. Their knowledge and backgrounds affect what they perceive. The participants will have a different view than the observers, and all those within each group will perceive different details or parts, though some parts of the whole may be mentioned by all or several observers.

---

[4] For illustrations of report abstracts, see pages 608 to 610.

Even authorities on certain subjects humbly admit they don't know all the answers, and they sometimes disagree among themselves on various topics. So do conscientious open-minded business executives, government leaders, educators, students. The more we delve into some subjects, the more we realize that there is so much more to learn and to consider. Semanticists suggest that we at least mentally add "etc." to remind us that statements are incomplete. We should not yield to the "allness" fallacy—with the attitude that what we know or say about something is all there is to know or say about it. (This caution applies also to the chapter you are now reading, for it too is necessarily an abstract.)[5]

Unfortunately, it is true of some people that "the less they know, the more sure they are that they know it all." Perhaps you have worked with such persons?

> A conspicuous example is that of the high school sophomore chatting casually with a man who (unknown to the student) was a distinguished scientist devoting his lifetime to studying botany. The smug sophomore commented, "Oh botany? I finished studying all about that stuff last semester." As Bertrand Russell stated, "One's certainty varies inversely with one's knowledge."

An important point to remember about abstracting is that a statement is not the whole story. Whenever you abstract material, try to make your abstract a fair representation of the whole situation or area from which you are abstracting and realize that other communicators may choose different ideas than you do.

Slanting. Alert communicators—as both senders and receivers of messages—also realize that possibly the parts they are acquainted with may not be representative of the whole. They should welcome other facts and consider them as objectively as possible. The communicator should try to determine whether the facts are "slanted" with intentional bias or opinion. Slanting is unfair in factual reporting. The reporter should be careful to include quoted statements in context and exclude expressions of personal approval or disapproval of the persons, objects, or occurrences being described. For example:

---

[5] If you wish to read more details about communication and human relations, semantics, processes of speaking, listening, writing, reading, or group dynamics, you might begin with the following books plus any bibliographies they contain: David K. Berlo, *The Process of Communication: An Introduction*, Holt, Rinehart and Winston, Inc., New York, 1960; Richard W. Budd and Brent D. Ruben, *Approaches to Human Communication*, Hayden Book Company, Inc., Rochelle Park, N.J., 1972; James H. Campbell and Hal W. Hepler, *Dimensions in Communication: Readings*, Wadsworth Publishing Company, Inc., Belmont, Calif., 1970; Stuart Chase, *Power of Words*, Harcourt, Brace and Company, New York, 1954; William V. Haney, *Communication and Organizational Behavior*, Richard D. Irwin, Inc., Homewood, Ill., 1973 (comprehensive bibliography pp. 529–570); Thomas A. Harris, *I'm OK — You're OK*, Avon Books, New York, 1973; S. I. Hayakawa, *Language in Thought and Action*, Harcourt, Brace and Company, New York, 1949; Richard C. Huseman, Cal M. Logue, Dwight L. Freshley, *Readings in Interpersonal and Organizational Communication*, Holbrook Press, Inc., Boston, 1969; Wally D. Jacobson, *Power and Interpersonal Relations*, Wadsworth Publishing Company, Inc., Belmont, Calif., 1972; Alfred Korzybski, *Science and Sanity*, Institute of General Semantics, Lakeville, Conn., 1948; Irving J. Lee, *Handling Barriers in Communication*, Harper & Brothers, New York, 1957; Gail E. Myers and Michele T. Myers, *The Dynamics of Human Communication*, McGraw-Hill Book Company, New York, 1973; Bess Sondel, *The Humanity of Words: A Primer of Semantics*, The World Publishing Company, Inc., Cleveland, 1958.

The reporter is not permitted to write: "A small crowd of suckers came to hear Superintendent Jones yesterday noon in that rundown hotel that disfigures the central area." Instead, the write-up may state: "Between 100 and 150 people heard an address yesterday noon by Superintendent Jones in the auditorium at the Edgemont Hotel on Center Street."

Too often people tend to identify a person or a group by the obvious, undesirable, or worst attribute. If a man sometimes drinks heavily, he is labeled as a drinker, though he may also be a helpful neighbor; kind, generous father; neat gardener; dependable accountant. If a company has one executive who is convicted of fraud and extortion, that individual's misdeeds may harm the reputation of the entire firm though its other executives and thousands of employees may be honest and law-abiding. Likewise, one insulting letter writer may adversely affect the image of the company that person represents.

Thus, it is best for us all to try not to judge the whole by a part. Otherwise we will have an inadequate, erroneous impression of the whole, as did the six blind men who each felt only one part of an elephant. The one who felt only the swinging tail thought an elephant was like a rope. The others' ideas of an elephant—based on the part they felt (shown here in parentheses)—were: a spear (its tusk), a wall (its broad side), a snake (its trunk), a tree (its knee), a fan (its ear).

Inferring. Every day most of us find it necessary to act on some inferences. We make assumptions and draw conclusions even though we ourselves do not (or cannot) directly see, hear, feel, taste, smell, or otherwise immediately verify the evidence or premise. Statements that go beyond the facts our senses report and conclusions based on facts are called *inferences.* Some inferences are both necessary and desirable; others are risky, even dangerous.

When we drop an airmail envelope into a mailbox, we infer it will be picked up, flown by plane(s), and ultimately delivered to our intended reader(s). We assume that the gas station attendant pumps gasoline (not water) into our car's tank, that the restaurant's kitchen is sufficiently sanitary (and free from poisons!), that the elevator in our building is capable of taking us to the desired floor, and so on.

Such inferences are necessary and usually fairly reliable—if we base them on reasonable evidence; but even so there have been disappointing exceptions.

Also, inferences are essential and desirable for business and professional persons when they analyze materials, solve problems, and plan procedures. Systems analysts, marketing specialists, advertisers, architects, engineers, designers, and numerous others all must work on various premises and make inferences after they have gathered as much factual data as possible. Even our legal procedures allow inferences from experts as acceptable evidence. However, when nonexperts attempt to argue on professional matters about which they have no facts, they—deservedly—get into communication troubles.

As intelligent communicators we must realize that inferences may be incorrect, unreliable, and the cause of miscommunication. We need to anticipate risks before acting on the basis of inferences.

> Suppose that a personnel manager notices that Sue Jones, a new management trainee, has been staying at least an hour after closing time every evening for the past two weeks. He might infer that Sue is exceptionally conscientious, or that she is incapable of doing the required work within the regular time, or that she has been given more responsibility than should be expected of a new trainee, or even that Sue is snooping around for confidential materials after others have left the office. Before acting on any of these inferences, the manager should get more facts!

In some industries executives may make a disastrous decision that ultimately causes loss of lives as well as money if they assumed wrongly that an inference in a report was a verifiable fact.

On any job you do—for an employer or others—be sure to consider the bases of inferences. Inform those who may be acting on your inference what portions of your statements are mere assumptions. If you are presenting or receiving a report on which an important executive decision may rest, be especially careful to distinguish clearly among verifiable facts, inferences based on facts, and mere "guesstimates."

Making Frozen Evaluations. Another drawback to effective communication is the "frozen evaluation"—the stereotyped impression that ignores significant differences or changes. To help assure that your comprehension of reality will be correct, you need to recognize that any person, product, or event

> May be quite different from others in the general group
>
> May have significant differences today when compared with characteristics yesterday or some time ago
>
> May deserve more than a two-valued description

Allowing for individual differences is necessary because in reality no two elements of a general group or classification are exactly alike. Customer_1 is not customer_{632}. Even manufactured assembly-line products differ under a microscope. Flashlight $\#F320_1$ is not the same as $\#F320_2$ or $\#F320_{102}$. When people find a common similarity in a group and ignore the numerous significant differences, they have formed a frozen—unfair—evaluation. Often such people adhere to their faulty stereotypes and communicate them to others. You have probably heard statements that all politicians are undependable, students are slow-paying customers, redheads are hot-tempered, fat people are jovial, people with close-set eyes are stubborn, and so on.

Allowing for time differences is also essential. A tendency of some people is to downgrade (or praise) all products of a certain brand simply because they have used one item once. They disregard not only differences in individual characteristics of items within the general classification but also possible changes because of time.

> Perhaps you've known a customer who asserts "I'll never again buy any coat with the Realex Label! The one I bought last year came apart at the seams." He should

realize that (1) probably not all Realex coats last year ripped at the seams; Realex coat$_1$ is not exactly the same as Realex coat$_{10,500}$; also (2) Realex coats last year maybe are not the same as Realex coats this year or next year.

Neither is a customer's payment record this year necessarily exactly the same as last year. Nor can you be sure that a successful sales campaign this year will again be successful next year. Everything and every person changes with time. No one or no thing remains static.

Allowing for differences in degree is a third essential for avoiding frozen evaluations. The communication practice of making only a strict two-valued "either-or" evaluation may be a source of miscommunication. If communicators designate people, products, or statements as either good or bad, strong or weak, honest or dishonest, hard or soft, large or small, fast or slow, black or white, true or false, they may be *polarizing.* They are overlooking important middle areas in between the extremes. To be fair and accurate, communicators should be specific in each case, with details and figures whenever possible.[6]

In short, to be discerning communicators, we must consider significant differences for a unit of any group—and also changes in any one unit during a period of time. We must ask *which* person, *which* product, *which* event, *to what extent* and exactly *when* any particular statement was true. This caution is useful for all communicators. It is also especially applicable for report writers, who must be able to identify their sources, dates, and specific details of important facts.

Influence of Attitudes, Opinions, and Emotions

The effectiveness of communication may be strongly influenced also by the attitudes, viewpoints, prejudices, and emotions the communicators already have in their mental filters.

Attitudes and Opinions. When the information we read or hear agrees with our views and attitudes, we tend to accept it and react favorably toward it. The accepted information fits comfortably in the filter of our mind. On the contrary, when the information disagrees with our views, habits, and attitudes—or appears to be disadvantageous to us—we tend to react negatively toward it and/or toward the informer.

Rejecting, distorting, and avoiding are three common undesirable negative ways that a receiver reacts to unfavorable information. For example:

> Suppose an employee perceives that a recently announced change in company policy is contrary to his beliefs or benefit. In reacting, he may reject or resent the company and/or his boss, perhaps falsely accusing them of being unfair. Or he may, instead, distort the meaning and misinterpret the true purpose of the policy change. Or he may avoid the message, situation, or people by putting off acceptance, hoping that his delay will somehow prevent the change and protect him.

[6] For examples of ways to be specific, see Concreteness in Chapter 5, pages 81–86, and in Chapter 15, pages 533–534.

Another significant truth is that people tend to react according to their attitude toward a set of facts, rather than to the facts themselves. For instance, a customer may be happy over an adjustment or a loan which a company extends to her, but angry when she learns that a neighbor received a better deal for what the customer assumes (perhaps wrongly) to be the same circumstances.

An added problem occurs if the receiver has a suspicion about or a prejudice against the message sender. People tend to react more according to their attitude toward the *source* of facts than to the facts themselves. A staunch Democrat will be less likely to accept an idea from a Republican than the same idea from a fellow Democrat. A conservative executive may be less likely to accept statements from the "office grapevine" than from the department manager. Stated positively, it is true that employees, customers, and people in general will react more favorably when a communicator has credibility—when they respect, trust, and believe in the communicator.

If you can predict the probable attitude, opinion, or prejudice that the receiver already has about a certain matter or person, you can better focus your communication in ways to reduce tension and resistance. Also, if you are the receiver, try not to let your personal biased viewpoints affect your perception of a message. Observe, read, and listen to various sources, because useful information may come from almost anyone. In the words of an old Indian prayer, "Let me not criticize my neighbor until I have walked a mile in his moccasins."

Emotions. Another influence on communication effectiveness is the emotional state of the communicator's mind at the time the message is sent or received. When personal or business upsets occur, people sometimes unjustly take out their problems on others.

Undesirable emotions—such as worry, anger, fear, despondency, hatred—even when due to circumstances entirely unrelated to the particular message, can adversely affect it. On a day when everything at home is wrong and disturbing, a person's written and oral communications at the office might sound unusually gruff, gloomy, or uncooperative. On the contrary, when everything is rosy in an individual's personal life, that person's business communications may also reflect this better emotional condition.

To be good communicators we must realize that people may react inconsistently when they are influenced by their emotions. We will have better communication when we catch people in the right frame of mind. Admittedly, it is often difficult or impossible to know just when is the best time. We need also to try not to allow our own personal emotions and sore spots to affect our messages.

The Closed Mind. One of the most difficult persons to communicate with is the one who seemingly has a closed mind on a certain subject, refusing to consider any new facts, no matter how objectively and tactfully the sender presents them. Typically, this person has only inadequate and mainly incorrect knowledge of the subject. Yet this type of individual vehemently rejects additional information, even from an expert who has made a long, careful study of the problem and the proposed change. The closed-minded person says in essence, "My mind is made up. Don't bother me with facts. I want what I want." Sometimes he or she goes a step farther and—even before reading or hearing the documented facts—unjustly labels them or the sender's views as distorted. In all, closed-minded individuals completely reject, distort, and/or avoid a viewpoint even before they know the facts.

Unblocking the mind of such people in an attempt for effective communication is far from easy. They may be reluctant to make any changes, yet they will not state why. They may argue, wrongly, that because something was good last year, it will be all right this year; or because a store or procedure or machine has been operating satisfactorily one way for X years, why change now?

Sometimes there is hope for better communication if these adamant persons can be encouraged to state their reasons for rejecting a concept. They may reveal deep-rooted prejudices, opinions, and/or emotions. However, if they react only with anger and refuse both to give reasons as well as to consider the other person's facts, effective communication will be impossible. To settle such a dispute, the intervention of a mediator or even a court of law may be necessary.

Summary

Effective communication depends to a large extent on insights into human nature and on the ability to get desirable responses. For most people, effective communication does not come naturally. It is a skill, to be learned and practiced. This chapter has included merely an introduction to the complex process of communication. Its aim has been to give you helpful ideas of why communication problems can occur and how, in general, they may be decreased or avoided.

To be an effective communicator, realize that human beings' mental filters differ. Try always to consider differences in word (and sentence) interpretations, keep an open mind for getting as many accurate facts as possible about reality, admit there is always more that could be said, and allow for the influences of attitudes and emotions. Above all, try to better understand the people with whom you communicate. This ability will be useful and developed further as you apply the principles in the remainder of this book.

Exercises

1. Review the factors of the communication process, and discuss where errors are likely to occur.

2. Select an object that you are familiar with; then look for characteristics you have not noticed in it before. How can you explain your discovery in terms of a communication principle?

3. The comment "Gerald Joiner is a member of five business clubs and two athletic clubs" may be intended as a compliment. Why might some listeners interpret it as derogatory?

4. Suppose you see Alice (the tenant who lives alone in an apartment directly above you) leaving at 8 p.m. from the front of the building. You have observed that she

leaves at the same time each weekday evening. Last week she told you she is a nurse in a downtown hospital and her shift started at 8:30 p.m. Tonight at 8:55 p.m. you hear footsteps in the apartment above you. You might infer spontaneously that a burglar has entered. Will you call the police? the apartment house manager? the hospital? Discuss reasons why your inference may be right or wrong.

5. Describe the room in which your class meets. How does your description differ or agree with those of your classmates? Why might an electrical engineer, interior decorator, and a flooring salesperson select even more and different details than any of the students?

6. Give two examples of how the opinions and prejudices in your mind affect your communication.

7. Yesterday you attended a banquet at which the speaker was a state senator. You liked what she said. In this morning's newspaper you read a quotation from her speech, and you consider it contrary to the main point the speaker was making. Explain the discrepancy in terms of topics discussed in this chapter.

8. On television this morning you and a friend heard a public officer confess that he had lied both under oath and in his recent popular book. Your friend commented: "You just can't believe what you read in books these days." Using communication principles, discuss the truth of this statement.

9. Discuss: "Communicators with similar mental filters are more likely to communicate effectively." Why? Give examples from your own experiences.

10. Assume you are assistant sales manager for the Widget Company. One of your new sales representatives, a recent college graduate, won top place last year selling the most tickets to a special campus event. Now she wants to use the same tactics she used for that college campaign. You are skeptical. Who's right? Discuss the viewpoints as part of the communication process.

11. A popular humorist and actor has stated that sometimes the same jokes which cause one audience to laugh spontaneously don't even get a chuckle another night in a different town. Discuss in terms of a communication principle.

12. Suppose your boss asks you to revise parts of a 70-page report because of various minor errors and omissions in two sections. You and Harold Lazybones worked together on that report the past two weeks. Harold is on vacation now. The portions to which the boss refers were written entirely by Harold, although the boss doesn't know this. (Incidentally, Harold's salary is $100 a month more than yours.) How will your reaction to the boss's request be influenced by your attitude toward the set of facts rather than to the request itself? Explain.

13. Discuss the advantages and risks of making inferences in business.

14. Discuss whether each of the following statements is an inference or a verifiable fact based on observation:
   a. The boss is a "swinger."
   b. Employees under twenty and over sixty-five are inefficient.

    c.   The union requested double pay for each hour of overtime.

    d.   The union requested too much money.

    e.   XYZ skis are no good.

15.   What general communication principles do the following statements and incidents illustrate? Discuss each briefly.

    a.   A friend of yours states: "I'll never buy our groceries from Tiptop Market. Haven't been there since the first week after they opened four years ago. Their produce department is a mess and prices are too high."

    b.   In a public utility, an order went out setting up a new procedure; on the basis of that order, five different powerhouses set up five different procedures.

    c.   This comment made to each of two employees caused one to be pleased and the other hurt: "Your report is very good today . . . what there is of it."

    d.   An article in tonight's newspaper states that a nationwide strike appears all but certain after union negotiators walked out of contract talks and accused management of forcing a strike. But the chief negotiator said he couldn't "conceive how anyone could say what we gave them was a provocation for a strike."

16.   Bring to class a picture, cartoon, or an intricate gadget. Show it to your class one minute (if possible, use an overhead projector); then hide your illustration. Ask three volunteers to leave the room. One at a time each will reenter the room and describe to the class what you displayed. Does any one student cover *all* the details? How many more can the rest of the class add to the three students' descriptions? Discuss reasons for differences in perception.

3 Planning before Communicating

The language used in business communications must get the message across effectively to gain the recipient's desired reaction. Whether you are preparing an oral or a written communication, you need to plan before presenting your message.

Your letter on company stationery or your telephone call as a company representative to a customer can create in the receiver's mind a favorable or unfavorable attitude toward your entire organization. Even after you have communicated orally on an important matter, you are often asked to "put it in writing." Your message then becomes a permanent record, which the recipient can reread anytime. Also, if geographical distance separates you and the person with whom you are communicating, or if the material is complex, technical, or lengthy, writing is often the only effective means of communication. A well-organized letter is like a bridge that spans the gap between you and the receiver of your message.

This chapter discusses the planning steps, the basic organizational patterns, and openings and closings—all essential to good business communication. Though the ideas presented here and in later chapters can be useful for both written and oral communication, the discussion and examples focus on written messages, because most communicators need more help on them.

Six Planning Steps

To communicate effectively, you should go through the following six steps before you transmit your message:

1. Know the purpose of the message.
2. Visualize your reader (or listener).
3. Choose the ideas to include.
4. Get all the facts to back up these ideas.
5. Organize your ideas in the most effective order.
6. Revise and proofread.

Know the Purpose

When you receive a letter, what runs through your mind—even before you begin to read? Usually you're wondering what the writer wants or what the purpose is. In fact, it's rather difficult for you to grasp all the various ideas of a particular message until you do know the purpose.

Following are excerpts from a form letter that is baffling because its purpose is obscure.[1] As you read the message, try to figure out why the writer sent it. Notice how frustrating it is not to be able to orient yourself or to figure out what purpose the various facts are supposed to support.

---

[1] Form letters are identical messages reproduced from one master draft and sent to two or more persons.

```
Friends:

Since the new administration took over in January, I have personally
visited the majority of our customers throughout the major cities of
the 11 western states.  In January, as agreed by all, we were suffer-
ing from a downturn in our economy.  Generally this has been appar-
ent through January and February of this new year. However, as we
approach spring--March and April--there appears to be a return of
confidence and optimism for the balance of 197_.  I am happy to re-
port that this change has been reflected by a heavy increase in
orders both for immediate delivery and for fall.  I share the feeling
that this year will again end in a banner year of prosperity.


As I move from city to city, I cannot help but feel what a great
privilege it is to be in America.  Yes--we have our problems.  But
let me remind you that as our nation matures we are overcoming
them. . . .
```

(Three more paragraphs mention, in general, labor disputes, strikes, segregation, religious tolerance, Americans' responsibilities for change. Then comes the last paragraph):

```
My business, of course, is to sell hosiery, underwear, and knit
goods.  Please think of me when you have need for these products and
let us not forget our obligation to every other fellow American.
                        Sincerely yours,
```

Do you know what the writer of that letter had in mind? Is it a newsy bit of chit-chat sent to customers to keep the company's name fresh before them? If so, why doesn't the letter say so? The letter could have started, "Here is another newsy message to keep you posted on the crucial domestic happenings of our times," and you would have known why the message was being sent. At least you wouldn't be in a quandary as you read the rest of the letter.

Like you, your reader appreciates knowing the purpose of your message. As you will see later when studying organizational plans for various types of messages, you should mention the specific purpose of most, but not all, letters and memos in or near the first paragraph. For all reports, state the purpose in the introduction.

In addition to the specific purpose of each message, all communications have, of course, an underlying general purpose—to build goodwill. For example, in a refusal or a collection letter, the purpose should be twofold—not only to refuse a request or ask for money, but also to maintain the customer's goodwill.

Thus, be sure to keep both your specific and the general purpose in mind as you plan every message.

Visualize Your Reader

After reading about the communication process (Chapter 2), you realize how important it is to better understand the people with whom you communicate. If you are well acquainted with your readers—or even if you have met them at least once—you can actually visualize each individual as you write. And you can better adapt your message to fit each individual's filter.

Most of your writing, however, will probably be directed to people you have never met. If you are sending a message to one person, you should try to classify that person the best ways you can—business or professional person or laborer; superior (boss), colleague, or subordinate; man or woman; single, married, or widow(er); young, middle age, or elderly; new or long-time customer; and so on. If you are addressing a form message to many people, remember the caution that every person within any group has a unique filter and special interests! But you should try to discover characteristics common to all of them and then imagine you're talking to one individual within that group. For example:

1. In upward communications (to your superiors), tact is important. Also, you should support factual statements with detail (but not to the degree that the boss becomes impatient), curb personal opinion, and give only conclusions unless you're requested to include recommendations.
2. In downward communications (to your subordinates), be diplomatic—never overbearing nor insulting. When you give instructions, be sure you supply all needed information clearly and give reason(s) for an order whenever desirable. Also (if you can) point out how your order benefits those it affects.
3. Successful retailers know their business well. You'd insult them if you talked down to them by saying, for example, that the right markup and an adequate turnover of merchandise will give a profit.
4. If you write to strangers for information, you must tell them how you intend to use it, particularly if the information is confidential or tends to be confidential.
5. An older person may be especially interested in security, while a younger person looks more toward the future.
6. Some people are more sensitive to tone (cutting words, negative words, and curtness) than are others.
7. To anyone not familiar with terminology of the business, you need to use easy-to-understand words and explain any technical terms.

To help get the desired response, you must also be sensitive to the feelings of your readers, as the following examples illustrate:

1. A Chamber of Commerce president included this sentence in his reply to a woman who had inquired about accommodations in and near his resort town:

   ```
   You can wear anything you choose and wearing nothing is approximated
   so closely at times that I think you could get by with that if you
   were so inclined.
   ```

   The woman who received this reply was a business woman in her fifties who was anything but a "swinger." She definitely forgot about staying at that place.
2. Then there was the university professor who received from the chairperson of a leading corporation a stockholder's letter that explained the company's pension program. Because the letter seemed so complicated, the professor wrote the chairperson and suggested the need for simplifying communications to the average stockholder. Here's part of the chairperson's reply:

```
Yours is the first criticism we have had from the many thousands of
stockholders who have already sent in the proxies saying that the
purpose of the meeting was not understandable to them.  I do not see
how I can state the facts any more clearly and simply than was done
in my letter of January 18.
```

No doubt the professor is still feeling the mental slap in the face and smarting from the implication that she must be stupid. Not only did the chairperson insult the professor but the reply itself was unclear. The wording gives the reader the impression that the *proxies* said "the purpose of the meeting was not understandable."

3. Finally, there's the man who reacted angrily by letter to a mail-order house that sent him a collection letter. But this fellow forgot that the person receiving his message was perhaps innocent of everything relating to the mix-up and misunderstanding:

```
I just mailed to you bunch of idiots a check in the amount of $42.00.
This morning from L.A., Cal, I received this piece of paper similar
to the pile of junk I received yesterday from the same source.  I am
getting plenty tired of all this boloney you knotheads are pulling
off because I have cancelled checks from away back 20 yrs.  I also
have a copy of the last contract and my payments are not due til the
25th of the month.  I have typed a copy of that contract and along
with other proof I am mailing the whole package to Chicago to see if
I can't talk them into tying the can to about half of you numbskulls.
```

This disgruntled individual should have realized he was insulting innocent people who, in turn, had to act upon his message! Being called an idiot, knothead, and numbskull hardly makes a person willing to go all out to help someone.

In short, when you write you must visualize your reader as well as you can, and write with the individual in mind.

Choose the Ideas

After you have decided on the purpose and visualized the reader, you can begin to choose the ideas that go into the message. And if you let only the purpose and reader govern what is included in your letter or report, you're more likely to avoid irrelevant ideas and overall wordiness.

In simple messages that discuss one or two points, you can make mental notes of the subjects you want to include. In more complex messages, you'll probably want to underline key words in the letter to be answered or jot down suggestions in the margin or on a memo pad. In a complicated letter or report, you may need a full outline of the major headings and subheadings.

Naturally the ideas that you will include in your communication depend upon the type of message you're considering. For example, take a welcome letter that a savings and loan association sends to a new customer. What is the purpose of this kind of letter? If you say the only purpose is to welcome the customer, then one or two sentences should suffice. They might merely thank new customers for selecting your association and welcome them. But should the purpose of this message be *only* to welcome? Shouldn't you also help them know your policy concerning savings accounts, the overall services available to them, and your association's eagerness to be their financial headquarters? If so, then the following ideas should be included in your welcome letter. (List ideas as they come to you; rearrange them after you choose the right organizational plan.)

1. Welcome them and thank them for opening an account.
2. State some of your services—free parking, save-by-mail, mortgage loans, special accounts.
3. Tell them the hours you're open to serve them.
4. Mention percentage of interest they earn.
5. Assure them you're ready to help with their problems or wishes.

After you have decided on these ideas and completed the other planning steps, you can mail a good welcome letter. See, for example, letter 2, page 78.

Get All the Facts

Having determined what ideas to include, ask yourself if you need any specific figures, facts, or quotations you don't have at the tip of your tongue. Be sure you know your company policy, procedures, and product details if this message requires them. Perhaps you should check with your boss, colleague, subordinates, or the files for an exact percentage, name of an individual, date, address, figure, or statement. Also, in reports that include tables or other illustrations, you should have these visual aids finished (or at least in rough draft form) at this stage.

You'll find further discussion on this planning step in Chapter 5 under Completeness.

Organize Your Ideas

The order in which you present your ideas is often as important as the ideas themselves. "The discipline of translating thoughts into words and organizing these thoughts logically has no equal as intellectual training. . . . Disorganized writing reflects a disorganized, illogical (and untrained) mind."[2]

Choose the organizational plan after you have determined your purpose, collected all needed facts, and asked yourself "How will the reader react to these ideas?" The basic plans are discussed later in this chapter.

Revise and Proofread

For the routine, short communications, you will usually be able to dictate (or write) quite easily with little or no revising. However, for much other writing—especially complex, longer messages and reports, new form letters, and any writing that is to be

---

[2] John Fielden, "What Do You Mean I Can't Write?", *Harvard Business Review*, May–June 1964.

published—you should expect to revise, sometimes substantially. You will want to make sure that the message meets all principles of good business writing. An ineffective message is a waste of everyone's time.

Top correspondents and authors have confirmed again and again that the best writers rewrite and rewrite and rewrite. Tolstoy revised *War and Peace* five times; James Thurber rewrote his stories as many as fifteen times.

> A business writer can't and needn't rewrite everything 15 times. . . . But he does have an obligation—to his reader and to his employer—to reread what he has written before it is mailed and to rewrite it when necessary. . . . It may take time, but it's part of his job. . . . The hardest part is making each word and sentence say exactly what you want it to say so that your reader will interpret it correctly and react as you want him to.[3]

To revise effectively, you must read your draft objectively, from the viewpoint of your recipient. Whenever desirable, consider suggestions from knowledgeable associates. At times you may feel like the doubtful report writer who remarked to his supervising editor: "You mean you want the revised revision of the original revised revision revised?"[4]

Careful proofreading is also essential. After your best revised business message is typewritten—and before it is mailed!—you or other dependable persons should read it. Any error should be corrected so that your paper will reflect favorably on you and your company. (See also Correctness in Chapter 4.)

Basic Organizational Plans

Your choice of organizational plan depends upon what you expect your reader's reaction to your message is likely to be. And that reaction, of course, depends to some extent upon what is already in your reader's mental filter, as well as on the content of your message.

Business letters, memos, and reports can be arranged by the direct (deductive) approach or the indirect (inductive) approach. For letters and memos you can choose one of four basic organizational plans: The Good-News, Direct-Request, Bad-News, and Persuasive-Request Plans.[5] The first two of these use the direct approach; the last two, the indirect approach. All these plans are to be considered as flexible guides only, not as rigid patterns. Your own judgment must help you decide the best organization and content for each message.

---

[3] Adapted from *Dear Sir:*, vol. 4, no. 1, Correspondence Improvement Section, Public Relations Department, Prudential Insurance Company of America, Newark, 1962.

[4] Time-wasting retypings can be eliminated by using a machine such as the magnetic-card or magnetic-tape typewriter on which you can make changes or additions easily without having an entire report draft retyped. Text as originally draft-typed is "played out" automatically to each point of revision. Changes or additions are typed manually, and then automatic playout of the corrected copy resumes.

[5] See Chapters 15–17 for discussions on organizing reports.

Direct (Deductive) Approach

When you think your reader will consider your message is favorable or neutral information (without any obstacle), you can use the direct approach. You begin with the best news or the main idea. *After* the opening, you include all necessary explanatory details and then end with an appropriate, friendly paragraph.

The Good-News Plan and the Direct-Request Plan both have three basic parts, shown in the following brief outlines:

ORGANIZATIONAL PLANS USING THE DIRECT (DEDUCTIVE) APPROACH

Good-News Plan	*Direct-Request Plan*

1. Best news or main idea	1. Main idea
	  a. Request, main statement, or question
	  b Reason(s) if desirable.

2. Explanation
  a. All necessary and desirable details
  b. Resale material*
  c. Educational material
  d. Sales promotion material*
	2. Explanation
	  a. All necessary and desirable details
	  b. Numbered questions, if helpful
	  c. Easy-reading devices

3. Positive friendly close, including, if appropriate:
  a. Appreciation
  b. Clear statement of action desired, if any
  c. Easy action
  d. Dated action when desirable
  e. Willingness to help further
  f. Reader benefit
	3. Courteous close, with motivation to action
	  a. Clear statement of action desired
	  b. Easy action
	  c. Dated action when desirable
	  d. Appreciation and goodwill

*Resale material is usually favorable information about a product or service the reader has already bought or is planning to buy. *Sales promotion material* usually includes suggestions for additional products or services the customer may find useful.

Use the Good-News Plan for messages that grant requests, announce favorable or neutral information, or exchange routine information between companies. In Chapters 8 and 14 you will have opportunities to study numerous examples of good-news messages that are favorable replies or favorable unsolicited messages.

Use the Direct-Request Plan when the main purpose of your letter is to make a request that requires no persuasion. Chapter 7, devoted exclusively to direct requests, gives you a variety of examples for such letters and memos. Chapter 13, on collection messages, also includes direct requests.

Indirect (Inductive) Approach

When you think your reader will probably react unfavorably (negatively) to your request or information, you should not spring the main idea in the first paragraph. Instead, you will need to begin, preferably, with some relevant pleasant or neutral or reader-benefit statements and then give adequate explanation *before* you introduce the unpleasant idea(s). You will also need to be especially careful of your word choices and tone, which will influence the reader's reaction.

The Bad-News and the Persuasive-Request Plans both use the indirect approach. Notice that each has four instead of three parts. You need to take a little longer to present bad news and to persuade!

ORGANIZATIONAL PLANS USING THE INDIRECT (INDUCTIVE) APPROACH

Bad-News Plan

1. Buffer (pleasant or neutral statements to "get in step" with reader)

2. Explanation
   a. Necessary details, tactfully stated
   b. Pertinent favorable, then unfavorable, facts
   c. Reader-benefit reasons

3. Decision (implied or expressed), along with offer of additional help or suggestions

4. Positive friendly close
   a. Appreciation
   b. Invitation to future action
   c. Clear statement of action desired
   d. Easy action
   e. Dated action when desirable
   f. Willingness to help further
   g. Reader benefit and goodwill

Persuasive-Request Plan

1. Attention
   a. Reader-benefit
   b. Reader-interest theme

2. Interest
   a. Descriptive details
   b. Psychological appeals
   c. Reader benefits

3. Desire
   a. Statement of request
   b. Conviction material to help create reader's desire to grant request

4. Action
   a. Clear statement of action desired
   b. Easy action
   c. Dated action when desirable
   d. Special inducement
   e. Reader-benefit plug

The bad-news message is one of the most difficult to write because your reader will consider it unfavorable. In Chapter 9 you can study various problems and examples that handle bad-news replies and unsolicited messages.

Use the Persuasive-Request Plan when you feel that your readers will probably find obstacles and react negatively unless they are persuaded. Thus you try to show them how they or someone in whom they are interested will benefit from the granting of your request. In Chapter 10 you will find a variety of uses for this plan. In addition, Chapters 12 (job applications) and 13 (collections) also illustrate persuasive requests.

Openings and Closings

Two of the most important positions in any business message are the opening and closing paragraphs. You have probably heard the old sayings "First impressions are lasting" and "We remember best what we read last." Whenever possible, place the main favorable ideas at the beginning and ending of a message. (This advice applies also to business sentences and paragraphs.)

Later chapters of this book—when discussing specific ways to organize various business messages—include examples of good openings and closings. However, because these parts are so significant, this section gives you an overview so you can concentrate on common essentials even before studying special types of messages.

Openings

Often the opening determines whether the reader continues reading, puts the message aside for later study, or discards it. The first paragraph should preferably (1) be reader-centered, (2) make a favorable impression, and (3) orient the reader to the subject and purpose of the message. The following are some specific suggestions for good openings.

1. **Get the reader into the picture**; don't emphasize the writer. Although an acceptable opening can begin with "I" or "we," try starting with "you" or "your."

Poor:	We have your letter of June 10 and we have referred it to our legal department and they tell us we . . .
Good:	Good news! Your insurance does fully cover the entire . . .
Poor:	We are pleased to announce our new bank-by-mail service.
Good:	Now you can enjoy the convenience of banking by mail.

2. **Begin directly with the subject** when doing so does not unfavorably affect the relationship between reader and writer. This type of opening is especially effective in a good-news message or a direct request.

Granting:	You will be pleased to know that your recent application for open credit has been approved.
Good news:	Three copies of *Brown's Garden Book* were sent to you today by parcel post as you requested.
Request:	So that the account of Mr. A. B. Smith, deceased, can be transferred to your name as Executor, will you please return to us the following:

3. **Use a buffer when you must refuse the reader.** Don't spread gloom with your first words; at least get in step.

Poor: We regret your loan application did not meet our regulations and board policies for approving a loan.

Good: Your application for a loan has received our careful attention. It is evident you are doing your best to provide a comfortable home for your family.

4. **In a persuasive request** (sales letter), **get the readers' attention** by saying something that will make them want to read further. Remember that the average person dislikes a "sales letter" and will throw it away on the least provocation.

Good: A college education today is worth more than ever before—but it costs more too! The lifetime expected income for a working person without a college education is $875,000; with four years of college the expected earnings are $1,125,000. This is an income advantage of $250,000, or a return of $62,500 for each year of college. (To a customer who has children.)

Good: Like most conscientious dog owners, you know that proper food is just as important to a dog as it is to a human being. And you know, too, that if you are trying to make up a scientifically balanced diet for your dog, it involves more time and effort than you can spare. And that's where Muskies can help! (Naturally, to a dog owner.)

5. **Be positive.** Talk about the pleasant—not the unpleasant. Say what you can do—not what you cannot do. And avoid mentioning anything that you do not want the reader to think about. In the following examples the undesirable words are italicized:

Negative: We *regret* to learn from your letter of September 10 that you found a *foreign object* upon opening a can of Seacrest oysters.

Positive: Thank you for taking the time to tell us about your experience when opening a can of Seacrest oysters.

Negative: We are *sorry* that, having *closed* your savings account, your name will be *missing* from our long list of satisfied customers. We sincerely *hope* that, despite the best efforts of our fine staff, there was *no occasion* on which you felt we *failed* to serve you properly.

Positive: We noticed that you recently *closed* your savings account with us. It was our pleasure to serve you, and we want you to know that your account was very much appreciated.

6. **Keep the first sentence and the first paragraph relatively short.** The first sentence should average about 17 words and not exceed 20 or 25 words. The first paragraph should be short enough—five or six typewritten lines or less—to entice the reader to start reading. You want to introduce the good news, get in step, orient the reader—not get involved in details. Examples of over-long opening sentences are:

a.   As doing so may be of possible service to you, I take sending the enclosed on-press tear sheet of your sketch as a convenient opportunity to recall to you that the privilege—

as a biographee who has cooperated with our compilers by supplying and checking data published in it—

which you now still have to an advance of publication subscription discount of 25 percent from the regular retail price of the shortly-to-issue new edition of *Who's What in the United States*

will soon expire on the formal announcement of the actual date of publication, for thereafter the standard price at retail must, as a matter of inflexible trade usage, invariably apply. (113 words)

    b. I realize that it is the responsibility of the underwriter in the department office to determine when an insured shall be blacklisted, but Mrs. A. B. Jones has expressed the opinion that we are not doing enough of this, and certainly if we do not file a report on a man like Mr. P. P. Peterson after the trouble he has caused us, then we are making a farce of the whole reporting program, a thought with which I am sure you in the Claim Department are in full accord. (90 words)

7. **Use a peg opening** (if desirable). As in a newspaper article, tell the highlights of the story in a nutshell. The other paragraphs will then merely expand this "peg" beginning. Occasionally include the five W's (who, what, when, where, and why) in the opening.

    Good: You and your family (who) are invited to a machinery demonstration (what) next Saturday from 10 a.m. until noon (when) in the ballroom of the Statler Hotel (where). The purpose of this demonstration is to show and explain to management the operation of the latest data processing equipment (why).

8. **Avoid beginnings that merely tell readers what they told you.**

    a. Your letter of June 13, 197–, requested comments and suggestions regarding proposed working papers for the second Technical Panel, 6023.
    b. I have your letter of the 21st, in which you informed me that Mr. John Smith called on you for the first time a few weeks ago and that he appealed to you as a capable and intelligent young man.

9. **Avoid trite beginnings.** Don't "date" yourself by using worn-out expressions. Use conversational words—as if you were talking to the reader.

    Poor: *Attached herewith please find* sketches for control panels.
    Good: Attached are sketches for the control panels.

    Poor: *Please be advised that* we have written the *above-captioned* policy for this *party.*
    Good: You'll be glad to know that effective March 15 Mrs. Mary Ryan's fire and theft policy is in force.

10. **Avoid an irritating opening**, or one that might anger the reader.

    Poor: I have your letter of (date) and I can't understand why you had difficulty in seeing that our action was correct.
    Good: Thank you for your courtesy in letting us know your candid feelings regarding action on your claim.

11. **Include the date of the letter you're answering** if the date is *beneficial* to either the reader or writer—*but don't stress the date.* The first five or ten words in your opening should begin to unfold the most important idea(s).

Poor: Replying to your letter of September 16, I wish to thank you for your approval for me to use your name as a satisfied user of X product.

Good: Thank you for your approval to use your name as a satisfied user of X product.

Poor: As per your letter of October 10, we have shipped your order today by Railway Express.

Good: The five dozen Conform hats you ordered October 10 were shipped to you today by Railway Express.

12. **Make sure the opening sentence is complete.** Here are examples of incomplete openings:

   a. Reference your letter of September 4, 1971, to Mr. Yokohoma of Japan Air Lines Company, Ltd.
   b. Received your letter of September 26, 1971, concerning Ms. Helen M. Smith's application for Associate Membership in the Society of Real Estate Appraisers.

Closings[6]

The closing is more likely to motivate the reader to act as requested if it is appropriately impressive. Here you have the opportunity to bring final focus on the desired action and leave a sense of your courtesy with the reader. What you say in the closing depends upon the purpose of the letter and the ideas in previous paragraphs. The following points give suggestions for various letter situations.

1. **If you want your reader to do something, clearly ask for action**—don't hint—*and*, if possible, *show how the reader will benefit* by complying. Use specific dates when you want an answer by a certain time. Say tomorrow, next week, next month, on January 17, rather than at your convenience, promptly, immediately, soon, in the near future. In sales letters you can offer a special inducement to action by offering a special price until a certain date, for example, or by emphasizing that the supply is limited.

   Weak: I would appreciate an interview to discuss my qualifications with
   (hinting) you in greater detail.
   Better: May I have an interview to discuss my qualifications with you in greater detail?

   Poor: Please take care of this matter at your earliest convenience.
   (indefinite)
   Better: So that you can bring your account up to date before the first of the month, please send us your check for $102.20 today in the enclosed envelope.

2. **Make action easy**—especially to someone who is likely not to reply. Include an addressed card or envelope if the occasion warrants it and perhaps put a stamp on it. Be sure the reader has your phone number and knows your office hours if you are asking for a phone response.

[6] See also pp. 80–81 on completeness in closing paragraphs.

3. **End on a positive note.** Include your apologies before the last paragraph. Negative endings weaken your presentation and may give your reader the choice of two decisions (one of which can work against you). Beware especially of four words that can be negative—if, hope, trust, and may.

Negative: I regret we cannot be more helpful in the study you are making.
Positive: The best of success with your term paper. You have an interesting topic to research.

Negative: We do hope this has not caused you any inconvenience.
Positive: Thank you for taking the time to explain . . .

4. **Be friendly.** Offer to help the reader further or again if that is appropriate. Remember this is the last thought you're leaving with the reader. An abrupt, demanding, commanding, or angry remark causes unfavorable reaction.

Good: Should you have further questions concerning this procedure, Max, please write or call me. My number is 555-4422.

Poor: Send us your check today.
Good: To keep your credit in good standing, please send us your check for $123.94 today.

Poor: I am sorry you had to write two letters, but of course you realize this action wouldn't have been necessary if you had supplied all the necessary information the first time.
Good: Thank you for giving us the opportunity to explain . . .

5. **Show appreciation.** Everyone likes sincere praise when it has been earned, but don't thank in advance. As a rule, it is presumptuous to ask people to do something and then thank them for doing it before they agree to do so.

Poor: I thank you in advance for your cooperation in informing your employees of these tours.
Good: I will appreciate your cooperation in informing your employees of these tours.

6. **Avoid trite expressions.** (In the examples below, the trite expressions are italicized.)

Poor: *Enclosed you will find a self-addressed* stamped envelope *for your convenience.* (It's okay to mention the envelope, but tie it in with a more important idea.)
Good: Please fill out this form and return it in the enclosed envelope by (date).

Poor: If we can be of service to you in the future, please *do not hesitate* to contact us as *we stand ready* to serve you.
Good: Whenever we can assist you again, please let us know.

7. **When appropriate, include a final "punch" line** to remind your readers of benefit to them or to other people involved.

a. You will find, in the enclosed pamphlet, helpful details to give you added enjoyment of your new Matrix recorder.

    b. When you are ready to make your reservation, please call (number) and give me the date and flight you prefer. Then you can be sure you'll leave on the plane and day of your choice.

8. **Occasionally you might wish to add a personal note**—unrelated to the subject discussed in the messages. Such a note is appropriate as a last paragraph or preferably as a handwritten postscript.

    a. You're fortunate to be at Estes Park this month. The thermometer registered 103 at 3 p.m. here yesterday.

    b. We wish you and Rudolph a wonderful wedding on June 13 and an exciting life together.

    c. Congratulations on the excellent paper you presented to our group last week. I thoroughly enjoyed what you said about. . . .

9. **Avoid incomplete endings** (statements)—especially those that begin with an "ing" participle and end with "we are" or "I remain."

    Poor: Trusting this information will prove helpful, I remain
    Good: Please let us know if you need additional information.

    Poor: Hoping to hear from you in the affirmative, I remain (or I am)
    Good: Please sign and return the enclosed form. Then you can soon begin to enjoy the comfort of . . .

10. **Avoid a long final paragraph.** Complete your discussion beforehand. Then you can confine your ending to five or fewer lines.

11. **Stop when you have finished.** Don't tack on a worthless "hoping to hear from you soon, I remain . . ." or a statement already mentioned in the message.

    Poor: With kindest regards, we are (or I remain)

    Poor: Again, we thank you for your inquiry.
    Good: Please let us know when we can help you again.

Summary

Before transmitting any message, consider carefully the six planning steps; they furnish the basis for an effective message. Choose a direct or indirect organizational plan, depending upon your reader's probable reaction to the message. And when expressing your ideas, pay particular attention to the opening and closing paragraphs because of their strategic importance.

Exercises

1. What is your reaction to each of the openings below: Is it good, fair, or poor? Why? If there is more than one opening to consider (indicated by *versus*), which do you prefer? Why?

    a. I have your letter of the 21st, in which you inform me that our new representative, Mr. John Smith, called on you for the first time a few weeks ago and that he appeared to you as a capable and intelligent young man.

b. Jean Doe, about whom you inquired in your letter of July 6, has kept an account with us since August 13, 1955.

c. As requested in your letter of June 3, we are very pleased to enclose herewith three copies of our latest administrative directory.

versus

Enclosed are three copies of our latest administrative directory that you requested in your letter of June 3.

versus

It is a pleasure to comply with your request and enclose three copies of our latest administrative directory.

d. Our concern about your mortgage payment is not altogether selfish—we see too many people who practice paying late suddenly having to face unexpected bills, and then before they realize it, they are two months past due. Many never fully recover and eventually lose their home.

versus

You have failed to correct the existing delinquency on the above-captioned loan, and furthermore you have made no arrangements for repayment.

versus

No reply has been received to our letter of November 8, and your above-numbered loan is in default since October.

e. We are in receipt of your memo regarding the four (4) No. 1111 Cragston wheels which you say are defective.

f. Good news! After reviewing the facts again, we are issuing the desired policy.

versus

This is in reply to your letter of March 19 requesting us to review the application which was previously declined.

g. We will be pleased to consider issuing the desired policy provided you submit a new application by November 15.

versus

A new application must be submitted by November 15; otherwise we cannot consider issuing the desired policy.

h. Congratulations on making the final payment on your home improvement loan No. 4-5555. We are sure that you had a real happy feeling of satisfaction when you could finally say to yourself, "Well, that debt is paid in full."

versus

Our records show that the balance on the loan account above has been paid off.

2. What is your reaction to each of the closings below? Is it good, average, or poor? Why?

a. Thank you for coming to see us. We are sorry we could not be of service.

b. We hope our error has not inconvenienced you too much.

c. When it is convenient, please let me know your decision.

versus

I trust you will avail yourself of the opportunity of making either of these changes and when your decision is reached, notify me at your earliest convenience. I await the pleasure of your reply.

d. You are never too young or too old to begin savings for a comfortable, financially worry-free retirement. Start today by opening a Check-A-Month Retirement Income savings account at State Federal and let us help you reach a sound retirement goal.

e. We are sorry that we are unable to be of service to you and hope that we can help you at some time in the future.

f. Please let us know when we can help you again.

g. When you opened an account here, this became your bank. Please let us serve you in any way which will add to your convenience.

h. We appreciate your interest and will keep you informed of all developments.

i. Hoping to hear from you, I remain

j. Fill out this form and return to me.

k. Trust that this will answer your question.

l. We regret that we are unable to be of further assistance to you.

m. As soon as you return the four completed proposals, I'll airmail one to Chicago for prompt rating. In this way you will receive the renewal as quickly as possible.

n. Again let me repeat how sorry I am to have not answered sooner.

3. A college administrator refused to answer the following inquiry from Mr. Lukas, whose letterhead stationery states "Law Offices, Irving A. Lukas." Try to figure out what missing information caused the receiver not to reply.

Dear Sir:

Will you please be good enough to advise me of the following, either by separate letter, or, for your convenience, by inserting answers in the spaces allotted for same alongside or below my questions.

1. Does your curriculum contain a separate and distinct course solely devoted to: chain store (retail) operation, organization, and administration?
2. Is this course given to undergraduates, postgraduates, advanced students?
3. Is this course also given: in the evening_____; summer extension_____?
4. What is the duration of this course?
5. May this course be taken without any other courses?
6. What are the requirements for an applicant to qualify for this course?
7. What are the names of the professors or instructors in charge of, or teaching this course?

The above data will be greatly appreciated. Please respond to my residence listed below my signature.

4. The following set of letters consists of an inquiry from a church to a bank and a reply to the inquiry.

    a. Which organizational plan does the inquiry follow?
    b. Evaluate the opening and closing of the inquiry.
    c. What is the purpose of the reply? What organizational plan should be used?
    d. Evaluate the opening and closing of the reply.
    e. Does the reply include the ideas necessary to fulfill the purpose? Are the ideas organized effectively? What improvements can you suggest?

Inquiry

Gentlemen

We would like to request your permission to post a church directional sign (Seventh Day Adventist Church) with directional arrow at the edge of your property-parking lot on First Avenue, near Central.

This is an attractive small sign on a neatly painted post. This is very important to our church because of the fact that Central Street is probably the shortest street in (city). The size of the sign is about 15" x 15".

The exact location of the sign will be specified to us as soon as we bring written permission from you from our office to Mr. Smith at City Hall. He will then advise us as to how and where to place the sign so that it will give a good appearance and not interfere with either traffic or your business operations.

Please indicate your permission hereon and return your reply to this office as soon as possible.

We appreciate your cooperation.

Reply

My dear Reverend Glouster

Thank you for your recent letter requesting permission to post a church directional sign in the corner of our parking lot on First Avenue near Central.

Unauthorized parking in the lot during our business hours has been a continuous problem for our bank. The parking lot already has several signs posted for different purposes. An additional sign in this corner of the parking lot could cause the public confusion regarding the use of the parking area. We, therefore, find it necessary to decline your request.

Your parishioners are welcome to continue to use this parking lot on Saturdays and at other times that you have church services which do not conflict with the business hours of the bank. We appreciate and wish to continue the cordial relationship with you and members of your church.

5. The following reply is from the Blank Oyster Company, Anytown, to an out-of-state customer who complained that she found two "ugly specimens" in her favorite brand of canned oysters.

    a. What is (should be) the purpose of this message?
    b. What organizational plan should be used?

c. Evaluate the opening and closing paragraphs and the explanation.
d. Point out the portions that are "resale" material and "apology." Are they well placed? Discuss.
e. Do you think the letter helps restore the customer's confidence? Why?

Thank you for giving us the opportunity to reply to your experience with Blank Brand oysters. We appreciate your thoughtfulness in writing.

Your enclosure turned out to be small pieces of the root section of a common seaweed which grows on the oysterbeds in great abundance. We are stumped how this substance could stick to an oyster through three successive washings and inspections in the canning process and still escape detection by our packers. But it did, and we are sorry that it happened.

It is of little help to explain that this harmless vegetable substance became totally sterile when the oysters were cooked in the can. You did exactly the right thing when you wrote about the incident.

Today we are sending you by parcel post two cans of Blank Brand oysters with our compliments. You are the discriminating consumer we want to please.

6. An office supply firm sends the following letter to parents of graduating high school seniors who have completed college entrance requirements. (For parents of a daughter, the word "son" is changed to "daughter.")

a. What is the purpose of this letter?
b. What organizational plan does the message use?
c. Evaluate each paragraph in terms of the suggested organizational plan for this type of letter.

Dear Mr. and Mrs. (Name)

With high school graduation just four weeks away, you may be searching for an appropriate present for your son. The Butler portable typewriter is a practical gift for the college-bound student, one which will provide him with continuous benefits throughout his college years.

Your son will find that a typewriter, like paper and pen, is a necessary part of his college equipment. Nowadays, instructors usually demand that written assignments be typewritten. Typed reports are neat and legible, and they accurately reflect student effort. Furthermore, a typewriter can work to reduce the time pressure students experience by enabling them to complete notes and outlines more rapidly than they could by hand. And, of course, a portable typewriter is especially well-suited for campus use simply because it's portable.

Unlike other machines, the Butler portable combines the quality features of an office typewriter with the storage and transportation convenience of a portable. Your son will find that the Butler copy-set dial will allow him to make up to 10 clear carbons; that the extra large carriage will enable him to type on oversize paper; and that changeable type bars will permit him to include a variety of technical signs and symbols in his typing. You'll find these and many additional Butler features fully described in the booklet enclosed.

The Butler portable is a value in price as well as features, for it costs just $100. And, if you like, we'll be glad to arrange the payment plan that best suits your budget.

For your convenience our offices will remain open to nine each week night from now until May 28. Ample parking is available on the west side of the building. We would enjoy meeting both of you and showing you why more people choose a Butler portable than any other make--and why it is a most useful and timely gift for your son.

7. Collect two or more business letters (that you or friends or relatives have received)—each preferably 100 words or more. If possible, try to get messages that are individually typed—not processed form letters. Study the body of each message for the following:

   a. Purpose—is it clear?
   b. Organizational plan—does the message use the right plan?
   c. Are opening and closing paragraphs appropriate?
   d. Notice the length of paragraphs. Do the first and last each have fewer than seven lines? Are other paragraphs under ten lines in length? What improvements, if any, are needed?

Be sure to keep these letters after this assignment is completed, because you'll be using them again and again for other purposes. For example, you'll check them for trite expressions, clarity, correctness, and other areas as you study these particular topics.

Business Writing Principles I

To help you choose the right words and sentences for your letters, memorandums, reports (and oral communication), you need to consider—after the planning steps—certain specific writing principles. Commonly called "the seven C's," they are: correctness, conciseness, clarity, completeness, concreteness, consideration, and courtesy. This chapter covers the first three C's: correctness, conciseness, and clarity. Chapter 5 discusses the remaining four C's.

Correctness

Some people have a distorted concept of the correctness principle. They think it comprises only proper grammar, punctuation, and spelling. The truth is that you can be correct grammatically and mechanically in every respect and still insult or lose a customer.

In its broadest sense, the term *correctness*, as applied to a business letter or report, means the writer should:

1. Use the correct level of language
2. Include only accurate facts, words, and figures
3. Maintain acceptable writing mechanics
4. Apply correctly all other pertinent C qualities[1]

Use the Correct Level of Language

As Figure 4-1 shows, there are three overlapping levels of language.[2] The first two—formal and informal language—are both correct; but they are quite different from one another, have different uses, and should not be interchanged.

The formal level of language is used for writing a scholarly dissertation, a legal document, or other material for which formality is expected. The expressions used are often long, unconversational, and impersonal—just what the term "formal" implies.

In contrast, the informal level refers to the language of business—the language of letters, reports, newspapers, and other business communications. Such language is alive and ever-changing. Instead of formal words, you will use short, well-known, and conversational words, as the following list illustrates:

Formal	Informal	Formal	Informal
anticipate	expect	endeavor	try
ascertain	find out	interrogate	ask
conflagration	fire	procure	get
deem	think (believe)	remunerate	pay
domicile	home	terminate	end
edifice	building	utilize	use

---

[1] See also Appendix B for check points on correctness.
[2] These levels overlap because of our ever-changing language. Some words once considered substandard have moved into the informal level, and some once informal words are now acceptable on a formal level.

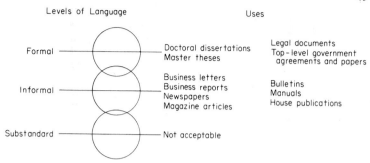

Figure 4-1

Phrases and sentences should likewise be expressed in conversational, informal language. For example, compare the stiff, wordy expressions in the *Formal* column below with the shorter *Informal* expressions.

Formal	*Informal*
Will attain the age of eighteen years.	Will be eighteen years old.
We will institute a mail search.	We will ask the post office to send out a tracer.
We thank you in anticipation of this courtesy and assure you that it will be a pleasure to serve you in a similar manner.	I'll appreciate your helping us. Let me know when I can return the favor.
Inform me of your intentions as to the liquidation of this balance.	Let me know when you can settle this account.
Should the supply of stickers sent you not be sufficient to meet your requirements, application should be made to this office for additional copies.	Pete, if you need more stickers, ask for them.
In order to substantiate our desire to accommodate our guests, we would appreciate your cooperation to anticipate your credit requirements before departure.	Please let us know in advance if you want us to cash a check as you leave.

The following poem by Enid C. Stickel provides a humorous example of how people try to put on airs.

Readability Gap

Colleges aren't schools,
They are learning institutions;
Problems don't have answers,
They have viable solutions.
People don't spend money,
They re-allocate resources.
Newsmen don't use tipsters,
They rely on informed sources.

Speakers don't make speeches,
They give oral presentations.
Bosses don't set quotas,
They just indicate objectives.
Workers don't take orders,
Though they implement directives.

Machinery can't break down,
But components can malfunction.
A court does not command
It just issues an injunction.
Programs don't have failures,
They have qualified successes.
And jargon doesn't hurt you—
It just constantly distresses!

The third level of language—substandard—is the one you want to avoid, because people generally don't accept it. If you use words on this level in writing (or in speaking), your reader(s) will begin to question your ability to use good English. Here are a few examples:

Substandard	Acceptable	Substandard	Acceptable
ain't	isn't, aren't	haven't got	don't have
between you and I	between you and me	in regards to	regarding
		irregardless	regardless
can't hardly	can hardly	nohow	anyway
hadn't ought	shouldn't	should of	should have

The following sentences illustrate the three levels of language discussed above—formal, informal and substandard:

Formal: Although Item 21 is enumerated in the report, the writer has ascertained that it is currently not in the organization's inventory or in the writer's possession.

Informal: Although Item 21 is listed in the report, it's not in our stock now and I don't have it either.

Substandard: Irregardless of the report that item ain't on our shelves now, and I haven't got it either.

Include Only Accurate Facts, Words, and Figures

Doubtless you already know how important absolute accuracy is for written messages. One erroneous digit (for example, $65,000 instead of $75,000) can make a difference of thousands of dollars. Even small errors of a few cents can be annoying to customers and undermine goodwill, as various examples in this text will show. And a wrong figure in an account number muddles up records and leads to untold problems.

Perhaps you recall reading about a telephone directory error involving two firms in a city of over a half million persons. The directory mixed up the phone number of one firm with that of a competitor. To make matters worse, each of these firms happened to have a department head with the same name. You can imagine the confusion that telephone-listing error caused! It was also costly for the telephone company because the firms demanded that the company individually inform all customers and potential customers of the correct numbers—at its own expense.

To be sure of the accuracy of your facts, you should verify all statements before writing and again before you sign or approve the message. Of course, you also need to be up-to-date on laws that affect your organization. Guessing or assuming that you are right can be costly. Just because a certain fact was true about a customer last year—or even last month—does not assure it is true now, as the following case illustrates:

> Mr. Henry Simson sent in a claim for medical benefits to his insurance company. In turn, the correspondent handling the case wrote back to Mr. Simson, saying, "We are pleased to enclose a check for $277.54 for benefits due you because of your confinement at the Mountain View Hospital." Unfortunately this correspondent shouldn't have sent the check because that hospital was not certified as a full "general" hospital, a requirement under the terms of Mr. Simson's policy. Innocently, Mr. Simson cashed the check.

> A month later the mistake was discovered and a notation made on Simson's file to the effect that no future payments were to be made because of confinement to the Mountain View Hospital.

> Two months afterward Mr. Simson again sent a claim for medical benefits because he once again had been a patient in that same hospital. The person who handled the claim this time consulted Simson's file, found the notation, and wrote a letter refusing the claim.

> However, this refusal was wrong because between Simson's two admissions the Mountain View Hospital had been certified as a full "general" hospital. Had the correspondents at the insurance company checked all the facts, such a mix-up would not have happened.

The good business writer must be continually alert to accuracy because of changing rates, regulations, laws, and conditions both locally and nationally.

You should also realize that, like most things in life, English is alive and ever-changing. Even the dictionaries can't keep up with its fast pace, but they can usually help you choose correct words to convey your intended meaning. Below are a few of the many words that are often confused in usage.

a, an	Use *a* before a word that begins with the consonant sound or long "u" sound. Use *an* before a word that begins with a silent "h" or a vowel sound.
agree to, agree with	You *agree to* a plan and *agree with* a person. One thing *agrees with* another thing.
all ready, already	*All ready* means entirely ready; *already*, previously.
advise, tell	You give counsel when you *advise*, and you inform without counseling when you *tell*.

a.m., A.M.	*a.m.* is easier to type and seems less noticeable than the capital letters. Save A.M. and P.M. for headlines and tables.
amount, number	Whenever you count the units, use *number*. *Amount* refers to bulk, weight, or sums.
anxious, eager	*Anxious* implies worry, whereas *eager* conveys keen desire.
between, among	As a rule, *between* involves two people or two groups; *among*, three or more.
claims, says	*Claim* as a verb means "to ask for what is due one": He claimed his baggage at the station.
continual, continuous	*Continual* means to occur frequently. *Continuous* means without stopping.
data	You can safely use a singular verb (data *is*) with this word when you are considering all the facts as a unit.
different from different than	Although both are acceptable, *different from* is preferred.
effect, affect	In business usage only *effect* is a noun; it means result, condition or influence. Both words are verbs—to *effect* is to bring about, to *affect* is to influence.
fewer, less	If you can count the items, use *fewer*; *less* refers to amount or quantity.
healthful, healthy	*Healthful* means giving health; *healthy* means having good health.
imply, infer	*Imply* means to insinuate, or suggest; *infer* means to conclude. A writer *implies*, whereas the reader *infers*.
lay, laid, laid lie, lay, lain	A person or a rug *lies* on the floor, but a person *lays* the book on the table or *lays* oneself on the floor. If you can substitute "place(s)," use the proper tense of *lay*.
loan, lend	Although these words are interchangeable as verbs, some people prefer to use lend as a verb and loan as a noun.
party, customer	A *customer* is an individual or person. *Party* is a legal term for an individual or a group of people.
please, kindly	As a rule, use *please*. *Kindly* means "in a kind manner." If you say, kindly tell me, you are really asking someone to tell you something in a kind way.
principal, principle	*Principal* means "chief" or "main." Whenever you can substitute "rule," use princi*ple*. In all other instances, use princi*pal*.
provided, providing	*Provided* means "if"; otherwise use *providing*.
we, I	*We* refers to the organization; *I* refers to the individual.
which, that, who	*That* refers to persons or things; *who* to people; *which* only to things.

Maintain Acceptable Writing Mechanics

This principle of correctness includes effective use of the parts of the letter and memo (covered in detail in Chapter 6) and of reports (shown in Chapters 15-17). *Mechanics* also includes acceptable spelling, sentence structure, punctuation, capitalization, and appearance. Envelopes, too, must be correctly addressed; if not, they may cause enormous wastes. See, for example, pages 125 and 126.

This book does not attempt to teach you grammar and the numerous other components of mechanical correctness. Years of training in English throughout grade school, high school, and college should have taught you to write grammatically acceptable sentences and paragraphs. But if you need review on the dangling participle, numbers as words or figures, punctuation, and other details that seem to plague writers, you'll find helpful suggestions in Appendix B. And if you need help on the parts of speech and sentence structure, be sure to consult an excellent, up-to-date grammar book.[3]

One of the most common weaknesses in writing mechanics is the inability to spell correctly many everyday words—such as convenience, questionnaire, receive, accommodation, stationery, and dessert. Business executives and customers expect you to spell correctly and may begin to question your overall ability if you misspell—especially such simple words. Don't embarrass yourself the way one graduate did when he stated in his application letter that he had a Batchelor of Arts degree. The receiver encircled the misspelled word with a red pencil and pinned the letter on the company bulletin board for every passerby to see.

The following letter is an example of a communication that led the receiver (Lt. Booser) to doubt the ability of the sender (a motel manager) and even assume that carelessness is the reason for many mistakes that occur in the motel office.

```
Dear Lt. Booser

I'am writing this letter telling you how sorry I'am about the mistake
this office and myself made concerning our business tranaction on May
30th and the letter wich was send to you.

Please accept my apology for the mistake made to you.  Your bill was
paid in full, but the two checks tranaction were mis-led.  My nite
cashier remembers very clearly that you paid the bill, but my nite
man did not sign the bill paid, which was place on the bookkepper's
deck.

Again I'am sorry about this situation, and will you please come in
the next time you are this way, and wish to thank you personally
about the whole deal.
```

---

[3]You will find any of the following helpful: Erwin Keithley and Margaret Thompson, *English for Modern Business*, Richard D. Irwin, Inc., Chicago, 1972; Arno Knapper and Lola Newcomb, *A Style Manual for Written Communication*, Grid, Inc., Columbus, Ohio, 1974; Glenn Leggett, C. David Mead, and William Charvat, *Handbook for Writers*, Prentice-Hall, Inc., Englewood Cliffs, N.J., 1970; Porter G. Perrin, *Handbook of Current English*, 1968, and *Writer's Guide and Index to English*, 1972, both Scott, Foresman and Company, Glenview, Ill.

If you are one of the many educated men and women who are better able to solve complicated business problems than spell correctly, you can take two precautions: refer to a dictionary often, and hire a top-notch assistant who's a whiz at spelling! English spelling does have many inconsistencies, as the following anonymous poem entitled "Pluralistics" highlights:

Pluralistics

We'll begin with a box and the plural is boxes,
But the plural of ox should be oxen not oxes.
Then one fowl is a goose but two are called geese,
Yet the plural of mouse should never be meese.
You may find a lone mouse or a whole set of mice,
But the plural of house is houses not hice.
If the plural of man is always called men,
Shouldn't the plural of pan be called pen?
If I speak of a foot and you show me your feet,
And I give you a boot would a pair be called beet?

If one is a tooth and whole set are teeth,
Why should not the plural of booth be called beeth?
Then one may be that and three would be those,
Yet hat in that plural wouldn't be hose.
And the plural of cat is cats and not cose.
We speak of a brother and also of brethren,
But though we say Mother we never say Methren,
Then the masculine pronouns are he, his, and him,
But imagine the feminine, she, shis, and shim.
So English I fancy, you all will agree.
Is the funniest language you ever did see.

Correctness in writing is important because it influences the reader in various ways. In the first place, the reader *expects* you to write correctly, and you create a bad impression when you abuse the language. In the second place, a poorly constructed sentence, a misspelled word (especially a customer's name!!), incorrect punctuation, and faulty diction distract the reader's attention. When the letter is opened, you want the reader to concentrate on the message—not on the blunders. Finally, incorrectness frequently results in ambiguity, misleading statements, or misunderstandings, as illustrated below:

Mr. Jones visited the school yesterday and lectured on "Destructive Pests." A large number were present.

From a newspaper column on advice to teenagers: "Keep jewelry to a very minimum—and leave errings to your older sisters."

Sign in a New York drugstore: We Dispense with Accuracy.

Pierce Eugene Puckett, B.A., M.A.—Assistant Professor and Aching Head, Department of Education.

Enclosed are your contracts and Gary Greenwood in triplicate.

Your Memorial Day speech will be followed by the firing squad.

You should always watch for the little things in writing—for correctness in grammar and mechanics—as well as for the big things. And never leave the mechanical principles of correctness solely to your secretary. Once you sign your name or initials to the message, you assume the responsibility for everything on the page—including correctness.

For a truly correct message, remember to also include—in addition to the accuracy elements already discussed—all the other pertinent C qualities that are covered in the following pages.

Conciseness

Many business executives believe that conciseness is the most important writing principle, because a wordy message requires more time (and money) to type and to read. Conciseness is saying what you have to say in the fewest possible words without sacrificing *completeness and courtesy*.

To achieve conciseness—the opposite of wordiness—try to observe the following suggestions.[4]

1. Omit trite expressions.
2. Avoid unnecessary repetition and wordy expressions.
3. Include only relevant facts . . . with courtesy.
4. Organize effectively.

This section discusses the first three points. Succeeding chapters cover organization.

Omit Trite Expressions

Trite expressions (also called hackneyed words, clichés, stereotyped expressions, deadwood, whiskered words) are usually longer than necessary and have become stiff, formal, and relatively meaningless because of overuse.

How or why does one begin using trite expressions? If you had to write a letter at work and didn't have the training you are acquiring now, you'd probably begin by studying the wording of messages in existing files—and probably the writers of those old letters used the same language, full of colorless, worn-out expressions.

The left column below lists some of the many clichés that should be avoided in business letters, memos, and reports; the expressions in the right-hand column are generally shorter and certainly more conversational.

Not this	*But this*
above-captioned loan	this loan, Mr. Smith's loan
advise (unless you mean to counsel)	tell, inform
enclosed herewith	enclosed
enclosed please find	enclosed is
it has come to my attention	I have just learned (or) Mr. Jones has just told me

---

[4] See also Appendix B for check points on conciseness and for additional trite expressions.

Our Miss Smith	Miss Smith, our credit manager
please be advised that	(4 wasted words)
please don't hesitate to call upon us	please write us
pursuant to your inquiry	as you requested
under separate cover	by June 1, tomorrow, separately, by parcel post, by Railway Express
the undersigned (the writer)	I (or me)

A letter loaded with trite expressions can give the reader an unfavorable impression of the sender. Compare, for example, these sentences:

Trite: In accordance with your request of recent date, we are enclosing herewith our cashier's check in the amount of $103.60, representing a withdrawal of said savings account No. 12345.

Improved: It's a pleasure to fulfill your request of July 19 by enclosing our cashier's check for $103.60. This amount represents a withdrawal from your savings in Account 12345.

Some expressions—for example, *for your convenience, per,* and *for your information*—can be trite in some situations and acceptable in others, as shown below.

Trite	*Acceptable*
Enclosed is an envelope *for your convenience.*	During December we're open Monday through Friday until 9 p.m. *for your convenience* in late afternoon and evening shopping.
As *per* your request, I am glad to tell you . . .	This car was speeding 80 miles *per* hour at the time of impact.
For your information, I wish to state that . . .	This material is *for your information* only. There is no need for you to consider any action.

Avoid Unnecessary Repetition and Wordy Expressions

Sometimes repetition is necessary for emphasis. But when the same thing is said two or three times without reason, the letter becomes wordy. The following letter from a business executive to a firm the company had dealt with for five years shows unnecessary repetition at its worst:

Will you ship us sometime, any time during the month of October, or even November if you are rushed, for November would suit us just as well, in fact a little bit better, 300 of the regular 3" by 15" blue felt armbands with white sewn letters in the center.

Thanking you to send these along to us by parcel post, and not express, as express is too stiff in price, when parcel post will be much cheaper, we are

The writer took 81 words to say what is said in 25 below:

```
Please ship parcel post, before the end of November, 300
regular 3" by 15" blue felt armbands with white sewn letters
in the center.
```

Here are three additional ways to eliminate unnecessary repetition:

1. Use pronouns rather than repeating nouns: Instead of "The East Coast Fire Insurance Company, Inc." again and again, use "it" or "they."
2. Use a shorter name after you have mentioned the long one once: Instead of "The Inter-Allied Johnson Manufacturing Company," use the Johnson Company."
3. Eliminate unneeded articles, prepositions, and conjunctions.

The evidence we have ...	Evidence we have ...
He said *that* he agreed	He said he agreed
The date *of the* policy	The policy date
and	Omit "and." Use a semicolon or a period.

Some expressions are wordy "gobbledygook," with unnecessary words that waste the reader's time. Notice how examples in the following *Concise* column save words without changing meanings:

Wordy	*Concise*
a long period of time	a long time
along the line of (salary)	about (salary)
at this time	now
consensus of opinion	consensus
due to the fact that	because
during the time that	while
during the year of 1971	during 1971
endorse on the back of this check	endorse this check
for a price of $200	for $200
for the purpose of	for, to
for the reason that	since (or because)
from the point of view of	as
have need for	need
in accordance with your request	as you requested
in due course	soon
in many cases	often, frequently
in most cases	usually
in order to	to
in some cases	sometimes
in spite of the fact	although
in (for) the amount of $200	for $200
in the city of Chicago	in Chicago
in the event that	if
in the neighborhood of	about
in view of the fact that	because
under date of	dated

Conciseness contributes to emphasis. By eliminating unnecessary words, you help make important ideas stand out, as in the following sentences. [Notice that the concise sentence eliminates from half to two-thirds of the unnecessary words in the sentence. (Figures in parentheses are the number of words.)]

Wordy: I am writing you at this time to enclose the postage paid appointment card for the purpose of arranging a convenient time when we might get together for a conference. (30)

Concise: Will you please return the enclosed card and name a convenient time for an interview? (15)

Wordy: The picture which is enclosed will give[5] you an idea of the appearance of this home. (16)

Concise: The enclosed picture illustrates[5] this home. (6)

Wordy: We hereby wish to let you know that we fully appreciate the confidence you have reposed in us. (18)

Concise: We appreciate your confidence in us. (6)

Wordy: Resolved, that appropriate steps be taken by the American Medical Association to encourage recruitment into the health professions of health-oriented personnel released from the armed services, that the cooperation of allied health professions and vocations be sought in this effort, and that such action be referred to the Board of Trustees and its Council on Health Manpower for implementation.[6] (60)

Concise: Resolved, that the Council on Health Manpower work with other health organizations to attract former military medical corpsmen into health careers. (21)

Include Only Relevant Facts . . . with Courtesy

A third way to be concise is to include only those ideas that develop the purpose of the message. How long should a message be? Just long enough to do the job effectively. The relatively short letter about armbands was quite wordy. Yet a two- or three-page letter can be concise. Furthermore, a short letter may be brief but not concise— if it lacks completeness and courtesy.

Given below are two extremes. The first example shows how writers can be so concise that they become absurd. The second is an example of excessive wordiness.

Example 1

Once upon a time, a fish dealer was planning a new sign for his store. It was to read *Fresh Fish for Sale Here Today.* A critical friend, however, had some suggestions:

"You don't need the word 'here,' " he said. "People can see where the store is. And you don't need 'for sale' either. They know you're not giving things away."

The friend continued: "And how about 'fresh fish' and 'today'? Do you want customers to think this is the only day you have fresh fish? That you sell old fish

---

[5] Whenever possible, talk in the present tense.
[6] Eddie Miller, "Quotables," *Civil Service Journal,* October–December 1970, p. 23.

on other days? Take out 'fresh.' And while you're at it, take out 'today.' People know you wouldn't be open if you weren't selling something today.

"You might as well drop 'fish' too. Anyone within half a mile can smell what you're selling."[7]

The moral of our fish story? Write concisely but don't destroy your message.

Example 2
The following very wordy letter is from a person who graduated from a university the previous year, and has had difficulty since graduation in finding a satisfactory place in the business world. As you read this letter to the Placement Office in the School of Business Administration, try to figure out why he's having so much trouble.

The university Placement Office has sent me at periodic intervals a form inquiring as to my current employment status. As you may recall from our discussion last spring I was most desirous of making a favorable change in vocational locale. After following up several recommendations made by your office (Goodwin, etc.) I was unable to negotiate an immediate change, and upon receiving suave assurances of rapid promotion from my superiors promptly regressed into the torpid complacency which characterized my thinking upon graduation. However my present intention to move is more than a harbinger of that most fragrant of seasons but rather stems from a feeling of disillusionment and inadequacy with my vocational environment.

[7] From *Effective Letters Bulletin*, New York Life Insurance Company, Spring 1967, p. 1.

```
May I once again prevail upon you to assist me in this undertaking
by informing me at your convenience of any job opportunity for
which you think I would be well suited.  As indicated in my last
reply to your office, I no longer look to accounting as my forte
but instead am seeking a selling situation which is both challeng-
ing and remunerative.

Thank you for your patience and understanding in this matter.  You
may reach me at 555-1234 during the day or at 564-4321 in the
evening.
```

Few employers would risk hiring this person because he might talk and write to customers in the same way he did in this letter. The reader or listener reacts negatively toward him because he uses pompous words and irrelevant material.

In contrast to this unfavorably pretentious message, the message could be informal and relevant if it read as follows:

```
Will you please tell me about any sales opening which is both
challenging and remunerative?  I am no longer interested in an
accounting job.

You can reach me at 555-1234 during the day or at 564-4321 in
the evening.  I shall appreciate your suggestions.
```

The major causes of irrelevancy include:

1. Not sticking to the purpose of the message.
2. Including information obvious to the reader—such as regurgitating at length what the reader told you.
3. Using big words to make an impression.
4. Beating around the bush—not coming to the point.
5. Using excessive adjectives (good writing uses concrete nouns and verbs that show action, but avoids excessive numbers of adjectives and adverbs).
6. Being excessively polite.
7. Writing long, involved introductions.
8. Not limiting the scope of the material.
9. Including too much explanation.
10. Not revising the first draft of a long, complicated message.
11. Including unnecessary background information.

As stated before, the effective concise letter must be complete and courteous. If completeness and courtesy are omitted, the result is abruptness—not conciseness—as the following examples illustrate.

Abrupt letter

```
Have you emptied your safe deposit box?  If you have, sign the
enclosed cancellation form and return it with the keys to the box.

If you are using the box, send us your check for $6 to pay the
rent from September 15, 1975, to September 15, 1976.
```

Concise letter

```
This is just a reminder that the rent on your safe deposit box
has expired.

If you wish to use the box another year, please send in your check
for $6.  You'll then be paid up until September 15, 1976.  If you
have no further use for the box at this time, just sign and return
the enclosed form with the keys.

Whenever we can help you with any of our other customer services,
please let me know.
```

It is true that the concise letter just given requires more words than the brief, abrupt message. But the end result is what counts—how the reader reacts. A reader might respond to the first sentence of the abrupt letter mentally by saying it's none of your business, but would not respond that way to the other message. Also, the "please" in the revision helps keep the reader from feeling he or she is being ordered to do something. Always keep in mind that the reader expects sufficient facts and courteous treatment.

In summary, conciseness is a writing principle that the business executive considers especially important. It saves time, and time is—or should be—scarce to anyone who spends a large part of the work-day dictating and reading letters, memos, and reports.

Clarity

Clarity involves most of the other principles of business writing—especially correctness, conciseness, completeness, consideration, and concreteness. Clarity means getting across your message so the reader will not misunderstand what you are trying to convey.

You want your reader to interpret your words with the same shades of meaning that you have in mind. And accomplishing that goal is difficult because, as you know, individual experiences are never identical; and words have different meanings to different persons.[8]

Here are some specific ways to help make your writing clear:

1. Choose words that are short, familiar, conversational.
2. Construct effective sentences and paragraphs.
3. Achieve appropriate readability.
4. Include examples, illustrations, and other visual aids when desirable.

Choose Short, Familiar, Conversational Words

The section on conciseness has already emphasized that good writing eliminates trite and wordy expressions. Omitting these expressions usually helps not only conciseness but also clarity. Furthermore, when you have a choice between a long word and a

---

[8]See Chapter 2 and the check points on clarity in Appendix B.

short one, use the short word, since you can usually be more sure that your reader will understand it.

Winston Churchill was a masterful writer who knew the secret and effectiveness of using simple words. After the disaster at Dunkirk in 1940, he (as Prime Minister of Great Britain) reported to Parliament in a message heard around the world. Below is a small part of what he said:

> We shall defend our island, whatever the cost may be. We shall fight on the beaches. We shall fight on the landing grounds. We shall fight in the fields and in the streets. We shall fight in the hills. We shall never surrender.

He said what he meant and his message came across loud and clear to millions of people. But what if he had used language like the following?

> We shall oppose the aggressors through the optimal mobilization and implementation of all existing defense-oriented modalities.[9]

Certainly, those words would be long forgotten.

Besides being short, the words you use should be familiar to your reader. Remember that your reader is busy and doesn't have time to run to the dictionary for meaning. Instead, the reader will guess what you mean (sometimes incorrectly) or will disregard some or all of the message.

Here is a story that involves clarity. A plumber wrote the National Bureau of Standards to tell them hydrochloric acid is good for cleaning out clogged drains. (Before you go any further into the story, visualize the plumber. Assume you don't know him or have never exchanged correspondence. It is a pretty good guess he isn't a college graduate—maybe he didn't finish high school. But he probably is a good plumber—at least conscientious—because he's writing to the Bureau to tell them something he thinks will help them.)

In reply to the plumber's message, a technical specialist of the Bureau wrote:

> The efficacy of hydrochloric acid is indisputable, but the corrosive residue is incompatible with metallic permanence.

The plumber then wrote to thank the Bureau for agreeing with him—when, of course, the Bureau was actually disagreeing with him. Sensing the plumber didn't understand, another member tried to set the man straight by writing:

> We cannot assume responsibility for the production of toxic and noxious residue with hydrochloric acid and suggest you use an alternative procedure.

Again the plumber thanked the Bureau. Then in desperation the head of the department wrote:

> Don't use hydrochloric acid. It eats hell out of the pipes.

[9] Eddie Miller, "Quotables," p. 23.

The moral of this story is to write on—not above or below—the level of the reader's understanding.

Avoid professional jargon. Your professional vocabulary contains words you've been accumulating since you began your business career, and these words are quite clear to you. Furthermore, your colleagues easily understand you when you use technical terms; and it's perfectly okay to use them when talking or writing to people who also use them. But avoid this professional jargon when you talk or write to a person who is not acquainted with such words. Notice that the sentences below (with the technical words in italics) are much clearer in the revision.

1. The *conversion privilege* of this term policy *terminates* June 5, 1977.

versus

Your right to change this policy to permanent insurance ends June 5, 1977.
2. *Days of grace* under this policy *expire* May 15, 1977.

versus

The extra 31 days allowed you to pay your premium without interest end May 15, 1977.
3. To *reinstate* your policy will require *proof of insurability* . . . .

versus

To get your policy back in good standing, you must (1) pass a satisfactory physical examination, (2) . . . .

If you must use technical words that the reader may not understand, define them briefly and clearly. If you don't, you'll confuse, embarrass, or irritate the reader, and perhaps be forced to explain later. Here are a few technical words and the synonyms that a layperson is more likely to understand:

Technical jargon	*Expressions familiar to the layperson*
abstract	history of the property
accrued interest	unpaid interest
annual premium	annual payment
assessed valuation	value of property for tax purposes
charge to your principal	increase the balance of your loan
compound dividends	dividends earned on your deposits and added to your account, which then earns more dividends on the dividends and deposits
conveying title	signing and recording a deed
easement for ingress and egress	agreement allowing passage in and out
escrow account	reserve account for taxes and insurance
hazard insurance	fire and windstorm insurance protection
interest compounded quarterly	interest added to your account every three months
maturity date	final payment date
per diem	daily

A politician—using "big, unfamiliar words to fool little people"—helped defeat the opponent by telling audiences:

> Are you aware that this candidate is known all over Washington as a shameless extrovert? Not only that, but this man is reliably reported to have practiced nepotism with his sister-in-law and he has a sister who was once a thespian in wicked New York. He matriculated with co-eds at the University, and it is an established fact that before his marriage he habitually practiced celibacy.

To help make your business writing clear, use short, familiar, conversational words.

Construct Effective Sentences and Paragraphs

Arranging your words in well-constructed sentences and paragraphs is also an important task that requires adaptation to your reader. Generally, the *average* length for sentences should be about 17 to 20 words; for paragraphs, about four to five lines in letters and eight to nine lines in reports. Even more important than length is quality. Aim for unity, coherence, and emphasis.

Unity. In a sentence—whether simple, complex, or compound—unity means that you have one main idea, and any other ideas in the sentence must be closely related to it. "I like you" and "George Washington died in 1799" obviously don't belong together. Also, in a complex sentence, the main idea belongs in the main (independent) clause.

In a paragraph, unity likewise means that you have one main idea or topic. It should be expressed in a topic sentence, usually at either the beginning or the end of the paragraph. (Sometimes it is somewhere near the middle.) The following sentence from an insurance letter is confusing primarily because the main point is not emphasized clearly. Isn't the revised paragraph—with topic sentence at the beginning—clearer?

> We have been advised that the allotment for the above-numbered policy was filed effective April 1976, but inasmuch as the premium due March 1, 1976, of $1.91 has not been remitted and inasmuch as allotment payments are not applicable to premiums due and payable in advance of the effective date of allotment, we hereby request that you contact the insured directly and request payment of this premium due.

Revision:

> Allotment payments can be applied only to premiums falling due after the effective date of allotment. Since the allotment did not become effective on this policy until April 1976, it cannot pay the March 1976 premium of $1.91. May we ask you to collect it?

In most business writing the preferred position for the topic sentence is at the beginning, where it receives the best emphasis. The sentences that follow it contain details to help develop the main idea. However, if you think that your main topic will be considered unfavorable or unclear by your reader, you may be wise to place the supporting details first and then lead up to the topic sentence at the end.

Coherence. In both sentences and paragraphs coherence is the quality of hanging together in such a way that the intended meaning is clear. It involves showing the reader the relationships within a sentence, as well as pointing the way from one sentence to another. Place every modifier as close as possible to the word it is supposed to modify; otherwise, the meaning may be unclear.[10]

Unclear:	The car is in the garage that he smashed.
Clear:	The car that he smashed is in the garage.
Unclear:	Being a top accountant, I am sure you can help us.
Clear:	Being a top accountant, you can surely help us.
	or
	As you are a top accountant, I am sure you . . .
Unclear:	Walking into your office, a bus hit the east wall.
Clear:	Walking into your office, I saw a bus hit the . . .
Unclear:	She wanted a policy for her house that cost $100 a year.
Clear:	For her house she wanted a policy that cost $100 a year.

Lack of coherence in a classified newspaper ad caused embarrassing problems for the poor fellow mentioned below.

For sale: R. D. Smith has one sewing machine for sale. Phone 543-1111. Call after 7 p.m. and ask Mrs. Kelly who lives with him, cheap.

Naturally, the paper was more than willing to clear things up. Next day's retraction read:

We regret having erred in R. D. Smith's ad yesterday. It should read: For sale, R. D. Smith, one sewing machine for sale. Cheap. Phone 543-1111 and ask for Mrs. Kelly who lives with him after 7 p.m.

Still trying gamely, the paper printed another clarification:

R. D. Smith has informed us he has received several annoying phone calls because of an error we made in his classified ad yesterday. His ad stands corrected: For sale, R. D. Smith has one sewing machine for sale. Cheap. Phone 543-1111 after 7 p.m. and ask for Mrs. Kelly who loves with him.

Final version:

I, R. D. Smith, have no sewing machine. I smashed it. Don't call 543-1111; the phone has been taken out. I have not been carrying on with Mrs. Kelly. Until yesterday, she was my housekeeper.

[10]See also Dangling Participles in Appendix B.

Emphasis. The quality that gives force to important parts of your sentence is *emphasis.* You can emphasize by position, space, and repetition. For instance, important ideas deserve the most important position in the sentence—at the beginning or at the end; they should not be buried in the middle. You can also emphasize important ideas by giving them extra space or by repeating significant words or phrases. Too much repetition, however, can result in a wordy sentence; too little repetition or the use of indefinite words such as "it" and "there is" can result in an unclear sentence.

Unclear: Our association recommends Mr. Johnson's article on credit, but *it* says that in *it* he makes *it* seem easier than *it* is.

Clear: Our association recommends Mr. Johnson's article on credit, but says that in the article he makes credit seem easier than it is.

Unclear: (In a letter promoting a laundry's special dry cleaning process that practically eliminated ironing by the customer) When your clothing is returned *there is* very little left to iron. . . . We don't mangle your clothes by machinery; we do *it* carefully by hand.

Unclear: It is necessary, for technical reasons, that these warheads should be stored upside down. That is, with the top at the bottom, and the bottom at the top. In order that there may be no doubt as to which is the bottom, and which is the top, for storage purposes it will be seen that the bottom of each warhead has been labeled with the word "TOP."

Achieve Appropriate Readability

Besides aiming for qualities of unity, coherence, and emphasis, you should adapt your business writing so that its readability will be appropriate for your recipient's general education level.

Among several guides that measure readability is Robert Gunning's well-known Fog Index.[11] It is based on two factors: length of sentence and percentage of hard words. By using the Fog Index, you can determine the educational level of your writing— whether it is for a reader who has an equivalent of a ninth-grade education (first-year high school), twelfth-grade (senior in high school), thirteenth-grade (first-year college), and so on.

To find the Fog Index of a passage, take the following three simple steps:

1. *Determine average sentence length*
   Use a passage of words (beginning preferably with the first word of a paragraph) in consecutive sentences which end nearest the 100-word level. Divide the total number of words in this passage by the number of complete thoughts. (A simple or complex sentence has one complete thought; a compound sentence contains two complete thoughts.) Your quotient gives the average sentence length.

2. *Figure the percentage of "hard" words*
   Count the number of words of three syllables or more in the passage, but don't count words:

[11] Robert Gunning, *The Technique of Clear Writing*, McGraw-Hill Book Company, Revised Edition, 1968, p. 38. Used with written permission of author, copyright owner.

   a. That are capitalized
   b. That are combinations of short, easy words (like bookkeeper, butterfly)
   c. That are verb forms made three syllables by adding *ed* or *es* (like *created* or *trespasses*)

3. *Add the average sentence length and the percentage of hard words and multiply by 0.4.*

This readability formula is especially useful when you want to determine if "Average Americans" will clearly understand what you are writing to them. Who are these persons? They are the cross section of all the people in the United States. They have finished the eleventh grade—maybe even graduated from high school. They are probably typical customers. Therefore, your level of writing should be no higher than the twelfth grade—perhaps even lower. Whether highly educated or not, everyone appreciates easy reading. If your level of writing to this average person is on the thirteenth level or higher, your message runs the danger of being ignored or misunderstood.

As you read the following portion of a letter, try to guess its readability level. (The underlined words have three or more syllables.)[12]

Thank you for your nice letter of March 1, 1976. Since you will be moving back to Pomona in the future, we look forward to meeting you then. To answer your questions <u>regarding</u> a savings plan, we have two types for your <u>consideration</u>.

1. <u>Regular</u> passbook savings yield 5 1/2 percent <u>dividends</u> compounded <u>quarterly</u>. You can make <u>deposits</u> and <u>withdrawals</u> by mail, with postage paid by us both ways.

2. Our Savings Certificates yield 6 1/4 percent <u>dividends</u>. <u>Minimum</u> amount for <u>opening</u> this type account is $5,000 and then upward in amounts of $1,000. They can be six-month or twelve-month Certificates and are <u>automatically</u> <u>renewable</u> unless you advise us to the <u>contrary</u>. (110 words)

This example has 110 words in the first 7 sentences, or an average sentence length of 15.7 words. The 13 "hard" words (underlined) are 11.8 percent of the 110 words. From these figures, you can compute the Gunning Fog Index—11, the educational level of a high school junior.

Words in example	110
Sentences	7
Average sentence length (110 ÷ 7)	15.7
Percentage of hard words (13 ÷ 110)	11.8
Total	27.5
Multiplier	0.4
Grade level (Fog Index)	11.0

[12] These additional guides from Robert Gunning may help you: (1) Count anything as a word that has space around it. Thus *March 1, 1976*, is 3 words; *one thousand dollars* is 3 words; *5 1/4* is 2 words; *five and one quarter* is 4 words; but *5¼* is 1 word; *twelve-month* is 1 word; *$5,000* and *$9,752,461* are each 1 word; if spelled out, the latter figure is 10 words. Exception: Do not count the numbers (I, II, 1, 2, 3,) or alphabetic letters (A, B, a, b, c,) that precede items or paragraphs. (2) Count hyphenated words as polysyllables only if one part is a word of three syllables or more. For example: *seventy-two* is 4 syllables. (3) Do not regard numerals as polysyllables regardless of pronunciation. Example: $987,652,431.50 is 1 syllable.

In contrast to the letter paragraphs shown above, the following from a letter to certificate depositors has a Fog Index of nearly 27—fifteen school years beyond a high school graduate:

> RESOLVED, That in <u>accordance</u> with the <u>provisions</u> of Section 545.3-1 of the rules and <u>regulations</u> of the Federal Savings and Loan System, and the charter and by-laws of this Association, there be and hereby is <u>established</u> this date a <u>separate</u> class of savings accounts <u>evidenced</u> by Separate Certificate <u>designated</u> as Class "C" which accounts shall be in a <u>minimum</u> amount of $10,000 and in <u>additional</u> <u>multiples</u> of $1,000. Said Class "C" accounts shall have earnings for the <u>period</u> <u>beginning</u> October 1, 1976, and ending December 31, 1976, and maintained for a <u>continuous</u> period of at least six months, declared <u>payable</u> at the rate of 6 1/4% per annum. (108 words)

Words in example	108	
Sentences	2	
Average sentence length (108 ÷ 2)		54.0
Percentage of difficult words (14 ÷ 108)		13.0
Total		67.0
Multiplier		0.4
Grade level (Fog Index)		26.8

Though average sentence length should be about 17 to 20 words, a pleasing variety of length is desirable. You can use a range of, say, from 3 to 40 words; but when a sentence exceeds 40 or 45 words, ask yourself how you can rewrite it into more than one sentence. Also, if *all* sentences are short (for instance, under 10 words) the result is monotonous primer-like language—choppy and undesirable.

Mr. Gunning considers his Fog Index a "simple warning system"—not a cure-all for any writing problem. He wants you to use this formula "to check to see if your writing is in step with that which has proved easy to read and understand."[13]

Readability formulas are popular and helpful in improving clarity, but there are limitations and cautions. First, a writer must be careful not to use too many simple words and short sentences, for the writing would be monotonous, elementary, choppy. Second, some "long" words really aren't as difficult as some two-syllable words (for example, *employee* versus *avid*). Also, you must count the same word as many times as it appears in the passage. Finally, a message with crude, harsh, unethical, insulting words may still get a desirable Fog Index. Used with discretion, however, the formula will serve the purpose of a *guide* to the readability of letters, reports, books, magazine articles, or any other business writing.

Include Examples, Illustrations, and Other Visual Aids, When Desirable

When you have a complicated and/or lengthy explanation to make in a letter or a report, you'll often find that you can improve the clarity of your message by giving your

---

[13] Robert Gunning, "The Fog Index after Twenty Years," *Journal of Business Communication*, vol. 6, no. 2, p. 3, Winter 1968.

reader an example, an analogy, or an illustration. Furthermore, visual aids—such as headings, tabulations, itemizations, pictures, charts—are definite aids to clarity and easy reading.

Whenever you have more than one set of figures, you'll make them much clearer to your reader if you itemize, tabulate, or set them off in some attractive way. Throughout this text—especially the section on reports—are examples of writing that uses illustrations and visual aids to help clarify the material for the reader.

In summary, make your writing clear by using words that are familiar to your reader. Watch the quality and length of your sentences. Organize paragraphs and your entire message so that the purpose is clear. Itemize and tabulate figures to make them stand out clearly. And give your reader helpful examples with appropriate easy-to-read headings whenever you need to explain complicated material.

Exercises

1. Revise the following sentences so that the reader can grasp the correct meaning clearly and quickly. If necessary, use more than one sentence.
    a. Although working full time on an outside job, Tom's grades remained good.
    b. Thank you for your letter concerning the ten pianos we received by airmail this morning.
    c. When only four years old, this customer's mother died.
    d. (From the mayor of a city to the county engineer):
        I have reviewed the plans of Metro, their ability to finance, and in some areas, realizing a great number of years may elapse, because of financial conditions and the build-up of areas, before construction is warranted of sanitary trunk lines for sewers, I think it is very appropriate at this time that the county enter into a study and possibly use their ability given to them under the County Services Act of operating lagoons and serving areas that can develop only if sanitary sewers are constructed.
    e. (From one insurance company to another insurance company):
        Frankly, the information we have while it may disclose some contributory negligence on our assured's part which, of course, is questionable, we still feel that your assured had he not been driving at the high rate of speed that he was could have swerved to his right and avoided our assured's vehicle but due to the fact he was coming down a hill at such a tremendous rate of speed with no control over his car and struck our assured, there was enough room to the right of your assured to have turned slightly and, therefore, avoided the accident.
    f. Working in a grocery, several professors chat with him daily.
    g. (To a retail store from a customer):
        On December 26 I returned these pajamas to the same store and after I was unable to find the correct size which I wanted in the same style, I requested a cash refund from the clerk who told me that the store didn't give cash refunds but that I could have a credit slip to apply to a later purchase.

2. Check the Fog Index of two pieces of business writing—one that you consider easy to read and one that is difficult. Then tell the class how the Fog Index of each agrees with your readability level. Use examples from this list:
    a. Letter from a company to a customer
    b. Annual report

c. Magazine read by the masses or members of a certain profession
d. *Wall Street Journal*
e. Article on front page of your daily newspaper
f. A report or a textbook

3. Assume you are writing to the average citizen. What synonyms for the following words would be better understood?

contingent   validity
rescind   default
accelerate   concur
aggregating   discrepancy
accrue   allegation

4. Assume the following words appear in the letters and reports that your secretary has typed for your signature. Without the help of any source, determine which words are misspelled and correct the errors. Then check all words (in a dictionary or in class) to see how many you had right.[14]

1. accomodation
2. aquainted
3. assistance
4. attatched
5. attornies
6. batchelor's degree
7. benefited
8. brosure
9. compliment (meaning supplement)
10. catalog
11. childrens'
12. colledge
13. consede
14. concensus
15. corps
16. congradulate
17. convience
18. correspondant
19. defendent
20. descendant
21. desert (meaning cake)
22. develop
23. dissadvantage
24. disatisfaction
25. envelop
26. excellant
27. existance
28. Febuary
29. heighth
30. incessent
31. insistance
32. interupt
33. it's (possessive)
34. knowlege
35. labled
36. manageing
37. mispelled
38. occured
39. oppurtunity
40. payed
41. paralel
42. personnel
43. pertinent
44. preceed
45. prefered
46. proceedure
47. proceed
48. questionaire
49. recieve
50. referance
51. referred
52. recind
53. reccomodation
54. resistence
55. salesbility
56. seperate
57. sargeant
58. servicable
59. stationary (paper)
60. writting

[14]If you need a handy pocket-size dictionary to help you spell correctly, try *20,000 Words*, compiled by Louis A. Leslie, Gregg Division, McGraw-Hill Book Company, New York, 1972.

5. Revise the following wordy sentences.

   a. You will note when you study the cost of stationery that the expenditure of stationery gradually and steadily increased for 1968, 1969, 1970, and 1971.
   b. I have your letter of October 14 and wish to say that we'll be glad to give you a refund for the blouse you bought here last week.
   c. Permit me to take this opportunity to call your attention to the fact that we have brought your account up to date.
   d. For your information we are attaching hereto a carbon copy of the letter sent to Mr. Ava Knocash under date of April 25.
   e. Please find enclosed herewith a copy of the report which is 15 pages in length.
   f. I wish to take this opportunity to sincerely acknowledge receipt of your order for one bushel of Washington Red Delicious apples and thank you for placing it with our company.
   g. Please be assured that we are now rechecking and reviewing all of our specifications as it is our earnest and most sincere desire to be certain and for sure that this machine gives you satisfaction and good service in every possible way in the future.
   h. In addition, will you please permit me to state in this letter that we will welcome any suggestions or comments that you may have at any time if you think of any methods for the improvement of our service to our customers.

6. Encircle the correct choice of "a" or "an" before each entry in the following list.

a an hotel	a an heroic effort
a an honorary degree	a an hour
a an unit	a an heir
a an historical event	a an union
a an honest opinion	a an unanimous decision
a an unique method	a an humble opinion

7. Correct the errors in the following message from a savings association to a real estate corporation:

   In rgard to your letter of the fifteenth, let me explain our policy on our Certificates of deposit. Your certificate comes due on November 9, 197_. At this time the interest check will be dispersed as you indicated at the time of your initial deposit and the certificate will be automaticly renewed unless you give us instructions to the contrary.

   In your letter you asked that the certificate be "rolled over for another 30 days." As I have explained our certificates have a life of 6 months, if you want the certificate renewed it will automaticaly be done. If you wish the certificate to be dispersed please contackt us prior to the experation date.

8. Assume that the following letter is a reply to a customer who asked for a copy of the free booklet the company had advertised on television a month ago. Is this reply concise or abrupt? Improve it in every way you can.

   This is to inform you we cannot comply with your request regarding booklets. We're out of stock and in the process of revising same.

9. Below is a wordy memo from the auditor of disbursements in Seattle to a colleague, who is the auditor of disbursements in Los Angeles. Both people work for the same organization. A *rear support* is a metal holder for a large ledger or dictionary you usually find only in libraries. Your job is to revise this monstrosity. The revision should be no longer than four or five sentences.

We previously sent you copies of our correspondence with the Albert M. Hunter, Inc., relative to the Hunter Wage Charts. Particular attention is directed to our comments relative to the rear supports 4 1/2 inches in length, which in our opinion were too long, in our letter dated April 8. As a result of our comments, Albert M. Hunter, Inc. developed rear supports 2 1/2 inches in length which they furnished us to replace supports 4 1/2 inches in length.

On July 19 we sent you by express 26 sets of the rear supports 2 1/2 inches in length. We are of the opinion that the rear supports 2 1/2 inches in length are a considerable improvement over the rear supports 4 1/2 inches in length and have accordingly replaced the rear supports 4 1/2 inches in length on the Hunter Wage Charts in use by us with rear supports 2 1/2 inches in length.

We assume that you will also wish to replace the rear supports 4 1/2 inches in length on the Hunter Wage Charts in use by you with the rear supports 2 1/2 inches in length. If you make the replacement, please return the rear supports 4 1/2 inches in length to us in order that we can return them to Albert M. Hunter, Inc., in accordance with their request.

For your information, the rear supports 2 1/2 inches in length to replace the rear supports 4 1/2 inches in length were furnished by Albert M. Hunter, Inc., free of charge with the understanding that the rear supports 4 1/2 inches in length would be returned to them.

If you prefer to continue using the rear supports 4 1/2 inches in length, please return the rear supports 2 1/2 inches in length to us in order that we can return them to Albert M. Hunter, Inc.

10. Assume the following letter is addressed to the president of Purple Shield, an honorary activity group on your campus. It is from Mrs. Gertrude Buffington, a stranger to the president. Revise it wherever necessary. Place the purpose near the beginning and apply especially principles of correctness, conciseness, and clarity to the rest of the letter.

Dear Henry

I got your name from the office in the Student Union Building the other day as being President of the Society of the Purple Shield.

I am at present, president of the Inter-Fraternity Mothers Conference and at a recent luncheon we had an honoured guest, Mrs. James P. Manson, whose husband sparked the founding of I.F.M.C. in 1943. We had a most pleasant visit and during the conversation she mentioned she had also actively supported and was interested in Purple Shield and that many years ago there was a Mothers Club or some such organization of this group. She was once the treasurer and she said she has a small amount of money which she would like to turn over to some sponsored group of Purple Shield. In other words, she was the treasurer or custodian of this money for the P.S.

Mothers club which apparently is non-existent nor do I hold much hopes for its reincarnation. But I think if the matter were presented correctly to her, she would give this group these funds or if necessary perhaps a group of Mothers of Purple Shield could meet together once a year or something. I think this money is over $300--more around $350 I believe--well, anyway, if you need the money or a small scholarship could be made in the name of James P. Manson or something of a memorial--Perhaps Dr. Fish, your faculty advisor could suggest what you should do. It seems a shame to have the money just sitting uselessly in the bank when there is a need for it or it could be working for the good of someone. You may use my name when and if you discuss this matter with Mrs. Manson.

11. Revise the following letter—from a college book store to a small manufacturer. Though the purpose is stated at the beginning, the letter rambles and seems artificially friendly. Improve it wherever desirable.

Once again with your kind permission, will you please make for us four armbands, blue felt, white sewn letters and white chain stitching as per the attached layout, and if you please Mr. Cowell, we have marked on the layout for the operator to kindly make these up just as we show them, and not change them. What we mean by that, in a most friendly way, this is a little order which you made up for us a few days ago, and the operator, thinking it would be perfectly all right, transposed the position of some of the lettering, so that they were not uniform all the way, and too, inadvertently on one or two of them left one or two of the letters out, and we are not complaining about that at all, all we want to say sincerely is that we are grateful for your taking care of these little things for us, and we are not registering any complaint at all, for we are using them for samples and do not expect you for one moment to do this again without your regular charge, for you make nothing on it, and you are just like us, we know, doing this to satisfy a customer, we being a customer, for other things, and if we weren't we would not have the nerve to ask you to make these, so therefore, if you please, this is for a bunch of women and they are a little bit more particular then men, and if the operator will just follow what we have laid out everything will be fine.

Thanking you so much, and with best wishes and kindest regards, we are

12. *Exercises on choice of words:* Choose the word or words that should be used in each sentence listed below. (For choice of words in some sentences you might need to consult a dictionary or grammar book in addition to the rules for word usage in this chapter.)

 a. While attending school, (a, an) university student might run (a, an) one-person business and still be (a, an) honor student.
 b. This act will not (effect, affect) my confidence in you.
 c. I am (anxious, eager) to (tell, advise) you that you are correct.
 d. Make your customers feel (its, it's) a pleasure to do as they suggest.
 e. This (party, customer) is (well known, well-known) in town.
 f. I (shall, will) be glad to handle the order (providing, provided) the firm is willing.

g. We have a large (quantity, amount, number) of suits on hand.
h. It will be (all right, alright) if you come later.
i. The dissension (between, among) the five departments has been settled.
j. The man (who, which, that) was crossing the street was struck by a car (who, which, that) Mr. Smith was driving.
k. Will you please see that (the undersigned, the writer, I) (is, am) notified of any changes in prices.
l. We sold (fewer, less) fans last month.
m. We had (already, all ready) received the dress when your letter arrived. I am (already, all ready) to write this customer.
n. Your rug should (lie, lay) (smooth, smoothly) on the floor. Please (lay, lie) the files on my desk.
o. The (principal, principle) officer of this company is Ms. Jones. The (principal, principle) of honesty should be evident in our letters. Now that you've been paying on your house for three years, how much (principle, principal) have you accumulated? The (principle, principal) of the school criticized the boy because he didn't know the (principal, principle) river in the United States is the Mississippi.
p. Of the two plans, the second is (least, less) expensive.
q. Do you know (who, whom) the manager promoted yesterday?
r. The credit for this sale goes to (you, yourself).
s. The chief engineer and (myself, I) inspected the factory.
t. I never knew anyone could be so slow in answering when a person wrote to (them, him/her).
u. Be courteous to (whomever, whoever) comes to your desk.
v. A large number of bills (is, are) outstanding.
w. The large number of employees (prevent, prevents) us from adhering to this suggestion.
x. We understand (you, your) wanting to be a sales representative.
y. Enclosed (please find, is) my check for ($100.00, $100).

5

Business Writing Principles II

The preceding chapter discussed three of the seven business writing principles: correctness, conciseness, and clarity. To give your writing content, force, and friendliness, you should also apply the remaining C principles: completeness, concreteness, consideration, and courtesy.

Completeness

Your business message is "complete" when it contains everything the reader needs for the reaction you desire. To achieve both the specific purpose of your message *and* the long-term purpose—maintaining goodwill, you need to consider carefully just how much information is enough for each reader. Remember that communicators differ in their mental filters; they are influenced by their backgrounds, viewpoints, needs, attitudes, and emotions.

Completeness is necessary for several reasons. First, complete messages are more likely to bring the desired results without the expense of additional messages. Second, they do a better job of building goodwill. (Incomplete messages can lead to ill will, lost customers, and hence decreased sales income and profit.) Third, complete messages can help avert costly lawsuits which may result if important information is missing. Finally, papers that seem inconsequential can be surprisingly important if the information they contain is complete and effective. In high-level conferences, in courtrooms, and in governmental hearings, the battle often centers around an ordinary-looking message that becomes important because of the complete information it contains.

As you strive for completeness, keep the following guidelines in mind:

1. Answer all questions asked.
2. Give something extra, when desirable.
3. Check for the 5 W's and any other essentials.

Answer All Questions Asked

Whenever you reply to an inquiry containing one or more questions, answer all questions—stated and implied. A prospective customer's reaction to an incomplete reply is likely to be unfavorable. The customer may think the respondent is careless or is purposely trying to conceal a weak spot. In general, "omissions cast suspicions," whether you are answering an inquiry about your product or recommending a former employee for a new job. If you have no information on a particular question, you must say so clearly, instead of omitting an answer. If you have unfavorable information in answer to one or more questions, handle your reply with both tact and honesty.

In the three situations described here, ineffective communication developed from messages in which the writers failed to answer all the questions.

Situation 1
A distributor of model trains, when replying to an inquirer's letter, answered only three out of seven questions. Because they were unnumbered and somewhat buried in five long paragraphs, the respondent apparently overlooked or disregarded four

questions. The reply, which was both incomplete and unfriendly, caused the distributor to lose the business and goodwill of a potential customer.

Sometimes, in answering an inquiry, you need certain specific information from the inquirer. It is then a good idea to list the needed details on a reply form which the inquirer can fill out and return to you. In this way both your answer and that of your respondent will be complete. In situation 2, had the bank supplied a reply form, the desired sale could have been completed with four, instead of eight, messages: the first inquiry; the bank's reply with an enclosed form to be filled out; the owner's authorization (on the form); and the bank's final liquidation notice and check.

Situation 2
On August 8 the owner of mutual-fund stock wrote to a New York bank's investment department that he wanted to sell his shares. He asked, "Just how does your bank want me to authorize this sale?" and he received the following reply.

```
If you wish to terminate Account #99998 and liquidate the shares held
by this bank, we need a letter of instructions signed by both you and
your wife just as the account is registered.  Please be sure to give
us the name of your fund, your account number, and to whom proceeds is
to be mailed.
```

This letter brought from the customer a second letter, signed by both himself and his wife. They included the fund name and account number and ended with this statement, "Please sell our 37 shares effective this date (August 23, 197_) and send proceeds to us." On August 28 they received the following telegram:

RE MLF FUND A/C 9999 UNABLE ACCEPT INSTRUCTIONS TO LIQUIDATE ON A SPECIFIC DATE FORWARD NEW SIGNED INSTRUCTIONS.

After asking for clarification from a local broker, the Browns wrote essentially the same letter as their second; however, this time they omitted the words "effective this date." A week later they received from the bank another request—this time to include in their reply both the name *and address* to which the proceeds were to be mailed! (The bank had not *asked* specifically for the address, and the customer assumed the proceeds would be mailed to their home address.) The next day they wrote their fourth letter. Finally—On October 8, two months after their original question—the Browns received a formal notice of liquidation with an attached check for the proceeds. However, during the delay, the price of the stock had fallen considerably and they lost money on their sale.

The replies in situations 1 and 2 were incomplete because the respondents omitted the answers to one or more questions or omitted important information in an explanation that answered a question. The next situation is an example of an incomplete response that *entirely* ignores the writer's real request. Be sure to avoid such gross carelessness in answering inquiries.

Situation 3

An insurance policyholder had read and studied her policy but could not understand the meaning of a particular paragraph. She inquired about its meaning and in doing so quoted the entire paragraph in her communication. In response to her letter she received one from the company informing her that if she would refer to paragraph 4, page 3, of the policy (the one she quoted!), she would find a complete explanation. (The correspondent added that the paragraph was clear and unambiguous.)

Give Something Extra, When Desirable

In writing letters you must sometimes do more than answer the customers' specific questions. They may not know what they need, or their questions may be inadequate.

For example, suppose you are president of the regional business executive's league for your industry and receive the following inquiry from an out-of-town member:

> I think I'd like to attend my first meeting of the League, even though I'm not acquainted in your city. Will you please tell me where the next meeting will be held?

If you answered only this one question, your letter would be incomplete. Realizing that your reader is a newcomer to your city and to your League's meetings, you should include in your reply a welcome plus such needed details as directions for reaching the building; parking facilities; day, date, and time of meeting; and perhaps also the program for the next meeting. Your message will then have the "something extra" that a reader really needs and appreciates.

Sometimes the "something extra" is a detailed explanation instead of a mere brief statement. The last paragraph of letter 1, below, contains an invitation that is meaningless for any new depositor who does not know what "facilities" are at his or her disposal. Letter 2, on the contrary, clearly explains the services offered and thereby makes the invitation meaningful. (If a writer can enclose a descriptive brochure, the letter can be shorter and still complete if it merely mentions the services and refers to the enclosure for details.)

Letter 1

Incomplete letter to a new savings depositor.

```
Thank you for the confidence you have shown us by the account you
recently opened.

All our facilities are at your disposal, and any time we can be of
service please feel free to call upon us.  Our appreciation is best
expressed by our being of service to you.
```

Letter 2

Revised, complete letter to the new savings depositor.

```
Thank you for the confidence you have shown in First Federal by the
savings account you recently opened.  Our goal is to make all our
services to you both pleasant and helpful.
```

Among the conveniences and services available to you at First Federal, you may be especially interested in these:

10-DAY GRACE PERIOD each month on your deposits means that your savings earn 5% interest from the 1st day of any month if they are deposited by the 10th day of that month.

SAVE-BY-MAIL POSTAGE-PAID SERVICE helps you to add to or withdraw from your account entirely by mail.

SPECIAL PURPOSE ACCOUNTS such as Christmas and Vacation Clubs enable you to save for a special purpose.

MORTGAGE LOANS help you to buy, build, or refinance a home or to borrow for property repairs and improvements.

FREE CUSTOMER PARKING is provided in the lot north of our office. The teller stamps your parking check, entitling you to free parking while doing business here. Office hours are 9:30 a.m. to 3:00 p.m. weekdays except for Friday when the doors remain open until 6:00 p.m.

You are most welcome to come in whenever we can assist you. Please consider this association your financial headquarters for your savings and borrowing needs.

Check for the 5 W's and Any Other Essentials

Another way to help make your writing complete is to answer the "5 W" questions— *who, what, where, when, why*—and any other essentials, such as *how.*

This method is especially useful when you write requests, announcements, or other informative messages. For instance, to order (request) merchandise, make clear *what* you want, *when* you need it, to *whom* and *where* it is to be sent, and *how* payment will be made. To reserve a hotel banquet room, specify type of accommodations needed (*what*), location (*where*), sponsoring organization (*who*), date and time (*when*), function or event (*why*), and other necessary details (*how*).

For some letters—especially those that bring bad news or make an unusual request— answering the question "why" may be important. Remember this general communication principle:

A message that answers the question "Why?" is more likely to motivate the receiver to take the desired action than one that does not explain why. But not everyone is motivated for the same reasons.

When you must say "no" to customers' requests for a refund or ask them to pay a higher bill than they expected, they will probably be less angry if you explain *why*, from *their* viewpoint.

To sell a product by mail, you need also to answer these 5 W's and the H (*how*). The example below shows the embarrassment and needless expense that can result when an omitted essential fact makes the action request of a sales letter incomplete. In fact, in this case a costly sales campaign failed because of incompleteness.

The sales department of a retail company decided to sponsor a direct-mail campaign to 100,000 prospects. The sales letter was to be personalized with a typed inside address and personal salutation. A special price offer was to be good for a limited time only. The letter ended with this request:

So that you can enjoy the advantages of (product) at this special price, send your order--but no money--today. Just take these two easy steps--

Write your initials in the upper right-hand corner of this letter.
Then mail it back to us in the addressed, stamped envelope that is enclosed.

However, to save the expense of having typists insert the 100,000 inside addresses and personal salutations, a budget-minded official requested that the entire message be printed and that all inside addresses be omitted. And the salutation was changed to the general, printed, "Dear Customer." The result was that the company received over 11,000 of the letters back, but no one had the slightest idea to whom the 11,000 initials in the upper right-hand corners belonged! Because all inside addresses had been omitted, the letters were incomplete for the action requested; they failed to answer the questions *who* and *how*.

An attempt to find out from whom the orders had come would have necessitated the expense of a second letter to the same 100,000 people and the embarrassment of admitting the serious slipup. Instead, the decision was made to abandon the entire campaign. No one knows the resulting disappointment and perhaps ill will caused among the 11,000 prospects who received neither a reply nor the product they had ordered. In addition, the company wasted the cost of the first 100,000 letters and lost the profits from 11,000 orders.

To make your *action request* complete, try these suggestions concerning the 5 W's and the H:[1]

1. *What and Who?: Clear statement of the action you desire your reader (or someone else) to take.*
   Should the reader: Phone your office for an appointment? Sign a card or a document? return it? to whom? Come to your office in person? Send you certain details? (Be sure you get the respondent's name and address, too.) What questions should the reader (or someone else) answer?
2. *How and Where?: Easy action.*
   Include your phone number (and area code) and extension if you want the reader to phone you. If you are often away from your desk or office, you might mention the best times the reader can reach you.
   Enclose a form (card, order blank, questionnaire, document) and an addressed reply envelope (perhaps with postage paid) if you want the reader to furnish information or sign and mail something.
   Give complete instructions regarding *where* and *how* if you don't include a form and/or an envelope.
   Enclose an envelope large enough to hold and protect the contents whenever you want the reader to return something bulky, confidential, and/or valu-

[1] See pages 39 to 41 for further suggestions regarding closing paragraphs.

able (a document, a check). Have your secretary address the envelope and, if desirable and possible, affix the necessary postage.

State your office hours and location if you want the reader to come to you in person. When, if at all, is your office open evenings? Do you have a free parking lot? Where?

3. *When?: Dated action.*

Name the date (and the time, if pertinent) whenever you need the reply by a certain time. Tactfully state the reason you need it then. (Perhaps you need to meet a printer's deadline, or the reader's opinions are necessary for a speech you are giving at a certain meeting.)

4. *Why?: Special inducement to act by a specified time.*

When appropriate, mention some benefit(s) the reader will gain by prompt action. A reader-benefit plug in the ending paragraph(s) is a stimulus to action.

Concreteness

Writing concretely means being specific, definite, and vivid rather than vague and general. The following guidelines should help you write concretely:

1. Use specific facts and figures.
2. Put action in your verbs.
3. Choose vivid, image-building words.

Use Specific Facts and Figures

Whenever you can substitute an exact fact or a figure for a general word to make your message more concrete and convincing, do so.

Vague, general, indefinite	*Concrete and convincing*
These *brakes* stop *a car* within a *short* distance.	These *Goodson power brakes* stop a *2-ton car* traveling *60 miles an hour*, within *240 feet*.
Please send your check for the *full amount soon*.	Please send your check for *$753.50 on or before June 5*.
A *quick* shave.	A *3-minute* shave.
Our product has won *several* prizes.	(Name) product has won *first prize* in *four national contests within the past three years*.
Your savings earn *high compound* interest.	Your savings earn *5 percent* compound interest (*added to your account every three months*).
After traveling an *enormous distance*, the lunar module landed *almost on time*.	After traveling *240,000 miles* and circling the moon *18 times*, the lunar module landed *within 1 minute 17 seconds* from the preplanned time.
This computer reproduces sales *campaign letters fast*.	This computer types *1,000 personalized 150-word campaign* letters *in one hour*.

Often vague, general words are "opinion" words, which may have different meanings to the sender and the receiver. For instance, how fast is fast? A bicycle rider and a racing car driver will have different meanings for this word. How large is large? A person reared in a village of 150 people may consider a population of 15,000 large; yet to a native of a city with 10 million inhabitants, 15,000 is very small. The list that follows gives words which can lead to uncertainty, misunderstanding, or confusion.

a few	low	nice	slow
a small number	many	quick	small
high	more	several	soon
large	most	short	tall

Using plenty of examples, prefixed by phrases like "for instance," "for example," "such as," also helps make your writing concrete as well as clear. (You will notice that this book uses this technique often.)

In certain cases it is, of course, permissible—and even desirable—to use general expressions. Exceptions to the "facts and figures" rule occur:

1. When it is not possible to be specific, for you may not have nor be able to get definite facts or figures.
2. When you want to be diplomatic. Thus, instead of writing, "We have sent you *five* notices of your overdue payment," you may be more tactful (to a usually prompt paying customer) by writing "We have sent you *several* reminders of this. . . ." Also, when refusing credit to a potential consumer, you may feel it is more diplomatic to give a general rather than a specific reason.
3. When you want to allow the reader to form his or her own opinion, or when exact figures are unimportant, as in: "A *few* (or *many*) of our employees attended the parade."

Put Action in Your Verbs

Strong verbs can activate other words and help make your sentence definite. To write strong sentences, you should (1) use active rather than passive verbs and (2) put action in your verbs instead of in nouns or infinitives.

Active versus Passive Voice. When the subject *performs* the action which the verb expresses, the verb is said to be in the *active* voice. In "Mr. Jones *repaired* the computer" the subject (Mr. Jones) did the repairing; the verb *repaired* is active.

When the subject benefits from or otherwise *receives* the action the verb expresses, the verb is said to be in the *passive* voice. In "The computer *was repaired* by Mr. Jones" the verb *was repaired* is passive.

A passive verb has three characteristics: (1) The subject doesn't do the acting; (2) the verb consists of *two or more* words, one of which is some form of "to be" (is, is being, am, are, was, were, will be, has or have been, had been, or will have been); and (3) the word "by" is expressed or implied ("by whom" or "by what"). The examples below show the difference between passive and active voice.

Passive	*Active*
Tests *were made* by us.	We *made* tests. (OR: Tests *showed* that . . .)
A full report *will be sent* to you by the supervisor.	You *will receive* a full report from the supervisor. (OR: The supervisor *will send* . . .)
An account *was opened* by Mrs. Simms.	Mrs. Simms *opened* an account.
It *is suggested* that . . .	We *suggest* . . .
It *is contemplated* by the committee . . .	The committee *thinks* . . .
Your figures *are checked* by the research department.	The research department *checks* your figures.

Generally you should use active rather than passive verbs because active verbs help make your sentences more:

1. *Specific.* "The Board of Directors decided" is more explicit than "A decision has been made."
2. *Personal.* "You will note" is both personal and specific; "It will be noted" is impersonal.
3. *Concise.* The passive requires more words and thus slows both the writing and reading. Compare "Figures show" with "It is shown by figures."
4. *Emphatic.* Passive verbs dull action. Compare "The child ran a mile" with "A mile was run by the child."

Occasionally, however, you may prefer the passive voice instead of the active, as in the following situations:

1. When you want to avoid personal blunt accusations or commands. "The July check was not included" is more tactful than "You failed to include . . ." "Attendance at the meeting is required" is less harsh than "You must attend. . . ."
2. When you want to stress the object of the action. In "Your savings account is insured up to $40,000" you have intentionally stressed "your account"—not the firm that does the insuring. Also "you are invited" is better than "We invite you."
3. When the doer isn't important in the sentence. In "Three announcements were made before the meeting started," the emphasis is on the announcements, not on who gave them.

Action in Verbs, Not in Nouns. Seven verbs—*be, give, have, hold, make, put,* and *take* (in any tense)—might be designated as "deadly" because the action they introduce is hidden in a "quiet noun." The examples below show how these "deadly" verbs can be changed to action verbs which shorten the sentences.

Action hiding in a "quiet noun"	*Action in the verb*
The function of this office is *the collection* of accounts and the *compilation* of statements.	This office *collects* accounts and *compiles* statements.
Mr. Jones will *give consideration* to the report.	Mr. Jones will *consider* the report.
The contract *has a requirement* that....	The contract *requires* that....
They *held* the *meeting* in the office.	They *met* in the office.
He *made* his first installment *payment.*	He *paid* his first installment.
The chairperson *puts* her *trust* in each committee member.	The chairperson *trusts* each committee member.
We will *take a look* at your record.	We will *look* at your record.

Action in Verbs, Not in Infinitives. Action can also be concealed by infinitives. Notice, in the following example, that both main verbs in the left-hand sentence belong to some form of "to be," which is a verb that doesn't convey much action or meaning.

Action hiding in infinitive	*Action in the verb*
The duty of a stenographer is *to check* all incoming mail and *to record* it. In addition, it is his responsibility *to keep* the assignment book up to date.	A stenographer *checks* and *records* all incoming mail and *keeps* the assignment book up to date.

Choose Vivid, Image-building Words

Among the devices you can use to make your messages forceful, vivid, and specific are comparisons, figurative language, concrete instead of abstract nouns, and well-chosen adjectives and adverbs.

Comparisons. Sometimes adding a comparison helps your reader to build a meaningful picture. Consider the vague "sense" images you get from the sentences in the left-hand column below as contrasted with the vivid impressions gained from those at the right.

Abstract	*Vivid*
There are a great many solder joints in the spacecraft, and each must have just the right amount of solder.	The spacecraft has 2½ million solder joints. If an extra drop of solder had been left on these joints, the excess weight would have been equivalent to the payload of the vehicle.

| This is pure clover honey, made by honeybees. | Honeybees have gathered nectar from approximately 4½ million clusters of clover and traveled about 150,000 miles—or equal to six times around the world—to deliver this package of Bradshaw honey to you. |

Figurative Language. Figures of speech often express an idea more vividly than literal language.

Literal (and dull)	Figurative
She is usually the one who gets things started in the organization.	*Jean Jones* is the *spark plug* of the organization.
X product helps you lose your double chin in four weeks, if you use X as directed.	If *two chins quarrel constantly for a place on your collar*, X product *helps settle the argument. Only one chin remains* after you use X just four weeks as directed.

In employing figurative language, however, beware of mixed and inconsistent figures of speech, for they may confuse the reader, or seem foolish and corny:

At the meeting, our president's remarks *hit the bull's eye right on the nose.*
You deserve a *nice bow* for *sticking to your guns right down the line.*

You must also be careful not to use figurative speech which can be interpreted literally or negatively or which sounds inappropriate:

As you enter our new lobby, your *eye* will first be *struck* by the bright stainless steel lighting fixtures. (Does this make you think, "Ouch"? Better: Your eyes will first *notice. . . .*)

Good roasts are tough to get, but we have them.

If you want new dollar bills for Christmas gifts, come to us. We have as many as a dog has fleas.

Concrete instead of Abstract Nouns. Still another way to enliven your writing is to use concrete nouns instead of abstract nouns, especially as subjects of your sentences. Concrete nouns represent subjects your reader can touch, see, smell, feel, hear, or taste.

Abstract	Concrete
Consideration was given to the fact that . . .	The *committee* considered . . .

Termination of the insurance contract will be in June.	The insurance *contract* ends in June.
Analysis of the situation suggests that Mr. Smith is right.	*I* think Mr. Smith is right.
The *impression* your living room carpet gives is one of elegance.	The *Worthman carpet* adds elegance to your living room.

Be exact in your titles, subjects, and references. Don't force your reader to guess. One more caution: If you are referring to an inanimate object, avoid using the neutral word "thing" whenever possible. Use a more specific word that is related to the "thing"—such as event, element, fact, idea, condition, method, plan, purpose, principle.

Adjectives and Adverbs. You can often build a more realistic and interesting word picture by adding well-chosen adjectives and adverbs. In the list below, adjectives are in italics; adverbs, in capitals.

Colorless	*Realistic, vivid, interesting*
The camera has a system that gives you *good* pictures.	The *Poney* camera has an UNCANNILY *precise metering* system that assures you PROPERLY *exposed, true-color* pictures.
Notice the *smooth* finish and the *grained* leather.	Feel the *satin-smooth chrome* finish and the RICHLY *grained* leather.
This cookware is guaranteed to withstand changes in temperature.	Because *Creston* cookware can withstand *extreme* changes in heat and cold, the guarantee assures you that you can SAFELY move any piece from your freezer to your *microwave* oven.

In your search for vivid picture-building words, be careful not to go to extremes with either adjectives or superlatives. Choose forceful, specific words and use sparingly such statements as "the most," "the largest," "the greatest," and "the best." Good writing includes concrete nouns, action verbs, and a minimum of adjectives and adverbs.

Consideration

You'll recall that the second planning step you should take before you start to write any business message is to visualize the reader. Consideration—also called "you attitude," empathy, the human touch, and understanding of human nature—means that you write every message with the recipient in mind. Try to visualize your readers— their desires, problems, circumstances, emotions, and probable reaction to your request. Then handle the matter from *their* point of view. In a broad but true sense, consideration underlies the other six C's of good business writing. To make your message correct, concise, clear, complete, concrete, and courteous, you adapt your language and message content to your reader's needs. However, in four specific ways you can show that you are being considerate of your reader:

1. Focus on "you" instead of "I" and "we."
2. Show reader benefit or interest in reader.
3. Apply integrity in your messages.
4. Emphasize the positive, pleasant facts.

Focus on "You" instead of "I" and "We"

Your readers are usually more concerned about themselves than about you or the company you represent. They appreciate seeing personal names instead of merely "Dear _____" in the salutation of your letter, and they like seeing personal names again in the body of a long letter. Also, they are more likely to read your message when they see the pronoun "you" rather than "I, we, us." Remember that the word b-u-s-i-n-e-s-s contains both U and I, but the U comes before the I. This is a good sequence for you to remember.

When you write your next letter, try to get your reader in the first paragraph; if possible, begin with "you" or "your."[2] And keep your reader in the message until you finish. The opposite of "you" attitude is the "we" attitude, in which the writer views every matter from his or her own (or the organization's) standpoint rather than from the reader's:

"We" attitude	*"You" attitude*
We allow 2 percent discount for cash payments.	You earn 2 percent discount when you pay cash.
I want to send my congratulations . . .	Congratulations to you on your . . .
We have enclosed a reply envelope.	Just mail your check in the enclosed envelope.

The department store letter below contains 20 "we-our-us-I-my" pronouns and only three "you's" and "your's" (underlined).

Letter 1
"We Attitude"

May I take this opportunity to express my thanks for the account you recently opened with our store. We are pleased to furnish a wide variety of products for the home or individual.

We want you to take full advantage of our store services, for we have the largest stock in the city. Also we make deliveries of

---

[2] Though a good letter may begin with "we," "I," or "our," you still need to get the reader into the first paragraph whenever possible.

our customers' purchases free of charge within thirty miles of our store.

We always like to receive visits from our customers, but we also fill orders by phone. Our Customer Service Department aims to fill every order within the same day we receive it.

When shopping at our store downtown, customers are invited to use the free customer parking privilege provided just across the street from us.

We welcome you to Bekinson's. If we can be of additional service in any manner, please call on us.

In contrast, letter 2—rewritten for more you attitude—contains 18 "you's" and "your's" (underlined) and only two "we-our-us" pronouns (underlined):

Letter 2
"You Attitude"

Thank you for the account you recently opened at Bekinson's. Serving you with your needs for clothing and home furnishings is a pleasure.

You will find 32 departments at Bekinson's stocked with a variety of quality items. And courteous sales clerks are here to assist you in selecting the merchandise that best meets your requirements.

If you prefer to shop within the comfort of your home, instead of coming to the store, you need only to telephone 882-5555 and ask for "Personal Shopping Service." A Personal Shopper will gladly take your order for any number of items, answer your questions about brands and sizes available, and see that the goods you order reach you by store delivery within a few days.

When you shop at our store downtown, you are invited to use the free customer parking privilege provided just across the street.

You are always welcome at Bekinson's. Please call on us whenever you need additional service.

As the foregoing examples illustrate, a letter is likely to have better you attitude when it contains more you's than I's. But there are two situations when it is advisable not to use "you."

1. When the reader has made a mistake:

   Poor: Your contract tells you plainly that ...
   Better: I am glad to explain more fully about the contract terms.

   Poor: You failed to enclose your check in the envelope.
   Better: The envelope we received did not have your check in it.

2. When the reader has expressed an opinion different from your own:

    Poor: You are entirely wrong in your attitude.

    Better: The proposed plan has three aspects which are extremely important and which we need to explain now.

Show Reader Benefit or Interest in Reader

Keep in mind that the "you attitude" focuses on the reader—*and*, whenever possible, shows the reader how he or she will benefit from doing as the message asks.

Even a simple request gets better response when a reader-benefit plug accompanies it. For example, an insurance company that wanted to update its address files sent to one-half of its policyholders a double postcard with this message:

> Since we haven't written you in some time, please help us bring our records up-to-date by filling in and returning the other half of this card.

Only 3 percent of these cards came back. To the remaining half of its policyholders the firm sent the same request—reworded to show reader benefit:

> So that dividend checks, premium notices, and other messages of importance may reach you promptly, please fill out and return the other half of this card.

This request brought 90 percent of the cards back in a few days!

When you try to see a situation from your readers' point of view, you will find it easier to show them you are aware of and are doing something about their needs and interests. This concern for your reader should be in every letter—whether you are writing to one person or to large numbers.

Try to personalize the reader benefits (as in letter 2) instead of stating them in a general way ("our customers," as in letter 1).

You can use reader-benefit appeals to help bring back checks on your collection notices and to soften the blow in a turndown letter by pointing out your company's concern for the reader and his or her long-term advantages. In addition, reader-benefit appeals are helpful in sales letters, requests for favors, and announcements to your employees and customers.

Apply Integrity in Your Messages

Personal honor, truthfulness, and honesty are qualities brought to mind by the term "integrity." In our day-to-day living, in our jobs, in business transactions—in everything we do—integrity is indispensable. Without it business papers would prove worthless and our confidence in people would be shattered. Leadership demands integrity, be it leadership of a social group, a business, an athletic team, or a charitable bazaar.

The leader's ethical standards, naturally, reflect also on the organization he or she represents.

Because you are an agent of your company, always remember that your messages help build your company's image. And to make this image one of integrity requires consistently fair treatment of customers and emphasis on basic honesty instead of insincerity and bluffing.

Consistently Fair Treatment. As the preceding section indicates, when you snow concern for your readers, you try to let them know you are aware of and are doing something about their interests. This does *not* mean, however, that you yield to the temptation of showing favoritism or allowing deviations for one customer that you would not allow for all other customers in similar circumstances. Particularly troublesome (and tempting) are the demanding customers who threaten to withdraw their large-volume business unless they get special privileges (which they know are against company policy and not granted to your other customers).

High ethical standards are the basis of consistent, fair treatment and consideration for everyone. They may require "doing the harder right instead of the easier wrong." A paragraph from *Fortune* magazine published long ago is still completely true and applicable today.

Language is not something we can disembody; it is an ethical as well as mechanical matter, inextricably bound up in ourselves, our positions, and our relations with those about us. When a businessman doubletalks, for example, it is often for reasons deeper than mishandled prose—hypersensitivity to criticism, fear of the competition, fear of getting out of line with trade-association policy, fear of a government suit, a serious split in the corporation policy—or . . . lack of any policy.[3]

Honesty instead of Insincerity and Bluffing. Is business bluffing ethical? This question has been widely discussed because reputable business managers feel strongly on the subject of ethics. They realize too that many times there are gray areas involving fine decisions between what is the complete truth and a partial falsehood. An honest business writer needs a strong conscience as well as knowledge of writing principles and company policies.

The old values of honesty, sincerity and trust, sometimes dismissed as Sunday school sentimentality, are actually Monday morning business realism in the quest for better communications. They create the climate in which communications grow. Where they do not exist, communications will be faulty, no matter how they are fertilized with methods and techniques. A man's character seems to have more influence than his personality in improving communications.[4]

In writing your letters, memos, and reports remember that employees, dealers, customers, and stockholders have a right to expect and most DO expect honest dealings.

---

[3] "The Language of Business," courtesy of *Fortune*, November 1950, p. 138.
[4] A. W. Lindh, "Plain Talk about Communicating in Business," courtesy of *Business Management*, April 1964; copyrighted by CCM Professional Magazines, Inc.

In the long run, the ethical way to write a message is also the most effective way. Buyers have the right to expect that an item of clothing, food, or hardware will be as advertised; that insurance companies figure premiums honestly on up-to-date actuarial tables, that a home they buy is as represented by the seller's agent and/or in the sales letter they received.

Consideration for others involves the Golden Rule—showing to others the same fairness and honesty that we expect for ourselves. Remember that both your own integrity and that of your company are revealed in the business messages you write.

Emphasize the Positive, Pleasant Facts

The fourth way to show consideration for your reader is to accent the positive. This means (1) stressing what *can* be done—instead of what cannot be done; (2) writing about the pleasant rather than the unpleasant; (3) avoiding emphasis on ideas your reader may view unfavorably.

Statement of What Can Be Done. The reader wants to know what you *can* do for him. By making clear what you can or will do, you also (by implication) often make clear what you cannot do, without using a single negative word. For example, compare the following two sentences:

> It will be impossible to open an account for you until you send us your signature card.

> *versus*

> Just as soon as you send us your signature card, we will gladly open an account for you.

The first sentence stresses what the official *cannot* do—instead of what can be done. The second message is far more positive and thus more effective.

The Pleasant instead of the Unpleasant. In the following examples the unpleasant (negative) and the pleasant (positive) words are italicized.

Unpleasant:	To *avoid* the *loss* of your good credit rating . . .
Pleasant:	To *preserve* (keep, maintain) your *good* credit rating . . .
Unpleasant:	We *don't refund* if the returned item is *soiled and unsalable.*
Pleasant:	We *gladly refund* when the returned item is *clean and resalable.*
Unpleasant:	To *avoid* further *delay* and *inconvenience*, we are sending this information by airmail.
Pleasant:	So that you will *get* this information *as soon as possible*, we are sending it airmail.

Ideas Your Reader May View Unfavorably. When a customer closes an account, do not begin your follow-up letter to the former customer with a negative paragraph, since such an opening emphasizes ideas you'd rather not have the reader think about. For example:

We *regret* that, since you *closed* your account, your name will be *missing* from our long list of satisfied customers. We sincerely *hope* that, despite the best efforts of our fine staff, there was *no occasion* on which you felt we *failed* to serve you properly.

A better opening would show appreciation for the customer's patronage and welcome him or her to other services, as in these two paragraphs:

```
It was a pleasure to have had you as a member of Federal Savings.
Thank you for giving us the opportunity to serve you.
```

```
We noticed recently that you closed your account with us.  Perhaps
you reached that particular goal for which you were saving, or it
may be that an emergency arose which called for a large outlay of
cash.  Whatever the reason, we are happy to have played some small
part in your financial program.  You are cordially invited to use
our other profitable, timesaving services as occasion may require.
```

After these opening paragraphs the letter could continue with a friendly mention of the convenient postage-free save-by-mail plan in case time or distance is a problem for the customer. An ending paragraph could wish the customer a happy future and welcome a return "whenever we can help you in any way."

Negative thinking is a habit—a bad habit. Avoid four words in particular—hope, trust, if, and may—when they carry a negative connotation. The following list shows how these and other negative-sounding words can be changed to emphasize the positive.

Negative	*Positive*
If we can help, *don't hesitate* to get in touch with us.	Please call on us *when* we can help.
I *trust (hope)* this is the information you wanted.	Should you need additional facts, *please telephone* me at 923-3333.
Thank you for your *trouble.*	Thank you for your *help.*
You *won't be sorry* you did this.	You'll be *glad* you did this.

Courtesy

"Everyone gains where courtesy reigns" is a good slogan for written as well as oral communication. Courtesy is even more important in business writing, than it is in face-to-face conversation. When you talk with a customer and see him frown over some expression you use, you can quickly redeem yourself by a smile, a twinkle in your eyes, your tone of voice, or perhaps a correction. In a letter, however, your words are on the paper forever, and you can't be with the customer when he reads the message. Your courtesy—or discourtesy—is there in black and white, and your reader will often form an impression of you or your firm from a single message. Courteous messages help to strengthen present business friendships, as well as make new friends.

Thus, courtesy is a goodwill builder. And the value of that goodwill, or public esteem, can be recorded on the balance sheet in thousands (or even millions) of dollars. Much money is spent in advertising to attract new customers and to keep desirable old customers. While advertising may bring buyers into the front door of your firm, discourteous letters—written carelessly by employees who do not care about or understand people—can drive customers out the back door!

Here are some of the more obvious ways to achieve courtesy in your business messages:

1. Be sincerely tactful, thoughtful, and appreciative.
2. Omit expressions that irritate, hurt, or belittle.
3. Answer your mail promptly.
4. Grant and apologize good-naturedly.

Be Sincerely Tactful, Thoughtful, and Appreciative

Courtesy stems from a sincere attitude that generates goodwill. A truly courteous person sincerely likes people, is thoughtful of their feelings, and tries honestly to help them.

One of the top copywriters in the advertising business, Walter Weir, has published a statement that is good advice for all letter writers as well as for advertising copywriters:

> I believe one best prepares himself for communicating by learning to love and genuinely loving all the countless other human beings with whom he inhabits the earth. I do not believe one can be a cynic and communicate effectively.[5]

The attitudes you have toward people influence the impression your messages will make. If you believe that most people want to pay their installments promptly, that people sometimes forget, and that most of them will try to pay when reminded, your tone should naturally be courteous. On the other hand, if you dislike people and suspect they are all out to get what they can for nothing, your writing is likely to reflect this thinking. The courteous writer is tactful, thoughtful, and appreciative.

Tact instead of Bluntness.   Though few people intentionally want to be abrupt or blunt, these traits are a common cause of discourtesy. Sometimes they stem from negative personal attitudes; sometimes, from a mistaken idea of conciseness. A time to be especially wary of bluntness is on those days when everything seems to go wrong. At such times, you are in danger of allowing your pent-up feelings to come through in your messages. Avoid expressions like the ones in the left-hand column below; rephrase such blunt or discourteous statements as shown in the right-hand column.

[5]Walter Weir, *On the Writing of Advertising*, McGraw-Hill Book Company, New York, 1969.

Tactless	*Tactful*
Your letter is not clear at all; I can't understand it.	If I understand your letter correctly, . . .
Obviously, if you'd read your policy carefully, you'd be able to answer these questions yourself.	Sometimes policy wording is a little hard to understand. I'm glad to clear up these questions for you.
Apparently you have already forgotten what I wrote you two weeks ago.	As mentioned in my May 15 letter (or memo) to you, (continue with the facts) . . .

Writing a letter to a customer generally requires more conscious "niceties" than writing a memo to a fellow employee. In letters to customers you usually avoid a one-sentence body like the following, because it sounds blunt.

```
Before we can replace the safety lock on the trunk of your 1976
Ford, it will be necessary that you give us the number of it.
```

Instead, you need to include a few additional tactful words, as in this example:

```
We will be glad to replace the safety lock on the trunk of your
1976 Ford.

So that we can know the right lock to fit your trunk, please
send us the casting number.  You'll find it imprinted on the side
of the lock.

Within the same morning we receive your reply, a new lock will
be on its way to you.
```

But in a memo to someone within your organization, you can omit the public relations pitch. A one-sentence body like the following is all right to an employee or colleague if it adequately covers your particular message:

```
Tom,
Please call me (Ext. 312) to tell me the casting number on the side
of the trunk safety lock you need for that '76 Ford.
```

When a reader has had sorrow, bereavement, or hardship, the writer should be especially considerate of feelings and emotions. Tactlessness may not only be blunt but also (unintentionally) cruel. For instance, when writing to a policyholder who had recently had one leg amputated, a heartless correspondent included this sentence:

```
Because you have lost only one leg, your policy doesn't entitle you
to the full $30,000 payment.  This amount is paid only when both legs
are amputated.
```

Tact also helps the tone of requests. Generally it is better to suggest and/or to show reader benefit with your request—rather than to command.

| *Commanding:* | You ought to . . . |
| *Tactful:* | Perhaps you could . . . |

| *Commanding:* | Please remit immediately. |
| *Tactful:* | To preserve your good credit rating, please mail your check by (date). |

| *Commanding:* | Tom, get your list to me pronto. |
| *Tactful:* | Tom, may I have your list by tomorrow at 10? Then I'll include it in my report at the meeting. |

Thoughtfulness and Appreciation. Writers who send cordial and courteous messages of deserved congratulations and appreciation (to persons both inside and outside the firm) help build good feeling and goodwill.[6]

An unpretentious, sincere courtesy note can bring the writer's company thousands of dollars of business. Remember, customers indirectly help to pay your salary, and you should let them know you appreciate their orders, their payments, and even their inquiries.

Even for routine payments a printed "Thank you" or "We appreciate your prompt payment" can be added to the flap or under the window of the company envelope in which you return to the customer your bill marked "PAID."

These principles of courtesy involving congratulations or appreciation also apply to colleagues or employees. For instance, what about the salespeople who made very high selling records? Or the office clerks who cheerfully worked overtime every night last month in the warehouse during a trying period? Employees do react favorably to a cordial note of thanks from "the boss."

You cannot measure courtesy by the number of "please's" and "thank-you's" or consideration by the number of "you's," as the following story indicates:

A young wife returning from her second session at a night-school business writing course, had just heard about the seven "C" principles. When she came home, her husband (who had never studied letter writing) asked her opinion of the collection letter he had "slaved over" all afternoon. He fumed, "I'm telling this guy what I think of him and I'll scare him into paying!" After his wife had read the letter, she commented: "I guess this meets six of the seven C's. It's complete, concise, clear, considerate (you have eight you's), and courteous (two please's and three thank-you's right next to the sarcasm and the threats). But I think it's not quite correct, because you've misspelled "louzy" and "bumm.""

Omit Expressions That Irritate, Hurt, or Belittle

The good business writer should avoid expressions that might offend the reader. Such expressions are discussed here in three groups: irritating, questionably humorous, and belittling statements.

Irritating Expressions. The following list contains irksome expressions to be avoided, particularly when used with "you" and "your."

[6] For examples of courteous goodwill messages, see Chapter 14.

contrary to your inference
delinquency (delinquent)
due to your questionable credit we are
    unable to
failed
failure
force
I'm sure you must realize
I do not agree with you
if you care
ignored
inexcusable
irresponsible
must
neglected
obnoxious
obviously you overlooked
simply nonsense
surely you don't expect
we are confused
we don't believe
we expect you to
we find it difficult to believe that

we must insist
we take issue
why have you ignored
you are delinquent
you are probably ignorant of the fact
    that
you claim that
you did not tell us
you failed to
you forgot to
you have to
you leave us no choice
you neglected to (overlooked)
you say
you should know
you surely don't expect
your apparent disregard of our previ-
    ous request leaves us no alternative
your complaint
your failure to
your insinuation
your neglect
your stubborn silence

Questionable Humor. Humor is often quite effective in business writing. However, before you try to be funny, be sure your humor is good-natured and appropriate for the situation. A flippant attitude can be in poor taste, as letter 1 indicates. Letter 2 conveys the same message informally but courteously.[7]

Letter 1—Offensive rather than humorous

Dear Mr. and Mrs. Smith:

  We were mighty happy to learn about the package the stork brought you. And what a distinguished tag you put on him . . . Joshua Gerald Smith II. You tell "Josh: that as soon as he's ready his Prudential agent will be around to help him set up his insurance program.

  In the meantime, I guess it's up to us to take care of the little fellow's insurance needs for a while--you know, educational funds and a little nest egg to help him start his journey through life.

  I'll phone you in a couple of days to find out when it will be convenient for you to talk about insurance for your new bundle of joy. Till then, keep his powder dry!

[7] From *Dear Sir*, vol. 3, no. 1, Correspondence Improvement Section, Public Relations Department, Prudential Insurance Company of America, Newark, N.J., 1961-1962.

Letter 2—Courteous

```
Dear Mr. and Mrs. Smith:

     Congratulations on the birth of your son, Joshua.

     Like other thoughtful parents, you no doubt want him to have a
happy, well-protected future.  It may seem early to be concerned
about financing his college education.  But we at Prudential have
seen too many youngsters miss out on college because their parents
put off the problem too long.

     If it is convenient, I would like to call at seven o'clock Friday
evening to show you how Prudential can help you solve this problem.
I'll phone Thursday to confirm the appointment or to arrange a differ-
ent time that you prefer.
```

Two other examples of humor in questionable taste are the following paragraph in a customer's letter to a department store and the store's reply. (The customer had received a lamp with the wrong base.)

```
The lamp I selected was sold to me by a highly untrained fellow in
your lamp department.  For some reason he was designated as salesman
number 1.  If it is impossible to send me the right base for my lamp,
perhaps you could send me salesman number 1.  That should help your
sales department, I would think, as he would make a better lamp base
than a salesman.
```

The store correspondent apparently tried to be funny too; here is the reply:

```
Our records show that the base you wished was sent to you on May 10.
We are surprised you have not received it.
```

```
Having examined salesman number 1 from all angles, we feel rather
reluctant to think he would make a good lamp base.  We are gratified
this didn't involve the cheese department, for you might have
suggested that we put him in the showcase.
```

```
We are sending you another lamp base.  If the one we originally sent
should reach you in the meantime, we would appreciate your returning
it to us.  We might have to use it in a pinch as a salesman.
```

Belittling Statements. Talking down to or belittling a reader is another form of discourtesy that can have a profoundly unfavorable effect. The following example is a flagrant case of discourtesy of this type:

To substantiate a railroad claim, the accountant of the AMC company needed the exact charges on certain returnable drums in which the XYZ Chemical Company annually shipped thousands of dollars worth of chemicals to AMC. AMC's accountant checked with the local representative of XYZ Company for this information, but was asked by him to contact Mrs. Lancaster at Diamond, California. After writing to her, the accountant received the following reply, which he said caused "a much greater explosion within our department than could have all XYZ chemicals combined."

```
In reply to your letter of October 10th addressed to Diamond,
California, attention Mrs. Lancaster, you made two mistakes.  In
the 1st place we have no Mrs. Lancaster and in the 2nd place Diamond
is not a place to send mail.

We make a charge of $8.50 on the Carbon Bisulphide-Carbon Tetra-
chloride Mixture drum to AMC Company, in your city.  That is for the
drum only.  We trust this is what is meant.
```

Answer Your Mail Promptly

For courtesy as well as better results one should answer a business inquiry promptly—in two or three days if possible. Even a reply on the bottom of the inquiry or a handwritten note on a postcard is usually better than a late (or no!) reply. If you need time to gather information, or have a stack of other urgent work, before you can answer a request, sending a short note like the following distinguishes you as a courteous person:

> I'll gladly send you the information you need. It may take a few days to assemble the facts. You will hear from me by . . .

The next two examples illustrate the value of promptness.

Example 1
A certain retailer in fine china tried an experiment in promptness. For one week he "dumped" all incoming inquiries (many inspired by his regional advertising) into two piles without sorting of any kind. One pile he answered within 24 hours; the others, in three weeks. Result? The prospects who had been answered promptly turned in almost 70 percent more orders than those who had to wait.

Example 2
Customers pleased with a company's courtesy often comment on the promptness of its messages. The following paragraphs quoted from *The Better Letter Gazette* of Teachers Insurance and Annuity Association illustrate well the effect that promptness had on a policyholder:

> But what impressed me still more was the extraordinary speed with which TIAA handled my claim. . . . It seems that special comment is called for when one of your policyholders sends in a claim one day, the check is made out the following day and he has it in his hands two days later. If this is typical of your operations, I can see why TIAA is regarded by the academic profession as a fairy godmother. So please accept my hearty congratulations along with my grateful thanks. . . .
>
> I want you to know that I have policies with several different insurance companies. In no other instance have I received the prompt, courteous attention given me by TIAA. . . .[8]

Sometimes promptness can be achieved by unusual methods. For example, when the owner of a retail men's store in the Dakotas asked a Chicago manufacturer to check his previously submitted order and let him know when it would arrive, the manufacturer sent the following message:

---

[8] *The Better Letter Gazette*, TIAA and CREF, New York, August 1960.

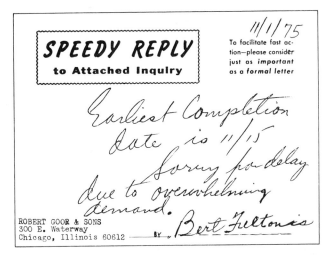

In this situation the manufacturer saved time by not dictating and sending a letter, and the retailer accepted the reply favorably. (Note that the printed explanation in the upper right-hand corner shows reader benefit.) If you are, however, writing to a new customer or if you don't know whether your customer would react favorably to such a reply, be safe and write a courteous card or letter instead!

Grant and Apologize Good-naturedly

Whenever you have occasion to comply with a customer's request, begin your letter with the best news first and inject a courteous, ungrudging tone. Notice the difference in tone of the following two paragraphs:

> **Grudging:**
> Your request causes a great deal of extra paper work to change monthly payments. However, in compliance with your request we hereby reduce your monthly interest and principal payments called for in our note to $ _____ , plus $ _____ for taxes and insurance; effective (month-day-year) your total monthly payment will be $ _____ .

> **Good-natured:**
> As you requested, we will reduce the monthly interest and principal payments called for in your note to $ _____ , plus $ _____ for taxes and insurance. Thus, starting (month-day-year) your total monthly payment will be $ _____ .

If a request has caused you extra work, you may tactfully tell the customer some-where in the letter—but not the first paragraph—to notify you by a certain time if he or she again wishes to change something.

Occasionally you may get a "nasty" letter from a customer, who is wrong in his or her accusations. A courteous reply can lead not only to an apology from the customer but also future staunch loyalty as a booster for your organization. For example:

> An irate father severely criticized a savings association for not paying dividends on his minor son's two deposits—30 cents and $10. He stated (discourteously) "Your

failure . . . is inexcusable. . . . I am calling this discrepancy to the attention of the State Banking Department." Instead of responding with anger, the bank correspondent mailed the following courteous letter:

Enclosed is your passbook for account #R 000 posted to date.

Your desire to have the account earn dividends is certainly natural and understandable. I am glad you've given me the opportunity to explain why the account has not yet earned dividends, so that you can bring the account to the desired balance in the future.

A little over six years ago, starting January 1, 1970, the Board of Directors of the Association raised the minimum balance required to earn dividends to $50. In the preceding month a notice of this change of policy was mailed to all savings account holders; and also posters and counter cards with this information were displayed in all our offices for the entire year of 1970. In addition, in April of 1970, another letter was sent to all savings account holders whose balances were less than $50 reminding them of the change in policy.

You can see, therefore, that we really tried to convey this new information to our savings members. We're sincerely sorry that for some reason you were unaware of this policy change. It has always been our practice to fully inform savings account holders of any changes that take place.

Your continued loyalty to the association is very much appreciated. We invite you to continue adding to this account; one of these days soon your son will see that his money does grow when deposited with Ninth Federal Savings Association.

When someone in your organization makes a mistake, you can apologize and correct the error perhaps even before the customer discovers it. Sometimes a small, printed form like the following (used by a bank) is useful to admit an error promptly and courteously.

Date _____ 19_____ Account No. _____

PARDON US . . . IT WAS OUR ERROR!

An incorrect entry was made. Please return your passbook in the enclosed envelope for the following reason:

Interest
not entered ☐   Balance incorrect ☐

Thank you.

By _____
(Name of bank)

Of course, if the matter is more serious, a special letter may be more appropriate, as you will see in later chapters.

Summary Checklist

The C qualities are closely interrelated; in fact, some overlap. For example, to be *correct* a letter should have all the other C qualities; the same is true for *consideration* and *completeness*. To achieve the seven C qualities in your writing, try to follow the principles on this checklist.

CHECKLIST OF BUSINESS WRITING PRINCIPLES

Correctness: Use the correct level of language
Include only accurate facts, words, and figures
Use acceptable writing mechanics
Apply correctly all other pertinent C qualities

Conciseness: Omit trite expressions
Avoid unnecessary repetition and wordy expressions
Include only relevant facts . . . with courtesy
Organize effectively

Clarity: Choose short, familiar, conversational words
Construct effective sentences and paragraphs
Achieve appropriate readability
Include examples, illustrations, and other visual aids when desirable

Completeness: Answer all questions asked
Give something extra, when desirable
Check for the 5 W's and any other essentials

Concreteness: Use specific facts and figures
Put action in your verbs
Choose vivid, image-building words

Consideration: Focus on "you" instead of "I" and "we"
Show reader benefit or interest in reader
Apply integrity in your messages
Emphasize the positive, pleasant facts

Courtesy: Be sincerely tactful, thoughtful, and appreciative
Omit expressions that irritate, hurt, or belittle
Answer your mail promptly
Grant and apologize good-naturedly

Exercises

1. Discuss orally what is needed to make each of the following postcard requests complete. (Some lack other C qualities in addition to completeness.)

    a. The red coat you had in your window last Thursday is exactly the style I would like to have. Please send it to me on my charge account.
    b. I am interested in the portable TV you advertised in yesterday's newspaper. Will you please tell me more about it? (The firm advertised one television set in the city's morning paper and a different set in the evening paper.)
    c. Please reserve three seats for the opera *Turandot* on Saturday evening.
    d. My daughter and I wish to repaint two bedrooms, each of which is 10' x 12'. Please send us the right amount of paint—in pink—to do this job, and charge my account.
    e. The next meeting of the chapter will be held Monday at 8 p.m.
    f. Please send me c.o.d. five more shirts exactly like those I bought from you three months ago. (From a cash customer)

2. Choose an active verb to replace each "deadly" verb hiding in some of the following nouns.

    a. Be of assistance.
    b. Make substitution.
    c. Have intention.
    d. Become an imposition.
    e. Improvement in quality has been made.
    f. Evaporation of the liquid takes place.
    g. Make a decision.
    h. Take action.
    i. We will give thought to your proposal.

3. Which of the following verbs are passive and which are active voice?

    a. Each member was given a copy of the annual report.
    b. The printer is planning to expand operations on Monday.
    c. Each courteous clerk wins goodwill for Mace Department Store.
    d. Final preparation will be made by the planning committee.
    e. The finance committee has been making a careful study.
    f. By January, the committee will have interviewed all applicants.
    g. Mr. Thom's secretary has completed the assignment.
    h. The contract will be signed next week.
    i. A farewell banquet has been planned in honor of Miss Bray.
    j. Many customers are reached by television advertisements.

4. Revise the following sentences to eliminate the negative aspects.

    a. We are looking forward to pleasant business relations with you.
    b. This information is being sent to you now so that we will avoid later misunderstandings about our credit terms.
    c. We know you will agree that our prices are not any higher than those of competitors.
    d. On c.o.d. orders we require a 20 percent deposit to safeguard ourselves against loss in case of refusal of merchandise.
    e. We will hold shipment of this hardware until we receive your confirmation.
    f. Unfortunately, I will not be able to give you any definite price until you let me know the size and quantity of cartons you need.

g. We are sorry that we cannot add a car to the policy without a specific description of the vehicle.

h. There will be a delay of four days in filling your order because the material for your coat has to be ordered from Chicago. We are sorry about this delay, but there is nothing we can do about it.

i. Because of shortages of material, we will not be able to ship before June 10.

j. I am sorry I cannot send you the booklet you requested as we have not received it from the publishers.

k. Your bicycle has been repaired and we hope you will have no further trouble with it.

l. We regret that we cannot extend your payment date for more than two months.

5. Change the following sentences so that they emphasize "you attitude" instead of "we attitude."

a. This is just the kind of job I am looking for, since it offers me a chance to get practical experience in personnel work.

b. We hope to have the pleasure of showing you what we think is the finest assortment of Italian boots in the city.

c. We value your patronage, for satisfied customers are the foundation of our success.

d. Since we have our own obligations to meet, we must ask your immediate attention to your past-due account.

e. We do not send receipts because of the extra work involved for us; of course, you have your canceled checks anyway.

f. Our pamphlet is designed to help its readers get the most out of raising beautiful roses.

6. Two months before his honorable discharge from overseas military service, a college graduate wrote to the largest university in your state asking about requirements for entrance into its law school. He said he wanted to make his home in your state and practice law there; therefore he preferred to take his law training in the area. Evaluate the following reply he received from that university. The letter was signed by "Director, Program for Servicemen." What improvements does it need?

Blank University does not have a law school. If you are interested in such training, you should apply to a university where such work is offered.

7. Assume that letters A and B were written by two correspondents in your insurance company to the widowed mother of a young man who was killed in an airplane crash. Which do you like better? Why? Revise the better of the two letters to make it excellent.

Letter A

The policy under which you have filed claim contains aviation restrictions which limits the Company's liability if the insured's death occurs under certain circumstances.

As the evidence received indicates the insured's death came within these restrictions, the Company's liability is for the restricted amount. Our check representing the Company's liability will be sent shortly to our Chicago office for delivery to you.

Letter B

May I extend to you my sincere sympathy in your bereavement.

When your son applied for his insurance, he was a pilot in the RCAF. He stated he did not want to pay an extra premium for the additional aviation hazard. Thus, the policy provided for payment of a restricted amount should his death result from nonpassenger travel or flight in any kind of aircraft. The restricted amount is a sum equal to the premiums paid to the Company, together with compound interest at the rate of 2½% yearly.

Because the evidence received shows that your son was pilot of the plane that crashed, I am sorry to say the Company's liability is for the restricted amount.

Our check for the Company's liability will be sent shortly to our Chicago office for delivery to you.

8. The sales manager of Right Fite Hanger, Inc., recently wrote to three television stations asking if they would like to handle her product on a commission basis. She had heard that some stations occasionally used their open time in this manner. Which of the three replies below do you think adheres best to the writing principles for business? Why? Compare your choice with the other two replies.

Reply A

I don't know where you got your information as stated in the opening sentence of your letter, "I have been informed that your station promotes items on a commission basis.", and we don't appreciate it. If you want to do business with us, buy; if you don't, don't write us.

Reply B

This will acknowledge your recent letter of offering your ladies' all plastic dress hanger on a commission basis.

I am quite sure that you did not run your advertisement in the Sunday newspaper supplement on a commission basis. By the same token we will not accept business on a percentage or per inquiry basis.

For your information, I am attaching our rate card.

Reply C

Your information must have been somewhat misleading inasmuch as NUTZ has never promoted items on a commission basis.

We would be delighted to handle the Right Fite hanger, and I personally think it is an item of great demand.

Enclosed is our rate card so that you can choose the time, frequency, and length of message which will promote your product as you wish it.

As soon as your reply to these points reach us, we will be glad to put all our resources at your disposal.

9. Discuss the purpose and weaknesses in each of the following letters. Then rewrite one to improve it in every way you can.

Letter A
Reply from a motel manager to a husband and wife who requested accommodations for two weeks starting one month from today.

Dear Sir and Madam

Your letter of the 23rd. inst was received on the 25th, and in reply will say, I can give you two rooms for time you desire them, and can make you very comfortable with the exception of hot water.

My wife is away on a vacation and shut off the gas water heater, but the few guests here at present find the water warm enough for a shower bath. Sea bathing is close by, and we are in a very desirable location and very central. You could come and stop with me for a day or so and if it meets with your approval stay for the two weeks.

The price would be $15.00 per person per day or $99.00 per week each. Please let me know if you decide to be my guest and the time you expect to arrive. Thank you kindly.

Letter B
Reply from a sardine cannery in Canada to a college student who wrote that he especially liked the sardines but please improve the can.

We thank you for your letter of April 28th and might say that we have a letter before us from our broker in Seattle wishing to purchase a carload of our sardines. After we received your letter we were a little uneasy about shipping him another car; however, on thinking the matter over if you had not liked our sardines we presume you would not have taken the trouble to write us.

We know the cans do not open right; it seems they will go alright for awhile and then we get a run of cans that everything seems to be wrong; the last thing we found out was that the grain in the tinplate had been changed without our knowledge. We have a special dye maker chasing this trouble all the time but let me tell you it is a headache. Don't think for a minute that you are the only one that writes in; we have good customers all over the country and when we get a run of cans that don't open right you can bet your life we get a lot of letters but we are going to keep trying and we hope in the meantime our customers will not be too hard on us.

We are going to send you a few tins from the new pack and will just pray that the dye maker has got the cans opening alright. With kindest regards.

10. Rewrite the following letter so that—in spite of the Congresswoman's limit on number of free booklets she may send—she can still retain (even build!) goodwill.

Inasmuch as I have had so many requests for Botanical Yearbooks
from students of your college who should look to their Representative from the State and Congressional District in which
they or their families are registered voters, and in order to
give the legal residents of my District their rightful share
of these books, I find it necessary to ask for the registered
voting address when I do not find it listed in the Register.

Because of this, may I ask you for the above information and if
you do know the name of your Representative I shall refer your
request to him or her for fulfillment. However, if you are a
constituent of mine I shall be glad to send the book.

11. For the following, refer to the letters you collected and have been studying for
various purposes. (Or use any other letters as your instructor directs.) Evaluate
each message by:

    a. Underscoring once all trite and wordy expressions
    b. Underscoring twice all technical language that the reader might not under-
stand
    c. Placing parentheses around all negative expressions
    d. Encircling all words and expressions that produce an unpleasant tone—such as
cutting words and abruptness
    e. Checking for violations of mechanics—misspelled words, confusing punctua-
tion, vague or incomplete sentences, number of sentences exceeding 45
words, "goozling" words (unnecessary big words when shorter words accomplish the job better), and incorrectly used words.

6

Appearance and Uses of Business Message Media

Among the various media you can choose for your written messages are letters and memorandums—plus such special timesaving media as memo-letters, postcards, Mailgrams, telegrams, radiograms, and cablegrams.[1] This chapter focuses on the appearance and uses of these media and on form messages—discussed from the writer's viewpoint.

Business Letters

The medium used most often for written messages to persons outside the firm is the business letter. It is judged on content, presentation, and physical appearance. Planning the content and presentation is your responsibility; typing the message so that it is neat, accurate, and attractive is usually your secretary's job. But when you sign your name at the bottom of the letter, you assume final responsibility for everything—mechanics, proper layout, content. If the message contains misspellings or grammatical errors, or if its appearance is poor, the reader judges you, not your secretary. Therefore, you and your secretary must work as a team to produce effective and attractive messages.

Recipients of your business letters form their first impressions even before reading your messages. Elements of appearance that help produce favorable reactions are appropriate stationery, correct letter parts and layout, and properly addressed envelopes. (In addition to these elements, neat typing also helps make favorable impressions. Poor appearance caused by strikeovers, dirty keys, light ribbon, smears, or poor erasing reflects on you as much as on your secretary.)

Stationery

Although your organization's stationery may be selected by your purchasing department and thus not be your concern, if you have an opportunity to make a choice or suggest a change, keep the following guidelines in mind.

Quality and Size. To help build an image of quality and stability, the paper you use should have at least 25 percent rag content. Good-quality paper is not only more attractive, but it permits easier and neater erasing. The difference in price is nominal. Even the best stationery costs usually less than two cents a sheet—very little, considering the average cost of a letter. The standard size sheet is 8½ by 11 inches, but other sizes are also appropriate for various uses.

Color and Weight. White is the most popular color, although many firms achieve a distinctive and warm touch by using stationery and envelopes that are pastel. The weight of general correspondence stationery ranges from 16 to 20 pounds; and of airmail, from 13 to 15 pounds. (Each of the figures is the actual weight of four reams of standard-size paper.)

Letterhead. Every business, even if it is a one-person operation, should use letterhead stationery for the first page of a letter. Only when you are writing a

[1] For reports, see Chapters 15–17.

Figure 6-1 Illustrations of modern letterheads. (All these letter-heads are printed in black, except the following: TWA initials, circles, and horizontal lines, in red; Weyerhauser outer triangle, in dark green; Allenite, all printing in medium green.)

business letter for yourself (not as an agent or representative for any organization) will you use paper without a letterhead.

The modern letterhead (see Figure 6-1) usually occupies no more than two inches at the top of the page. Printed, embossed, or engraved in this area are name and complete address of the firm, including ZIP code, and sometimes the telephone number, cable address, nature of the business, and name of the department or branch office sending the correspondence. Optional details are names of officers and directors, trademark or symbol, slogan, starting date of the firm, and an appropriate picture— perhaps of the building, product(s), or a familiar landmark.

Parts of the Letter

Most business letters have seven standard parts: (1) heading, (2) inside address, (3) salutation, (4) body, (5) complimentary close, (6) signature area, (7) reference section. (See Figures 6-2 to 6-7.)

When appropriate, any of these optional parts can be included: (1) attention line, (2) subject line, (3) file or reference number, (4) enclosure(s), (5) carbon copy notation, (6) mailing notation, and (7) postscript.

Heading. The letterhead and typewritten date comprise the heading. It shows where the letter comes from and when it was written (or dictated). Usually the date is typed two lines below the last line of the letterhead—at left margin, centered, begun at center, or placed so it ends with the right margin.[2] (The letter style and

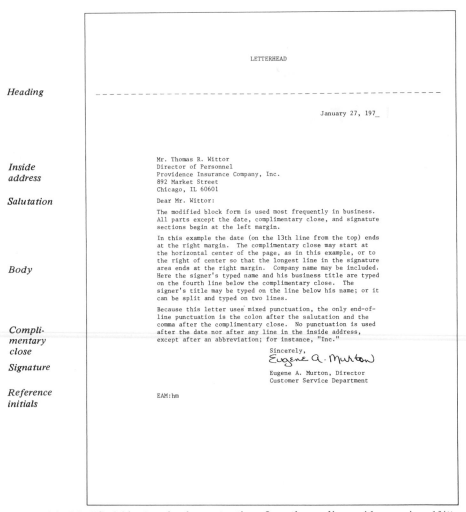

Figure 6-2 Modified block; mixed punctuation. Length, medium; side margins, 1¾″; line length, 5″.

[2]The date sequence in American business letters is always month, day, year. The names of the months should be spelled out, and the days (in figures) following the month should not be followed by st, nd, rd, or th. The same rule applies in the body of the letter. But when the date of the day stands alone, add st, nd, rd, or th; for example, "The goods arrived on the 15th of this month."

letterhead help determine which placement to choose.) When you type a business letter on blank paper (for yourself, not for an organization), type both your return address and the date, but *not* your name (see Figure 6-7).

Inside Address. Always blocked at the left margin, the inside address includes the title, name, and address of the person or persons and the organization to whom the letter is directed. (Whenever possible, address your letter to a person or persons rather than to an organization alone so it seems more personal.)

A courtesy title should always precede the addressee's name (full first name or two initials plus surname). If the addressee has no professional title—such as doctor, professor, superintendent—use Mr., Mrs., Miss, or Ms. If you are not sure from the name or initials whether the reader is a man or a woman, use Mr. If you don't know the marital status of a woman, use Miss or Ms., which stands for either Miss or Mrs. If your letter is addressed to two or more men, use Messrs. (plural of Mr.); if to two or more married women, use Mesdames (plural of Mrs.); and if to two or more unmarried women, use Misses (plural of Miss).

The business or executive title of your addressee should be included in the inside address. It is a matter of judgment (depending upon the relative length of lines) whether this title is typed (1) on the same line with the addressee's name, (2) on the second line preceding the company name, or (3) on a line or two by itself. Any of these is correct:

1. Mr. William Stassen, President
    Western Construction Company
2. . Miss (or Ms.) Marietta R. Worthington
    Treasurer, Ace Credit Company
3. Mr. Harry M. Fitzsimmons
    Vice President and General Manager
    Building Services, Inc.[3]

Avoid duplication of titles.

Wrong: Dr. Herbert Moore, M.D.

Right: Dr. Herbert Moore *or* Herbert Moore, M.D.

The order of arrangement for the various elements of the inside address is comparable to a pyramid. On the top line you place the smallest unit (an individual's name). The remaining items progress downward to the largest unit, as the pyramid below illustrates:

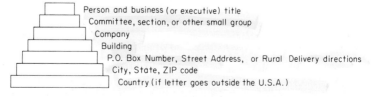

Person and business (or executive) title
Committee, section, or other small group
Company
Building
P.O. Box Number, Street Address, or Rural Delivery directions
City, State, ZIP code
Country (if letter goes outside the U.S.A.)

[3] If you need suggestions on when to spell out and when to abbreviate words, see **Abbreviations** in **Appendix B.**

The number of lines usually ranges from three to six, as the following five-line address illustrates:

Mr. James Bengstone, Manager
Southwest Title Company
1601 Tower Building
2973 Lerpson Boulevard
Los Angeles, CA 90020

Salutation. The salutation is the friendly greeting that precedes the body of the letter. It is typed two spaces below the inside address and even with the left-hand margin.

Popular salutations in use today are:

1. Dear Mr. (Mrs., Ms., Miss) Doe—when writing to a customer, acquaintance, prospect, stockholder, supplier, or stranger.
2. Gentlemen[4] (not Dear Gentlemen or Dear Sirs)—when writing to a company or P.O. Box, or Ladies (not Dear Ladies or Dear Mesdames)—when you're sure that all employees are women.
3. Dear John (or Mary or nickname)—when writing to an individual you'd address this way in person and when it is appropriate for you to do so in your letter on this occasion.

Such salutations as Dear Sir and Dear Madam are impersonal and should be avoided whenever possible.

The first line of the inside address determines the salutation. For example, if it contains the name of a group, committee, or company, the salutation is plural—"Gentlemen" or "Ladies." If it contains the name of an individual, the salutation is singular—"Dear Mr. (Mrs., Miss, Ms.) Smith" or "Dear John (Mary)." An intervening attention line does not change the salutation:[5]

```
Midwest Office Equipment Company
(Street address)
(City), (State)  ZIP

Attention: Mr. (Mrs., Miss, Ms.) Jones

Gentlemen
```

The "Salutopening" is preferred by some business executives. If you feel that a salutation such as "Dear Mr. Brown" is not appropriate, because he is a stranger to you, or the "Dear" just seems unnatural, you might prefer a *salutopening*. This

[4] Salutations such as "Gentle Persons" and "Dear People"—advocated by the National Women's Commission—are also being used by some (especially government and university) offices in letters to organizations consisting of men and women. Some writers use "Ladies and Gentlemen" for social organizations, "Gentlewomen" to groups consisting of all women.

[5] Some business executives do not use this rule. If they must begin the inside address with the organization name, and must also have an attention line to an individual, they personalize the salutation, using, for instance, "Dear Mr. Jones" instead of "Gentlemen." As an alternative, if you feel strongly that you want to use Mr. Jones's name in the salutation and it's agreeable with your firm, then add his full name (first name or initials and surname) on the inside address, above the company name, and omit the attention line.

is typed on the salutation line, but it omits "Dear" and begins with the first few words of your opening paragraph plus your reader's name. After the name the sentence continues a double space down to the first line of the letter body, as in these examples:

Salutation line What do you think, Mr. Brown,

Body of the enclosed suggested arrangement for . . .?

and

Salutation line Thank you, Miss Smith,

Body for writing us so promptly about your new address.

Most business executives have not yet accepted the salutopening in their daily writing. They use the conventional salutations already discussed.

The "simplified letter" (see Figure 6-5) uses instead of a salutation the reader's name near the beginning of the first sentence.

Body. This book discusses in detail the content and presentation of the body; thus only general guidelines are summarized here. In the body you try to:

1. Organize according to an appropriate plan.
2. Keep your first and last paragraphs short—preferably less than seven lines.
3. Vary the intervening paragraph lengths.
4. Make the average length of your sentences about 17 to 20 words.
5. Achieve the C qualities.

Generally all letters should be typed single-space, with double spacing between paragraphs.

When the body of a letter is two or more pages, each page beyond the first is headed by a combination of addressee's name, page number, and date. This information is typed 1 to 2 inches from the top of the sheet in any of the following ways:

Mr. John Jones
Page 2
May 3, 197–
 or
Mr. John Jones   2   May 3, 197–
 or
Mr. John Jones–2–May 3, 197–
 or
General Supply Corporation   2   May 3, 197–
Attention Mr. John Jones

Complimentary Close. The complimentary close should agree, with respect to formality or informality, with your salutation. Most business letters use one of three key words—"sincerely," "truly," or "cordially." The following salutations and complimentary closes are appropriate together:

Dear Mr. (Mrs., Miss, Ms.) Smith Gentlemen (Ladies)	*and*	Sincerely, Sincerely yours, Yours sincerely, Very truly yours, Yours very truly[6]
Dear John (Mary, or a nickname)	*and*	Sincerely, Cordially, or some more familiar phrasing in good taste— such as Best regards

At times, you may want to use a complimentary close that ties in with your message or product, for example:

Warmly	Yours for fashion	Yours for extra profits
Gratefully	Yours for cleaner air	Season's Greetings

[But avoid inappropriate "gimmick" complimentary closes, like the following: "Gastronomically yours" (from a restaurant), "Hopefully yours" (from a collector), or "Saltily yours" (from a salt processor).]

Signature Area. You can include in the signature area four separate identifications—name of your company, your signature, your typewritten name, and your business title.

Your company name, if printed on the letterhead, need not be repeated after the complimentary close (except in legal documents and negotiable instruments).[7] However, if you wish to include the company name (many firms require it, for various reasons), type it in capital letters a double space under the complimentary close.

Your typed name appears three to five lines under either the company name (if included) or the complimentary close.

Your signature is usually written in blue or black ink—never pencil—above the typed name.

The typed business title usually follows the typed name.

Very truly yours,	Yours sincerely	Cordially yours,
Thomas L. Sutton	THE PRONSON COMPANY	*Roy Layton*
Thomas L. Sutton Manager, Plant 2	*Mary P. Tracy*	Roy Layton, President
	Mary P. Tracy Personnel Manager	

[6] Business executives' views differ widely on the use of "yours" and "very" in the complimentary close. Many writers prefer to omit both these words with "sincerely" and "cordially," because they feel that adding them makes these friendly closes sound stilted or inappropriate. On the contrary, with "truly" many prefer both "very" and "yours," for just plain "Yours truly" has fallen in disfavor because of jokes about this expression. Thus they use "Yours very truly" or "Very truly yours." Still others dislike all the "truly's." The choice is up to you.

[7] Even though the firm name is not typed in the signature lines, the firm is considered responsible for the content of a message written by one of its agents about business the agent is *authorized* to handle.

If you prefer, instead of having your name typed under the complimentary close, it may be typed flush with the left margin, usually on the same line with your title, which appears four lines under the complimentary close. You sign above your title. (See Figure 6-3.)

If you are a man, "Mr." is omitted before and after your name, unless your first name is used by both men and women (for example, Robin, Chris) and you want to be sure the respondent addresses you "Mr."

If you are a woman, you might want to add "Miss," "Mrs.," or "Ms." to your name in the signature section. Usually parentheses enclose the title when it is included in the handwritten signature, but not when it appears with the typed name. For business and professional women, the following signatures are commonly used:

Unmarried woman:

Sara Jones   (Miss) *Sara Jones*   *Sara Jones*
                            (Ms.)
Miss (or Ms.) Sara Jones   Sara Jones   Sara Jones

Married woman or a widow: If Sara Mae Jones married Albert B. Smith, she may use her first name and husband's surname, or insert for a middle name or initial her maiden surname or her middle name. However, many married women, especially professionals, do not use their husband's surname; their signatures continue as before marriage.

Sara Jones Smith   (Mrs.) *Sara J. Smith*   *Sara M. Smith*
                       (Ms.)
Mrs.   Sara Jones Smith   Sara J. Smith   Sara Mae (or M.) Smith
(or Ms.)

Divorcee: same form as for a widow unless the court has restored her maiden name, in which case she uses the style of the unmarried woman.

Reference Section. Your initials as dictator of the message, and those of your typist, usually appear at the left margin on the same line with the last line of the signature area (your name or title) or one or two lines below that. If your name is typed at the left margin instead of in the signature area (Figure 6-3), the typist's initials follow it. Among the common forms used are:

```
KLM:tr            KLM:TR          klm/tr
K.L.Morning:TR    KLMorning-tr
```

If someone other than the signer of the letter composes it, practice varies regarding reference initials. Many firms show at least on the file copy the initials of signer, writer, and typist (KLM:JC:tr); the original, to the addressee, may omit all or the writer's initials, to avoid showing that the signer did not dictate the letter.

Attention Line. Considered part of the inside address, the attention line directs a letter to a particular person or title or department when the letter is addressed to a company. It is useful when the writer doesn't know the name of an individual but wants the message to go to a particular title (Sales or Adjustment Director) or department (Personnel). It is also useful when the writer knows only the surname of an individual and thus cannot use the name on the first line of the inside address.

The usual placement of the attention line is between the inside address and salutation (a blank line before and after it), flush with the left margin, indented with the paragraphs, or centered. (See Figure 6-3.)

ATTENTION PURCHASING MANAGER   Attention Miss Erickson

Subject Line. Considered part of the body of the letter, the subject line helps to tell your reader at a glance what your letter is about. It also helps in filing. The subject line may include or omit the word "subject" or "about." It is usually placed either on the same line with the salutation or double-spaced below the salutation and centered. (See Figures 6-5 and 6-7.)

File or Reference Number. To aid in filing and quick recognition for both the sender's and the reader's company, some firms require that file, loan, or account numbers be typed above the body of the letter in a conspicuous place.

Enclosure Notation. To remind whoever prepares your envelope for mailing that something is to be enclosed, the enclosure notation is usually typed a single or double space under the reference initials. This notation also alerts the addressee's incoming mail department to check for enclosures. An enclosure is anything in the envelope other than the message itself. One enclosure is a unit that can consist of one or more pages (for example, a two-page résumé with an application letter is only one enclosure). When more than one item is enclosed, your secretary should indicate the number: "Enclosures 3" or "Enc. 3." When the enclosures are especially important (checks, legal documents, or blueprints), it is desirable to list in the enclosure notation exactly what the enclosures are.

Copy Notation. When you want other persons to receive a copy of the letter you have written to the addressee, the names of these persons (arranged in order of importance or alphabetically) should be typed after "cc" (carbon copy) or a similar notation just below the reference initials or the enclosure notation (if any):

cc: Mr. Sims   Copies to A. E. Brown and R. J. Sims

If you do not want the addressee to know that other recipients are getting a copy of the letter, your secretary can type "bcc" (blind carbon copy) and the recipients' names *on the carbon copies only.*

Mailing Notation.[8] Words such as "Special Delivery," "Registered," or "Certified Mail," when applicable, may be typed either below the carbon copy notation (or whatever is the last notation) or on the second line below the date.

Postscript. To emphasize a point already in your letter or to include a personal brief message unrelated to the letter, a postscript (typed or handwritten) may be added—below everything else typed on the page. However, if you forgot to include an important idea in the letter body, it is usually better to retype the letter than to add the information in a postscript. (See Figure 6-7)

Letter Layout

Although the layout of the letter is primarily the typist's responsibility, it is covered briefly here to give you a basis of choosing the style(s) you prefer. Many progressive companies have adopted a format used throughout the company, so that all their letters contribute to an attractive, uniform image—regardless of dictator, department, or stenographer.

Punctuation Styles. The two forms of punctuation most used in business letters are *open* and *mixed.* In open punctuation, no line of any of the seven standard letter parts (except the body) has any punctuation at the end unless an abbreviation requires a period. Mixed punctuation—the most popular style today—is like open except that a colon follows the salutation and a comma follows the complimentary close.

Letter Styles. Business letters are usually arranged in one of the letter styles described briefly below. You will find additional details discussed within the letters illustrated in Figures 6-2 to 6-7.[9]

1. *Modified block* form is currently the most popular style. All parts are blocked; there are no paragraph indentations. The date, complimentary close, and signature sections begin near the center of the page; the other parts, at the left margin. (See Figures 6-2 and 6-7.)
2. *Modified block with paragraphs indented* is also popular. (See Figure 6-3.)
3. *Full block* begins every line at the left margin. (See Figure 6-4.) This is the fastest style to type, especially when used with open punctuation. To offset a lopsided appearance at the left, some firms use a letterhead with most of its printing at the right side.

[8]If you have occasion to use several notations after the signature area, the initials RECMP indicate the proper order for arranging them vertically at the left margin: reference initials, enclosures, copy notation, mailing notation, postscript.

[9]The discussion in these letters is adapted from *Reference Manual for Stenographers and Typists,* Ruth E. Gavin and William A. Sabin, Gregg Division, McGraw-Hill Book Company, New York, 1970, and from *The Secretary's Handbook,* Doris H. Whalen, Harcourt Brace Jovanovich, Inc., New York, 1973. For additional details about typing mechanics and numerous other helpful tips, consult these or similar manuals.

4. *AMS simplified style,* adopted by the Administrative Management Society, uses full block and open punctuation; omits the salutation and complimentary close; and includes a subject line without the word "subject," typed in all capital letters a triple space after the inside address. The first paragraph contains the reader's name. (See Figure 6-5.)
5. *Hanging (or inverted) paragraph style* is unsuitable for daily correspondence, but distinctive for a sales or advertising letter in which you want to emphasize the first words of each paragraph. All lines of the letter body are indented except the first line of each paragraph. (See Figure 6-6.)

Public and government officials—as well as business persons writing formal messages—often use what is called the *official letter style.* Its general layout may be blocked or semiblocked, but the inside address—instead of being placed above the salutation—is typed at the left margin two to five lines below the last line of the signature section. Reference initials and other notations, if any, then appear after the inside address. (Some writers also use this style with informal letters that begin with a first-name salutation.)

Tips for Letter Placement. The easiest way to achieve pleasing appearance for all your letters is to have a competent secretary. However, most students—and even many young businesspersons—find it necessary to type some letters themselves. Though there are other good placement guides, the following table is easy to use. It assumes a fixed vertical position for the date—on about the 14th line from the top of the page. Notice that line length of a letter is about 4, 5, or 6 inches, depending on letter length.[10] Before using the guide, you should:

1. Estimate the approximate number of words in your letter.
2. Know whether your typewriter has elite (E) or pica (P) type.[11]
3. Place the typewriter paper guide at zero.

(The letters in Figures 6-2 to 6-7 are based on this guide, for elite type.)

		Line length in		Margins		
Letter length	*Words in body*	*Inches*	*Spaces*	*Width in inches*	*Machine settings**	*Number of lines between date and inside address*
Short	Under 100	4	40 P	2¼	22–62 P	6–10
			50 E†		26–76 E	
Medium	100–200	5	50 P	1¾	17–67 P	3–8
			60 E		21–81 E	
Long	200–300	6	60 P	1¼	12–72 P	2–6
			70 E†		15–85 E	
2-page	Over 300	6	60 P	1¼	12–72 P	2–6
			70 E†		15–85 E	

*To allow for the ringing of the typewriter bell and to avoid frequent use of the margin release key, add five spaces to the settings for the right margin. For suggestions on how to divide words correctly at the right margin, see Syllabication in Appendix B.
†Rounded off.

[10] To save time and money, some firms use the same line lengths for all messages regardless of length.
[11] With pica type you get 10 characters to the horizontal inch and 85 across the 8½-inch page; with elite, 12 to the inch and 102 across the page. Both have 6 vertical lines to the inch.

LETTERHEAD

----

2 blank lines

December 1, 197_

Accounting Department
Eastern Register Company
1969 Fourth Avenue NE
Sometown, Anystate 99999

Attention Mr. Johnson

Gentlemen:

This modified block form is like that in Figure 6-2 except that its paragraphs are indented five or more spaces. The date may be centered or placed so it does not extend into the right margin. In this example the date begins at the horizontal center of the page.

The attention line here is at the left margin, two lines below the inside address, and underlined. It could also have been centered and typed in all capital letters without underscoring. If you wanted Mr. Johnson's name in the salutation, you would type his first name (or two initials) and his surname above Accounting Department. Then you would omit the attention line and use "Dear Mr. Johnson" in the salutation. If you know him well and address him by his first name (Bill), your salutation could be "Dear Bill."

In this example the complimentary close, like the date, begins at the center of the page. The company name is omitted, but it could have been included. Also the signer's name--instead of being at the left--could have been typed above the "General Manager" and reference initials (like "MM:hw") could then have been used at the left margin.

The term "Enclosures 3" in the reference section shows that three additional items are being enclosed in the envelope. Each different item is counted as one, regardless of the number of pages it may have. The notation "cc" indicates that a carbon copy is being sent to Mr. Jami and Miss Krown. Names are in alphabetical order or by rank. The address of each may be included if doing so will help the typist in sending the carbon copy or if it is needed for filing information.

Very truly yours,

Millard M. Morrison

3 blank lines for signature

Millard M. Morrison/hw   General Manager

Enclosures 3
cc: Mr. Thomas Jami
     Miss Helen Krown

Figure 6-3 Modified block with paragraph indentations; mixed punctuation. Length long; side margins, 1¼″; line length, 6″.

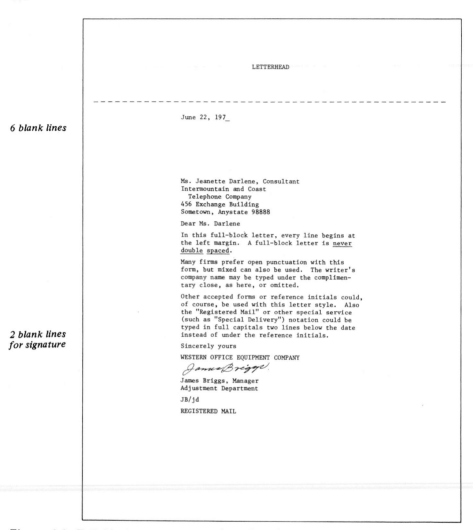

6 blank lines

2 blank lines
for signature

Figure 6-4 Full block; open punctuation. Length, short; side margins, 2¼″; line length, 4″.

3 blank lines

*4 blank lines
for signature*

LETTERHEAD

- -

July 26, 197_

Mrs. Gary Hurlbut
P. O. Box 9152
Sometown, Anystate 66666

FORMAT FOR SIMPLIFIED LETTER

This letter form, Mrs. Hurlbut, has been recommended by the
Administrative Management Society (formerly NOMA) as an
important timesaving step when typing business letters.
This letter setup saves about 19 key strokes. Here are its
features:

1. It uses full block form and open punctuation.

2. It omits the salutation and the complimentary close, but--
    to personalize--the reader's name is used at least in the
    first sentence.

3. The subject line is in all capitals, omits "subject,"
    and has at least one blank line both before and after it.

4. The signer's name and business title are typed in all capi-
    tals, starting at the left margin at least four blank lines
    below the last line of the letter body.

5. The typist's initials are typed at the left margin two lines
    below the signer's name. Enclosures are indicated below the
    initials. Names of persons receiving carbon copies are typed
    below the initials and enclosures.

Mrs. Hurlbut, the efficiency of this Simplified Letter suggests
that it is especially desirable where output must be increased.

PAUL A. MULLINS - RESEARCH DIRECTOR

hm
Enc 4
Messrs. Ronald Scharf, Mike Luberts, Erich Wittor

Figure 6-5 AMS simplified style; full block and open punctuation. Length, medium; side margins, 1¾''; line length, 5''.

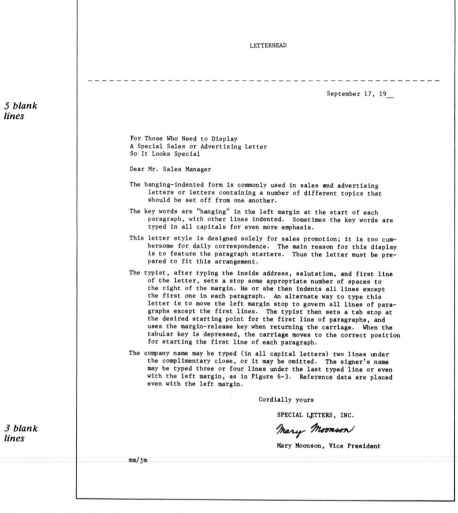

*5 blank
lines*

*3 blank
lines*

Figure 6-6 Hanging (or inverted) paragraph style; open punctuation. Length, long; side margins, 1¼″; line length, 6″.

1½″ from top

3 blank lines

                                                    4524 17th Avenue
                                                    Seattle, WA 98102
                                                    October 4, 197_

Mr. Joseph M. Albrecht
Manager, Jupiter and Jones, Ltd.
815 Fourth Avenue
Vancouver, B.C.
Canada

Dear Mr. Albrecht:

          Subject: Letters with Quotations and Tabulations

The subject line (if given) is typed on the second line below the salutation. It may be at the left margin, indented the same as paragraphs, or
centered--as in this example It may be typed either in all capital
letters or in capital and small letters that are underscored. The word
"Subject" often precedes the actual subject.

When you have quoted matter, numbered paragraphs, tabulations, or other
material that you want to emphasize in the body of your letter, your
secretary should always double space before and after such material. For
instance, here is a quotation from an article in a handbook:

               When a quotation occupies more than three lines, give
               it special display (use a shorter line length than
               that used for the remainder of the material) and type
               it single spaced, instead of using quotation marks.

When you want to set off listed items or tabulated material, your secretary should indent the left and right margins equally and single space
such material.

                              1975   1976

          Gross income............$550,972 $588,974
          Expense and taxes....... 390,004   392,593

          Net income..............$160,968 $196,381

To bring out points more forcibly, the items may be indented an equal
number of spaces from the left and right margins and numbered. These
methods help to bring material to the reader's attention quickly and
artistically.

          1. Your profit will increase 10 percent.
          2. Your savings are insured up to $40,000.

1½″ from bottom

Figure 6-7 Personal business letter, modified block with mixed punctuation. First page of a two-page letter typed on blank paper (with no letterhead). Side margins, 1¼″; line length, 6″.

*1" from
top*

*2 blank
lines*

*4 blank
lines for
signature*

Mr. Joseph M. Albrecht
Page 2
October 4, 197_

Letters over 300 words in length usually require two pages, particularly
when typed on a pica-type machine. The right, left, and bottom margins
on the first page should be balanced. The second-page heading begins at
least six line spaces (1 inch) from the top and consists of the name of
the addressee, "Page 2," and the date. The letter continues on the
second or third line below the heading--with at least two or more lines
of the body.

Tabulations, quoted material, and enumerations in the body of any letter
affect the working out of the letter-placement rules. It is often necessary to adjust the marginal stops for a longer line of writing and very
often to raise the letter on the page.

A postscript is typed at least two spaces below the reference initials
or enclosure notation. The "P.S." may be omitted.

Sincerely,

Franklin G. Worthington

Franklin G. Worthington

FGW:re
Enclosure--Insurance Policy #95991

P.S. The signer of this letter has no title. He is writing on blank
paper, not on a company letterhead.

Figure 6-7 (continued) Second page of a two-page letter. Length, two pages; side
margins, 1¼"; line length, 6".

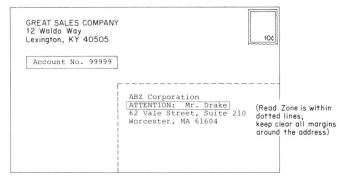

Figure 6-8   Sample envelope.

Envelopes

Your organization's envelopes not only get your messages to their destination, but help, indirectly, to advertise your company. The quality of the envelope paper (preferably the same as the letter stationery) and the pictures and slogans, if any, all contribute to your organization's image. Each envelope should show the sender's return address, which is usually printed (in a format identical with that of the letterhead), or typewritten if necessary, in the upper left corner.

The inside address of the letter is the outside address on the envelope. To speed the processing of your mail at the post office, your company should keep up to date on Post-Office-recommended location and legibility of the address on the envelope and the layout of information within each address.

Recommended Address Location and Legibility.   Your return address should be printed or typed in the upper left-hand corner of the envelope, about one-half inch from the top and left edges. The addressee's name and address must be completely in the LOWER RIGHT QUARTER SECTION—the "read zone"—because the Post Office electronic mail sorters (Optical Character Readers, OCR) are programmed to scan this specific envelope area. (See Figure 6-8.)

To be read by the OCR, the envelope address should be clearly imprinted with dark print (or typewriter type) on a light background. The address should be parallel (within five degrees) with the bottom edge of the envelope; slanted or crooked lines can confuse OCR recognition.

Recommended Address Layout.[12]   To be processed quickly and accurately by OCR, the envelope address should meet these requirements (see also Figure 6-8):

---

[12]Most information in this section is adapted from *Addressing for the Optical Character Reader*, United States Postal Service, Publication 114, January 1971.

1. **The format** must be single-space and blocked, not indented.

Good	*Poor*
Mr. John Smith	Mr. John Smith
6 Vale Street	6 Vale Street
Worcester, MA 01604	Worcester, MA 01604

2. **City, state,**[13] **and ZIP code,** in that sequence, must all be on the bottom line.
3. **Street name—correctly spelled—or box number** should be on the line immediately above the city, state, and ZIP code.
4. **Number of an apartment, room, suite, or other unit of multiunit unnamed building** should appear immediately after the street address on the same line—never above, below, nor in front of the street address.
5. **On-arrival instructions** such as "Confidential," "Attention Mr. Drake," "Please forward," and account numbers should be typed either (a) outside the read zone (as shown in Figure 6-8 for the boxed account number) or (b) inside the read zone on any line above the second line from the bottom of the address (as shown in Figure 6-8 for the boxed attention line).

To give you an idea of the wastes that occur from inadequately addressed mail, here are some figures from the Postmaster General's Office:

45,300,000   pieces of mail went to the dead-letter office and its branches in 1974

$538,000   in checks, drafts, and cash was found in letters sent to the dead-letter offices during this year.

$358,000   could not be restored to rightful owners because of lack of information on or within the envelope.

$6,000,000   —approximately—is spent by the Postal Service each year trying to find correct addresses for inadequately addressed mail.[14]

---

[13] Although you can use any of the traditional spellings and abbreviations for states, the Post Office recommends use of the following two-letter abbreviations—two capitals without periods or spaces.

Alabama . . . . .AL	Louisiana. . . . . .LA	Ohio . . . . .OH
Alaska . . . . .AK	Maine. . . . . .ME	Oklahoma . . . . .OK
Arizona. . . . . .AZ	Maryland. . . . . . . .MD	Oregon . . . . .OR
Arkansas . . . . .AR	Massachusetts . . . . .MA	Pennsylvania. . . . . . .PA
California . . . . .CA	Michigan . . . . .MI	Puerto Rico . . . . . . .PR
Colorado. . . . . . . .CO	Minnesota . . . . . . .MN	Rhode Island . . . . . .RI
Connecticut . . . . . .CT	Mississippi . . . . . . .MS	South Carolina . . . . .SC
Delaware. . . . . . . .DE	Missouri . . . . .MO	South Dakota . . . . . .SD
District of Columbia . .DC	Montana . . . . .MT	Tennessee . . . . .TN
Florida . . . . .FL	Nebraska. . . . . . . .NB	Texas. . . . . .TX
Georgia. . . . . .GA	Nevada . . . . .NV	Utah . . . . .UT
Hawaii . . . . .HI	New Hampshire . . . .NH	Vermont . . . . .VT
Idaho. . . . . .ID	New Jersey. . . . . . .NJ	Virginia. . . . . .VA
Illinois IL	New Mexico . . . . . .NM	Washington . . . . . .WA
Indiana . . . . .IN	New York . . . . .NY	West Virginia . . . . .WV
Iowa . . . . .IA	North Carolina . . . .NC	Wisconsin . . . . . . .WI
Kansas . . . . .KS	North Dakota . . . . .ND	Wyoming. . . . . . . .WY
Kentucky . . . . . . .KY		

[14] E. V. Dorsey, Senior Assistant Postmaster General, Washington, D.C., and Lawrence J. Williams, Budget Officer, Seattle District Office of United States Postal Service, April 1975.

Memorandums

In contrast to the letter, which is directed outside your organization, the memorandum (memo) goes within your organization. It is an informal written communication from one person or department to another person, persons, or department. The stationery, parts, layout, and envelopes of the memo are somewhat different from those of the letters described in the preceding section.

Stationery

Memorandum stationery often differs from letter stationery in quality, color, size, and printing.

Quality, Color, Size. Because the memo goes to employees within the firm, consideration of public relations is not necessary. Memo stationery is usually of a much less expensive quality paper than that for regular letters; also, instead of white, memo paper is often in pastel colors—yellow, cream, pink, blue—for easy identification. Sometimes each color indicates the department to which a particular copy should go. Sizes of sheets range from the standard 8½ by 11 inches to small slips 4 by 5 inches.

Printing. At the top of the full-page memorandum are usually printed such words as OFFICE MEMORANDUM and the company's name (but not address). Along the left margin (or in various other locations) are printed: TO, FROM, SUBJECT, DATE—and sometimes also MESSAGE. In some memos FROM is omitted and the writer signs at the end—as on a letter. Some memos also include such printed words as File number; Telephone; For your: approval, information, comment (see Figure 6-9). Printing at the bottom sometimes includes various instructions and reminds employees of the risks of oral messages (Figure 6-9).

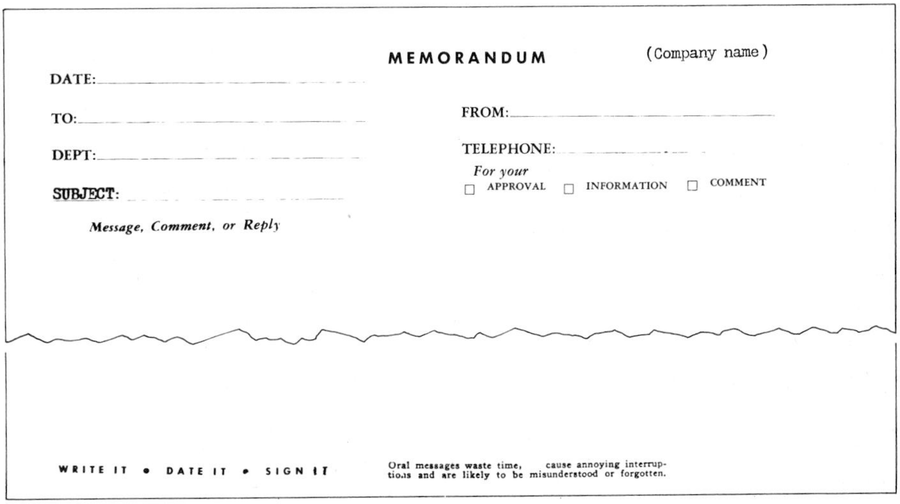

MEMORANDUM (Company name)

DATE:_____

TO:_____ FROM:_____

DEPT:_____ TELEPHONE:_____

SUBJECT:_____ *For your* ☐ APPROVAL ☐ INFORMATION ☐ COMMENT

Message, Comment, or Reply

WRITE IT ● DATE IT ● SIGN IT Oral messages waste time, cause annoying interruptions and are likely to be misunderstood or forgotten.

Figure 6-9 Office memorandum. (Jagged line indicates a portion of actual sheet removed here only to save space.

The combination *message-and-reply memorandum* form is an especially good time- (and expense) saver for both sender and recipient. A packet of three or more sheets of paper (white and colored), plus carbons (unless special "carbonless" paper is used), makes up a message-reply packet. Printed instructions at the top or bottom tell the sender and the reader how to use the sheets. Printed lines may aid those who communicate in handwriting. Each packet is perforated near the top for easy removal of sheets, and each sheet is divided into two sections—one labeled MESSAGE, for the sender, and one marked REPLY, for the recipient. These two sections may be side by side or one above the other. (See Figure 6-10.)

Parts of the Memorandum

The standard parts of the memorandum are: to, from, subject, date, and body. Optional are such items as reference initials, enclosure(s), file number, routing information, and department and telephone number of sender. Most of these parts are printed on the memo stationery, as illustrated in Figures 6-9 and 6-10. Unlike the letter, the memo requires no inside address, salutation, complimentary close, or full signature. The combination message-reply forms do, however, provide lines for both the writer's and the reader's signature. (See Figures 6-10 and 6-11.)

INTEROFFICE COMMUNICATION

TO _____ PLANT/DEPARTMENT _____

FROM _____ PLANT/DEPARTMENT _____

SUBJECT _____ DATE _____

M E S S A G E

SIGNED _____

R E P L Y

DATE _____ SIGNED _____

PERSON RECEIVING COMMUNICATION - RETAIN THIS COPY FOR YOUR RECORD (1st page: white)

ORIGINATOR: DETACH THIS COPY. SEND REMAINING SET, CARBON INTACT, FOR USE OF REPLIER. (2d page: yellow)

RETURN THIS COPY TO SENDER (3d page: pink)

Figure 6-10 Interoffice memorandum packet containing carbons under sheets of paper (white, yellow, pink) with sections for both the message and the reply.

```
- - - - - - - - - - - - - - - - - - - - - - - - - ┌───────────────────────────────
                                                   │ FROM
  ┌─                          ─┐                    │    RELIABLE Furniture Mfr's., Inc.
  │                            │                     │         1742 FIRST AVE.
  TO      Best Products Co.                          │      SEATTLE, WASHINGTON 98104
          PO Box 0000                                │         MUtual 3-1440
          Sometown, Somestate 47777
  └─                          ─┘
```

SUBJECT: __Our order No. 8203 of March 2__   DATE: __March 26, 197__

FOLD ▲   **M E S S A G E**

On Mar. 2 we placed an order for 36 #2000-RR's, 24 #2900's, and 36 #500-CLS's,
and sent it along with a note to Tom Jears in Los Angeles (asking to ship either
WASH-ORE. SHIPPERS COOP ASSN - Chicago or E. St. Louis, whichever was less
expensive for your truck or auto freight to deliver to the above depots).

As of this date we have had no confirmation. PLEASE ADVISE.

J D:hw

                                        John L. Doe

PLEASE REPLY TO ──────► SIGNED   John L. Doe

        R E P L Y

We have been temporarily out of rug rollers. However, we should be
able to ship your order this week by Washington Oregon Shippers.

                                        Jim Rebessa

DATE   March 31, 197__ SIGNED   Jim Rebessa

GRAYARC CO., INC., BROOKLYN, N.Y. 11232   **THIS COPY FOR PERSON ADDRESSED**   (1st page: white)

GRAYARC CO., INC., BROOKLYN, N.Y. 11232 **PERSON ADDRESSED RETURN THIS COPY TO SENDER**   (2d page: pink)

                                                                       (3d page: yellow)
DETACH THIS COPY — RETAIN FOR ANSWER. SEND WHITE AND PINK COPIES WITH CARBONS INTACT.

Figure 6-11 Memo-letter stationery for routine short messages. (Jagged lines indicate a portion of actual sheet removed here only to save space.)

What you write after the TO, FROM, and DATE will vary with the situation and your organization's practices. A courtesy title— Mr., Mrs., Miss, Ms.—before your reader's name (after TO) may be used or omitted, depending upon your relationship with the reader (superior or subordinate) and the degree of informality within your organization. You omit the title before your name. Also, if the memo is a temporary message, not to be filed, and if you and the writer work together regularly, you may merely use initials, first name, or nickname after TO-FROM, and all figures or abbreviations for the date:

TO: J.E.H.   TO: Jack
FROM: T.R.M.   *or*   FROM: Ted
DATE: 2/10/7_   DATE: Feb. 10, 197_

However, if the memo will be filed, these parts should be spelled out:

```
TO:     Mr. (optional) James E. Hill, Personnel Manager
FROM:   Theodore R. Murdock, Accounting Department
DATE:   February 10, 197_
```

If you are sending the same message to several persons, their names and/or titles should be typed after TO. If you write to the same persons often, you might have a form prepared with their names printed (or dittoed or mimeographed) after the TO. When you have only one copy of a document, book, or other important papers that you want everyone in a certain group to read and comment on, circulate a covering memo—the single original, with no copies for readers to keep—among those on your list. Brief instructions (printed or typed) tell the readers what to do:

```
DATE:     May 2, 197_
TO:       Tom Brown_____        Please initial and pass on; last
          James Brown_____      reader please return memo and attach-
          Anita Jones_____      ment to sender.
          Searl Lichen_____
          Harry Green_____
FROM:     Kermit Hobson, Personnel  K. H.
SUBJECT:  Your suggestions on attached Procedures Manual
```

The body of the memo, as for the letter, is its most important part because it contains your message. In general, you can use the same guidelines and organizational plans for the memo as for the letter; the few differences are pointed out in succeeding chapters.

Layout of the Memorandum Body

The memo body, unlike that of a letter, is not centered on the page. The first line usually begins a double- or triple-space under the subject line regardless of the length of the message. Left margins are usually lined up evenly below the TO.

For memo pages beyond the first, headings are the same as those for the business letter; namely, reader's name, page number, and date. Reference initials are typed a few spaces below the body, at the left margin. If only your title appears in the FROM line, or if the FROM line is omitted, you should sign your name a few spaces below the body of the memo. If your typewritten name follows FROM above the body, you may place your handwritten initials above or to the right of your name, to indicate that you have read the memo.

Carbon copy (cc) notations in memos may be placed after the reference initials (as in letters) or near the top of the memo between the TO and the FROM.

Envelopes

How your memo is routed to the addressee depends partly upon where you and the reader are located. If you are in the same building, the memo might be inserted into the reader's mailbox, put on his or her desk by a messenger, or routed through compressed-air tubes. If you are in different buildings, your memo may be mailed in a manila or regular company envelope. The envelope address contains your name and department in the upper left corner and the reader's name, department, and address according to your organization's procedures.

Special Timesaving Message Media

Included in this section are various message media that save time for both the sender and recipient. They can be useful in certain situations when speed is essential *and* the messages are relatively short (though, of course, there are exceptions). The media that merit at least a brief discussion here are memo-letters, postcards, Mailgrams, telegrams, cablegrams, and radiograms. (Form messages are also time-savers, their advantages and types are discussed in the next section.)

Memo-letters

In the interest of speed and lower costs, many firms (especially wholesalers, publishers, and manufacturers) use a combination message-reply or memo-letter form for routine short messages directed *outside* their organization. Compare the reply message memo-letter packet in Figure 6-11 with the interoffice memorandum shown in Figure 6-10. The main differences are that in the memo-letter: (1) after the FROM, the full name and address (perhaps also phone number) of the sender's company are printed (sometimes in the same format as for the firm's regular letterhead); and (2) after the TO, a larger space is provided so that the typist can insert the full name and address of the recipient, because he or she is outside the sender's firm. Some firms have the words "memo-letter" printed near the top of the sheet.

A further time-saver is the printed request-for-information form, as illustrated in Figure 6-12. Notice that besides the printed 28 requests this firm commonly uses, the form leaves spaces for six others to be inserted if desired. The bottom of this memo-letter form allows space for comments by both the sender and the receiver. This form, like the interoffice memo packet shown in Figure 6-10, is a packet of three sheets with carbons preinserted.

The memo-letter is mailed in the same kind of envelope as a regular business letter or in a window envelope (in which the address after the TO serves also as the envelope address).

Postcards

For short messages that are not confidential you can often save time and expense by using postcards. These media do not require folding, sealing, or inserting in envelopes, and the postage is less than for letters sent first class.

J. W. MICROELECTRONICS CORPORATION
REGIONAL TECHNOLOGY PARK - BLDG. C
4901 STENTON AVENUE • PHILADELPHIA, PENNSYLVANIA 19144 • PHONE 215-329-8681

REQUEST FOR INFORMATION

TO: _____ DATE _____ REQUEST NO. _____

_____ P.O. NO. _____ INV. NO. _____

_____ INV. DATE _____ INV. AMOUNT _____

PLEASE REPLY TODAY VIA ☐ THIS FORM ☐ WIRE ☐ TELEPHONE ☐ RETURN ENVELOPE ENCLOSED

☐ 1. PLEASE ACKNOWLEDGE OUR ORDER AND GIVE SHIPPING DATE

☐ 2. PLEASE CHANGE ORDER AS NOTED BELOW AND ACKNOWLEDGE

☐ 3. PLEASE ADVISE WHEN ORDER WILL BE SHIPPED

☐ 4. MUST HAVE MORE SPECIFIC SHIPPING DATE

☐ 5. CAN YOU MEET OUR SHIPPING DATE?

☐ 6. GOODS NOT RECEIVED, PLEASE TRACE SHIPMENT

☐ 7. IF SHIPMENT HAS BEEN MADE, PLEASE MAIL INVOICE TODAY

☐ 8. WHEN WILL BALANCE OF OUR ORDER BE SHIPPED?

☐ 9. PLEASE RUSH PRICES REQUESTED

☐ 10. PLEASE SEND A SHIPPING NOTICE

☐ 11. PLEASE SEND A RECEIPTED FREIGHT BILL

☐ 12. PLEASE SEND A CERTIFIED WEIGHT SLIP

☐ 13. PLEASE SEND ACCEPTANCE COPY OF OUR P.O.

☐ 14. RELEASE SHIPMENTS AS SHOWN UNDER "REMARKS" BELOW

☐ 15. PUT OUR P.O. NUMBER ON ALL SHIPMENTS

☐ 16. SHIP THIS ORDER TO ADDRESS BELOW

☐ 17. WE HAVE NO RECORD OF TRANSACTION COVERED BY YOUR INVOICE. PLEASE GIVE US ORDER DATE, DATE SHIPPED, P.O. NUMBER, NAME OF PERSON PLACING THE ORDER AND/OR SIGNED DELIVERY RECEIPT.

☐ 18. YOUR INVOICE IS RETURNED FOR REASON CHECKED:

☐ 19. WE REQUIRE _____ COPIES OF EACH INVOICE

☐ 20. PRICES DO NOT MATCH YOUR QUOTATION

☐ 21. TERMS DO NOT MATCH OUR P.O.

☐ 22. QUANTITY DIFFERS FROM OUR P.O.

☐ 23. UNIT PRICE IS INCORRECT

☐ 24. EXTENSION PRICE IS INCORRECT

☐ 25. OUR P.O. NUMBER IS LACKING OR INCORRECT

☐ 26. SALES TAX DOES/DOES NOT APPLY

☐ 27. ORDER SHOULD BE BILLED F.O.B. DESTINATION

☐ 28. ORDER MUST BE SHIPPED VIA _____

☐ 29. _____

☐ 30. _____

☐ 31. _____

☐ 32. _____

☐ 33. _____

☐ 34. _____

OUR REMARKS   YOUR REPLY

Figure 6-12 Printed request-for-information packet (three sheets) with numbered requests for easy check-off; also spaces for remarks and for recipient's reply.

On the stamped side of the card, usually only the reader's name and address are typed. The message side includes the name and address of the sender, the date, salutation, message, complimentary close, and signature. (To save both space and time, some business firms have their name and address *printed* in one line, usually across the top of the postcard's message side.)

As a customer you can use a postcard, for example, to inquire, to request a free advertised booklet, or to order a product that is to be charged to your account. As a representative of a business firm you can send postcards and reply cards for a wide variety of uses, three of which are illustrated in Figures 6-13, 6-14, 6-15.

ORDER CARD

Please send me

    copies of *Two Studies in Automobile Franchising*   @ $9.50 = $

    copies of *Institutional Holdings of Common Stock*   @ $9.00 = $

    copies of *Antitrust Policy and Economic Welfare*   @ $6.00 = $

                                         total $

Name

Address

City   State   Zip

Payment enclosed   Bill me

Prepaid orders are sent post paid. Foreign orders must be prepaid.

Figure 6-13 Business reply order postcard. The reverse side is addressed to the seller; the firm's name, address, and postage permit number are printed in appropriate places for address and stamp.

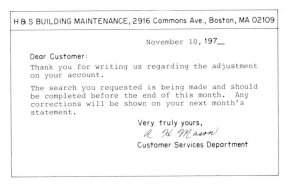

Figure 6-14 Seller's postcard acknowledgment of a customer complaint.

Figure 6-15   Seller's "miss-you" postcard, asking to serve the customer soon.

Mailgrams

When you need to reach any number of people predictably, simultaneously, in writing, with impact, the *next business day*–you can use Mailgrams. These media have urgency and prestige value similar to telegrams, but at much lower cost.

Uses and Appearance.   You can use Mailgrams in many ways–to announce important news to sales representatives, distributors, stockholders, employees–speedily, simultaneously; quote special prices; acknowledge orders; congratulate; collect delinquent payments. Figure 6-16 illustrates Mailgram format and tells some advantages in the words of Western Union's Vice President John E. Cochran.[15]

Methods of Sending.   Your Mailgram can originate from a telephone, IBM Communicating Mag Card or Redactron Communicating typewriters, Telepost terminal, Telex, TWX, computer, or tape. Each message is routed electronically by the Western Union network to a post office near your addressee and printed out individually. It is delivered in a Western Union blue and white envelope (Figure 6-17) the next regular mail, usually the day after it's sent, sometimes the same day.

To send one or a few Mailgrams, you can phone Western Union toll-free, day or night. An operator types each message, as you dictate it, onto a cathode ray tube, makes any corrections electronically, and presses a button that transmits your message

---

[15] Additional information in this section is from Western Union brochures and courtesy of William Deilke, Area Mailgram Coordinator, Seattle, Washington.

```
MGMNWKB NWK
2-205617E158 06/07/74
ICS IPMMTZZ CSP
2018251100 MGM TDMT UPPER SADDLE RIVER NJ 100 06-07 0929A EST
ZIP 07834
```

western union **Mailgram**

```
MR.ACTION COMMUNICATOR
1 MAIN STREET
ANYWHERE U.S.A. 07384




DEAR MR.COMMUNICATOR:

MAILGRAM IS THE ACTION COMMUNICATION.

MAILGRAM'S TELEGRAPHIC FORMAT AND IMPACT GET QUICK READERSHIP.
IT'S EASY TO USE, MAY BE PERSONALIZED,GETS ATTENTION, AND MOST
OF ALL IT GETS RESULTS.

WESTERN UNION WILL GLADLY ASSIST YOU IN PREPARING YOUR MESSAGE
AND LIST FOR TRANSMISSION IN VOLUME ORDERS SO THAT YOU MAY OBTAIN
THE LOWEST RATE POSSIBLE.

THE WRITTEN RECORD MAKES YOUR MEANING CLEAR. MAILGRAM MAKES SURE
THAT EVERYONE GETS NOTIFIED IMMEDIATELY. THE MEDIUM SAYS THE
MESSAGE IS IMPORTANT.


JOHN E COCHRAN
VICE PRESIDENT, MARKETING
WESTERN UNION TELEGRAPH CO.
ONE LAKE STREET
UPPER SADDLE RIVER,NJ 07458

0932 EST

MGMNWKB NWK



THIS SAMPLE MESSAGE IS 700 CHARACTERS IN LENGTH (OF 110 WORDS).
```

Figure 6-16 Mailgram.

to the computer. Then the computer automatically switches your message to the appropriate post office.

If your company has a Telex, TWX, or Infocom system your operator can type your messages directly from your teleprinter into the Western Union computer. To send 100 or more Mailgrams at a time, you can get Western Union assistance regarding computerized address lists and messages—for lowest tariff rates.[16]

---

[16]Cost of a Mailgram originating by phone is $2.50 for 100 words or less ($1 each additional 100 words). For a Mailgram originating from Telex, TWX, or computer, costs are significantly less —depending on the sending method and length of message. Words in the message plus the address and signature are counted in Mailgrams.

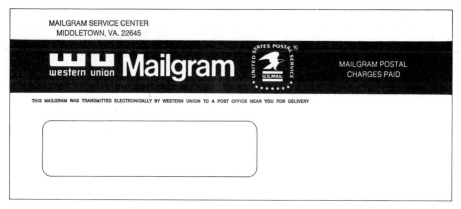

MAILGRAM SERVICE CENTER
MIDDLETOWN, VA. 22645

western union Mailgram
 MAILGRAM POSTAL
 CHARGES PAID

THIS MAILGRAM WAS TRANSMITTED ELECTRONICALLY BY WESTERN UNION TO A POST OFFICE NEAR YOU FOR DELIVERY

Figure 6-17 Mailgram window envelope (3¾" × 9").

Telegrams, Cablegrams, Radiograms[17]

You can send a message by telegram within the continental United States; by cablegram or radiogram for overseas communication. The format of telegrams and cablegrams is similar to that of the Mailgram. Most telegrams today are delivered by telephone; cablegrams are transmitted by transoceanic cable; radiograms are wireless messages (usually delivered to ships).

Telegrams. For domestic telegraphic service, you can choose full-rate telegrams or overnight telegrams. The fastest domestic service, for transmission within two hours, is the full-rate telegram. The minimum charge is for 15 words. The more economical overnight telegrams are messages accepted up to midnight for delivery not earlier than the following morning.[18] The minimum charge is for 100 words between points within the United States. If your firm sends numerous telegrams, you should be sure to get a copy of Domestic Telegraph Service Rules. These sheets contain highly useful, money-saving specific details on how to count words, figures, forms of money, symbols, and punctuation.[19]

---

[17]Information and examples in this section are included by courtesy of Ms. Marlene D. Parry, Administration Supervisor, Western Union office, Seattle, Washington.

[18]Cost of an interstate 15-word telegram (in 1975): $4.95, if delivered by telephone; $7.95, by messenger; 12 cents for each additional word over 15 up to 50 words; 8 cents, each word over 50. Cost of an interstate overnight telegram: $4.20 for 100 words or less, if delivered by telephone; $7.20, by messenger; 3 cents for each additional word over 100. Only words in the message (not the address or signature) are counted.

[19]Chargeable words in a domestic telegram are a total of (a) dictionary words, (b) full words in proper names, and (c) matter subject to the 5-character word count. Under the five-character rule, combined figures, signs, or alphabetic letters count one word for each five characters or fewer. For example: these are each one word: urlet (your letter), 9-16-76, #415(A). Punctuation marks, though transmitted, are neither counted nor charged for. Spaces automatically separate matter into word groups: AT&SF is one word; A. T. & S. F. is five words.

Cablegrams and Radiograms. Because transmission of messages outside the continental United States is necessarily costly, it is extremely advisable to be well informed on rules for international word count. If you communicate frequently with representatives overseas, you might develop mutually understood code symbols to save costs. For example, notice how the following cable text from an insurance agent in Greece to his home office in the United States can be cut from a word count of 25 to only 10 words. (Words in the address count extra.)

(25 words)   CUSTOMER HAS TODAY ACCEPTED A NEW INSURANCE POLICY INCLUDING FIRE EXTENDED COVERAGE AND VANDALISM ALSO PUBLIC LIABILITY AND PROPERTY DAMAGE AS WELL AS WORKMENS COMPENSATION

(10 words)   CUSTOMER TODAY ACCEPTED NEW POLICY INCLUDING FECVM PLPD AND WC

Form Messages

Whenever you want to send an identical message to at least two persons, you can write what is called a "form letter" or a "form memo," based on a master draft.

Uses and Advantages

Form messages are useful when you need to (1) announce news to customers, employees, stockholders, suppliers; (2) seek information on credit or job applicants; (3) answer often-recurring inquiries; (4) acknowledge orders; (5) make simple adjustments; (6) acknowledge payments; (7) sell a product or service by mail; (8) collect payments on charge accounts; (9) promote goodwill.

Why use forms? The main advantages are these:

1. **They save time.** After a master draft is prepared, it can be duplicated (by automatic typewriter or other timesaving machines), used again and again, and thus help speed correspondence. If the form is designated by a code number, marked in the customer's folder, an actual copy of the form need not even be filed in the folder. Thus forms can save time of executives, secretaries, and (in some cases) file clerks.
2. **They save money.** Mainly because they save time, messages processed from a master draft may cost only a few cents each, instead of several dollars for individually dictated and typewritten messages.
3. **They can be better quality.** Sometimes if routine messages are prepared by inexperienced, hurried, or disgruntled writers (and overworked typists), they are mediocre or poor both in content and appearance. In contrast, when one or more experts prepare the master forms, they can be of higher quality and more effective.
4. **They make possible wider mass mailings.** If desired, thousands of copies can be duplicated quickly from a master draft and mailed the same day to persons over a wide area. The impact of such a mailing campaign could not be achieved as quickly (or economically) without forms.

Kinds of Forms

Four kinds of form messages are: complete form, fill-in form, guide form, and paragraph form.

Complete Form. Messages identical in every word are "complete" forms, especially useful for announcements, some collection reminders, and large-scale campaigns when being *impersonal* is desirable. They may be reproduced on a printing press, computer, multigraph, mimeograph, ditto, or other types of duplicating machines.

In a complete form *memo* the word TO is followed by such terms as "All Employees" or "Management Personnel." In *letters* a general salutation (Dear Customer, Homeowner, Sports Buff, Student) is chosen to fit the type of individuals getting the letter. Sometimes the first few words of the first sentence are placed where the inside address and salutation usually are:

Faked *inside* *address*	The last time you had a chance like this to get World and Home News
Faked *salutation*	at a big savings . . .
Body	. . . business was coasting along without any serious worries, the war in Asia seemed to be cooling off, the President had . . .

Fill-in Form. A message prepared in advance to meet a specific kind of situation may have spaces left for filling in variable information. The date, customer's name and address, account number, payment due date, and so forth are inserted in the right spaces on each individual letter. The fill-ins should be made on a typewriter with matching type and ribbon.

Some fill-in forms—like, for example, Figure 6-12—are obvious forms. They are useful in routine situations when both the writer and reader consider forms acceptable.

However, when it is desirable to personalize each letter, fill-in forms can be reproduced by computer, automatic typewriter, or other high-speed automatic machines with magnetic tape capacity for inserting variable information at the time each form is reproduced. Thus, each person on your mailing list will receive a letter containing his or her name in one or more places and all the specific variables that apply to his or her case. The "fill-ins" are almost unnoticeable.

Guide Form. Sample letters prepared in advance for various situations can be kept on hand (usually in an office correspondence manual) and referred to whenever a communicator writes similar messages. The communicator uses any sample as a guide only, inserting personal phrasing wherever desirable.

Paragraph Form. An office booklet of paragraphs to meet various situations is often an efficient way to save the letter writer's time. The writer does, however, need to use good judgment in selecting right paragraphs.

The booklet usually contains various sections covering the frequently written messages. An airline, for example, may group its paragraphs under: Passenger Fares,

Flight Schedule Inquiries, Air Cargo, Adjustments, Charter Flights, and Goodwill. Each section contains numbered pages with various opening, closing, and intervening paragraphs that answer often-asked questions. Each paragraph is marked by the page number and a letter of the alphabet.

Thus, after choosing the appropriate paragraphs for your message, you need merely dictate the paragraph numbers; for instance, "2C, 5A, 9C, 15E." If you need a special paragraph that is not in the booklet, you dictate it. Your transcriber copies the designated paragraphs from the book and adds your specially dictated paragraph in the right order. (If an automatic typewriter programmed with magnetic tape or card is used, a letter can be completed in a few seconds.) Each customer gets an attractive personalized letter composed of form paragraphs that exactly answer his or her questions and needs.

Summary

Letters and memos are the most used written business message media. In addition, for special situations, memo-letters, postcards, Mailgrams, plus other telegraphic and wireless media are also effective.

Attractive appearance of a business letter is an important aid to the reader's favorable first impression. Stationery, parts and layout (format), and envelope addressing should follow certain guidelines. For memorandums (sent within the organization) the stationery, parts, layout, and envelopes are different from those of letters. Memo-letters have a format more similar to a memo than to a letter. Postcards have certain timesaving features. Though the formats of Mailgrams, telegrams, and cablegrams are similar, these messages differ in methods of transmittal, word count, and costs. All convey the impression that your message is important and urgent. To get the most economical rates, study the telegraph company's rules governing these services.

The four kinds of form messages offer advantages in time, cost, quality, and quantity mailings; but they must be used with good judgment.

This chapter is your guide for *formats* of business letters, memos, postcards, telegraphic media, and form letters and memos. In Chapters 7-14, which focus on *content,* most illustrations include only the message *body*—to save space. Therefore, when typing your complete messages, you may want to refer regularly to this chapter for correct layouts.

Exercises

1. What are the standard and optional parts of a business letter?

2. a. What is the most popular layout style for business letters?
    b. Describe it and compare it with four other popular styles.
    c. Which do you prefer and why?

3. How do the standard parts of the memo differ from those of the letter?

4. What are the advantages of using postcards, when desirable, for business messages? What disadvantages can you name?

5. What are the advantages—and possible disadvantages—of (a) form messages? (b) Mailgrams? (c) telegrams? (d) cablegrams?

6. Each of the following parts of a letter has one or more faults. Treat each part as an independent unit. Correct errors and change all obsolete forms.

In the heading (stationery that doesn't have a letterhead):

a. 3 April 197—
   15,447 E. 5th St.,
   Seattle, Wn. 98155

b. Mr. John F. Slyfield
   15 Mt. Vernon Ave.
   New Orleans, La. 52345
   Jan. 5th, 197—

In the inside address:

c. Mr. John E. Henning, Esq.
   4317-18 Avenue N.E.
   Chicago,
   Illinois

d. Professor Lee Stephenson, Ph. D.
   School of Business Administration
   University of California
   BERKELEY 94900

e. Campbell and Morris Furniture Co.,
   1,496 Westlake Ave.
   City

In the signature and reference section

f. (open punctuation)   Very Truly Yours,
                               State Federal Savings Assn.,
   D.E.S./A.R.F.   Mr. Donald E. Smith
   INCLOSURE   President

g. (mixed punctuation)   Sincerely Yours,
   Richard E. Scroggs:ab   Credit Manager

h. (mixed punctuation)   Cordially yours
                               MEURER & HOHANNES, INC.
   RAJ:AF   Raymond Jensen
   cc: Thomas Brown   Prod. Mgr.

In the inside address, salutation, and complimentary close (assume mixed punctuation for parts i through n):

i. Veterans Adm.
   Detroit, Mich. 23456

   Attention: Dr. Chester Allen Powers

   Dear Dr. Chester Powers

                     Respectfully yours,

j. Dr. William Knapp, M.D.
    618 Wrigley Bldg.
    Chicago 14, Ill. 34567

    Dear Carl,

                            Sincerely yours

k. Byron Renshaw
    17,672 3rd St., N.E.,
    New York City   11111

    Dear Sir:—

                            Yours

l. Gladyne Lucchesini
    644a Liberty Bldg.
    Des Moines, Ia. 2222

    Dear Miss Gladyne Luchesini

                            Yours truly

m. Northwest Company, Inc.
    Accounting Department
    Phila, Penna. 33333

    Dear Miss Swanson

                            Your faithful friend

                            Pasco & Co.

    Incl.   Clifford D. Bergerson
    al; cdb:TR   Personnell Mgr.

n. HAVDAHL MANUFACTURING COMPANY
    Attention: Miss Helen Burgess
    Eleven South Fifteenth St.
    Kansas C'y, Mo. 76543

    Dear Sirs: RE: February Sale

7. Which of the following three memorandums is best? Why? How does even this
    memo need improvement? In your evaluation, be sure to consider the probable
    purpose of the message and whether the memo is likely to be filed.

a.
```
Jack to Bob, 4-23-7_

B O O K L E T   S C H E D U L E

Johnson now says Saturday sure.
```

b.

```
TO:      RJL
FROM:    JS
April 23, 197_
HEALTH BOOKLET SCHEDULE

I checked with Johnson and now have a definite promise that
the 6000 Standard "Your Health" booklets will be delivered
Saturday, April 26.

This rescheduling will not affect our other production
schedules.
```

c.

```
TO:            Dr. Robert Lawson, Vice-President

FROM:          John Spam, Managing Editor

April 23, 197_

RESCHEDULING OF STANDARD "YOUR HEALTH" BOOKLETS

I talked with Thomas Johnson this morning in an effort to
reschedule production of 6000 Standard "Your Health" booklets
to permit delivery Saturday, April 26.

He indicated at first that such a rescheduling would delay
either the "Travel Plans" or the "Vacation Hints" booklets,
but after talking with his production manager he agreed to
make the schedule change without delaying our other pro-
duction.

Thus we can definitely count on delivery of "Your Health"
Saturday.
```

8. If you have an employer or know an organization that is willing to furnish the following specified materials, ask for them and then answer the questions:

   a. Bring to class a sample of a firm's letterhead stationery and envelopes and be prepared to evaluate them orally. If the firm has several sizes, qualities, and colors of stationery, evaluate them all and discuss briefly the uses of each.

   b. Bring to class a sample of memorandum stationery and any intracompany envelopes used for memos. Be prepared to evaluate them orally. Can you suggest improvements—perhaps timesaving additions or changes?

   c. Which of the standard styles of letter layout does the firm use? If the firm has not adopted a uniform style for all letters, try to collect—from various secretaries—as many different styles and layouts as you can. Be prepared to:
      (1) Illustrate those you like best and tell why.
      (2) Discuss those you like least and tell why.
      (3) If possible, find out why the secretaries and/or their bosses prefer the style they use.

    d. Find out from two or three secretaries in the firm what their pet peeves are concerning their bosses' use of letter parts or manner of dictating these parts.

    e. Be prepared to discuss the following aspects of memos in the firm you visited:

        (1) How frequently are memos used rather than telephone conversations?

        (2) Who writes memos? Only department heads? Nontitled employees? Others?

        (3) To whom do employees write memos?

        (4) Are memos usually routed through a superior? If so, through whom?

        (5) What is the average length of memos?

        (6) What standard and optional parts do the firm's memos contain?

9. Evaluate (in writing or orally, as your instructor assigns) the following, using the letters that you have already collected and been studying:

    a. Regular parts of each letter

    b. Optional parts

    c. Appearance—layout on page, strikeovers, type alignment, ribbon lightness

    d. Spelling accuracy

PART

MAJOR
LETTER PLANS

7

Direct Requests

When the main purpose of your message is to ask the reader to do something, you are writing a *request* letter or memo. Whether you organize your message according to the direct- or the persuasive-request pattern depends upon the nature of the request and, most of all, upon how you think the reader will react to that request. Generally when you make a simple inquiry or a routine request, you will *not* have to persuade your reader to do what you ask. You can usually handle the following types of messages with the direct-request plan:

Inquiries
Claims (complaints) and requests for adjustments
Requests for action related to routine business procedures
Invitations, orders, reservations
Requests pertaining to civic causes or public officials
Early-stage collection messages

This chapter presents the direct-request organizational plan, discusses the first five types of requests, then compares them briefly in capsule checklists. Chapter 13 discusses early-stage collection messages.

Organizational Plan

For a routine inquiry or request you assume that the reader will do as you request once he or she understands what you want and why you want it. Thus you use the direct approach—introduce your main idea in the first paragraph. The direct-request plan has three basic parts:

---

1. Main idea
   a. Introduce your request, major statement, or question.
   b. State reason(s), if desirable, justifying the request.
2. Explanation
   a. Include details necessary to help the reader respond to your request correctly.
   b. Consider numbering your questions (if more than one) for easy reading and answering.
3. Courteous close with motivation to action
   a. State clearly what action you want the reader to take—and when.
   b. Make action easy, if appropriate, by including a reply envelope, your telephone number, office hours, or any other appropriate helpful information.
   c. Express appreciation and, if appropriate, include a statement of goodwill or reader benefit.

Inquiries

To get facts that you need and cannot conveniently or economically obtain yourself, you write inquiries requesting information. Because the questions asked are important in all inquiries, this section begins with suggestions about phrasing and arranging questions. Then follows a discussion of direct-request messages that seek information about persons and messages that ask about products, services, and other matters requiring no persuasion.

Wording and Arrangement of Questions[1]

So that you can get exactly the information wanted, you must be especially careful when planning the questions to be included in your inquiries. The following suggestions apply to all kinds of direct-request inquiries:

1. Make your questions specific. If the product about which you inquire is technical, include specific physical dimensions, technical specifications, exact intended use of the item, architectural drawings, or whatever else will help the respondent. A single general question such as "Will you give us any information you can on this applicant (or product)?" will probably bring an inadequate reply or one so general that it will be almost useless.

   The more penetrating your questions, the more likely you are to get the information you need. Most respondents who would not *volunteer* unfavorable facts (especially about a person) will, however, be frank when asked specific questions provided you promise confidential treatment.
2. Use a separate paragraph for each main question if the questions require explanation.
3. If you have more than one question, consider numbering them. If you have only two or three questions, you may place them in the body of your letter, but it is generally better to list your questions on the same sheet below the body. Then the respondent can answer directly in the spaces provided and need not write a separate letter.
4. When you have more questions than space at the bottom of your letter page, or when your questions require lengthy answers, place them on a separate sheet and be sure to allow enough space for adequate answers.
5. Keep your questions to a minimum and make them clear. A long or vague questionnaire decreases the number of returns.
6. Word your questions to get more than "yes" or "no" answers if you need a detailed opinion or description. For example a yes or no answer to: "Did the applicant have duties that required responsibility?" would probably be inadequate. To obtain a more helpful answer, you might ask: "What kinds of duties requiring responsibility did the applicant perform especially well?" In contrast, a yes or no answer would be adequate for such a question as: "Does the applicant have an account with you?"
7. Word some questions for simple checking of "Yes," "No," or "Don't know" if you plan to tabulate numerous answers (say, 50 or more).
8. If you wish the respondent to "rate" a person, product, or service, it may be better to define each category on your rating scale. For instance, the following example shows one of eight questions on an employer's questionnaire about an applicant for employment. Notice how both the squares and the definitions make responses easy. The best choices may be at the right (as in the example) or at the left, but consistent placement of best choices is more convenient for both the reference and you—especially if you must compare many replies.

[1]See also Stanley L. Payne, *The Art of Asking Questions* (especially Chapter 14, which lists 100 considerations), Princeton University Press, Princeton, N.J., 1951; and Lyndon O. Brown, *Market Research and Analysis,* Ronald Press Company, New York, 1969.

ABILITY TO GET ALONG WITH OTHERS:
Is the applicant a likable, friendly, and tactful individual, or an egotistical, unpleasant, or thoughtless individual? Will he draw to him the people with whom he deals or keep them at a distance? Is he well-poised in normal social situations? (Check one)

☐   ☐   ☐   ☐   ☐

| Egotistical, unfriendly or tactless | Somewhat neutral, does not easily attract friends | Approachable | Likable, friendly, and tactful | Exceedingly pleasant and agreeable; will draw others to him |

9. Carefully arrange your questions—generally with the easiest to answer first.
10. Word your questions in a neutral way so you will not influence the answers.
11. Consider sending to your reader two copies of the questionnaire if you think he or she might need one for personal records.

Inquiries about Persons

When you need information about a person, you usually direct your request to a reference—a responsible source of information. The person about whom you ask the reference to give information may be an applicant for a job, a loan, credit, membership in an organization, an award, or for some kind of special training or insurance protection.

Inquiries to a reference may be written by the applicant or, more frequently, by the person who seeks information about the applicant.

Applicant's Request to a Reference. Sometimes an applicant asks references if they will send a recommendation direct to someone who needs confidential information about that applicant. For instance, suppose you are seeking admission into a graduate school that requires at least four confidential recommendations. Perhaps you can approach some of your selected references in person or by telephone. To others, however (if they are out of town or if you have a questionnaire they need to fill out), you will have to write a letter.

Because your request to a reference is asking a favor, it is best to state courteously in the first paragraph why you are writing to this person and what the recommendation is for. If you haven't been in touch with the references for some time, you may need to refresh their memory about who you are.

The explanation section of your request should include a brief summary of pertinent facts about yourself. Consider carefully the references' relationship to you and decide what facts they will need to grant the favor you are asking and to give a fair, helpful recommendation. (Sometimes an attached data sheet is useful.) If, for example, the reference is a former professor, you might include the following information:

1. The course you studied under the reference—when, where, and your grade.
2. Your major, and your grade-point average (GPA) in the major.
3. Your overall GPA in college. If the professor will or might recall that you made poor grades, include perhaps an honest brief explanation as to why your college GPA wasn't higher (for instance, number of hours each week you

worked to provide finances; a bad first year or first two years, but higher GPA the last year; or whatever is pertinent).

4. Difficult related courses you studied (if grades are good), from whom you took the courses, and the grades you received.

5. Test scores—graduate record exam, law school admission test, admission test for graduate study in business or medical school, or any other pertinent scores.

6. Honors, honor societies (Phi Beta Kappa, Beta Gamma Sigma, etc.), studies in any special honors programs.

7. Scholarships awarded.

8. Leadership qualities; for example, offices held in living group, on campus, in political groups.

9. Activities—College Bowl, tutoring, United Nations Model Congress, etc.

10. Guidelines, if possible, for the recommendation. Enclose, if you can, a form or letter from the graudate school stating what information it seeks from the reference about you—distinguishing intellectual traits or abilities, leadership capacity, quality of work done, character, integrity, or other personal traits.

Your closing paragraph should state to whom the letter or form is to be sent; be sure to state the full name and address, unless this information is printed on the form. And, of course, include a statement of appreciation.

If it is necessary for you to obtain recommendations about your work in specific courses or jobs in which your work was just mediocre, be sure to provide an explanation regarding the quality of your work, if possible. In inquiry 1 the applicant shows consideration for the reader by courteous tone, by the facts included about courses he studied, by mention of factors that influenced the quality of his chemistry studies, and by the reasonable time allowed for response.

Inquiry 1
An applicant's well-written request to a former professor.

Dear Professor Brown:

Introduction of request and reason
This letter is to reintroduce myself to you and to ask a favor of you. The University of Montana's Dental School has asked for a recommendation from my Organic Chemistry professor.

Explanation, tion, details about past relationship
Almost four years ago--in Winter and Spring Quarters of (year)--you were my chemistry professor here at the University of Montana. The courses I took from you were Chemistry 241 and Chemistry 242, both of which met at 3 p.m. daily. The grades I received were C's, but I believe I could have done better if circumstances had been a little different that year. Besides the lapse of two years between my inorganic and organic studies, there was also my part-time job in the Applied Physics Laboratory until 3 p.m. four days a week. Because this work caused me to come to your class about 15 minutes late, I sometimes missed important laboratory work, a fact which necessarily affected my grade. In our several conferences, however, you often commented very favorably on my work.

More details, leading to reason for this request   Currently I am a senior, graduating this quarter with a grade point average of 3.02 (out of 4.0) in Business Administration. I am applying for admission to the Dental School at the University of Montana. To this date I have completed successfully all the predental requirements, and would like to begin dental studies next fall.

Easy and dated action   The enclosed form is one the Dental School requires regarding my studies in organic chemistry. Professor Brown, will you please fill out and return this form in the enclosed enve- lope to the Admissions Officer? I will appreciate very much your mailing this information within the next two weeks-- before the admissions deadline, March 1.

Inquirer's Request to a Reference. The most frequent requests to references are those written by persons who need confidential information about the applicant. Suppose, for example, that you are the employer, lender, creditor, insurance under- writer, or officer of any organization that is considering an applicant for a special reason. The letter of inquiry you write to each reference the applicant has listed can be organized according to the direct-request pattern.

Your opening paragraph usually includes the full name of the applicant you are considering, why you are considering the applicant, and why you are writing to the reader.

The explanatory section should include:

1. Sufficient details about the requirements of the job, loan, credit, scholarship, or membership for which the applicant is being considered. Such facts help the reference to visualize whether the applicant can meet the requirements.
2. If appropriate, a few pertinent facts the applicant has already told you—such as length of time worked for the reference, job title, achievements. This way you can check on the applicant's accuracy and honesty.
3. Clearly stated questions (preferably numbered) asking exactly what you want to know about the applicant.

The ending paragraph usually includes appreciation, promise of confidential treat- ment of the reply, and (if appropriate) provisions for easy action[2] and an offer to reciprocate.

Obviously, the content and processing of your inquiry to a reference will depend upon your purpose and your reader. If, for example, you are writing to references about an applicant for a unique position, you will no doubt compose a special message with special questions. Not only will your letter be individually typed, but also you will usually expect a letter reply from the reference. The letter below (inquiry 2) from a hardware store manager to a department store manager, is an example of such an inquiry.

---

[2]When you write to a business executive at a business address, you can usually omit the en- closed reply envelope because many business executives prefer to use their own firm's stationery. However, when you write to a reference at home (for instance to a personal reference whose busi- ness address is unknown to you) or to someone who may be in a one-person office or in a non- profit organization, it is appropriate to enclose a stamped reply envelope.

Inquiry 2
Personalized request listing numbered questions in the letter[3]

Name, why being considered, and a few facts he has told
Mr. Morton L. Dryer, one of your former employees, has applied here as assistant manager of our electrical supplies department. He states that he was in charge of your electrical appliances section for about a year, and he has given your name as a reference.

Request
We need a qualified person who can, in about two years, become department manager. I will appreciate your frank answers to the following questions and any other pertinent facts you can include:

Questions
1. When was he in your employ and why did he leave?
2. How satisfactory were his services as a section head in your store?
3. Do you know of any personal habits or characteristics that might hinder or help his success in a position of responsibility?

A promise
Your statements will, of course, be kept confidential.

Inquiry 3 below is an exceptionally thorough individually typed inquiry which interweaves explanation and unnumbered questions for each qualification. It is reproduced here as an example of the care that a reputable firm takes in placing an outstanding candidate.

Inquiry 3
Personalized request interweaving explanations with questions in the letter.

Full name; reason for request
We are seriously considering Barbara Rankin for a position in our Research Department here. She has given your name as a reference.

Details— applicant's work
As you may know, Barbara has been working in a clerical position for us part time for about a year in our branch office in your city. Now she has expressed interest in getting into more professional work and pursuing her career in writing for our head office.

Details; specific request and explanation
Because of Barbara's outstanding record in college, to say nothing of the fine work she has done for us, we are making every effort to find, or create, a position for her here. And for that reason I am asking for help in finding out as much as possible about her relative strengths and weaknesses. In this way we can do a better job of fitting her talents to our needs and in assigning her work which is not either beyond her present capacity or out of line with her interests and skills.

---

[3]To save space, most examples in this and succeeding chapters include only the body of each message. You can assume the salutation is the usual "Dear Mr. (Mrs., Miss, Ms.) plus the reader's surname" unless otherwise indicated.

*Two
implied
questions*
I understand that Barbara worked about two years part time in your advertising office, and I will welcome information about how effectively and concisely Barbara writes, particularly how readily she can compose business letters to advertisers.

*More
questions
with
details*
In addition, we would like to have your impressions of the attitudes and skills that Barbara can carry over from school to the business world--her ability to organize her work, her originality, initiative, reliability, and ability to work smoothly with others while under pressure. Under what degree of supervision and guidance is she likely to do her best

*A
promise*
work? Any and all comments you may care to make will be a great help and, of course, confidential.

*Easy
action
(phone)*
Your schedule is probably particularly heavy at this time of year--and I hesitate to call you when you may be busy. Perhaps it would be simplest for you to telephone me collect (area code and phone number) when convenient for you. I am usually at my desk between 9:00 and 11:30 Monday through Friday.

If you (for example, as personnel manager) need references on hundreds of new applicants, sheer volume will force you to plan a duplicated form that you can use again and again. For instance, inquiry 4, used by a national business machines firm, is printed with lines for typewritten fill-ins, including name and city of the applicant, in the opening. The questions on the lower half of the same sheet ask the reference to evaluate the applicant—from superior to unsatisfactory—on various personal qualities; also there is a small space for comments. (If you prefer to define each rating category, use a form with questions similar to that illustrated in suggestion 8, page 149.) As is customary and desirable, the last question gives the respondent additional space for "other comments." The information obtained from such open-ended questions can be extremely important and helpful.

Inquiry 4
Printed inquiry adaptable for any reference about any prospective applicant; evaluation form on same page below the request.

*Name and
reason*
M_____(name)_____ of ___(city)___ states that he/she was employed by you as _(type of work)_ from _(date)_ to _(date)_ . He/she has listed your name as a reference.

*Type of
work*
We are making a careful study of the qualifications of this applicant to determine whether it would be in his/her best interests to consider a position as Sales Representative in our business of furnishing a complete line of (type of machines are named here).

*Request
and
easy
action*
Will you please give us your answers and comments on the following points and any other comments which you feel will be helpful to the applicant in choosing a life's work? Just mail your reply in the enclosed stamped return envelope as soon as possible.

	Superior	Good	Average	Below average	Unsatis-factory	Comments
Potential ability to sell a quality product (your estimate)						
Personality						
Industry—determination						
Aptness in learning						
Creative ability—resourcefulness						
Dependability—cooperation						
Disposition—balance						

For what type of work do you think applicant is best fitted? _____

Would you strongly recommend that applicant enter sales work? _____

Other comments (you may also use reverse side): _____

(Signed) _____

Date _____   (Title) _____

Inquiries about Products or Services

Both as a consumer and as a business or professional person, you will have many occasions to seek information from the seller of products and services or from customers, employees, and others.

Direct Request to the Seller. When your inquiry goes to a seller—whether a manufacturer, retailer, investment broker, or hotel clerk—the addressee's self-interest should make him or her glad to comply with your wishes. Perhaps you want a free catalog, price list, or booklet about products, deliveries, or payment plans. At such times your complete direct request need be only one sentence, such as:

> Please send me your latest sporting equipment catalog and the descriptive folder you advertised in the April issue of *Sportsman Illustrated.*

If, however, you have a unique individual problem, you may need to ask questions for which the recipient does not have prepared answers. Following the direct-request plan, present your main idea (request and/or reason) in the first paragraph. Deciding whether to place your reason or request first depends upon your request and reader. In most inquiries to a seller concerning a product or service, it is entirely optional whether to present request or reason first. But if you think your request is somewhat unusual or will be time-consuming for the reader to answer, state the reason first. After the opening paragraph, include all needed explanation and/or questions. The final paragraph contains the action request.

Inquiry 5 is written by a purchasing manager requesting information from a manufacturer about a product he is considering buying. Notice that the letter begins with the major request; but if you prefer to begin with the reason, you might interchange paragraphs 1 (request) and 3 (reason).

Inquiry 5
Inquiry about an advertised product; numbered questions within the letter.

Major request	Your ads in <u>Good</u> <u>Business</u> magazine have attracted our attention, and we will appreciate your answers to the following questions:
	1. What is the price of each Quiktyper?
	2. How long does it take an average typist to learn to operate this machine?
Specific numbered questions	3. To what extent can your experts estimate about how much money a company can save in a year with Quiktyper, if it uses--for instance--25 different one-page form letters and mails a total of 270,000 letters a year?
	4. What guarantee do you offer?
Reason for request	Before deciding whether our firm should invest in one or more automatic typewriters, we should like as much information as possible about leading brands.
Suggested action	If you have a factory agent in this area, we welcome a demonstration any time within the next two weeks, preferably after receipt of your written reply to these four questions.

Direct Requests to Customers, Employees, and Others. As the seller of products or services, you can often use inquiries to win back "missed" customers who have not bought from your firm for some time or to obtain information about your firm's products or services.

"Miss you" messages can be either simple requests (as discussed below) or persuasive requests (see Chapter 10). Many firms have revived hundreds of unused accounts by mailing a series of direct requests—ranging from colorful postcards to form letters on specially designed stationery. Such messages concentrate on telling readers that they are missed, appreciated, and important, and asking them to come back. Specially designed letterheads and colors often aid in making visual the word pictures expressed in miss-you messages.

Inquiry 6, from a firm of auto service specialists, includes a touch of humor on a descriptive letterhead that introduces the theme of the message.

Inquiry 6
A "miss you" request designed mainly to get the customer to come back. A picture at the top shows a home hallway, a lighted lamp, a clock with hands at 2:15, and a

*person entering the front door cautiously on tiptoe while carrying a pair of shoes.
A voice from upstairs calls:*

"WHERE HAVE YOU BEEN?"

*Main
idea*

We've missed you too! And we've been asking about you,
because it's the repeat appearances of good customers like
you that play the leading part in our business.

Reason

In fact, customers like you are the balance wheel, the
spark plugs, the drive shaft that keep us going. With us,
customers are about the whole works.

*Suggested
action*

That's why we've been wondering about you. Remember that
our door is always open for you--from 8 a.m. to 6 p.m.
Mondays through Fridays. You won't have to tiptoe in.
Every appearance you make in our shop is sincerely appre-
ciated. DRIVE IN SOON, won't you? WE'LL DO OUR BEST TO
PLEASE YOU.

Inquiry 6 is designed simply to get the customer to come back. Other miss-you
letters may go a step further and ask what is wrong. Then if the former customers
have a complaint, they feel they can express it; if they have none, they will probably
say so and perhaps place another order. Either way the silence has been broken, and a
dead account may be revived. Also, your firm may have gained useful information
about its products or services.

When you ask your customer what is wrong, you have several ways to make replying easy. Some messages, like inquiry 7, merely ask the reader to jot down the reason
on the margin or back of the letter. Others invite the reader to phone, and still others
list a few possible reasons for the reader to check off. (This list may include also some
humorous unlikely reasons. See, for example, Figure 6-15, page 134. A later sentence
then asks for another chance to serve the customer soon.)

Inquiry 7
A "miss you" inquiry aiming mainly to get a reply that answers "What is wrong?"

*Main
idea*

Perhaps you have the answer to a question that has worried us.
For a long time we have received no order or mail from you;
and as we do not know why, we are concerned.

Explanation

We have missed the privilege of serving you--a good business
friend. Often we have asked ourselves, "What did we do or
say to offend this good customer?" What causes this absence?
We've checked all the orders and correspondence from you plus
our shipment schedules and prices to you--and everything
looks OK.

*Suggested
reasons*

But something must be wrong, to keep you from us so long.
Please tell me about it frankly. If in any way our merchandise or service did not come up to your expectations, let us
make amends. There may be some other reason why we have not
heard from you; and if so, will you please tell us?

<table>
<tr><td>Easy
action</td><td>Just write your note on the margin or back of this letter and mail it in the prepaid envelope addressed to me. I'll very much appreciate your reply.</td></tr>
</table>

Other inquiries about your firm's products or services can also be in the form of direct requests. Besides asking lost customers what is wrong, you can ask steady or new customers for their comments about your products which they have bought or returned. Then not only will you obtain valuable information, but you will also help build customer confidence in your genuine desire to maintain good service. (For examples of messages showing continuing concern see Chapter 14.)

Often you will need information from employees, colleagues, or other persons *within* your organization. Inquiry 8, a memo launching an employee survey, can be adapted so that it is suitable for other types of readers—inside or outside your organization—whenever your questions are easy to answer and no persuasion is necessary.

Inquiry 8
A memo seeking employee needs and preferences about parking on company premises; questionnaire attached.

TO:	All employees Date: May 1, 197_
FROM:	Parking Division, Personnel Department
SUBJECT:	<u>Your preferences about parking permits</u>

Reader-benefit reason	In an effort to improve the parking situation for all employees, your Parking Division is conducting a survey of your needs and preferences.
Request and dated action	Will you please fill out the attached questionnaire and return it, unsigned, to your supervisor by Friday, May 1, at 5 p.m. Then you will be sure that your feelings are included in the survey. The results of employee opinions and suggestions will be tabulated and announced at the next employee meeting, May 15.

Claims (Complaints) and Requests for Adjustments

Whenever you are dissatisfied with a product, service, or policy, it is to your advantage—and the company's—to communicate with the right person promptly about the desired correction. Oral complaints to sales representatives or clerks often do not bring results; a much better procedure is to write an effective letter to the proper company official who does care when a problem exists and who can and will do something to correct it.

When you state your complaint, you usually make a claim or request for some kind of adjustment. All such requests are grouped together in this section and labeled *claim letters.* Claim letters should be organized by the direct-request pattern whenever they involve a routine matter that is covered by a guarantee or by established procedures for customer relations.

Typical situations for direct-request claims about merchandise involve defective materials or workmanship, malfunctioning parts, soiled or shopworn items, or products not as represented. Claims about services include delivery mix-ups, broken promises, discourtesy, carelessness, clerical or bookkeeping errors, and minor inconveniences relating to violation of published company policies. (For those claims that involve controversial issues, substantially large sums of money, repeated errors, and other serious matters you will need to write a persuasive request, as discussed in Chapter 10.)

Characteristics of Well-written Claims

To be fair to the seller, to the product or service, and to yourself—write promptly. Also, be sure your letter has all the C qualities. Show by your attitude and wording that *you have confidence in the readers' fairness*—confidence that they will make the adjustment after they get the facts. Omit any statements that sound like appeals or threats.

When you complain about the poor condition of a product, for instance, state all the pertinent facts logically, courteously, and impersonally, without exaggeration or irrelevant material. Guesses and opinions about who may be to blame for an error are unwise and unhelpful. Let the reader determine causes; you present facts as you see them. And when your purpose is to call attention to an employee's poor service, make clear you are doing so because you think the behavior is not representative of the firm's usually good customer relations policies.

Anger and name-calling are, of course, taboo. Remember that the reader is not the person who made the mistake. The purpose of your claim letter is to get as satisfactory an adjustment as possible. A writer who antagonizes the recipient merely lowers the chances of satisfactory adjustment—or at least of being considered a reasonable individual. One extra caution: When you write as an agent for your employer or business, you must be even more careful to avoid tactless, intemperate accusations. Such outbursts not only reflect unfavorably upon you *and* your company, but they also may place you in danger of a libel suit.[4]

It is often a good idea to state both sides of the case—for example, you might comment on something you *like* about the firm's products or service. Such a statement can be in the opening paragraph or in the explanation. Even humor (not sarcasm) is appropriate when the matter is relatively small.

Organization and Content of the Simple Direct Claim

Begin your direct claim with the main idea—namely, the need for an adjustment or correction of an error. Do not waste the reader's time by giving lengthy details or background information in the first paragraph.

In the explanatory paragraph(s) of your letter, include all facts the reader will need to understand your claim clearly. For instance, if you wish free repairs on an item that is malfunctioning within the guarantee period, present evidence of the date of your

[4]See Appendix A, about legal aspects of letters.

purchase, make clear that you followed carefully the operating instructions (if you did), and state clearly what is wrong.

In your action paragraph, ask for what you want or leave the decision to your reader. Depending on circumstances, you will usually request one or more of the following. (The numbers in parentheses after each request refer to the claim-letter examples illustrated in this section.)

1. Refund—for all or part of purchases price (1)
2. A new shipment with the correct item(s) ordered (1)
3. Free replacement of the defective part(s), the whole item, or the whole shipment, or service (2)
4. Free repairs (3)
5. Reduction in the price (because of a product or service defect) (3)
6. Free inspection, leading to redecorating, complete overhaul, etc.
7. Explanation and/or change in policy or procedure (4)
8. Credit to your account (or a credit slip) (4)
9. Cancellation of an order or part of an order.
10. Correction (and perhaps explanation) of a billing error

If you need the adjustment by a certain time, state why, as in the last paragraph of the following claim. You should also consider (and perhaps ask) whether the defective or incorrect product should be returned to the seller. Although the claimant in the letter below returned the wrong-size item without asking, often it is better not to return goods until you have the seller's instructions.

Claim 1
A courteous claim (dated June 9) to a sportswear department manager from an out-of-town cash customer who needs an exchange or a refund.

Main idea *—request*	Enclosed is the sweater which Nelson's delivery truck left yesterday and which I wish to exchange for the correct size or a refund.
Explanatory details	When I selected and purchased this Hudson sweater in your department last week (for $20.38 cash), I asked that a size "L" be sent to my home. The size I received is only an "S", and of course I can't wear it. My sales check is #7902, dated June 4, written by salesclerk #801.
Specific request	Will you please send me the correct size "L" in exactly this same style and color or, if this is not available now, a cash refund of $20.38. As I am leaving on a one-month trip
Dated action	June 17, it is necessary that I receive the sweater or the check before that date.

Sometimes you may have to present your direct-request claim a second time. A second request usually goes to a higher official, and your letter will probably have a dual purpose—to obtain the desired action and to complain about the lack of response (or incorrect response). For example, suppose that instead of receiving the sweater or cash refund you requested by letter in claim 1, you receive only a credit slip which you don't want. Or suppose that instead of writing your first claim, you returned the sweater in person to the sportswear department, and there both the salesperson and the department manager rudely insist that you accept a credit slip. If you know the refusal is contrary to the store's published policy, you will justly feel that a higher official should know about the situation.

For such a dual-purpose direct-request letter, you might begin with a paragraph like one of the following:

> The purpose of my letter is to ask you for a cash refund which I am unable to obtain through normal channels. Also I'm sure you will want to know about the discrepancy between the treatment I received in your sportswear department and your advertised company policy of customer satisfaction or a full refund.

or

> You will be interested, I think, in the experience I had with a wrong-size sweater I received from your store June 8. I believe I am entitled to a cash refund, though two of your employees refused to give it to me.

Your explanatory paragraph should tactfully present all pertinent facts about your purchase and the department employees' statements; you should also enclose a copy of the credit slip or its date and number. The ending paragraph will be a forthright request for the refund.

The next two examples are written by business executives for claims concerning their companies. Claim 2 concerns faulty products; claim 3, faulty service. Notice that in both letters the writers present all needed facts without anger and with good you-attitude.

Claim 2
A considerate complaint from a gift store owner to a wholesaler, about faulty merchandise.

Main idea; request

Our shipment of Swedish tumblers was checked in yesterday and put on sale, then hurriedly withdrawn when the stock room reported it to be a completely defective shipment. We are asking you for an adjustment on these tumblers.

Details

The news about this shipment was especially disappointing to me because we had already advertised that the sale was to begin today. I personally washed and examined a dozen glasses of each size, four each (and not necessarily the worst) of which we are sending you by express for your examination and comment.

There is no regularity in the mars, scratches, and abrasions, or whatever the defects should be termed, to indicate faulty moulds. In fact, I've never seen anything in domestic or imported glass to equal the variety of imperfections apparently present in some degree in every glass of this shipment.

You-
attitude

I realize fully that you had no opportunity to check this merchandise and that it is only through your customers that you learn of its condition and can in turn seek an adjustment from the factory.

Action

We are withholding sale of the glasses and payment of the bill until we hear from you.

Claim 3

A considerate complaint (May 18) from a restaurant manager to a laundry about faulty service.

Main idea—
something
is wrong;
compliment
too

What has happened to Spic's starching and mending service? You may recall my April 19 letter complimenting you on the neat appearance of the uniforms Spic sent then. But the last three shipments have contained both torn and incorrectly starched garments.

Details

On May 10, nine of our twenty waitresses' uniforms came back as limp as though they had not been starched at all. Though our girls were disappointed, we decided that "accidents will happen" and surely next week they'd be as good as ever. But on May 14, all 20 uniforms came back again limp--in collars and cuffs. Also four had unmended rips on the pockets. That morning on our outgoing laundry bag I pinned a note for the driver asking if the laundry would please again observe the following request, which had been overlooked the previous week:

EXTRA HEAVY STARCH ON ALL COLLARS AND CUFFS

More
details

Today--same thing happened. All collars and cuffs were limp as though they had no starch! BUT this time five of the cotton slacks of our men waiters had extra heavy starch in them. They were so stiff they stood up alone! It took a bit

Good-natured of persuading to get the men to wear them; we had a good
attitude laugh each time.

More you
attitude

Yet all this mix-up hurts the image of our restaurant. We like our employees to look neat. As you know, I'd much rather compliment than complain. But the change has been so abrupt that I'm sure you want to know. I ask that you please:

Specific
request

Reduce your charges for the 49 unstarched uniforms and the overstarched five pairs of slacks, and

Make free repairs on the four torn uniforms, which we will return to your driver on his next call.

In the future, can we count on the usual good mending as well as starching service?

The last example of a direct-request claim (claim 4) is a customer's somewhat humorous, but effective, complaint to a loan company.

Claim 4

Humorous complaint about a premium computation error; directed to a computer, not a person.

Dear Computer #   :

Main idea It seems you're trying to take my bank account and home away from me, and you haven't even told me your number yet. You have my number--Social Security #99-81-9999.

Detailed explanation On 12-1-74 (I'm using figures as you do, Mr. Computer) I obtained mortgage loan #999,9999 from the company you run. On 2-2-75, I received notice that because of real estate property tax rate increases, my monthly mortgage payments were increasing. You asked whether I wanted to continue my $164.20 monthly payments and pay an annual sum to the escrow account of $108.12, or add 1/12 of the tax amount to each monthly payment. My choice was #2.

On 3-1-75 you billed me for a monthly payment of $17,321. Now obviously, computer, since I didn't have enough money to make the lump sum payment to the escrow account, I don't have enough to make a monthly payment of $17,321. My old-fashioned arithmetic makes $164.20 + $9.01 = $173.21. Perhaps the remainder, $17,321 - $173.21, is interest? In my opinion, such an interest charge is excessive, even though computers may be exempt from usury laws. Since you are the only one from your department who ever writes me, I suspect there are no human workers in your employ who could help me.

Action request Anyhow, I'm enclosing my check for $173.21, which I think should be credited as a full monthly payment on my loan. If you can't accept it, please ask your president to explain the company policy to me. And please do not bend, fold, mutilate or punch all your little holes in this letter until your president has a chance to read it.

In this pleasantly witty letter, the customer reveals not only a premium computation error, but also woes in getting computerized replies to inquiries.

Requests for Action Related to Routine Business Procedures

The messages in this section include business or professional people's requests that are directly related to routine business procedures within their firm. The discussions and examples are grouped in two categories—according to whether the requests go to persons outside or within the organization.

Requests to Persons outside Your Organization

As a business or professional person you may need to ask your customer, supplier, transportation company, or others to sign an enclosed signature card or form or document. Or you may need missing answers on a customer's credit application, or the return of a budget payment book, or a correction of an irregularity in a check sent to your firm. These and numerous other routine matters can be handled by direct-request messages.

You can use form letters, either processed or individually typed, but it is often a good idea to personalize the letter by individual typing as in request 1 below. However, even processed form messages—like requests 2 and 3—are satisfactory when the messages are clearly the same for all members (customers) in a group.

Notice that all the following letters are concise, clear, and courteous. And they all begin with the reason or the request (or a major statement that leads to the request) either in the first paragraph or at the beginning of the second.

Request 1
A bank's trust department asks the executor of an estate to return an affidavit, signature card, and passbook; individually typed message.

Reason and request

So that we can transfer the account of Mr. R. S. Roe, deceased, to your name as Executor, will you please do the following:

Numbered specific requests

1. Sign the enclosed affidavit.
2. Fill out the enclosed card and sign it.
3. Return to us the signed affidavit, card, and your passbook No. 222-222.

Reader benefit and easy action

The same day these important materials reach us, we will transfer the funds to a new account with no loss of earnings. Please use the enclosed airmail envelope to speed your reply.

Request 2
Request from a mortgage loan company to a borrower regarding increased loan payments; personalized form letter signed by the company's president.

Main idea

The valuable benefits your Homeowner's Mortgage Protector Plan provides become effective on the date the Certificate indicates--if you have paid the insurance premium for the plan.

Request with specific payment amounts

In case you have already mailed your mortgage installment for the month in which your protection is to become effective, please send the premium--$ --to us now so that you will be fully protected for the month.

Next month and for all future payments please be sure to combine your mortgage and insurance payments into one check for $

Reader benefit

We are pleased you have secured this protection for yourself and family. Many of our customers have found this is a very valuable and worthwhile program. After you have read the Certificate carefully, please file it with your other valuable papers.

Whenever common errors—for instance in checks, order forms, registration—occur frequently among your customers, a well-worded form request is a time-saver. Request

3 illustrates a simple, concise form. See also Figure 6-12 for another timesaving form for handling routine requests.

Request 3
Multipurpose printed form (7" x 3½") to inform customers of needed check correction.

Request	Your check is being returned with the request that you please make the correction(s) as indicated below. This check . . .
Details (what should be done instead of what's wrong)	__Should be signed by maker. __Should be properly endorsed. __Needs an individual endorsement. __Must have the written amount agree with the figure. __Should be made payable to us. __Needs the correct date.
Action reader benefit	As soon as you have made the correction(s), please return this check or a new check, and we will be glad to credit your account.

Requests to Persons within Your Organization

The memos included here are straightforward requests exchanged between employees, colleagues, supervisors and subordinates, and others, such as stockholders, who are part of an organization. (Most memos of authorization for special studies and reports also fall in this direct-request group.)

The next two examples illustrate well-written requests to persons within the writer's organization. As you read request 4, notice its good features—the six numbered details for easy reading and the definite, courteous instructions about the desired action. Enclosed with the memo was a two-page sample report with detailed discussion of each of the six headings.

Request 4
A division manager's memo asking field representatives to send monthly reports.

TO:	Jim Inkley	Emma Koontz
	Ruth Lindquist	Dick Dubuque
	Tom Sedlock	
CC:	Ralph Smith	
	B. J. Loners	
FROM:	James Pearson	
SUBJECT:	Monthly Reports	DATE: September 10, 197_

Request	Starting October 1, will each of you please submit to this office on the 21st of the month a monthly report including:

Numbered details

1. Major orders received during the month
2. Anticipated major orders for the following month
3. New business activity
4. Lost orders
5. Industrial trends
6. General comments

Helpful sample

A copy of the form I would like you to use is attached.

Clear statement of where and when report should be sent

By no later than the 21st of every month, please mail your monthly report to me, with copies to the following:

1. Each of the other sales representatives
2. Gail Rankin, Sales Manager

I will appreciate your cooperation.

Request 5, to stockholders, includes both a reader-benefit reason and two suggestions for easy action. Notice the "faked inside address" and omission of salutation.

Request 5
A corporation secretary's second request to stockholders for a proxy; printed message

Second Request
For Proxy for
Annual Meeting of Stockholders May 9, 197_

Main idea

At the close of business on April 25, we had not received a proxy from you for the Annual Stockholders Meeting to be held May 9.

Perhaps you have already mailed that proxy. If so, we thank you and ask that you disregard this request.

Request; easy action

If you have not yet returned your proxy, however,--or are doubtful whether you did so--will you please fill out either the enclosed proxy form or the one we sent to you April 8 along with the meeting notice and invitation.

Reader benefit; easy action

So that you will be represented at the meeting, please mail your proxy today in the enclosed reply envelope.

Invitations, Orders, Reservations

Though quite different from each other, invitations, orders, and reservations are similar in that the reader is asked for participation, merchandise, or facilities.

Invitations

Invitations that require no persuasion can be both good-news announcements and simple requests. Regardless of how you classify them, they are organized according to the same three-part plan: main idea, explanation, action.

The main idea in the first paragraph is the invitation request, and you should try to include in it as many of the 5 W's as you can. The following sample openings are representative of two kinds of invitations you may need to send in business.

Memo
To all employees (from the company's house-organ editor):
Do you have an item of news or a suggestion you would like to share with other employees in our company? If so, you are invited to submit it for inclusion in our Semi-annual Company House Organ before March 1.

Letter
To all customers (from an administrative officer):
You are cordially invited to attend the Open House of our Topname Airplane Company . . .
Sunday, June 10, from 2 to 5 p.m.
in Plants 2 and 3.

In the explanation paragraph of your direct-request invitation, include all details that your reader(s) will appreciate and need. The ending paragraph clearly states the desired reader action and makes the action easy. If you need a reply by a certain date, be sure to say so.

The letter below invites business executives to a luncheon meeting.

Dear ALTRUA member:

Request	The next meeting of ALTRUA is one you are especially invited to attend. As your yearbook shows, this is the
What *Who*	FORUM LUNCHEON, sponsored jointly by the Chamber of Commerce and our club to be held
Where	at Lake City Community Hall, (address)
When	on Thursday, April 21, 197_ 12:15 p.m.
A detail about the program	A highlight of the program is the panel discussion on the topic, "Problems of the Small Business Executive in K County." You will find the discussion timely, challenging, and thought-provoking.
Easy action	To make your reservation, please call either Trish Norden (823-7777) or Mike Browne (349-9999) before Tuesday, April 19, 5 p.m. How about phoning right now while you think of it?
Reader benefit	We look forward to seeing you April 21 at the luncheon. For your convenience, free parking is available on the north side of the Hall.

Orders and Reservations

When you are ordering supplies or equipment and do not have an order blank or purchase form of the company with which you are placing the order, you can accomplish your purpose by writing a letter according to the direct-request plan. The same is true when you wish to reserve hotel accommodations, a meeting room, parking facilities for a conference, or any other premises.

Order letters include three kinds of facts: details about *what you are ordering or reserving, directions for shipment,* and *manner of payment.* In both order and reservation messages, the main idea in the first paragraph is that you are ordering or reserving something. Your explanatory paragraphs give whatever details the order or reservation requires—about quantity, color, style, size, price, payment, location, shipment date, place—plus any special instructions your reader might need. The last paragraph invites prompt shipment and dated action, if desired.

The following letter illustrates the organization and content of an order letter with items tabulated for easy reading. You can use a similar organization plan for reservations.

Request	Please ship the following supplies to reach our main office at 9251 Grand Avenue (City, State, Zip) by Wednesday, June 3:			
Details	Quantity	Description (and or catalog number)	Unit Price	Total
		Total		$

Payment — These items are to be charged to our account on the usual 2/10, net/30 terms.

Shipment *Courtesy* — As we plan to distribute the ball-point pens for customer gifts on the opening day of our new branch, June 5, it is imperative that this shipment arrive on time. We count on your company's usual promptness in filling orders.

Requests Pertaining to Civic Causes or Public Officials

Public officials need and appreciate suggestions from enlightened business executives, professionals, and concerned citizens. Often, when an important issue is up for debate, they welcome direct communications that are not part of an organized drive.

When you have a request, plan, or information that you sincerely believe is in the best interests of the community—or at least of your business or industry—remember the power of a good letter to the proper officials. As former President Kennedy said, "Everyone's vote counts in America, but those who write letters to express their opinions make their vote count more often."

Messages regarding civic causes or to public officials can involve any of the previously discussed four types of common situations—inquiries, complaints, requests for action related to routine business procedures, or invitations. But because of their special nature, they are grouped together separately in this section. Letters of this type are generally best handled by the direct-request plan. The busy official receiving your letter will welcome the message that states the purpose in the first paragraph. The following opening paragraphs about various issues should give you ideas on how to begin your request with the main idea:

1. *From a business executive to a Senator in Washington, D.C.:* The proposal to increase the truck weight and sizes on the interstate highway system deserves your serious consideration. I believe such an increase would be extremely unwise and wish to join the many others who ask that you oppose such a measure.
2. *From a store owner to the City's District Engineer:* This letter protests the proposed underpass at 60th Street and Highway 409. This change would cause an undue hardship on small-business owners who have invested their savings to build businesses convenient to the community in this area.
3. *From a citizen to a county highway commission:* The newspapers have stated that your department is installing numerous directional signs, in an attempt to help people (especially strangers) find their way around (city name). This action is a tremendous and useful job. My suggestion concerns how to help the many people who miss the right exits and need to get back to the freeway again.
4. *From a member of the Armed Forces to a home-state senator:* This letter respectfully requests your assistance for my early release to accept employment because of family hardship.
5. *From a citizen's committee favoring a certain bond issue:* To help keep public education in this area sound, we urge your support of Special Levy 102.

As with all other direct requests, after you have introduced your main idea (request and reason), continue with adequate explanation. You may also find it desirable to enclose drawings, printed summaries with documentation, or any other visual material pertinent to your explanation. End with a forthright request such as, "we will appreciate whatever you can do to urge that Congress will legalize . . . during the current session."

The Capsule Checklists on pages 184 and 185 provide a quick summary of each type of direct request discussed in this chapter—inquiries, complaints, requests for action related to routine business procedures, orders, and invitations that require no persuasion.[5] As you study these direct-request plan lists, notice that you introduce your main idea at or near the beginning, include whatever details your reader needs, and end courteously with easy and dated action, if appropriate.

Exercises

Inquiries about Persons, Products, Services

1. Comment orally on the good and poor qualities of the following inquiries about persons (sent to references). Which ones do you think will best accomplish their purpose? Why?

    a. From a national oil company:

    > We are considering Mr. Larry R. Terrill, for a position with this Company and he has given your name as a personal reference.
    >
    > May we have your frank comment both as to his ability and personal qualities? Do you know of any reason for our

---

[5] For every direct request pertaining to a civic cause or public officials, follow the checklists on whatever type of situation best applies. If you prefer, merely follow the "direct-request general plan" in the first column and use your good judgment about what details to include.

not giving him full confidence? We shall appreciate any additional comments which will help us in reaching a correct decision, and also in adapting him to our organization in the event of our employing him.

Since this matter is very active at present, we shall appreciate a prompt reply and are enclosing a stamped and self-addressed envelope for this purpose.

b. From the Big Brother volunteer service organization of a city: (This is an obviously processed form letter.)

Dear Mr. Willman:

About: Robert Zurbach

The above-named gentleman has applied to us to serve as a Big Brother. He has given your name as a reference.

We feel you, in your contacts with him, would be able to advise us as to his stability and moral character. As a Big Brother, he will be working with a young, fatherless boy, establishing a friendship and offering moral and character guidance to the boys.

We would like your frank appraisal, which will be held in strict confidence. Since your evaluation is necessary to complete the application, we will appreciate hearing from you soon.

c. Night letter telegram from an agency of the United States Government:

PATRICIA M. MONELL DATE OF BIRTH 5/18/52 BEING CONSIDERED FOR EMPLOYMENT AS VETERAN'S CLAIMS EXAMINER QUASI-LEGAL POSITION HAS GIVEN YOUR NAME AS REFERENCE. REQUEST EVALUATION BY RETURN NIGHT LETTER COLLECT WITH APPLICANT'S DEMONSTRATED POTENTIAL TO PERFORM SUCH DUTIES, AND PERSONAL CHARACTERISTICS EXHIBITED DURING EMPLOYMENT WITH YOU. DO YOU HAVE ANY ADVERSE INFORMATION? WOULD YOU RECOMMEND FOR FEDERAL EMPLOYMENT?

2. Messages a and b are forms used by two law schools to get information about the many applicants who seek admission. Compare them for completeness, clarity of questions, information sought, and ease of action. Which will probably be more effective?

a. The above named person has applied for admission into (school name) Law School. Because your name was listed as a reference, we will appreciate a letter of recommendation from you.

No special form is required. Letters should be detailed and frank appraisals of the applicant as to (1) qualities of intellect, (2) communication skills, (3) character, (4) maturity, and (5) personality. Comparisons of the applicant with other students known by the writer to have been admitted to the Law School are helpful.

b. Mr.
Ms.
Mrs. _____

Miss (LAST NAME)   (FIRST NAME)   (MIDDLE NAME)
is an applicant for admission to the (school name) Law School. Each year the

number of applicants to the School far exceeds the number that can be accepted. You will greatly assist this applicant and the School by providing specific and candid answers to this inquiry. The information you provide will be treated as confidential. Prompt completion of this form will be appreciated by both the applicant and the School, for the application cannot be acted on until this form is received from you. Thank you for your cooperation.

1. How well do you know the applicant? _____
2. Has the applicant performed in an honorable and trustworthy manner in

   academic work and social relationships? _____
3. Has the applicant been the subject of disciplinary action or proceedings

   (for misconduct) or of academic censure (for deficient scholarship)? _____
   If so, please explain. (Please use the reverse side if this space is insufficient.)

   _____

   _____

4. Has the applicant any physical handicap or any illness, physical or mental,

   that in your opinion bears on his or her ability to do law school work? ___
   If so, please explain. _____

   _____

5. In classes with you, how have you graded the applicant's academic perfor-

   mance (percentile, if possible)? _____
6. What is the applicant's approximate rank for all work taken in your

   college? _____

7. To what degree did the applicant's scholastic achievement measure up to

   capacity? _____
   ☐ Fully realized capacity.   ☐ Had capacity to do considerably
   ☐ Performed reasonably in view   better.
     of capacity.   ☐ No basis for judgment.

   Remarks: _____

   _____

   _____

8. Please furnish any other information that will be of assistance to a consideration of the applicant's transcript and college record as a whole. Helpful remarks can relate to, but need not be limited to, unusual time-consuming extracurricular activities, leadership performance, motivation, capacity for interpersonal relations and significant participation in outside employment. We will also appreciate your estimate of the applicant's grades, courses taken and major field as a reliable measure of academic

   capacity. (Please use the reverse side if this space is insufficient.) _____

   _____

   _____

9. Do you recommend the applicant for admission to the (name) Law School?
   ☐ I recommend with enthusiasm.   ☐ I recommend with reservation.
   ☐ I recommend.   ☐ I do not recommend.

Signature _____

Name (Please type or print) _____

Title _____

Date _____ Address _____

3. Prepare to discuss orally the strengths and weaknesses of the following letters designed to get information. Comment particularly on organization, clarity, completeness of explanations, and motivation for action.

   a. To subscribers of a magazine: (salutation is "Dear Journal Reader.")

   > You're right. Another questionnaire.
   >
   > But we feel it's an important one, and the short time required to complete it should be well spent, for it will help shape the course YOUR magazine, the Journal, will take in the important years ahead.
   >
   > We say YOUR magazine because it's written and edited with readers like you in mind. That's why the editors would like to take stock of what you like and dislike about the Journal. What parts are good? What needs improvement? What might be cut down or eliminated? What might be added?
   >
   > Your answers will help the Journal keep step with the rapidly changing field of (name of field).
   >
   > You will note that we have not provided a space for your signature. This is by design. We believe that anonymity will produce more straight-from-the-shoulder opinion and constructive criticism. Thank you for your help.

   b. From a firm of research counselors in New York to an addressee in a state 2,500 miles away. Addressee is an employee of a city light company (letter is an obvious form with a "Dear Sir" salutation):

   > May we ask a favor that takes only a minute of your time?
   >
   > We are conducting a special study to help determine how familiar people in industry are with one of our clients.
   >
   > We would appreciate it very much if you would answer the questions on the attached sheet and return the questionnaire to us in the enclosed stamped envelope. Your reply will be confidential, of course, and the results of the study will be shown in statistical form only.

   c. To a real estate agent: (Salutation is "Dear Mrs. Aimes.")

   > I have clients who are very much interested in the Sand & Surf in (town name).
   >
   > They are prepared to make an offer of $110,000.00. This seems to be in line for a restaurant that grosses between $115,000.00 and $118,000.00 a year.
   >
   > My clients have a background in this type of business, restaurant and lounge. They have been wanting to locate this side of the mountains and preferably in (town name) area.

4. As purchasing manager of the Fidelity Department Stores, you need to replace 10 electric typewriters that are beginning to show their age. They have been good machines, but lately they have been breaking down frequently.

   Already you have asked for and received bids on four makes. Each of the four distributors has quoted you practically the same price on the 10 new electric machines and offered you just about the same allowance on your 10 old typewriters. Thus, you don't favor one distributor over another because of price.

   Since you don't know enough about typewriters, you decide to write to a college chum who now heads the business education department at a distant university. He teaches typing and his classroom should contain a good representation of all leading makes. He certainly should know the good and bad points in the latest models he has available for his students. His name is Dr. Robert Grippe, Professor of Business Education, College of Arts and Science, University of (state), (city, state ZIP).

   Write a letter to Dr. Grippe explaining your problem and asking which of the four brands you should select. Be specific. So that he can help you, you must explain what you expect from these machines. You can do so by asking specific questions and/or explaining what the machines will be used for. If you use questions, decide where they should go—in the body of the letter, at the bottom of the sheet the message is on, or on a separate enclosure?

5. As a management trainee of an exporting firm, you have become interested in preparing yourself for work in one of the company's South American offices. To qualify you need to learn Spanish. The local community college and the university both offer courses in Spanish, but you wonder if a correspondence course might serve your needs better, provided you have enough time for study. You want to learn how to read and write the language fluently enough for business use.

   Write to Verlits Schools of Languages in New York City, asking for all the facts you need. Today is August 1 and the new position you'd like to fill opens September 1 next year. You want to know how long it would take by correspondence to get the equivalent of a year's university Spanish course. You also wonder whether Verlits Spanish instructors are natives of Spanish-speaking countries, and/or former Verlits students, and/or former university students? Also you wonder about costs, examinations, certificates, home study assignments, and tempo of the work.

6. You are director of employee training in a large industrial organization. One of your jobs is to secure up-to-date pertinent training films. In a professional magazine advertising products related to your industry (assume one related to your major), you have read about a new film on "Comparative . . ." (select your title). The ad mentions only one rate: "Rental fee as low as $9." Before ordering the film, you need to know if the rental charge is $9 for each showing or on a time basis. If on a time basis, you wonder how long you may keep the film; you'd like to show it at all three of your production plants to about 100 employees at a time; you have 2,000 employees altogether. Other matters to inquire about include: length of film; need for special screen, amplifier, or projector; age group or educational level for which film is produced. Write to the film producer, Top Grade Films, Inc., St. Louis, MO 63101.

7. You are personnel director in charge of training for Hanson Stores, Inc., a chain of retail hardware stores with headquarters in San Francisco and with branches in Arizona and Oregon. Yesterday you interviewed Thomas Brandon (24), who seeks to join your management training program. His application form indicates he graduated from the University of Ohio three years ago and that he served in the Coast Guard for the next two years. He says he worked "for a

while" at the Midwest Appliance Company in Cincinnati. He thought he wanted to work up to top management with that firm, but finally decided he'd rather live on the Pacific Coast, because he enjoys the ocean and water sports. He seemed to be very enthusiastic about working up into a branch-store management position with your firm.

His application letter—and his comments during the interview—indicated that he also worked part time as a sales representative in a men's clothing store two months, while attending the university; one-half year in a service station, part time; and "also in several other places."

His scholastic record—with a major in marketing—is excellent (he says), although you don't have the transcript of his work. You are more concerned right now about his disposition to stick with a two-year training program. Your company's usual procedure is to place young trainees in the smaller towns, most of which are inland. (Some are over a hundred miles from the ocean.) You wonder if Brandon would stick with the company during the years (perhaps up to six or seven) that he would be situated inland. Also, as you talked with him you noticed that he interrupted you several times to tell you about his views, and he knocked two of his former employers, including Midwest Appliance Company. One of the references to whom you will write today is Mr. Bronson Quill, personnel director at Midwest Appliance Company. Try to find out whether his experience with Brandon indicates that he has the qualifications to do effective work—first as a management trainee and later as a branch store manager. He'd also be in the Customer Service and Adjustment Departments for a while. Is he sufficiently tactful and courteous?

8. As executive administrator of staff personnel at City Hospital, you are currently searching for the right person to be Chief Pharmacist. One of the applicants you interviewed yesterday is Wilma Bunsell (age 34), who worked at the Toprank Pharmacy in Omaha from January 1973 until July 1975. She has given the name of Maureen Riekerk, Chief Pharmacist at Toprank, as a reference.

Your hospital, one of the leaders in the country, established a new 300-bed teaching and research wing two months ago and now plans to open a new pharmacy five months from today. Both personal qualifications and technical skill are important for the responsible job of Chief Pharmacist. You need to know whether Ms. Bunsell has the ability or potential to organize from scratch a pharmacy in your modern, well-equipped hospital. You need a frank evaluation of her as a worker, because this job will demand a tremendous amount of initiative, drive, and sustained working capacity. Also, because she will have people working under her direction, she must be able to organize them into a tightly knit and happy working group. You'd like to know if she is liked and respected by subordinates, associates, and supervisors. Also it would be helpful to know what duties she performed at Toprank Pharmacy. Write a tactful, well-organized inquiry to Ms. Riekerk for the information you need.

9. You are planning to enroll for graduate work at the American Institute of Foreign Trade, Phoenix, Arizona. It will be necessary for you to earn part of your expenses while attending there.

Write to the registrar to get the necessary information. You need to know how much money must be paid in advance of attendance, what kind of lodgings are available for families, and whether any part-time jobs are obtainable. Also you'd like to know if the placement office at the Institute places the school's graduates in domestic or foreign opportunities, whichever the graduate may prefer.

10. You are assistant credit manager in the mortgage loan department of a savings and loan association. You need information from credit references that Thomas Plicant has given you on his application for a mortgage loan. Write to the Topcraft Department store's credit manager asking about the applicant's credit record with that store. You need to know (1) how long the applicant has been a customer there, (2) how well he has paid his account balances (3) what the terms of sale have been, (4) any credit limits imposed on him, (5) frequency of purchasing, (6) whether his buying and paying habits have changed within the last 10 months, and (7) whether Topcraft knows any reason for the change, if any.

Claims (Complaints) and Requests for Adjustment

1. Evaluate the following opening paragraphs of claim letters, and tell how to improve the poor ones. Which one(s) do you consider effective? Why?

   a. In the past year I have ordered nearly $200 in goods from your store, by mail. Two weeks ago I came there in person and bought a gray overcoat. As I was heavily loaded with packages I asked the clerk to send the garment to me by store delivery. When the overcoat arrived, I was busy and so I didn't open the package until two days ago.

   b. Never in my life have I been treated so rudely as I was the other day in your store, by two jerks you call employees. I tell you, the way I was insulted gave me a good indication of what kind of people you're hiring these days. I'm so mad I will never go back to your store again.

   c. You should be interested in an experience I had in your store recently.

   d. To the adjustment-department manager:
   In line with your policy on consumer satisfaction published in your recent catalog, I am requesting a cash refund of $35.38 for a toaster I purchased two weeks ago for cash. The reason I have directed this request to your office is that your department manager indicated that such a refund would not be possible.

   e. From a gift-shop manager to a newspaper about a desk lamp advertised: Please stop the presses for a second to take a quick look at the Bramhall classified ad in your September 4 issue of the (city) *Times*. Its form is excellent, but it is in the wrong pew "sitting" under the "for rent" caption. Will you set it straight, please, by rerunning it without charge?

2. Comment on the following claim letters. Consider tone, organization, clarity, accuracy, and probable effectiveness in getting the desired result. What changes, if any, do you recommend? Please be specific. Try to determine first what each writer really wants.

   a. From a business firm in Detroit to Air Freight Corp. in Pittsburgh, PA.:
   Re your Airbill No. 54663, we originally shipped this same amount of mdse. to Cincinnati UPS (United Parcel Service), got overnight delivery, and it cost only $6. Now your shipment from Cincinnati to us took over 15 days to get to us and you want $27.38. Now if you want to rebill and charge ICC surface rates, we will pay you, but if you think 15-day delivery is Air Express. . .better check the rubber bands on your airplanes or start feeding those pigeons better.

   b. From a charge customer to a department store with five branches: This handwritten letter had merely the date at the top and the writer's signature (Mrs.

Joan M. Smith) at the end. Her envelope had no return address. (The store has 150 Smiths and no Joan M. Smith.)

I cannot understand your statement each month showing that our account has a past due payment. This is very irritating since our payments have been:

```
3/10/7_ - $25.00
4/3/7_  - $30.00
5/ /7_  - $25.00
6/3, 7/6, 8/2, 9/10/7_ each $50.00
```

It is my understanding that our payments each month are to be only $10.00 per month. As you can see ours have been much more than that--so where do you get this "overdue" bit.

I am at this time sending another $50.00 check, which I'm sure you will agree does not make my account past due. Please get my records straight as I don't believe this makes my credit rating look too good.

c. From a landlord to apartment tenants:

It seems some of your typing late at night disturbs some tenants. Perhaps when all is quiet it is easier to hear.

I was wondering if you type on the nook table--as that is bad because the table is fastened to the building. A felt pad will help if you do not already have one. The University Book store has them just for that purpose.

I know your typing is important to your schoolwork, however I would like to keep everyone happy.

d. From a college student in a small town to a discount house in another state:

To whom it may concern:

I don't know who packs your boxes but they sure blew this order. (A) I ordered ice bucket 86103NF gld w/blk trim, & received ice bucket 86-118NF Tahitan Holiday pattern w/ivory trim. (B) I ordered a trip nip bottle tote 416VT & get a Deluxe Carry-all Diaper bag 516HR.

Now listen I'll keep the ice bucket OK. But the diaper bag has got to go. I'm a senior in college & single. I don't have a wife or baby.

Please send me my trip nip bottle tote & advise me on what to do with the diaper bag. Come on give me a break; this is a small campus what are you trying to do--start rumors?

3. Last Saturday you took a 7:30 a.m. Transcontinental bus to Mount Vernon, a city 200 miles from where you live. The bus was scheduled to make five stops along the way and to arrive in Mount Vernon at 11:30 a.m. This would be just in time for you to attend an important regional luncheon at the Marlborough Hotel starting at 12 noon. (You had planned two months ago to attend this function and to return the same afternoon on the 5 p.m. bus.)

At about 10 a.m. the driver of your 7:30 a.m. bus, after making four sched-uled stops to pick up passengers, turned off the freeway for an *unscheduled* stop at a roadside snack bar—a 6-foot open-air counter with no chairs and no roof. He told passengers they would be there "a few minutes to stretch and have a snack if they wished." As your hands were sticky after eating a candy bar, you stopped in the rest room to wash them. About two minutes later when you came outside, the bus was gone! The driver had apparently left without a warning toot or a count of noses! Thus you were stranded off the freeway, 15 miles from any scheduled bus stop; and no other bus was to pass on the freeway one-half mile from the snack bar for three hours. You would surely miss the entire function. What could you do?! (You're not a hitchhiker.) The snack bar operators stated this was the second time in a week that the same bus driver had left a passenger stranded at the same place. Rather than have you miss your luncheon, one of the operators generously offered to drive you in her car until she caught up with the bus. You both hoped it would be just a few miles, because she had to get back to her job. However, after 25 miles you reached the next town—the fifth scheduled stop—just as the bus driver was starting the motor ready to leave for the last lap of his trip. You hurriedly pressed $7 cash into the hand of your good Samaritan and hopped on the bus. Not one word of apology came from the bus driver! At the luncheon all your friends agreed with you that the driver should be reported.

Write an effective letter to the customer service manager at Mount Vernon requesting whatever adjustment (and explanation) you think is fair. Send a copy to the bus company's head office in Dallas, Texas. Make your message as concise as possible; assume whatever is necessary for completeness.

4. You are purchasing agent for a large company that has its own employee lounge and library. Recently you bought, by mail order, five copies of a certain book ($12 each) related to your industry and placed them in the company library. One of your employees has just discovered some serious page discrepancies in one of these books. In checking all five books you find that two of the five have the same inaccuracies:

   On the back of page 92 is page 121
   On the back of page 94 is page 129
   Pages 120, 252, 255, 341, and 395 are missing entirely.

   Write to the Hall Book Company, New York City, to get the needed adjust-ment.

5. Last Tuesday you took an interesting tour with a group of 15 other business people through the Ace Lumber Mills. All of you had attended a conference and the tour was scheduled as part of the conference. After walking from one building to another, you happened to be the target for a glob of tar that dripped from a roof of one of the mills as you entered. It fell on your left shoulder, on your new suit. One of the employees suggested that after the suit is cleaned you should send the bill to this lumber mill. Now you have had the suit cleaned and you want reimbursement. Write a courteous letter to get the desired refund.

6. The person who delivers your daily newspaper folds the paper and hurls it at your home as she speeds past on her bicycle. Last summer you had to replace the wire on the screen door because of the repeated impacts. You spoke to the girl about the damage, and she promised to be more careful. Now, on January 18, you find that she has broken a pane of glass in one of your living-room windows.

Write to the North End News Agency and endeavor to have the situation righted. You cannot speak to the girl directly because you are away from home at the time she delivers the paper. Telephoning from your office would mean a long-distance charge.

7. You are accounting department manager of Flowers by Hardley, a reputable florist. Today (April 2) you received a $104.50 bill from Airway Freight Corporation, 947 Columbus Building, Indianapolis. The bill shows two deliveries—Airbill #18692 and #25479—unpaid since January 15 and February 5 respectively. You have cancelled checks and invoices showing that both these shipments were paid when delivery was made. In fact, your firm always pays freight when it arrives. You resent the computerized statement across the bottom of today's bill: "THIS IS OUR FINAL REQUEST BEFORE REFERRING THIS TO A COLLECTION AGENCY. REMIT NOW." This is the first billing you have received. Your firm's general manager has decided that as of today he is switching to another airfreight company that takes better care in bookkeeping. He says that any company this careless in keeping records probably is no less careless in handling freight. Write to the general manager of Airway Freight Corporation after you have determined your purpose and what evidence you need to enclose with your message.

8. Assume you bought a new automobile last month. You garage it during the week because you live in a big city and want the car mainly on weekends. But whenever you planned a trip and got the car out on Saturday morning, the valves have stuck. The service garage each time refused to fix them until the following Monday or Tuesday. Four weekends in succession have been ruined this way. Each time you had to leave the car until the following Tuesday.

Last Saturday morning (the fifth week) you planned to drive your son to summer camp. You loaded the car with camp equipment, got into the driver's seat—and the valves stuck again. You finally had to rent a car for your 300-mile round trip. Send your claim letter by registered mail to the vice president of the auto company factory, with a copy to the head of the company's sales division. The service garage to which you have taken your car is an authorized dealer for the auto company. You want the valves replaced without charge, reimbursement for the car-rental expense, and some kind of assurance of better service in the future.

9. Assume that your new neighbors—an elderly couple who have had no college or business training—asked you today (May 20) to please write an extremely important letter for them. They have offered to pay you for your help. Here is their story (somewhat long, but facts are crucial).

We have a contract with Americana Encyclopedia Company to purchase their 30-volume set for $399.50. The contract was made out on the 20th of January this year and the terms read $15 a month until paid for. They informed us we were to make these payments to the Fairname Credit Corporation, New York City by the 7th of every month, starting with March of this year.

We are buying this house here and by mistake we began sending our monthly house payments to the Fairname Credit Corp. The person we are buying the house from (Mrs. Max Jones) told us that an agency in New York City would be collecting our monthly payments and that this agency would be sending a booklet, etc., to use for further correspondence. We received the Fairname Credit Corporation Booklet and mailing address February 15, and since there was no mention of the Americana Encyclopedia, we took this to be the house payment book. When we did hear from Americana we thought it only a coincidence that the same New York agency was collecting for house and books—since the party we are buying the house from lives in New York—so we continued to make house payments and our encyclopedia payments to the Fairname Credit Corporation.

As of now we have sent Fairname $417.33 in house payments and $45.50 in encyclopedia payments. This makes a total of $462.83. If our house payments are being applied to the encyclopedia, this means then that we have overpaid Fairname $63.33 over the total cost of the encyclopedia. Nothing has been mentioned about this so far; in fact we have never received a receipt from Fairname and we wrote them about the last payment last month (April 28). It seems odd to us that no one in their office wondered why we would send two separate checks—one for $15.00 and the other for about $140.00 per month—when the encyclopedia contract calls for $15.00 per month.

We want our house payment money back as soon as possible before June 1. We have made three monthly house payments to Fairname. Our check No. 493 on March 1 amounted to $140.25; check no. 498 on March 25 was for $138.00; and on April 28 we sent another check, no. 524 for $139.08. That is a total of $417.33. If we don't pay Mrs. Jones as promised in our house contract to her, she takes the house back. So we hope you will urge the Fairname Credit Corporation to send our money back and in the future to send receipts for money they receive. We must send $417.33 for our house to Installment Credit Assn., New York City, by June 5.

Following principles stressed in this course, write an effective letter to the Fairname Credit Corporation for the signature of Mr. Leonard Nolittle. Assume, of course, that your letter will be typewritten. Indicate in the correct way that copies are being sent to all persons concerned.

Miscellaneous Requests, Orders, Invitations

1. The following messages deal with routine business situations. Analyze each situation and then decide whether the message is adequate. Suggest improvements.

    a. A printed form letter from the president of a savings association to customers; it has no salutation, but the customer's name and address are inserted at the top.

    _____ Please sign the enclosed withdrawal slip and return to us.

    _____ Would you please send us your signature card. _____

    _____ Would you please send us your social security (reporting) number.

    _____ We need your *original* hazard (fire) insurance policy (with extended coverage) in at least the amount of $_____ .

    _____ An error was made on your last transaction which has already been corrected on our records (we'll correct your passbook the next time we have it).

    _____ We are returning your check because _____ .

_____Your construction interest payment starts _____, 19 _____ .

in the amount of $_____ ; thereafter, interest payments will be

$ _____ until regular payments ($_____) start

_____ , 19 ___ . YOU MAY MAKE FULL PAYMENTS AT ANY TIME AND RECEIVE CREDITS TOWARD FUTURE PAYMENTS.

Thank you.

b. Memo from the company's social director to all supervisors.

Subject: Christmas gifts for our departmental secretaries

With Christmas just around the corner, it's time for me to raise my ugly head above ground once again to remind you it's time to consider our departmental secretaries.

If you wish to contribute toward a gift for each gal, please leave your donation in my box by December 10. A dollar from each of you will be adequate.

2. Assume you are the new assistant manager of Apex Life Insurance Company's office in your city. Your company will be holding interviews on a nearby college campus January 30 for winter and spring quarter graduates. You want to send a concise personalized form letter to graduating seniors inviting them to sign up for an interview (whenever you specify) or to call you for further information. You will also grant off-campus interviews. You believe your company has jobs that graduates should be interested in. They can build a business career with no capital investment, they can get comprehensive training to develop their talents, and a monthly life income after 20 years of qualified service. Is there anything else you should include?

3. Your employer encourages young executives to enroll for additional university training whenever possible, and the firm pays tuition for desirable programs. You (assistant personnel manager) would like to attend the Graduate School of Business Administration Management Program at the State University (in the same city). Because most classes meet Monday evenings and a few on Saturdays, they will not interfere with your job. You believe the course will definitely make a graduate more knowledgeable in the management field, thereby increasing his or her worth to the company. Some of the topics you foresee as particularly valuable to your present job are: Management Communication, Performance Appraisals, and Basic Human Motivation. The course, over one academic year, costs $1,500 with $300 required to be submitted with your application and the remaining $1,200 by October 8. Today is August 13. Enclose your application with your memo to Mr. D. J. Heinrich, Executive Vice President.

4. You are area coordinator for your company's blood bank. Last year, through the cooperation of various departments, your book bank had ample credits to provide the 289 withdrawal units requested by employees. Now the annual drive is approaching again. On March 3 your company's employees are to participate in this worthwhile cause from 10 a.m. to 4 p.m. (You decide on the place and on other necessary details.) You want donors to sign up for the time most convenient

for them. Provide sign-up sheets in convenient places, and write a memo to all employees, attaching a folder about the blood bank and on donor qualifications.

5. The following is the first draft of a form letter request from a mortgage loan company to borrowers. The improved revision which was mailed is illustrated in request 2, page 164. Which do you think should be more effective and why? Compare the two letters in organization, openings and closings, paragraphs, action requests, clarity, completeness, and consideration. Be specific.

Dear Homeowner:

We wish to inform you that the Homeowner's Mortgage Protector Plan Certificate which you recently received is to be read carefully and then filed with your other valuable papers. The benefits provided by the Plan are very valuable.

The protection will become effective on the date indicated on the Certificate after the premium has been paid. The premium which is shown on the enclosed Certificate should be added to your future monthly payments.

If your mortgage payment has already been made for the month the protection is to become effective, the premium should be sent now so that you will be fully protected for the month. Next month, combine the payments.

We are pleased you have secured this protection for yourself and family. The acceptance of this Plan by so many of our customers indicates to me that it is certainly a valuable and worthwhile program.

6. To conserve fuel, because of the current fuel shortage, you—as operations manager —want to request all employees to observe certain simple fuel-saving steps. Without fuel your plant cannot operate; so it is to everyone's interest that as much gas and diesel be saved as possible.

   You ask that all vehicles must be shut off when idle. Examples include: lunch periods and break times; when chip trucks are under bunker for any time (diesel manufacturers recommend engines should not idle more than five-minute periods); when trucks are being loaded with lumber, logs, or other materials; when trucks are standing idle at any other times not in use. Also you want all employees having company cars to obtain fuel at outside sources. And you request that operators run machines in such a manner as to conserve fuel without loss of efficiency. Excessive speeds where not necessary consume more fuel. You believe that cooperation of all employees could result in 5 to 10 percent savings. Ask the superintendent and shop stewards to make sure proper steps are being carried out. Mention in your memo that you will make personal inspections periodically. Plan an attractive easy-to-read format for your requests.

7. Evaluate the following memo from the general manager to the superintendent of manufacturing department. Consider format, organization, tone, and clarity.

SUBJECT: PURCHASE REQUISITION PREPARATION

As you are aware, Manufacturing's requisitioning and purchasing techniques have recently been scrutinized. This examination has pointed out several discrepancies that were the result of typing errors.

Reviewing these errors and how or why they occurred has convinced me that some of them could have been avoided by more careful preparation of requisitions. To minimize these kinds of errors will you please consider having your department do the following:

    a. Prepare all requisitions in ink
    b. Print in large, bold, and distinct letters
    c. Double space between multiple line items
    d. Use only one brand name/supplier per requisition

Your incorporation of the above suggestions will go a long way to improve the final results for which Manufacturing will be held accountable.

8. As administrative assistant to the president of Benson Savings Association, write a letter inviting customers and their families to be your special guests at a grand opening of your new quarters on Thursday, Friday, and Saturday, the last three days of this month. There will be handsome gifts for both ladies and gentlemen, special door prizes with drawings every two hours, and refreshments. Children will receive balloons. Also, each current passbook holder will receive a special present. Your new building is graciously furnished, with a number of authentic period antiques. A SPECIAL GUEST name tag which you will enclose with your invitation letter entitles customers to their gifts.

9. You are director of the regional general manufacturing office of your company. You need to write a memo to all plant managers asking them for a report by July 30 this year. In this report—for the past fiscal year—you want them to be sure to cover the following points:

The major accomplishments of their plant during the past year, major problems facing them for next year, objectives for their plant for next year, plans for accomplishing them, and anticipated difficulties. Also you want a brief summary—one paragraph on each subject—covering their plant's operations last year in the areas of: organization planning, quality performance, production and scheduling performance, community relations, personnel management, costs of operation, health and safety, product development, and any other matters they think significant. If they will please organize their report in this manner, they will be especially useful to you in preparing your Annual Division Report and in making plans for next year. You feel the company has had a good year and you look forward to an even better one next year.

Arrange your request in an easy-to-read format (perhaps consider some tabulating?) and achieve a pleasant tone.

10. As customer relations director of Custodial Services, Inc., you have the pleasure now of announcing your firm's three-day Housekeeping Seminar in your area. Your letter is to be a form, individually addressed to local and regional directors of large firms that have custodial supervisory personnel. Make clear that from

each firm one or more custodial supervisors may attend. Enclose with your announcement a formal seminar folder, giving cost and detailed program. Make clear in your letter the place, dates, and highlights of the training sessions, and leave a pleasant goodwill-building tone.

CAPSULE CHECKLISTS FOR

I	*II* *Inquiries about Persons*		*III*
Direct-Request General Plan	*To Reference by Applicant*	*To Reference by Person Interested in Applicant*	*Inquiries about Products or Services*
1. MAIN IDEA 　a. Request, main statement, or question 　b. Reason(s) if desirable	1. Main idea 　a. Reason for writing to this person 　b. Introduction of request 　c. Memory refresher	1. Main idea 　a. Applicant's full name 　b. Why you are considering this applicant 　c. Why you are writing to this reader	1. Main idea 　a. Major request and/or 　b. Reason(s) for interest in product or service
2. EXPLANATION 　a. All necessary and desirable details 　b. Numbered questions, if helpful 　c. Easy-reading devices	2. Explanation 　a. Summary of pertinent facts about yourself: courses, major, GPA, outside work, tests, scores, honors, scholarships, leadership 　b. Guidelines for the recommendation: kinds of information the inquirer needs 　c. Enclosure of form(s), if helpful	2. Explanation 　a. Requirements for job, loan, credit, scholarship, membership 　b. A few pertinent facts applicant told you about him/herself 　c. Specific questions: 　　(1) More than "yes, no" answers 　　(2) Explanations if necessary 　　(3) Itemization—in body, underneath, or on separate questionnaire	2. Explanation 　a. Specific questions 　　(1) More than "yes, no" answers 　　(2) Explanation whenever necessary 　　(3) Itemization if more than one and desirable for clarity and/or ease of response 　b. Promise of anonymity, if desirable
3. COURTEOUS CLOSE. WITH MOTIVATION TO ACTION 　a. CSAD[1] 　b. EA[2] 　c. DA[3] 　d. Appreciation and goodwill	3. Courteous close 　a. CSAD;[1] to whom recommendation should be sent 　b. EA[2] 　c. DA[3] 　d. Appreciation	3. Courteous close 　a. Appreciation 　b. Promise of confidential treatment 　c. EA[2] 　d. DA[3] 　e. Offer to reciprocate (if appropriate)	3. Courteous close 　a. Suggested or specific action desired 　b. DA[3] 　c. EA when appropriate[2] 　d. Appreciation and courtesy

[1]CSAD = clear statement of action desired
[2]EA = easy action
[3]DA = dated action, if desirable

DIRECT REQUESTS

IV *Complaints,* *Claims, Requests* *for Adjustment*	V *Requests for Action* *Related to Routine* *Business Procedures*	VI *Invitations*	VII *Orders and* *Reservations*

1. Main idea
  a. Purpose(s)
    (need for
    adjustment or
    correction of
    error or
    procedure)
	1. Main idea
	  a. Reason and
	  b. Request (inter-
	    changeable)
		1. Main idea
		  a. Invitation
		    request with
		    all pertinent
		    5 W's—who,
		    what, when
		    (day, date),
		    where, why
			1. Main idea
			  a. Statement of
			    order or
			    reservation

2. Explanation
  a. Something good
    about reader or
    product or serv-
    ice, if true
  b. All relevant
    facts pertinent
    to the claim
  c. Omission of
    anger, threats,
    sarcasm,
    exaggeration,
    persuasion
  d. Desirable quali-
    ties: prompt-
    ness, faith in
    reader's fairness;
    good humor
    (when appropriate)
	2. Explanation
	  a. Desired details
	    and, if helpful,
	    instructions
	  b. Itemization
	    preferably when
	    more than two
	    items are
	    requested
	  c. Reader benefit,
	    if any
		2. Explanation
		  a. All necessary
		    details—if to a
		    function:
		    program, time,
		    apparel, costs,
		    refreshments,
		    location, direc-
		    tions, parking;
		    if to submit
		    material:
		    length, method,
		    format, etc.
		  b. Setup and
		    enclosures as
		    needed for
		    easy reading
			2. Explanation
			  a. Details about:
			    (1) Needed items
			      or facilities—
			      quantity, size,
			      color, style,
			      catalog num-
			      ber, price
			      (or rate)*
			    (2) Payment—
			      method,
			      time, deposit
			      (if any)
			    (3) Shipment—
			      date and place
			    (4) Special instruc-
			      tions, if any
			    *If reservation:
			    function, number
			    in expected attend-
			    ance, requirements

3. Courteous close
  a. CSAD:[1]
    Free replacement,
    free repairs,
    refund, credit,
    price reduction,
    inspection, expla-
    nation, apology or
    change, new ship-
    ment, or adjust-
    ment left up to
    reader
  b. EA[2]
  c. DA[3]
  d. Appreciation
    and courtesy
	3. Courteous close
	  a. CSAD[1]
	  b. EA[2]
	  c. DA[3]
	  d. Courtesy
		3. Courteous close
		  a. CSAD[1]
		  b. EA[2]
		  c. DA[3]
		  d. Courtesy
			3. Courteous close
			  a. CSAD[1]
			  b. EA[2]
			  c. DA[3]
			  d. Courtesy

[1]CSAD = clear statement of action desired
[2]EA = easy action
[3]DA = dated action, if desirable

Good-News
and Neutral
Messages

A message that conveys good news is usually easy to write, because you are giving or telling your reader something that is pleasant. A neutral-reaction letter is also relatively easy to write, because the message is about something that the reader considers neither good nor bad news—just information that may be useful.

You can adapt the good-news plan to a variety of situations. Use it whenever you answer a request or when you initiate an unsolicited message yourself—if the news will be favorable or at least not unfavorable to your reader. Among the many kinds of letters and memoranda you can organize with the good-news plan are the following:

Favorable replies

Answering inquiries for information related to sales
Answering inquiries for information unrelated to sales
Granting adjustments on claims and complaints
Approving credit
Acknowledging orders
Granting favors
Accepting invitations
Granting any other requests—pertaining to business, government, and organizational procedures or individual needs
Accepting job offers, franchises, and other negotiations

Favorable unsolicited messages

Announcements about:
    Sales and events
    Procedures, policies, and responsibilities
    Honors and activities of people
Transmittals
Congratulations, appreciation, and other expressions of goodwill

This chapter discusses the good-news organizational plan, the first six types of favorable replies listed above, and all the listed favorable unsolicited messages except the last entry (Congratulations, etc.). Additional illustrations of messages adaptable to the good-news pattern are included in Chapters 12 and Chapter 14.

Organizational Plan

The direct approach—putting the best news or the main idea (if it is favorable or at least not unfavorable) in the opening paragraph—is the most effective plan to use for good-news and neutral messages. As with direct requests, the organizational structure of these messages has three parts. Hereafter this good-news and neutral pattern is called simply the "good-news plan":

1. Best news or the main idea
2. Explanation, which includes one or more of the following, when desirable:
   a. All necessary details
   b. Educational information
   c. Resale material
   d. Sales promotion
3. Positive, friendly ending
   a. Appreciation
   b. Clear statement of action desired and motivation to action
   c. Willingness to help further

Because the items in the explanation section form the basic core of your message, you must use good judgment in deciding which items to include. The following discussion highlights the content and uses of these four items:

a. *All necessary details:* Include whatever facts, terms, reasons, and other explanations pertain directly to the best news or the main idea. Consider, for instance, whether the reader needs specific details on the why, what, when, who, where, and how of the news or main idea.

b. *Educational information:* Include instructions for use and other educational facts about a product or service the customer has bought if such information is necessary to help the customer get the utmost benefit from his purchase or his relationship with your firm. If you enclose an instruction booklet, a short paragraph within the letter may call special attention to certain pages in that booklet.

c. *Resale material:* Include appropriate favorable information about a product or service the reader has already bought or is planning to buy, or about your organization. Such material usually answers the question "What will this do for me?" and strengthens the reader's confidence in your product, service, or organization. Write concisely and with restraint. Avoid exaggeration and superlatives (such as "sensational," "perfect," "out-of-this-world value" because most readers react negatively toward them. Good resale keeps the customer "sold" on the product and company and helps to encourage repeat orders.

d. *Sales promotion:* Include suggestions about other products or services related to those the customer has bought or is considering buying—whenever doing so indicates your desire to be of further service to the customer or whenever it seems appropriate. This material should be presented without sales pressure; the emphasis should be on what the customer may need or appreciate and not on a desire to get more business. Also you need to consider the reader's probable mood before you decide to include or omit sales promotion. For instance, near the end of a good-news message—when you are fairly sure the customer will be in a receptive frame of mind—sales promotion may be quite appropriate.

Favorable Replies

To help build goodwill, any progressive organization replies to all reasonable requests courteously, helpfully, and promptly (within two days, if possible). If you know there will be a delay, a brief acknowledgment should state why and then tell the inquirer approximately when to expect a complete answer. Even in such a message you can begin with the best news first—with information that is useful to the reader or shows you are doing something. Don't start with such negative statements as: "We are sorry we cannot answer your request here. . . ." Emphasize the positive, for example:

> Your request for information about solenoids has been forwarded to our Chief Systems Analyst, Mr. Richard Hacket, in our Chicago offices.
>
> You can expect to receive his helpful comments regarding your special needs soon after he returns from Alaska next week.

In every good-news reply your compliance with the reader's request is more important than any expression of gratitude or pleasure. Depending upon circumstances, you can begin by saying that you have done it (the preferred beginning), that you are doing it, or that you will do it. Thereafter the material you select for the explanation and ending varies significantly with the circumstances.

The discussion in this section includes guidelines and examples of favorable replies to requests for information (both related to sales and unrelated to sales), adjustment, credit, orders, and favors, and provides a basis for deciding how to answer all other types of good-news replies.

Answering Inquiries for Information Related to Sales

Requests for information about services or products you sell are inquiries related to sales. Included are questions about catalogs, prices, terms, discounts, deliveries, products, manufacturing methods, types of accounts available, sources of supply, and similar information.

Replies to many of these inquiries are actually sales letters and are often called *solicited,* or *invited,* sales messages.[1] The inquirer is often already your customer, or a potential buyer, who may become a steady, satisfied customer *if* you send a reply that impresses favorably. This section discusses content of the three good-news parts and suggestions for handling inquiries prompted by advertising.

Positive Opening Paragraphs. The best way to begin these letters is by courteously doing one of the following:

1. *Sending the requested material*
   Enclosed are three samples of the nylon materials you asked about. We are glad to send these to you with our compliments.

[1] For a discussion of *unsolicited* sales messages see Chapter 10.

2. *Answering favorably one of the inquirer's questions*
   a. Yes, Ms. Jones,
      You can use Latex Enamel paint in your bathroom with complete assurance that it is washable.
   b. You're right! Model XL2, about which you inquired, can easily become an exceptionally good profit-maker for you. Our dealers have reported it to be their most popular do-it-yourself maintenance kit.
3. *Introducing the main idea(s)* that your letter will cover
   a. Thank you for giving us the opportunity to tell you about the two insured savings plans available for you at First Federal.
   b. I am glad to explain to you the differences in the three Portable Vibration Monitors you asked about in your January 5 letter.

Answers to All Questions.[2]   In your explanation section, you should answer all questions—direct or implied. In many cases, you will also provide educational, resale, or sales promotion information. Arrange your answers so that the favorable responses are at the beginning and end of your explanation section, to accent the positive and "embed" the negative aspects. Maintain a you attitude; keep the reader in every paragraph if possible.

Embedding the negative does not mean that you should omit or twist the truth. It means that you can emphasize what something *is* rather than what it is *not*. Like a good salesperson, you try to determine what the customer really needs. Sometimes this need enables you to handle favorably an answer that seems to you at first to be negative. Contrast, for instance, the negative and the positive answers to the following four questions:[3]

1. *Question:* Is the raincoat sprayed with ABC liquid so that it will be waterproof?

   Negative reply: No, I'm sorry to say the raincoat is not sprayed with ABC liquid. However, the material itself is made of durable vinyl which is completely waterproof.
   Positive reply: The material in this raincoat is made of a durable vinyl which is permanently and completely waterproof. Thus you need never bother with any spray even after the garment is cleaned many times.
2. *Question:* Do you carry the Bronson tape recorder? If so, how long would it take for you to send one to my office if I should decide to order it? (inquirer lives 500 miles from seller, and only 100 miles from the factory. Seller is out of the item today, but notice that the inquirer has not yet ordered it.)

   Negative reply: We are temporarily out of stock of the Bronson, and so we couldn't send you one right away. If we reorder especially for you, it will take 10 days after we receive your request.
   Positive reply: Yes, we do carry the Bronson tape recorder, and we can usually send it to you within one day after we receive your order. As it is an extremely popular model, we sometimes run out of it temporarily. In such a case, we will gladly reorder immediately so you can expect delivery within 10 days. Occasionally, for a rush order, we could have the item sent to you direct from the factory within two days after your request reaches us.

[2] See also the section on answering all questions asked, pages 76–78.
[3] You may also wish to reread examples on stressing positive and pleasant facts, pages 91–92.

3. *Question:* Do you send these washing machines c.o.d.?

Negative reply: No, we don't send c.o.d.
Positive, helpful reply: Instead of c.o.d., which would require you to pay the full amount upon delivery of the machine, you have a choice of several payment plans. With every purchase the required down payment is 10 percent sent at the time of the order; the balance is payable in convenient monthly installments which you can arrange with our representative, Mr. Jepson.

4. *Question:* Will you refund our money if we buy these draperies by mail and then find they don't blend with our other room colors?

Negative reply: No, we don't refund all your money; you must pay for shipping charges.
Positive reply: If you should wish to return the draperies within two weeks from the invoice date, you will get a full refund less shipping charges.

When quoting prices, be sure to use the same positive psychology by considering your reader's needs and circumstances. Unless the price of a particular product is a bargain, mention it only *after* you have stated most selling points and reader benefits. (For additional suggestions on methods of handling price quotations honestly as well as effectively, see Chapter 10.

Effective Action-getting Paragraphs Leading to Sales. To get the desired action from your invited-sales reply, remember to make action clear, easy, dated if necessary, and beneficial to the reader when possible.[4] Sometimes itemizing the steps that the reader should take is effective, as in the following example:

To start either account, you need take only three easy steps:

Action, clear and easy

1. Complete the enclosed application card. Be sure to check which plan you prefer, indicate which name or names should appear on your account and what address we should send your mail to, add your social security number, and sign your name at the bottom of the card.
2. Enclose--in the prepaid envelope provided--both this application card and your money order or check that you wish to deposit.
3. Drop the sealed envelope into the nearest mailbox. As soon as your application card and deposit reach us, we

Reader benefit

will open an account which will begin earning 5% or 5 1/2% dividend immediately for you.

Letter 1[5] below is a helpful reply to an inquiry related to sales. A potential customer who planned to cover both kitchen and concrete basement floor with linoleum wrote to a manufacturer of nationally known flooring products asking for "any booklet that will help us choose the right linoleum." She also asked, "Please tell us how much the product you recommend for us would cost per square yard." The reply, from the supervisor of the customer information bureau, not only sends

---

[4]To refresh your memory about other suggestions for all good closings, you might wish to reread pages 39–41 and 80–81.
[5]Courtesy of Armstrong Cork Company, Lancaster, Pennsylvania.

the requested booklet but also answers each implied and direct question in a positive reader-benefit way. Instead of stating that the customer's choice of linoleum for her basement is poor, the writer emphasizes that, while linoleum is an excellent flooring for some areas of the home, other kinds of flooring are more suitable for use in basements. Also, instead of stating that he can't quote prices in one letter, the respondent suggests how a nearby resilient flooring retailer can help the inquirer.

Letter 1

A well-written reply that answers questions tactfully, encloses a booklet containing decorating ideas, and suggests where to go for additional help. [6]

Best news first and reader benefit
We appreciate the interest you have shown in Armstrong's products and are sending you a copy of our latest decorating booklet showing how resilient flooring can be used to make your home more attractive, more comfortable, and easier to care for.

Educational information
In your letter, you mention plans for a basement family room and ask about linoleum for this purpose. It's important here to make a distinction between linoleum and other types of flooring, such as vinyl. Even though linoleum is an excellent flooring for kitchens and some other areas of the home, it should not be used in basements or in any room where it would be installed on concrete that is in direct contact with the ground.

Several other kinds of Armstrong flooring are highly recommended for use in basements. Many homemakers prefer one of the vinyl floors that come in sheet form, because these can be installed with virtually no seams in a typical room. If you're planning a do-it-yourself installation, though, you should consider Excelon Tile, a vinyl-asbestos flooring that is much easier for the home handyman to install.

Further help available
An Armstrong flooring retailer near you will be happy to discuss your ideas with you when you call on him. He is familiar with conditions in your locality, and he can help you choose the flooring that will give you the most satisfaction. Also, he can show you the styles and colors that are available and can provide you with price information.

Suggested action
For a list of Armstrong retailers near you, please consult the Yellow Pages of your telephone directory, under "Floor Materials." Visit one of these stores soon to see what's new in flooring. Again, thanks for writing. We wish you every success with your new family room.

Suggestions for Handling Inquiries Prompted by Advertising. Whenever a firm advertises, it should be prepared in advance for various kinds of inquiries. To save time and expense, you can compose pertinent form paragraphs, and even entire messages, as guides for answering the most-often-asked questions. Some messages should look personalized and individually typewritten (as letter 1), even though the body may be essentially the same for other inquirers who asked the same questions.

---

[6] Regarding salutations for examples in this and following chapters, please see footnote 3, page 153.

(The cost of personalized messages can be decreased considerably by using automatic typewriters or computers.)

On the other hand, many favorable replies do not need to be personalized—especially in routine situations when you are sure your reader will not object to a processed form. Most readers would rather receive promptly a high-quality courteous form that is complete than a poor personalized letter that is late, incomplete, or perhaps even inaccurately—and hurriedly—typewritten. Letter 2 is typical of the well-written processed sales-oriented replies that accompany booklets or samples or other free information sent in response to a coupon or inquiry.

Letter 2
Processed sales promotion reply (without inside address) with easy action order form.

Good news with courtesy; no salu- tation	Here is your . . . Foremost Radio catalog to aid you in your selections. Thank you for requesting information on Foremost communication receivers.
Resale *Reader benefit*	You will find much useful data in the section on "precision construction and advance design." Other sections show you why Foremost sets are the world's finest receivers. In war they met the most severe military requirements and in peace they are the choice of radio amateurs, shortwave listeners, industrial and scientific users. A Foremost set places the whole world at your fingertips.
Reader benefits	All communication receivers listed in your catalog are in stock now for prompt shipment at the prices shown. You can get liberal trade-in allowances on standard communications receivers (Hallicrafters, National, Apex, and Howell). If you prefer a time-payment plan, the attached sheet gives you details.
Easy action	To assure delivery within 10 days, just enter your order on the enclosed order form and mail it now in the postage-free envelope. Your order may be accompanied by a deposit as low as 10%, with shipment to be made c.o.d. for the balance due, or you may include full remittance if you prefer.
Reader benefit	You can begin to enjoy the unusual reception of a famous Foremost set by placing your order now.

Answering Inquiries for Information Unrelated to Sales

Among the most frequent nonsales inquiries you might need to answer are requests for information about personnel and credit applicants. Other inquiries may be from students, researchers, educators, and the general public—about a variety of subjects. The following section focuses on recommendation letters (about personnel and credit applicants), but also briefly discusses other replies to nonsales inquiries.

Letters of Recommendation. When you furnish pertinent information about an applicant's qualifications, character, and/or general conduct, you are writing a recommendation. It should preferably be addressed to the specific person interested, instead of "To whom it may concern."[7] You have a threefold responsibility when you write recommendations. You must be fair—(1) to the applicants, so they can get what they are best qualified for, (2) to the inquirers (prospective employer, creditor, landlord, or whoever), for they are depending upon your frank comments, and (3) to your own conscience and reputation for integrity.

Basically, a recommendation is a confidential report.[8] Recommendation letters are included in this section, however, because they are important good-news or neutral replies to nonsales inquiries. Discussed below are the expanded good-news outline, recommendation letters on outstanding candidates, and recommendations on candidates with shortcomings.

The following expanded good-news outline serves as a basis for a recommendation letter.

1. Main idea
   a. State the applicant's full name and what his relationship was to you— employee, customer, friend, tenant, club member. Mention dates, length of time, and type of job, credit, tenancy, or whatever is pertinent that he held under you. Use facts; don't guess.
   b. Work in an expression of pleasure, if sincere, combined with your statement of purpose for writing the letter. (A subject line can cover part of item b with such words as "Confidential report by request on Thomas W. Jones as a prospective field representative.")
2. Explanation
   a. Answer all questions—direct or implied. (Omissions cause suspicions.)
   b. Arrange answers in the best psychological order, depending upon facts.
   c. Back up your statements of evaluation (excellent, outstanding, and so on) with specific facts about performance. For a job applicant:
      (1) Tell specific job duties that applicant performed.
      (2) If the inquiry states requirements of the job for which the applicant is being considered, talk about those duties that will be significant.
      (3) When desirable, tell work habits that show personality characteristics.
   d. Be honest and fair with negative material.
      (1) Include it only if pertinent to the inquiry and likely to affect the applicant's success.
      (2) Imbed and subordinate it through amount of space and word choice.
      (3) Know the legal aspects of recommendations (see Appendix A).
3. Ending
   Include if possible a candid statement of your personal opinion about the applicant's probable fitness for the position (or whatever the applicant is being considered for—lease, credit, membership) and your recommendation, qualified or unqualified.

[7]A to-whom-it-may-concern letter is sometimes given to a satisfactory employee before he or she leaves the company; but because it must necessarily be general and not confidential, it carries much less weight than the confidential specific recommendation.
[8]See Chapter 16 for additional discussion on letter reports.

Recommendation letters for outstanding candidates are easy to write, because everything you want to say is favorable, as in letters 1 and 2 below.

Letter 1

A Marine Corps Commanding Officer writes a good solicited recommendation to the Regional Manager of a nationally known business firm about a Corporal seeking a management trainee position.

Pleasure, purpose, name, job, length of time
    I am glad to answer your inquiry about Wayne S. Prochas. Because Wayne has worked with me nearly two years as a correspondence clerk, I know him well.

Answers to questions
    During this time he has demonstrated outstanding abilities in both general office and management work. In twenty years of military service I have only once before made such a high recommendation, and presently I have over 800 officers

Duties performed
and men in my command. With speed and efficiency Wayne has attended to the administrative correspondence of more than 800 men attached to this command, and he has never once complained of the work load or poor conditions under which he has had to work.

    I recognize in this man a great potential because he is intelligent, industrious, and so well liked by all who come in contact with him. Corporal Prochas does his work with

Personality
no supervision and can be relied upon to deliver a finished product at all times. Also I get the very definite impression that he could, if placed in a position to do so, generate

and
ideas as well as process those of others.

character
    As to conduct, personal habits, and ability to handle himself properly this man has no faults, to my knowledge. He doesn't appear to have to work at being a gentleman. It seems to come natural to him. His loyalty is unquestionable and by his practices he has influenced others to a great extent.

    I have two regrets: first, I can not take this man to my

Unqualified recommendation
next command and, secondly, I do not possess the word power necessary to describe this man. But I do say this; my information is accurate and I am sincere. He will make a real contribution to any organization which he may choose to join. I recommend him very highly without any reservation.

Though the statement following "secondly" in the last paragraph above seems overdone (and could be revised), this commanding officer is to be commended for his sincerity and for including more than mere glowing adjectives to describe a man he considers outstanding.

Letter 2

A retailer courteously answers an inquiry about a credit applicant.

Name and relationship
    Mrs. George L. Wardman, about whom you inquired in your May 2 letter, has been a customer of ours for the past eight years.

Answers to questions
> She has used our credit facilities with a limit of $400. Her orders have been placed, on the average, about twice a month. I am pleased to report that she has always paid her bills promptly according to invoice terms.

Candid opinion
> We consider Mrs. Wardman one of our preferred customers, thoroughly responsible with her financial obligations.

Notice that in letter 2 the reference correctly refrains from making unwarranted statements about the applicant's probable ability to shoulder any other debt. He merely reports on Mrs. Wardman's past credit record with his (the reference's) firm; he does not (and cannot) promise future payments elsewhere.

Sometimes an inquiry will contain a question which you can't answer—either because you don't know or because you can't reveal the information. In either case be sure to tell the reader why, instead of ignoring the question.

In recommendations for candidates with shortcomings you must decide whether to include or omit negative material. If the candidate has the needed good qualities, you may be able to give a qualified or even an unqualified recommendation. In any case, you should mention the weakness only if it meets these conditions:

1. You are sure it is true (not hearsay or the result of personal prejudice or jealousy).
2. It occurred often enough to be worth mentioning.
3. It is pertinent to the job (or credit, etc.) for which applicant is being considered.
4. *It is sufficiently serious* to affect applicant's probable success.

For instance, an applicant who was discharged because he was caught twice stealing from the petty cash drawer should probably not be employed in a job that will require him to handle company funds. Likewise, such serious shortcomings as the following should usually be mentioned tactfully: habitually disagreeable temperament, excessive drinking or drug use, poor health causing frequent absences, unwillingness to cooperate or to obey laws, dishonesty, extreme emotional instability. If you prefer not to present them in writing, you can write a short letter acknowledging the request and inviting the reader to call you. To protect yourself whenever you must make negative statements, you should know the legal aspects of recommendations (see Appendix A).

If you are writing a recommendation letter about a candidate who has one serious shortcoming, but who was otherwise satisfactory (or excellent), organize your letter so that you establish the applicant's more favorable characteristics before you mention the defect. In letter 3, for example, the negative information is imbedded and the former employer ends the message with a candid qualified recommendation.

Letter 3
A department manager comments on a former employee who had a serious short-coming. (This letter answers inquiry 2, page 153).

Full name and brief summary	<u>Confidential Appraisal by Request on Morton L. Dryer</u>
	Mr. Dryer worked hard for us as a salesman in the electrical appliances section for about a year. He was such a dependable salesman that when the section manager resigned to go to the East, we placed Mort in charge and found him well quali-
Answer to part of question 1	fied for the job. He was with us 22 months--until last November.
	As section manager, Mort had much responsiblity. Besides ordering all merchandise for the section, he was also in charge of the eight salespeople working under him. He was exceptionally well liked by both subordinates and customers.
Answer to question 2	He had a knack of being genuinely tactful and thoughtful with every customer. Because of his personality and his knowledge of the stock, he pleased a good many steady patrons and increased the total sales within his section by over 15 percent in his first half-year as manager.
Favorable comment before and after the negative answer to part of questions 3 and 1	Mort's work at the store was entirely commendable for about 18 months. Then he developed a drinking problem, which gradually affected his disposition and his attendance. When I talked with him about the change, he mentioned home problems and serious worries. He tried hard to stop drinking and did so for several weeks. But after he had missed a day's work every week for three months, I regretfully had to let him go. Often I have wished I had kept him, for he was such a good worker and a pleasant friend.
More about question 3	Mort's other personal habits are good. His pleasant personality, honesty, and fine physical appearance are an asset to any company. He takes an active part in outdoor sports and, except for the problem I mentioned, is in fine health. It is quite probable that his move to your town will be a definite advantage to his family and himself.
Qualified recommendation	Mort is intelligent and well educated (a marketing graduate of Broadway College). Because he knows the electrical appliance business well and has so many other fine qualities, I would definitely give him another chance to lick his problem, if I had the opportunity. He can be a top-notch department or section manager especially in the electrical field.

Other Replies to Nonsales Inquiries. Answering the nonsales inquiries that business executives receive from various people often takes a good deal of time. Nevertheless, to build goodwill and give genuine service, helpful replies like letter 4 are desirable.

Letter 4
A collection manager replies with a personalized letter to a college student who requested information.

	Dear Mike:
Courtesy and best news	It is a pleasure to return to you the completed form as requested in your letter of April 12.

Comments	I was very favorably impressed with the sample collection series you enclosed. As a whole, the letters are courteous and also appropriately firm. Achieving the right tone in this type of letter is very important, and I believe you have done so.
Offer of further help	Any further information you may need from us will be gladly forwarded.
Interest in survey	The recap you offered to send showing your survey results should be interesting. I will appreciate receiving a copy.

If your firm in its advertising offers free information pamphlets not related to sales, you can handle replies with processed form messages, which cut costs substantially.

Granting Requests for Adjustment

An adjustment letter is the reply to a complaint (called a claim letter). In general, the best attitude is to give the customer the benefit of any doubt. Most persons are honest in their claims, and it is usually better to make the desired adjustment than to risk losing a customer.

Even though your firm's adjustment policy may be generous, the ultimate success of your good-news adjustment letter depends not only upon what you say but also upon how you say it. The discussion in this section concerns (1) the tone of adjustment-granting messages, (2) organization and content when the seller is at fault, (3) variations when the buyer or a third party is at fault, and (4) organization when the fault is not yet determined and will be investigated.

Tone of Adjustment-granting Messages. Consideration and courtesy are exceptionally important when you grant an adjustment. Because your reader has been inconvenienced, irritated, and perhaps angered, he or she is especially sensitive to the tone of your message. Even when the letter grants a request, it can lose a friend and destroy goodwill if its tone is poor. Compare, for example, the following "poor" sentences (in which the antagonizing expressions are italicized) with the suggested "better" versions:

Poor: We are *amazed* that you are *dissatisfied* with the range you ordered from us. (Amazed is overdone; dissatisfied is negative.)

Better: You have every right to expect top quality performance from the range you ordered from us, and we will see that you get it.

Poor: Nevertheless, *so that we can keep you as a satisfied customer,* we are *willing to allow you* to exchange these toys. (The motive sounds selfish; "willing to" and "allow you" sound condescending and grudging; the sentence lacks you attitude.)

Better: Because we want you to be completely pleased, we will gladly exchange the toys for you.

When you (or anyone else in your firm) are definitely at fault, saying "I'm sorry," "We apologize," or even "Please forgive us" is quite disarming. You are more likely to lose face by *not* apologizing than by doing so. One apology (preferably in the *explanation* section) is enough, however, for most situations.

Organization and Content When Seller Is at Fault. When your company is at fault, you should, of course, always grant the adjustment. In general, the best organization is:

Begin with the best news—what is being done about the claim.

Include whatever explanation and details are desirable concerning cause of the mistake; resale on the product, service, or your firm; sales promotion and/or educational material.

End courteously, showing a desire to cooperate, please, and assist.

The following discussion aims to help you avoid common pitfalls and plan carefully. After reading about various parts and paragraphs of adjustment grants, you will see examples of complete letters.

In the opening paragraph, try to begin with whatever you think the reader will consider best news. Your choice depends upon the customer's request and sometimes upon his or her attitude. If the customer asked for something specific—like a refund, exchange, credit memo, or speedier service—you should grant or promise immediately. However, if the nature of the request or attitude makes a "granting" opening inadvisable, you will try to get in step with the customer in some other appropriate way. For example, if a customer has found a bug in a jar of oysters and vows never to buy your products again, you can't very well *begin* by saying you're sending another jar of oysters to replace the faulty one! Instead, you might express appreciation for the thoughtfulness in writing and/or agree with a comment made in the complaint.[9] In the following examples, the first three grant immediately and the last three open with various statements to get in step with the reader.

Customer's request or complaint	*Suggested opening*
1. That you refund the purchase price.	You are certainly entitled to get back the $6.80 you paid to telephone us—and here's the check.
2. That you "eliminate the delays" in your merchandise shipments or risk losing business.	You will be glad to hear that we have found a new way to speed deliveries of fresh vegetables to you. From now on your produce can reach you within two hours after we receive your order.
3. That you replace immediately 10 defective copies of a book needed by May 15.	Today 10 copies of (book title) were sent to you by airmail, shipping charges prepaid. You should receive them three days before May 15.

[9]Later in the letter, after appropriate explanation and resale, you can tell the customer you are sending a gift replacement. See, for example, letter 1, pages 203–204.

Customer's request or complaint	*Suggested opening*
4. That you refund to a friend the $30.50 purchase price because of your firm's "inexcusable error." (Your customer bought a wedding gift for a friend. Instead of charging it to your customer's account, your store incorrectly sent the "gift" to the friend c.o.d. That was two months ago; the friend does not yet know about the mix-up.)	(To the customer's friend) You have had the unusual experience of paying for your own wedding gift–much to the embarrassment of our mutual friend, James L. Lamson. The mix-up is due entirely to our inexcusable error, for which we extend to you our sincere apologies. (Note: In this case the refund check is mentioned only after the explanation.)
5. That two special toys ordered four weeks ago did not arrive in time for Christmas.	We have disappointed you and your children at what is usually the happiest time of year, and we are truly sorry! Now I want to do everything possible to make amends.
6. That the service of a certain waiter in your restaurant was disappointing, and the customer's guests were embarrassed.	You are perfectly right to feel that you should receive prompt and courteous service from our waiters. That is exactly our goal for every guest, and we thank you for taking time to write us.

Explaining what caused the mistake requires tact and judgment. When your firm is at fault, admit it frankly without blaming "a new employee" or the enormous volume of your business. (If you're so big, maybe you should improve your methods.) How much explanation to include depends upon the kind of mistake and the customer's probable interest, but generally it is desirable to include at least *some* explanation. (See, for example, letters 1 and 3 pages 203 and 205, which include careful explanation plus resale.) Paragraphs such as the following–from three different adjustment grants–help the reader understand how the error occurred:

You guessed correctly. Apparently all the shipping papers, including the original ones that should have been kept for our use, were sent to you. As a result, we have no record of the ordered paint. We are certainly sorry that you were inconvenienced by our slipup. We always try to be careful in processing every customer request accurately and promptly.

I am distressed to learn that you have not received our shipment of Volumes 3 through 20 and that your previous correspondence received no reply. During the past few months, we have been converting our accounts to computer; and you should have been sent a letter informing you of the delay in processing our files and asking your cooperation. I cannot explain why our announcement missed you.

Sometimes we find that a package miscarries in the mails. This occasionally happens because of a stenographic error in addressing the label, or damage to the label in the mail, obliterating the address. Apparently that's what happened with your parcel.

Avoid the following pitfalls in your explanations:

1. Don't blame an inexperienced clerk. Your firm should have trained the clerk adequately; thus it is better that the company (we) assumes the mistake rather than the individual.
2. Don't suggest that your employees are careless or inefficient. Describe your normal businesslike methods to indicate that this error was an exception.
3. Don't say "mistakes are bound to happen" or that because of the size of your firm there will naturally be frequent errors.
4. Don't promise the error will never happen again. If it *does* happen again, the situation will be doubly embarrassing. Better show the care you are taking to assure correct service in the future.

Sometimes an explanation isn't necessary, for example, when the mistake merely involves a small routine clerical error between two business firms. Also, if the matter is complicated (or perhaps even confidential), or if for no good reason someone just "goofed" several times, no explanation at all is sometimes better than a lengthy discussion which may sound like an alibi or which will be filled with negatives.

Resale is necessary if the person complaining seems to be losing faith in your firm. If possible, include concrete evidence of your efficient service, safe and correct shipments, and/or your care in producing or selecting high-quality products. If certain steps have been or will be taken to prevent recurrence of whatever the customer is complaining about, mention them. Sometimes you can honestly state that a new procedure is developed "on the basis of helpful comments like yours" (see letter 2, page 204).

When you grant a customer's request to exchange unsatisfactory goods, you can strengthen confidence in the replacement you have sent by including a resale paragraph similar to these (from a nursery and a hardware store, respectively):

This new flowering quince is a choice plant from our sturdy Penbrook stock. It is hardy enough to withstand zero temperatures and requires little care. You will be delighted with its deep-pink blossoms twice each year—at Christmas and in midsummer. In size it fits beautifully with the other trees you selected last month.

You can use this (name) cleaning solvent safely and successfully on cloth materials, painted surfaces, and even on your varnished furniture. The easy-to-follow directions on the box label help you to remove any spot confidently without rubbing.

Sometimes it is desirable to resell the customer on keeping both the replacement you are sending *and* the original slightly defective shipment. (You save return-shipping charges and the bother of processing the damaged merchandise.) A consumer may be glad to keep slightly damaged articles if you substantially reduce their price. Likewise, a dealer customer may be willing to accept a below-average shipment which can be used for a special sale and quick profits if you give sufficient inducement— price reduction, consignment terms, or perhaps longer payment time.

Sales promotion material is usually helpful in adjustment grants, but there are exceptions, depending partly upon the type of product or services involved and partly upon the type of adjustment granted. If, for instance, a retailer sells only one type of costly product (like furnaces, home insulation, or roofing), which the average consumer buys only once in a great while, sales promotion material would be out of place. On the other hand, if the seller carries a variety of often-replaced items, sales promotion may be desirable. Without sounding greedy, you want to encourage the customer to continue to buy other goods from you.

Also, if the customer returned the original shipment and is receiving credit or a refund, he really needs a different replacement. Sales promotion material is then appropriate, as in the following paragraphs from different firms:

> Your nephew Tommy may be happier with toys designed especially for his age group. Tillman's carries many toys just right for four-year-olds, as the enclosed folder illustrates—on pages 12–14. Tommy may enjoy our alphabet puzzle (#R-6322), which is sturdy, entertaining, and educational. Other toys he will like are the plastic set of modern cars (M-8909), the metal boat kit (B-6222) that can be assembled easily, and our small-size sing and play piano. All these and others shown are educational toys to help Tommy learn as he plays with his friends.

> For your customers who want to do their own wallpapering, you'll find the ready-pasted product an especially good seller. Walton Cedar Closet Wallpaper containing a mild insecticide is not only an effective protection for all homes in your area, but also easy and convenient to apply.

With a genuine desire to serve the customer well—and *not* mainly to make a sale—you can sometimes also include informal, no-pressure sales talk regarding products useful with goods you have just shipped. This information focuses the customer's attention on your thoughtfulness and gives a feeling of a pleasant future relationship.

The ending paragraph of the adjustment grant should bring the message to a logical, pleasant close. It may (1) tie in suggested action with sales promotional material; (2) comment on the pleasure the reader will gain from the high-quality new article you have sent; (3) express your appreciation that the reader took time to write; and/or (4) issue a cordial invitation that the customer continue to come to your firm for top service. Be sure not to include any negative thoughts, such as an apology or a reminder of the inconvenience the mistake caused. Don't suggest future trouble or imply that the customer may stop buying from your firm. Now that you have read about the parts of adjustment grants when the seller is at fault, you are ready to analyze and compare complete messages.

Letter 1 concerns a situation in which the seller is at fault. The disappointed customer has stated the intention of never buying a canned food product again. Notice that the writer does not begin by "granting" or even giving the free assortment; instead the main idea is a statement of appreciation and resale. The assumption is that only after reading the explanation—and more resale—will the customer be in a mood to accept the replacement. The last paragraph effectively ties in a gift with a hint of sales promotion.

Letter 1
A good adjustment-granting letter from the Assistant Manager of Quality Control Department of a national packing corporation to an out-of-state customer who found a fly in the can.

Main idea: thanks and resale	Thank you for writing us of your experience upon opening a can of DeMona Spinach. We are very concerned about this because of the particular care taken in the preparation of all DeMona Products to assure you of receiving a wholesome and high-quality food item.
Explanation with resale	Upon arrival at the packing plant, the spinach is run through a large perforated cylinder where it is tumbled and shaken apart to eliminate particles of soil, etc. From there, it is transferred to wide traveling belts where inspectors remove all imperfect leaves and any other defects present. The spinach then goes into the washers in which a series of paddle wheels keeps it in a state of constant agitation while high pressure jets of water wash, rewash, and rewash again. After that, it is subjected to a further careful inspection as it is placed in the cans; therefore, you can see we do everything possible to produce a clean, wholesome product.
Easy action and apology	To further investigate this incident, we will appreciate your sending us the code mark which was embossed on the lid of the can in question. This will enable us to refer the matter directly to the plant where the spinach was packed. If you made a note of it, please send it to us on the enclosed reply card. We appreciate your bringing this situation to our attention and offer you our sincere apology.
Gift to regain goodwill and promote sales	Within a few days you will receive an assortment of DeMona Fruits and Vegetables. We want you to enjoy them so thoroughly that you will continue to be a regular DeMona satisfied customer.

Letter 2 brings good news to a customer who is irritated because there is no "right turn only" sign in a bank's parking lot. No resale is necessary in this reply because the customer isn't losing faith in anything relating to the bank. Sales promotion is also unnecessary here.

Letter 2
A banker, courteously grants an irritated customer's request for a parking-lot sign.

Best news first	Because of your excellent suggestion, we plan to install the "right turn only" sign to improve the parking lot exit at Emmett Street. Thank you for your interest in suggesting a practical way to help traffic move smoothly.
Explanation (details)	We have been concerned with the traffic flow problem caused by the congestion on Emmett Street. This exit problem has interested us from a long-range point of view, as well. As you probably know, we acquired holdings to enlarge the parking lot and provide both an entrance and exit on Ravenna Avenue. Our new parking and traffic plan should be in operation in about one year's time.
Friendly close	We invite you to make further suggestions which will help First National maintain the finest banking service in the Ravenna District.

In letter 3 the customer service manager's main purpose is to regain Mrs. Larson's confidence in the store's desire to serve promptly. Thus the manager begins with an idea calculated to please this, or any, reader—a sincere indirect compliment and appreciation.

Letter 3
A tactful reply to a department store customer's complaint about not being waited on in turn.

Compliment implying granted request
You were thoughtful to write us about the service you have received in our store. Your letter helps us in our constant effort to improve and make Gill's a place where you and others can enjoy shopping.

Explanation
Your friendship and goodwill mean a lot to us and we have thoroughly investigated the incident about which you write. Miss Simkins feels her error keenly, Mrs. Larson, because she has always assisted our customers to the utmost of her ability. In all sincerity, she said she did not know you were ahead of the other customer at her hosiery counter. Miss Simkins will be most appreciative if you permit her to see and talk with you, for she feels a personal apology is the least she can offer you.

Sincere apology and resale
Though an apology will not take the place of the good service you should have received, we do want you to know that we are sorry the incident happened. Prompt and courteous service is Gill's pledge--a pledge every salesperson in the organization must follow.

Courtesy and forward look to service
My office is on the third floor, Mrs. Larson, to the left of the elevator. On your next trip to Gill's, won't you stop in just for a minute or two. Your interest in Gill's is highly valued, and we look forward with pleasure to seeing and serving you again soon.

Variations When the Buyer or a Third Party Is at Fault. A few differences may be desirable in the organization and content when someone other than the seller is at fault. In many cases you may, of course, be justified in refusing—instead of granting—the request. Nevertheless, firms will occasionally grant a buyer's claim even though the buyer or a third party is at fault.

When the buyer is at fault and you decide to grant the adjustment claim, you have two choices for letter organization. You can begin with the best news (granting the claim) and continue with the usual pattern or you can begin with a statement that gets in step with the reader, then explain the mistake, and after that grant the claim. The reason for the latter alternative is that sometimes the psychological effect on the reader is better if you allow the claim *after* you have shown tactfully that the buyer, not your firm, is at fault. The next two letters handle the same situation in these two different ways: Letter 4 begins with the refund, and letter 5 begins with a buffer. Both have a "Dear Mrs. Hamilton" salutation.

Letter 4
A salesmanager grants a refund on a blouse that faded because someone washed it incorrectly; best news first.

<table>
<tr>
<td>Best news, refund</td>
<td>We were very concerned to hear of your experience with the "Lady Marlow" blouse you purchased recently at our downtown store. As a result, you are receiving the enclosed cash refund for the original purchase price, plus sales tax, totaling $11.50.</td>
</tr>
<tr>
<td>Resale with tactful (impersonal) explanation of necessary washing care</td>
<td>The "Lady Marlow" is one of the finest lines of ladies blouses made. The synthetic fibers and the special dyes which make possible the beautiful colors in these blouses do, however, require special care. Whenever these blouses are laundered, washing in a solution of very mild detergent and lukewarm water gives the best results. As the instruction tag on every blouse states, these garments are very sensitive to heat and should therefore always be dried at room temperature, never in an automatic dryer. Furthermore, any staining substance which comes in contact with the material must be loosened in cold water, because hot water often causes a chemical change that loosens the dye and results in fading.</td>
</tr>
<tr>
<td>Resale and additional emphasis on care; educational enclosure</td>
<td>Although the "Lady Marlow" line does require special care, I'm sure you will agree that its beauty and elegant fashion lines outweigh the special care required by the fine fabric. Because of the many new materials on the market, I think you will find the enclosed booklet on the laundering of all types of synthetics both interesting and educational.</td>
</tr>
<tr>
<td>Sales promotion with implied action and courtesy</td>
<td>As you are one of our regular customers, we invite you to our upcoming June sale. A complete line of summer fashions, including new pastel and print blouses, will be waiting for your inspection. The sale begins June 12, but the general public will receive an announcement on June 14.</td>
</tr>
<tr>
<td></td>
<td>It's been a pleasure to help you.</td>
</tr>
</table>

Letter 5
An alternate for letter 4; explanation before the best news.

<table>
<tr>
<td>Resale on the firm (buffer)</td>
<td>As a regular customer of Finestein's, you know that we are proud to guarantee the quality of each of our garments. In light of this, we were very concerned when we received your "Lady Marlow" blouse in the mail.</td>
</tr>
<tr>
<td>Resale on the blouse, and explanation</td>
<td>(Resale and explanation paragraph may be similar to paragraph 2 in letter 4, but the resale portion usually goes after the explanation and granting.)</td>
</tr>
<tr>
<td>Tactful statements showing seller not at fault

Best news— refund, with sales promotion</td>
<td>Since our laboratory tests show that the fading in the trim of the blouse is not due to defective dye, the stripes have apparently come in contact with some other chemical agent, or water that is hotter than lukewarm, or with excessive heat. Although we cannot assume responsibility for the fading in this blouse, we are glad to give you the opportunity to replace it. Enclosed is a check for $11.50, covering the purchase price plus sales tax.</td>
</tr>
</table>

Sales promotion and invited action We invite you to visit the blouse department again soon to select your choice from any of the newest arrivals. Besides the popular "Lady Marlow" you will find also several other famous-name brands. And of course you may also be interested in the new summer fashions in dresses and coats.

If a third party (say the transportation company) is at fault, many firms accept responsibility for adjusting claims and seek reimbursement from the third party. This method is customary with wholesalers shipping to small dealers or retailers sending to individual customers who are unfamiliar with claim-filing procedures.

Letter 6
A gift-shop owner replaces a lamp damaged in shipment.

Best news— replacement A new Brighton lamp should reach you in a few days to replace the one you received in damaged condition. We sent it today by prepaid express.

Explanation showing seller not at fault As the (name) Railroad gave us a receipt acknowledging that they received the original lamp perfectly crated, the porcelain base must have been cracked in transit. We are sorry this happened, for we know how much you want this beautiful gift for your cousin's wedding anniversary. Although our responsibility ended when the railroad accepted the package, we are glad to make this replacement for you.

Suggested action to help claim with carrier Will you please give the original lamp to the express driver when the second lamp is delivered. We will then enter a claim with the railroad.

Courtesy and resale Thank you for writing promptly. Our main concern is that you receive the lamp in time for the anniversary, and in perfect condition.

Organization When the Fault Is Not Yet Determined. Sometimes the final adjustment decision cannot be made until the seller determines who is responsible for the mistake. In such cases, let the buyer know promptly that you want to investigate the claim. Your letter should have a neutral effect on the reader, for you are neither granting nor refusing the request. The best organization is: express interest in the problem, assure the customer you are looking into the matter, include brief resale if desirable, and courteously state that you will give the facts as soon as they are available.

Letter 7
A hatchery manager promises to investigate.

Interest in problem Thanks very much for your report on the N&H "Nick Chick" Leghorn pullets delivered to you on March 29. I sympathize with you, for pullets you buy from Nerving's should meet the high standards of previous lots. We want to do everything possible to cooperate with you.

Possible causes of problem; promise of investigation

Tints, egg size, broodiness are characteristics both genetic and environmental. That fancy phrase simply means pullets can be influenced by both breeding and rearing, management, etc. Because there are so many factors involved in the conditions you describe, we are asking our Oregon field representative, Mr. Vern Jackson, to call on you within the next few days. You will find him cooperative and helpful.

Resale

Most hatcheries would be satisfied if 90% of their stock was good 90% of the time. Not Nerving's. We are aiming for 100% on both counts and won't rest until we reach that goal. Of course, when you are dealing with "life" there are numerous variables making this difficult. But, we keep trying. That's why letters such as yours help in pointing out where improvements can be made.

Courtesy

We want you to be a satisfied customer, Mrs. King. If we are at fault in any way, you are assured we'll do our level best to make amends. Thanks again for writing; you help us take steps to make things right.

Approving Credit[10]

The message telling the customer of your granting of credit often includes all parts of the basic good-news plan—best news first, then terms,[11] resale, sales promotion, and appreciation.

Decision or Shipment in First Paragraph. If the customer has not yet ordered any merchandise on credit, begin with the credit-grant decision and a cordial welcome. If an order was sent with the request for credit, begin with the date and method by which the goods are being shipped (thereby implying the credit grant). Make clear the purchase details (name and quantity of goods sent, item prices, freight, and total charge); for more than two or three items, attach an invoice copy. Mention cordially that the shipment has been added to the customer's new account.

Explanation of Credit Terms. In your explanation section, mention briefly the basis on which credit was earned, and clarify the terms. If, for instance, an applicant's references all speak highly of prompt-pay habits, it is psychologically a good idea to mention them. The applicant is then encouraged to continue to live up to this good reputation in dealing with you.

Your explanation of the credit terms must be clear and concrete to help reduce collection problems later. Suppose, for example, your wholesale firm's terms are 2/10, net/30. You must be sure that every new credit customer (dealer) knows whether your terms are based on invoice date, shipping date, delivery date, or from the end of the month (e.o.m.). Misunderstanding on this important detail can cause

[10]Every city has a Credit Bureau—an association of credit grantors (stores, banks, car dealers, credit unions, and so forth). The function of the Credit Bureau is to collect the credit records of their customers and consolidate the information of each individual. Then, when a credit grantor receives a request for credit, it asks the Credit Bureau for the applicant's record and forms its own conclusions. The larger credit grantors are linked to the Bureau by teletype, which enables them to get a printed record in seconds.

[11]You can place the terms either before or after the resale and sales promotion. If before, you're more certain the reader will notice them because you're emphasizing the terms; if after, you seem to be stressing the other person and not "what's in it for me."

a customer's payments to be as much as a month off. Compare these vague and clear statements regarding credit terms:

Vague: Our credit terms are the usual 2/10, net 30.
Vague: Under our credit terms of 2/10, net 30, you earn a 2 percent discount if your payment is made in 10 days. (10 days after what?)
Clear: Our credit terms are the usual 2/10 net 30, based on invoice date.

To an *inexperienced* business owner, or one whose payment record has been shaky, you might write:

> Under our credit terms of 2/10, net 30, you earn a 2 percent discount if your payment is postmarked within 10 days of invoice date; the full amount is payable in 30 days. On the enclosed March 28 invoice you save $12.40 by mailing your check on or before April 7—a saving to you almost equivalent to the cost of two shirts.

Of course, if all wholesalers within your industry abide by the same standard interpretation and your new customer is experienced in this industry, you need merely state your terms.

Besides stating terms clearly, you need also to use positive wording about a credit limit, if any, as these examples show:

Negative: We are limiting you to $500 maximum credit each month (each credit period).
Positive: In any credit period you are welcome to (you may) purchase up to $500 of merchandise on your new account.

If you are in a retail firm, you must likewise make your billing and payment obligations clear to the consumer. Are you opening a monthly charge account,[12] a budget account,[13] or a revolving credit account.[14] Do all statements (bills) from your firm go out on the same day each month or do you have cycle billing? Be tactful in telling the customer when payments are due. Compare, for example, the poor tone in "We expect you to pay" or "You are expected to pay" with the improved tone in "Payments are due within 10 days after the billing date" or "Please send your payment within 10 days."

Resale and Sales Promotion. The credit-granting message should include customer-benefit resale information on the firm's services. Also, it is sometimes desirable to

---

[12] With a monthly charge account the customer may charge purchases during any month and is required to pay for them in full usually upon receipt of a statement (or within 10 days of its receipt) the month following the date of charge. Some retailers mail all statements the same day each month. Others use *cycle billing*, which helps to level out the billing department's load over a 30-day period. For example, customers whose names begin with A–C may be billed for 30-day purchases through the 5th of a month and statements may be mailed on the 10th; those whose names begin with D–F may be billed through the 8th and statements mailed on the 14th; etc.

[13] With a budget account (a time-payment plan) the customer makes a down payment (usually 10 percent) on the purchase and agrees to make monthly repayments on the unpaid balance. Purchases on home furnishings, appliances, and electronic equipment usually must be paid within 18 months; apparel and other "soft" items; within 12 months.

[14] With revolving credit the customer and the store agree on a maximum amount of credit, and then the customer agrees to pay a certain monthly amount according to the store's established terms (ranging from $10 to $25, usually, on account balances from $100 to $150). The customer usually pays an interest and service charge on the unpaid balance. Additional purchases may be made at any time, provided they do not raise the total balance beyond the agreed limit.

include sales promotion material (in the next-to-last or last paragraph) about such news as a forthcoming sale, new seasonal merchandise, or products allied to those ordered (if any). Such news encourages the customer to use credit.

To keep your letter short, you can enclose a leaflet describing departments and services such as the following:

For the consumer
Free parking, mail and telephone shopping, personalized services for men, home-planning bureau, bridal consultants, tearoom and other restaurants, child-care services, gift wrapping, free and frequent deliveries, special discount or purchase privileges.

For the middleman (retailer or wholesaler)
Nearby warehouses, factory representatives, quantity discounts, free window or counter displays, national advertising, cuts and mats for newspaper and other advertising, repair services, manuals, factory guarantees, prompt and speedy deliveries, research department.

Future-Service Ending. Close your credit grant with statements which indicate your desire to serve the customer well in the future, or which specify particular services. Inviting readers to a special sale, for example, helps to get them to use their accounts. The tone must in no way sound greedy for orders, and you must observe the usual suggestions for easy action and courtesy.

Each of the following two letters establishes a pleasant and clear relationship with the new credit customer—letter 1 to a consumer and letter 2 to a wholesaler.

Letter 1
A retailer uses a processed form letter to grant credit to a consumer; applicant's name and address are typed in the inside address and salutation.

Best news: welcome and new account
We welcome you as a Bon and Nelson credit account customer. Your new charge plate is enclosed and we invite you to use it often. This plate will identify you at all Bon and Nelson stores; so please sign it in ink before putting it into your wallet or purse.

Credit terms
You will receive your statement soon after the first of each month, showing purchases up to the 23rd of the preceding month. Bills are payable by the 10th of each month. (Unpaid bills are subject to a 1 percent finance charge.)

Resale on store services
As one of our regular charge customers, you will receive announcements of all our sales before they are advertised for the public. If you should wish sometimes to shop in the comfort of your own home without a trip to town, you can do so conveniently by phone. Just ask for "Personal Shopping Services," tell your needs to the shopping assistant, and then just say "Charge it to my account."

Invitation to future use of account
The enclosed leaflet explains the numerous Bon and Nelson services available for your convenience. Do use them often to save yourself both time and money. We look forward to giving you friendly, courteous service in any of our colorful stores . . . for many years to come.

Letter 2

A wholesaler grants credit (and ships merchandise) to an established hardware store owner; the letter is individually typed.

Best news: shipping goods; new account
The Topskill tools you ordered April 3 are on their way to your store today by B&L Motor Freight. You can count on having them for your gardening customers by Saturday. This merchandise, as itemized on the enclosed invoice, has been added to your newly opened account.

Explanation of terms

Resale on products
We are pleased to extend to you our most favorable terms of 2/10, net 30 (based on invoice date). The information we received about you is completely complimentary to you personally and as a business owner. We appreciate your choosing us to supply you with our nationally advertised hardware and gardening products.

Resale on wholesaler's services
Packed with your order is our latest assortment of window display materials with full directions for making them attractive. Our representative, Mr. Carl Webber, will call on you about twice a month and gladly assist you in answering any questions you may have about Topskill. If you would like free envelope stuffers to mail to your customers and mats for your newspaper advertising, indicate your wishes on the enclosed illustrated checklist.

Resale on product
You will notice the enthusiasm customers express for your new line of tools. Their durability and precision is appreciated by both the craftworker and the amateur do-it-yourselfer.

Easy action for orders
To place your future orders, just use the easy-mail order forms at the back of your catalog. You can expect deliveries within three days after we receive your orders. You may be assured of our cooperation at all times.

Acknowledging Orders

An order acknowledgment performs several important functions. It lets the buyer know that his or her order has been received, is appreciated, and is given attention. It helps to build goodwill. Furthermore—and very important—by identifying and accepting the order, the acknowledgment completes a valid contract between buyer and seller. For these reasons the acknowledgment must be definite and complete, in keeping with the situation.

Orders that your firm can fill immediately fall into two types—first orders and repeat orders. Although the acknowledgment for both types should identify the shipment and show appreciation, the message contents will be quite different.

Acknowledgment of First Order. The new customer needs to know that his or her order is being filled promptly and correctly, that it is appreciated, and that—because of your products and services—dealings with your firm will be pleasant and profitable.

Sending the ordered items on their way is usually the best beginning for your first-order acknowledgment to the new customer. State what, when, and how you shipped, and if possible state approximately when the shipment should reach its destination. Express appreciation for both the order and remittance (if you received it).

Then take care of any needed details about shipping charges and payments. If you opened a new credit account for this customer, you will of course explain the credit terms.

Here are a few overworked expressions to avoid in first-order acknowledgments; they are followed by comments and or suggested revisions:

Vague, trite, and a little inaccurate: "We have shipped your order. . . ."
Comment: The order is really a piece of paper on which the customer authorizes you to send requested items; your firm fills the order and ships merchandise, groceries, livestock, or whatever was ordered.

Better: "The bedspread (No. 204) and the electric blanket (No. B43) which you ordered September 4 were sent to you today by parcel post. You can expect them in a few days. Thank you for your order and your enclosed $50.20 check in full payment.

Trite: "Welcome to our long list (or family) of satisfied customers."
Comment: Omit such statements and show elsewhere in your letter by actions—prompt service, reader-centered resale, sincere thoughtfulness—instead of by empty words that you appreciate the order and want to please the customer.

Trite: "Thank you for your order, which we are glad to have."
Comment: The customer is more interested in when you're sending the goods than in your thanks; also, the "glad to have" may seem a bit greedy to some customers.

Specific resale material should be adapted to the purchaser. Resale on company services (as listed on page 210) is appropriate for both the consumer and the retailer. Resale on the products ordered is usually more desirable for the consumer than for the retailer. Before ordering, the business manager who will resell your products has usually studied their merits carefully—through sales literature, catalogs, and perhaps information from your sales representative—and you generally need not repeat what has already been read. However, the manager may appreciate a few additional facts and any special product features he or she can emphasize to customers.

To a consumer, resale material from the "home office" is sometimes extremely helpful. After placing a first order with a firm (either by mail or through a house-to-house sales representative), the consumer may regret signing the contract—especially when the item purchased is a luxury. For example, suppose that you bought a 20-volume deluxe encyclopedia for $400 and gave the traveling sales representative a $20 down payment. Afterward you have "buyer's remorse," and feel that you can't really afford such a purchase. Now, suppose you receive from the publisher a three-paragraph order acknowledgment devoted entirely to your payment obligations. Such a letter would hardly be reassuring!

On the other hand, suppose that instead of the letter just described, you received one like letter 1 below. Notice that eight of its nine paragraphs contain reader-benefit and resale material and only one mentions payments. Don't you agree that such a letter would help reinforce your confidence in your purchase? Depending upon circumstances, adequate resale may range from one sentence to several paragraphs.

Letter 1
Resale in a completely processed acknowledgment to a consumer purchaser of an encyclopedia (and perhaps other educational materials)[15]

Contract acceptance; thanks; resale
With sincere thanks we accept your contract covering the items listed on the enclosed Summary of Purchase. By placing your order with us, you have joined hundreds of thousands of parents, teachers, and children to whom these outstanding educational materials have become an important part of daily living.

Resale
In addition to these fine products that you will soon receive, there are several important and exclusive supplemental benefits and services that we want to tell you about:

Summary of purchase; payment details
Your Summary of Purchase lists all of the items that you ordered on your contract and the total price of the order less the amount of your down payment. If you have chosen our budget plan, it also states the payment terms of the contract. If you paid for your order in full, this Summary will serve as your paid-in-full receipt.

Reader-benefit suggestions; resale
Also included on your Summary of Purchase is your Account Number. This number is our primary means of identifying your account. If you should have occasion to write to us, we would appreciate it if you would use your account number. It will help us quickly identify your account and give your inquiry prompt handling. So that your account number is always handy, we suggest you record it on your Quality Guarantee (enclosed with your order shipment) and keep it with one of your sets.

Reader benefits; resale and sales promotion
The enclosed Exchange Certificate offers you the opportunity to purchase at a discount, another set of World Book under the conditions specified. In addition, you can choose other learning and teaching aids prepared for children and adults.

Reader-benefit suggestion
Be certain to look at these enclosures very carefully, and then put them in a safe place. They are most valuable and important to you, and will be helpful if it is necessary to answer questions about your account.

Reader benefits
As a World Book purchaser you will be able to keep your set up to date with The World Book Year Book, an annual supplement which reviews the important events of the preceding calendar year. You will also find our Science Year Annual very helpful and informative. You'll receive an announcement regarding these supplements before they are published each year.

[15]Courtesy of Field Enterprises Educational Corporation, Chicago, Illinois.

Resale

We congratulate you on your decision to purchase this marvelous encyclopedia which has been serving American education for more than five decades. The present World Book is the result of years of planning under the supervision of an editorial advisory board of specialists and was produced by more than 1400 noted scholars and authorities. It includes all the features on which the World Book has built its reputation.

A confidence-building close

A year from now, I feel certain, you will agree that this purchase has proved one of the most satisfactory investments you have ever made. It will serve you well for many years to come.

Looking forward to future orders and reader satisfaction is usually the best way to end the first-order acknowledgment. You can tie your suggested action in with resale or sales promotion; be sure your reader has order blanks or whatever else is needed for easy action. If you wish, you may invite the cash customer to fill out and return a credit application form; but avoid suggesting that credit will be automatic.

Letter 2 on page 211 is typical of a good first-order acknowledgment to a dealer buying on credit. With a few changes, that letter could be adapted for a dealer who sent a check with a first order. Letter 2 below, to a cash customer, includes a credit application form.

Letter 2
Personalized acknowledgment of a first cash order from a dealer.

Restatement or order

You can expect to receive the two dozen Topskill lawn edgers, #L592, and the five manual mowers, M 687, in time for your garden sale Monday, May 15. They were shipped by prepaid express this afternoon.

Appreciation and check acknowledgment

Thank you for your order and for your $425.50 check, which exactly covered the items as priced in your new dealer catalog. As you know, the suggested markup on these items is 30 percent.

Resale on services for dealer and customer benefit

Your customers will be pleased with these highly popular Topskill tools. Currently they are advertised in 1/2-page two-color ads in House and Home and Western Garden magazines, April through July. You can assure your customers that every Topskill is factory guaranteed according to the contract that accompanies each tool. A special feature of the Topskill edger is its ability to trim neatly within one inch of flower beds and rockeries. On the mower, a simple twist of the Dial knob adjusts both wheels and roller for precise cutting height and ease of operation.

Services to dealer

Illustrations of counter and window displays and other free sales helps are sent with this letter. Just let us know your needs on the enclosed checklist.

Suggestion
for credit You may be interested in our regular credit terms of 2/10, net 30 on future orders. If so, just fill in and return the enclosed form; we will gladly consider your credit application. Also, if you have any questions with which we might be able to help, just write us. We'll do our best to serve
Courtesy you promptly.

Acknowledgment of Repeat Orders. Most orders come from repeat customers who know and like a firm's products and services, and who don't expect a typewritten letter acknowledgment. Usually the goods can be sent as quickly as an acknowledgment can be mailed. In some cases standard purchase order forms give complete instructions about terms and delivery date, and they stipulate that the buyer will be notified only if the order cannot be filled as requested. In others, an adequate good-news order acknowledgment is an inexpensive (perhaps printed) form, a carbon copy of the shipping invoice, or a postcard as illustrated here. Various rubber stamps enable clerks to insert pertinent comments, such as the one shown referring to the will-call.

Though most repeat orders are filled without letter acknowledgments, an unusually large order may occasionally warrant a personalized letter. This message may include appreciation, a statement of how the order is being handled, and perhaps a few cordial comments about your past relationship and future plans to supply the customer's needs.

Granting Favors

Whenever you decide to grant a favor, you have a comparatively easy letter to write. Whether the favor is serving on a committee, speaking without pay at a convention, donating money, or lending your firm's equipment without charge, the good-news plan is the best to use. Usually all you need is the acceptance first, pertinent comments or explanation, and a cordial ending—as in the following letter in which a business executive accepts an appointment:

Acceptance	I will be glad to serve as a panel member on the program of the National (name) Association's 197_ regional convention in Chicago.
Comments	The date--March 25--has already been circled on my calendar. Also, my employer warmly approves of this participation. Arrangements have been made so that I can be away from the office three days.
Comments on the assignment and participation	The topic you suggest is one I've been interested in for some time. If they will work in, I might bring several charts which our company has been using this past year with some success. With four members on the panel, however, and one hour allotted to us I know I should limit my comments to no more than 12 minutes, as you suggest. Then we'll have time for questions and answers.
Courtesy	I'm looking forward to working with you and the other panel members toward putting on a stimulating panel discussion.

By following the good-news plan plus the suggestions and cautions discussed in this section, you can also write effectively favorable replies to all other kinds of requests—from customers, employers, employees, friends, government officials, or anyone else.

Unsolicited Favorable Messages

The previous section considered messages that are written because someone inquired. This section discusses *unsolicited* favorable and neutral-reaction messages—specifically announcements and transmittals. Good-news unsolicited messages that congratulate, thank, welcome, and show continuing concern are covered in Chapter 14.

Announcements

Like all other good-news messages, favorable announcements should follow the good-news plan—best news or main idea first; then adequate explanation, resale, or educational material; and, finally, the appropriate ending.

Though some announcements are written for one person only, most are intended for members of various groups. If the same processed (printed, mimeographed, dittoed) letter goes to each member of a group, the salutation is usually general—such as "Dear depositor" or "Dear (company name) customer." Those announcements that are directed to persons within your organization usually have memo format with "All employees" (or members) after the TO.

Included in this section are group and personal announcements about sales and events; procedures, policies, and responsibilities; and honors and activities of people.

Announcing Sales and Events. Whenever you wish to announce a sale or an event (luncheon, conference, celebration, meeting, or other function) about which you need merely to inform your readers, you can use the good-news plan. The opening paragraph usually includes as many of the 5 W's as possible.

An excellent way to build and strengthen goodwill with regular customers is to let them know—by various special announcements—that you appreciate them. For example, message 1 announces a sale before newspaper publication.

Message 1
A store's preannouncement to charge customers about a forthcoming sale; processed form without insertions.

Reason and best news; 5 W's

Because you are a regular (store name) customer, we are glad to announce to you a special sale of an unusual collection of winter coat values . . . in one of the Designer Room's greatest coat events. This announcement comes to you now so that you can make your selection during a three-day period before newspaper ads appear.

Displayed items for emphasis

PREANNOUNCEMENT SELLING
Wednesday, Thursday, and Friday
November 6, 7, and 8
NEW WINTER COATS BY OUR FOREMOST MAKERS
all priced far below regular
$69 $109 $149

Details

FINE COATS FROM OUR BEST MAKERS . . . IN MISSES AND PETITE SIZES. Coats such as you'll see at much higher prices after this great selling. Every one a new, just-arrived 197_ fashion!

EXCITING FASHIONS AND COLORS including shiny black coats, neutrals, and bright colors, fur trimmed coats, town tweeds, dressy and casual styles, various shapes, coats that wrap or button.

LUXURY FABRICS by Forstmann and Stroock. Silken fleeces, plush textures, imported and domestic tweeds.

Easy action

TAKE ADVANTAGE OF THIS OPPORTUNITY FOR FIRST CHOICE! For three days . . . November 6, 7, and 8, you may come in and choose your coat in advance of newspaper announcement. We consider this one of our most outstanding coat events of the year. Come in early . . . prices will return to regular immediately after this event.

Whether you call your message an announcement (as in the above example) or an invitation (as in the example on page 167), you use the same three-part organizational structure.

Announcing Procedures, Policies, and Responsibilities. You will have numerous occasions to announce procedures or policies and to explain reader responsibilities to customers, employees, and others. Though some of these announcements may be good news, many may simply contain neutral information. Whenever you do have good news to announce, it is desirable to begin with a statement of pleasure or reader benefit (the "why" of the 5 W's).

Throughout the message try to keep the reader in each paragraph, if possible and desirable. Use resale and show reader benefits whenever possible.

Many announcements about procedures, policies, and responsibilities can be processed form messages, like the following memo—message 2. Others—like message 3—must be individually typed with a personal salutation.

Message 2
Announcement to all employees about enrollment for company insurance plans.

TO: All Kenmore employees   DATE: November 22, 197_

FROM: John K. Wood, Retirement and Insurance Officer[16]

SUBJECT: <u>Open Enrollment Period for Company Insurance Plans</u>

Why, when, for whom where, what (itemized)

The annual open enrollment period for employee insurance plans will be between December 4 and 27 at the Retirement and Insurance Office. During that time, you may

1. Enroll in medical, life, salary continuation, or accident insurance plans for the first time
2. Transfer from one basic medical plan to another, or
3. Add previously uninsured dependents to medical insurance plans.

Effective date

Changes and additions made during the open enrollment period will take effect next January 1, 197_.

Enclosure and instructions

Please refer to the attached individual "Insurance Program Summary" which shows the premiums, company contributions, and payroll deductions for the plans in which you are presently enrolled. Then refer to the rest of the attached material which explains just what to do if you wish to make changes in your coverage.

Offer of more help

Brochures describing the plans and individual counseling services are available at the Retirement and Insurance Office, 4th floor; or phone extension 3-9876 if you wish one mailed to you.

Message 3
A lending officer's message to a new loan customer about payment responsibilities; individually typed. (Salutation: Dear Mr. and Mrs. Mooney)

Congratulation and main idea

Several days ago it was our pleasure to congratulate you on your plans to improve your home. Now we are pleased to give you details concerning the loan you received from Central Loan Association to provide the funds you need.

---

[16]Some officers omit the FROM line and sign above their typed signature and title at the bottom.

Here is the important data pertaining to your Home Improvement Loan:

Details tabulated for easy reading

Date of Loan	June 15, 197_
Amount of Loan	$1,349.88
Number of Payments	60
Monthly Installment	$25.40
First Payment Begins	July 1, 197_

Offer of further help

Should you have any questions or inquiries as to any of our services, please come in, or just give us a ring at 222-2222. We are always glad to help you.

Though the preceding message is individually typed, it can be based on a guide form, since all paragraphs except the figures and dates in paragraph 2 will be the same for every borrower.

Announcing Honors and Activities of People. To inform customers and employees about promotions, awards, new appointments, and other activities of various persons, it is thoughtful to send announcements.

Announcement of a promotion can be similar to message 4, which informs employees of a colleague's promotion to managership. Similar announcements can be sent when a new officer has joined the staff or when one or more employees have been shifted to new departments, been elected to noteworthy offices, or won any other honors deserving recognition.

Message 4
Announcement of an employee's promotion to an office.

Memo to: All employees

Copy to:[17] Elaine B. Wells
Richard W. Bram
W. M. Glass

From: James T. Camp

Date: February 15, 197_

Subject: Bernard S. Galston, new St. Paul Manager

Best news first

We are very pleased to announce that Bernard S. Galston has been promoted to the position of St. Paul Manager. He will be responsible for all aspects of the St. Paul–Minneapolis Warehousing and Trucking operations.

Details about the new officer

A native of St. Paul, Mr. Galston was graduated from the University of (name) in (year) with a BA Degree in Business Administration, emphasizing transportation. He has had extensive experience in all phases of transportation and in all phases of our own company's operations. Also he is a a Captain in the United States Army Reserve and a member of the National Guard Association.

Suggested action

We know you will all join us in congratulating Mr. Galston on his promotion and in wishing him success in his new position.

[17]Though the usual position for copy notations is at the end of the message (a double-space under the reference initials), some firms have a standard procedure to indicate the copy routing in the memo heading, especially if the persons receiving copies are officers.

A letter of introduction announcing a new field representative who will be calling on customers is often printed on the company's letterhead or on a special card. Another use for this type of letter (individually typewritten, usually) is to introduce a friend or acquaintance to a business executive you know in the city the friend is moving to or visiting.

Message 5
Letter of introduction from a business executive to a business acquaintance.

Full name and why being introduced	This note is to introduce to you Rhoda M. Parker, the daughter of a dear friend and customer of ours. Rhoda is doing a survey among business firms in your city. Her interest concerns problems of the small business executive.
Explanation	She has just finished college and is expecting to enter the Graduate School of Business at the University of (name in another state) next fall. In the meantime, Rhoda is donating her summer to this voluntary study.
Request and courtesy	I would consider it a great favor if you would give this young woman a few minutes of your time and open the door for her to meet other business leaders in your community. You'll find her appreciative and bright. Both her father and I will be grateful to you for any courtesy you show to Rhoda. I really think you'll find her quite interesting.
Courtesy	The next time you get to our city, give me a call. I'd be delighted to have you as my guest for lunch or dinner.

Transmittals

Transmittals differ from announcements in several ways. Announcements always include an explanation whose main purpose is to convey information. Transmittals may or may not include explanation; their main purpose is to transmit something, which is usually mentioned in the first paragraph. This section discusses two types of transmittals—those without discussion and those with discussion.

Transmittals without Discussion. Many times you will need to mail something, such as a check, document, form, passbook, booklet, or map, to a consumer or a business house. If your action is routine, you can transmit the item without explanation. Such transmittals don't even have to be individually typewritten, or even in the format of a letter. They can merely be in the form of a cordial, short note. Given below is an example of an acceptable processed fill-in transmittal to which a typist adds the missing usual parts.

Transmittal 1
Document transmittal letter.

Dear

Subject:

Main idea: We are enclosing the following instruments for your file
transmittal   regarding the above property:
and reason

        ( ) Owner's Policy
        ( ) Warranty Deed conveying property to your name
List for   ( ) Cancelled Note and Deed of Trust, Loan #_____
easy   Payable to _____
checking   ( ) Copies of Closing Papers
        ( )

Courtesy   Thank you for allowing us to be of service to you.

Transmittals with Discussion.[18] When you include discussion in a transmittal, your message may be quite similar to favorable replies to requests. The main difference is that in the transmittal the writer is sending the enclosure of his or her own volition, not because the reader asked for it. These messages may be personally typewritten or processed, depending upon the circumstances. Transmittal 2 is individually typed.

Transmittal 2
Individually typewritten form transmittal of savings certificate's first dividend.
(Salutation: Dear Mr. and Mrs. Briggs)

Best news: Six months have gone by and your Savings Certificate has
transmittal   earned its first dividend. Enclosed is a check for the
           amount earned.

           As agreed, your certificate will be renewed automatically
Explanation for another six-month period. At the same time, we are
and news of glad to announce that as of January 1, 197_, dividends on
increased   Savings Certificates will be computed at the rate of 6½%
earnings   instead of 6%. Because each account is now insured up to
           $40,000, you might want to increase your account.

Easy   If you wish to purchase another certificate--and saving by
action   mail is more convenient for you--just state your wishes on
and   the enclosed signature card and mail it with your check in
thanks   the postage-paid envelope. Thank you for saving here at
           State Federal.

Whenever you answer favorably a request or announce news that will be favorable or neutral to your reader, keep in mind the three-part organizational good-news plan. The Capsule Checklists on pages 236 to 239 give you a review of both the basic plan and various adaptations when you answer requests for information, adjustment, credit, order filling, favors, and when you announce or transmit something.

---

[18]See also the discussion of transmittal letters with reports, Chapter 17.

Exercises

Favorable Replies to Inquiries for Information Related to Sales

1. Letters A and B below are replies to routine, direct requests. Suggest improvements where needed in opening and closing paragraphs, you attitude, and adequacy of resale material. Which of the two do you like better? Why?

   A. Individually typed reply from a steam specialty company:

   Gentlemen:

   Replying to your letter of 30 Sept. 197_, please be advised that we are mailing to your attention, under separate cover, four copies of our current #57 General Catalog describing products of our manufacture, at no charge to your company.

   Appreciating your inquiry and hoping to be favored with your orders, we remain

   B. Processed form reply from a clock manufacturer;[19] personalized address and salutation:

   Here is the Seth Thomas booklet which you recently requested.

   As you look over the wide variety of styles offered for your choice, we are sure you will find the Seth Thomas clock you have always desired--either for your own home or for that certain someone who appreciates an outstanding gift. There are distinguished Period designs, charming colonial reproductions and smart moderns for those who appreciate this mode of furnishing.

   All clocks illustrated represent the finest in designing achievement and are truly the creations of experts in the craft of fine clockmaking. Their friendly presence in your home is a tribute to your appreciation of fine living.

   May we suggest that you visit your local Seth Thomas dealer. Many appliance stores handle Seth Thomas self-starting electrics--while keywound and electrics are offered by better jewelry and department stores.

   For gifts that will surely become treasured possessions, select Seth Thomas clocks--they are always appropriate. And, for finer--friendlier living in your own home, be sure to choose an authentic Seth Thomas--"The Finest Name in Clocks."

2. The following is the reply a motel manager in a small resort town sent to a young man who inquired about rates and accommodations. He wrote that he and his wife were planning a three-week automobile trip and they expected to stay five nights in the town (Lagina) "sometime in July."
   Comment orally on the good and poor qualities of this reply. How many

[19]Courtesy of Seth Thomas Clock Company, Thomaston, Connecticut.

errors can you find? (The crossed-out words appeared that way on the mailed letter.) Rewrite it so that it is accurate and contains appropriate you attitude and resale material. Make any necessary assumptions.

>   Thank you for your postal card regarding rates for
> Summer.
>   Our rates for two are $110.00 per week & ᴍᴋᴋᴀᴀᴠᴋ̶ᴋ̶
> ᴋ̶ᴀ̶ᴋ̶ᴋ̶ᴋ̶ᴋ̶ᴘ̶ᴋ̶ Oceanview are $120.00 per week.
>   These Apartments consist of Bed Sitting room, fully
> equipped kitchen, bathroom and Shower and Garage.
>   We are located in the North section of Lagina about
> a mile from the main business District. The market is a
> block away and we are about two hundred yards from Crescent
> Bathing Beach.
>   We do not allow Pets.
>   On receipt of $10.00 deposit we will be pleased to
> reserve the accomodation you require.
>   Thanking you for your courtesy, I am,

3. The inquiry in problem 6, page 173, has been referred to you, the Booking Department Director of Top Grade Films, Inc., St. Louis, Mo. Write the reply, to James Jepson, National Products Corp., (assume address), giving specific answers to all questions, plus any other information you consider desirable. Your firm sends films to any state in the United States for a rental of $9 for three days, plus shipping charges. Transportation time is not counted in with these three days. Usually shipping time takes about five days to adjoining states; across the continent, it may take as much as ten days. If a customer wants a film for a whole week, the charge is $18 for the week. If he rents it for two weeks (the maximum you allow), the charge is $35. Each customer is expected to return the rented film promptly. If, for instance, it is rented for three days but kept for five days, a full $9 per day for each day over the rental is charged; Saturdays and Sundays are not counted, however. Assume any other pertinent details about the film (related to your major). You have a complete film catalog that you can send free of charge.

4. As correspondent for the Patton Electric Products Company, manufacturers of electric mixers, toasters, and other kitchen appliances, you need to answer an inquiry from Mason Electric Company, one of your new distributors in Phoenix, Arizona. They carry your complete line of eight products in their two stores, and they need the free newspaper mats to use in their local advertising campaign and also window display materials. Also, they would like to see a sample of the envelope stuffers (illustrative sales leaflets) that they might enclose with their customers' monthly statements. These leaflets are not free, although of course the one sample you're sending today is free. These colorful leaflets cost $6.60 a thousand but customers get good ideas from them. This is the first inquiry you have had from this new distributor since the welcome letter you sent 10 days ago.

5. You, manager of the customer service department of your savings bank, have received the following inquiry from Robert Gibbens in a nearby town:

As I have a six-months savings certificate with you and six
months are up, will I have to renew that or will it automatically go on? Will the interest be added to the capital
or will it be mailed to me? Is there any way I could earn
higher interest? Would like to hear from you.

Mr. Gibbens' certificate now has a principal of $9,000. If he increases this
amount by $1,000 (to $10,000), he'll be eligible to purchase a one-year certificate which earns at the rate of 6¼ percent. It's important that he recognize
the difference between the certificate he has and this one-year certificate.
The one-year certificate pays ¼ of 1 percent more per annum, but it does not
contain the automatic renewal clause that his present certificate has. If he
should desire not to make any change, his present certificate will automatically
go on at the rate of 6 percent a year. The interest is mailed to him and does
not add to the certificate. He should already have received the dividend check,
which was mailed five days ago. If he would like his dividends to earn for him
also, he can open a passbook savings account and endorse his dividend checks
to your bank "For Deposit Only" to his savings account, and send them to you
together with his passbook. The deposit will be made and the passbook returned
to him immediately. Write your courteous reply to Mr. Gibbens' inquiry.

6. Assume you work in the passenger department of Central Airlines, whose planes
   fly in and out of your city, Houston, Texas. Answer the following letter from
   Mrs. Metilda Oldtimer, who lives in a rural area about 60 miles north of
   Houston.

For several years now I've been wanting to get up courage to
take an airplane trip from Houston to Los Angeles. I have
saved up the money and the bus to downtown Houston goes right
by our house. Now I'm 78 and I guess that is supposed to be
old. My family has been urging me to come. My favorite
grandson is getting married in L.A. and I want to attend his
wedding, and I want to go the safest and fastest way. How
long does the plane take?

There are a few things I want to know first. I've heard that
lots of people get sick on airplanes. I also hear that you
serve alcohol and I can't drink anything but milk or tea. I
suppose, too, that nothing but cold food is served, and I
have to have hot meals. Oh, and one more thing, would we be
too high up to see objects on the ground?

If you can clear up these points, I think I'd like to take
the trip.

Here are the facts: Fewer people get airsick than get sick in trains or autos. You
don't serve cold meals. Hot meals are prepared and served individually by the
stewards—not just lunches but full dinners. Also, there is no charge for the
meals. You don't serve alcohol free in economy and tourist classes. Champagne
cocktails are served free in first-class travel, but for those who don't want
champagne, there's tomato or fruit juice. Jet planes between Houston and Los
Angeles fly at between 30,000 and 39,000 feet altitude, from which passengers
can see the ground when weather is clear. One stop is made in Phoenix, Arizona—the plane swoops down smoothly before it lands. Scenery is gorgeous
along the way. Flying time is about three hours. Airport bus picks up passengers

at Sleepeze Hotel in downtown Houston and takes them to the Houston Airport in 35 minutes; the charge one way to the airport is $2.50. Give all the information Mrs. Oldtimer needs to make a reservation. Your goal is to try to encourage her to travel by air *on your line*. Skillfully combine reader-benefit sales talk with your answers to all her questions, implied and stated. Assume any other needed pertinent details.

Favorable Replies to Inquiries for Information Unrelated to Sales.

1. Rewrite the following reply to remove the negative tone, inaccuracies, and unnecessary repetition. Also arrange the material for easier reading. Sign it as Assistant Chief of your state's Fishery Management Division. Assume today is September 29.

   Dear Mr. Fowler:

   Your letter of August 21st addressed to the State Department of Fisheries was misplaced, hence we have not had an opportunity to answer it sooner. We regret the delay a great deal.

   Following is the information you requested. It concerns only plantings made in comparitively recent years.

   Heather Lake was stocked in 1961 with 19,600 rainbow trout fry. It was stocked again in 1971 with 6,240 rainbow fry. Bear Lake was stocked in 1967 with 10,305 rainbow trout fry. It was stocked again in 1976 with 6,000 rainbow fry. Canyon Lake or Lake Twenty-two was stocked last in 1969 with 16,170 rainbow trout fry.

   We hope this information still had some value despite the lateness with which it is reaching you.

2. As staff supervisor in the test support division of your factory, you have been asked by the personnel department to write your recommendation on Steven J. Barkman, Clock No. 2409. Today is August 31. Your resume of Steve's summer employment will become part of the permanent personnel records. A carbon copy of your memo is to be sent to Janet Bore and M. D. Taylor, both department heads in your firm. Steve arrived in your department on June 15 this year and was assigned to your most tedious job—No. 5377 (you can decide what this job is)—which lasted two months. Steve is returning to college next month, as agreed when he was hired in June. Steve reasons well and has the ability to organize his work load. Should he apply for reemployment next summer, you would gladly welcome him into your group. Steve learns quickly and has adapted himself to your methods with minimum difficulty. His attitude, attendance, and cooperation are excellent. He is highly thought of by his lead personnel and supervisors. Write a recommendation, using correct *memo* format.

3. You—personnel manager for Aceline Insurance Company—have just received the night letter telegram in Exercise 1c, page 170, about Patricia M. Monell. Pat worked in your Claims Department 20 hours a week for two years while attending the university, in the School of Business Administration. She was meticulously accurate, unusually conscientious, and tactful with customers. Although only a part-time employee, she earned two promotions during the two years. She thrives on responsibility. From the telegram inquiry you don't

know what duties she will be expected to do in a quasi-legal position. You do recall that she took three university courses in Business Law, and she happily told you she received two A's and a B. You know no adverse information (except that while working in the claim filing section she dressed quite shabbily; her interest was not in clothing). Write your night letter telegram in 100 words, choosing only pertinent facts. (See footnote 19, page 136, for chargeable words.)

4. Assume you received from the Big Brother Volunteer Service Organization the same letter that was written to Mr. Willman in Exercise 1b, page 170. Robert Zurbach is one of your best friends. You've know him nine years and have the highest regard for his stability as well as his moral character. Assume pertinent details and perhaps a specific example showing why you believe he would be ideal for giving character guidance to a fatherless boy. Add any other needed details to make your letter complete and effective.

5. You are Assistant Manager of the Loan Department of the Merchant's National Bank, your city, and you have received a letter of inquiry from Mr. Lawrence Park, Public Relations Director of the National Environmental Council. He is considering Nathan Baro for a field representative job and asks your recommendation of Baro, who worked for your bank as a field collector of unpaid loan installments. Baro's job was to call at debtors' homes and collect their payments which are past due. In the new job he would work with business executives to upgrade environment conditions.

   Nathan worked for your bank from May 19 to December 20 last year and quit on impulse with one week's notice after a disagreement with an immediate supervisor. This supervisor happens to be the most strict of all your supervisors in his collection policies. He insists that every item of property should be promptly repossessed when a debtor is delinquent in his payments. Nathan Baro, on the contrary, believed in the gentle "soft sell" method. He was pleasant, honest, and extremely patient with customers, often much more so than the supervisor wanted. With one customer in particular, Nathan and the supervisor clashed; it was finally the cause of Nathan's leaving. The customer had borrowed $5,000 to lease a fleet of trucks for an out-of-state construction job. Although he was financially able to pay the monthly installments, he was habitually late; furthermore he threatened to transfer all his business—including his checking and savings account—to a competing bank unless the collection department quit harping about his late payments. Baro sided with the customer, arguing that as long as the customer cheerfully paid extra interest on all his late payments and because he always did pay (though late), the bank should "go easy" in its dealings with him, to save his goodwill. One day the supervisor angrily told Baro to repossess this customer's trucks or quit; Baro chose the latter, for he refused to compromise with what he thought was the right course of action.

   When you heard about the incident, you called Nathan back to your office and tactfully told him that his record has been very satisfactory with the bank and you hoped he would reconsider and stay. Nathan's collection record for the six months he was with your bank was second to the top for your twelve collectors in the field. He was exceptionally well-liked by customers and fellow employees. Baro thanked you for your invitation to return and said he would like to; but, because he would have to remain under the same stern supervisor, he thought it best to return full-time to his university studies and give up the job until another opening might occur the following summer.

   Nathan is a sociology and English major at the university, and an ardent supporter of social justice. He spoke occasionally about his desire to do something worthwhile in the community to help improve environment and help the underprivileged. You honestly believe he will be happier in the type of work for which Mr. Park is considering him. Write a tactful, frank recommendation, after you have sorted out the important and the irrelevant facts.

6. You are Credit Manager of Topcraft Department Store. Answer the credit inquiry in Exercise 10, page 175 assuming that it requires a letter because no questionnaire was enclosed. The applicant is Mr. Thomas M. Plicant, whose credit record with your store has been excellent ever since he opened the account seven years ago. He has bought an average of $90 monthly, under terms that require payment by the 10th of the month following purchase. Assume any other pertinent, necessary facts, and answer the six questions from the assistant credit manager of the savings and loan association. (You may assume a negative answer to one of the assumed questions.)

Granting Adjustments

1. Evaluate the following adjustment letters. What do you like and dislike about each? Suggest specific improvements where needed—in the tone, organization, accuracy, and adequacy of explanation and resale.

   A. This letter, dated January 27, from a department store, accompanied a gift box of assorted cheeses which a charge customer had bought and asked the store to send for Christmas to a Mrs. Greaves, in another state.

   Dear Mrs. Greaves:

   We are replacing the box of cheese which was purchased by Miss Mueller in December. This original purchase was returned from the Post Office because the label was not legible. Due to an error in our shipping department, the second box of cheese was not mailed. However, this third box of cheese should reach you in a few days.

   We are sorry for the inconvenience this has caused you.

   B. From the Chicago (head office) Service Department of a national electrical appliances firm to a customer in a city 1,000 miles away. The letter is mimeographed; the customer's name and "coffeemaster" are obvious typewritten fill-ins.

   We are concerned with your report about your appliance.* Our service work is guaranteed and if our service man failed to repair the appliance correctly, we want to see that the proper repairs are made without further expense.

   We would suggest that you return the appliance* to us and use the enclosed shipping label on the package so that it will be connected with this correspondence when it arrives here. If we failed to make the correct repairs, we will not only take care of that for you without charge, but we will also pay the postage both ways.

   *Coffeemaster

C. From a manufacturer to a retailer.

```
Thank you for telling us of the problem you have had with the
the coats you purchased.

Sometime ago, a batch of material having bad formulation
escaped detection by our quality control people.  The line
inspectors caught most of the finished coats before they
were invoiced.  However, some were shipped.  Apparently
your order was among them.

The situation has since been corrected and we don't believe
you will have this problem with a replacement.  Accordingly,
a special shipping label is enclosed for returning your
defective merchandise to us.  It will be promptly exchanged
upon receipt.  Please let us know if we may be of further
service.
```

2. Assume that two months ago Mrs. James Long, one of your long-time good customers, bought a dual-control four-slice chrome-plated electric toaster from your store and asked that it be sent as a wedding anniversary gift to her out-of-state friends, Mr. and Mrs. Horace Benson. Since then she has found no charge for the $36.50 on her monthly statements from your store; neither has she received a thank you from the Bensons. Last weekend, as a guest at the Benson's home, she noticed they were using the exact toaster she had sent them. To her chagrin they called it their "mystery toaster" because it had reached them c.o.d., although neither of them had ordered it. Because they needed one they kept it. Mrs. Long then told them of her gift. She is furious with your store and wants you to make a proper adjustment immediately. This situation requires two letters—one to the Bensons and one to Mrs. Long. Will you send her a copy of your message to the Bensons? Also, should your letter to the Bensons mention the refund in the opening paragraph? Why or why not? The salesclerk forgetfully omitted Mrs. Long's name on the sales slip. Finding only the name and address of the Bensons (who have no account at your store), the shipping department sent the toaster to the Bensons c.o.d.

3. You are adjustment correspondent for the R. L. Buck Co., a mail-order firm with nationwide distribution. Three weeks ago today Mrs. John Norton, of your city, placed an order (in person) for one galvanized steel Tower Climber with flying trapeze (#79 FP 3077, priced $25.99, shipping weight 51 pounds). She wanted your store to send it to her grandson Donald Brown, 417 North Sixth Street, Billings, Montana. She paid you $25.99 plus 94 cents sales tax. She left emphatic instructions with your mail-order department to bill *her* for all shipping charges, because at the time the clerk who waited on her could not determine the exact charges to Billings.
    Today you received the following letter from Mr. Dennis Brown, 417 Sixth Street, Billings, Montana:

```
If the enclosed material exemplifies the efficiency of
your operation, I'm glad I don't patronize your firm!  You
sent this bill to Donald Brown, our 5-year-old, who can't
write you himself.

Enclosures:
     Order blank
     Due slip for $3.03
```

Across the address on the order blank is clearly written "Send due to customer Mrs. John Norton, 1439 East Spruce Street (your city)" Under the caption "shipping charges" at the bottom of the order blank is another notation: "Send due to cust." Both these notations were made at the time the clerk first took the order. Therefore, it's quite obvious that someone slipped up. Since you want to try to keep the goodwill of Dennis Brown (he may trade at your Billings store), write a letter trying to erase the bad impression he no doubt has of the efficiency with which your store seems to operate, especially regarding the $3.03 due slip.

4. As assistant manager in the customer service department of A. B. Atlas Company, "jewelry's finest craftsmen" in Hartford, Connecticut, you need to answer today (January 2) a special delivery complaint from Olaf Lampson, vice president of Beta Gamma Sigma, business honorary, at the University of Ohio chapter. He asks what happened to the order he mailed to you almost three months ago (October 5). The chapter needs 35 crested pins for an initiation to be held three weeks from today. Your records show you received his official order and that the pins were shipped to him November 9 by first-class mail. Since the package has not been returned to you unclaimed, you can only assume it was lost in the mail. Company procedure requires that the customer complete the enclosed insurance affidavit so that you can file a claim and tracer with your insurance company. Upon receipt of the affidavit properly executed, you will immediately enter a no-charge replacement order. Write a goodwill-building adjustment. (This chapter has bought jewelry from you for many years.)

5. As circulation manager of the North End News Agency in your city, answer the complaint in Exercise 6, page 177. Because the newsgirl who broke the customer's pane of glass is one of your employees, you assume responsibility and agree to pay for replacement of the living room windowpane. You've also taken the necessary steps to see that the paper deliverers understand how they should deliver papers in the future. Make clear what the customer is to do so that you can pay for the glass promptly.

6. Step into the position of Customer Service Manager of Transcontinental Buslines. Today you are to answer the complaint in Exercise 3, page 176 from the passenger who was left stranded at an unscheduled stop. You are very disturbed about this matter and glad the customer wrote to you. You did not know that this particular driver had left another customer stranded last week. The company has strict rules for bus drivers and for safety of passengers. One of them is that they stop only at scheduled places. Another is that they make sure each passenger is back on the bus if he or she should be. This driver is usually very dependable, and he regrets the inconvenience he caused the passenger. Make whatever reasonable adjustment you think will please the passenger. Try to keep her goodwill for future trips on your busline. (Remember she also has friends who have heard of the incident.)

7. From Ms. Marlene Aimes you (customer service manager) received today a complaint letter that the boots your store sent by mail last week are too small. These boots were on special sale for $19.50. The usual store policy is to accept no returns on special sale merchandise. (This rule is one reason that you can offer goods at such low prices.) However, in this case you will make an exception to the rule because she did not know (and your store did not inform customers) that this style of boot must be larger than for dress shoes. You'll

be glad to take the boots back and you will credit her account for $19.50. Ask her to pack them in the same box in which they came and to mail them with your name on the address label. If she wants a larger size, you will send it to her for the sale price.

Other Favorable Replies about Credit, First Orders, Favors

1. You are a correspondent in the credit department of the leading department store in a city of 100,000 population. Several weeks ago Mrs. Ima Rich wrote you, saying she just moved to town from a distant city and wants a credit account with your store. In turn, you sent her an application form to fill out because the local credit bureau had no information available on Mrs. Rich. She filled out the form and returned it to you promptly. In turn, you checked her facts—including the references—and find she has an excellent credit reputation. The references complimented her for prompt payment throughout the years she traded with them. Your assignment is to notify her that you have granted her credit with your store. Assume your department store has the services you'd expect in a city of 100,000. In preparation for this assignment, you (or a representative from your class) might want to find out what services are available at a comparable department store and also the type of message the store sends to an individual like Mrs. Rich.

2. Mr. and Mrs. Grayson Tilly, 924 Malaki Street, Eugene, Oregon, have applied to your savings and loan association for a $14,500 mortgage home loan. Through the local retail credit association, and other references they gave you, you have checked their credit record and found it to be excellent. Also, all other conditions regarding their home and neighborhood are fine. Thus you have decided to approve their loan application. Write the appropriate letter, telling them what they need to know. The length of the loan is 17 years. Monthly payments will be $105, plus 1/12 of the annual real estate taxes and fire insurance premium. The interest cost of the loan is 7 percent yearly. Closing costs are $250. This loan commitment by your association is good for only 30 days. It is necessary that these borrowers sign and return a form which you are enclosing. By signing it, they will formally notify you of their acceptance of the loan. If they have questions, you'll try to answer them. Of course, their reply must come within the 30 days.

3. You are credit manager of the National Athletic Supply, Inc., a wholesale firm in Bloomington, Illinois. Today (January 25) you approved a credit request from Mr. Robert Rainsdale, owner-manager of Bob's Sporting Goods in Muncie, Indiana. He has ordered:

20 Little League baseball bats, Catalog #BB987	$2.25	$ 45.00
30 baseballs with cork centers, BC 0716	1.75	52.50
10 Deluxe table tennis sets, #TT 8106	8.00	80.00
Total		177.50
Shipping charges		6.00
		$183.50

This is his first order to your firm. It came to you through your field representative Lana Browne, who reports an exceptionally favorable location of Bob's Sporting Goods—within two blocks of both junior and senior high schools and in the heart of a residential shopping area catering to young families with children. Mr. Rainsdale (a college graduate six years ago, majoring in Recreation) bought the store three years ago with savings and a small inheritance. Although his capital investment is limited, he is a well-liked manager with progressive ideas. As a former captain of his college football team and as a Little League coach for four years, he is widely known and respected in the community. His character and ethical standards are above reproach. His references report that he has always paid his bills, although often payments have run past the 30-day periods. You decide to grant him credit on your usual 2/10, net 30 terms and to give him a little "education" (tactfully) on what he gains from paying within the discount period. You are setting a credit limit of $200 until you see how well he keeps his account up to date. The items he ordered were sent by Railway Express today; delivery will be within two days. The Little League bats (of white ash) are approved by the American Baseball Association; the Deluxe table tennis sets (with 5-ply basswood paddles and sure-grip vinyl handle bindings), as well as the bats, are nationally advertised in *Sports Parade* and *Parents* magazines. You're enclosing with the shipment some counter and window displays, plus the needed order lists and blanks and your new spring catalog.

4. You are sales manager for American Wholesale Office Supplies Mart, Cincinnati, Ohio. Acknowledge a first order from Carson's Office Equipment and Supplies, 898 Second Avenue, Scranton, Pennsylvania. Mrs. John Carson, owner-manager, has ordered by letter the following from you:

30 cartons of standard mimeograph stencils (MS952) @ $1.50	$ 45.00
50 reams MP 621 mineograph paper @ $1.60	80.00
50 reams easy-erase typing paper EP 632 @ $1.90	95.00
	$220.00

Mrs. Carson enclosed her check for $235 saying she was estimating the shipping charges and would forward more if necessary. You must refund the excess paid, because shipping charges are only $8.50. These supplies are being wrapped and shipped tomorrow afternoon by motor freight, and should get to Scranton the next morning. From her order, it appears that Mrs. Carson has only your Paper and Duplicating Supplies Catalog. Send her your folder illustrating your new line of other office supplies, which ranges from letter scales and portable envelope sealers to typewriter erasers and 10 different colors of pens and pencils. Can you think of anything else you should send or tell her to make this retailer's future ordering from your firm easy and profitable? (Credit terms to charge customers are 2/10, net 30.)

5. Assume that in the five years since you graduated from college you have become active in the local chapter of a national business organization relating to your major work. (Assume a pertinent name.) Last month you were presented with the "Executive of the Month" award, and a short article appeared about you in this organization's national magazine. Today you receive a complimentary letter and invitation from the president of the organization's chapter in another city (100 miles away) to be dinner guest (7 p.m.) and banquet speaker (20 minutes) on Thursday evening, one month from today. Your spouse or a friend will also be a welcome guest, and the organization will provide for your car expenses and hotel overnight costs. There is no fee for speaking. After thinking the matter over, you decide to accept, even though you must be back at your office at 8 a.m. the next (Friday) morning. The topic suggested for your talk is one that's dear to your heart. Write your pleasant acceptance and make clear

any details the president will need to know. Assume any additional necessary facts. The chapter's publicity will go to press 10 days from today, so of course you need to respond fairly soon. The earliest you can get to the banquet is 7 p.m.

6. As customer relations manager you have decided to write a personalized form letter that your firm (a chain of retail department stores) can send to each customer who reports that his or her credit card is lost or stolen. Acknowledge receipt of the notification and assure the customer that he or she will be protected from the date you received it against loss arising from its use by persons not authorized by the customer. Here is how your new security system works for the customer: You will mail a new set of credit cards to the customer as soon as they can be prepared. They will have a code number after the regular account number, but otherwise they are the same as before. Once the new cards are received, the customer is to use only these cards and return any remaining old credit cards in an envelope which you have provided.

To reduce possible loss to your firm, you have in the meantime placed a "stop credit" notice on the customer's old credit cards, which means they will be accepted by all stores without question but only for charges under $10 each. The customer should therefore not attempt to make individual purchases larger than $10 between now and the time the new cards are received. The new credit cards may, of course, be used normally. For the time being, the customer will receive (as before) only one statement from your stores, and it will combine purchases made on both old and new cards. The customer is to examine the sales slips carefully. Should there be any discrepancies, the customer is to return the slips to your office at once for crediting to the account. Let the customer know that you appreciate the opportunity to be of service.

7. Assume you are the newly elected vice president and membership chairperson for your college Alumni Association. Your first form letter is to the alumni who have paid their membership dues for the current year. Welcome them and express your personal appreciation for their interest and support. Encourage each member of participate to the fullest in the various alumni programs available. Solicit suggestions at any time concerning your association. Address your sample form letter to Harold Harms, 983 Summit Avenue North, your town (city). All future letters you mail to members for this same purpose will have a body identical to the one you write today, but each will be typed on automatic typewriter and have a personalized inside address and salutation.

Good-News and Neutral Announcements

1. You are chairman of the Chamber of Commerce second annual spring luncheon, and you've been working hard on plans for the past two months. A senator of your state, the Honorable Denise J. Doe, has accepted your invitation to be principal speaker. Because you anticipate that recent events in the state capitol will generate a high level of interest, you have moved the luncheon to a larger room at the local athletic club. You have decided to permit a member to bring one nonmember guest. The purpose of these luncheons is to provide an opportunity to get reacquainted with other business executives in your community and to hear a challenging and provocative message from a

prominent public figure. The program this year should provide both. The date is Thursday, May 20, 197–. The total number you can accommodate is 175. Your cutoff date for reservations is May 17. Luncheon will begin at 12 noon. Write the letter announcing this event and make action easy for reservations. Be specific.

2. You are accountant for R&H Distributors. Today (February 28) you have discovered an error you made regarding freight bill #730015, dated November 11 last year, from Howard Carloading Company, 908 Utah Avenue, Salt Lake City, Utah. Through your oversight you have not yet paid this bill, though payment was due last November 18! Your firm tries always to pay its bills on time. It was an honest mistake and you want to apologize for it. You received freight bills 730015 and 72119 from Howard on the same day. Since these two freight bills were identical except for the bill number, you had put them together assuming that one was a copy of the other. You hope this incident will not hinder any future good relations your firm may have with Howard Carloading. Write an appropriate letter with which you transmit your check for the $20.98 that was due three and one-half months ago.

3. Design an eye-catching announcement memo for all your employees to take part in your company's annual blood bank drive. You are assistant personnel manager. The date is Friday, March 15, from 10 a.m. to 4 p.m. in the company's health annex, room 84-A. Your memo goes to each of 500 employees. You are providing donor sign-up sheets that will be posted on bulletin boards in 10 areas, two on each of five floors. Because of the recent flu "epidemic," donors have been light and demands for blood have been heavy. Ask the employees to give this drive their full support and to sign up by a certain date.

4. As executive assistant to the president of Topeak Life Insurance, Tulsa, Oklahoma, you have the pleasure of writing an announcement today (March 1) to all Topeak stockholders. (It will be signed by the president.) The Board of Directors voted to declare a 10 percent stock dividend payable to all stock holders of record on April 15 this year. This is the first stock dividend declared by the company. It can be attributed mainly to the outstanding combined efforts of the Board of Directors, Home Office, and Field Marketing Personnel. Since its inception, Topeak has been dedicated to growth, not for the sheer sake of growth alone, but recognizing growth as the primary instrument to be used in building a successful and progressive company. The president feels that stockholders can look upon the company's past growth with justified pride and toward its future growth with great optimism.

    Tell the stockholders that if the home address has changed recently, they should notify the Home Office to prevent delay in receiving dividends. If a stockholder is currently holding Topeak stock which is not in his or her name, the stock should be forwarded to the Home Office so a transfer can be made before April 15. Right after that date the dividend will be computed and sent directly to each stockholder of record. The stockholder need not send any verification to the Home Office. Your announcement is to be a complete form with the same salutation for all recipients.

5. Revise the following memo announcement so it has better you attitude and more active than passive verbs. Correct any other errors.

Date: March 9, 197_
To: Customer Service Personnel
From: Ron M. Jensen
Subject: Deposit and Cash Receipt Books

Effective March 9, 197_, the following changes will be made
in the use and care of deposit and cash receipt books by
sales people.

1. The deposit and/or cash receipt book(s) issued to a
    salesperson will be used only only by the person to
    whom the book is issued.

2. Whenever a deposit or other monies are collected, the
    salesperson will remove from the receipt book(s) the
    customer's copy(s) and give this to the customer as is
    now done. In addition, at the end of their shift,
    salespersons will no longer turn in their receipt
    book(s) with the money and tickets. Instead they will
    pull the accounting copy(s) and put these in the
    envelope provided with the cash and tickets for those
    transactions.

3. Deposit and reciept books are not to be left laying
    around in a vehicle or other places. They are to be
    under the strict control of the individual the
    book(s) is issued to.

Normally a sales person will have one deposit book and one
cash receipt book. Additional books may be issued by a
service supervisor. All used up books are to be returned
to the supervisor for forwarding to the accounting department.

*(Capsule Checklists for Good-News
Messages begin on page 236.)*

CAPSULE CHECKLIST FOR

I Good-News (and Neutral): General Plan	*II* Answering Inquiries for Information Related to Sales	*III* Answering Inquiries for Information Unrelated to Sales—Letter of Recommendation

1. BEST NEWS or MAIN IDEA	1. Best news or main idea
	a. Positive opening with one of these:
	  (1) Requested material
	  (2) Favorable answer to a question
	  (3) Introduction of main idea(s)
	b. Courtesy; appreciation
		1. Best news or main idea
		a. Applicant's full name and relationship to you; job(s) held
		b. Pleasure; reason for writing

2. EXPLANATION
a. All necessary details
b. Resale material
c. Educational material
d. Sales promotion
	2. Explanation
	a. Answers to all questions—direct or implied
	  (1) Positive, helpful tone
	  (2) Imbedded negatives
	  (3) Emphasis on what something *is*, what you can do or have
	  (4) Reader benefits
	  (5) Prices after most selling points (unless price is a bargain)
	b. Resale (with reader benefits) when appropriate
	c. Educational material on product use, if pertinent
		2. Explanation
		a. Answers to all questions—direct or implied
		b. Best psychological order for threefold responsibility to:
		  (1) Applicant
		  (2) Person considering applicant
		  (3) Your conscience
		c. Specific facts about
		  (1) Applicant's job, duties, conduct
		  (2) Applicant's work or other habits
		  (3) Personality, etc.
		d. Honesty and judgment about negatives
		e. Caution to know legal aspects; establishment of confidential nature of reply "by request"

3. POSITIVE, FRIENDLY ENDING a. Appreciation b. CSAD[1] c. EA[2] and motivation d. Willingness to help further e. DA[3] f. RB[4]	3. Courteous close a. CSAD[1] (sometimes) Itemized steps, if desirable b. EA[2] c. DA[3] d. RB[4] and courtesy; offer of further help, if appropriate	3. Courteous close a. Candid statement of your personal opinion about applicant's probable fitness for whatever he or she is being considered for b. Positive (not negative) attributes at end

[1]CSAD = clear statement of action desired
[2]EA = easy action
[3]DA = dated action, if desirable
[4]RB = reader benefit

GOOD-NEWS MESSAGES

IV
Granting Requests for Adjustment

Seller at Fault (A)	*Buyer or Another at Fault (B)*
1. Best news	1. Best news or buffer
a. Whatever will please buyer most	a. Same as IV, 1,a
	or
b. Courtesy	b. Get-in-step-with-reader, courteous comment and concern
2. Explanation	2. Explanation
a. Brief resale with tactful explanation of error (if desirable)	a. Brief resale with tactful explanation of error, showing seller not at fault
b. Instructions for buyer action if needed	b. (If use of 1,b above, best news after explanation)
c. Concrete resale on firm, services, or goods if desirable	c. Concrete resale same as IV, A, 2,c
d. Cautions	d. Cautions
e. Sales promotion on replacement of returned item(s) or on allied goods	e. Sales promotion same as IV, A, 2,e
3. Courteous close	3. Courteous close
a. Suggested action and forward look to future pleasant use of goods and services	a. Same as IV, A, 3, a–d
b. EA[2]	
c. Positive idea; help	
d. RB[4]	

CAPSULE CHECKLIST FOR

V *Approving Credit*	*VI* *Acknowledging First Orders*	*VII* *Granting Favors*

1. Best news
  a. Credit grant (if no purchase)
  b. Shipment (if goods ordered)
    (1) Description
    (2) Quantity
    (3) Prices, costs
    (4) Method, charges
  c. Courtesy
	2. Best news
	  a. Shipment details same as V, 1, b (1)–(4)
	  b. Thanks for remittance and/or order
		1. Best news
		  a. Acceptance of favor, request
		  b. Courtesy

2. Explanation
  a. Basis for credit; compliment
  b. Concrete, positive statements of credit terms; payments, dates, discounts, limits
  c. Resale on services—
    (1) Consumer: parking, shopping services, department, conveniences, deliveries, price benefits
    (2) Middleman: warehouses, discounts, selling aids, advertising, factory guarantees, repairs, deliveries
  d. Resale on product choices
  e. Sales promotion sometimes—allied goods
	2. Explanation
	  a. For credit customer same as V, 2, a and b
	  b. For cash or credit: Resale on services same as V, 2, c
	  c. For cash or credit: Resale on products ordered; highlights on special features— adapted to buyer
	  d. For cash customer: Perhaps credit application form enclosed, with invitation to return it for consideration
		2. Explanation
		  a. Pertinent comments and details regarding favor— what is being or will be done, etc.
		  b. Questions, if necessary, pertaining to favor

3. Courteous close
  a. Forward look to pleasant service and orders (no greedy tone)
  b. Suggested action
  c. EA[2]
  d. RB[4]
  e. Courtesy; suggestion of further help, if pertinent
	3. Courteous close
	  a. Forward look to pleasant service and orders (no greedy tone)
	  b. Suggested action
	  c. EA[2]
	  d. RB[4]
	  e. Courtesy; suggestion of further help, if pertinent
		3. Courteous close
		  a. Cordial, pertinent comment; perhaps a forward look, a good wish, a compliment, or a request

[1] CSAD = clear statement of action desired
[2] EA = easy action
[3] DA = dated action, if desirable
[4] RB = reader benefit

GOOD-NEWS MESSAGES (Continued)

VIII *Announcements*	*IX* *Transmittals*

1. Best news; main idea
  When appropriate:
  a. 5 W's (all or most);
     reader in first and all
     other paragraphs
  b. Statement of pleasure,
     compliment, con-
     gratulations
  c. Admission of error;
     with good news
	1. Best news; main idea
	  a. Transmittal of
	     specific item(s)
	  b. A concise reason
	  c. Courtesy

2. Explanation
  a. Details to emphasize,
     reader benefits, if
     possible
  In admission of error:
  b. Explanation and
     apology; emphasis on
     sincere desire to serve
     well
  c. Resale on firm, prod-
     ucts, or services, as
     appropriate
	2. Explanation
	  If needed:
	  a. Comments
	  b. Instructions

3. Courteous close
  a. CSAD[1]
  b. EA[2]
  c. DA[3]
  d. RB[4] and/or offer of
     further help
  e. Courtesy
	3. Courteous close
	  a. CSAD[1]
	  b. EA[2]
	  c. DA[3]
	  d. Offer of further help
	     or other items or RB[4]
	     about items trans-
	     mitted

 **Bad-News Messages**

Whenever you must write a message that your reader will consider disappointing or unfavorable in some way, the situation requires special planning and careful choice of words. A competent letter writer can actually win or keep a friend for his or her company even when refusing an inquirer's request or transmitting other unfavorable facts.

Most of the bad-news letters and memorandums you may have to write can be grouped under the following unfavorable replies and unfavorable unsolicited messages:

Unfavorable replies

Answering sales-related inquiries when the information is undesirable
Answering nonsales inquiries when the information is undesirable
Refusing adjustments on claims and complaints
Refusing credit
Acknowledging orders you can't fill now or at all
Declining requests for favors
Turning down contract or work offers

Unfavorable unsolicited messages

Announcing bad news about prices and/or services
Requiring minimum orders and/or deposits
Penalizing for nonconformity with rules and procedures
Conveying other bad news

This chapter discusses the right attitude for transmitting bad news, suggests plans for bad-news messages, presents various examples of unfavorable replies and unsolicited messages, and provides capsule checklists. Additional illustrations of bad-news messages are in Chapters 12 and 13.

The Right Attitude

Everything you learned in preceding chapters about the communication process, consideration, and courtesy toward your reader applies to bad-news messages.[1] In such messages it is especially important that the *tone* of your letter be appropriate. Because the right attitude toward your recipient will improve the tone and thus the effectiveness of your letters, keep the following additional suggestions in mind when you write bad-news letters:

1. *Remember that every letter you write can be considered a sales letter.* With bad-news letters, you are trying to sell your reader on the idea that your decision, though contrary to his request or action, is fair and reasonable—and possibly even to his advantage in the long run.

2. *Try honestly to see things from the other person's point of view.* Show him why your suggested plan or requirement is needed and/or to his advantage. A statement such as "It will be advantageous to you if you work it out this way. . . ." is much more effective than the selfish "It would be inconvenient for us (or against our policy) to do as you ask."

[1] See especially pages 21–22 regarding attitudes and opinions and pages 86–92 about consideration and courtesy.

3. *Avoid leaning on company rules or policy;* it seldom soothes your reader. Include, if possible, the *customer-benefit reasons* that are behind your rules and procedures.

4. *Look for the best in the other person.* Although a customer may be mistaken, try to have confidence that he honestly wants to do the right thing. The following expressions show faith in the reader:

   We are confident that you . . .
   You are probably wondering how you can . . .
   You will agree, I believe, that . . .

5. *When praising a person, single him out; when criticizing him, put him in a group.*

   Single out: You certainly made the right decision, Mr. Brown.
   As a group: Sometimes customers, unknowingly, make the wrong decision.

6. *Shield the reader's pride.*

   Tactless: If you had read the instructions I gave you, you would have noticed that they specifically state you had to sign the acceptance form within 30 days.
   Tactful: Our commitment was good for 30 days. In the instructions that you received with the . . . you will find . . .

7. *Talk* with *the reader, not down to him.*

   Condescending: We are willing to look into this matter for you.
   Agreeable: Thank you for taking the time to tell us about . . . We always appreciate . . .

Plans for Bad-News Messages

The underlying purpose of every bad-news message is to present the unpleasant facts with *you* attitude—in such a way that the reader will consider you fair and reasonable and will preferably remain a friend of the organization you represent. Your choice of message plan is influenced by the circumstances—your purpose, your relationship to the reader, and the particular facts in each case. You have two choices of plans: the indirect or the direct.

Indirect Plan

Before you read the suggested indirect pattern for stating bad news, try an experiment on yourself. Suppose you as a customer have been waiting for a reply to your request for something you want very much from a business firm—a refund or perhaps a loan important to you. How would you react if the reply began with a negative statement similar to these:

We regret (are sorry, wish to state) that we are unable to refund the $300 down payment you made on the car.

or

Your application for a loan (refund) has been denied (refused, rejected).

Wouldn't you feel more receptive toward the firm and its bad news if the reply had opened with at least a brief agreeable statement—like the following—and then presented an explanation *before* the bad news?

> We appreciate your letter telling us how you feel about the 197_ hard-top Mercury you purchased from us three months ago.

> Thank you for giving us the opportunity to consider your loan application for financing your proposed home purchase.

Most people appreciate hearing at least some explanation before the bad-news decision, especially if it seriously affects them. Usually a good rule to consider is "Be quick to give good news, but take longer to tell the bad news." Thus, whereas the good-news message uses a direct approach, the bad-news message usually follows the indirect approach. Using this approach, the bad-news plan has the following four-part suggested organizational structure:

---

1. Buffer
2. Explanation and analysis of circumstances
3. Decision—implied or expressed—with resale and/or constructive suggestions
4. Friendly, positive close

Under each part of this bad-news basic pattern you have several alternatives, as shown in the expanded list below.

1. Buffer. If possible, fill your first paragraph with mainly reader-interest —to get in step with your reader. However, your buffer must begin close to the general subject of your letter; avoid irrelevant material. Also, avoid statements that might mislead the reader into thinking you are granting the request; such statements merely build the reader up for a sad letdown! Apologies are unwarranted if your firm is not at fault. One or more of the following buffers can help put your reader in a more receptive attitude:

a. *Agreement.* Agree with the reader on something, if possible (perhaps a matter-of-fact comment on which there is general agreement—business conditions, costs, or any other pertinent item).
b. *Appreciation.* Thank the reader (for a check, information, application, request, inquiry, cooperation, or whatever applies).
c. *Assurance.* Assure the reader of careful consideration and explanation of all available facts about the problem.
d. *Compliment.* Try to compliment the reader on something good about his or her past record or request (sincerity, careful listing of all pertinent facts, etc.).
e. *Cooperation.* Show a sincere desire to be as helpful as possible.

f. *Good news.* If you can grant any part of a request and you think your reader will be pleased, begin with that good news.
g. *Neutral courtesy.* Keep your opening paragraph noncommittal. For instance, if you must announce an unfavorable price increase or service decrease, use neutral words such as "needed change."
h. *Resale.* Begin with brief, appropriate resale (on your merchandise, services, or organization).
i. *Sympathy.* Express sympathy—if the matter is very serious and likely to be greatly disappointing to the reader.
j. *Understanding.* Show understanding of the reader's needs and problem (desire to have a dependable product, to pay at least a partial amount due, etc.).

2. **Explanation and Analysis.** Include honest, convincing reasons why under the circumstances the matter must be different from the way the reader wants it. In two types of situations, however, stating a reason is unnecessary: (1) when the matter is routine and obvious (clerical error) and (2) when you'd get mired in negative or confidential material if you tried to explain. When you decide to include an explanation, place it *before* the decision and remember these suggestions:

a. Try to convince the reader that you are acting in his or her best interests in the long run, or at least according to a law that is enforced equally for all. Avoid the insincere: "Much as I would like to . . . however . . ." Also avoid reasons that suggest benefit only to your firm.
b. Explain courteously all pertinent facts behind your decision. Mention first the favorable factors, then the less favorable ones.
c. Don't dodge with such statements as "our policy prevents . . ." State, if possible, specific reasons (especially customer-benefit reasons) for your policy.
d. If the reason is confidential or too complicated to explain, then show—as a substitute—that the request has been carefully and sincerely considered (for the reader's benefit as well as your company's).

3. **Decision—Implied or Expressed with Resale and/or Constructive Suggestions.** Make the decision clear, positive, concise; and embed it in favorable material if possible. You have these alternatives:

a. If the reasons are so sound that your reader will conclude you *must* refuse the request, payment, or such, you can omit the negative entirely and make the bad-news decision clear by implication. For example, if you are already scheduled as luncheon speaker in Chicago May 6, omit saying, "Therefore, I cannot attend your luncheon in St. Louis that same day."
b. If an implied decision might be misunderstood, express your decision briefly and clearly, near the end of the explanation. Be careful never to mislead or cause your reader to be uncertain about your decision. The best place for a negative decision is in the middle—not the beginning—of a paragraph, and never in a paragraph by itself. Avoid *must refuse, cannot grant,* and similar negatives.
c. If you can, offer a constructive suggestion, state a counterproposal, an alternative course of action, or a ray of hope for the future. By emphasizing what *can* be done, you may clearly imply what can*not* be done without actually using the negatives. For instance, if you must refuse requested credit, you can offer a layaway plan; instead of a requested personal interview, you can enclose a helpful booklet to answer questions.

  d. If a compromise is desirable, suggest what your firm can do and what the customer can do.
  e. If desirable, resell the reader on your company's services and/or practices and policies.

    4. Friendly, Positive Close. End on a positive note, with one or more of these ideas:

  a. Assure the reader he is appreciated as a customer (or as an interested inquirer and possible future customer).
  b. Invite future patronage, cooperation, suggestions, and/or compliance with the decision. Include mild, no-pressure sales promotional material if you think your reader is in the right mood for it. (See page 189.)
  c. If you are awaiting his approval, or he should take some action, make clear exactly what he is to do, when he should do it, and how he can do it easily. (See pages 80–81.)
  d. Express continued interest, service, and reader benefit.

Genuine sincerity must underlie whatever words you use to express your message. The writer who has a true feeling of goodwill toward every customer will find it easier to convey a bad-news message effectively and at the same time protect the interests of the company.

Direct Plan

Though you can use the indirect bad-news plan for most unfavorable messages, there are situations that may warrant the direct approach. Again, the choice depends upon the particular circumstances. You may decide to begin directly with the bad news if you have:

A routine or small matter on which your reader is likely not to be seriously disappointed or personally emotionally involved—especially a message between employees of two business firms or within the same firm (and perhaps also to a person who is known to prefer reading the bad news in the first paragraph!).

or

An urgent message that should be called to the reader's attention forcefully—as in the late stages of a collection procedure.

If you use the direct approach, the pattern is essentially the same as the direct good-news plan, except that the opening contains bad instead of good news.

---

1. Bad-news decision (with or without a brief buffer)
2. Explanation
3. Appropriate courteous ending

Most of the bad-news replies and unsolicited messages in this chapter are organized by the indirect approach (hereafter referred to as the bad-news plan), but you will also find examples of messages organized by the direct plan.

Unfavorable Replies to Requests[2]

This section focuses on unfavorable replies to requests for information (sales-related and nonsales subjects), adjustment, credit, orders, favors, and some kinds of contract offers.

Answering Sales-related Inquiries When the Information Is Undesirable

If you have no honest favorable answer to your reader's direct question(s) regarding catalogs, prices, terms, products, and similar sales-related information, your reply should be organized by the bad-news plan. In some situations all four parts of such a message may be expressed adequately in four or five sentences. For example, in letter 1, the district manager of a national tire manufacturing firm answers a rancher's two-page letter about her pet lion.[3] The lion had outgrown pet-store rubber dog bones, and the rancher asked if the rubber company could make a 12- to 14-inch heavy rubber toy with a hidden bell inside.

Letter 1
A concise, helpful bad-news reply about a product the writer's firm does not manufacture.

Buffer: *thanks*	Thank you very much for your interesting letter concerning Little Tyke.
Explanation; implied decision	Goodyear does not make rubber sundry items such as balls, and toys, and we have no molds with which to make up the item you need for Little Tyke.
Helpful suggestion	Some rubber company specializing in rubber drug sundries may be able to help you. You might try the Miller Rubber Company, Division of Goodrich, in Akron, Ohio.
Pleasant close (good wishes)	The best of success to you in finding just what you need for your famous pet.

When the inquiry is about a complex or more serious matter, much more detail may be necessary, especially in the explanation and resale portions. The next example—from the president of a wholesale cement firm to a contractor who had asked why the firm's prices were so high—illustrates how tact and specific details can help to retain a reader's goodwill despite bad news.

[2] To embed negative material in replies that are chiefly good news, see pages 191–192 and 197–198.
[3] Adapted from a letter by Goodyear Tire and Rubber Co., Akron, Ohio.

Letter 2
A goodwill-retaining bad-news reply to an inquiry about high prices.

Buffer: *thanks for* *inquiry and* *business*	Thank you for your inquiry and concern over the amount we charged you for your concrete. Because your business is very much appreciated and valued highly, it is important to me as well as to you that you understand why we billed you $525.08 instead of $463.13.
Explanation *Decision* *Fairness to* *all and* *reader* *benefit*	Due to the $1.44 hourly employee wage increase, the increase in the price of cement, and overall increases in direct and indirect operating expenses, it was necessary to increase the price of our concrete. For the past 11 months our prices for 5 sacks of our concrete have been $17.90 to individuals and $17.40 to all contractors. If we lower the price to one contractor, all others would rightly expect equal treatment. By maintaining our price, we treat everyone equally and can assure you that you are getting the quality of material you order and expect.
Resale	I realize that you were able to buy concrete at a lower price in the past, but the company that you bought the concrete from is no longer in business just because their price was not sufficient to cover their direct costs and expenses. Neither you nor we would want this condition to happen to us. We are proud of our reputation for quality products and service and want to continue to serve you in the future.
Pleasant *close* *(thanks;* *further* *service)*	Your letters are always welcome. Also, if you have questions or need supplies, please call me between 7:30 a.m. and 5:30 p.m. at 999-3333, or call evenings at 666-6666.

Answering Nonsales Inquiries When the Information Is Undesirable

Occasionally you may have to write bad-news answers to nonsales inquiries. Whenever you send bad news to anyone outside your firm, it is usually better to follow the bad-news plan.

When you receive a request for a recommendation on a person about whom you have only unfavorable information, and whom you honestly cannot recommend, you have four alternatives:

1. Call the inquirer on the telephone and discuss the matter.
2. Write a brief refusal similar to the following:
    On the basis of my experience with Tom Dawson, I am sorry to inform you that I do not have sufficient favorable information to recommend him for the position (credit) for which you are considering him.
3. Omit the applicant's name throughout the reply (use "the person about whom you inquire in your letter of April 10")[4] and include whatever facts are pertinent regarding employment, credit, or personal record.

[4]Omitting the applicant's name is acceptable if you are sure your reader knows whom you are writing about. However, such a practice could be extremely confusing and lead to mix-ups if the same two firms happen to correspond about two or more persons on the same day! Employers who exchange information frequently might set up a file number for each person on whom they seek information. Replies would then be about a file number (known to the employer and respondent as a specific person).

4. Include both the applicant's name and an honest, frank report, as in letter 3. Because of libel laws it is imperative to be cautious and scrupulously accurate. Though you can use the direct plan, similar to that discussed in Chapter 8, pages 197–198, the following letter uses the bad-news plan. Notice that the first paragraph is basically a buffer of neutral courtesy; it does not reveal the bad news. Only after stating facts does the writer state a decision.

Letter 3
A frank nonrecommendation of an unsatisfactory former employee.

Full name and work	Tom Zoe, about whom you inquire, was on our payroll five months—from April 197_ until two months ago. He was hired as a messenger and a sign painter's helper.
Facts	Because his job with our firm was his first since he quit high school, we tried to be more understanding about his personal problems that affected his work. I must tell you confidentially that Tom had been victimized by unfortunate home experiences which caused him to drift into careless habit patterns from the standpoint of responsibility and regularity.
Unfavorable work	His attendance record with us shows an average of one absence every six days. Both as a messenger and as a helper he abused rules and privileges. Because each time he promised to do better, we gave him several extra opportunities to straighten himself out. Unfortunately the pattern became worse instead of better and we finally had to replace him.
Decision	Thus, on the basis of our experience with him, I am sorry I cannot recommend him for responsible work. I am glad to see that he is now getting the help of your counseling service and sincerely hope he will develop right attitudes.
Hope for the future	Perhaps in time he will be able to establish himself with really worthwhile activities. You have my sincere good wishes.

The best overall policy is: be honest, tactful, and aware of your threefold responsibility—to the applicant, to the addressee, and to yourself.

When you're writing to someone in your own organization about a relatively small matter with which the reader is not emotionally involved, you probably should use the *direct* refusal plan, as in the memo below.

Letter 4 (Memo)
A bad-news direct-plan memo about company equipment.

	TO: Ann Brown, Purchasing
	FROM: Harry Mills, Plant 2
	SUBJECT: New ventilating fans needed
Bad news	Today Jake Jones, representative of Ace Electric, told me that the noisy fans you asked about can't be repaired or adjusted again. He says they're a total loss. The only thing possible for ventilation is to buy new fans.

Details
> Three fans, model XA22, should do the job well. They'll cost us $80 apiece installed. Jake says he can install these fans this coming Saturday.

Action request
> If you approve, I'll go ahead and make arrangements. Jake needs two days' notice, because he'll order what we need from the factory. Will you give me a jingle by Wednesday afternoon?

If your firm is a nonprofit organization that gets large numbers of requests for free information—and if you often need to send bad-news replies—you may, to cut correspondence costs, even devise a form letter listing the most recurring negative facts, as in letter 5.

Letter 5
Printed form letter to handle a nonprofit organization's multiple inquiries for which many answers may have to be bad news.

Buffer: thanks
> Thank you for your recent inquiry. In the interest of economy your request is being answered by this form letter. Check marks and the comments below indicate the action taken.

Facts and implied decisions
> 1. The item or information you requested is
>   (a) enclosed.
>   (b) out of print. Copies are in many libraries.
>   (c) not yet available; (___ will be sent later),
>   (___related material is enclosed).
>   (d) not a publication of this organization.
> 2. Your request will be filled as soon as our supply is replenished.
> 3. The free supply of this report is exhausted. Copies may be purchased from (name and address) for ___ cents a copy.
> 4. Your request has been referred to _____
> _____

Suggestion for future action
> If you write us again in regard to this request, please return the enclosed correspondence since we have retained no record of it.
>
>   (Printed name and title of writer)

> Comments:

Refusing Adjustments on Claims and Complaints

When you refuse a request for adjustment, realize that the customer is probably disgruntled and even irritated, and be particularly tactful when "selling" on the fairness of your refusal. Especially important material to include—besides your buffer and explanation—is resale material, constructive suggestions, and even sales promotion when appropriate.

This section discusses three kinds of unwarranted customer claims on which you may have to write a refusal: (1) when the customer is at fault regarding a product, (2) when the customer is mistaken in a complaint about an account or a service, and (3) when the customer makes an unjustified policy complaint.

When the Customer Is at Fault regarding a Product. Often customers who claim free replacement or repair of a "malfunctioning" product are at fault because they violated instructions for using it. Also, many customers seek a refund or credit on items simply because they have changed their mind. Or a customer might return as "new" an article which cannot be resold because of something the customer did wrong. The next three examples illustrate satisfactory adjustment refusals in such cases.

Misuse of a product is the basic reason for the refusal in letter 1. Notice that the writer calls attention to the user's mistake indirectly and that she shields the reader's pride. She doesn't say, "You violated the instructions" or "You obviously failed to read the directions." Instead, the message includes a tactful logical explanation and an implied but clear refusal, followed by a constructive suggestion and easy-action reader-benefit ending.

Letter 1
A mail-order house refuses to replace free a broken, misused garden hose.

Buffer: agreement and appreciation	When you buy a Widgeon product, you are right to expect high quality. We appreciate your returning the hose for our inspection so that we can meet our goal--satisfying your needs.
Resale and assurance about honoring guarantee	To provide each of our thousands of Widgeon customers with the specific hose he or she needs, we carry a wide selection. Each type of garden hose described in the Widgeon catalog is guaranteed to give you the service it was designed for. We are always glad to replace a hose provided its defect lies with assembly or materials.
Reason for Opaque hose breakdown *Implied refusal*	As stated in the catalog, the Opaque Plastic Hose you bought is recommended only for use in mild climates and also it is not to be shut off at the nozzle. Since Mount Vernon's weather ranges in temperature annually from -15 to $+105^{\circ}$F, you can see how these extremes may have affected the splitting of the hose. Laboratory analysis indicates that the damage was caused by excessive water pressure resulting from either shutting the hose off at the nozzle or from water pressure greater than that normally found in most cities. Because Mt. Vernon has the normal water pressure of 60 pounds per square inch, the split occurred because someone shut the hose off at the nozzle.
Constructive suggestion	Two Widgeon hoses--the Gold-Line Plastic and the Neoprene Rubber--are especially recommended for shutting off at the nozzle. In addition, you can use the Neoprene Rubber Hose even in harsh weather. Both are described on the enclosed copy of catalog page 977.
Easy action and reader benefit	After you have decided which hose best meets your needs, fill out the enclosed order form and mail it in the envelope with your check or money order for $8.47 or $10.58, which include shipping costs; or indicate that you wish c.o.d. shipment. Either way you can be watering your garden again just three days after we receive your order. And you can be sure of many years' dependable service.

Unsalability of the returned product is another common reason for adjustment refusals. The customer who claims a purchase is no longer wanted may be trying to return an item he or she has damaged or kept out so long that the store can no longer resell it. Letter 2 is a retailer's refusal to a consumer; letter 3, a wholesaler's refusal to a new dealer.

Letter 2
A retail clothing store adjustment manager refuses to accept a returned evening gown for credit.

Buffer: assurance and thanks	To please our customers is the foremost aim of Bon-James. Thank you for writing us explaining your wishes about the evening gown you purchased here last month.
Reader-benefit facts about exchange policy in general	We want you and all our other customers to enjoy the confidence of knowing that any purchase from us is for merchandise of outstanding quality and style and that it is absolutely clean, fresh, and new. Wearing apparel may be returned for full credit anytime within 30 days provided the garment is in clean, resalable condition.
Findings in this case	To maintain the high standard on the goods we sell, we carefully check returned merchandise before it is again placed for sale. This examination of the gown you mailed to us disclosed facial makeup at the neckline and several brown spots near the hemline. Because cleaning would render the garment "used" to anyone wishing to repurchase it, the gown is unacceptable for resale.
Implied decision	
Helpful suggestions	You can be sure that the skillful touch of our fitter will make the sleeves of your Dior evening gown just the length you like best. For this reason, we suggest that you stop in to see Mr. Davis, who served you when you purchased the gown. He will hold it for you until you can come in for a fitting; or, if you want us to send it to you without any changes, he will arrange its prompt return.
Easy action	Please check and mail your preference on the enclosed card. You can depend upon us to do everything possible to help you feel pleased with the gown. You can wear it several years with confidence that it is a highly fashionable evening garment. As you may recall, it was an outstanding success in the Designer Show held in New York on June 2.
Resale	

Letter 3
A wholesaler refuses to accept returned out-of-season clothing from a new small retail shop owner (who started in business six months before). Letter is dated December 13.

Buffer: courteous, neutral opening	The three suits and two coats which you returned to us arrived today. We appreciate the business you have done with us and, as you are new in the apparel field, we would like to inform you again about our policy of returns.

Explanation about wholesaler require- ments; reader benefit

Women's clothing is highly seasonable merchandise and items move very fast. No wholesale firm accepts returned clothing when it is out of season. As we explained in our first letter to you, we must ask that any retailer who may wish to return anything on open order, do so within two weeks of purchase. Such a system of merchandising benefits you in the long run, because you are assured of top quality fashion clothing at lower prices.

Specific facts on this case

All the five garments we received from you today have been out of our house almost seven weeks. You purchased them October 23 when we were selling fall and winter goods. Now in the present time of year we in the wholesale business are going entirely into spring merchandise. Thus you will under- stand why we cannot accept these garments for credit and are

Decision

returning them to you.

Suggestion

You will surely find appreciative customers for these suits and coats through a specially advertised sale before Christmas. As they are in popular colors and materials, your customers

Resale

can get several years of good wear from them.

Future orders and service

When you are ready to select your spring stock, use the handy order blanks in the back of your Marco Spring Catalog. You can choose from a wide variety of leading spring fashions and expect deliveries within four days after we receive your order.

When the Customer Is Mistaken in a Complaint about an Account or a Service. In addition to refusing adjustments on returned merchandise, you may also have to write bad-news letters to customers who make erroneous claims resulting from a variety of intangible grievances. Among them are unwarranted claims about their account bal- ances or payments and unjustified gripes about various aspects of your firm's service.

Unwarranted claims about account balances or payments may arise when the cus- tomer thinks you have made an error because your statements do not agree with his records. If you find your records are correct, you must give the customer the bad news that he owes more than he claims. In your response, be sure to explain each additional charge clearly, for your reader may have forgotten that a purchase or that late charges were added or that some past checks were returned by the bank for various reasons. A tabulation of figures, as in letter 4, or a photostatic copy of the record may be helpful to your customer.

Letter 4

A loan company's credit manager explains why a borrower owes more than she thought.

Buffer: assurance, cooperation

As you requested, I have rechecked all your loan payments back to the first one you made after our company purchased your loan in June 1970. I'm glad to give you this summary so that it will help you reconcile your record with ours.

Detailed explanation

Your $87 check just received was credited as follows: Interest $1.50 and principal $85.50. The amount still past due is $138.93, made up of the following:

1974	August payment missed	$82.93
	October and December payments each short $2	4.00
1975	February payment short	10.00
	March, April, May, June, July, August, September, October payments each short $2	16.00
	December interest	23.00
1976	February payment short $3	3.00
	Balance past due	$138.93

Suggested action

To make payment of this amount easier for you, you may add $11.58 each month for the next 12 months. In this way your monthly payments of $94.51 ($82.93 and $11.58) will help you pay the overdue balance within a year.

Insurance policyholders sometimes make unwarranted requests which the claims department must refuse. In these and similar instances, if you can grant any part of a claim, be sure to begin with that good news. After a positive good-news opening, the reader will be in a better frame of mind to accept whatever refusal is necessary. For instance, compare the following two openings to a policyholder who requested both an $825 refund (which she could not have) and a $55 annual reduction in future premiums (which she could have).

Negative: We are sorry to inform you that we cannot refund the $825 you have paid us in extra premiums the past 15 years. As you were rated a substandard risk because of high blood pressure, the additional premium was mandatory.

Positive: The good news from our medical examiner's report that you no longer have high blood pressure now makes you a standard risk in all respects. We are glad to tell you that you will no longer need to pay the $55 annual extra premium.

Even if a situation has no good news or alternative, careful organization and wording can help soften the blow. For example, notice how letter 5 (excessively negative and organized by the direct plan) can be improved by emphasizing positive ideas and using the indirect plan, as in letter 6.

Letter 5
A poor, negative liability denial sent by a death benefits division.

Bad-news decision

I regret to have to inform you that it is the Company's position that no liability exists for this benefit.[5]

It cannot be found that we have been furnished with the due proof required by the policy contract that death resulted

---

[5] Though the blunt bad-news opening in letter 5 was undesirable for the policyholder, a similar direct opening *could* be used in a memo to the agent or to other employees concerned with the case.

Negative explanation

directly and independently of all other causes from bodily injury effected solely through external, violent, and accidental means. On the contrary the proof of death furnished by you indicates that death was due solely to disease. Furthermore, the denial of the authorization for examination and autopsy has deprived the Company of one of its rights under the policy contract.

Negative decision

On these grounds liability for double indemnity is denied. The amount of single indemnity already paid represents the Company's entire liability.

Letter 6
Improved revision of letter 5.

Buffer: assurance, careful consideration

Your claim for double indemnity has been given careful consideration. Our study included the evidence you submitted and information obtained by the Company through investigation.

Explanation of policy's coverage

The policy provides for the payment of the double indemnity benefit upon receipt of proof that the death of the insured resulted directly and independently of all other causes from bodily injury solely through external, violent, and accidental means; and, furthermore, that double indemnity shall not be payable if the insured's death resulted directly or indirectly from infirmity of mind or body, illness, or disease.

Facts in this claim

The certificate of death you submitted in support of your claim gave the cause of death as disease. It does not refer to any accident. Moreover, information obtained through our investigation appears to confirm that death was was due solely to natural causes. Also, refusal to furnish authorization for an autopsy deprived the Company of substantial rights under the policy. In these circumstances, the Company denies that it has any liability for double indemnity. I am sorry, Mrs. Smith, that our

Decision

decision could not be more favorable to you.

Positive thoughts

The single indemnity payment that you have already received represents the Company's entire liability under the policy. I am glad it is of some help to you, and wish you many years of continued good health.

Unjustified gripes about company services deserve careful and tactful explanation that establishes your company's accuracy and resells the reader on its usual high-quality service. For instance, the printer who is wrongly accused of misspelling a name on the customer's stationery may have to enclose a copy of the customer's original handwritten order showing the identical spelling.

An unusually knotty problem concerning an unjustified gripe is handled by letter 7. A customer had told a rug cleaning company's driver that though she had had the rugs 12 years, they had never before been cleaned professionally. The rugs were badly worn and extremely dirty; the cleaner devoted about four times the amount of care and time given the usual carpet. Yet the first time the rugs were delivered to the customer she refused to pay for the cleaning, saying they were "not clean enough." She paid after the second cleaning, but then asked for a refund, saying she was still not satisfied.

Letter 7
A rug cleaner refuses a request for refund.

Buffer: an agreeable comment

It is often said that a carpet will more than double the comfort of a room, and a clean carpet does even more. It gives you longer service and is more attractive.

General educational facts about carpet care

Carpet experts agree that the best care for a rug is to have it professionally cleaned about once in three years. The hardest wear and tear on a rug comes from grinding the dirt into it over a period of time. Sometimes it is hard to realize how worn and spotted a rug can become from 12 years of normal wear--especially with growing boys in the family. Some spots and dirt get ground in and just won't yield to even the best cleaning methods like ours.

Specific facts on cleaning customer's rugs

I well remember your carpets as they were brought in. It was determined by our experts that to give you the best job possible, we would double the time and care given the usual carpet. When your carpets were returned to us we were somewhat surprised, but nevertheless we indicated to you on the phone that we would do the second cleaning free of charge.

More facts about service; resale

Altogether your rugs received four times the amount of time and care given the usual carpets, and we only asked that you pay for one cleaning. With experienced workers skilled in modern cleaning and spot-removing processes, we try to satisfy all our customers. Because we have well earned the charge of $51.72 on your rugs--and in fairness to our other customers--we must charge you for an honest, reasonable

Decision

cleaning job.

Sales promotion; easy action; reader benefit

Please allow us to place your name on our customer calendar, from which we automatically send you a rug cleaning reminder every third year. Just fill in and mail the enclosed postcard if you wish this exclusive service. We are glad to be able to give you free pickup and delivery and prompt dependable service to keep your rugs in the best of condition through the coming years.

When the Customer Makes Unjustified Policy Complaints. Customers' incorrect complaints about company policies cover a wide range—from prices to employees' activities to merchandise displays. The main purpose of your reply is to explain and justify whatever policies and procedures the complainer finds undesirable, and to resell on your company. The suggestions in this chapter should help you handle such situations effectively with the bad-news plan.

Often a "soft" answer can not only placate the customer, but even lead to an unexpected happy relationship. For instance, one new customer had the audacity to write a sarcastic complaint to a company president because a welcome letter to the customer referred to his friend, the salesman, as Mr. R. Brown instead of Ragmar Brown. Letter 8 is the courteous reply from the president, Mr. Plumb.

Letter 8
A good-natured reply to a sarcastic policy complaint.

Buffer: agreement and partial explanation
>I agree with you that the name R. Brown sounds rather abbreviated. But in preparing these welcome messages to new customers, we abide by the wishes of each field representative concerned. Mr. Brown, in asking us to welcome you, directed us to refer to him as R. Brown.

More explanation
>Now, if I had changed R. to Ragmar because I prefer it or because I surmised you might prefer it, then Mr. Brown might have informed me he detests "Ragmar" and thus requests that we use his initial.

A few "human" comments
>I'm sorry the abbreviation upset you. You can be sure that "rushing off to a golf course" which you mention, is not within my day's activities. I haven't found how to run a nationwide company and still find time to play golf at all.

Pleasant resale
>Please don't feel too unhappy toward us. At least we <u>tried</u> to welcome you as a new customer. I believe you'll even like us as time goes on.

The president's courtesy paid off. The customer wrote a pleasant apology, which ended with this paragraph:

>If you should ever visit my town, I would be honored to have you as my guest at the golf course. I'm going to take up that sport and discontinue writing nasty letters.

Mr. Plumb did visit the customer (Mr. Simpson) one day. The happy ending of this story is that Mr. Simpson later became an employee of the company—as field representative.

When customers write anonymous complaint letters, you usually have no way to reply. However, some business executives receiving anonymous complaints about matters that should be cleared up for all customers run both the complaint and the reply in local newspapers, or even magazines. Among complaints adaptable to such a procedure are, for example, those about store hours ("Why aren't you open evenings and Sundays?") or service ("Why do you have a self-service policy?"). A business executive's display reply underneath such a complaint can be an effective, excellent advertisement, filled with resale, customer-benefit explanations, and sales promotional material.

Refusing Credit

Even when you are refusing a credit application, you want to try to keep the reader's goodwill. A person's credit reputation is quite important and personal; therefore a credit manager must be careful about what he writes and how he expresses his reasons.[6] Refusals of both retail and mercantile credit are organized by the bad-news plan, but since their content can differ, they are grouped separately in the following discussion.

Retail Credit Refusals. To an individual consumer, a refusal usually begins with a buffer that refers to the firm's appreciation or careful consideration of the reader's request for credit and/or to his or her interest in the store.

Explanation portions of retail credit refusals vary considerably, but four ways of handling the reasons for refusal are in common use:

1. Reason is omitted entirely (see letter 1 below).
2. "Insufficient information" is the only reason given (see letter 2).
3. Factors generally considered in evaluating credit applications are stated without indicating specifically which apply to the reader (letter 3).
4. Specific reasons are stated (letters 4 and 5).

The first three of these methods can be easily adapted by credit departments that find it necessary to use form letters because of a large number of applications (often over a wide geographic area)—for example, chain stores, national oil companies, travelers' card services. Because of similar names among the thousands of individual requests, mix-ups and errors do occur. Thus credit managers for firms handling numerous requests find it safer to omit specific reasons, especially those that pertain to undesirable character and poor-pay habits. However, from the customer's standpoint the refusal which omits the reason entirely is the least helpful (although it may save some embarrassment). The "insufficient explanation" reason is considered by some customers to be artificial and insincere; nevertheless both methods 2 and 3 are popular and usually acceptable under certain circumstances, provided the constructive suggestion is tactful and helpful.

The fourth method—stating specific reasons—is desirable when the following conditions exist:

The situation requires an individually typed reply (as in an application for a large loan).

The reason does not involve poor (dishonest, unreliable) personal character.

The desired relationship between the credit department and the applicant is somewhat personal.

The applicant cannot come for a personal interview and is likely to be offended with anything but an individual helpful letter.

Such letters are usually longer—and harder to write—than the first three types, but when tactful and accurate they are highly appreciated by the recipient because they indicate what must be done to earn (or restore) a good credit standing.

---

[6]Some credit departments use the telephone for all their refusals. Even if you work in such a department, you will find that you can apply many of the writing principles of this chapter to your oral refusals.

In stating your decision, try to use positive words and, if possible, stress what can be done. Avoid such negatives as "not able," "did not approve," "unfavorable," "does not meet," "must decline." Instead of stressing what is wrong, suggest (whenever possible) how the situation can be improved. Often you can combine resale and constructive alternatives with either the decision or the ending paragraph. In line with circumstances, the applicant may be invited to take one or more of these steps:

1. Come to an office to discuss the case if he has questions or thinks an error has been made
2. Examine his record at the Credit Bureau and write any needed corrections.[7]
3. Apply again later when conditions have improved
4. Contact another lender or credit agency that you name
5. Use the lay-away plan or another suitable credit plan
6. Continue buying from the company on a cash or c.o.d. basis

The ending usually ties in with one of these suggestions and, if possible, includes a reader benefit. Compare the next five examples for methods of handling reasons and for application of other suggestions on credit refusals to consumers.

Letter 1
No stated reason. An unhelpful retail credit refusal.

Buffer: *appreciation*	We sincerely appreciate your confidence in us as expressed by your recent credit application.
Decision	After careful consideration, we find that at this time it would be better for you to continue your purchases from us on a cash basis.
Forward look (weak)	We hope you will give us frequent opportunities to serve you from our wide selection in each of our stores.

Letter 2
Insufficient-information reason. A popular retail credit refusal inviting a conference as well as cash purchases.[8]

Buffer: *thanks*	Thank you for the preference you have shown Bon-Frederick by your application for a charge account.
Explanation: *insufficient* *information* *Decision*	As you know, the usual custom before opening a new account is to get information which will serve as a basis for credit. Such information as we have thus far obtained is insufficient (or: does not permit us) to pass favorably upon your request at this time. If you feel there are other details which would favorably affect your credit, you are welcome to call
Suggestions: *conference,* *cash buying*	on us so that we can consider all the facts.

[7]See Footnote 10, page 208 about functions of city Credit Bureaus. It is customary that for 30 days after applicants have been refused credit because of a Credit Bureau report, they can see their report free. But they are charged a fee ($3.50 to $5) if they merely want to check its accuracy. If you are moving from one city to another, it is an excellent idea to check your current report, then request that it be sent to the Bureau nearest your new home.

[8]The last paragraph of letter 2 refers to buying on a cash basis. Because some customers consider this suggestion obvious—maybe even offensive—you can avoid reference to cash by wording the last paragraph in a way similar to that in letter 3.

Resale

In the meantime, please let us supply your needs on a cash basis. We will make every effort to serve you well with high quality merchandise and friendly service.

Letter 3

List of factors usually considered (general reasons). A popular retail credit refusal inviting reapplication and lay away (with no reference to cash buying).

Buffer: thanks

Thank you . . .

for your recent inquiry regarding the status of your credit application.

Explanation: list of factors considered

A number of factors are taken into consideration when reviewing an application. Length of time at one residence and employment are of vital importance to us as well as income, assets, age, number of dependents, and the paying record of current and past obligations.

Implied decision; assurance and invitation

You are assured that all the above available information has been carefully analyzed in your case. Circumstances may change in the future, at which time we would be pleased to reconsider your new request for credit.

Invitation to purchase; no mention of cash

In the meantime, we invite you to save on your household and clothing purchases at Ranney's regular everyday low prices and frequent sales. Also, of course, you're welcome to use our easy lay-away plan for bigger purchases.

Letter 4

Specific reason—inadequate income. An individually typed loan refusal.

Buffer: compliment and favorable aspects

You are to be complimented on your desire to provide the best possible housing for your family. Also, both your loan application and credit report indicate that you have maintained a steady employment record. This too is commendable.

Explanation: reasoning from general to specific

In mortgage lending, however, extensive studies have revealed that a certain relationship between a person's income, fixed monthly expense, and loan amount should exist to make a loan advisable. Our maximum loan is two and one-half times the annual income, or payments may not exceed 20 percent of the monthly income. Since your income at present meets neither

Reader-benefit decision

of these requirements, you can understand why we feel that an additional financial burden will not serve your best interests.

Suggestion

If you would like to stop in my office, I will be glad to go over with you the minimum requirements for a smaller loan. This discussion might help you in setting and planning your desired goal for home ownership. As time goes on and your income increases, you will be able to improve your financial position to the point where we can help you buy a newer and larger home.

Future help

Feel welcome to come in any day between 9 and 5. We sincerely want to help you reach your desired goal.

A credit manager can provide helpful "education" to an applicant. For instance, when a charge-account applicant with sufficient income has a miserable poor-pay record, some credit managers tactfully state the reason somewhat as follows:

> Customarily we make a routine check on credit applicants according to three factors—ability to pay, character, and record of prompt payments. Since you have such a fine record on two of these factors, I know you will want to establish a good-pay reputation too. Lampson's can then gladly reconsider opening an account for you sometime in the future. In the meantime, may we continue to serve you on a cash basis?

Letter 5
Both general list of reasons and specific reasons. A processed form retail credit refusal by a firm handling a large volume of applications. (Salutation: Dear Customer)

Thanks	Thank you for your recent request for a charge account at Berry's.
Decision	Because of the reasons checked below, we regret that we cannot open an account with you at the present time.
Specific reason(s)	_____ under age 18 _____ age not indicated on application _____ short time on present job _____ unemployed at present time _____ unable to verify employment _____ application incomplete (returned once to be completed) _____ insufficient information for credit bureau to work with _____ inadequate response from credit references _____ references given are too new to rate _____ overextended _____ no banking
Forward look	When the checked condition is changed, please give us the opportunity to reconsider your application.

Mercantile Credit Refusals. Wholesale or mercantile credit is that which is extended by one business firm to another. The preferred organizational pattern for mercantile credit refusals is the bad-news plan.

For the buffer you have choices similar to those used in retail refusals—appreciation, assurance of careful consideration, brief resale on products or services. If the firm sent an order, refer to it only incidentally, because you are not filling it now and should not detract attention from the main concern—credit.

The most noticeable difference between retail and mercantile credit refusals is that the latter are generally more forthright in the reasons for refusal and of course are individually typewritten. The decision is based on the firm's financial statement plus other credit ratings (by Dun and Bradstreet, special rating agencies, creditors, and sales agencies of the wholesaler or manufacturer considering the applicant). As with retail credit, the emphasis should be on the positive—the desirable goal—rather than on what is wrong now.

A credit refusal can include one or more reader-benefit suggestions:

1. Reduction of apparently excessively high inventory by special means
2. Ways to build up customer's volume of sales (and working capital, if pertinent); perhaps offering assistance of your firm's sales representative
3. Advantages of modest buying, local financing, and cash discounts
4. Cash purchases—smaller, more frequent orders
5. Cash on delivery or cash with orders earning discount privilege
6. Review of the applicant's credit situation again at a future time

Which of these suggestions do you find in the following refusal?

Letter 6
Credit refusal from a wholesaler to a retailer.

Buffer
Thank you for promptly forwarding the credit information we requested on January 15. The statements provided by trade references are essential to our evaluation of each request for an open account.

Explanation
Without exception, the reports we've received strongly attest to your excellent character and integrity. Information regarding the operations of the hardware store, however, has been somewhat less encouraging. The intense local competition which you face apparently has had an adverse impact on your profit position.

Implied refusal
Understandably, meeting existing obligations as they fall due has been no easy task. Though these difficulties are only temporary, any additional credit purchases at this time would increase your obligations to an unhealthy level. Of course, we want to do everything possible to help you regain the competitive position that will allow us to arrange an open account.

Offer of additional help
I've asked our area representative, Mr. Eric Wittor, to visit your store and discuss with you the programs you can use to increase your volume of business. Our experience with hardware outlets has enabled us to assist many customers with their merchandising problems. For instance, effective promotion of leader items can quickly expand store traffic, increase the turnover rate of general merchandise, and help dispose of excess inventory.

Offer of additional help
In the meantime you'll need to maintain your stock of necessary merchandise. By reducing your present order about one-half, you should be able to obtain the essential items your store requires. Of course, you will be entitled to the 2% discount that applies to all cash purchases. Just use the enclosed order form and mail it in the envelope provided.

Friendly, positive ending
Your shipment will be on its way within a few hours after we receive your instructions.

One good test for any letter is what your reaction to it would have been if you had received it. Would you feel offended if you were the retailer? Would you buy from the wholesaler? True, you're not getting credit, but the writer seems sincere and interested in you.

Acknowledging Orders You Can't Fill Now or At All

Whenever you get an order which you cannot fill immediately, your acknowledgment will be at least temporarily bad news to your customer. The customer is expecting the goods ordered and any intervening message from you may delay delivery and cause some inconvenience. This section discusses bad-news acknowledgments regarding: incomplete or vague orders, back orders, substitution orders, and diverted or declined orders.

Many firms handle routine and repeat orders by preprocessed forms. These are acceptable when the firm sells cataloged, small, or low-profit items and when the situation does not require much detailed explanation. One common timesaving way to indicate portions of routine orders that cannot be filled as requested is to use rubber-stamped (or typewritten) comments inserted on printed acknowledgments (like the stamped S7 comment regarding a substitution in "letter" 1 that follows.

"Letter" 1
A printed order acknowledgment with stamped comment, used by a national retail mail-order firm.

COMPANY NAME OF SELLER		INVOICE NO. ____		
Thank you for your order. It received our careful attention. Any changes necessary in filling your order are explained by stamp impressions or by letters.	Catalog Number Current Price L5021 $3.85	VALUE OF GOODS		
		TAX		
PLEASE DO NOT DESTROY THESE PAPERS until you are satisfied that your order is all right in every respect.	Catalog Number Current Price L5053 $4.95	SHIPPING CHARGES		
IF YOU WRITE US about this order, please be sure to return ALL of these papers with your letter. It will help us give you prompt service.	(S7) OUR SELECTION IS THE NEAREST TO YOUR CHOICE THAT WE CAN FURNISH. IT IS BETTER MERCHANDISE AT NO INCREASE IN PRICE.	TOTAL AMOUNT		
IF YOU RETURN ANY PART of this order, please glue the envelope containing these papers and your letter to the outside of the package and apply additional mailing postage for the envelope.	This is the amount charged by the Postoffice for C.O.D. service. The Delivering Postmaster also collects a fee to pay for the money order sent to us. You can save the C.O.D. fee expense by including total remittance with future orders.	←U.S. MAIL C.O.D.–FEE		
		TOTAL AMOUNT OF C.O.D.		

Though processed form letters are time-savers, they are impersonal and cold. Many times the customer expects or deserves a more detailed explanation. Situations that require personal letters are discussed below.

Incomplete or Vague Orders. If an order that omits necessary information comes from a customer who has never before ordered the items in question, you probably cannot guess what is wanted. It is always better to write (or phone) the customer than to risk errors and annoyance. Your main goal is to keep the customer sold on your goods and to get whatever information is missing so you can fill the order soon.

If the order lists some items that you are sending now, mention them first, of course. If not, begin with a buffer—usually short resale on the product about which the order is incomplete, appreciation for the order, and, if a first order from a customer, welcome. Then, before you request the missing information or payment, state a reader-benefit reason—that you want to be sure to send exactly what will be liked best. Shield the reader's pride by omitting such words as "you forgot" or "you failed to." Be sure to include explanatory facts the customer needs to complete the order, such as sizes or color choice available. Include pictures, catalog numbers, sketches, swatches, and other helpful items when appropriate. Make the action easy and clear for the customer, and assure him of prompt shipment (if true), as in letter 2.

Letter 2
Acknowledging an incomplete rush order from a charge customer.

Buffer: *resale*	You have made a perfect choice in ordering the fashionable three-piece Adrien suit for your vacation. Smart styling, combined with sophisticated simplicity, gives you a suit you can wear for many activities in Alaska and elsewhere.
Reader- *benefit* *request* *Facts*	So that we may send you the exact suit you have in mind, let's double check on the style and color. The enclosed leaflet pictures the two models available. You may choose each of these suits in pink, aqua, light green, or white. Presently we have your size 12 in all of them.
Easy *action*	To help you get your reply to us easily and quickly, we are enclosing a telegram order form addressed to me, with spaces for your choices. Just fill in the model number and color you want and wire it to us collect. Your suit will be sent air express the same day I hear from you.
Prompt *delivery,* *resale,* *courtesy*	In less than two days you will be enjoying the use of your smart crease- and soil-resistant no-iron Adrien for your pleasure in vacationing and traveling. Thank you for giving us this opportunity to serve you.

Often incomplete-order acknowledgments are much shorter—perhaps even postcard size. The opening might omit the resale and begin with "Thank you for your order for . . . ." The second paragraph then states the available sizes (or colors or whatever is pertinent); the last paragraph makes action easy and perhaps states a reader benefit.

Orders for Out-of-Stock Items to Be Back-ordered. If your stock of an ordered item is temporarily depleted and you expect a new shipment within a reasonable time (one or two weeks), you can ordinarily back-order and assume that the customer would rather wait than cancel the order.

As with the incomplete-order acknowledgment, your main goal in the back-order letter is to keep the customer sold on your goods and to serve him or her well. Because of the necessary delay in waiting for the return of the out-of-stock item, your message should again be organized by the bad-news plan.

Your buffer can be resale on the ordered item (to reinforce the customer's confidence in his choice), appreciation, and (if appropriate) a welcome.

Your explanation should focus on the positive aspects—the date the goods will or can reach the customer. Be sure to omit such negatives as "cannot send," "out of stock," "exhausted," "Won't have any . . . until." Instead, word your idea something like this:

> We will be able to ship these radios to you by May 15, when our reordered new shipment from the factory is expected here.

Your explanation should preferably include a reason for your being out of the item, so the customer won't think your firm is inefficient. If such reason(s) pertain to high popularity or exceptional demand, they even strengthen your resale and the customer's desire for the item. In your action-getting close, positive suggestion is again useful. The easiest way for the customer to "show" approval of the back order is to take no action. Thus back-order acknowledgments often include the positive:

> Shipment will be made as soon as we receive the new supplies, unless you instruct us to the contrary.

If the wait might be unreasonably long, you should ask the customer to let you know (perhaps by an easy-action reply card) whether he or she approves of your shipping on the later date. Your emphasis whenever possible should be on acceptance, not cancellation. Sometimes a bit of sales promotion material on seasonal or related goods is appropriate, if it is included clearly for the customer's benefit—as a service to the customer rather than just another sale for your firm.

A short message such as letter 3 is sufficient on an order for one temporarily out-of-stock item. Letter 4 shows how to mention the same item in a combination order.

Letter 3
Acknowledging an order from an "old" charge customer on an item to be back-ordered.

Buffer: thanks and acknowledgment
Thank you for your order for one dozen Perkup 26-inch Window Fans, at $36 each.

Resale and explanation
The demand for this newest three-speed reversible fan has far exceeded our most optimistic expectations at this time of year, with the result that we have twice reordered from the factory. The manufacturer has assured us that our new supply will be delivered within ten days.

Decision:
expected
delivery date
Reader
benefit

You may plan on receiving a rush shipment of your fans before March 20. Your customers will like the way these automatic thermostatically controlled Perkups enable them to enjoy cool breezes indoors regardless of the heat outdoors.

Letter 4

Acknowledging a combination order that includes an out-of-stock item to be back-ordered for a business firm (old charge customer).

Items shipped

The following items you ordered March 8 are being shipped to you today by National Motor Freight:

```
10 Bellman Door Chimes, walnut grain      @ $10.50
 5 Hassock Fans, four-speed, woodtone     @  30.95
```

Resale and
explanation
on out-of-
stock item;
expected
delivery date

Thank you for your order. You can expect to receive the one dozen top quality Perkup 26-inch Window Fans ($36 each) before March 20. The demand for this newest three-speed reversible fan has far exceeded our most optimistic expectations at this time of year, with the result that we have twice reordered from the factory. The manufacturer has assured us that our new supply will be delivered within ten days.

Resale

We will rush your fans to you as soon as they reach us, so that you'll have them a good while before the usual hot weather spells in your area. You can assure your customers that these automatic thermostatically controlled-Perkups will enable them to enjoy cool breezes indoors regardless of the heat outdoors.

Orders for Out-of-Stock Items on Which You Suggest a Substitute. When you get an order for a certain model or brand that you cannot supply soon enough by back-order or that has been discontinued, you can often suggest a substitute—provided you honestly think it will meet the customer's needs.

Usually it is safer to ask permission to substitute before you ship, as in letter 5, especially if the customer must pay a higher price for the newer line and if the items are breakable or otherwise costly to ship. (Unfortunate shippers who have sent large substitute shipments without permission have sometimes had to pay many dollars in express charges both ways for rejected merchandise returned by a displeased customer.)

Letter 5

Suggesting a substitute in place of an ordered discontinued item.

Buffer:
thanks and
brand resale

Many thanks for your order on June 27 for a Semco office storage cabinet. You can be sure that your decision to buy a Semco was a decision to buy the finest.

Explanation
for new
model
(substitute)

Early this year, in line with business executives' increasing need for better internal security, the Semco factory came out with a new model storage cabinet, the C-402. Because it has all the features our customers have been asking for, we now stock this model exclusively. Though it's possible that

Where
ordered item George's Supply in North Center may still have the model
might be C-302 your ordered, we are sure you will want our newest
obtained after you check these improved features of the C-402:

√. . . HEAVIER GAUGE STEEL than any other cabinet on the
market assures extra heavy duty for extra safety.
√. . . REINFORCED DOORS and BASE provide added sturdiness.

Reader-   √. . . A DEPENDABLE YALE LOCK makes the cabinet tamper-
benefit   proof for stored articles.
features of   √. . . ADJUSTABLE SHELVES--six of them--allow easy
substitute   storage for almost any size supplies.
√. . . NEW COLORS blend with your office decor:
mint green, fog grey, or walnut brown.

For all these advantages the C-402 is inexpensively priced[9]
at only $89.95 delivered to your office. To give me your
Easy action "OK" for shipment, just call me at 873-9999 any weekday
between 8 and 5. I'll have your new Semco cabinet on its
way to you the same day.

Reader- We'll be happy to deliver it on open account giving you a full
benefit 30 days for payment. You'll be glad you bought the newest
resale Semco 402.

Letter 5 exemplifies well the desired organization for the substitution letter. Notice
that the buffer begins with appreciation and general resale—emphasizing the strongest
point of reader appeal that the two articles have in common—the Semco brand. It
omits any point of difference (model number, in this case) between ordered and substitute items.

The explanation and bad-news decision stress what the firm *does* have instead of
what it does not carry. The new substitute—Model 402—is introduced with one of its
merits *before* the bad news that the ordered item—Model 302—is unavailable. One
good way to do this is to state that you now stock the substitute *exclusively* (if true),
but don't use the word "substitute" in your letter because of its negative connotation.
If the substitute is a different brand instead of merely another model of the same
brand (as in letter 6), do not mention the ordered item by brand name more than once
(or at all), because you want the reader to focus attention on your product. However,
don't knock your competitor's product; sell your product on its own merits. You can
mention where the ordered product may be obtained, but subordinate your statement
in a dependent clause, as in letter 5. If the price of the substitute is higher, be sure to
state adequate selling points to justify the difference. If your substitute is lower in
quality but an excellent value because of price or other reasons, stress these benefits.

Your ending paragraph asks for authorization to send the substitute—or tells why
you have already sent it, as in letter 6. In the latter case, make clear that the item
comes to the customer on trial or subject to approval. Although you are safer to get
approval before sending a substitute, many sellers (such as mail-order firms) substitute
quite regularly in orders from repeat customers whose preferences they know. Sometimes substitution is also made in rush orders for very similar same-price inexpensive

---

[9] Instead of "is inexpensively priced at" you might write "is well worth the small additional
$5," or "is an excellent value even at $5 more than the older model," if you think your reader
would appreciate knowing the price difference.

items or when the company absorbs the price difference. The writer of letter 6 mailed the substitute because it was identical to the customer's order in every way except the print, and he felt sure this buyer would like the one sent.

Letter 6
Sending a substitute before asking permission.

Buffer: thanks	Thank you for your order of May 20 for a Hailani Hawaiian sport shirt, size 40.
Facts about the substitute	We are sending you today by parcel post a Hailani shirt of the same high quality, casual style, and bright colors as the one specified. Though the printed design on the fabric is a little different from the one you described, we feel sure you'll be delighted with it as soon as you see it.
Resale	As you know, one of the distinctive features of Hailani Sportswear is the great variety of fascinating exotic prints, with only a few in each size. We are fortunate to have the gay "tropic garden" pattern in your size. It is being sent
Return privilege	to you on your account for your approval, of course, on a money-back guarantee.
Resale	You'll appreciate this wash-and-wear shirt, we're certain, on many carefree days this summer.

Orders That Must Be Diverted or Declined. Some orders you will have to divert or refuse because the customer has come through the wrong marketing channel, does not meet your standards as to payment or other requirements, or has ordered goods or services that you cannot supply as soon as needed.

For instance, if your firm is a manufacturer or a wholesaler and you cannot sell to an ultimate consumer, your refusal should preferably keep this consumer's goodwill. Convince the customer to buy your products from your authorized dealers. Your buffer thus will be basically resale, to build the customer's confidence in the choice of product or brand. Your explanation will give reader-benefit reasons for your merchandising policy—stressing how you do market your products (exclusively through authorized dealers) instead of how you don't. Make your refusal clear and combine it with a reader benefit. Among consumer benefits for local dealerships are:

Customer's privilege to see all goods before buying
Faster deliveries
Lower shipping costs—or none
Personal services

Provide for easy action, by returning any check the reader sent you and including names and addresses of nearby dealers plus a reassuring statement about them. A last reader-benefit bit of resale will help keep customers sold on the product and encourage them to buy it.

Letter 7
Diverting a consumer's order from the factory to an authorized dealer.

Yes, Ms. Janette,

Buffer resale   all those nice compliments you've heard about TOWER musical instruments are true. And you're right to insist on buying a TOWER for the first--and every--guitar you own.

Explanation for local marketing   One of the reasons that so many musicians are enthusiastic over their TOWER instruments is the special individual care they received before selecting just the right guitar for their own particular preferences. This is why we market all TOWER instruments exclusively through authorized music stores instead of by mail from our factory。

Easy action   The name and address of the authorized music shop that handles all TOWER products in your city is:

> Polk Music Supply House
> 422 Broadway East

Reader benefit   Any of their experienced music representatives will gladly show you the different styles and sizes of TOWER guitars. They range from the slim, fast-action flat-top guitars to the mellow-sounding classic-type and electric guitars.

Motivation to action   So that you can select your favorite personally, we are returning your check. Do stop in at Polk's soon--to hear, feel, and buy the TOWER guitar you like best.

Sometimes you must refuse an order because you have no other choice. If you cannot supply the customer's needs now but want him to return to you for future orders, you will of course include resale on your product or service. In addition you will mention where the customer can get what he urgently needs now—*if* you think such suggestion will be helpful. For instance, a hotel manager can mention to out-of-town customers other hotels (competitors) if her own hotel will be filled during a certain weekend. However, she should also include some resale on her own hotel and invite the customer to stay there on his next visit to the city. In contrast, the orchard owner in the situation handled by letter 8 finds it both unnecessary and unfeasible to mention where his repeat customer might buy apples elsewhere. Instead, he concentrates on reselling his own apples.

Letter 8
Refusing an order from an orchard's repeat mail-order customer.

Thanks and resale   Thank you for your order of one crate of Wilfred Orchard's red delicious apples. We are pleased that the popularity of our fruit extends into the Eastern states to good customers like you.

Resale and reason   As a steady customer for five years, you understand the care we take in shipping our fruit nationwide. You may have heard that eastern Washington experienced a heavy storm during blossomtime, and an unusually cool summer. As a result, the

Decision   fruit in our orchards is not up to the quality you have a right to expect. Therefore, I am returning your check at this time.

Forward look and resale   Next year I will notify you when the apple crop is ready. Then you can order the delicious apples you and your friends have enjoyed in the past.

Declining Requests for Favors

Customers, noncustomers, and employees may request various privileges or favors, other than information, which you have to refuse. The bad-news plan is usually the safest to use in most favor refusals. However, in some instances you may use the direct plan, placing the refusal in the first paragraph. This section illustrates a variety of favor refusals, both business-related and personal.

Declining Business-related Favors. Among the numerous favors that customers ask and that you may have to refuse are: changing requirements or payment due dates, transferring from one type of account to another, seeing your firm's confidential material, getting special reduced rates, or skipping several payments on a contract (as handled by letter 1 below).

Letter 1
A loan officer refuses a customer's request to skip several loan payments.

Buffer: thanks   Thank you for telling us your viewpoint regarding your loan payments during the summer.

Explanation and appeal to fair play   Accommodating customers is one of our main objectives. This service involves fair treatment to every borrower with accepted business practice that also protects the investments of our depositors. Exceptions granted to one customer could rightfully be expected of others too, and thus eventually disrupt the entire credit structure. Therefore, the long-established rule is that all payments not made within ten days of the due date are subject to an added "late payment" charge. When a loan becomes 90 days past due, the law requires that foreclosure action be started.

Implied refusal   Mr. Howe, when you obtained the loan last December, you agreed to repay it in regular monthly payments. Though you were a schoolteacher then there is no indication in our file that you requested any deviation from the usual 12-month payment schedule. Because most of the high school teachers in this area get their salary each of 12 months, we assumed the same was true for you. However, even on a 9-month basis a teacher does know in advance that he will receive no paychecks during the summer. Many other people have little or no advance indication when their source of income will cease.

Reader-benefit suggestion   The enclosed leaflet was prepared for persons who need to allocate earnings over a 12-month period. You will find it useful, I believe. For the present, you will save the late-payment surcharge if your check reaches us by June 10.

Action request If you feel that mailing your June check before that due date would impose an extreme hardship on you, please call me at 772-7222. At that time we can make an appointment so that we can work out your problem with you.

When you must refuse to lend your company's supplies or premises or other valuables, you should also use the bad-news plan (letter 2). Remember to consider your reader's feelings and be as helpful as possible.

Letter 2
A tactful goodwill-building refusal to lend a bank's lounge and parking facilities for a Cub Scout area meeting.

Buffer: appreciation, agreement, compliment Your letter extending us the opportunity to contribute to the activities of your Cub Scout group is warmly received. As a Den Mother, you surely must share our high esteem for scouting and all it stands for.

Reasons On November 20, the date of your scheduled meeting, our Main Office will host a group of visiting bank managers and board members from throughout Illinois, Missouri, and Indiana. Thus, for most of that day our lounge will be filled with

Implied refusal business leaders. May I suggest, however, an alternative location for your meeting.

Suggestion When I spoke to my friend, James Scott, building manager of the Lakeside Eagles, about your needs he said he could offer their hall November 20. The room is large enough to easily accommodate 40 to 50 scouts and chaperones, and parking space is adequate. Mr. Scott suggests that you phone him soon

Easy action (683-9992) weekdays between 7 a.m. and 4 p.m. to confirm your plans and discuss necessary details.

Cooperation and good wishes You may be assured that we at First National are sincere in our desire to help you and your group whenever we can. Best of success always with your group of scouts!

On somewhat routine matters between departments of the same firm it is quite permissible to begin directly with the bad-news decision, as in letter 3:

Letter 3 (memo)
An acceptable direct-plan refusal of a specification change; message between two departments of a commercial airplane manufacturer

To: J. R. Lander
From: T. M. Jepson
Subject: Food and Beverage Elevator
Reference: RPD-5244-12 dated 6-15-7_

Refusal As shown on page 5 of the specifications, paneling for elevator walls remains a valid requirement. Thus the referenced request to use paint instead of vinyl paneling is unacceptable.

Explanation	Because of the particular uses for this elevator and the expected altitudes for flights, it is necessary that all walls have the extra protection of the exact vinyl as in the specifications instead of mere coats of paint.
Request	Will you please, therefore, see that the paneling requirement is met, according to specifications.

Declining Nonbusiness and Personal Favors. Requests concerning nonbusiness activities may involve donations of your time, money, property, or other assistance. In refusing a nonbusiness favor, include an appropriate buffer, reason(s) before your decision, and (if possible) a helpful suggestion.

Letter 4
A refusal to accept the office of regional director.

Buffer: agreement, compliment, appreciation	XYZ Club has a great deal to offer for both businessmen and women. I've always found it worthwhile. And so I appreciate even more the compliment you expressed in nominating me for the office of Regional Director.
Reasons	To perform this job adequately, I realize I should travel to the three State Days this coming year and to correspond regularly each month with the 22 chapters in this region, before sending monthly reports to our national office. I've given your invitation a good deal of thought, in the light
Implied refusal; emphasis on positive	of my present responsibilities as executive trainee at the ABC Company here. My job requires that I devote long hours to the program daily. Often I work Saturdays, too. In addition, Sally and our 3-month-old son have also been very demanding on my time. Considering everything, I'm convinced the job would be better filled by someone else for the coming year.
Suggestion	If you'd like a suggestion, you might find Herbert J. Smith would be interested in this type of chapter office. He's been active in XYZ for 10 years, two of them as our excellent president. He's an established accountant at the National Gadget Company and is unmarried. Herb enjoys being involved and in my opinion would be a perfect regional director. I'm enclosing a card with Herb's address in case you would like to contact him.
Cordial wishes	You have my best wishes, Jim, for getting the right man. You're doing a terrific job for the organization.

At times you may honestly feel that a request is extremely unreasonable and you're tempted to tell the reader so. If you must get some negative thoughts off your chest, go ahead and write the grumpy letter. But don't mail it immediately. Chances are that the next day you'll decide to soften the tone (which writer of letter 5 didn't do but should have done, as in letter 6).

Letter 5
Untactful refusal from a manager of a marketing research firm to a college student.[10]

I have your request for advice and booklets regarding the practices and experiences of this Company in consumer research and market testing. You list seven questions, each of which is so broad in scope that an adequate answer would require at least a written chapter. A comprehensive answer to all seven questions would comprise a thesis on marketing research. I would like to ask you a few questions:

1. Do students think a manufacturing company has any responsibility to contribute to their education? Do they think the company should help students prepare their thesis for the sake of building goodwill? or for securing a possible future customer?

2. If an affirmative answer is given to #1, what do students regard as a reasonable amount of cooperation?
   a. To check a few Yes or No questions?
   b. To furnish available and pertinent literature if available?
   c. To write a dissertation for them on one subject? on seven subjects?
   d. To write a thesis for them?
   e. To teach them by mail?

3. Do university instructors advise their students to request commercial companies to contribute their knowledge of market research to the students? Cannot your instructors answer most of the questions you ask? For example, you ask "What effect do consumers' desires and needs have on the adoption of specifications and designs for a product?" Is this not in your textbook, or can it not be answered by your instructor?

4. If the answer to #3 is affirmative, how do university instructors think commercial companies would justify the time and expense involved in writing educational material for students in answer to specific but broad scope questions?

You need not answer the above questions nor reply to this letter. My questions are rhetorical and I have no intention of writing a reply to your questions. My contribution to your education is this letter, and in my opinion it should be more valuable to you than an answer to your questions would be.

Letter 6
An improved version of Letter 5.

Buffer:
thanks   Thank you for your interest in our practices and experiences in consumer research and market testing.

---

[10] Though letter 5 (which was actually mailed) is untactful, its questions may deserve serious consideration by those who seek detailed information. Requests like "Please give us information about all the goods you sell" are so broad that they are impossible to fulfill.

Desire to help *Decision*	We definitely want to share with you this requested information, and it's possible to do so if you limit yourself to specific questions which permit answering in a few minutes. Preferably a questionnaire form that allows us to fill in
Alternate	answers seems to be the best format. The seven questions you submitted to us are so broad in scope that each one requires a lengthy reply to cover the subject adequately.
Suggested action and reader benefit	Please send your one- or two-page questionnaire to Mrs. Michael Leach, vice president of research in our organization. She is our authority on consumer research and market testing. Since she will not be starting on her three-week survey trip for another month, she will probably have time to fill out and mail your material to you the same day she hears from you.

Turning Down Contract or Work Offers

Grouped in this category are the refusals you may have to write to business firms, clubs, and individuals that propose various jobs and services for a fee. Letter 1 illustrates a refusal to enter a bid on a business firm's project; letter 2 turns down a nonprofit organization's idea for raising money. Both use the bad-news plan. Refusals by and to individual job applicants are covered in Chapter 12. Letters of resignation are discussed in the section on bad-news announcements, pages 281–282.

Letter 1
Declining to bid on a construction job.

Buffer	Thank you for the opportunity to bid on the plumbing work for the 50 homes in the Highland Park development.
Reason *Refusal*	Because of other large commitments we have lined up for the coming year, our time schedule is such that we must reluctantly pass up the opportunity to compete on your job this time.
Suggestion and cordial close	Please keep us on your list for your next project. Best wishes for your satisfactory completion of the Highland Park plan in time for occupancy next fall.

Letter 2
Refusing a nonprofit organization's proposal to earn funds by subcontracting services for an out-of-state management corporation. (Letter was mailed to the president of a university business honorary. Salutation is "Dear Ed.")

Buffer	We appreciate very much your letter inquiring about the possibility that Milton Management Corporation might be able to subcontract some of our handwork through your chapter.
	Ed, if we were to ship any of our large mailings to your city from St. Louis in order for your chapter to complete the necessary work, we would encounter many difficulties.

Explanation   To give you an example, an annual report mailing for Milton Funds weighs approximately 18 tons. You might also be interested to know that we no longer mail our annual and semi-annual reports in envelopes because of the terrific expense involved with hand-stuffing. We now pack each report in a polyethylene bag which is electronically sealed, thus saving us a considerable amount of money each year.

Refusal   I do want to assure you that your request for obtaining work from our corporation has been given very careful consideration; but because of the distance involved between our Home Office and your University, it is not feasible. You might contact some of your larger printing companies or firms that do mailings in your local area and subcontract work from them. You might also consider such fund raising

Suggestions   projects as tuition dances, car washes, or bingo games.

Forward look   With your good leadership and your chapter's cooperation, you will surely reach your very commendable goal.

Unfavorable Unsolicited Messages

You may sometimes have to send unpleasant messages which are not in response to an inquiry. This section illustrates unfavorable announcements about prices and services, orders and deposits, rules and procedures, plus miscellaneous bad news. You are generally wise to use the bad-news plan whenever you think your readers will be seriously disappointed or even angered by your bad news. However, when you write to employees or other business associates on routine matters, you may use the direct plan.

Announcing Bad News about Prices and/or Services

When your firm finds it necessary to increase prices and/or curtail services to customers, a buffer opening followed by reasons before the unhappy decision will help break the news gently, as in messages 1 and 2.

Message 1
A well-written bad-news announcement about a laundry's increased prices. (Salutation is "Dear TRIM customer:")

Buffer: comment   Yes, "Times have changed!" A quarter century ago when TRIM first started lending homemakers a hand with the family laundry, you could buy good quality ladies' blouses or men's shirts for two or three dollars. Now they cost seven to twenty dollars.

Reasons   During the same period soap prices rose from 15 to 69 cents a package and wrapping paper from 6 to 37 cents a roll. Wages too have at least tripled in many instances. To continue giving our customers high quality service, we too had to increase our prices twice, the last one eight years ago. In the meantime, all these and other items--taxes and costs we cannot control--have also risen substantially.

Reasons   So that we can continue to assure you the same twice-a-week
pickup and delivery service with the same top standards of
careful laundering and cleaning of your clothing, our new
prices will go into effect as listed on the enclosed card.

Decision   The starting date is May 1, 197_.

Forward   You can count on TRIM to do everything possible to continue
look;   giving you the same high quality service you have enjoyed
resale   through the years. We appreciate your confidence and your
patronage.

Message 2
A clear, acceptable announcement by a wholesaler regarding limitations in services.

Buffer: In reviewing 197_ business and trying to plan for a future
neutral   in which we can continue to give you good service, it has
courtesy   become evident that some modifications must be made.

Reasons   Our problems are not unlike yours or anyone else's in
business today. All items of expense in business have been
constantly increasing without a corresponding increase in
profit margin on goods and services. Rather than increase
prices in general, the following changes as an alternate
Decision   plan will become effective July 1 this year:

(1) Free local delivery will be continued only on orders of
at least $15. Orders for a lesser amount, if received by
1 p.m. can be delivered the next business day by United
Parcel Service or can be sent by our regular delivery service
if the customer wishes; but the actual cost of this service
will be added to the invoice.

Details   (2) Out-of-town shipments will continue to be shipped as
on the   instructed by the customer, or instead of instructions, will
decision   be routed by the least expensive of Parcel Post, United
Parcel Service or Auto Freight. Actual shipping costs will
be added to the invoice.

(3) Collect telephone calls will be accepted only in cases
where we have been in error.

A decision on these three changes was made after a very
Fairness to   careful analysis of our costs in relation to service. We
customers;   are sure you will agree that these changes are minimal and
courteous   fair to our customers. If you have any suggestions on how
invitation   we may improve our service to you, we will greatly appreciate your writing or calling us right now.

In contrast to the *buffer openings* of messages (letters) 1 and 2 to customers, you
you can use *bad-news direct-approach openings* similar to the following when you announce the same decisions in memos to your employees. The first is an opening for a
memo about the laundry's increased prices:

Because of increased costs of all materials and operations, TRIM now finds it necessary to increase prices of laundry services. The following new prices will go into effect for all customers May 1, 197_:

And an opening for a memo about the wholesaler's limited services might be:

> So that Gray's can continue to give good service without a general increase in prices to our customers, the following restrictions in delivery and telephone services will become effective July 1 this year:

Even for employees, however, you should follow the bad-news plan and begin with a buffer when they are likely to be personally affected or seriously disappointed by your bad-news decision. Suppose, for instance, that your company management has decided to close the employee cafeteria food service mornings and evenings and to keep it open only during noon hours. To partially offset this decrease and to provide for changing employee food preferences, the snack-bar service will be increased. Message 3 illustrates a poor way to announce these changes to employees; message 4, a good way. Notice the difference even in subject lines.

Message 3 (memo)
A poor negative, incomplete bad-news announcement to employees about decreased cafeteria service; direct plan.

TO: All employees of ABC   January 25, 197_

FROM: Karen Whitson, Food Services Director

SUBJECT: Closing of Cafeteria for Breakfasts and Suppers

Starting next Monday, February 1, there will be no more breakfasts or suppers served in the cafeteria. This facility will hereafter be closed every morning and afternoon. Lunches will will be served in the cafeteria only between 11 and 2 p.m.

However, to provide continuing service to our employees, the snack bar will be open from 8 a.m. to 5:45 p.m. and offer a wider selection of food.

Message 4 (memo)
An improved version of the preceding bad-news announcement to employees; indirect plan.

TO: All employees of ABC   January 25, 197_

FROM: Karen Whitson, Food Services Director

SUBJECT: Changes in Company Snack Bar and Cafeteria Service

Buffer: reader-benefit noncommittal statement To keep food prices at their present level, in spite of rising costs, and to meet your changing needs—the snack bar and cafeteria services will be modified starting Monday, February 1.

Reasons Changes are necessary because during the past three years fewer employees have been eating breakfasts and suppers in the cafeteria and costs of operating it have steadily increased. So that you can continue to benefit from both low *Employee benefits* prices and good quality food, we are altering the services and we believe you will like them.

Decision: favorable changes first

Snack Bar Services--The snack bar will be expanded to offer a wider selection of food than ever before. From the semi-self-service counter and the vending machines you can choose:

Packaged Cereals	Fruits and Juices	Sandwiches
Doughnuts	Soft Drinks	Hamburgers
Rolls	Ice Cream	Salads
Coffee, Tea, Milk	Pies and Cakes	Potato Chips
Hot Chocolate	Candy Bars	Soup

Decision: emphasis on the positive

Cafeteria Service--Each day a lunch special consisting of a hot main course, salad, dessert, and drink will be served, as before, for less than $1. The cafeteria will serve only lunches.

New Hours--The new hours effective February 1 are:
Snack Bar   -   8 a.m. - 5:45 p.m.
Cafeteria   -   11 a.m. - 2:00 p.m.

Employee benefits

In addition, the cafeteria doors will remain open, however, between 8 a.m. and 6 p.m. for those of you wishing a meeting place during work breaks or to enjoy food brought from home or the snack bar.

Forward look; employee benefits and invited action

You are invited to use these facilities whenever you can. They are available to you at no extra price on snacks or lunches. If you have any suggestions on the new cafeteria or snack bar services, please jot them on a slip of paper and drop them into the Suggestion Box at the cafeteria door.

Occasionally for a relatively small matter you can put across a bad-news decision effectively by using good-natured humor:

Message 5 (memo)
Humorous price-rise announcement to employees.

TO: All employees

FROM: Cafeteria Management

SUBJECT: An Invitation to a "Funeral Service"

Sad(?) news

On Friday, September 30, 197_, your company cafeteria will bury a very dear servant, a veteran of 20 years whom most of you enjoy every day.

Details

There will be no music, no solemn ovations, no (we hope) violent outbursts of emotion. Instead, there will be FREE COFFEE for everyone in the cafeteria during the lunch period September 30. We hope you will attend the last rites

Decision

of the 10-cent cup of coffee. On Monday, October 3, the price will rise to 15 cents. It has been decided that coffee service should no longer be subsidized and the current cost of producing and selling a cup of coffee is more than 10 cents.

A happy thought

We're sorry. We loved that 10 cent cup of coffee too. But here is a cheery thought: Your pennies still buy more when you use them in your company cafeteria!

Requiring Minimum Orders and/or Deposits

At times you may need to tell a customer that he or she must either give your firm more business or lose former privileges. For instance, a manufacturer may require his authorized distributors to sell at least a certain minimum amount or lose their franchise; a retailer may discontinue sending free catalogs if she does not receive orders; a publisher may want to cut costs by decreasing the length of his "free" mailing list; and a bank may have to announce bad news about minimum balances on dormant savings accounts. For such messages the bad-news plan is advisable. Letter 1 erroneously follows the direct plan, while letter 2 correctly uses a buffer.

Letter 1
A poor bad-news announcement from a large producer of fully prepared baking mixes to a wholesale firm.

We are sorry to see that your business with us has fallen down so that it does not pay to have you on our books any more, as we can only afford to have accounts on our books who sell merchandise right along.

We appreciate the Alaskan situation where it is seasonal buying, but your business has fallen off so that now there is practically nothing.

We would appreciate a line from you as to whether you think you could build this business up, or whether it would be best for all concerned for us to discontinue your company as one of our jobbers.

Will you please advise us by return mail so we will know what to do.

Letter 2
An improved version of letter 1 (asking a wholesaler to increase his orders or drop off the list).

Buffer: favorable past	In the past five years we have had the pleasure of filling your orders for prepared baking mixes. We have also appreciated the prompt manner in which you have always paid your account.
Explanation: minimums and reasons	When you first started trading with us, we extended jobbers' prices to you--on the condition that a minimum amount of merchandise be bought during the year. Setting our price structure on this minimum for jobbers enables us to sell at lower prices. In spite of seasonal buying from Alaskan customers, you have in the past sold the product well.
Concern; implied bad-news decision	Because during the last year your purchases fell far short of the agreed minimum of $500, we are concerned about ways that we might help you, rather than assigning your territory to another jobber. Pasty Cake Mixes are nationally advertised
Suggestions	to help create a demand at grocery stores, and orders should be flowing your way. Housewives use cake mixes the year 'round. Perhaps you would like to work out with our representative, Barbara Hempstead, a special plan adapted to your particular situation. During the busy summer season your volume could be higher to offset the decreased size of orders during the slack winter months.

Requested action	Will you please let us know, in the enclosed envelope, within a week if you plan to continue to represent Pasty Cake Mixes. We want to have your firm distribute our products provided you meet your jobber's quota regularly.

Penalizing for Nonconformity with Rules or Procedures

Announcements about penalties for deviating from required procedures or disregarding previous notices quite often begin with the bad news. The direct plan should be used, especially when the situation is urgent or when the writer wants the reader to be sure to read the main idea, as in this letter:

	Dear Saver
Main idea	A new federal ruling will drastically affect the status of your inactive account #111-1111.
Explanation

Decision | Effective August 28 of this year, federal regulations governing our operations were revised regarding a service charge on inactive savings accounts of less than $10. We are now permitted to charge $1 each year to maintain each account that has not been used in the last three years. As you realize, this minimum charge permits an association to just about break even financially in maintaining these small inactive accounts year after year. |
| *Suggestion* | May I suggest that you arrange to convert your account into an active one before (date) so that you earn a high 5% dividend with complete safety of your money. By doing so, you also avoid the $1 yearly charge on an inactive account. But, if you do not wish to add to this account, then you should close it immediately to avoid this charge. |
| *Pleasant close* | Please come in or call me at 222-2222 if you have any question concerning your account. We are here to serve you. |

Conveying Other Bad News

You may have to write other bad-news unsolicited (and solicited) messages. As a rule, you can handle most of them well by the bad-news plan.

However, one exception to the usual rule for customer bad-news letters is when you must announce that you made a mistake which is not in the customer's favor. In such cases it is often better to admit your error in the opening, as in the next example.

Letter 1
Announcement of an error that unfavorably affects the reader.

Tactful lead to bad news	We always appreciate the opportunity to be of service to our customers, but I'm sorry to tell you that last month we did you--and ourselves--a disservice.
	The correct amount of your February, 197_ premium was $125.61, and we billed you for only $120.55, a difference of $5.06.

Details	We overlooked the difference in insurance premium between your former policy and the new policy which has given you additional coverage since January 1.
Request and easy action	May we ask you to sign the attached form and send it to us with your check for $5.06? Just slip it into the enclosed envelope and mail it.
Goodwill	You can be sure we'll do our best to see that you get accurate service in the future.

The letter of resignation is another bad-news announcement you may have to write. Whether you resign from a job for which you have been paid or from an elective office, you consider your reader(s) and your relationship to them before you decide to organize by the direct or indirect plan. Your letter should include your reason for resigning (ill health, better position, or whatever), appreciation and pleasant comments about the people you are leaving, perhaps a statement of regret, a definite effective date for the resignation, and a sincere cordial ending. The following two letters of resignation are both well written. In letter 2 the writer felt that the busy board of directors would prefer reading the main idea (though it is bad news) in the first paragraph. Letter 3 gives the bad news *after* the reasons.

Letter 2
A direct-plan letter of resignation (to a board of directors).

Main idea: bad news	With much reluctance and regret I must ask to be released from my position of State Director of Civil Defense.
Reason	Because I have developed a heart condition, my doctors have instructed me to move on a slow bell and particularly emphasized my giving up Civil Defense. While the condition is not dangerous at present, it is of the "warning" type.
Pleasant comments	As you may guess, this is pretty much of a blow to me, but it isn't smart to ignore the advice of our doctors. During the past four years I've greatly enjoyed working with the many fine people of our state organization. It is thus difficult for me to request that you accept my resignation
Date of resignation	to become effective immediately after your next month's board meeting.
Good wishes	I'm convinced of the importance of our Civil Defense cause and assure you that my good wishes will continue to go with you and the great work you are doing.

Letter 3
An indirect-plan resignation (to a college senior's employer for whom he worked five years); dated May 1.

Buffer: agreeable statement	Just as each business must chart its course for the future, so must every individual ask himself: Where am I going? and Where do I want to be 15 years from now?

Appreciation	Over the past five years I have given serious thought to these questions. I will always remember how much your company has meant to me. You have given me not only valuable experience and a sense of perspective, but also work and earnings that helped pay my expenses through the University. As both you and I realize, however, my chances for long-run advancement
Reason	necessary to satisfy my goals are limited here at Ace Sign Company.
Reason	To make full use of my college training and in an effort to provide better benefits to my family, I am accepting a position in the Finance Department of the International Products in (city). As my reporting date will be June 11, please
Resignation	consider this resignation to be effective June 5. In the meantime I am willing to work any necessary overtime, at no additional cost to you, to ensure an effective transition for my successor here.
Cordial close	Again, thank you for your many kindnesses during the years I have worked in your firm. I hope that you and all my co-workers at Ace will continue to be my personal friends in the years ahead.

In summary, whenever you must write unfavorable news—whether you are replying to a request or initiating an unsolicited message—you are usually safe to follow the indirect, four-part bad-news plan. If you use the direct plan, be sure that the type of message, the situation, and the relationship between yourself and your reader warrant that approach. The Capsule Checklists on pp. 300–307 review both plans (column I) and adapt the indirect plan to 10 kinds of bad-news messages.

Exercises

Answering Inquiries When the Information Is Undesirable

1. Your new assistant has just laid on your desk the following letter he wrote (to a long-time customer) for your signature as customer service manager of your firm, Research Consultants. He admits he hasn't had much training in letter writing and says he'd appreciate your comments on his attempt. You decide to rewrite this one for him and let him compare the two versions of this bad-news message. Improve the letter in every way you can—especially the organization and you attitude. Emphasize positive instead of negative aspects, and maintain goodwill toward your firm. Because you aim to assist this good customer as much as possible, you have asked your staff to contact other sources in addition to your own company files. Those sources may have some materials on plans that do fall into the class the customer discussed. As soon as they have something definite, you will write the customer again.

> I am sorry to say that, unfortunately, our editors did not find anything in our plan files that would apply to your problem regarding pension plan summaries for trade association staff employees.

We have also not yet found any plan elsewhere that would fall into the class you discussed.

I wonder if, when you looked through the Reports, you did not notice that there is a pension plan for the Employee Association League of New York State? I found this plan on pages 106-112. I am not certain whether this is the type of plan you are interested in.

2. Assume you are manager of the Jay-Fraser Sales Corporation for an automobile manufacturer in Michigan and that your new assistant has just written the following reply (dated May 4) to an inquirer 2,000 miles away. What improvements can you suggest? Rewrite the reply so that it will be a goodwill builder even though you cannot at present give the information asked for in the "four points." He wants to know about the Jay convertible automobile because he is interested in owning one some day.

Dear Mr. Stewart:

This will acknowledge receipt of yours of April 23. At the time of this writing we are not in a position to give you any information on the four points which you mentioned in your letter since no information is available to us for release at this time.

We are sure, however, that your local dealer will be only too happy to keep you informed as to when the Jay convertible will be made available to the public.

We would like to thank you for your interest in our cars.

3. Letters A and B are replies from two state colleges to a university junior living in another part of the same state. On June 2 she wrote to each college the same inquiry about admission requirements for a transfer student currently majoring in Business Education and intending to teach in elementary or junior high schools. Compare these replies for opening and closing paragraphs and for helpful explanation. Which letter do you like better? Which is more helpful? Why? What improvements can you suggest for each reply?

A.

Dear Miss Hopson:

We are happy to hear of your interest in attending Central State College. Enclosed you will find information on admission requirements and application procedures for transfer students. At your request, an application for admission is also enclosed.

Your particular combination of elementary education with a business major cannot be endorsed for teaching at Central. I would suggest that you give me a call at 963-4214 so that I may further explain our program to you.

If I can be of further assistance, do not hesitate to contact me.

B.

Dear Miss Hopson:

In response to your letter of May 21, we are sending you the catalog for the academic year just completed. The new catalog is in the process of preparation but will not be available until some time in July.

On page 40 of the catalog, you will find the professional education sequence of 36 credits required of all candidates for a B.A. in Education and provisional certificate. On page 41 are listed the programs for elementary teachers and secondary teachers. You will see that Business Education is not an approved major for elementary or junior high teachers and that Business Education majors planning to teach in the senior high must complete a minor in Economics. Thus, if you were to transfer to Western to become an elementary teacher, you would have to develop a new 45-hour major. You could continue with your major for teaching senior high and would then need to complete the Economics minor. Requirements for the Business Education major are listed on page 70 in the catalog and course descriptions follow. Descriptions of the Education courses begin on page 76. Dr. Elaine Palm is adviser for the Business Education program, and Dr. Stewart Van is chairman of the elementary domain. If you have specific questions for either of these professors, it would be well for you to include a copy of your college record to date so that they would be better informed to answer your questions.

An application for admission with advanced standing is enclosed for your use if you decide to make the change.

4. As purchasing assistant for a national life insurance company, answer Miss Linda Mond's courteous request for literature about attitudes of drivers. She needs this material for a speech she will give at a community meeting of taxpayers. Your company does not handle any other insurance except life insurance. Therefore you do not have any material which will help her. What constructive suggestion(s) can you add to aid her? Can you name two or three firms that specialize in accident or car insurance? State and local law enforcement officers may also have useful information.

5. Point out the negative expressions in the following form letter. Then rewrite it to emphasize the positive aspects, instead of the negative, keeping the basic facts the same. This form reply was sent from the Government Printing Office to a business executive who requested a copy of the $9 text on the summary and conclusions of FTC *Reports on Coffee Price Investigation.* Is the direct plan usable here? Why or why not?

Thank you for your inquiry which is enclosed. We are sorry the publication you desire is not in stock at this time. However, we hope to have more definite information concerning the availability of this publication in a short time. We have recorded your interest and will notify you just as soon as definite information is available. We regret that factors beyond our control make it impossible for us to be more definite at this time and hope you understand that we act merely as a distributor of Government publications and not as the author or the issuing agency. For this reason, we sometimes cannot be specific as to when or whether or not a publication will be available.

The large number of orders and letters of inquiry received each day by this Office makes it impossible for us to write you a personal letter. We hope this reply is satisfactory and that you understand that we value your inquiry none the less highly despite the necessity of our answering in this form.

6. The following letter from a national manufacturer of party favors has several weaknesses. Rewrite it (to Jim Brown, chairperson of a college football banquet) to improve it in every way you can. Assume additional pertinent facts, if necessary, and try to be more helpful to this banquet chairperson. He wants individual souvenirs ("about 2 or 3 inches wide") to use as favors or place cards for the 250 persons expected to attend the banquet five weeks from today. Although your factory does not have any such souvenirs in stock, you do manufacture special items to order. All you need is a design and three to four weeks' time; your skilled workers turn out really attractive novelties. Assume that your reader (the chairperson) lives 2,000 miles from your factory. Time is short. It is possible that the L. G. Baldwin Company (a retail supplier about 1,000 miles from Jim Brown's city) may have football souvenirs in stock. What can you say to be helpful?

Dear Sir:

We have pleasure in acknowledging your letter of 20th September concerning your inquiry about small individual football souvenirs for your banquet. Though we note that you had been advised by Marcus Company to approach us in this connection, we are sorry to inform you that we do not have football novelties and thus cannot supply the material which you need.

We regret we cannot be of service to you for this occasion.

Refusing Adjustments on Claims and Complaints

1. The following goodwill-killing message is a processed form letter sent by a state-wide hospital service association to customers who hold a certain hospital insurance policy. Mr. Alton Grimshaw, a business executive who received this letter, was angered by it and considered it a "horrible letter." How many reasons can you find for agreeing with Mr. Grimshaw? (His wife had been rushed to the hospital in an ambulance; he had paid cash for this service, and now included his receipt, along with other hospital bills which he thought his hospital insurance policy covered.) Suggest specific ways to present the bad news tactfully in this form letter.

Dear Mr. Grinshaw:

We are returning your receipts for ambulance service.

We realize when you know you are not paying a rate for such service, you can understand our reason for rejection of this bill.

We are sorry we are unable to be of assistance to you with this charge.

2. Compare the following two letters for tone, organization, and content. Discuss specifically why the revision is better than the original. (The messages are individually typewritten from the home office of an insurance company to an insured policyholder who claims that certain illness expenses incurred should be covered by the policy.)

Original

I would like to acknowledge the application for benefits and itemized bills which have been referred to us through the Vermont Office. I regret to find that we will be unable to be of service to you on your claim.

The primary purpose of your hospital expense policy, as its name implies, is to provide protection to help defray the high expenses usually resulting from those conditions which are serious enough in nature to require hospital confinement as a result of accident or sickness, emergency treatment, maternity, surgery, and polio.

As you can see, there are no benefits provided for out-patient services in a hospital incurred as a result of sickness, nor does it provide for the payment of doctor's fees in the absence of surgery.

Inasmuch as the bills you have presented indicate that no losses covered by the policy have been sustained, the Company has no alternative to disallowing your application for benefits. I am sorry that the circumstances do not permit giving you more favorable advice.

Revision

Thank you for the opportunity to explain the Company's position on the August 3 statement from the ABC Hospital.

The main point is that the primary purpose of your Hospital Expense Policy is to cover in-patient hospital charges and surgery. An in-patient is one who incurs at least one-day room and board charges. The policy also covers maternity, polio, and emergency treatment as an outpatient from accidental bodily injuries.

Your claim is for outpatient care at the ABC Hospital for treatment of a sickness. Also, the doctor's bill does not show any surgery was performed. These charges are not covered by the premium being charged, and no provision is made for them in the benefits. Therefore, we cannot approve benefits for these particular expenses.

If you should present another claim in the future, benefits will be considered in accordance with this explanation. And if you have any questions, please contact me.

3. As consumer service assistant manager of the Bleachex Company in Worcester, Mass., you have today received a complaint from Mrs. E. A. Leyton, of Spokane, Washington. She writes that after using your Bleachex liquid to remove a stain from her new white nylon car seat belt, she found the belt turned "an ugly yellow." She wants you to pay the $8 for a new belt. However, from her description of the yellow discoloration, it appears that the nylon had been treated with a resin (for soil resistance and "body") that is not compatible with any dry or liquid chlorine bleach. Your label states that Bleachex removes fruit, vegetable, etc., stains from washable cotton, linen, nylon, and other synthetic materials. But you do not advocate Bleachex for stain removal unless the entire item can be immersed in the properly mixed solution and then rinsed well, which is important to stop the bleach action. Thus, Bleachex should not be used on a car seat belt because of the inconvenience of removing the belt and all metal trimmings before immersing the material in the right solution. Though you can't guarantee 100 percent results, she may wish to immerse the belt for a few minutes in a solution of 1 gallon water, 2 tablespoonfuls of sodium sulfite (from a drugstore or photo supply shop), and ½ cup of white vinegar, and then rinse thoroughly. Although you must refuse her claim, make your reply tactful, helpful, and positive.

4. You are customer service director for the telephone company in your region. One of the letters you must write today is a refusal to Sam Winter, a student at Central Community College (about 50 miles from your office). Here is his complaint letter:

The enclosed bill from you for $75.80 contains long distance calls that I won't pay for. Apparently someone in your office got numbers screwed up and charged my account instead of someone else's. I know I made eight of the calls on this bill, but the other two I didn't make. I don't know anyone in those towns and therefore I refuse to pay the $15.95 charges on them.

Your bill says I supposedly made those calls on March 19. Well, that day I'm sure I didn't make any long-distance calls, because I was busy planning for the little celebration party I had that same night. It was a special event. I didn't see anyone using my phone that night, either. Anyway, whoever made the calls should have to pay for them, not me.

Enclosed is my check for $59.85, which I think is in full payment of what I owe you.

Your Operations Staff members have thoroughly investigated this claim. Your highly accurate equipment registers every call—whether it is directly dialed, or placed through an operator as a collect call. If it is the latter, the operator makes a definite, written report on each call. The two calls Mr. Winter questions were placed at 9:30 p.m. and 10:05 p.m. March 19; each was directly dialed; one was 15 minutes long, $7.10, and the other, 20 minutes, $8.85. The number from which these calls originated is definitely that of Sam Winter. As every phone book states near the front under "long distance information and rates," any calls dialed must be billed to the number from which the call is made. Thus Sam must pay for the entire bill, including the $15.95 unpaid balance. Can you include one or two helpful suggestions for him? (Perhaps, now that he knows the date, time, town, length of each call, and the cost of each, he should check among his March 19 guests to see who placed the calls.) Your staff members even checked all equipment and operations records, and found no equipment problems recorded for March 19.

Write Sam Winter a tactful refusal that will keep his goodwill and, hopefully, get his full payment before your company has to disconnect his telephone! Remember to emphasize positive aspects.

5. Your firm repairs cameras and electronic equipment. One of your out-of-town customers sent you for repair a GRAPHLIX camera, Model 512, bearing the serial number 49866. She claims the camera is defective and asks for free repairs, because she has had it only six months on a one-year guarantee. Examination shows that the camera is not defective, but it has been dropped and badly misused. These repairs are needed: replace broken lens, $32; repair range finder, $4.50; repair and readjust electronic eye, $4. These repairs will put the camera in first-class shape; it cost originally $165. Write to the customer, Ms. Jean A. Murdock, letting her know why she will have to pay for these repairs. You are customer service manager. Your guarantee accompanying all cameras states they are guaranteed for workmanship and materials under normal operating (use) conditions, but *not* when emersed in water, dropped, or given other unusual "shock" treatment.

6. As adjustment department manager of Otis Radio Company, manufacturers of portable radios, you need to write a refusal letter today to Mr. Swen Swenson. He sent his portable Bike Radio #95432 to you for repair because it ceased to function. He enclosed a copy of his $15.95 purchase slip dated six months ago and asks that you repair the radio free because the year is "not yet up." He lost the guarantee, but assumes it was for one year. Actually, however, these radios were guaranteed—on workmanship and materials—for 90 days. During that time you gladly make all repairs free of charge. However, since the guarantee period expired on this radio three months ago, Mr. Swenson will have to pay the $14.95 repair charges. You can get the radio into like-new condition.

    Because your newest tiny portable radio costs only $16.95, you wonder if he wouldn't rather purchase the newer one instead of repairing his own. This new radio is guaranteed for one year. Though it is a little smaller than his present radio, its large controls assure adequate volume and tuning. The high-impact case clamps on the handlebar easily; it fits most bikes. It uses only one 9-volt battery. Though battery costs (45 cents) usually are extra, you would send one free of charge, if he should wish this new radio. Do not in any way high-pressure him, however; he'd be $2 ahead if he chooses to keep his present radio. But the new one is solid-state AM; measures just 5 x 6 x 2 inches; weighs less than 1 pound; and it can be detached from the handlebars and used as a portable to carry indoors whenever he wishes. It is your factory's newest model, and, you think, it's the best you have turned out for this low price. Write the letter that will be truly helpful to this customer, who must choose between paying $14.95 repairs or $16.95 for a new radio, even though he had thought all repairs would be free.

7. You are the manager of a reputable appliance store in Cleveland, Ohio. You sold Mrs. Lotta Moneybags a new washing machine which was a gift for her daughter

who recently got married. Mrs. Moneybags is a very wealthy widow and Clara is her only child. Mrs. Moneybags also is a very influential person in the city and a very good customer of yours. She is very narrow-minded, however, when it comes to her daughter—Clara can do no wrong. Just today you received this letter from Mrs. Moneybags, who is currently vacationing two weeks at a resort in another state:

```
I purchased from you six months ago a brand new 197_ Jetwash
washing machine for my daughter.  You assured me that this was
the best machine on the market and that it would give years of
trouble-free service.  You even guaranteed it for 3 years.

My daughter has been using this machine and she informed me
that last week it quit running.  She had a repair person from
your store come in and look at the machine to see what was
wrong and he told her that the motor had burned out as a
result of a bearing in the spin mechanism burning out.  I was
very upset to learn of this trouble so I talked to the repair
person myself by phone.  He told me that the damage to the
bearing could have only resulted from improper loading of the
machine, and it appeared to him that Clara grossly overloaded
the machine every time she used it.

I don't believe your repair person, and it is perfectly
apparent that this machine was defective and he is trying to
shift the blame to my daughter.  Now I know that you are a
rational man, Mr. (your name), and I am sure that you agree
with me that this machine is defective.  Therefore, I would
like your store to replace this machine at once, as it is
a terrible inconvenience to my daughter not to have a washing
machine in good working condition.
```

To be fair to both Mrs. Moneybags and to yourself, you telephoned Clara and made an appointment to go to her home to examine the washer. After observing the condition of the motor and talking with the daughter, you realized that the repairman told the truth. The machine is not defective and the breakdown was the result of improper use. The instructions for using are printed on the inside of the lid of the washer, giving all the details for loading the washer properly. Furthermore, anyone ought to be able to understand these instructions. The tub has a clearly marked red line over which you are not to load clothes. Overloading causes the tub to spin in an irregular manner, which in turn places undue pressure on a particular bearing located just below the tub agitator. This bearing—the one that burned out on Clara's machine—receives the full weight of the load, plus the centrifugal force when spinning. This bearing was badly burned and melted in several places. Because the lubrication around the bearing is still sealed in, the only thing which could have caused the failure was improper loading. If a burned-out bearing isn't replaced right away, the motor also burns out because of the excessive strain exerted as it tries to spin the tub agitator.

Write a letter to Mrs. Moneybags denying her request as tactfully as possible. You would like to keep her business. Also, she is very influential in your community, and you do not want her hurting your market with malicious gossip. You will have to charge her $31.45 (including tax) for the needed replacement parts to put the machine in top-notch working order again. Furthermore you will have to keep the machine in your shop for three days for repair. But you will not charge her for labor that would amount to another $30, or for a $15 service call. Giving her a new machine is ridiculous.

8. Assume that you are customer service department manager of the Ketchum and Pleasam Department Store in your city. Today you get a letter from Mrs. James Gleason, 919 North 20th Street, in a small town about 20 miles from your store. Attached to her letter is a package containing three pairs of ($6.60 each) faded blue jeans that she bought from your store when she was there in person. She describes exactly from which of your basement departments she bought the jeans, and she's right. Her complaint is that they have shrunk and faded so that she will not wear them. She wants you to send, without extra charge, three pairs of sanforized navy blue jeans that won't shrink or fade. She complains that she's surprised your store's merchandise doesn't stand washing.

   Here are the facts: To meet the demands of the numerous young people who insist on wearing jeans skintight, who prefer to cut them off at odd places, and who want them to look "grubby" soon, you carry a special brand that pleases these customers. On the counter at several places are signs stating: "These jeans are guaranteed to shrink and fade!" This is the counter from which Mrs. Gleason bought her jeans. Clearly she just didn't read or see the signs, and you can't be responsible for her error. From your third-floor sports department you can send her three pairs of Topco brand sanforized navy blue jeans ($6.90 each) in her size, and they're guaranteed *not* to shrink. Of course, she'll have to pay for them. If your instructor approves, you may suggest a compromise to Mrs. Gleason; perhaps she won't suffer a complete loss on the faded jeans she returned. If you make no compromise, be sure to return the unwanted jeans and add a constructive suggestion.

Refusing Credit

1. As credit manager of a national oil company, you receive hundreds of applications for credit cards. One refusal which you must write often is to young people under legal age. Draft a goodwill-building form letter (which can be processed) to handle such refusals. If the applicant could get an adult who would be willing to guarantee his account, you'd do your best to accommodate him. Enclose a necessary form together with a second credit card application. The guarantor is to sign both forms and the applicant is to return them to you with a reference to his original application.

2. Compare the following processed credit refusals used by three national large retail credit firms—mail-order, banking, and travelers' aid, respectively. Notice that each has the refusal in or near the opening paragraph.

   a. From the standpoint of a credit applicant, discuss your personal reaction to each of these letters. Consider the opening, adequacy of reasons, and constructive suggestions.
   b. Rewrite either letter B or C, placing the decision *after* the reasons (and revising the wording as needed).
   c. Do you like your rewrite better than the original? Why or why not?

   A.

   ```
   We sincerely appreciate the opportunity you gave us of con-
   sidering your recent credit application but find we are
   unable to accommodate you on a credit basis at this time.

   We hope you will continue to shop at (name), taking advantage
   of our everyday low prices and grant us the privilege of
   serving you again.
   ```

B.

Thank you for your application for a (name) credit card.
Your interest is appreciated, but we sincerely regret that
we are presently unable to approve your request.

Because of the many uses of (name) card, the requirements for
obtaining a card are different than those for many other
types of credit, and these requirements cover many areas of
consideration. From the information given to us in your
application, we are unable to issue a card at this time.

However, if you have additional information which you believe
would warrant a review of your application, or if you believe
that there may be a misunderstanding, we would be pleased to
have you contact us.

C.

We are genuinely sorry that we cannot comply with your request
for a (name) credit card at this time.

Any one of a number of factors may be responsible for this
decision. The unique nature of the (name) credit card--
offering as it does virtually unlimited credit at over
150,000 service establishments throughout the world - obliges
us to place unique requirements on its availability. Consequently, a large number of applications fail to qualify.

Some of the factors considered in evaluating applications are:
job longevity, length of residency, number of dependents,
income as reported to us, net worth, ratio of income to
liabilities, nature of employment, credit references, credit
history, and property ownership. As much as we regret to
decline an application, we are compelled to do so if it does
not meet the requirements in any one of these categories.

It has been our experience that persons who do not meet our
requirements at one time may qualify later on. You are cordially invited to reapply at a later date, if you feel your
circumstances have changed.

Thank you for your interest in our service.

3. You are the manager of a wholesale fabric business. You distribute fabrics to many stores in your state. You allow them 30 to 90 days to pay for goods and sometimes longer if necessary. Just recently you have run into a very difficult situation. You extended credit to one small fabric shop that was run by a very personable fellow, Mr. Greenfab. He has come in several times to your warehouse and ordered and picked up fabric. He seems quite at home with all the personnel in your company and everybody likes him. For these reasons when he was unable to pay his bill in 90 days you gave him an indefinite extension. He continued to place orders and his bill has become larger and larger. It has now been a year since he has paid for anything. Of course part of the blame is yours for letting it go on as it did, but you have decided that you can no longer extend credit to this man until he starts paying his past bill. You had explained that you had to stop credit and he said he understood, but when he called up on what he termed "emer-gency" situations, you always said, "Well, only this time." The situation is now

out of hand, and you want your money. Decide on a course of action and write an effective letter.

4. As credit manager of the Regis Department Store, you have received a credit application from Mrs. George Bann, who seems to be doing a noble job of making the family ends meet on her $450 monthly wages. She and her husband and four children rent a $90-a-month cottage. Her husband has been unable to work for three months because of illness, but he hopes to get a job within two or three more months. You honestly feel that a charge account is not what this family should have now. Unexpected emergencies in their financial position could cause them serious problems. Cash purchasing from your complete catalog, where they pay as they go, lets them know where they stand at any time. Also you have end-of-month sales regularly, with savings up to 50 percent. Send Mrs. Bann a catalog supplement with all the news about your sales. Perhaps when Mr. Bann is working you will reconsider her application for your monthly payment plan. Make your letter specific and genuinely helpful.

5. Among the credit refusals on your desk today is one you must write to Harrison Noteworthy, a 28-year-old attorney in your town. He has been a regular cash customer of your hardware store for the past two years and now has applied for a revolving charge account. Though you do not know him, you have read about him in local newspapers and thought there would surely be no problem at all in granting him credit. Since moving to your town four years ago, he has become prominent in sporting events and has a good reputation socially.

However, in checking his credit records on file at the City Retail Credit Bureau, you are surprised to find that he has a very poor credit reputation. His past-due payments at six stores total almost $9,000. One of his creditors is suing him because of a $2,300 debt that is 10 months past due. According to the Credit Bureau, all his other creditors report him as "slow" or "poor pay." He formerly had a steady position and regular income in the state attorney general's office. But four years ago he quit because he wanted to start his own private law practice. A handsome bachelor, he apparently has spent money lavishly and saved very little.

You decide that a charge account with your store is definitely out. Perhaps some other time after his law practice in this town gains a stronger foothold, you may be able to open an account for him. He is invited to come in to talk to you (or your assistant, Miss Lavaun Sutter) for a confidential discussion of his credit picture and how he might change it. You do want to keep him as a satisfied regular cash customer. And you'll go to any reasonable lengths to assure that your customers are pleased. However, because of the current business conditions, you are tightening your requirements and safeguards in all your credit granting. Write Mr. Noteworthy the kind of letter that will achieve your goal of keeping him as a friend of your firm.

6. During the past 18 months you, credit manager of Lifetime Building Materials, Inc., have noticed that Thomas Wright—a contractor customer of yours—has been running later and later in his payments. Instead of discounting his bills each month (paying them within 10 days and receiving 3 percent discount) as he had always done previously, he has been taking the full 30 days and longer. In fact, the last seven payments have been 60 to 90 days late. You realize that many buyers in the construction industry have been experiencing higher operating costs and fewer contracts. Nevertheless, it is essential to keep accounts receivable current. You must refuse to sell any more materials to Mr. Wright on credit until his

past statements are paid up and his condition has improved. Hopefully, this is only a temporary situation. Suggest smaller orders and cash payments—with the 3 percent discount to help him reestablish his former excellent credit standing. Any other suggestions to show that you want to cooperate with him?

Acknowledging Orders You Can't Fill Now or At All

Incomplete Orders

1. As customer service representative for Lipman Department Store, Los Angeles, California, you have today (July 8) received an order from Mrs. Rose Fairmont, 135 Third Street, Gardena, California 90247. She writes that last Saturday evening on her way to a theater in Los Angeles, she happened to pass your store windows on the west side. In the center window she saw a pantsuit that she would like you to send her in size 12: in "red, white, and blue. I think the price was $29.50; just charge it to my account. It's just the thing I'd like to take with me on a trip; we'll be leaving Tuesday, July 15. Will you please send it to reach me no later than Monday?" In checking with your window decorator, you learn that six pantsuits were displayed in the center-west window last Saturday. Worse yet, three of them were in red-white-blue prints—(1) horizontal stripes in the jacket top, with navy blue slacks, (2) vertical stripes for both the jacket and slacks, and (3) plain red jacket with navy trim on the collar, and white slacks. Which does she want? Your secretary tried four times today to phone Mrs. Fairmont, but received no answer. You must now write her a letter which goes in the 5 p.m. mail pickup and should reach her tomorrow or Thursday morning. If she will get her answer to you by no later than Friday noon, you can be sure to send the right suit to her on the store delivery truck Monday morning. Devise easy action for Mrs. Fairmont, and also make sure you will get all the information you need to fill her order immediately.

2. From Mr. Marvin Randall, assistant manager, Midwest Marine and Pool Supply, 910 Jetson Avenue, Detroit, Michigan 48214, you receive an order for:

10 Boarding ladders, 3 steps	@ $8.50
50 ft. #6314 Marine Mat and Dock Runner, red	@ 3.00 per ft.
3 doz. deluxe #98145 Chaise pads, floral	@ 2.00 each

    These items are to be shipped freight charges collect and billed on the firm's usual credit terms of 2/10, net/30. You can't ship two of these items, however, until you get more information. The boarding ladders come with 7-inch and 11-inch hooks—so they can clamp securely to boats, rafts, pools, or docks. Which size does he want? It is even possible that he might want five of each, but you think it is risky to guess. The ladder prices are the same for both sizes of hooks. These white vinyl-covered hooks turn a full 360 degrees for fast and easy fitting, and they fold so that the ladder is flat for convenient storage. The steps are varnished oak hardwood, 15 inches wide.

    The Mat and Dock Runner #6314 is in aqua color, not red. The red is listed in your catalog (which Midwest Marine has) as #6316. Though he probably wants the red and just wrote the wrong catalog number, you want to be sure before you ship this heavy roll. (Shipping weight is 3 pounds per foot!) This is an excellent runner for deck or dock. It is made of all-weather nonslip brush-action polyester pile with heavy rubber backing and is 36 inches wide.

    You do have the chair pads and can ship them today. They are a durable waterproof vinyl floral pattern, ideal for outdoor patio use. Today is May 10.

Decide whether you should ship the pads today or wait until you can send the other items too. Write for the needed information, make action easy, and cover all pertinent details. You are assistant sales manager for Pool and Patio Wholesale Company, San Francisco, California 94101.

3. You are assistant research director of Travel Service, International. Members pay annual dues and get travel assistance as well as discounts on trips they book through their local chapters. Your organization publishes and mails (free) a *Quarterly Newsletter* to all members across the United States. Also you publish (for sale at cost) a few reports and booklets on various phases of travel. Because your organization has no credit department, none of these published booklets can be sent unless the member sends cash with the order. You do not send c.o.d. Part of the back page of every *Quarterly Newsletter* is devoted to announcements about new publications and their cost (which includes postage for mailing to any town in the United States). There is a clear statement on this back page about the cash-in-advance policy. Nevertheless, today you received an order from Mrs. Susan Land, Shelby, Illinois, asking that the following reports be sent c.o.d. (or that you bill her later):

2 "Money-saving Hints for Modern Travelers"   ($3 each)
1 "The Incredible Paradox of the 70's"   ($2.50)

You must hold up shipment of these booklets until you receive her remittance. Write a tactful acknowledgment of her order, explaining both your policy and the reason for it. Your prices on the pamphlets are at cost; the saving that your organization makes by operating without credit and collection procedure is passed on to members in lower prices.

Back Orders

4. Mr. Lawrence Meisner, a charge customer at 854 Glenwood Drive, Eugene, Oregon 97401, orders five more rolls of the #TG3772 gold color flocked raised damask wallpaper ($15.95 a roll). He writes that he just finished papering the dining room with this pattern and his family likes it so much that they now want the hall to match. Your store (Galli's Interior Design Shop, Portland, Oregon 97208) is completely out of this pattern; you sold your last roll three days ago. You are the exclusive dealer for these distinctive wallpapers in Oregon and get them direct from the Mayberry Mills in Massachusetts. A wire from the mills yesterday promised that your special order of #TG3772 would reach your shop in 10 days. Write Mr. Meisner the appropriate letter to keep him convinced that this choice wallpaper is well worth waiting for. It is one of the most elegant you carry. Its beautiful flocked damask pattern has the lovely look and feel of velvet. Textured to simulate fine silk, all on tough vinyl, it is strong and won't tear even when wet. Also, it's prepasted and pretrimmed, and can be cleaned with soap and water. Shipping time between Portland and Eugene is one day.

5. In your Wholesale Camera Supply Company (Norman, Oklahoma 73069) you have just received an order from Angel's Photo Shop, 931 Wabash Avenue, Shawnee, Oklahoma 74801, for parts to repair a Model #25 box camera. Mr. Angel stated that his customer cherishes this old camera as an heirloom and wants to get it into good working order. Facts: This model of American camera is obsolete and new parts are no longer available. If Mr. Angel's customer desires, you will try to obtain these parts on special order; however, there will be a delay from

three to four weeks and the part may be used. The price also may be considerably higher than current material prices on similar parts for newer models. At this moment you have no way of knowing just what the prices may be. Write to Mr. Angel to get his approval of the back order and some kind of understanding about what his customer considers the maximum he would be willing to pay for the parts. You will, of course, try to get them for the very lowest price possible and assure Mr. Angel that such an old-model camera in top working order will indeed be a possession to be proud of. Make action easy.

6. As a correspondent in the customer relations department of Publishers' Bureau, New York City 10001, it is your job to write Mrs. Sydney Cline, Director of Rocky Creek Camp, Great Falls, Montana 59401, that the new printing of the book she ordered—B9551 ($5.98)—has been delayed about one month. From your catalog she ordered three copies of this book, which she says she wants for her camp counselors. She enclosed a check in full payment, including $1.10 shipping charges. As it is still early in the summer (today is June 1), you wonder if she would like you to ship the books when they come off the press. In case she needs books sooner, you do have other titles similar to the one she ordered. Enclose a new brochure from which she can select other books at the same price, any of which you can send so they'll reach her within a week. Ask Mrs. Cline whether she wants you to back-order B9551 and if she'd like you to send any other books to tide her over. In case she wants to reorder instead of or in addition to waiting for B9551, enclose an order form and make clear what you'll do about her check.

Substitution Orders

7. From Ms. Verna Jackson, owner of Tip Top Variety Store, Macon, Georgia 31201, you (Acme Closet Accessories, Inc., wholesaler, in Hartford, Connecticut 06101) receive an order for:

3 dozen #25C538 12-pocket Todd shoe bags	@ $2.30	$82.80
2 dozen #25P862 16-garment Todd vinyl bags	@ 2.60	62.40

These are to be added to her account. You have today shipped by parcel post the shoe bags, but the particular garment bags she ordered are no longer manufactured by Todd Brothers. This item was discontinued last month. The new (#35P880) garment bag comes in three colors—sea green, sky blue, and pink—of electronically quilted vinyl instead of the clear plastic formerly used. The quilted vinyl wears better and is guaranteed to resist splitting at the seams. The zipper is 48 inches long instead of the former 40 inches and thus makes inserting garments easier. Because this bag was not included in last year's catalog, Mrs. Jackson of course did not know about it.

You are sending her the new spring catalog, just out. The bag in question is pictured on page 5. Its price is $3.20 each, but well worth the 60 cents difference over the clear plastic. A complete assortment of other color-mated closet organizers is also available. Her customers will like, for instance, the matching eight-suit bag and the five-shelf file, both with zipper front, sturdy steel frames, and see-through 1-foot square windows of clear vinyl. Though you're sure Ms. Jackson will be glad to carry the new #35P880 bags—and also the other accessories—you write to ask her approval before shipping the bags. Provide order blanks and any other information she may need.

8. Mr. Maurice Mitch, a senior at Central College in your state, writes to your Richards Men's Clothing Store (in his home town). He sends you the label from the all-weather coat he bought from you over four years ago and states he'd like another one just like it, for it has given him excellent service all this time. He says he couldn't find anything like it in the college town where he is. He ends with:

> Please send me this coat in tan color and just charge it to my account. I'd appreciate your rushing it to me by Saturday the 16th (that's 10 days from today), because I need something new for a special function that day.

Facts: You do still carry this same Ralston brand in the same handsome all-cotton poplin material—in both black and tan. Its sharp good looks, careful tailoring, welted seams, and reasonable price have made it a perennial favorite among college men. However, the style has been changed a little during the past year. Instead of the four exposed buttons, this year's style has a "fly front" that neatly covers a convenient 30-inch zipper. Instead of the former patch pockets, these pockets are set in, with an attractive lower flap. Like the former coat, this one is treated with Scotchgard Brand Fabric Protector to resist water and oily stains. The price, $30, is about $4 more than Mr. Mitch paid four years ago—but all prices have increased and this coat now has additional features. Decide whether you will send this coat before or after you get Mr. Mitch's approval. His college town is 400 miles from you; shipping time is normally two days.

9. You are sales manager of National Confectionery Supplies. Your assistant has just laid the following draft of a bad-news message which needs your signature before it is sent to Martina Roget, Roget Candy Company, Bedford, Indiana:

> Thank you for your special delivery letter of January 10 ordering a rush shipment of another supply of our Exel Cherry Syrup.
>
> May we suggest Item 12-B on page 10 of our catalog? This is in stock now and ready to be shipped to you immediately. Item 12 "Jumbo Ann," which you inquired about has been completely sold out and we will be unable to fill any more orders for this particular item until early February, about the 8th. The two syrups, 12-B and 12, are similar except that the former has a heavier syrup. We have found that many of our customers prefer the heavier syrup since, by dilution, they have been able to supplement their other syrups without appreciably altering the original. As you will note in the catalog, the price of item 12-B is 10 cents a case higher than the cherry syrup which was the subject of your inquiry.
>
> We believe you would be completely satisfied with the substitution and shall await further instructions from you.

Today is already January 12. This letter overlooks the fact that Miss Roget stated in her "rush order" letter that she needs the syrup by January 16 latest, because the factory has exhausted its supply and must fill large candy orders from stores before the Valentine Day rush. Shipment time between your warehouse and Bedford is two days minimum. Thus there is insufficient time for an exchange of information by even special delivery. You need to get your message to her faster. If you can get Roget's reply of approval by January 13 (tomorrow), you will ship 12-B in time to reach her by the 16th. Now try your skill in expressing the above letter in these timesaving ways:

   a. A 15-word telegram. (See Footnote 19, page 136 for word-cutting sugges-
       tions. Remember also the 7 C's.)
   b. A 100-word Mailgram. (See pages 134–136.)

Declining Favors, Invitations, and Miscellaneous Requests

1. Assume you receive the following letter from Mrs. Harry Gaylord, chairperson of
    the local United Way Campaign for this year:

    ```
    Dear Mr. (or Ms.) (your name)

    As you know, our city conducts a United Way Fund Drive
    annually.  Many people volunteer their help to coordinate
    the campaign.  Will you be willing to serve as a captain
    this year?

    Captains are responsible for a particular geographic area.
    Yours would be a 10-block area bounded by _____ Street on
    the west, _____ Street on the east, _____ Street on the
    north, and _____ Street on the south.  You would be respon-
    sible for selecting workers in each block, who in turn will
    canvass each house in their particular block.

    Needless to say, your effort will be for a most worthy
    cause.  Will you drop me a line . . . soon, saying you'll
    accept?
    ```

    Unfortunately you must decline the request. Since the campaign is kicked off in
    October and you will be out of the state on vacation (or company business) that
    month, you won't be around to do your duty. Write a considerate reply.

2. Mr. John Field, 425 Ninth Street, North Platte, Nebraska 69101, writes to you—
    loan officer of the Second Federal Loan Company, Lincoln, Nebraska 68501—
    requesting a favor. He would like you to let him change the due date of his loan
    payments from the 1st of each month to the 10th, but you have to refuse his
    request. Mr. Field borrowed from your company on a Government Guaranteed
    Loan and signed a Deed of Trust Note. The due date on such mortgage loans is
    determined by the date the mortgage is signed. It is written into the mortgage
    contract that his payments must be received within 15 days of his due date,
    which is the 1st of each month. His remittance must arrive by the 15th of that
    month to avoid a late charge. It is possible, of course, for him to use the payment
    date of the 10th of the month, but he would have to prepay one month in ad-
    vance. You are unable to change due dates on Government Guaranteed Loans.
    Write the appropriate reply to Mr. Field.

3. As chief clerk of the traffic department of the Washington State Ferries, you have
    to answer a request you received two days ago from Miss Sally Harada, Star
    Route 3, Box 95C, Bremerton, Washington 98307. She asks if you would please
    make a special search for a pair of manicure scissors she lost on the ferry from
    Bremerton to Seattle, February 8. They were a gift from her boyfriend who is
    now in the Navy 3,000 miles away, and she will be heartsick until they are found.
    She was sitting by a window seat in about the middle of the ferry on the right-
    hand side and she thinks these scissors dropped either on the floor or into a crack
    along the wall. As she doesn't mention the name of the ferry nor the exact time
    of her trip—and as you have four ferries on this route—you had to search on all

four ferries. So far no scissors have been found. But you'll keep this a matter of permanent record and if the item is found or turned in, you will notify her immediately. Write the bad news to Miss Harada; send copies of your letter to: Information Booth, Colman Ferry Terminal; Dock Superintendent, Colman Ferry Terminal; and Agent, Bremerton—and indicate these copies on your letter to Miss Harada.

4. You are manager of the special service department of National Photographic News Service, 952 E. 45 Street, New York City 10017. Today you must refuse a request from Mr. George McVey, business manager of *The Engineer*, a magazine by and for college engineering students. (Address: 542 McKinley Building, University of Illinois, Urbana, Illinois 61801.) He asks if you would send him from time to time any news pictures which are related to the engineering field. Because his magazine has an extremely low financial budget, he asks if you will please allow the magazine substantial discounts on pictures. You can't allow any discounts to anyone. Your standard charge is $8, from which you are unable to deviate. Your news service has extremely high costs of production, as your staff covers a wide area both in types of pictures and in geographic location. If the $8 rate (for each picture) meets his budget, you suggest that he send you a list of specific subjects in which he is interested. This list will be turned over to your researchers who then will submit for his consideration all photos received which are in line with his requirements for editorial reproduction in his magazine. Pictures are sent on approval and he will be charged only for those he accepts from each shipment. All rejected photos must be returned. Write a goodwill-building letter, showing that you are interested in being of service to his magazine.

Bad-News Announcements

1. Your company cafeteria, built 16 years ago to serve about 1,000 employees, is definitely too small for your 1,900 employees. As a remedial step you (vice president for food services and finance), together with the board of directors, have decided upon a temporary solution. You will close the directors' lounge as a lounge facility—starting September 5, 197_—and will no longer serve just officers and guests there. The plan is to convert the directors' lounge—which is a table service dining room of very limited capacity and use—to an employee vending-machine food service room, supplemented by short-order counter service during peak demand hours. Present patrons of the directors' lounge are mainly a few officers and a few guests; the average patronage daily has been less than 30 during the three hours a day the present table service is open. Economically this is a marginal operation that cannot be justified. This lounge is conveniently located so that it can easily be used by your swing shift during evening hours without keeping the rest of the building open.

   This planned change will of course greatly alleviate the pressing demands for additional food service facilities for employees. But the table service will be missed by the few who enjoyed it before. To them this announcement will be bad news. Word your announcement so that every loyal officer will accept your decision with understanding, and even approval. The new plan should help decrease employee lunch-hour tardiness and improve morale. The officers still have the officers' dining room on the twelfth floor. To partially offset the loss of table service from the directors' room, this officers' dining room now has additional private seating space. The recent enclosure of the south porch has been equipped with comfortable lounge facilities in the latest decor and a modern sliding partition is usable for those officers who want a separate space for private conferences. Write your memo to all management members.

2. For many years your company has been sending free copies of a glossy magazine *Improving Your Correspondence* to anyone who requested to be on your mailing list. Seldom do you hear from your readers. The cost of this little publication is about $2 each. In an effort to try to pare unnecessary expenses, your firm's directors have suggested that the mailing list be revised to include only those persons and firms that still read and appreciate the publication. They realize that after a passage of years those who originally requested to be on the mailing list may no longer be reading the magazine. Write a pleasant, positive-sounding, processed message that will offend no one, even though it is basically bad news. Your goal is to find out out which readers wish to keep the magazine coming. They'll help you keep your mailing list up to date by taking a certain action that you request. Can you word your announcement in such a way that the readers will be dropped from your mailing list if you don't hear from them?

3. Announce to your employees in building B that all electricity will be turned off between 10 and 11 a.m. next Thursday morning, June 10. They will have to plan their work in such a way that they can get along without using any electric machines that hour; in fact they won't have any electric lighting either. However, as these are sunny days, lack of electricity for lighting should not be too much of a problem. Everyone will be responsible for getting out the amount of necessary work that day, and the electricity shutoff will not be an excuse for working overtime in the afternoon, for no extra pay will be allowed. The electricity shutoff is necessary while workers hook up a major power cable between building B and the highway. New fluorescent lighting will be installed within the next month. In organizing your memo, consider whether you should use the direct or indirect plan—and have reasons to defend your decision.

4. You are president of the Exchange Building Garage, Inc. Your company manages a 400-car garage used by business executives who occupy the Exchange Building. Because of steadily increasing operating costs (mainly wages) you have found it necessary to increase the monthly parking rates to $40 a month (instead of the former $35), plus the state sales tax. This increase will become effective January 1, 197_.
    For the past two years you have been absorbing the increased operating expenses, but cannot continue to do so any longer. After several conversations with Mr. J. L. Dorff, vice-president of Commercial Properties, Inc., and with Exchange Building owners who lease to the business firms in the building and from whom you lease your garage facilities, you received permission for the rate increase. Now that you have decided on the rate and date, you will write two messages:
    a. A letter to Mr. Dorff, telling him your final decision regarding the monthly rate and the effective date. Inform him that you will notify all your parking customers before a certain date. You might restate to him briefly the reason for this increase, refer to your previous conversations, and show appreciation for his understanding. Will you organize this message by the direct or indirect plan? Why?
    b. A letter to all customers who have been renting monthly parking space from your garage. This increase comes to them as a bad-news surprise. Give them whatever details you think they will appreciate having. Will you organize the same way as for message a? Why or why not?

CAPSULE CHECKLISTS FOR

I
Bad News

General plan (A) (indirect)	*Exception (B)† (direct)*
1. BUFFER 　a. Agreement 　b. Appreciation 　c. Assurance 　d. Compliment 　e. Cooperation 　f. Good news 　g. Neutral courtesy 　h. Resale 　i. Sympathy 　j. Understanding	1. Main idea 　a. Bad-news decision, some- 　　times with a brief buffer 　　and/or reason
2. EXPLANATION 　a. Necessary details—general to 　　specific 　b. Pertinent, tactful favorable 　　then unfavorable facts 　c. RB[4] reasons 　d. Emphasis on desired goal	2. Explanation 　Same as I, A, 2, usually a and d
3. DECISION—implied or 　expressed—WITH 　RESALE AND/OR CON- 　STRUCTIVE SUGGESTIONS 　a. Imbedded statement of bad 　　news—clear, tactful, positive, 　　(what CAN do), concise; often 　　tied to b (suggestion) 　b. Helpful counterproposal, 　　plans, alternates 　c. Resale 　d. Sales promotion	3. Decision omitted (already in 　I, B, 1) 　Resale and suggestions often un- 　necessary and omitted; some- 　times same as I, A, 3, b
4. POSITIVE, FRIENDLY 　APPROPRIATE CLOSE 　a. Appreciation 　b. Invitation to future action 　c. CSAD[1] 　d. EA and motivation[2] 　e. DA[3] 　f. Willingness to help further 　g. RB[4] 　h. Good wishes 　i. Courtesy	4. Positive, friendly appropriate 　close 　Sometimes same as I, A, 4, a–i

[1] CSAD = clear statement of action desired
[2] EA = easy action
[3] DA = dated action, if desirable
[4] RB = reader benefit

See also pages 39 and 80, discussing
complete action requests and the
five W's

BAD-NEWS MESSAGES*

II
Answering Inquiries When the Information Is Unfavorable

Sales-related (C)	*Nonsales Inquiries (D)*

1. Buffer
  a. Appreciation
  b. Assurance
  c. Resale
  d. Understanding
	1. Buffer
	Same as II, C, 1, a–d, for non-sales inquiries except unfavorable recommendations; for the latter:
	  a. Inclusion (or omission) of applicant's name, relationship to you
	  b. Reason for writing

2. Explanation
  a. Answers to all questions
  b. Pertinent facts and details
  c. RB^4 reasons for company policy
	2. Explanation
	  a. Answers to all questions
	  b. Pertinent facts (favorable and unfavorable)—record, duties, habits
	  c. Caution on legal aspects
	  d. Establishment of confidential nature

3. Decision—with resale and/or suggestions
  a. Same as I, A, 3, a
  b. Ideas for getting needed help
  c. Possible future changes
  d. Resale on firm, products, services if appropriate
	3. Decision—with constructive suggestions
	  a. Frank, honest statement on nonendorsement of candidate
	  b. Possibility of intervening changes since you last saw applicant

4. Positive, friendly close
  a. Good wishes
  b. Appreciation
  c. CSAD[1]
  d. Willingness to help further
	4. Positive, friendly close
	  a. Ray of hope for improvement
	  b. Willingness to help further
	  c. Good wishes

*All lists include possible content. For any one message, choose only pertinent and appropriate items.
†For uses of direct plan, see page 246.

CAPSULE CHECKLISTS FOR

III	*IV*
Refusing Adjustments on Claims and Complaints	*Declining Requests for Favors and Invitations*

1. Buffer
  a. Agreement on something
  b. Appreciation
  c. Assurance
  d. Cooperation
  e. Neutral courtesy
  f. Understanding
  g. If granting part of a claim is good news, opening is on the portion granted
	1. Buffer
	  a. Appreciation
	  b. Compliment (to reader)
	  c. Assurance
	  d. Agreeable comment

2. Explanation
  a. Tactful, logical statements of reasons
  b. General RB[4] procedure, policy, instructions, guarantee
  c. Resale interwoven
  d. Education on product use
  e. Impersonal specific facts about buyer's mistake
	2. Explanation
	  a. Facts and (sometimes personal) reasons leading to refusal

3. Decision—with resale and/or constructive suggestions
  a. Impersonal, expressed or implied, but clear refusal in positive language, perhaps tied with c (below)
  b. Clear indication if you are returning the product
  c. RB[4], constructive suggestion(s) for using rejected product and/or selecting another
  d. Resale on the product, service, and/or firm
	3. Decision—with resale and/or suggestions
	  a. Clear, tactful decision, implied or stated; emphasis on the positive aspects (desire to help, etc.)
	  b. RB, suggestions—when, how you *can* help
	  c. Alternate sources of help to reader

4. Positive, friendly close
  a. CSAD (tactful suggestion without urging)[1]
  b. EA[2]
  c. Positive forward look
  d. RB and satisfaction[4]
  e. Courtesy
	4. Positive, friendly close
	  a. CSAD[1]
	  b. EA[2]
	  c. DA[2]
	  d. Good wishes
	  e. RB[4]
	  f. Courtesy

[1] CSAD = clear statement of action desired
[2] EA = easy action
[3] DA = dated action
[4] RB = reader benefit

BAD-NEWS MESSAGES (Continued)

V
Refusing Credit

Retail Credit (E)	*Mercantile Credit (F)*
1. Buffer a. Agreeable comment b. Appreciation c. Assurance d. Brief resale on product and/ or firm e. Incidental reference to the order, if any	1. Buffer a. Same as V, E, 1, a–e
2. Explanation Choice of: a. No reasons b. "Insufficient-information" reason c. List of all usual reasons d. Specific reason(s): same as I, A, 2	2. Explanation a. Specific reasons b. Favorable, then unfavorable facts c. Emphasis on desired goal
3. Decision—with RB[4] counterproposal and suggestion(s) a. Same as I, A, 3, a b. Suggestions: Conference Other lenders Future review Other credit plans available Lay-away Cash or c.o.d. buying	3. Decision—with RB[4] counterproposal and suggestion(s) a. Same as I, A, 3, a b. Suggestions: Inventory reduction Sales or capital increase Local financing Cash or c.o.d. buying; smaller, frequent orders Help of sales representative Future review
4. Positive, friendly close a. Invitation regarding a suggestion; CSAD[1] b. Forward look c. Resale d. RB[4] and EA[2] e. Courtesy	4. Positive, friendly close Same as V, E, 4, a–e

CAPSULE CHECKLISTS FOR

VI

Acknowledging Orders You

Incomplete or Vague (G)	*Back Orders (H)*

1. Good news, if any, and buffer
  a. Shipment details on items you're sending, if any
  b. Buffer: short resale on vague item(s)
  c. Brief order acknowledgment (date, item)
  d. Appreciation
  e. Welcome, if new customer
	1. Good news, if any, and buffer
	  a. Same as VI, G, 1, a
	  b. Buffer: specific resale on ordered depleted item; no mention of depletion
	  c. Same as VI, G, 1c–e

2. Explanation
  a. RB^4 reason for requesting missing information
  b. Facts about choices available (sizes, colors, models)
  c. Descriptive enclosures
	2. Explanation
	  a. Approximate date goods expected to reach buyer
	  b. Reason unavailable now $(RB?)^4$
	  c. Resale

3. Decision—with resale and/or suggestions
  a. See G, 2, a above—implied decision
  b. Perhaps brief resale on the item(s) in general
	3. Decision—with resale and/or constructive suggestions
	  a. See H, 2, a above—implied decision
	  b. Possibly mild sales promotion on allied item(s) to be shipped with back-ordered item
	  c. Perhaps brief resale on back-ordered item

4. Positive, friendly close
  a. $CSAD^1$
  b. EA^2
  c. DA^3
  d. RB (prompt delivery?)^4
  e. Courtesy
	4. Positive, friendly close
	  a. If shipment in reasonable time: no action; assumption that back-order is OK
	  b. If longer:
	    $CSAD^1$
	    EA^2, DA^3
	  c. RB^4

^{1}CSAD = clear statement of action desired
^{2}EA = easy action
^{3}DA = dated action
^{4}RB = reader benefit
*S = substitute; O = ordered item

BAD-NEWS MESSAGES (Continued)

VI

Can't Fill Now or at All

Substitutions (J)	*Diverted or Rejected (K)*

1. Good news, if any, and buffer
  a. Same as VI, G, 1, a
  b. Buffer: broad resale embodies both S and O*; omits points of difference
  c. Same as VI, G, 1 c–d
	1. Buffer
	  a. Resale only if your products or services are to be bought elsewhere
	  b. Brief order acknowledgment
	  c. Appreciation

2. Explanation
  a. One or two merits of S before revealing unavailability of O
  b. Sales point on why we carry O exclusively
	2. Explanation
	  a. One or two RB's[4] for your sales policy: (selections, deliveries, shipping costs, extra services)
	  b. Any other pertinent facts

3. Decision—with resale and suggestions
  a. Unavailability of O—in positive terms (exclusively stock S)
  b. Passive statement on where O may be bought
  c. Price and quality justification of S, with RB[4]
  d. Sales promotion
	3. Decision—with resale and suggestions
	  a. Positive statement of your policy, to clarify what you can't and can do
	  b. Payment return, if any
	  c. Justification of price difference at local dealer
	  d. Help on where to get what reader wants

4. Positive, friendly close
  a. If substitute already shipped: assurance of money-back "shipment on approval"; RB[4]
  b. If substitute not yet shipped: CSAD[1] EA[2], DA[3] RB[4]
	4. Positive, friendly close
	  a. Resale
	  b. CSAD[1]
	  c. Future service
	  d. RB[4]

CAPSULE CHECKLISTS FOR

VII *Turning Down Job or* *Contract Offers*	*VIII* *Announcing Bad News about* *Prices and/or Services*

1. Main idea or buffer
  a. If routine matter be-
    tween businesses,
    maybe I, B, 1
  b. Otherwise, I, A, 1
    buffer:
    (1) Appreciation
    (2) Agreeable comment
    (3) Compliment
	1. Main idea or buffer
	  a. If routine (or reader
	    not emotionally in-
	    volved), I, B, 1
	  b. Otherwise, I, A, 1
	    buffer:
	    (1) Agreeable com-
	      ment
	    (2) Neutral courtesy
	    (3) Brief resale

2. Explanation
  a. Reasons leading to turn-
    down (already full
    schedule in writer's
    firm; usual requirements
    or qualities sought, with
    or without revealing
    reader's specific lack)
	2. Explanation
	  a. RB[4] reasons and analy-
	    sis of increasing costs,
	    etc.

3. Decision—with resale and
  suggestions
  a. Clear, tactful decision,
    implied or stated—em-
    phasis on positive
    aspects—(what your
    firm *is* doing about such
    work, etc.)
  b. Invitation for possible
    future reapplication
    and review
  c. "Filing" for future
  d. Alternatives
	3. Decision—with resale and
	  suggestions
	  a. Effective date of new
	    plan
	  b. Clear statement and
	    itemizing if needed
	  c. Enclosures or examples
	    if helpful
	  d. Resale on your firm's
	    products, services,
	    prices

4. Positive, friendly close
  a. Good wishes
  b. CSAD[1]
  c. Courtesy
	4. Positive, friendly close
	  a. Forward look
	  b. Resale
	  c. Invitation to action
	  d. CSAD[1]
	  e. EA[2]
	  f. RB[4]
	  g. Courtesy

[1]CSAD = clear statement of action desired
[2]EA = easy action
[3]DA = dated action
[4]RB = reader benefit

BAD-NEWS MESSAGES (Continued)

IX Requiring Minimum Orders and/or Deposits	*X* Penalizing for Nonconformity with Rules or Procedures	*XI* Conveying Other Bad News

1. Main idea or buffer
  a. If routine (or reader not emotionally involved), I, B, 1
  b. Otherwise, I, A, 1 buffer:
    (1) Agreeable comment
    (2) Neutral courtesy
    (3) Compliment on past
    (4) Hint of urgency or need for change
	1. Main idea or buffer
	  a. Same as IX, 1, a
	  b. Same as IX, 1, b
		1. Main idea or buffer
		  a. Same as IX, 1, a
		  b. Same as IX, 1, b

2. Explanation
  a. Tactful review of reader's record—favorable to unfavorable
  b. Emphasis on desired goal and helpfulness
	2. Explanation
	  a. Details about the requirements
	  b. Reasons leading to the penalty
		2. Explanation
		  a. Details on what is wrong

3. Decision—with resale and suggestions
  a. Clear tactful statement of what will happen unless reader meets requirements
  b. Suggestions (improved advertising or merchandising; assistance of sales representative
  c. Enclosures; aids
  d. Resale
	3. Decision—with resale and suggestions
	  a. Same as IX, 3, a
	  b. Suggestions for eliminating penalty in future
	  c. Forms and deadlines
		3. Decision—with suggestions
		  a. What needs to be done
		  b. How to do it

4. Positive, friendly close
  a. Same as VIII, 4
	4. Positive, friendly close
	  a. CSAD[1]
	  b. EA[2]
	  c. DA[3]
	  d. RB[4]
	  e. Assurance
	  f. Good wishes
	  g. Courtesy
		4. Positive, friendly close
		  a. CSAD[1]
		  b. EA[2]
		  c. Goodwill
		  d. Courtesy

10 Persuasive Requests

Besides situations in which mere *asking* is sufficient (routine direct requests), you will face situations in which you need to *persuade.* The favor or action you ask—the reader's time, money, support, or agreement—is such that you anticipate some objection. To persuade your reader to take the requested action, you develop rational and/or emotional appeals. Analysis of and consideration[1] for your reader's circumstances, needs, and emotions are especially important for effective persuasion.

You can use the persuasive-request plan for the following kinds of messages:

Requests for favors that—
    Require time, knowledge, or effort
    Ask donations of money or other valuables
    Urge cooperation on goals and projects

Other Nonroutine requests:
    Adjustment
    Credit
    Changes in policy or performance

Unsolicited Sales letters to—
    Make a direct sale
    Serve as stimulus to future sales
    Bring back lost customers
    Apply for a job

Collections (discussion and late stages)

This chapter discusses the persuasive-request plan and how you can adapt it to various requests for favors, other nonroutine requests, and sales. Job applications are covered separately in Chapter 11 and collections in Chapter 13.

Organizational Plan

The persuasive request, like the bad-news letter, uses the indirect approach. You assume that if your request were stated directly at the beginning, it would be bad news to your reader, who would then react unfavorably. Thus, before you mention the specific request, you will have to prepare the reader for it and, when possible, present facts to indicate that your proposal is beneficial or useful. Remember, your reader is not expecting your message, and you should attract his or her attention and arouse interest *before* revealing what you'd like done.

The basic structure for persuasive letters usually has four parts, commonly known as the AIDA formula for sales presentation:

A—Attract the reader's favorable *attention.*
I—Arouse the reader's *interest.*
D—Create *desire* and convince the reader.
A—Make clear the *action* the reader needs to take.

---

[1] For a review of general ways to show consideration, see pages 87–92.

Although attention, interest, and desire are listed here as distinct steps, they are usually combined or blended so smoothly in the well-written persuasive message that it is difficult—and unnecessary!—to separate them. Also, the parts do not always occur in the sequence given here; for example, it is possible to omit or deemphasize those points that have been covered in earlier letters, advertising, or personal contacts with the prospect. You-attitude content and reader benefits are most important. What you call the parts and whether you have three or four is unimportant. In fact, the persuasive-request plan is sometimes called the four P's—promise, picture, prove, and push— or discussed under *three* parts—star, chain, and hook. In the AIDA persuasive-request *general* outline below, the other names for the parts are indicated in parentheses.

1. Attention *(promise; star)*
Attract favorable attention with a reader-interest or a reader-benefit theme. Begin with a relevant statement or a challenging question that entices the recipients to read on because they want to know "What's in this letter for me?" Highlight a point that is close to the reader's interests or needs, instead of talking about yourself or your organization. Avoid exaggeration, foolish questions (Do you want a steady income?), and obvious statements (Money helps you pay your bills).

Because many people throw away envelopes that look like part of bulk mailings, even the envelope plays an important part in getting favorable attention. Among the devices used with varying degrees of success on envelopes are color, handwritten addresses, contest announcements, questions, and a few enticing words from the message printed on the envelope. Some firms conceal their identity on envelopes, omitting their name and address. However, because many people resent such tactics, this practice has questionable value.

The letterhead can also be an effective, important attention getter. For favor and sales letters that are sent to numerous readers, letterheads can and do deviate from the usual simplicity suggested for other business letterheads. Some contain different pictures and colors to tie in with each favor or sales message. (Advertising agencies and stationery design specialists can help you with these needs. The discussion in this text concentrates on the written message itself.)

2. Interest *(picture; chain)*
Build upon the theme started in the attention-getting opening. Begin to tell what your project, product, or service is and what it will do for the reader. Describe it clearly and specifically in two ways (not necessarily in this order):

    a. Its physical description—important features, construction, appearance, performance, beauty, functions (any or all of which may be omitted for a long-established subject well known to the reader).
    b. Its value or benefits to the reader (or others in whom the reader is interested). (Some writers call this material "psychological description.")

Of the various features and uses that the project, product, or service has, emphasize the central selling point—that point you think is most likely to make the strongest appeal to the prospect. For instance, will your proposal bring comfort? entertainment? health? recognition? security? Show the reader how your proposal gives one or more benefits like the following:

Appreciation (by others)	Pleasure
Approval (by others)	Popularity
Beauty or attractiveness	Position of authority
Cleanliness	Prestige
Comfort	Pride
Convenience	Profits
Cooperation	Protection for family, business,
Customer satisfaction	self, or others
Distinctiveness	Provision for the future
Efficiency	Recognition
Enjoyment	Reduced work
Entertainment	Respect
Extra earnings	Safety and security
Fair treatment	Satisfaction of helping others
Friendships	Savings
Good reputation	Self-preservation
Health	Solution to a problem
Improvement	Success
Love of home, family, others	Thrift habit
Money and other valuables	Usefulness
Peace of mind	

3. Desire and Conviction *(prove; chain)*

So that your readers will desire to do as you request and be convinced that they (or others in whom they are interested) will benefit from your proposal, you usually present proof. Give evidence that your statements are true. Include needed facts, figures, testimonials, tests, samples, guarantees, and any other proof that your proposal may call for.

A descriptive folder permits you to avoid cluttering your letter with many details. However, if you have an enclosure, mention it only after stating most of your selling points and then motivate your reader to read further details in the folder. Link your reference to the enclosure with a sales point. Don't depend on the enclosure to do your selling.

Emphasize positive aspects, but be honest about stating costs when pertinent; minimize negative aspects, and write from the reader's point of view.

4. Action *(push; hook)*

Clearly state what the reader should do to comply with your request and thus to gain the benefits. Make action easy—by including a reply form, envelope, phone number, office hours, location, and so forth. Induce the reader to act now or within a certain time, and end on a reader-benefit plug, which may tie in with your opening statement.

Persuasive Requests for Favors

As a conscientious business or professional person you probably participate actively in various committees and organizations. And you have numerous opportunities to write (as well as to answer) favor requests that seek the recipient's donation of something— time, knowledge, effort, money, or cooperation. The AIDA plan helps you to ask a favor effectively, as described below.

Getting Attention for Favor Requests

To begin your favor request with something close to your reader's interest or benefit, consider what appeals are likely to be most meaningful to her or him. Try to introduce a direct or indirect benefit that you can develop as a central selling point more fully later in the letter. You want to get the reader's attention *before* stating your request, but you need to use good judgment in introducing benefits. Be careful that your statements don't sound like high pressure or bribes, as in this poor opening for a letter inviting a political candidate to speak: "How much would it be worth to you to influence the views of 2,000 voters?"

Effective openings you can use—with discretion—for various favor requests are: (1) a sincere compliment, (2) one or more rhetorical questions, (3) an assertion with which the reader will agree, (4) a problem that is the basis for the favor request, (5) a statement of what is being done or has been done to solve or lessen a problem, and (6) a frank admission that your message is a request for a favor. Many good letters even combine one or more of these openings, as in some of the following examples.

Sincere-Compliment Openings
Request to speak, without fee, to a local chapter:
Ever since your stimulating speech last year to delegates at KSA national convention in Atlanta, our Tri-City chapter members here have wanted to meet you personally. We believe you could be a profound influence on our future program and growth.

Request to accept an important chairmanship:
Your exceptionally fine work in People-to-People projects, as well as your present Council position, emphasizes that you deserve a place on this year's East Coast conference program of the National Personnel Association.

Question Openings
Request to participate in a six-month research project:
Have you ever had the fun of participating in a market research study? As you know, market research is the study of consumer reactions and attitudes to products. This research is extremely useful to manufacturers in helping them to give you and your family products to better suit your needs.

Request to become a member of a University YWCA:
WHAT'S THE USE?
"What's the use of getting an education?"
    "What's the use of planning ahead?"
        "What's the use of living thoughtfully?"
            "WHAT'S THE USE OF ANYTHING?"

Agreeable-Comment or Assertion Openings
To speak to students majoring in advertising:
Advertising is the spark plug of any business and a challenge to the creative thinker. Yet what advice can you give to the many students who cannot decide what area of advertising to enter?

To join a campaign committee for preservation of a historic landmark:
Pike Place Market holds colorful memories of the early days in Seattle. It's a gentle reminder of an era that will soon be almost forgotten—unless responsible citizens like you show their concern.

To help in getting community support:
If there is one topic in which you and I share a special interest, it is the education of our children. The success of our school levy will determine the quality of education received by Bellevue students.

Basic-Problem Openings (sometimes introduced as stories and suspense)
To sign a pledge and contribute to a reward fund:
The bombing of the Center Building is an act of violence which has outraged many members of this community. Its significance lies only in part in the $300,000 of physical damage and in the gross inconvenience created during reconstruction.

   Certainly of greater significance for all is the fact that this incident is a blatant violation of the principle of common decency and of respect for the orderly and humane life of this city.

To contribute to a lab fund:
DIAGNOSTIC LABORATORY IN DANGER!
INDUSTRY STANDS TO LOSE $60,000!
Contributions for the new diagnostic lab in (town name) have stopped coming in. Unless we can immediately raise $11,000, we will lose the $60,000 appropriated by the last legislature on the condition we in the industry match it with $35,000. Only $24,000 of the necessary $35,000 has, so far, been pledged.

"What Has Been Done about a Problem" Openings
To send a gift to the Fund for the Blind:
Thousands of blind Americans wait eagerly each month for their copies of the Braille or Talking Book edition of *The Reader's Digest*. It is the only magazine of its kind they may receive in Braille or Talking Book form (long-playing records) which is exactly like the ink-print edition read by their sighted friends. This means something very special to them.

   With the help of friends like yourself, we can supply these . . .

To hire the jobless through the Millionair Club:
During the past year homeless and needy men, women, and children enjoyed 123,000 warm nourishing meals at Millionair Club; 3,088 adults and children received clothing; men and women received 9,321 jobs, 406 units of blood transfusion, emergency hospital treatment, and many other kindnesses.

"Frank Admission of Favor" Opening
(Disarming frankness encourages some readers to discover for themselves how they will benefit from complying. Though these frank openings are like those used in direct requests, the remaining paragraphs of persuasive letters contain meaningful appeals.)
To accept an honorary state appointment:
The state needs your help!
   As a prominent respected psychiatrist, you have been recommended to serve on the State Board of three to conduct oral Civil Service examinations of applicants for psychiatric work in State Rehabilitation Centers.

To be moderator at a national convention:

To get and keep our 197_ NRMA convention program on the beam, we shall need three top-grade people to serve as moderators. You can no doubt guess why I am making this appeal to you.

Yesterday, while our national president, Henry Gibson, visited me—I suspect mainly to see what I was doing about providing a good program—I said, "We need new faces to lead the show in New York City next December. How about Joan Murdock from ABC Company? He replied that he knew you and that we couldn't find a better NRMA dependable.

To fill out and return a questionnaire:

WILL YOU HELP DMAA?
—AND HELP YOURSELF, TOO?

I'd like to ask a favor of you. It concerns the gathering of important facts and information regarding postal rates. Here, in a nutshell, is the story:

Arousing Interest and Creating Desire to Do the Favor

Once you have decided on an opening that sets the theme and encourages the recipient to read on, you can continue to build on your idea. To get both the reader's interest and desire, you need to (1) include all necessary description—physical characteristics and value of the project, (2) present facts and figures through which the reader can determine direct or indirect benefits he or she may derive, and (3) handle negatives positively. This material comprises the greater portion of your persuasive request.

Physical Characteristics and Value of Project. If your reader is not a member of your organization or familiar with it, you need to give brief, but adequate information about its purpose, scope, and members. But be sure not to *begin* your letter by talking about yourself and your organization, especially if the reader is an outsider! Place this material after a you-attitude opening.

In addition, you need to describe to all readers the problem or project to which the favor relates and to establish its values. For instance, if you are asking for funds to send underprivileged children to summer camp, you might describe (perhaps with the use of a folder) the physical camp facilities, size and number of buildings, surroundings, recreation areas, and number of children and counselors. Then you show the value of these facilities to the children—character-building, friendships, appreciation of nature, fun, and so forth. Sometimes you can effectively get readers to visualize themselves in the shoes of those their funds can help and in this way arouse their interest in your project.

Direct and Indirect Reader Benefits. Usually near the middle of your letter you explain how the reader is to take part in the project. So that readers will desire to do as you ask, be sure to include all necessary facts and figures to convince them that their contribution will be enjoyable, easy, important, and of benefit to them (as much as is true and possible). Try to show direct and/or indirect benefits.

Direct benefits to a person who does a favor vary with the type of favor. For example, if a person is to speak (without a fee and perhaps even without a traveling expense allowance) at a widely publicized convention, he or she may gain direct benefit from the favorable publicity as well as from personal contacts with the audience. If other prominent speakers are on the same program, say so; for this fact is an additional compliment to your reader. Both the speaker and his or her employer (who perhaps pays traveling expenses) can gain directly from recognition, prestige, and popularity—plus increased future sales of products or services. However, it is better not to actually state these benefits, but rather to let the reader determine them from the facts. Be sure to tell the reader when he or she is to speak, where (date, day, hour), on what topic (or if the speaker is to choose it), for how long, to whom, and to how many people.

Direct benefit may also come to the company that donates merchandise to, for instance, a charity or well-attended event. The people who see the company's name on the donated product will feel goodwill toward the donor and tend to buy its products when they need them. Again, it is better not to state such benefits specifically, but to let your readers determine them themselves. Stating obvious benefits bluntly may make the favor request sound like a bribe.

If your reader is to become a member of your club or to take part in a project, describe that club or project and tell how it will (directly) benefit the reader. Try to keep the reader in each paragraph and write from the reader's viewpoint.

In some favor requests the direct benefit offered may be a premium or gift or other small reward or token of appreciation. Those who participate in a questionnaire survey may gain because the results will ultimately lead to improvements that make their work easier or help them to save money.

Indirect benefits may come to the participant who helps the members of a group he or she is interested in or a member of. For instance, you can use indirect-benefit appeals to get a sales manager to speak (without a fee) to your school's marketing club or an auditor to talk to an accounting club. In each case, your reader's contribution may benefit him or her or the profession at least indirectly, because he or she helps a group of listeners whose interests are in a field of work he or she is interested in. Similarly, when you want to urge a busy person to accept a time-consuming office without pay, you can appeal to a sense of loyalty to the organization and the good his or her leadership can provide. Such indirect reader benefits are often persuaders.

In still other cases you can get a reader's cooperation by appealing on the basis of altruism—selfless devotion to the welfare of other human beings (or even animals). When persons contribute to a charity drive, for instance, they benefit by knowing they have helped bring happiness and hope to less fortunate people.

Though there may be times when you honestly cannot see or show reader benefits, try always to present every favor request from the reader's point of view.

Positive Handling of Negatives. With the persuasive-request plan you must not only use appeals and stress reader benefits, but you need to ask yourself, "To what will my reader probably object?" Then stress the positive aspects—what *can* be done—to minimize the negatives, as in the following examples:

Probable Objection	*Possible Points to Stress*
1. Allowance for traveling expenses and/or speaker's fee is inadequate	a. Will you gladly meet her at the airport or any other station? b. Will she be guest of honor at a banquet? Maybe her spouse too? c. Will a car be available for her use in your city? d. Is her part on the program so important that her employer will want to take care of her expenses? e. Are other famous functions, exhibits, or attractions available in your city? f. Can you arrange overnight accommodations? g. If she lives in the same city, will someone pick her up at home or office? h. If she'll drive her car, how about parking and easy access to the place where she'll be speaking?
2. Expected pledge or contribution is too large	a. Will you accept contributions in small installments? b. May he pledge now and pay after a future date? c. Can you compare the donation to amounts spent on luxuries? d. Can you show the great relief his gift will bring to those who need it?
3. Requested questionnaire looks long	a. Are the questions easy to answer? Why? b. Is taking part in the survey fun because . . . ? c. Can the entire questionnaire be finished within x minutes? d. Will the ultimate gain or reward be an incentive?

Asking for Action

Having included necessary facts, benefits, and positive aspects, you can confidently ask for the reader's acceptance. Make action clear, easy, and dated if necessary. If you need the reply by a certain date, tie this request in with reader benefit whenever possible—prominent billing on the program, adequate time for publicity, and so forth. Omit such negative statements as "*If* you can donate anything, please . . . ." Better say, "To make your contribution, just return . . . ." Your last sentence often can tie in with an appeal or statement featured in the opening paragraph, as a last reader-benefit plug.

Asking Favors That Require Time, Knowledge, or Effort

By using the persuasive-request AIDA plan, you can urge a busy person to be speaker at an important banquet or conference for little or no pay—and even partly or entirely at his or her own (or employer's) expense. You can encourage people to accept time-consuming chairmanships or to serve without pay on long-term committees and boards. You can obtain answers to research questionnaires which require more than routine effort by the recipient. You can give employees or club members a pep talk about attending certain functions; and you can increase membership in a business, professional, social, or religious organization. All these favors require time, knowledge, and/or effort, as the next two examples illustrate.

Request for a Speaker. In letter 1, the president of an aircraft owners and pilots association invites an author (who is a member of the same nonprofit association in another city 500 miles away) to be principal speaker. The letter includes all needed details about date, time, place, audience, length and topic of talk. The underlying appeal or central selling point is the reader's ability to help in a serious crisis those of similar interests. Notice how paragraph 3 emphasizes the positive aspects and also makes clear that the group *can* pay transportation expenses (but is not offering a speaker's fee). If you are writing for a nonprofit organization to someone not a member, you should explain the club's purpose and nonprofit nature before you state what you *will* pay for the speaker. (For some very large functions—with an attendance of several hundred persons—even a nonprofit organization might assess each member a small amount to cover both a speaker's fee and traveling expenses.)

Letter 1
Inviting a speaker to address a banquet without an honorarium.

Attention, reader-centered; compliment

The article you wrote in the March issue of Flying has been of great interest to us in the Viewmont Chapter of AOPA. We are currently involved in a battle to acquire a surplus Naval Air Station for general aviation use and find your ideas on airport facilities just the approach we need to convince those not familiar with general aviation problems.

Interest; the problem

And the request

Three months ago we learned that the Highpoint Naval Air Station would be surplus in August of this year. It looked at first that general aviation would easily acquire this badly needed airport. But recently much opposition has developed. The area residents simply do not understand why another airport for "small planes" is needed. We have planned a banquet for the leaders of the community to convince them of the genuine need for this facility and would very much like you as our dinner guest and speaker. Your views on the general crisis of airport congestion would be extremely helpful in presenting our case. Will you tell us how you put the new program into effect last year in your city?

Reader benefit

Desire and conviction details

You will enjoy, I'm sure, the dinner and entertainment we have planned. The banquet will be held at the new Century Hotel, Monday, June 20, at 7 p.m.; but the time can be changed if another hour is more convenient for you. You will, of course, be reimbursed for your traveling and overnight hotel expenses; and I personally will see that you are picked up and returned to the airport at your convenience. We expect about 100 persons to attend. After two local speakers present their views, we would like you to speak for twenty to thirty minutes to conclude the arguments with an expert's opinion which will add much strength to our cause.

Dated action

A brief letter from you indicating acceptance will assure the success of this function. Also, please include your preference as to dinner hour. Because the program goes to press in three weeks, will you send your decision by May 20? The members in this area will sincerely appreciate the contribution you can make to our obtaining another urgently needed general aviation airport in this area.

Value of reader's talk

Request for Help in a Survey. Whether you are a student gathering firsthand information for a report, a business executive surveying your employees, or a research consultant working for numerous clients, you will get better cooperation from your readers when you write persuasively.

Letter 2, for example, stresses reader benefit throughout. This letter also illustrates one way you can save money if you have a slim budget and a long mailing list: in place of the personalized inside addresses and salutation, you can use a reader-centered attention-getting statement or question. A letter similar to the one below gained a 79 percent response.

Letter 2
A persuasive, effective request for return of a questionnaire by college teachers.

Attention; reader benefit

Would knowing what other college teachers are doing in their business communication courses help you?

Reader benefit or interest

Perhaps you, like many others, have wondered how the content, emphasis, and assignments of your basic course compare with those in other colleges that offer courses similar to yours in credit hours, size of sections, and prerequisites. Or you may have considered changing your courses and you could use tips on what others are including.

Interest; description of project

To gather this information about this rapidly expanding field of study, we are making a nationwide survey of business communication courses taught in schools holding membership in the American Association of Collegiate Schools of Business (AACSB). This study is planned to get specific details on the subject matter and written assignments in 1974-1975 courses.

Desire; facts and reader benefit

You are the only teacher in your institution receiving this letter and the enclosed form. All names of participants will remain confidential in the report of this study. By completing the questionnaire and returning it, you will be helping expand knowledge about the teaching of this vital subject matter. Also, you'll know how your courses compare with others. You will find the questions easy to answer, we believe, because most of them require only your checkmark.

Dated, easy action; reader benefit

To make sure that your college is included in this study, please mail the form by May 1, in the stamped envelope provided. In appreciation of your cooperation in this study, you will receive a summary of the findings, if you wish,[2] before the information appears in print.

---

[2]The respondent could indicate his or her wish—and also protect anonymity—by returning his or her name and address on an enclosed separate slip.

The benefits offered to the college teachers for mailing the questionnaire enclosed with letter 2 are mainly intangible, yet they are adequate because the readers are expected to have a keen interest in helping to improve their profession. On the other hand, when you ask information from persons who have no built-in interest in your questionnaire, you may—if your budget allows—also have to offer a tangible inducement. For instance, the director of consumer panels for a national market research firm, in a request to "Dear Homemaker," included a tangible gift (tableware), as well as intangible benefits (enjoyment, usefulness, safety, and anonymity). The following two paragraphs from the letter come after three paragraphs that describe this particular product study and how it helps manufacturers "to give you and your family products to better suit your needs":

> All we ask is that you keep a record of your purchases of these items. In addition to the fun you will have being a part of this interesting study, you will receive a place setting of International Silver Company's Rogers Cutlery Stainless Tableware from their "Modern Living" group—for every month of diaries we receive. It will be important, however, that you return every diary for each of the six months so that you can continue on the panel.

> You will never be approached by a sales representative as a result of your participation in this study, nor will the purchase information you send us ever be reported as coming from your family. Your information will be strictly CONFIDENTIAL.

Asking Donation of Money or Other Tangible Valuables

Many people are even more reluctant to part with material goods than they are to donate their time. Thus all you have learned about persuasiveness, appeals, factual presentation, and reader benefits is even more important for requests to donate valuables.

If you want your reader to donate money, describe the problem and tell what is being or has been done, what needs to be done, and what your organization is doing about the problem. After stating meaningful facts, tell what it will cost to do what your organization wants to do—and how the reader can help.

If the donation is for a cause from which the reader benefits directly—as in improved recreation facilities for a club of which he or she is a member—you can choose from appeals such as comfort, enjoyment, friendships, health, love of family. However, if the donation goes to charity, your main appeal is usually altruism. Action paragraphs like the following help the conscientious reader who wonders how much he or she should give:

1. A gift of $4 will buy vitamins for 25 children . . . $6 will provide a cup of milk to 500 children . . . $15 may keep a father and mother alive to care for their own children . . . $100 sends 1,000 pounds of medicines to our hospitals.
2. "What is a thoughtful contribution?" You can best answer this question, BUT we suggest that an amount approximating two hours' pay would be justified in light of. . . .

3. A sacrifice of $3, $5, $10 or more . . . whatever you can spare . . . represents your concern for men like Tommy's daddy. It can help pull a troubled man back to a life of respectability.

In the next two messages, notice how appealingly the boys' home director and the business executive present the problem, tell what has been done and needs to be done about it, and persuade the reader to help.

Letter 3

A persuasive request before Christmas for a donation to charity—unusually senti-mental, but especially appealing to readers who have a generous spirit at Christmas-time. (A colorful letterhead shows two homeless boys in the snow peering forlornly into a bright Christmas-decorated home living room in which a fire is glowing warmly in the fireplace.)

My dear Friend:

Attention: what has been done

HOW MUCH IS A HOMELESS BOY WORTH? Today thousands of proud, productive citizens who live in the cities and towns across the nation were, only a few years ago, homeless, destitute boys. Many are skilled mechanics in the various trades; others are farmers, business and professional men.

The problem

These men came to Boys Town as young boys, of all races and religious creeds. They all had the same qualification--they were homeless. They were sad, sensitive, with many heart-aches because some tragedy had robbed them of their home and parents. Some wandered along the crossroads of the nation, their only home in some empty freight car. Others, who had been in trouble, came to us with snarls on their faces, with eyes that were hard, sullen, and suspicious.

HOW MUCH ARE THEIR LIVES WORTH TODAY--TO THEMSELVES, THEIR WIVES AND CHILDREN, AND TO THE NATION?

What our institution does

Here at Boys Town we continue, year after year, to rebuild the lives of homeless, deserted boys. We give them a good home, good food, and a parent's rightful attention which they have been denied. I talk with them individually, dis-cuss their problems, and help them solve these problems. They are educated in our schools, and are taught a practical trade in our well-equipped trade school, on our farm and dairy. During their spare time they engage in athletics, music, Scouting, and many hobbies. Their mental and moral training, and our self-government system teach them to become stalwart, wholesome citizens.

What needs to be done

My boys need you, and there are many more to come. As Christmas approaches, won't you help me provide for more homeless boys who will come to Boys Town, and who have no other place to go? I am enclosing your 19__ Christmas seals. Most contributions I receive are in $2, $3, and $5 amounts, but any amount you care to send will let me serve as your Santa Claus to my family of almost 1,000 boys.

Action request; altruism appeal

Because they've already had life's share of grief and hard-ships, won't you help them to be happy now?

Reader benefit

God bless you, and may your own Christmas be doubly happy because you have brought happiness to a homeless, helpless boy.

(Complimentary close and signature area)

Reader benefit

Your contribution is an allowable income tax deduction. We employ no solicitors or fund-raising organization; we pay no commissions.

Letter 4 (Memo)

An executive's persuasive request to employees to contribute generously to an annual fund drive.

TO: All Members of the Wigget Staff

FROM: Alberta Jones, President

SUBJECT: An appeal for the UGN Fund

Attention: problem

All of you are aware that this year our community has a larger number of needy, desperate, afflicted people of all ages, creeds, and races.

What is being done

You know also of the fine work that the United Good Neighbors Fund does to provide community services through 82 Good Neighbor agencies. Hundreds of persons volunteer freely of their time and money to make this drive successful each year, with no thought of tangible rewards.

Reader benefit

Your one contribution helps in many ways, and you are spared from being dunned by separate agencies. I would like to make a personal appeal this year that all of us reassess our values of this program and make an honest effort to give just a little bit more. All contributions are voluntary, of

Request

course. Each of us sets the figure our conscience dictates, but I sincerely hope you can find it in your hearts to join me in increasing our donation this year. Our company's goal is $52,900.

Appeal to altruism

We are all most fortunate in not being on the receiving end of this program, and one way to count our blessings is by helping those less fortunate, as described in the enclosed leaflet.

Reader benefit and easy action

The home drive commences after the contributions are collected from business employees (November 2-6). When you contribute your entire amount through your Company solicitors, the sticker you receive, placed in a window at home, tells the story that you have given and you will not be again disturbed. Remember, UGN pledge cards make it possible to make contributions in small monthly or quarterly installments, or if you choose, you may make payments by payroll deductions.

Appeal to pride, altruism

Let's give serious consideration to the amount we contribute this year and try to make it one of which to be proud. Your support will be received with appreciation by the many agencies within UGN.

You can adapt the foregoing suggestions and illustrations to any persuasive request for donations—whether of money or of other valuables such as food, clothing, furniture, films, housing, or parking facilities. Whatever the request, remember to choose appropriate appeals and convince your readers that your project is worthy. Then include sufficient facts so they will want to do as you ask.

Urging Cooperation on Goals and Projects

As a committee chairperson or officer you may from time to time need to get your readers to support various goals and projects that your organization considers important. Letters 5 and 6, sent to members and voters respectively, illustrate how persuasive requests can help move readers to action toward which they would otherwise be indifferent.

Letter 5
A membership chairman appeals for help in boosting membership.

Attention: agreeable comment and question
NPRA MEMBERSHIP JUMPS 100%

Wouldn't you be delighted to see that headline in the NPRA Journal? And you can . . . for it can be done easily . . . without gimmicks or strings or expense to you.

Reader-benefit goal
Increased membership will strengthen our effectiveness and benefit each of us as well as the entire field of public relations. If you—each member—will find us one new NPRA member, our size can double.

Easy-action request
The method is simple and effective. Go over your firm's executive roster, your list of business associates. Think of everyone you know who might be interested in public- and customer-relations. Write the names and addresses on the enclosed card and drop it into the mail.

The follow-up
That's all you need to do! Our secretary, Jim Banks, will take it from there. He will check the names against our current NPRA member and prospect lists and write to those who haven't joined, or been invited before.

Tie-in with opening
Isn't that easy? Find one new member for NPRA . . . and look for that headline soon . . . NPRA MEMBERSHIP JUMPS 100%.

Letter 6
Four citizens (one expert each in engineering, medicine, business leadership, and law) persuade citizens to vote for a bond issue.

Dear Southside resident:

Attention: reader-benefit comment
Each of us has the opportunity on May 19 to leave a legacy for the future when we vote on the Forward Move bond issue—rapid transit. This program will substantially improve the quality of your environment for many years to come.

Interest: reader benefits Rapid transit will reduce traffic congestion and air pollution, both of which are becoming increasingly difficult problems in the Southside area. In addition, it will be of enormous benefit to you as a resident of Southside. To you and the employees in this area rapid transit brings easy access to plants and businesses plus increased mobility from the southside to all parts of the greater (city name) community.

More benefits The proposal was conceived with the environment in mind. In fact, one of the major goals of the May 19 rapid transit election is to win the fight against pollution by creating an attractive alternative to the automobile. One-third of the system will be entirely underground. The cost can be covered adequately by the 1.3 mill tax levy, which amounts

Easy breakdown of costs to about $20 annually per taxpayer on a $20,000 home. This is only $1.67 a month or less than 6 cents a day for each family!

Reader-benefit facts for interest and desire Access to the Southside area will be improved by express bus service to a new bus transfer station at East 65th Street and the Freeway. Service from the east side and north end will be vastly improved. When the electric rail network becomes operative, the Southside District will be served by two stations--25th Avenue SE and East 65th Street, and another in the vicinity of the Southside Hospital. These facilities will be entirely underground. Thus the beauty of Southside will be maintained while convenient access is enormously improved.

Reader-benefit request On the basis of the compelling need and an opportunity to preserve and strengthen your area, we ask you to vote "Yes" with us on May 19.

Other Persuasive Nonroutine Requests

You can also use the persuasive plan effectively when you must convince your reader to grant your request for adjustment or credit or for a change in a policy or performance. This section discusses how the AIDA parts can be adapted to these kinds of requests and then presents illustrative letters.

Adapting the AIDA Plan

For your attention-getting opening you can use any of the suggested six kinds discussed above for favor requests (pages 313 to 315). However, to present a concise logical argument, it is usually best to begin with an assertion. This statement often is a principle—a major premise on which both you and the reader agree or about which you wish to persuade the reader; for example, these two (which can also be considered agreeable-comment openings):

No doubt you expect your authorized dealers to uphold the good name of your products.

I am sure you want your company to have a reputation for fairness and honesty.

You will get the reader's interest and desire when you state all necessary facts and details—interwoven with reader benefits. Include whatever description the reader needs to see that his or her firm is responsible (if this applies) and that your request is factual, logical, and reasonable. Your action request should be a logical conclusion based on the major premise and the clearly stated facts.

Persuasively Requesting an Adjustment

When a product or service from a reputable firm is unsatisfactory but you know that your claim for an adjustment is outside the warranty or otherwise unusual, your message should follow the persuasive-request instead of the direct-request plan. You also need to be persuasive when your request is *not* unusual but the seller disregarded your first direct request.

In letter 1, because of unusual circumstances, the customer persuasively asks for a new camera and certain other expenses—even though the printed guarantee includes a statement that the firm will service the camera but "cannot assume responsibility for loss of film, for other expenses or inconveniences, or for consequential damages occasioned by the equipment." This is an unusually long letter, but the details included are necessary to achieve the goal. The writer did get essentially what he wanted, though in slightly different form—six free rolls of film with processing mailers and an exchange of his camera with one owned by the manager of the local Picturetronics, Inc.

Letter 1
A consumer writes persuasively to a manufacturer's adjustment manager requesting an unusual adjustment.

Attention: assertion of major premise

"Let your Wessman camera preserve those precious moments for you." This appealing advertising slogan, plus your company's good reputation, helped me to choose a Wessman camera for my once-in-a-lifetime trip to South America. Because of unusual circumstances I now find it necessary to appeal to you.

Interest; facts about purchase

Six months ago I purchased my Wessman "Instanshot" camera from a reputable store here. That was two months before my trip so that I would have time to become thoroughly familiar with the camera before traveling in a foreign country. (I was a member of a group representing the Foundation for International Understanding, and our long planned trip was a goodwill tour which I wanted to preserve in good pictures.)

Conviction facts; the problem

It soon became obvious that the electronic eye and the little black bar indicator were not functioning. The reputable dealer from whom I had bought the camera had retired a month later, sold out his business, and closed his store. Your authorized dealer--Picturetronics, Inc.--here in (city name), however, repaired these parts under your company's warranty. But the next time I used the camera the flash attachment did not work, though the batteries were new. Again Picturetronics had the camera for a week's checkup and repair. Finally, two days before my departure on the trip, they called to report that my camera was "now in excellent working order." Little did any of us guess the picture problems ahead.

More on the problem Nevertheless, the camera was again a disappointment only two days later--on my first attempt to take a picture with it before leaving the airport. Twice the flash did not go off and two pictures on my film were thus wasted. Because it was Sunday morning and only a few minutes before plane departure, there was of course no way to have further repairs then.

Reader in writer's shoes; writer's care and trust Perhaps you can imagine how you would feel at this moment. I had depended upon your authorized dealer's word that my camera was in excellent condition! (Incidentally, I always handle a camera with care according to instructions, for I know it is a delicate precision instrument.)

Tie-in with major premise Throughout my trip there were numerous "precious moments" I wanted to preserve with my new Wessman camera. Most of these were on indoor occasions--receptions, dinners, and other functions with people. I can buy postcards of buildings and nature. But no one sells pictures of the precious moments with other human beings who assembled just for our group!

Writer's losses Yet these moments are lost forever because the flash attachment failed numerous times. These failures also resulted in my ample supply of Wessman film being exhausted much too soon. I thus had to purchase additional film plus flashbulbs in foreign stores at much higher prices.

When my developed film was returned I found that 72 negatives were total blanks. In other words, 72 times that flash attachment failed: 72 precious moments are lost instead of preserved, as your slogan advertises.

Appeal to fairness and pride Picturetronics, Inc. have said they can't understand what is the matter with this camera and they've done all they can. Even they suggest that my camera must be one of the very rare defective products from your usually dependable high-quality stock. Thus I am returning this camera to you for your in-

Request spection. But after all the heartaches it has given me--in losing instead of preserving precious moments--I ask that you please keep this camera and send me instead a new dependable Instanshot camera. Also, will you please reimburse me for the $39.92 I paid for wasted film, processing, and flash-bulbs. Copies of sales slips are enclosed.

Tie-in with major premise By making these fair replacements you will help to restore my faith in Wessman. Also, not only I myself but friends who share my disappointments, will again believe that Wessman does "preserve those precious moments."

Letter 2—also long—is a persuasive request written after previous direct requests had failed. Because of the seriousness of the situation, this writer (the dealer) uses some negative appeals—*loss* of reader benefits—along with the positive benefits. The letter is addressed to the production manager.

Letter 2
A dealer persuasively requests better deliveries of a manufacturer's products.

<table>
<tr>
<td>Attention-
getting
assertion</td>
<td>Repetition is an accepted mechanism for achieving emphasis. Although we have stated to you before our situation with respect to Crown tools, we are writing again now to emphasize to you the probable sad consequences of your current performance and allocations.</td>
</tr>
<tr>
<td>Interest;
problem</td>
<td rowspan="2">Because of population influx in this area and the tremendous increase in construction here, we believe you are taking a serious hazard by overlooking your competitive position in _____ (name of state). Too many new users of electric tools and too many established Crown customers are finding it necessary to turn to other brands. Come the day when you have more tools than orders, you'll be sorry, and we with you will suffer in pride and pocketbook.</td>
</tr>
<tr>
<td>Risk of
losing
benefits</td>
</tr>
<tr>
<td>Reader
benefit</td>
<td>Our plea to you is certainly more deserving than most distributors you know, here or elsewhere. We sell Crown saws and no other hand saw; we sell Crown drills, not eight other kinds; your sanders, your grinders, your shear and even your good little nibbler are all we have. We have no connection nor do we seek one with any of your competitors.</td>
</tr>
<tr>
<td>Conviction;
facts that
affect reader
benefit

Description
of problem</td>
<td>Now, we have lots of lines, big equipment and small. We represent 84 manufacturers and we have 14 sales people outside, 4 inside. Whether on commission or on trainee salaries, these people get paid in direct proportion to the gross profit they bring the house and they know it. Their total mass sales effort is split in direct proportion to the gross profit. Our total allocation of tools for September was $2,400. Even if we had received these tools, which we didn't, each representative could have had $150 worth to sell; a maximum personal gain on Crown tools, about $13. What percentage of sales efforts do you expect to command for a maximum monthly potential of this amount, especially if the representative had to wait 6 to 12 months after the sale to get delivery for a, by then, irate customer?</td>
</tr>
<tr>
<td>Appeal to
fairness</td>
<td>From the viewpoint of management, how can we reasonably spend time training sales personnel in your line? Let me assure you that we do spend time and energy all out of proportion to our immediate profit. We took about 115 down payments on saws based on promises we made on your authority and in good faith. So far, we have refunded 68, you have lost 68 customers at least temporarily, and our expense of handling these and other Crown tool orders has been serious.</td>
</tr>
<tr>
<td>Reader
loss of
benefits</td>
<td>We have, to our present sorrow, booked a tremendous backlog on your saws. Should we keep booking orders even on extremely indefinite delivery? We wish you'd tell us.</td>
</tr>
<tr>
<td>Facts on the
problem</td>
<td>Yesterday we checked our customer orders against our backlog with you. It was a shock even to us. We have 6 of your tools in stock. Four are air saws; two are samples not to be sold. After heavy cancellations we have remaining now firm orders</td>
</tr>
</table>

Reader-
benefit
appeal

for 192% of the orders we have with you. Our backlog with
you slightly exceeds 12 times your intended (unmet) September
allocation.

We mentioned 192%. With a guaranteed promise of 60 days on
saws, we could run this to 300% in signed sales orders within
three days. Every man we have has a list of customers who
want to be informed of any break in the situation. Now, a
word about our customers. We have the best quality trade.
The major industrials and their responsible contractors in
(state name) comprise the bulk of our backlog in Crown tools.
They are our friends and can be yours! We want you to help
us serve them to ensure their helping us when there are more
tools than tool buyers.

More risks

In conclusion, a word about competition. It is public information that Rall brand has made us and you look pretty foolish here. We have heard some mechanical complaints about
Rall, but the difference of say 40% in the life of a saw is
not noticeable to the man who has only Rall saws. Because
of your unbalanced and locally unfavorable allocation flow
here, very few fellows we know have been able to compare new
Ralls with any but old Crown saws. We cannot in honesty
divert Crown saws to rental for the present, and the number
we have to sell doesn't allow many chances for comparison.

Request;
reader
benefit

Therefore, please do everything you can to step up your
shipments to fill the backlog of orders while you can still
save this excellent market!

Persuasively Requesting Credit

Most credit applications are direct requests, made in the routine course of business.
However, sometimes you may seek a special credit privilege which on the surface you
appear to be unqualified for. In such cases a persuasive request is more effective. For
instance, if you are just starting your own first store and your capital, inventory and
current income are barely adequate, you will need to convince prospective creditors
that they can depend upon you to pay regularly. Or you may wish to ask for 120-day
credit terms instead of the usual 30-day period. Whatever your unusual request may
be, be sure to include sufficient facts and figures to show how you have planned carefully and perhaps how the reader will benefit—for example, from your expected expanding market.

Sometimes credit applicants' first direct request is turned down and they cannot
understand why. If they still want credit with that firm, a persuasive request such as
letter 3 may help accomplish that purpose. This letter brought a prompt, pleasant
phone call, an apology, and the granting of a revolving credit account "gladly."

Letter 3
A persuasive request for credit after a turndown.

Attention:
assertion

Your form letter of January 31 refusing my request for the
Blank's Revolving Credit (BRC) account and suggesting I
consider an Easy Payment Account came as a mild shock.

*Interest;
applicant's
work and
knowledge*

Blanks, without a doubt, maintains certain policies regarding
credit applications from individuals. In my occupation as
a bookkeeper and assistant manager of City Paint and Hardware
Company, I process many applications for credit. Therefore,
I feel that when you considered my application, either sufficient information was not given or the fact that I am
renting a house, rather than buying, was regarded as grounds
for listing me as a person of "questionable" credit standing.
In either assumption, I believe the following information
will give you a clear picture of my "present circumstances."

Employment and Income
        (7 lines)

*Conviction
facts*

Assets and Liabilities
        (8 lines)

References
        (11 lines)

*Reader-
benefit
request*

The Easy Payment Plan you suggest is an expensive way to buy
merchandise. To buy on this plan partially defeats the
purpose of "SHOP AT BLANKS AND SAVE!" Small easy payments
do not appeal to me. Nor does dragging out payments over a
long period of time. Your BRC account would be one I would
use frequently. And you can be sure that you will receive
prompt payments. BRC fits my present needs and my ability
to pay. Your extending this privilege to me will be greatly
appreciated.

Persuasively Requesting Changes in Policy or Performance

Besides requesting nonroutine adjustment or credit, you may at times need to persuade a company to make other exceptions from its usual policy. Or you may wish
to persuade individuals to change their actions, or to give employees a written pep
talk hoping to improve their future performance. The basic persuasive-request pattern
is again applicable here.

Changes in Policy. In letter 4, an advertising consultant tries to persuade the
public relations officer of ABC Company to deviate from its usual policy of not giving away or lending products. An outstanding magazine feature writer (renamed Jake
Edlis in this example) had written for permission to borrow, free, ABC Company's
new XX boating equipment—to use, photograph, and mention in all or some of his
new series of feature stories on outdoor life. Because Jake knew ABC's usual policy,
he wrote a persuasive request to both the advertising consultant and the public relations officer (Mary) presenting to them numerous facts about the magazines for which
he writes and names of other large companies that regularly lend their equipment and
products to him.

Letter 4
*An advertising consultant's persuasive request to deviate from the usual no-loan
policy regarding equipment.*

Dear Mary:

Though I know it is ABC's policy not to loan or give away its products, I think sticking to it in the case of Jake Edlis would be a mistake.

Interest and
conviction There are very few writers in the recreation field for whom I'd take a stand on this issue. Among them are _____, _____, _____, and Jake Edlis.

Company
benefit First, lending your boating equipment is a relatively small expense for the publicity ABC is bound to receive in return. The space value could, conceivably, amount to tens of thousands of dollars. As you know, his write-ups reach about 16 million readers each month.

More
company
benefit Second, ABC is big league now. Big leaguers play the game by getting respected writers like Edlis to use their products (many of them carrying big price tags) and write about them.

More
company
benefit Third, as a member of the Outdoor Writers Association of America and a well-known feature writer, Edlis is bound to talk to a lot of other "influentials" in the field. He could, intentionally or not, start word that ABC is willing to take
Risk of
harmful
results if
change is
not made lots of free space, but unwilling to extend the accepted courtesy of letting legitimate feature writers try its products without charge. Ultimately, this could lead to poor press relations and a resulting drop in our publicity lineage.

Company-
benefit
request In the interest of maintaining exceptionally good press relations, please reconsider your company's "no give-away" policy when someone with the stature of a Jake Edlis offers his services. I'm sure you'll be glad you did.

Changes in Performance. Persuasion is necessary whenever you need to convince individuals to change their performance (which may include personal appearance and habits as well as business practices) and if direct requests have been or would be unheeded.

The next two examples[3] illustrate how important the right tone and use of appeals are for getting reader cooperation. As you read letter 5, note these faults:

1. Overemphasis on negatives—"disturbed," "horrified," "will have to be removed," "senseless," "punishing," "destroying"
2. Overuse of "we"—meaning Landlord, Inc., rather than all people (us) in the neighborhood
3. Manager's domineering, threatening, discourteous attitude, which places all parents on the defensive and seems to blame their children, although the vandals may have been outsiders
4. Total lack of reader appeals

[3]Courtesy of New York Life Insurance Company, *Effective Letters Bulletin,* Summer 1965.

Letter 5

A poor, negative, unpersuasive request from a building manager to tenants.

TO ALL PARENTS·LIVING IN 100 OAK AVENUE AND 50 ELM AVENUE

We have become seriously disturbed because of the recent vandalism in your neighborhood. Every day now, storage room doors are being broken, tires removed from bicycles, parts of baby carriages are taken off, etc. etc., but today we were horrified to see a beautiful living tree (in front of 50 Elm Avenue) completely cut in half. Now the tree will have to be removed.

We would like all the parents to have a good talk with their children in order to stop this senseless destruction.

We will start patrolling this section very closely from now on, and if necessary, we will call in the municipal and school authorities of Metropolis, in order to start punishing children who are found destroying property.

In contrast, letter 6 eliminates the main faults of letter 5. Its tone is friendly, courteous, and positive. Equally important, this letter emphasizes community spirit, mutual concern, and cooperation. Letter 6 appeals to the parents' pride, love of family, health, and desire for security; and it includes the young people as citizens instead of accusing them indirectly of being vandals.

Letter 6

An appealing, improved version of letter 5.

TO ALL FAMILIES IN THE ELM AVENUE SCHOOL DISTRICT:

Attention: a mutual problem

I know you will be as sorry as I was to learn that the lovely old elm tree which gave our school its name was destroyed today. Its beauty and grace are now lost to us forever, and all of us regret this tragedy.

Interest; need for mutual effort

The destruction of our landmark appears to be another in a recent series of acts of vandalism in our neighborhood--a problem which can affect all of us unless we make a mutual effort to rid ourselves of it.

Conviction; appeals to safety, health, security, and civic pride

A number of residents of our community have volunteered to do patrol duty in their off-hours, protecting the safety of our families and our property. Though we appreciate their desire to help, we need to ask ourselves if a patrol is what we really want. Do we want our neighborhood to be a prison for our children or a place of freedom and healthful growth?

Shall we instead face this problem frankly and constructively? Let us consider a few facts. Does our community have adequate provisions for recreational activities, or should we be contributing more to the creativity, growth, and culture of Metropolis? Have we done everything possible to make this the city in which our young people will be proud to grow up?

Request   It has been suggested that we discuss these things both in our own homes and then together as a community. Will you meet with us next Monday evening, January 18, at 7:30 in the auditorium of Elm Avenue School so that we may plan a constructive program of progress? Perhaps we can form a "Civic Pride

Appeals to pride and cooperation Committee" comprised of both young people and adults--a committee which can investigate our needs and help us plan a calendar of events to appeal to everyone. Our mayor and council members share our enthusiasm and have agreed to be present.

Reader benefits Let's make Monday evening "Family Night." Fill the auditorium with families, ideas, and appetites for cake, coffee, and cokes. See you at 7:30!

Unsolicited Sales Letters

Every year millions of dollars' worth of goods and services are sold through sales letters—both solicited and unsolicited—to consumers, businesses, and industries. Unsolicited sales letters are also known as "prospecting" and "cold turkey" letters. They are initiated by the seller for various reasons and are not direct answers to inquiries.[4] Direct mail[5] successfully urges people to buy products ranging from mail-order cataloged items to real estate. Not only large retail chains such as Montgomery Ward and Sears Roebuck, but also thousands of lesser-known big-city and small-town merchants, wholesalers, and manufacturers sell effectively by mail. (Many firms sell exclusively by mail.) Even managers of shops selling services (for home and auto repair, health, beauty, protection, and others) stimulate their businesses by sales messages.

Although you should be aware of the enormous potential income that is possible using well-written sales letters, you need also to be aware of the strong resistance that many people have toward such messages. Common criticisms from readers who look unfavorably on sales letters are these: insincerity, appeals to the wrong group, hidden gimmicks, lack of personalization, "Madison Avenue" approach, excessive length, exaggeration.

In general, your success in sales letters will depend upon three factors: the mailing list, the right appeals, and the presentation. The first two of these factors are *prewriting* steps. The remainder of this chapter discusses the steps to take before writing unsolicited sales letters, gives suggestions for writing them, and offers examples of various kinds of unsolicited sales letters.

Steps before Writing the Unsolicited Sales Letter

Because your sales letter may go to hundreds—even thousands—of people, you need to do exceptionally careful planning before starting to write it. The six planning

---

[4] For solicited sales letters—which are answers to inquiries about products and services—see Chapter 8, pages 190-194.

[5] In general, the term "direct mail" refers to any printed matter, other than periodicals, that attempts to sell or promote sales by mail. It includes—in addition to letters—postcards, manuals, brochures, order blanks, pamphlets, leaflets, gadgets, and reply forms. These items usually supplement the letter and help create a favorable seller-buyer relationship.

steps—about purpose, reader, ideas to include, fact gathering, organization, and revision—are especially important. You usually first gather facts on your product and your prospective buyer and then give extra thought to the purpose, appeals, and presentation of your entire sales message.

Gathering Facts about Your Product. Before you write a sales letter, you first analyze thoroughly the product you want to sell. (The word "product" as used here includes both tangible products and intangible services.) You gather information through reading, observing, testing, using, comparing, questioning, researching.

If yours is a tangible product, what are its physical characteristics—size, color, shape, content, composition? How is it made and where did raw materials come from? How does it operate? What is its performance record? How does it compare with and differ from competitors' products in durability, efficiency, appearance, price, terms? What are its weaknesses? Strengths?

For your future buyers, benefits (psychological description) are usually much more significant than physical description. What will the product do for each user? What human needs or desires does it fulfill? For instance, a magazine may be a certain size, with x number of pages, on glossy paper, with hundreds of half-page pictures. But what information and enjoyment—even profits—does it bring to the user? What good does it do the buyer in business, home, family, and community contacts?

A new real estate subdivision may consist of 100 six-room brick, ranch-style houses on one-quarter-acre tracts. But why should the reader purchase in this subdivision rather than elsewhere? Perhaps living here is unique because of the climate and scenic beauty which allow year-round sun, fun, and sports, plus a plentiful supply of fresh water and fertile soil? Perhaps a trend of prolonged rise in real estate values makes this property a good investment? Perhaps it is an exceptionally good place to rear children?

Your vinyl jackets may have the same "rich grain as expensive buckskin leathers" and be available in 10 sizes. But of special interest to your customer are these facts about what a jacket *will do for her*:

It is completely water-repellent, so she will be dry in any downpour.

Though the jacket is fully lined, she can wear it in any weather all year round.

It's soft and pliable and never needs costly dry cleaning; she saves money.

Dirt and stains come clean with a damp cloth and a little mild detergent.

Its classic style won't go out of fashion.

She saves money also by buying direct from the factory, and no salesperson rushes or pressures her.

She can try the jacket on at home and wear it 10 days without obligation.

Whatever your product, you must know all its physical features and its reader benefits before you can confidently and effectively sell it.

Knowing Your Reader and Obtaining Mailing Lists. To sell your product effectively by letter requires also a knowledge of your reader and a selective, up-to-date, accurate mailing list. You'll use the mailing list both for a test mailing and for the entire mailing of one or several sales letters. Testing means mailing the letter to a small percentage (perhaps 5 to 10%) of the names on your list to see whether the letter brings the percentage of response necessary for you to make a profit.

Previous discussions in this text on you attitude and visualizing your reader also apply to sales letters, and they need not be repeated here. It is especially important to remember that the sales letter must be adapted to the needs and interests of your specific group of readers. When your product has almost universal use, you may have several different, reasonably homogeneous groups of prospects. Thus if you want to sell lighting fixtures by mail, you need to know the tastes, problems, preferences, and conditions of your various prospective users–homeowners, architects, store or office managers, plant or hospital or school superintendents, and so forth,–and you'll write different letters to each group.

Selectivity in your mailing list is important because even an excellent sales letter about the best product in the world will not sell if the message goes to the wrong readers. You would not sell office filing cabinets to outdoor laborers or fishing boats to low-income people in a desert area, or Cadillacs to pensioners.

You can buy, rent, or make up a mailing list that includes the best potential buyers for your product. The more similar their characteristics and circumstances, the better. You can buy names and addresses of almost any kind of specialized group of people– classified by income level, age, marital status, sex, number of children, occupation, geographic location, color of eyes, height, education. However, you need to be cautious. For instance, even if your product is for people with above-average incomes, you must take other factors into account. For example, an individual with a $30,000 income and eight children may be less able to spend for luxuries than a childless person with a lower income.

If you wish to make your own list, you will find one or more of these sources useful: telephone books, directories, membership lists, vital statistics, newspaper articles, replies to your advertising, and–sometimes best of all–your own company records.[6] Your credit and sales departments can give you lists of present and former customers; other departments can furnish lists of stockholders, employees, suppliers. Any or all of these may be good for your own company-prospect list.

Up-to-dateness and accuracy can save a firm needless waste on costs of labor, postage, paper, and processing. Postal authorities tell us that over one-fourth of all addresses change within one year. Names and titles may change too. The mailing list must be correct in addresses, spelling of names, use of prefixes (Mr., Miss, Mrs., Ms., Dr.), and titles (vice president or executive vice president). No matter how selective the list may be, it is good only when it is updated and correct.

Deciding on Purpose. The purpose of an unsolicited sales letter may be to make a direct sale, to serve as stimulus for future sales, or to win back lost customers.

---

[6] Among the many firms that have compared the pulling power of rented versus their company-prospect names is Merrill Lynch, Pierce, Fenner and Smith. They found that 10,560 rented names brought a 7.4% response; 10,900 company-prospect names brought a 24.9% response. (*The Reporter of Direct Mail Advertising Newsletter*, November 1966.)

To make a direct sale is usually the purpose of a sales letter about a relatively inexpensive convenience item or a service that the prospect can buy without previously seeing or discussing it in person. Sometimes even for more expensive or complex items your purpose may be to sell with only one letter, as you will see later in this chapter. More often, however, for such products the direct-sale letter follows previous groundwork laid by former letters (in a campaign series), by demonstrations, by advertising, or by sales representatives. The requested action to clinch the sale is that the prospect send for the article.[7]

To serve as a stimulus for a sale sometime in the future is the long-range purpose of a variety of sales letters, many of which are known as sales promotion messages. They help to build goodwill, to supplement advertising that failed to bring desired results, to give a pep talk to distributors. Or they may serve as part of a campaign series involving complicated costly products (like factory machinery) or services (like mortgage lending) that require planning and/or individual consultation with a company representative before purchase. In these letters the purpose may be to introduce the product and then follow up with a salesperson. The requested action may be that the customer should: ask for a booklet, catalog, or other information; invite a representative to call; or come to the salesroom.

To win back lost customers is the goal of other sales letters. The purpose is to let customers who haven't bought anything for some time know you miss them, to find out why they haven't been buying from you, and to sell them on coming back. The requested action is usually that the customer return a questionnaire; often an enclosed order blank brings a direct sale. For dissatisfied customers, good follow-up can help bring in future sales.

Choosing Ideas and the Main Appeal. After you have collected facts on your product, obtained a mailing list of likely prospects, and determined your purpose, you are ready to decide on ideas to include in your sales letter. Instead of cluttering your letter with a long list of facts about your product, you should select for emphasis a *central selling point* and translate it into user benefits. You stress whatever appeal is most likely to convince the prospect that he/she should buy your product. Often this is the feature or benefit that differentiates your product from competitors'. After you have stressed the central selling point, you can introduce other appeals about your product. (For a second letter to the same prospect, you can stress a second central selling point.)

Your central selling point is always based on what you estimate are the prospect's needs. Will the product cut his/her costs? protect him/her? make him/her more attractive? If your product will appeal to different groups of prospects for different reasons, you will write a different sales letter to each group. In each letter you will feature the central selling point and appeals that you estimate are most pleasing to the readers for whom you write it. For example, to dealers who expect to resell your product, you will emphasize quick turnover and profits. To consumers you may feature comfort,

[7]In some letters—those offering a free trial or money-back guarantee—the requested action (sending for the article) is usually only a preliminary, conditional step. The sale is really not closed until the customer has examined and perhaps used the product within a specified time limit.

pride in personal appearance, safety, or any other appropriate appeals like those listed on page 312. Remember also that individuals within any group have different mental filters and situations, and may thus be motivated for different reasons (perhaps another central selling point which you stress in a later letter).

Suppose, for instance, you want to sell by mail the vinyl jacket described briefly on page 333. To readers living in rainy areas you might feature year-round comfort (dry in any downpour). To readers in arid regions your major appeal may be convenience (easily cleaned and wearable the year around). For students you might focus on both attractiveness (in style) and saving money (infrequent replacements, factory prices, no dry-cleaning bills).

Planning the Presentation and Making Revisions. The fifth and sixth planning steps —organization and rewriting—involve much more than deciding upon the organizational plan and final content of the letter itself. Consider your letter as part of an entire mailed sales presentation which includes the letter with all enclosures—whether it is to be a single sales effort or to be part of a campaign series.

Your presentation must move readers to take the desired action—and yield a satisfactory profit. The percentage of response needed for profitable returns may range from less than one percent to a much higher figure, depending upon various factors. For instance, the Mercedes-Benz letter mentioned in footnote 10 successfully achieved its goal, though only three-tenths of 1 percent of the readers purchased a car. The returns the mailing brings must be sufficiently greater than its total cost—for the list, plus planning, consulting (with direct mail specialists)[8], writing, revising, reproducing, testing, and mailing the letter with all its enclosures.

Ultimately, though the initial cost of these steps may be high, the cost per mailing may be as low as 10 to 50 cents or as high as several dollars each—and the resulting profits many times these amounts. Plans and decisions (by you and perhaps other executives and a consultant are essential. You need to consider enclosures and also the length, appearance, and timing of the entire sales message. Your budget and numerous other factors enter into this plan.

The number and kinds of enclosures that supplement your sales letter should be planned before you write it. Will the envelope contain any descriptive pamphlet, separate testimonials, pictures, samples, gimmicks, gadgets, order blank, and/or a reply envelope? Gadgets and gimmicks should be used only if they help to dramatize a point, not if they merely attract attention. (Some readers dislike them; others become absorbed in them and fail to read the letter.) The usual enclosures are leaflet, order blank, and reply envelope.

The length of the sales letter depends on various factors. For example, if the enclosures adequately take care of all needed details, the letter should preferably be only one page. This is especially true if its purpose is to get action other than a direct purchase. If a catalog or booklet is to be sent later upon request, or if a demonstration or sales representative is to follow, these methods will help make the sale. On the con-

---

[8]Many firms (except those with specially trained direct mail staffs) ask outside specialists to write their sales letters and plan the enclosures.

trary, if you do not have a separate enclosure—and especially if you want to make a direct sale—your letter may have to be longer than one page. Just be sure it is as concise as possible!

Many conflicting ideas exist about the desirable length of sales letters. Don Francisco, a former great in the advertising business, once gave a good answer to the question, "Why do all direct mail experts believe in long copy for their selling letters?":

> They find that it is better to have 20 people read the entire letter and be convinced than to have 100 merely see it.[9]

Direct mail experts have proved again and again that long copy works—if it catches and holds the reader's interest and is sufficiently convincing.[10]

Appearance of the sales letter may be coordinated with the letterhead, envelope, and enclosures in color, pictures, designs, and so forth. To a prospect a company is what it appears to be in its printed mailing. You need to decide (usually with the help of experts in direct mail, advertising, and/or processing) on the quality and color of paper to be used and also whether the printing will be in one or more colors. Other factors to be considered in your planning are these:

> Should special pictures, designs, handwritten "teaser" statements, or other attention-getting devices or gimmicks be used on the outside envelope and the letterhead?[11] If so, they will to some extent affect the wording of your letter . . . and your costs too.

> Should the letter be personalized with the reader's name and address? You will be well repaid for carefully comparing relative costs. If your mailing list is long, computerized letters with computerized matching fill-ins can be effective. Or you may have the name, address, and salutation processed in a different color from that of the letter's body. Another alternative is to insert a catchy appropriate statement in place of the inside address and salutation, as illustrated on pages 138 and 356.

> What about the sizes of the letterhead, envelopes, and other enclosures? Should any be oversize? Transparent? With what size and kind of type?

> Should the envelopes have windows? Should part of the letter's message show through one or more windows?

> Should you "dress up" the sales letter itself? You can add interesting variety and emphasis by occasional underscoring or capitalizing of important ideas, by indenting some sentences or paragraphs on both margins, by use of more short than long paragraphs, and by "inked" lines, arrows, or other marks to emphasize ideas.

---

[9]*Sam's Almanac of Direct Mail*, vol. V, no. 5, The Mail Advertising Bureau, Inc., Seattle, Washington, 1967.

[10]One of the more startling success stories is the case of the Mercedes-Benz company that sold 1,500 Model 190D Sedans for $4,068 each, one summer before Labor Day (1965)—entirely through a five-page letter which their advertising agency designed and mailed to 500,000 people. This letter's success was remarkable for another reason: these cars used diesel fuel, a hurdle because diesel fuel stations were scarce at the time. (Courtesy of Mercedes-Benz of North America, Inc., Fort Lee, New Jersey).

[11]See also page 311, regarding the attention-getting importance of envelopes and letterheads.

The reproduction of your mailing pieces should preferably be done professionally. Using your company's duplicating machine may be all right for some small sales efforts, but professional jobs make the best impression. Also it is best not to try to disguise direct mail with "cute" attempts to fool the recipient, for most people react negatively to them. The honest, well-written factual presentation that is reader-centered and pleasing always outpulls the others.

Timing of the sales message also affects its success and should be carefully planned. Consider what is likely to be the best time of the week, month, season, and year to launch a certain sales campaign. The time of your mailing will naturally affect the wording of your sales letter and sometimes your choice of appeals (as for certain seasons, holidays).

Figures released by the National Association of Manufacturers show that 80 percent of orders are placed after the sales representative's fifth call. Remember that a sales letter is a "sales representative" too. Some firms have effectively sent the same letter (perhaps on paper of a different color) to the same prospects two or three times and received orders only after the last mailing.

Suggestions for Writing the Unsolicited Sales Letter

After you have completed the prewriting steps—about your product, mailing list of prospects, choice of ideas and main appeals, and the planned presentation—you are ready to develop the sales letter itself. This writing (and revising) will probably take hours, even days. If time and budget permit, you may decide—with the help of a consultant—to prepare several versions of your letter to test their pulling power before mailing one to the entire mailing list.

Your basic guide is the AIDA organizational pattern discussed on pages 310–312. Although the discussion below focuses separately on each part of the AIDA plan, the parts need not always be in this sequence, nor need all parts be in every letter. Some sales letters begin with desire-creating material such as testimonials or guarantees. Some start with action-inducing statements such as special offers or free trial. Some may skip product description and uses (the interest section) and devote most of the letter to proof—if, for example, the reader already knows the description and uses but needs conviction material to reinforce interest and create desire to buy the product. Circumstances vary—and so do sales letter content and organization.

Attracting Your Prospect's Attention. The best way to catch the attention of a busy reader is by promising—or implying a forthcoming promise—*to benefit him or her by satisfying a need*. Mention what the reader gains from the product before you name it. (Using the reader's name in the salutation also helps get attention.) Though the letter may go to thousands of people, each copy must "talk" in a natural, sincere, friendly way to an individual human being. The opening should be appropriate, fresh, honest, interesting, specific, and relevant to the central selling point. Avoid tricky, exaggerated openings, which have been so overused that the American public is unmoved or annoyed by them. Of course, if you can think of a novel, catchy opening that honestly relates closely to your central theme, go ahead and use it.

Also be careful to avoid openings that may outdate your letter soon. For instance, one letter addressed to "Dear Graduate" began "Now that you are out of school for three months . . . ." Readers who had been out of school longer than that were of course annoyed by the inaccuracy.

For both *form* and *content* of the sales letter's attention-getting opening you have a variety of choices. But keep the first paragraph short, preferably two to five lines, sometimes only one. Short paragraphs look easy to read and thus are more likely to get the reader started. If unusual circumstances require you to have a long opening paragraph, it should be set up in an easy-to-read way—sometimes with double spaces between sentences or with some lines indented from both margins. (See, for instance, the first example under "Questions" that follows.)

Any of these forms of expression can begin your sales letter—command, direct statement, headline, hypothetical comment, or question.

Command
Try to tear up the enclosed paper.

Give your college student a head start toward financial security!

Direct Statement
Here is an opportunity to test a new product right at your own desk.

You probably have employees who would benefit greatly from R&L's low-cost Language of Business Course.

Headline
NOW YOU CAN GET
THE MOST COMPREHENSIVE BENEFITS EVER OFFERED THE FISHERMAN
—FOR LESS THAN 15¢ A WEEK!

Hypothetical Comment
IF THREE RADIATOR REPAIR EXPERTS
WALKED INTO YOUR SHOP THIS AFTERNOON . . .
(See letter 1, pages 350–351.)

Questions
How many records will $3.98 buy in your home town? Only one?
But . . .

 we'll send you 12 of the latest hit albums—
 up to $66.76 worth of new records—

 plus a transistor radio—for the same $3.98!

Are there ways to save far more money than you do now? Can you increase your capital significantly by shrewd investments? What are the smart ways to buy so that you spend less and have more? How do others free dollars from taxes in ways you'd never suspect?

For the content of your attention-getting opening, you can choose from any of the following 11 kinds (arranged alphabetically). As you read the examples, notice which *form* of expression they use.

1. **An Agreeable Assertion**
   Selling window units:

   Your new home that you are planning to build will probably last you for the rest of your life. Be sure when you build it that one of the four essential parts of your home will also last a lifetime.

   Offering a free brand-new handbook and a special magazine subscription:

   As a Westerner interested in boating, you know how different our yachting and boating activities and opportunities are out here.

2. **A Comparison or a (Short!) Story (Avoid a long story opening. It detracts from your main theme.)**
   Selling a secretary's handbook along with a free *kit:*
   (Pictures of a cluttered and a tidy desk at top of letter)

   It's really amazing! Betty and Sue work side-by-side in the same office. They have the same secretarial training and skills . . . both have identical workloads —yet Betty is usually putting away her typewriter by 4:45 everyday, while Sue usually can't even find her newspaper under the clutter of unfinished work still on her desk.

   And not only the janitor notices! Their boss has noticed the difference too. So besides the sheer delight of an easier day with much less pressure, let's face it, Betty will be in line for promotions, pay raises, and all the "fringe benefits" that go with them!

3. **An Event or Fact in the Reader's Life**
   Selling a savings account:

   Congratulations on the new arrival in your home! Your baby's first word . . . and that first step . . . are important events. So is the first dollar that goes into a child's own savings account.

   Selling car insurance:

   The fact that you are a college senior specializing in medicine and attend a well-respected university like (name) tells people about your character.
   For instance, it may qualify you for a special low-cost auto insurance program that might not otherwise be available to you.

4. **A Problem the Reader May Face**
   Urging use of a catalog to shop by mail:

   During the next few weeks you and people all over the country will be doing Christmas shopping. Some will be early birds. Others will wait until the last minute; and if they are shopping in the stores, they will be pushed around and have to take what is left instead of being able to purchase just the items they had in mind.

   Enclosing a booklet to a family and urging them to visit "your Ford Dealer":

   If you're like most families, you're probably comparison shoppers—who look for and get the most for your money. And you know how important comparison shopping is—when you're looking for a new rug, a couch, or a washing machine.

5. **A Quotation**
   Selling repair service:

   "A stitch in time saves nine."

   Selling correspondence study:

   "To be or not to be, that is the question."

6. **A Scare Opening**[12]
    Selling bank safe-deposit boxes:
    (Picture of a burning home. Letter is on a simulated document from which a corner has been burned off.)

    Let's JUST SUPPOSE
    This was a valuable document in your home, destroyed because of fire. Not only could it mean a severe financial loss but replacing it might take months as well as a considerable amount of inconvenience.

    Selling health and accident protection:

    And . . . how *lucky* can you be?
    Statisticians tell us that *one* out of every *six* persons will be sick, though not necessarily hospitalized, during the coming year. Can you count on your luck getting you by without a serious case of work-stopping, income-crippling illness?

7. **A Significant Fact about the Product**
    Urging professors to order multiple copies for class use:
    In 51 of 56 well-known United States colleges and universities, the Class of '7_ voted (name) magazine their first choice among 18 of America's leading magazines.

    Selling TV cable service:
    More than 4,000,000 viewers in the UNITED STATES . . .
    . . . and . . .
    over 10,000 people in the (city) area alone enjoy sharp, clear, multichannel television reception by means of C.A.T.V. (Community Antenna Television).

8. **A Solution to a Problem**
    Selling canned seafood:
    Here's the solution to your Christmas present problem. You will delight in giving this taste treat from the North Pacific to your relatives, friends, and business acquaintances.

    Selling hospital insurance:
    (Picture of a $935 check at top of letterhead.)
    You can receive a check like this, or even up to $5,000, when you or a member of your family goes to the hospital . . . *IF* you are protected by Hospital Plan.

9. **A Special Offer or a Gift**
    Selling book club membership:
    The extraordinary opportunity described in the big circular—for you to get this remarkable new major dictionary AT AN IMMEDIATE SAVING OF $20 (capitals in red print)—speaks pretty much for itself.

    Announcing a sale:
    Save!!! Purchase *any* one item at the White Front (city name) Store for 10% off!
    You, as a preferred customer, can purchase any one item beginning 10 a.m. and ending 9 p.m. Tuesday, September 30, at 10% OFF our everyday low discount price.

---

[12]Scare openings are usually *not* recommended—except for some kinds of insurance and other services treating accidents or crime *if* the idea of harm or danger is already in the prospect's mind and the letter offers a solution. If, however, the idea of danger or harm is not likely to be on his mind, the opening should be positive and pleasant, stressing the solution rather than the danger.

10. A Surprising or Challenging Statement
Selling a magazine subscription:

It's a waste of time, but try to tear up the enclosed order form that offers you Newsweek for about 13¢ a copy.

I'm sure you can't. It's printed on special paper that just won't tear. But go ahead—give it a try! (Although this opening is a gimmick, it relates well to the central theme—reliability.)

Selling a fund plan:

It's not the cost of a college education that really hurts . . . it's the cost of *not* having it.

Today, the college graduate earns, on the average, $175,000 more during his lifetime than the high school graduate.

11. Testimonials
Selling industrial cleaning compound:

"XX is by far the best cleanser we have ever used," says Mr. Tom Brown, building superintendent at ABC Company.

Arousing the Reader's Interest. Having attracted the reader's attention, you now arouse interest by beginning to "picture" your product and telling what it will do for the reader. You begin to develop the central selling point.

As stated in the general outline on pages 310–312, you can picture your product in two ways—physical description and reader benefits. You can place the benefits first—as in example 1 below—or later, but usually they are interwoven with physical description, as in example 2.

Example 1
Stating benefits before physical description.

When you use <u>Family Investments</u> you find hundreds of ways to make your money earn more and go further--for your home, clothing, food, travel, taxes, and pleasure. You get a rich source of advice from accountants, automotive specialists, real estate agents, tax consultants, life insurance experts, bankers, stockbrokers, lawyers.

This leatherbound book contains 467 pages, divided by subject into 15 chapters, 165,000 words. Sturdily built for continual use, the book has 310 drawings, graphs, and tables to illustrate points and clarify meanings. In essence, using the book will be like taking a fascinating course in managing your family's money--from highly paid professionals.

Example 2
Interweaving benefits and physical description.

The "heart" of your outfit is Bell & Howell's great Zoom-Lens Electric-Drive Super 8 Camera. You just pop in the Kodak cartridge of Super 8 color film (it's fast and simple) . . . <u>aim</u> . . . and <u>shoot</u>. That's all there is to it. And this camera is <u>electrically</u> powered--no winding whatsoever. Pop the cartridge in and you are ready to shoot a full 50-foot movie without interruption.

```
Just consider how every step virtually takes care of itself:  the
camera sets itself automatically for different types of film--it
even adjusts automatically for indoor or outdoor filming--and the
Optronic Electric Eye sets the lens (also automatically) measuring
only that light reaching the film.
```

Creating Desire and Convincing the Reader. After getting your readers interested in one or several of your product's benefits, you need to create in them a desire to own it. Furthermore, if your purpose is to make a direct sale, you need to convince them that they should buy your product. Like the personal sales representative, your letter leads the prospect buyers through a "mental demonstration" so they imagine themselves already the owner—and it offers proof whenever necessary.

The reader's progression from interest to desire to conviction is usually gradual. It is not necessary to worry about exactly where one step begins or ends; these steps are parts of an integrated whole. Together they develop your central selling point and help urge the reader to take the requested action.

To create desire for your product you usually continue with additional physical description and reader benefits. You describe the product specifically and clearly (unless the reader already knows its description because it is a well-known product or because you described it thoroughly in a former letter), and you show the reader the advantages to be gained from using this product.

The relative importance and length of discussion on physical features and benefits vary with the type of product and the overall sales presentation. Usually you should stress reader benefits more, and include only enough description to support the benefits. The length of desire-creating material within the letter ranges from one paragraph—in a one-page letter with descriptive brochure—to several paragraphs if the letter itself is two or more pages long, with or without an enclosed brochure.

The emphasis on reader use and benefits is especially important if your product is valued mainly for its use and/or your prospect is familiar with its appearance (for instance, an electric iron, a camera, or a television set). But if the product is valued mainly because of its appearance (for example, an ornament or a blouse), its physical details must be fully described; usually an accompanying brochure also includes a colorful picture. If the product is machinery or technical equipment, your letter must clarify its sturdiness of construction, fine crafting, and other technical details in terms that the prospect values and can understand—whether the prospect is an ordinary citizen or a professional. Whenever desirable, you enclose with your letter technical sketches and meaningful pictures, charts, graphs. In all cases, be sure to emphasize the central selling point and show how the reader benefits. Work in one or more appeals, such as those listed on page 312.

The following examples illustrate desire-creating paragraphs that develop the central selling point and benefits. Example 3 here follows Example 2. Notice how it continues to stress the central theme—convenience—in order to increase the reader's desire. These paragraphs are part of a three-page letter.

Example 3
Developing the central selling point and benefit—convenience.

Breathtaking ZOOM shots from wide-angle to close-up[13]

And with this camera, the special fingertip-control ZOOM lens makes
it possible for you to get the same kind of breathtaking zoom shots
TV and movie directors use--you can actually shift from wide-angle
shots to dramatic close-ups (and back again) while you're shooting.
And there is still another tremendous design advance: you actually
view through the lens while you're filming--you get exactly what you
see. And for extra fun, you can get in the act yourself: you just
set the camera's special "Automatic Run Control."

Bell & Howell Super-Bright Super 8 Projector Threads Itself

With this Bell & Howell Super 8 Projector, threading is, at last,
outmoded--this projector does it all for you--easily, in just 5
seconds! Just press a button, insert the film, and the film automatically winds itself through--and you sit back, relax and enjoy
your movies--up to 400 feet of film without interruption of any kind.

And this projector has other top-quality abilities: Imagine being
able to run your movies backward. You can! Simply flip a lever and
divers bounce backward onto the board or the family goes backward
into the car after just getting out.

Just flip a lever again and this projector practically turns into a
slide machine! Now you can view the hundreds of motion picture
frames you have taken one at a time--and look at them individually.

You get a complete HOME MOVIE "ENTERTAINMENT CENTER"--all these
extras are included:

(The letter continues to list nine extras.)

Example 4 is part of a two-page letter selling a "his and hers" car coat ensemble.
The central theme is the ensemble's attractive style, usefulness, and comfort along
with money-saving easy upkeep.

Example 4
Developing appeals of comfort, attractiveness, practicality, savings.

These coats look like "Buckskin" leather...have the same rich grain
as expensive leather--though the tough supported vinyl we use will
probably last longer than leather. They're completely water repellent
so you'll be dry in any downpour. Yet this fully-lined coat looks so
good, feels so good on you, that you'll wear it in any weather all
year round.

This wear-with-any-color "Buckskin" color coat is a practical coat for
driving, shopping, all your leisure activities. It never needs costly
dry cleaning. Dirt and stains come clean with a damp cloth and a little
mild detergent. This is a casual coat you'll LIKE wearing, in a classic
style that will look good on you...that won't go out of fashion.

---

[13] The headings in this letter were green, in contrast to the blue print used for the rest of the
letter; in a subsequent mailing of the same letter, headings were orange and the rest of the letter
print, brown.

And you'll like all the "extras" we build into these coats: the warm
quilt lining, the "stay buttons" to keep the buttons from falling out,
the extra interlining that gives you the practical "up-or-down" collar
for wind or sun comfort, the generous pockets, the action sleeves.

To convince you must present proof to your reader that the features and benefits
you describe are true. By convincing the reader you strengthen his or her desire to
have the product. Try to anticipate the reader's questions and objections—about the
product itself and/or its price—and answer them. You might not get another chance to
do so!

The main proof about your product's features and benefits comes preferably from
evidence that persons outside of your company determine. These outside sources
include satisfied users; recognized testing laboratories, agencies, and disinterested persons; and the prospect himself. Seven popular kinds of proof are illustrated below.

From Satisfied Users

1. **Facts about Users' Experience with the Product.** *These include verifiable reports and statistics from users.*

   The green page in the enclosed brochure itemizes the savings which 203 contractors have realized from EASI-POUR concrete mix. Notice that their actual
   savings range from 45% to 85%. As you study the table, note its specific facts
   about the size of each job. Then compare the figures with your own average
   costs for similar projects.

2. **Names of Other Buyers and Users.** *State how many persons or firms already are
   using the product. Better yet, when appropriate, give the names of satisfied
   well-known users, or offer to send names and addresses upon request.*

   This Fleet Management Service has enabled our clients to operate their sales
   representatives' auto fleets better and more economically. And it might do
   the same for you. Companies that are using our service include:

   > a food products manufacturer with a sales force of 625, a greeting card
   > manufacturer with a sales force of 130, a textile manufacturer with a sales
   > force of 96, a coffee processor with a sales force of 230. (Names furnished
   > on request.)

   Among the hundreds of business firms that are pleased with their use of ABC
   equipment are: Marshall Field and Company, Alcoa Aluminum, Ford Motor
   Company, United Airlines, and Chase Manhattan Bank.

3. **Testimonials.** *Because testimonials have been abused (with phony quotations by
   nonusers who are paid to make them), many people distrust them. To establish
   the credibility of the testimonials you use, select persons or firms that are bona-
   fide users of your product and whose judgment the reader respects. And be
   specific. Avoid exaggerations and vague generalities.*

   "Since we've been using EASY-POUR concrete mix, six of our workers can
   place and finish a section of concrete street with curb—12 feet wide and a
   football field long—in only *one hour.* Its paving ability and its quality surpass
   any concrete mix we've used during our twenty years of operation." Gene
   Aimes, Project Superintendent, East Contractors, Inc.

From Recognized Testing Laboratories, Agencies, Disinterested Persons

4. **Performance Tests.** *Whenever recognized experts, testing laboratories, or au-
   thoritative agencies in the field relative to your product have made satisfactory*

performance tests on it, their evidence offers convincing proof. Also effective are statements, reports, and statistics compiled by impartial, reliable witnesses.
Learnfun electric toys have earned the endorsement and Seals of Approval from Underwriters Laboratories, Good Housekeeping Institute, American Medical Association, and National Safety Council.

In every performance test by the United Automotive Association, ALERT batteries ranked at the top of the list. Read in the enclosed brochure the details of qualities tested, and decide for yourself why ALERT is the battery for you.

From the Prospect

5. **Free Trial.** *If you have so much confidence in your product that you're willing to let the prospect try it on a free trial basis, your offer provides a very effective form of proof. The mail-order customer thus has the same opportunity to examine the product carefully as he or she would have before buying in a store. In fact, the customer gets the added privilege of using it before buying or paying for it.*
   For your use alone, we have enclosed a Reservation Certificate giving you the privilege of using the *Bell & Howell Super 8 Complete Home Movie Outfit for 30 full days—free and without obligation.* We supply the color film—a 50-foot Kodak Cartridge—and the movies you make are yours *free*—to show and to keep.

   You'll have a full 10 days to use your new coats . . . to wear them walking, driving, working—without actually spending a single cent. . . . If for some reason, any reason at all, you don't like them, just send them back to me within 10 days, and we'll forget the whole thing. What could be fairer?

6. **Guarantee.** *With the guarantee, the customer pays for the product before using it, but gets a written promise that if not satisfied he or she will get a refund (or credit), or free repairs, or free replacement of the entire article.*
   With every ARTEX product you buy you get this firm, money-back guarantee: "All ARTEX products are Unconditionally Guaranteed to please. If you are not completely satisfied with any ARTEX, return it for full refund within 30 days."

7. **Samples.** *Let the prospect examine, try, and/or use the samples that you send (for instance, swatches of clothing or drapery materials; pieces of wire, rubber, or fireproof insulation) or that he calls for himself (such as gasoline for his car, or a food or beverage made fresh daily). The prospect is asked to perform some suggested action to convince himself that the product meets the writer's claims.*
   Look at the sample I've sent along. See the beautiful grain. Notice how soft and pliable it is. No jacket leather was ever softer—or more carefree. And notice the quilt lining. You'll be comfortable no matter what the weather.

   Just pick up the enclosed STICK-UP page, pull back the hardy Celanar protective sheet. Then place an assortment of odd-size clippings, ads, photos, memos on the STICK-UP sheet in any arrangement you choose. Finally, return the protective covering and press down gently.
   Note how *sharply* and *clearly* you see every word through the transparent sheet, every shading of the material you've mounted on the STICK-UP page. But note this too . . .

The placement of the proof section varies. Usually these statements come after the desire-creating description and benefits. However, if the proof involved possesses the necessary attention-getting qualities to justify placing it at the beginning, you may do so.

The price of your product may be one last hurdle you must surmount to convince the reader. Your presentation on the selling features, benefits, and proof may have convinced the prospect that your product meets the need and he or she should buy it. But is the product worth the price and can he or she pay for it?

If your price is a bargain, you might feature it as an attention-getting opening. If the price doesn't justify this degree of emphasis, state it only *after* you have presented most of the selling features, benefits, and proof. Of course, if your letter is part of a campaign series to sell a costly item, the price might not be mentioned until near the end of the series. Sometimes price is not mentioned in the letter at all. If the product or service varies with the customer's needs (as for insurance or a complex heating installation in an industrial plant), the exact price quotation is given only after consultations with sales representatives.

If your prospect is likely to consider your price a drawback, try to bring the price within reach. For example, in addition to stating the full price, you can use the following methods to deemphasize price and help convince the prospect that he can pay it!

1. Break it down into "easy" weekly or monthly payments.
2. State it in terms of unit prices ($4 each book) instead of case lots or dozens or sets ($160 for the encyclopedia set).
3. Interpret it on the basis of the benefits to be gained.
4. Emphasize its cost on a daily, monthly, or yearly basis—depending upon the product's estimated life and service (only 2 cents a day).
5. Compare it with the amount the average reader spends daily (monthly) for nonessentials or luxuries.

The discussion of price is usually presented just before the action paragraph(s)—if price and action are clear-cut and distinct. Sometimes, however, they blend, as do interest and desire. In some letters you will include price inducements with conviction details; in others, with action. Because offers of easy payment (as well as "no money down now" and credit card use) more often serve as special inducements to action, they are discussed in the next section.

Getting Action. Having convinced your reader that your product is valuable, needed, and worthy of purchase, you now must encourage the most important step—performing the action you request.

All previous discussions in this book about handling negatives, overcoming price resistance, and inducing action are applicable to sales letters and are not repeated here. You also already know that a complete action section should:

State clearly the action you desire.
Make action easy.
Date the action (when desirable).
Offer special inducement to act by a specified time (when desirable).
End with a last reader-benefit plug (when appropriate).

To induce the reader to act within a certain time instead of procrastinating, you can use one or more of the following methods (arranged here alphabetically):

1. **Credit Cards.** *The convenience of merely charging a purchase to a nationally accepted credit card—bank, national oil company, travel agency, diners' club, or other cards—is an effective inducement to action. The holder of such credit card(s) need not write a check or send a money order now, but merely return an order blank listing a credit card number.*

   Send no money now. To order, just check on the enclosed form that you wish this purchase charged to your account with one of the acceptable national credit firms listed. Then be sure to fill in your account number as shown on your credit card.

2. **Easy Payments and/or "No Money Now."** *A budget plan or a future-payment plan by which the prospect pays nothing down now may serve two purposes— to convince the reader that he can afford to buy your product and to induce him to take the requested action. Thus, though the prospect may not have the entire price of the product, he will be able to order right away if he need not pay the entire amount (or anything) at once.*

   For as little as $10 down you can begin to reap the benefits of this useful encyclopedia before school starts. Easy monthly payments as low as $8 a month can be arranged at your convenience.

3. **Free Gift.**[14] *If the prospect buys one item, she may receive two for the price of one; or she may receive a free gift that is different from the item you are selling.*

   Agree to try them for ten days on our No-Money-Down offer, and I'll send you a matching leather-look vinyl Tote Bag FREE. This gift is yours to keep, even if you later return the jackets.

4. **Free Trial.** *The free trial serves two purposes—to convince the reader of your sincerity about the product's merits, and to induce action now. The reader has nothing to lose; she spends no money now and she need pay later only if she finds the article satisfactory.*

5. **Last Chance.** *Be careful about telling your prospect that this is the last chance to buy your product. This idea has been abused and many readers react negatively because they think the writer isn't sincere.*

   Because of the growing shortage of materials and labor for these specially designed vases, this is the *last time* they can be offered at this extra low price. This offer is good until midnight, May 15, 197_ only.

6. **Limit in Quantity or Time.** *The warning here is the same as for "last chance." However, if you can honestly state that the supply of the product or the time for its production is limited, you have an effective inducement for prompt action.*

   The supply of this model is limited. When our current stock is sold out, no more will be available. That's why I urge you to complete and mail the Official Reservation Form before midnight of the date shown.

---

[14] Sweepstakes and other games of chance have been powerful action inducements. The prospect may be "eligible for winning any one of 5,000 prizes" if an enclosed card is mailed before midnight of a certain date. However, such methods are prohibited in some states. Furthermore, studies have shown gross inconsistencies between the prizes that some companies advertise and the number they actually award. See "Games People Shouldn't Play," *Sales Management*, December 1969, pp. 17–18.

7. **No Obligation to Buy.** *When the purpose of your letter is to get the prospect to ask for more information, to come for a demonstration, or perhaps to ask a sales representative to call, he is more likely to act if you promise he is under no obligation to buy.*

Mailing the enclosed card does not in any way obligate you to buy insurance, and no salesperson will call on you unless you invite him or her. To receive full details about this plan, with specific figures at your present age—and your free portfolio—just return the postpaid card above.

8. **Premium.** *A promise of higher earnings if the reader acts before a certain date is also a good incentive.*

By sending your deposits in the enclosed envelope, so they reach us by the 10th of May, you earn 5% dividends from the 1st of the month.

9. **Special Price for a Limited Time.** *Setting a time limit for bargain prices (perhaps on out-of-season items), or for introductory prices on new items or to new buyers, effectively induces action. Offer a discount on the purchase price if the reader buys before a certain date or if cash in full is sent with the order.*

This special introductory rate (for new subscribers only) brings you 40 big news packed issues of *World Reports* for only $4.97. That is down to half-price for 40 issues if you bought them a copy at a time. You get this special rate if your order is postmarked before November 1.

The complete action section in sales letters often (but not always) contains all five of the elements listed on page 347. As you read the following examples, see how many of the elements and special inducements each contains. Notice also that the third example contains a conviction element—guarantee.

1. Just initial this letter and return it in the enclosed postage-paid envelope, and a copy will be mailed without cost or obligation.
2. May we send you quotations on your next job? We will mail our price special delivery within 24 hours after your card reaches us. You will be delighted with our prompt service and even more delighted with the excellent results you will obtain with our expertly made, close tolerance dies.
3. GET THE NEXT 6 ISSUES OF *FITNESS FOR LIVING* FOR HALF PRICE— only $2.95. You don't even risk your $2.95. You *send no money* with the enclosed special Reservation Certificate unless you wish. Just mail it back, we'll enter your subscription and bill you.

   You save $1.55 on the single copy price of 6 issues. AND HERE'S OUR MONEY-BACK GUARANTEE TO YOU:

   > If at any time during the term of your subscription, you are not satisfied with FITNESS FOR LIVING for any reason, let us know and your *entire* payment will be refunded immediately. If you enter a "billed" subscription, all you need do is write "cancel" on the invoice you receive and that's it.

   Mail the enclosed postpaid order form. Get started today on the way to healthier, pleasanter, more zestful living.

Writing an effective sales letter is a lot of work, but it can be greatly rewarding. Many a sales letter mailed to thousands of prospects has brought thousands—even millions—of dollars in returns. Even the expert writers "agonize" over their copy. Good selling presents the benefits and the proposition in such a way that the readers become convinced and "sell themselves." On the other hand, if the letter sounds like high-pressure salesmanship, the readers may become defensive. To achieve your goal may require meticulous editing and rewriting, but the results will be worth the effort.

Examples of Unsolicited Sales Letter

This section illustrates letters that aim to: (1) make a direct sale, (2) serve as stimulus to future sales, and (3) bring back lost customers. As you read them, notice how description is mixed with and reinforces reader benefits, how the central selling point (labeled CSP in these examples) is developed, and how reader-benefit appeals are emphasized. Notice also which of the suggested ways these letters use to gain attention, interest, desire-conviction, and action.

Making a Direct Sale. When the product you want to sell is relatively inexpensive (from your prospective customer's viewpoint), you may be able to sell it effectively with one sales letter. (Even expensive items can sometimes be sold in this way.) All direct-sales messages ask the reader to buy now or within the near future.

The first letter below, sent to business owners, illustrates one way to sell relatively high-priced items successfully by one letter and detailed enclosures. The two items sold were priced at $170 and $295 (prices, though omitted in the letter were in the enclosures). On a mailing of 4,500 this one-page letter brought in $45 in direct sales for every single dollar of costs.[15]

Letter 1
Selling radiator cleaning tanks to service-shop owners.
CSP: Less time to clean tanks.
Appeals: Reduced work; higher profits.

Attention
```
IF THREE RADIATOR REPAIR EXPERTS WALKED INTO YOUR SHOP THIS
AFTERNOON . . .

And the first one, the owner of Midtown Auto Radiator Service
of New York City, said: "We are cleaning 10 to 12 radiators
in our tank and find that it requires only 20 minutes to get
them thoroughly clean."
```

Interest
```
And the second man, proprietor of the Bronx Radiator Service,
said: "We clean nine radiators in one tank in half the time
it used to take to clean two."

And the third man, owner of Goldberg's Auto Service of
St. Johnsbury, Vt., said: "We have found this the most
satisfactory way to clean radiators that we have ever used."
```

Desire
```
. . . you'd certainly feel that you owed it to yourself to
find out just what they used to bring those men such new
speeds and profits, wouldn't you?
```

---

[15] Courtesy of Aeroil Products Company, West New York, New Jersey, and the Darnell Corporation, *The Dartnell File of Tested Sales Letters.*

Well, here is how they--and YOU--are in a position to make such claims!

Conviction You will find their explanations of exactly how they do it (along with reports of other leading radiator specialists from coast to coast) in the enclosed Bulletin #308. In addition, you will find complete specifications on two sizes of radiator cleaning tanks that will enable you to clean up to 4 or up to 12 radiators at a time--<u>probably in LESS time than it now takes you to clean ONE!</u>

Conviction and action Don't just take our word for it - - - read the genuine letters and see the actual, unretouched photographs in the enclosed bulletin. Then prove these new speeds and savings in <u>your own shop</u> by mailing the Guarantee Order Form TODAY!

Letter 2 is two pages long and, like letter 1, also has an enclosed folder. To provide variety and emphasis, letter 2 uses variations in color, margins, and type.[16]

Letter 2
Selling "Stick-Up" album pages to business persons.
CSP: An exclusive easy-to-use plastic product, guaranteed, at factory-to-you prices.
Appeals: Convenience, quality, savings of money and time.

IT'S UNPRECEDENTED!

Attention <u>an opportunity to</u>
<u>test a new product</u>
<u>right at your own desk.</u>

Reader benefit Within the next few minutes you can prove to yourself, without leaving your desk, that our amazing new STICK-UP--the instant press self-adherent album page--does away forever with messy paste-up of clippings.

Interest and proof —by use of sample Just pick up the enclosed STICK-UP page, pull back the hardy Celanar protective sheet. Then place an assortment of odd-sized clippings, ads, photos, memos on the STICK-UP sheet in any arrangement you choose. Finally, return the protective covering and press down gently.

Note how <u>sharply</u> and <u>clearly</u> you see every word through the transparent sheet, every shading of the material you've mounted on the STICK-UP page.

<u>But note this, too</u>: If the arrangement you've set up doesn't please you, all you have to do is pull back the Celanar cover once again, pick up the clippings or photos, and rearrange them any way you desire.

Desire With STICK-UP, you can do this as often as you wish . . . and there's no mess, no fuss, no sloppy paste-pot! You save time, and save money, you do away with aggravation and frustration.

More reader benefits And, what's more, you always have a neat, clean, effective set of clippings or other materials for presentation or record purposes.

[16]The first line and paragraphs 2, 6, 7, and 11 are in light brown type; all others are black. The signature is brown.

STICK-UP is exclusive . . . you can obtain it only from
Transparent Industrial Envelope, Inc. And like other high
quality, famous T.I.E. products, it comes to you at great
savings, because--like the Hercules Page Protectors and
Price
advantages
Hercules Ring Binder Sets that are described on the back of
the enclosed folder - it is offered to you directly by the
manufacturer, at low, low factory-to-you prices.

T.I.E.'s direct sales technique means there's no jobber, no
retailer, no middleman. It means no mark-ups - and you reap
the benefits!

After you've product-tested the enclosed STICK-UP instant
press album page yourself . . . after you've proved to yourself how STICK-UP ideally meets your own needs . . . read the
accompanying folder carefully. It tells you in detail all
about three great products available to you from T.I.E., the
world's largest direct-to-you producer of transparent protective plastic products. Because we specialize in meeting your
requirements for mounting, preservation, presentation and
protection of your sample materials . . . because we do this
on a larger scale than any other firm in the world . . .
because T.I.E. adheres strictly to the highest standards of
design and construction, we offer you this firm, moneyback
guarantee:

Guarantee
"All Transparent Industrial Envelope products are
Guaranteed to please. If you are not completely
satisfied with any T.I.E. product, return it for
full credit within 10 days."

Plus gift
offer
You'll find this Guarantee repeated in the accompanying folder.
And you'll find there, too, a most unusual Personalized Free
Gift Offer, with full details of how you can obtain, without
cost, a practical, convenient, prestigious gift for use in
your office and at home.

Action
request
with
reader
benefit
So, take advantage now of T.I.E.'s low Factory-to-you prices
on STICK-UP, the new instant press self-adherent album page
with protective Celanar cover. For your 8 1/2 x 11" or
8 1/2 x 14" sheets, order Hercules Page Protectors, the
strongest page protectors available anywhere today; and
Hercules Ring Binder Sets, built to take the toughest punish-
ment you can give them.

Reader
benefit
Send in your order today; remember, every T.I.E. product is
fully guaranteed to give you complete satisfaction - or your
money back!

Sincerely,

Easy
action and
reader-
benefit
proof
P. S. There's a handy postage-paid Order Form enclosed for
your convenience. But before you fill it in and mail
it, pick up the material you've already mounted
on the STICK-UP sample sheet and rearrange it. Then
smooth the protective Celanar sheet back into position.

Isn't STICK-UP great?

In addition to prospective customers, you can also mail direct-sales letters like the preceding two to your present customers—about products they have not yet bought from you. Such letters can even get a "free ride"—thus saving you extra postage—if you enclose them with your monthly mailings to your customers. By this means hundreds of companies sell to their present customers goods ranging from books, magazines, and record albums to movie projectors, home furnishings, and clothing. Many of these letters are prepared by the manufacturer (with assistance of advertising consultants) for use by dealers on their own letterhead stationery. They are especially effective because action is made easy; customers can charge their purchases on their own credit cards instead of dealing with distant manufacturers direct. Repeated tests have shown that an offer mailed equally to customers and prospects produced many times more business from customers than from prospects. Furthermore, these special customer appeals can help counteract the attempts of competition to win your customers.

Another popular kind of direct-sales letter that stimulates present customers to buy "now" is the announcement about a special function "for our preferred customers only." Usually as a special inducement a substantial discount is offered on all items customers purchase that certain day or evening. Other effective inducements include inexpensive gifts, premiums, or refreshments. When these announcements do not require strongly developed appeals, they are really good-news letters[17] rather than persuasive requests.

Serving as Stimulus to Future Sales. Many sales letters urge action other than an immediate order for a direct purchase. Some of these sell products or services which are complicated or expensive, or which must be specially tailored to fit the buyer's particular needs. Others sell continual use of the customer's credit card which enables her or him to buy not only the firm's products but also other conveniences.

To sell complicated, expensive, or specially designed items, you usually expect that the buyer will need more time, information, and personal observation. In this category are real estate, industrial equipment, insurance, costly installations, pleasure boats, cars, and products or services the reader may have considered unnecessary.

A campaign series of letters is a popular means of stimulating ultimate sales of such products and services. You decide in advance how many letters you should send, the time intervals, and the content of each. Some might ask the customer merely to request further information, as in letter 3.[18] In other letters you might request that the reader call your office or store for a demonstration, or ask for a sales representative to visit, as in letter 4.

Letter 3
Urging a travel-policy purchaser to request free facts about a special insurance plan. CSP: New, low-cost substitute income plan that protects in case of accident or sickness.
Appeals: pride and security.

[17]See the section on announcing sales and events, page 217.
[18]Your replies to these respondents would be solicited sales letters—discussed on pages 190–194.

WHAT MAKES YOU WORTH $250,000 or MORE?

Attention   You purchased a Travel policy at one of our airport booths recently. That got us to thinking.

There's a good chance you have a potential fortune of $250,000 or more that you have left entirely, or at least partially, unprotected.

Let's take the example of a person age 30 who earns $600 a month. During his lifetime he will earn $254,400 . . . if he lives AND IF HE KEEPS HIS HEALTH.

So, depending on your age and monthly income, you can well imagine the value of your own health, your ability to produce that income. Would it be $300,000? Or $400,000?

Interest   The risks involved in leaving unprotected an asset so valuable as your health are numerous. An accident--any time or any-where--or a sudden illness can topple a career, break up your savings, bankrupt your entire financial future.

Yet, how can the wise person avoid such risk? How can he make sure he'll have an income every month--if sickness or accident strikes? It is possible. And it is easy for you

Desire   to find out how you can protect the fortune you will earn with a plan that can pay you up to $1,000.00 a month (up to $32.25 a day--tax-free) when an accident of sickness pre-vents you from working.

(1)   Just returning the enclosed card will bring you the free facts about this new, low-cost, common sense Substitute Income Plan.

Action

(2)   And because you do travel, we'll also furnish you information showing how this plan can include up to $50,000 in accidental death benefits. This is not only flight or travel insurance--but year-round, 24-hour-a-day coverage for just about any accident you can imagine.

There you have two good reasons for returning your card. Here is the third:

Inducement to action   (3)   Because this plan is suited to your particular needs, we would like to further encourage your interest by offering you as a gift the handsome Pocket Secretary and Card Caddy pictured here. This is such a handy and valuable item we know you'll appreciate receiving it.

And it's absolutely free, as is the information about the $1,000 Substitute Income Plan with the $50,000 accidental death feature. So--if you are worth $250,000 or more, you will appreciate the wisdom of protecting your most valuable asset.

Action   Mail your card today. We'll furnish the free facts and you'll receive the handsome pocket secretary we have reserved for you.

Depending upon the kinds of products you sell, you can sometimes get a highly satisfactory return by mailing only a relatively few letters. For instance, a manufacturer of bulldozing equipment mailed one sales letter to only 58 business executives. To the requested action "Write, wire, or phone for further details" 30 readers replied; they bought $250,000 worth of equipment. Another example of an effective single letter is letter 4. Though mailed to only 100 sales managers, the letter sold one million caps! Each letter was individually typewritten on one page.

Letter 4
Urging sales managers to request a sales representative to give more information about an advertising gadget.[19]
CSP: Adjustable, lightweight, low-cost Paperlynen service caps for distinctive advertising.
Appeals: appearance, savings, comfort, distinctiveness.

Dear Mr. Gates:

Attention Literally and figuratively you can <u>hit the top</u> with your advertising.

How? With Paperlynen Adjustable Service Caps.

Interest Paperlynen Caps offer the ideal medium for placing your name constantly before the public eye. Worn by storekeepers and your own employees, these caps will not only help sell your products but are a constant goodwill reminder. And, as a means of cooperative advertising, they're excellent. In addition, Paperlynen <u>Adjustable</u> Service Caps are preferred because of their:

<u>Appearance</u>
Adjustable to any and every head size; always fit; look like linen; sanitary-clean.

<u>Low Cost</u>
Cost less than expense of having ill-fitting cloth caps laundered; this saving in addition to saving of initial cost of cloth caps.

Desire <u>Comfort</u>
Light in weight; porous nature of crown permits free, filtered ventilation.

<u>Distinction</u>
Offer the opportunity of distinction through imprinting your firm's name or trade mark in a manner not possible on ordinary caps. With cooperative advertising or as a dealer help, the storekeeper's name may also be added.

[19]Courtesy of S. Posner Sons, Brooklyn, New York, and The Dartnell Corporation, *The Dartnell File of Tested Sales Letters.*

Conviction   Several samples of Paperlynen Caps are enclosed. Look at 'em, try 'em, test 'em. We're sure you'll like 'em.

Action   When you are ready for more information call XX3-628-1030 and one of our salesmen will be up to see promptly.

To sell continual use of the customer's credit card, you need from time to time to show the benefits that can be gained from it. One example of such messages is letter 5, which an oil firm's credit card promotion manager used "with a great deal of success."

Letter 5
Urging use of credit card for product purchases and other conveniences. [20]
CSP: Detergent gasoline for extra engine-life and mileage at no extra cost; also additional advantages of the credit card.
Appeals: savings, safety, convenience.

Attention

> $1 of Mobil gasoline . . . Free! . . .
> with the enclosed certificate and
> your Mobil Credit Card.
> Nothing to buy.

Dear Fellow Motorist:

Attention   It may be surprising, but it's nonetheless true: The biggest single expense we are likely to have in our lifetime is for our automobiles. If you're like most Americans you will spend even more money on your car (including insurance, depreciation, repairs and operating expenses) than on your home. And if your family has two cars, you'll spend a great deal more.

In either case, it's important to get the most for your money, to make your car serve as long as possible. One of the best ways to prolong the life of your car is to make sure the inside of its engine is clean.

Interest (in card and product)   This is why you should be happy that you carry a Mobil Credit Card. Because Mobil Premium and Mobil Regular both have a Detergent that not only cleans carburetors . . . but also helps clean a number of vital engine parts. And it does it faster·than gasolines without detergent action get them dirty.

If you keep on using Mobil Detergent Gasoline, its cleaning action will keep working for you automatically. And your cleaner engine will . . .

give you less frequent and smaller repair bills;
give you noticeably more engine power for safe
   acceleration;
give you faster starts and smoother running, both
   of which reduce wear and tear on your car.

[20]Courtesy of Mobil Oil Corporation, New York, New York.

Desire-
conviction   And there's one more bonus--cleaner air. . . . We learned
how to make this gasoline through a massive and continuous
research program on the automotive pollution problem.
(Four paragraphs, omitted here, explain how the special
detergent additive helps your car release less pollutants
into the air, cleans a dirty oil screen, and saves you
money.)

What does all this extra engine-life and gas mileage
with a cleaner engine cost you? <u>It doesn't cost one</u>
penny more . . . nor a stroke of work. It all happens
automatically, every time you drive with Mobil Detergent
Gasoline in your tank.

You can buy Mobil Detergent Gasoline at over 26,000 Mobil
Dealer Stations, coast to coast. But with your Mobil Credit
Card, you can do even better:

You can use it to pay for tires, batteries, and all
   kinds of auto accessories on Mobil's new convenient
   Revolving Credit Plan.
You can charge a stay at any one of some 2,200 really
   good motels all over America.
And if you ever run into trouble on the road, you can
   use it to charge car repairs up to $75 . . . and use
   Revolving Credit too.
You can reduce the amount of money you must carry,
   reducing the risk of loss or theft.

Action
(continued   Your Mobil Credit Card brings you greater motoring pleasure
use of   and convenience while Mobil Detergent Gasoline helps keep
card and   your engine clean (instead of making it dirty). We thank
product)   you for using them both and hope you'll continue to enjoy
these important dividends every mile you drive.

A postscript on letter 5 tied in with the offer made at the beginning and served as
a special inducement to action:

We're so pleased with Mobil Detergent Gasoline we'll buy your next
dollar's worth. Simply hand the enclosed certificate and your
credit card to your Mobil dealer, and he'll put $1 worth of Premium
or Regular gasoline in your car but not charge you a cent. It will
be your first step toward a cleaner engine.

Bringing Back Lost Customers. Many businesses spend thousands of dollars on
advertising to attract new customers and yet neglect regular customers. Studies have
indicated that *indifference* on the part of the seller is the main reason customers leave
one company for another. At least two-thirds of such customers drift away because
they feel their business isn't appreciated, because they are treated discourteously, or
because some grievances were unadjusted.

The best way to find out why customers haven't bought from you for, say, six
months or more, is to ask them—either in person or by mail. Warm, sincere, friendly
letters can help you to learn why you lost customers and can also help you win them
back. (Of course, it is important that after you know customers' reasons, you take
steps to correct any weaknesses!)

The secret for winning back lost customers is to tell them that you miss them—and to keep telling them. Patience and persistence do pay off. For instance, one department store in Chicago reopened 2,724 accounts with sales totaling $73,001.34; a retail store in Long Beach, California, brought in $30,000 from lost customers; and a Buffalo merchant regained 47 percent of his lost accounts with 30 mailings over a period of five years.[21] Numerous other firms have also had rewarding results (sometimes even with one letter!)

Your first miss-you letters may be simple inquiries (without appeals).[22] However, when direct inquiries bring no response, you need to mail persuasive requests that say, in essence:

We miss you
Here are the benefits you get by coming back to us
Please come back

Sincerity, imagination, appropriate appeals, and sometimes good-natured humor characterize these messages, as illustrated below in letters 6 and 7.

Letter 6
A unique letter to win back "lost" hotel guests.[23]
CSP: High standard of personal service to "special guests."
Appeals: Enjoyment, comfort, convenience, prestige.

Dear Mr. Morgan:

Attention Today we registered an ex-president, two senators, a congressman, several assorted corporation presidents, a foreign personage with party, generals by the one, two and three star, plus a group of tourists. But not you.

Interest I suppose you thought we'd be too busy to notice that you were among the missing. But that's not true. We haven't made The Mayflower the standard of personal service by forgetting our special guests the moment they leave the check-out desk.

What happened?

Desire Have you sworn off roast beef when it's as succulent as our Rib Room specialty? Are you punishing yourself by giving up really comfortable, handsome, air-conditioned guest rooms for lesser accommodations? Do you feel guilty about staying at a hotel so perfectly located and so completely dedicated to your convenience? Or have you just not been in Washington lately?

We hope it's the latter.

Action Please write and end our suspense as soon as possible. Or, better yet, come back for a visit. Old friends are best friends. And busy as we are, we miss one of our very best friends: you!

[21] *Reporter of Direct Mail Advertising*, September 1965, pp. 49–50.
[22] For direct-request miss-you letters, see pages 156–158.
[23] An award-winning letter created by Spiro & Associates, Inc., Philadelphia, for the Mayflower Hotel in Washington, D.C.

Letter 7
An unusual department-store letter that brought an "excellent response in revived accounts and much favorable comment," according to the credit manager.[24] Beneath the letter was a picture of a customer credit card, removed from Rosenfields Good Customer File.)
CSP: The magic of purchases and services through the credit card.
Appeals: Ease, convenience, friendly good service.

<table>
<tr><td></td><td>IF YOUR ACCOUNT CARD COULD TALK, HERE'S WHAT IT WOULD SAY . . .</td></tr>
<tr><td>*Attention*</td><td>I'm getting lonesome - you haven't used me or your charge account at Rosenfields in over 90 days.</td></tr>
<tr><td>*Interest*</td><td>Really I'm not fussing, but I'm not just an ordinary card. I'm full of magic!</td></tr>
<tr><td>*Desire-conviction*

Reader benefits</td><td>I can dress you up in clothes as glamourous as a queen or movie star, yet priced to meet any budget. I can supply you with beautiful lingerie, hats, shoes, accessories, and dozens of other clothing, household and personal needs, so easily and conveniently.</td></tr>
<tr><td>*More benefits*</td><td>I can bring you the service of friendly folk in a store which has served Baton Rouge for generations, folk who take a personal interest in your needs and in giving you good service.</td></tr>
<tr><td>*Action*</td><td>Use me this month--attached is your current Rosenfields Credit Card which enables you to charge your purchases without delay.</td></tr>
</table>

With good judgment, a bit of originality, and imagination, you can develop a variety of appealing miss-you letters. If you prefer, you can buy special-theme messages from advertising specialists, with or without gadgets symbolic of various holidays, seasons, products, and services. Be sure, however, that they relate closely to your company's business.

In summary, use the persuasive-request plan whenever you need to write a favor request, a nonroutine claim that requires persuasion, or an unsolicited sales letter. Begin with an attention-getting appropriate opening; arouse interest through physical description and/or reader benefits; create desire and conviction by developing your central selling point and benefits, by offering proof, and by handling price in a positive way; then ask for action. If appropriate, offer special inducements so that the reader will act within a certain time. The Capsule Checklists that follow the exercises give a summary of the general plan and the three main kinds of persuasive requests.

[24] Courtesy of Rosenfields, Baton Rouge, Louisiana, and the Dartnell Corporation, *The Dartnell File of Tested Sales Letters.*

Exercises

Requests for Favors

1. The following form letter asks the reader to fill out a questionnaire. Criticize it constructively regarding you attitude, tone, honesty, word choice, and the attention-getting and action paragraphs. What impression does the letter give you about the writer and his company? Would the letter persuade you to furnish the requested information? Why or why not? What improvements can you suggest? The letter was sent from a radio manufacturing company whose letterhead states "Offices: Tokyo, Japan and Hong Kong; United States Offices (address) Los Angeles, Calif. (zip)." The envelope was postmarked in Los Angeles. The processed letter had no inside address. Notice the comments about enclosures following the letter.

Greetings and Salutations.

We are sending this letter to a select group of people like yourself who have been recommended to us by an American research organization.

The courtesy we ask is that you read this letter and favor us with the answer to the enclosed questions. In appreciation for your cooperation, we shall do our utmost to reward you for your kind help. (Please read on.)

You can save us time and money in our marketing plans. We will be undertaking extensive advertising in the United States and are very anxious to place our advertising where it will best be seen by people like yourself--will you please help us by filling in and returning the enclosed questions in the free envelope--it is a two minute service that will be greatly appreciated.

We are enclosing a Brochure of the first selection of the (year and name) Portable Radio Models to appear on the American market. In return for your participating interest, we offer you a completely free gift of your choice of any nationally famous (name) Watch.

Please fill in the questionnaire and mail to our Los Angeles office in the enclosed envelope. On the back of the questionnaire is the order form to choose your reward.

We beg you not to delay or put off your reply. Your immediate answers to our market questions are needed to complete our survey, also the initial supply of watches forces us to limit this free gift offer only to that quantity now in our Los Angeles warehouse.

Comments about enclosures: The printed questionnaire contained four questions (about the name and address of the reader's "favorite" newspaper, magazines, and local radio stores). Above the questions was this request: "Please fill out this questionnaire and mail it to our Los Angeles office with your radio order." On the reverse side of the questionnaire was an order form for radios and tape recorders, followed by this request: "Select one free watch for each radio or tape recorder you order. We regret we cannot send your free watch unless the questionnaire is completed." An enclosed leaflet pictured two radios, one tape recorder, and nine men's and ladies' watches. ("Completed" meant answering the questions and ordering a radio or tape recorder.)

2. The following request was sent by the executive employment manager of a large national hotel corporation, typed (on hotel letterhead) by automatic typewriter, and addressed personally to the Director of University Placement Services. Evaluate the letter, commenting particularly on its tone, stated reader benefits, action request, and postscript; and state ways to improve it.

```
Dear Prof. (name):

No, we won't be recruiting on your campus this year . . .
sorry about that!

But, we ARE looking for the BEST college grads in the United
States (we would say the world, but there might be a language
problem), and feel you can help us.

The student we want would come to your mind quickly.  He's the
one who made you say to yourself, "This is the most promising
individual I've seen in years!"  (He may even remind you a
little of yourself at that age.)

Refer the right people to me directly and you can be sure we
will do right by them.

Just think, Prof. (name), some day you may be able to say you
know the President of (name of hotel chain) because you got
him his job.

P.S.  Whether or not you believe the enclosed "Careers Fact
Sheets" is up to you . . . we tried to modestly let people
know about career opportunities with the best and fastest
rising hotel chain around.
```

3. Assume that you are program chairperson for your college chapter of a national organization composed of students whose major is the same as yours. For the past two years the members have repeatedly mentioned their desire to hear this organization's national vice president, Mr. L. F. Kameron. He is known to be an outstanding, dynamic speaker. Two of your members who heard him at the organization's national convention last summer also have been enthusiastic about him. Because he lives 2,000 miles from your school and your chapter's treasury is small, however, everyone has just assumed that getting Mr. Kameron would be almost impossible. Nevertheless, in yesterday's newspaper you happened to read that Mr. Kameron will be attending a one-day business conference in Somecity (you insert a city name), which is only 250 miles from you—just the day before your chapter's annual Founders' Day Banquet.

Now you want to persuade Mr. Kameron to accept your invitation to be principal banquet speaker. You cannot pay him any speaker's fee, but your budget enables you to pay traveling expenses equal to round-trip plane fare from (Somecity) to yours. Six planes daily fly between these cities; if he prefers a bus, buses run on an hourly schedule. A scenic ride by freeway takes about four hours, in case he prefers to drive a private car. Mr. Kameron will, of course, be your chapter's dinner guest. Maybe you can think of an inexpensive, courteous way to take care of him if he wishes to stay overnight after his talk? Assume any other necessary details that will make your letter complete—with you attitude. Consider carefully the best appeal(s) to use.

4. Point out the weaknesses, errors, and good points in the following letter. Then—
   as program chairperson—rewrite it, applying the principles you have learned, to
   make your request so appealing that the reader will want to accept. Address it to
   Mrs. R. J. Milliman, Director of Public Relations, KMRO Television, in a city
   about 80 miles from you. If your instructor approves, you may choose another
   topic instead of air pollution.

> What are you plans for Saturday evening, March 20? The
> members of our (city name) Business Leaders' Club feel it
> would be a pleasure to us to have you as the principal
> speaker for our annual banquet that night.
>
> Ways to fight air pollution is a topic that our members are
> concerned and realize the need of practical advice from ex-
> perienced executives. Your many editorial comments on
> Channel 16 KMRO have shown us your sincere interest and
> extensive study on this subject. Our members and their
> spouses want to hear you in person. This banquet is our
> biggest function of the year, and we would be honored to
> have you and your spouse as our guests.
>
> The banquet will be held in the Marlboro Room of the Plaza
> Hotel at 7 and will be informal. A varied entertainment
> program and an excellent dinner at $6.50 per person have
> been arranged.
>
> Your traveling expenses would be provided, and I hope that
> you can take advantage of a visit to our city to settle any
> personal affairs you may have here. The Plaza Hotel is
> equipped with excellent facilities in the event you decide
> to extend your visit.
>
> I shall appreciate your assent to this request so that I can
> welcome you on your arrival if feasible.

5. Assume you graduated from the university five years ago and you have become
   an active member of a certain professional (or business or social or religious)
   group that owns the building in which meetings and activities take place.
   You have just been elected treasurer of your organization for a two-year term.
   For about 15 years this organization has been saving money to build a much-
   needed extension to its building. (Assume specific reasons why the addition is necessary and beneficial to members.) It has been planned that construction will
   begin next July 1—three months from today—and be completed by October 1.
   (Assume today is April 1.) The addition, as sketched by architects and approved
   by your executive board, will cost about $90,000. Your books show $39,000
   cash in the building fund; your organization can get a $46,000 mortgage. You
   need to raise $5,000 cash between now and about May 5 or construction cannot
   begin. Your task is to try to raise this money. After several meetings with the
   executive board, it is decided that, rather than asking your members to put on
   several fund-raising events (which are time-consuming), or assessing them a definite amount, you will urge them to make a donation. The board members want
   you to head this fund-raising campaign.
   Write a letter, remembering that it is a form letter, to be sent to all members.
   Assume a mailing list of 600. Try to keep your letter to one typewritten page.
   Select the appeals (loyalty, pride, self-interest, and so forth) that you think will
   be most effective in moving your readers to take the requested action. Set May 5
   as the deadline for donations, because adequate time must be allowed for making
   financial arrangements before construction begins. Make action easy and include

any reasonable inducements for your readers to act now. Naturally, you'd rather have checks returned with each reply; however, for those members who would rather sign a pledge now and pay later—before the completion of construction—plan an easy-action reply form, which you can depend upon in your financial calculations.

6. As the new systems manager for the National Casualty Associates, you have considered numerous ways to increase company efficiency and decrease costs. Recently, after checking correspondence procedures, you were surprised to find several wasteful, unnecessarily time-consuming methods that you'd like to change. However, before authorizing any changes, you have decided to survey the preferences of the management staff in your home office and 60 branch offices. You have prepared an easy-to-answer two-page questionnaire asking for their reactions to eight money- and timesaving suggestions. Now write a persuasive, courteous memorandum urging these executives to fill out your enclosed form and return it to you by a certain date, so that you can complete a needed report on their replies. Promise anonymity to all respondents. Include appropriate appeals to urge their cooperation. Three of your money-saving suggestions may require a little explanation and "selling" before your readers approach the questionnaire.

   a. You advocate using window envelopes instead of individually addressed envelopes for the approximately 150,000 monthly messages your company sends to policyholders, prospective customers, suppliers, and stockholders. You think window envelopes could save thousands of hours of typing time annually, because the inside addresses on the letters or forms within the envelopes could serve for the envelopes too.

   b. You are considering adopting a standardized companywide letter format—blocked, open punctuation, with or without salutation and complimentary close. Such standardization, you feel, would give the company an image of uniformity and at the same time save stenographic time.

   c. With each company letter that asks the recipient for a brief answer, you would like to enclose a courtesy carbon for his reply. The recipient would then merely type his reply at the bottom of your letter, return to you the carbon copy (showing both your letter and his reply), and keep the original for his files. Such an enclosure would bring speedier answers to company requests and would cut down the need for second or third requests to get replies, thus saving postage and labor costs.

   As you write your memo, remember that your readers are in management, just as you are, even if you do probably outrank many of them. Watch your tone and try to build pleasant relations and high morale.

7. The following request was sent (mimeographed, without inside address or date) by a district manager on the letterhead of a national insurance company. If you were the policyholder receiving this letter, would it persuade you to act? How does the purpose of this message affect your image of the company? Is the request clear as to kind of personnel wanted? What improvements can you suggest for this letter?

```
Hello:

The present and projected growth of our area requires that
we add additional personnel to our staff.  Rather than go to
an employment agency for help, the thought struck me, WHY NOT
ASK YOU AS A BUYER OF INSURANCE for recommendations of men
or women that you would like to see serve you.  I realize that
```

this is an unusual request to ask, but after all, you are the
best judge of the type of people that you want to deliver our
Fast-Fair-Friendly service.

We are seeking someone who may have reached a "peak" in their
present job or someone anxious to establish a career and
business of their own. They may perhaps be a neighbor, a
sales acquaintance who is dissatisfied, your son or daughter,
a widow having trouble making ends meet, or perhaps a man or
woman at your place of employment. Someone who wants to
advance themselves.

Since I don't know this friend of yours, I am counting on you
to help by writing their name on the enclosed card and mailing
it to me. Should they be interested in learning about our
career opportunity, I'll show them how we train our representatives, our opportunities for advancement, and how we give
them the right atmosphere for permanent success.

Please send me your recommendation as soon as possible as it
may well be the "turning point" in the life of your friend.
I will let you know the results following our interview.

8. You are vice president of the Greater Greenwood Community Council. (Greenwood is a residential area of a large city.) Your council members want you to
write a letter to every taxpayer (about 12,000) in your community to raise
money for a worthy cause.

Fred More, your State Senator from the 49th District, initiated and won a class
action taxpayer's suit against the state in a precedent-setting case. Because he
went well beyond the call of duty in taking this action in behalf of the community, he has personally incurred a financial burden of no small proportions.
Senator More expended over three months of legal time on this case, having tried
a six-day trial in Superior Court and having argued the matter twice in your State
Supreme Court. He received no fee for his services and in addition personally incurred some $2,000 of out-of-pocket legal expenses. The Greater Greenwood
Community Council has unanimously passed a resolution supporting a money-
raising effort in behalf of the Senator. All residents (taxpayers) of this area in the
city together saved over $6 million on their property taxes last year because of
this one man's efforts in their behalf.

Your Council hopes to get at least small personal donations from most people in
the entire Greenwood community, as an indication of their appreciation of Senator More's help. You all would rather have such donations than a few large contributions from business firms. Write an appealing, persuasive message that will get
a large favorable response.

9. As building manager of your company's three-story structure, you have just received an unusual report from your sanitation engineer. He has found that at least
one rat has been attracted to the building recently. The employee practice of
leaving food on bookshelves, desks, and other open locations will have to be discontinued or watched very carefully. Each office occupant must be made aware
of the problem and the possibility that he or she is part of the cause. As rats will
not bother to infest an area unless there is good reason to do so (food), the best
way to maintain rat-free premises consists of denying them food, water, and
safety. It would be economically unfeasible to make the needed structural

changes for rat-proofing the entire building. (The cafeteria is, however, rat-proofed.) About four months ago you wrote a simple announcement (without appeals—merely a "direct request") to all employees. But apparently some (or most?) have forgotten about it. Now again one rat was seen, but many more, still unseen, could come into the building. Thus you must write a persuasive request in a memorandum to all employees, urging them to cooperate on preventive action. Instruct them to exercise utmost care with lunches or other food brought into the building. Instruct them not to leave any food in their offices overnight. Also request them to be alert for signs indicating rodent or insect activity: droppings; gnawed food, odor; dark rub marks along wall, ceiling, under door, ventilator, which indicate a runway. Request that employees inform a certain office as soon as such evidence appears. Watch the tone of your memo, and be sure to consider the attitudes of your readers.

10. Assume you graduated from college two years ago and became an active member of a business, professional, social, or religious organization. You have just been elected vice president and have been asked by the executive board to see if you can increase attendance at meetings for next year. Assume that the organization has a potential membership of 200, but that during the past three or four years only 15 to 25 have been attending monthly meetings regularly. You would like to have at least 50 or 60.

Plan a letter to send to the 200 potential members aiming to find out in a friendly, tactful way why so many have not been attending meetings and what types of programs, arrangements, or methods would get them to the meetings. Be careful to keep the tone positive and cheerful, filled with you attitude. Suggestions: Perhaps more would come if they had transportation, or if the meetings were held at a more central location, or if the business portion were shorter and the programs more entertaining, or if someone would phone them shortly before meetings. In the past, written announcements have been sent to all members a week before a meeting. Devise some method which will make it easy for each member to answer your letter giving you specific information about what is preferred in topics, speakers, activities. Assume that your letter will be mimeographed.

Nonroutine Requests for Adjustment, Credit, or Changes

1. Assume you have just received a credit turndown for a charge account with a local store. The reason stated for the refusal is correct. (Assume a legitimate reason such as under age 18, presently unemployed, or a similar one). However, for various other reasons—perhaps a steady trust fund income you receive from a regular source, or a verifiable record of integrity, or any other good reason(s) that might outweigh the shortcoming, you know that you will be a prompt-paying customer. You always take care of all obligations you have. Write to the store's credit manager an honest, persuasive request for credit. Make your reasoning logical and appealing, so that your reader will be convinced that she should make an exception for you and grant you a charge account.

2. You are manager of Vernie's Men's Wear in Sometown, South Dakota. You have two stores—one situated in the downtown area and one two blocks from a college campus. For years you have carried exclusively Van Doser shirts, which you buy direct from the manufacturer. On June 5, only four days after this firm's fall catalog came out, you again ordered a complete Van Doser line for your two stores. You asked for delivery by September 10. But now you have noted with

alarm the many changes the manufacturer made in your fall order. Back-to-school goods scheduled by your sales staff for early delivery have been pushed to October and November. You haven't a stripe in stock and college opens next week. You've had to switch to other brands because you can't get all the Van Doser merchandise you'd like. You have faith in Van Doser merchandise; it's your preference of all brand shirts on the market. But this is the third time in four years that they have changed delivery time on your orders.

While you were in Minneapolis just a few days ago, you noted that the Custer Men's Store (a retail store for this shirt manufacturer) was stocked with everything in the Van Doser book, and Custer could not have ordered any sooner than you did. Just how does this manufacturer expect to keep good customers like you with that kind of treatment? Unless they can find some way to supply your stores adequately and promptly, you may have to find a replacement for Van Doser shirts. You feel you have helped considerably to build this manufacturer's business the past five years. Right now you feel like giving your business to a competitor. Address your message to Mr. Thomas Newsom, sales manager of Van Doser Manufacturing Company, Chicago. Be tactful, firm, and appropriately persuasive.

3. As the new office manager and accountant of Jessup Realty you have just encountered a situation that you think needs to be handled by a good persuasive letter. Six months ago the owner-manager (Nick Jessup) bought, for one of the two secretaries in the office, a steel secretarial desk and a secretarial posture chair —from the ABC Office Equipment Company. When they arrived, he was displeased with them both, but never bothered to write anyone to request an adjustment. He did talk to the ABC sales representative, Claire, however. Here are the facts as Mr. Jessup tells them: "I've been doing business OK with ABC for a number of years, and I always pay my bills promptly. But not this one! They can just wait."

"For the first three months after this desk and chair arrived, I refused to pay anything on them. After receiving collection letters, I decided to send only a $5 payment each month, although they wanted $20 a month. You see, these items have given us troubles from the day they were delivered. The secretarial steel desk costing the exorbitant price of $289 isn't worth a damn. First of all, I wanted a secretarial desk with a deep-well drawer. Both Claire and the ABC manager stated that there were none available. A week or so later I learned that there were any number of them available in other office equipment stores. That burned me up! Secondly, the typewriter arm (which is a big factor in the cost of the desk) has not worked properly since the day the desk was brought into my office. Claire attempted to give the typewriter arm 'emergency first aid' by the use of a piece of wood, which kept the arm outstretched at all times. We finally found it necessary to discontinue the use of the typewriter arm. This means that considerable valuable space of the desk is wasted. I also have a gripe in connection with the posture chair, which cost $58. One of these days someone will find their "posture" on the office floor, since the back-rest bar that goes underneath the seat works itself loose every second or third day. So do you see why I don't want to pay for this stuff on time? I still want a properly operating secretarial desk with a deep-well drawer plus a posture chair that is not defective. It is my belief that a proper adjustment can be made. However, if they don't see fit to do anything regarding this matter, I'll continue my practice of small ($5) monthly payments. Frankly, I suppose I should have written Jerry Bean (the ABC manager) a letter long ago, but I've been too mad to write. If you think you can give him the whole story in a letter and get the adjustments I want, go ahead and try! I yelled at him once on the phone, but it didn't do any good."

Now that you know the facts, you have a good opportunity to show your new employer what you can accomplish with a well-written persuasive letter. Write your letter for either Mr. Jessup's signature or your own, whichever you think will be the psychologically better way to get a favorable reply to this request for adjustment.

4. Your wholesale firm has a policy of granting a 2 percent discount for bills your customers pay within 10 days of invoice date, and the full amount is due in 30 days. One of your customers paid a $560 invoice (dated October 11) with his check mailed on November 9. But he deducted $11.20 discount. Consequently, you wrote him a courteous direct-request letter, asking him to pay the $11.20. Today (November 20) you get an angry protest from the customer, stating that his cashier was in the hospital last month and so a number of bills accumulated that otherwise would have been paid within the 10-day period. He added, "Your company is the only one out of about fifty that has attempted to chisel us out of this discount. We can buy plenty of watches, equal in quality to yours, from folks who are willing to meet a customer halfway—and who realize there are always just exceptions to any business rule. Of course, if you insist, a check will be mailed; but it strikes me as a small amount to cause the severing of business relations between us."

To your company, a discount of $11.20 involves a long-standing company principle—that of impartial treatment of every customer. You maintain the "2/10 net/30" policy because it enables you to earn similar savings by paying your own bills promptly; then you pass the savings on to your customers in lower prices, as a reward for their promptness. When customers pay after the 10-day period, you make no savings. You do not want to grant special privileges to some concerns, because such inconsistencies involve much more than a small discount. Write a persuasive request to this customer (Flatwood Jewelry Shop) urging him to pay this honest debt.

Unsolicited Sales Letters

1. Your new assistant laid the following sales-letter draft on your desk for your approval before it is mailed to 10,000 homeowners in your community. Obviously, it needs a good deal of revision. Rewrite it, making all needed improvements. Choose a central selling point and include good appeals, persuading the reader to take your desired action. (The salutation is "Dear Home Owner":)

I am writing this letter to offer the services of Inca Millwork and Construction Company in the remodeling of a home.

We are primarily in the business of kitchen and bath remodeling. We can furnish custom cabinets and any type of built-in appliance using such name brands as General Electric, Frigidaire, or Hot Point.

Our customers are given the latest selection of floor coverings and counter top materials.

We maintain our own craftsmen to do the specific job and we guarantee all of our work.

We offer customers bank financing, F.H.A. or conventional with nothing down and no monthly payments until sixty days after completion of the job.

Our company is not the largest in the home improvement field and we do very little advertising. The bulk of our business is acquired through the recommendations of satisfied customers, low prices and quality work.

Please use the self-addressed, stamped card for a free estimate or call 904-8888.

2. As sales manager for Lamson Manufacturing Company, Columbus, Ohio, you want to send—to retail store managers who have been your regular customers—a letter that ties in with your national advertising campaign. During November and December your company's all-purpose folding card tables with four matching folding chairs will be featured in two consumer magazines in full-page three-color ads. These ads will be read by 24 million people. You consider this the most powerful selling story you have ever put across. Now (October 1) you want to be sure that the 590 retail store managers that carry your products are sufficiently well stocked with a variety of these table-chair sets to meet the expected consumer demand. Wholesale price of each five-piece set is $31.80. Retail price is $53; separate folding tables are $16 each and each chair is $10.50. Thus, by buying the combination set, consumers save $5. Each table is 36 inches square, with vinyl covered top and bronze-tone finish steel frame 28 inches high; shipping weight, 21 pounds. The matching folding chairs have padded vinyl seats, steel legs; shipping weight, 12 pounds each. Colors for both tables and chairs, green or mushroom beige in plain or floral patterns. These beautiful, practical, and low-priced items are just what consumers will need for Christmas. In your sales letter, provide easy-action order blanks and promise prompt shipment; be as specific as possible. Orders you receive by October 18 can be filled and the sets shipped in time for your customers to have them in stock by November 1.

3. Assume that last month you ran three advertisements in a local newspaper announcing the opening or remodeling of your business. You sell a service—such as transportation, advertising, tax consulting, traveler's aid, or restaurant. Write an unsolicited letter selling your service to a select list of (imaginary but probable) prospects who you are sure can benefit from what you can do for them. The goal of each letter is to bring your prospect to your business for his first "purchase" or (if more appropriate) for a consultation. Select a central selling point and build your letter around it. For instance, if you write for a restaurant, perhaps you will want to emphasize a food specialty or a special plate for which your chef is famous. Perhaps you will also want to mention your speedy service, exotic decor, music, prices, or extra-generous servings. Your letter should contain strong reader-benefit appeals. If you want to offer some special inducement such as a free gift or a reduced rate for the first visit, that's fine. If yours is a service that customers use repeatedly (such as a restaurant or transportation facility), figure out an appropriate way to determine which customers are calling for the first time.

With your sales letter submit a complete "assumption sheet" that includes a brief statement on each of the following:

a. The nature and location of your service
b. Your reason for choosing this service
c. Your central selling point
d. The specific purpose of your message
e. Any unique assumptions you have made (special letterhead, season)
f. The kind of enclosure(s), if any, you would have

4. Compare the following two letters,[25] both of which are designed to sell the same excellent service for top executives. Which one would you mail to management personnel if you had the choice and why? In your analysis of each, consider specifically: (a) you attitude, (b) attention-getting opening, (c) interest and conviction material, (d) action request.

A.

CAN YOUR CUSTOMERS REALLY AFFORD
THE DEBT THEY ARE CARRYING?

Dear Sir:

Debt presents an attractive means of financing. But--since assets have a way of melting away when a concern encounters troubles--the decision to extend bank or merchandise credit involves the balance of expected return and increased risk.

This is cash flow analysis.

The concept and procedure for determining cash flow is fully presented in the Dun & Bradstreet Advanced Credit and Financial Analysis course.

Throughout the course, the credit function is approached as a managerial function with profit responsibility to the entire organization. The objective is to develop managerial judgment that will be of value to both the organization's advancement and the individual's advancement.

While the course employs some of the most advanced techniques of financial analysis, great care is taken to have it remain completely practical. The advanced materials are fresh enough to remain current practice for many years.

An outline of the content of this new Dun & Bradstreet business course is shown on the following page. The course can be both a challenge and a reward to men and women in your organization who are concerned with growth and profits. To enroll just fill in the registration form on page 4 and return it to me.

B.

Your management personnel should know
    . . . how to read a balance sheet between the lines

The ability to judge a financial statement accurately--to predict credit responsibility and avoid unusual risks, can be a tremendous asset to your firm.

Balance sheets can hide the facts you need to make a sound credit judgment. The facts are there to the man who knows what to look for, who knows how to interpret what he sees.

[25]Courtesy of Dun & Bradstreet, Business Education Division, New York; and *Direct Marketing*, April 1970.

The D&B Advanced Credit and Financial Analysis course is built around authentic business credit problems. The executive learns by dealing with financial facts. His solutions are compared with real life situations--he follows the action as it happened and sees into the why and how of credit decisions.

> Twelve sections cover business credit, financing, debt, management, investment techniques, bankruptcies and dozens of other aspects of business money management.

This is a home study course completed in six months, with the student's progress checked regularly and reported to management.

Thousands of top business leaders have completed this up-to-the-minute training and are using their sharpened financial know how to improve the earning performance of their firms. The men you select for this instruction can do as well, and within six months.

Read the enclosed detailed description and then list the executives you want to enroll. Their training can begin at once, with their new skills put to work quickly to protect company earning potential.

Select your personnel today and we will get them started at once. It's never too soon.

5. You are a part-time employee for Mod Man, Inc., a men's clothing shop. "For men who think young." Your employer, knowing you are a college senior and that you're studying business communications, has just offered you a challenging opportunity to try your skill on a sales letter. After you write it, he will pay all expenses for reproducing and mailing it—plus a 10 percent commission to you on the direct sales your letter brings in.

   Here is his proposition: The store's men's formal wear rental department is sponsoring a special Senior Ball promotion. Your letter is to be mailed to all men in your college senior class. Assume at least 1,000 on your mailing list. All your readers need to do is to stop in at Mod Man and register. Your employer has made arrangements with a local automobile dealer to have a brand new 197_ customized convertible on display right in the store starting this weekend until two days before the Senior Ball. Someone who registers will win the free use of this car for the night of your Senior Ball, courtesy of Tom Tolaf Auto Sales, Inc. In addition, there will be four other big winners, each of whom will get: Senior Ball tickets for two; a corsage of their choice; a $20 gift certificate for dinner for two at (name) restaurant (the best in your city); and their formal wear rental at no charge. All the seniors have to do to get a chance to win is to register and choose their formal wear from your store. You have the largest and most fashionable collection in the city: everything from white dinner jackets to full-dress tails, with 23 styles in between including double-breasted coats, turtlenecks, and ruffled shirts, and all at Mod Man's standard low rental rates.

   Your one-page letter will be processed in any way you choose—mimeographed, by computer, or dittoed—and will be on the store's letterhead. There is to be no enclosure. You may send the letter over your own signature, if you wish. Design its layout in any way you choose. If you wish, you can give this promotion a special name (such as "Your Prom Night On Us").

6. Assume you are sales manager of the Armo Products Company, which manufactures do-it-yourself tools and home building supplies. To get your company's name before the public and at the same time to help your exclusive dealers, you

have developed a special-offer plan for the dealers. By taking advantage of your cooperative plan, the dealers can buy—at half price—book matches to give away to their consumer customers as goodwill builders. This week you need to send a letter to your 600 dealers telling them about your plan. Each dealer can have his or her name imprinted on one side of the book matches. The other side shows the Armo insignia and identifies the dealer's store as headquarters for Armo products.

These matches enable the dealer to tie in with your firm's national advertising, which sells Armo products all over the country. You have placed a large advance order with your match manufacturer. However, initial orders from dealers who have recently visited your plant indicate that the demand will soon exceed the supply, so it's a good idea for your dealers to place their orders right now. You can sell them 4,800 book matches in the new double size for only $20. This is less than ½ cent per book match. The 4,800 books contain 192,000 matches, each a reminder of the dealer's business. In your letter provide a convenient order blank and remind the dealers to specify the imprint they want.

7. You are general manager of the Uptown Auto Sales and Service. Your body shop department gets numerous opportunities to make repair estimates on automobiles damaged in accidents. Usually, prospective customers get estimates from three different repair shops. You have good reason to know that your shop's prices and bids are very similar to those of your closest competitors. Thus prospective customers who must choose one of three shops often have very little except price to guide them.

You want now to draft a form letter—on your company's letterhead—for your or your foreman's signature. It is to be sent from time to time to each customer on whose car the shop makes an estimate. Typed on automatic typewriter, each letter will have a personalized inside address and salutation. Its purpose is to persuade each reader to bring his car to your shop because of the benefits he gets in addition to the reasonable price. Your facilities are complete. Everything is done in your shop: paint, metal, mechanical, glasswork, frame straightening. Your personnel are hand-picked factory-trained specialists. They take pride in their work. You use only genuine factory parts, and you guarantee satisfaction. Your policy is service, quality, and integrity. You'll also consider a customer's credit for a budget account, so he can have his car repaired now and pay later. Write the sales letter that will help each prospective customer to decide that your company is where he should have his car repaired.

8. Assume you have been out of college 10 years. Recently a group of your former classmates persuaded you to be chairperson of the class tenth anniversary reunion. The date chosen coincides with your college homecoming, at which the classes that graduated 10, 25, and 50 years ago are especially honored. You have rented the Horizon and Rainier Rooms of the Plaza Hotel for Saturday evening of homecoming weekend, and committees have been working on plans.

Now it is your job to write the "sales letter" to urge former classmates to buy tickets and attend. It's to be a new-fashioned get-together of cocktails, dinner, dancing, and reminiscing. For an orchestra you found three persons who play the kind of music that was popular when you all were in college. For those alums who need tickets for the homecoming football game against UCLA, you've managed to reserve a few. But they must get their requests and money in immediately. The seats aren't quite on the 50-yard line, but they're inside the stadium, which is pretty good, considering the limited supply. You already have a reservation from Fairbanks, Alaska, and you're hoping for many others from distant places. A prize will be given to the classmate traveling the longest distance.

Write a convincing letter that will urge—and get—an excellent turnout. Provide a good way for readers to make their reservations and make clear that $10 must accompany each reservation.

CAPSULE CHECKLISTS FOR

I *Persuasive Requests—General Plan*	*II* *Persuasive Requests for Favors*

1. ATTENTION (promise; star)
   a. Introduction of relevant reader-benefit or reader-interest theme—centered on reader, not on writer's organization
   b. Envelopes and letterheads sometimes specially designed for the message
	1. Attention
	   a. Sincere compliment
	   b. Questions
	   c. Agreeable comment or assertion
	   d. Basic problem
	   e. What has been done about a problem
	   f. Frank admission of a favor

2. INTEREST (picture; chain)
   b. Introduction of project or product's physical description, benefits, central selling point
   c. Appeals: appreciation, approval, beauty, cleanliness, comfort, convenience, cooperation, customer satisfaction, distinctiveness, efficiency, enjoyment, entertainment, extra earnings, fair treatment, friendships, good reputation, health, improvement, love of home and others, money and other valuables, peace of mind, pleasure, popularity, position, profits, recognition, safety, satisfaction of helping others, savings, self-preservation, and others
	2. Interest and
	3. Desire
	   a. Necessary physical description of project
	   b. Facts, figures, and reader benefits to convince reader that his or her contribution will be enjoyable, easy, important, beneficial—directly or indirectly
	     (1) In request for speaker: date, day, hour; place; function; topic; talk length; audience size, interests; honorarium, expenses; special attractions; appeals.
	     (2) In request for donation: problem; needs; past, present methods of meeting needs; costs; reader contribution: benefits, appeals.
	     (3) In request for cooperation: problem; facts, suggestions, committee, etc. to help meet goal; reader's part; benefits, appeals.

3. DESIRE (prove; chain)
   a. Desire: development of description, benefits, central selling point, appeals; perhaps with an enclosure
   b. Conviction:
     (1) "Outside" proof; perhaps with enclosures
     (2) Price and terms when needed and appropriate; perhaps in enclosure
	c. Positive handling of negatives and probable objections for favors that:
	     (1) Require time, knowledge, or effort
	     (2) Ask donations of money or other valuables
	     (3) Urge cooperation on goals and projects
	   d. Enclosures (brochures)

4. ACTION (push; hook)
   a. CSAD[1]
   b. EA[2]
   c. DA when desirable[3]
   d. Special inducement when desirable
   e. RB (often tied in with opening statement)[4]
	4. Action, same as I, 4

*Lists include possible content. For any one message, choose only pertinent and appropriate items.
[1]CSAD = clear statement of action desired
[2]EA = easy action
[3]DA = dated action, if desirable
[4]RB = reader benefit

See also pages 80–81 for W's on complete action requests.

PERSUASIVE REQUESTS*

III Other Persuasive Nonroutine Requests	IV Unsolicited Sales Letters

1. Attention
    Same as II, 1; preferably an agreeable assertion or a principle which is used as a major premise.
	1. Attention
	  a. Agreeable assertion
	  b. Comparison or short story
	  c. Event or fact in reader's life
	  d. Problem reader may face
	  e. Quotation
	  f. Scare opening
	  g. Significant fact about product
	  h. Solution to a problem
	  i. Special offer or gift
	  j. Surprising or challenging statement
	  k. Testimonials

2. Interest and
3. Desire
  a. All necessary facts and details pertaining to request for adjustment, credit, or changes in policy or performance—interwoven with reader benefits and appeals
  b. Description as needed by the reader to see that his or her firm is responsible (if applicable) and that the request is factual, logical, and reasonable
	2. Interest
	  a. Beginning development of physical description and product benefits, geared to prospect's needs; meaningful appeals
	3. Desire-Conviction
	  a. Full development of needed description, reader benefits, central selling point
	  b. Proof by users, laboratories and agencies, prospect:
	    (1) Facts about users' experience with product
	    (2) Names of users (5) Performance tests
	    (3) Testimonials (6) Guarantee
	    (4) Free trial (7) Samples
	  c. Price presented in psychologically favorable way(s)
	  d. Enclosures to strengthen desire-conviction

4. Action
  a. Logical conclusion based on the major premise and the clearly stated facts; then same as I, 4
	4. Action
	  a. CSAD[1] c. DA[3]
	  b. EA[2] d. RB[4]
	  e. Inducements
	    (1) Credit cards
	    (2) Easy payments or no money down
	    (3) Free gift
	    (4) Free trial
	    (5) Last chance
	    (6) Limited quantity or time
	    (7) No obligation to buy
	    (8) Premium
	    (9) Special price for limited time

PART **3**

SPECIALIZED MESSAGES

11 The Written Job Presentation

I. "PRODUCT" ANALYSIS—EVALUATING YOURSELF
II. MARKET RESEARCH—FINDING WHO CAN USE YOU AND WHAT THEY PREFER
    A. Information Sources for Careers and Jobs
    B. Desirable General Qualifications of the Applicant
    C. Desirable General Qualities for the Written Job Presentation
III. RESUME
    A. Opening Section
    B. Education
    C. Work Experience
    D. Activities, Achievements, Awards
    E. Personal Data
    F. Other Relevant Facts
    G. References
    H. Examples
IV. LETTER OF APPLICATION
    A. Opening for Favorable Attention
    B. Middle Paragraphs for Interest, Desire, Conviction
    C. Last Paragraph
    D. Sample Letters of Application
V. EXERCISES

Sometime in your life—perhaps several times—you will probably seek a job through a written presentation. If you answer advertisements or choose companies that do not send recruiters to your campus, you will usually need to write and mail your application. Also, even if you interview a firm's representative on your campus, you may still be asked for additional, written infromation. Furthermore, several years after you graduate from college—if you desire to change jobs—the ability to write a good presentation of yourself will help you get a better, more satisfying job. Thousands of applicants have found that the best way to get interviews and desired jobs is through the direct-mail approach.

Actually, when you apply for a job you are selling a "product"—yourself. The research before you write, as well as the planning and writing of your "sales promotion" job presentation, should be as thorough as for selling any other product by direct mail. This chapter discusses the "product" analysis, market research, résumé, and application letter.

"Product" Analysis—Evaluating Yourself

Whenever you are selling something, you want to be sure you are representing the product fairly. You need to analyze it to know *what* you are selling before you can start investigating *where* and *how* to sell it. The same is true when you are selling your services. To appraise yourself adequately, take an inventory of your employment qualifications. Begin by listing—on several sheets of paper or cards—your specific achievements and capabilities. You might write them under various general headings like the following:

Work experience, skills, aptitudes
Your part-time and full-time jobs since high school—dates, employer and supervisor names and addresses; your title(s), duties, successes, promotions.
Your specific skills and aptitudes; also machines (office, industrial, craft) you can operate well.

Education
Schools (colleges, technical, military, high, other) you attended—dates, names, locations; your degrees, major(s), scholastic standing in each.
Courses—in major, core, and useful electives; grades.

Activities and achievements
Extracurricular and professional organizations—memberships, offices held, and noteworthy accomplishments in clubs related to your major, or in sports, church, social, community projects.
Achievements, honors, awards—scholarships, honor rolls, and other recognitions.
Travel, foreign language facilities, hobbies, personal business ventures, publications, and so forth.

Next, write your answers to the following questions to determine your:

Interests, preferences, and attitudes
Which courses in my schooling did I enjoy most? In which did I earn high grades? (Place a check mark before favorites of courses you listed under Education.)

Which duties and responsibilities did I like best? In which was I most successful or do I have a continuing interest? (Place a check mark before the areas that indicate your preferences under Work Experience and Activities.)

Do I prefer to work with people, figures, machines, or ideas?

Would I rather sell, create, or design? Lead or follow?

Am I more comfortable in a large or a small organization?

What values do I consider most important in my career—salary, prestige, friends, family, material goods, leisure, travel, others?

In which locality do I prefer to live? Have I strong preferences?

What are my obligations to my community, family, employer?

Last but by no means least, you can rate yourself on the following personal characteristics considered important by employers who seek college graduates:

Your Self-appraisal Checklist on Personal Characteristics

	Excellent	*Good*	*Fair*	*Poor*
• Integrity				
• Ability to think logically				
• Enthusiasm, initiative, drive				
• Dependability				
• Ability to communicate orally and in writing				
• Intelligence				
• Maturity				
• Analytical ability				
• Ability to get along and cooperate with others				
• Emotional stability				
• Evidence of good judgment				
• Ability to make decisions				
• Health				
• Physical appearance				
• Capacity for leadership				
• Bearing, poise, self-confidence				
• Courtesy, tact, diplomacy				
• Adaptability				
• Sense of humor				
• Neatness of work				

An objective self-analysis like the foregoing inventory is strictly for your own use. It will not be mailed to anyone, but it helps you see patterns emerge regarding your capabilities, desires, interests, and achievements that are unique to you. Fortunately, no one else has exactly the same qualifications you have! Sort out your strengths (perhaps by double check marks) and try to determine your best salable qualifications.

Market Research—
Finding Who Can Use You and What They Prefer

The next phase of your job-getting campaign is to determine which jobs and employers require what you have to offer.

Perhaps you know right now the kind of career work you want and even the organization you will work for; if so, you are fortunate. More likely, however, you are one of the thousands of young people who are not sure which of several interests or careers they should pursue, where the job opportunities are, or what general and specific qualifications they must meet. Various information sources can be helped in this situation. Bear in mind, of course, that because supply and demand in the employment market change from year to year, it is best to get the most current information.

Information Sources for Careers and Jobs

To get ideas about various occupations and career opportunities, you will find useful printed materials such as the following in libraries and perhaps your campus career placement office:

Reference Books
Career Planning Handbook; A Guide to Career Fields and Opportunities, U.S. Civil Service Commission, U.S. Government Printing Office, Washington, D.C.

Dictionary of Occupational Titles, U.S. Department of Labor, U.S. Government Printing Office, Washington, D.C. Summarizes characteristics, abilities, and skills contributing to success in various occupations and careers.

Occupational Outlook Handbook, U.S. Bureau of Labor Statistics, U.S. Government Printing Office, Washington, D.C. Highlights employment opportunities in various fields.

Magazines and newspapers
American Journal of Sociology, total issue, January 1973

Fortune magazine, various issues.

M.B.A. Magazine, total issue March 1971, February 1975, and others.

Wall Street Journal, various issues.

Periodical indexes
Applied Science and Technology, Business Periodicals, Public Affairs Information Service, Readers' Guide, Standard and Poor's Industrial Index, Standard Register of Advertisers. These may list recent articles on the career you are considering.

Books in the 1970s
Choice and Challenge: For American Women, by Gladys Harkson; Schenkman Publishing Co,. Inc., Cambridge, Mass., 1971.

Go Hire Yourself an Employer, by Richard K. Irish; Doubleday Anchor Press, Garden City, N.Y., 1973.

Guide to Career Education, by Muriel Lederer, Quadrangle/The New York Times Book Co., N.Y., 1974.

The Professional Job Changing System—World's Fastest Way to Get a Better Job, by Robert J. Jameson, Performance Dynamics, Inc., Verona, N.J., 1974/75.

What Color Is Your Parachute? A practical manual for job hunters and career changers, by Richard Bolles; Ten-Speed Press, Berkeley, Calif., 1972.

SRA Occupational Briefs, Science Research Associates, 259 East Erie Street, Chicago. Consists of 210 four-page briefs (of which 70 are revised each year) about major job areas.

After deciding on the kind of career you want, you will need infromation about employers and various types of jobs available in your chosen field. Many published materials inform you about openings, products, services, geographical locations, sizes, problems, and/or other facts regarding employing organizations. Among them are:

College Placement Annual, College Placement Council, 35 East Elizabeth Street, Bethlehem, Pennsylvania. Contains an alphabetical list of United States and Canadian firms seeking college graduates; includes brief information on openings and the proper persons to contact; also includes alphabetical lists by majors and geographical locations.

Moody's Manuals of Investment, Moody's Investors Service, 99 Church Street, New York. Contains financial and background information and locations of banks, insurance firms, financial agencies, municipals and governments, railroads, public utilities, industrials.

Poor's Register of Directors and Executives; United States and Canada, published annually by Standard and Poor's Corporation, 345 Hudson Street, New York. Has an alphabetical list of over 27,000 leading business firms, their addresses, principal products, number of employees, directors, and key officers.

Thomas' Register of American Manufacturers, Thomas Publishing Co., 461 Eighth Avenue, New York.

Company annual reports, brochures, pamphlets, house organs, newsletters. (Get them in placement offices or by writing to the firms.)

Professional journals, business magazines, newspapers. Often periodicals have columns for both help wanted and position wanted. Sometimes special ads publicize openings. Also, occasional articles discuss companies' new ventures, expansions, additional products, and so forth. Such leads may suggest employment possibilities for you.

Besides these printed materials, you can get helpful advice and sometimes tips about good openings from persons familiar with work or firms in your chosen career. These may be useful sources of information:

Business people in your chosen field or firm(s)

Chambers of commerce

Company representatives—traveling for book publishers, insurance companies, office supply firms, public relations departments

Counselors—in your school, business, sports, or activity programs

Employment agencies—including national, state, city, and private bureaus

Friends and relatives

Personnel departments—sometimes provide application forms and leads if you telephone or call in person

Professors and instructors

School placement offices

Desirable General Qualifications of the Applicant

An important part of your research about the job market is learning what the employers' (your buyers') needs and requirements are. You will then be better able to focus on jobs that are in harmony with what you can contribute as an employee. Desirable general qualifications all employers look for usually include—in varying degrees, depending on the job—the following areas:

Evidence of education and intelligence

Work experience and skills

Activities, achievements, social development

Personal characteristics, interests, desires, attitudes

These areas, as you have probably noticed, are similar to the headings above the questions you asked yourself if you made the inventory self-appraisal suggested on pages 378 and 379. All the personal characteristics in the checklist (page 379) are desirable general qualifications. In addition, employers also look for proper attitude toward employment and a few other desirable personal traits.

Proper Attitude toward Employment. You will more likely make a favorable impression when your attitude shows willingness to learn and work, interest in the field of your choice, interest in the company, and reasonable attitude toward salary.

Willingness to learn and work includes accepting beginning or routine work within your chosen field—especially if you are a recent college graduate. Although you may have attended school 16 years or longer by the time of graduation, many facts you've learned have been general enough to be useful for all students going into all types of businesses. On the job you will need to learn specific duties; procedures, and practices of the company that hires you. As the newspaper correspondent Hal Boyle once wrote: "You have to learn how to saw wood before you can make a cabinet."

Yet the majority of employers receive many applications from recent (21-year-old) graduates for jobs that require years of service or training. These unrealistic requests— which indicate an unwillingness to learn and work—include applications to be a personnel director, store manager, editor, comptroller, foreign correspondent, account executive, and so on. It is true that a college degree opens doors to employment, but you still have to prove your worth in your written application, interview, and actual performance on the job.

Interest in the field of work you have chosen is important because usually it stimulates greater effort and leads to greater accomplishment on the job. Employers expect you to know the type of work you prefer for a career and to have chosen a career you will enjoy. Don't expect the employer to decide the type of work you are best fitted for. You must arrive at your own conclusion about your estimated part in the world's work.

A broad educational background is definitely an asset, no matter what field you have chosen, but extensive academic training without a goal or objective is pointless. Whether you apply for a specific job or an opening in a more general area depends upon the type of work involved. For example, if you are interested in a particular job, such as selling, teaching, or accounting, you will apply for that specific assignment—and nothing else. On the other hand, if you want to get into a field, say advertising, you will indicate that area, and *not* a specific job. And a graduate wanting managerial work in the personnel department will probably get there through the firm's management training program.

Interest in the company should be genuine, after you've studied the company and know it is the type of organization in which you can do your most productive work. In your résumé and letter you will try to show *how you can be helpful to the employer.* Do not emphasize your own self-interest, such as what fringe benefits the employer will offer *you.*

Reasonable attitude toward salary implies that you consider a challenging opportunity more important than a large beginning salary. Emphasis on salary—in the first written job presentation—creates an unfavorable impression. In general, especially if you are just beginning your career, it is best not to mention desired salary in the letter or résumé. (This matter can be discussed during the interview.)

Other Desirable Personal Traits. Heading the list of desirable personal characteristics is integrity (see page 379). This trait and three others not listed—sincerity, self-confidence, and determination—deserve special comment here regarding general qualifications desirable for every applicant.

Integrity and sincerity instill confidence. No employer can become interested in an individual who is deceptive. For example, most personnel executives can detect when an applicant is insincerely praising a company or mechanically stating a desire to work only for that particular firm. Another type of insincerity—or even dishonesty—is exaggerating and padding qualifications. Sincerity doesn't mean, however, you need to expose your shortcomings. If you haven't had work experience or don't have a good grade-point average, you need not mention these negative aspects at all in your written presentation. Instead, you should stress—honestly—other positive qualifications that strengthen your presentation.

Self-confidence involves the ability to sell yourself without high-pressure tactics and egotism or timidity. Employers appreciate the applicant with you attitude, who tries honestly to show how he or she can be helpful to the employing firm. Overuse of the word "I" makes a negative impression. As one executive of a nationally known company said: "The word 'I' is used so frequently in some application letters that we get the general idea the applicant has become overawed by his accomplishment of having earned a degree."

Determination requires initiative, drive, and tenacity to get work done. If you don't have the ability to carry projects through to the end, you won't be of much use to the company.

You can show determination through your background. For example, if you had to drop out of school because of finances or poor grades, but managed to get your degree by attending night school, you are certainly a determined person. Or if you quit school voluntarily and then returned to complete your degree—only through sacrifice on your part—you have determination to succeed.

Later in this chapter, the sections on "Résumé" and "Letter of Application" illustrate specific ways to present your various qualifications effectively to the employer.

Desirable General Qualities for the Written Job Presentation

Many personnel directors have commented that only a small percentage of the hundreds of applications they receive each month are well-written and appealing enough to warrant interviews. The rest must be discarded, for readers haven't time to figure out what the applicants have to offer. A sloppy, inaccurate message from an applicant supposedly trying to make a good impression causes the employer to wonder about that person's overall capability.

Your written job presentation—the letter and résumé—will make a more favorable impression on the prospective buyers if it has the seven C qualities. In general, try to follow these suggestions:[1]

1. *Present your message concisely, clearly, honestly, with consideration* for the reader. Desirable length is usually a one-page letter and a one- or two-page résumé—unless your background includes years of valuable experience. The employer is busy and doesn't want to waste time on irrelevant details or minor points. Remember, your aim is to get an interview—not to give your life history, Be sure your résumé is up to date (and indicate this fact clearly).
2. *Give specific and pertinent information* relative to the position sought. Generalities are not only confusing; they imply the applicant is trying to conceal a weakness or is insincere. Include enough facts to be convincing.
3. *Be yourself and don't use canned messages.* Your résumé and letter should reveal your individuality. Personnel executives easily recognize and react negatively toward canned messages that sound as if they've been copied from a textbook or written by an employment agency.
4. *Use an appropriate, businesslike approach.* You should sound serious, rather than smark-aleck or "cute." Avoid slang and novelties like: a burnt corner (to show "a burning desire" to work), an upside down letter (saying applicant is not afraid to start at the bottom), or reference to yourself as "a product originating only 21 years ago"! However, discreet originality is desirable for an applicant interested in a job—such as advertising—involving a high degree of creativity.

---

[1]You will find additional, specific suggestions in sections on the "Résumé" and the "Letter of Application."

5. *Triple check for accuracy of mechanics*—grammar, sentence and paragraph structure, organization, desirable headings, parallelism of items under each heading, punctuation, and spelling. Employers place heavy emphasis on spelling accuracy for these reasons:

> If you have *spelling* errors on the important job application, you'll probably continue having errors in letters to customers; and many customers judge the overall ability of a writer by spelling accuracy. Further, transposing letters within words—such as "teh" for "the"—shows carelessness in proofreading Maybe (so the employer thinks) the writer is also careless in other aspects of work performance. Be especially careful about spelling names of persons, firms, and job areas. (Commonly misspelled words include "J. C. Penny" for "J. C. Penney," "Weyerhauser" for "Weyerhaeuser," and "personel" for "personnel.")

6. *Make appearance attractive.*

   a. Paper for the letter and résumé should usually be 8½- by 11-inch bond, at least 16- to 20-pound weight, and 25 percent rag content. White is safest (but some readers consider beige or off-white desirably distinctive).
   b. Typing of both letter and résumé should be with neat, black type (if desired, on an IBM Selectric machine with variations in type sizes and styles); margins, ample for easy reading of uncrowded data; erasures or corrections, unnoticeable.
   c. Duplicating—by offset (such as multilith), print, xerography, or other neat professional methods—is permissible for résumés, but *not* for letters. Each application letter must be individually typewritten.

7. *Personalize your presentation as much as possible.* Tailoring a résumé for a specific job or company is desirable. It's like a rifle shot instead of a shotgun blast. However, even if you are sending out numerous general-purpose résumés (neatly reproduced), you should preferably address each accompanying *letter* to a specific person *by name* and use that name in your salutation. Address your letter to the person (chief accountant, sales manager, personnel director) who is in charge of employing applicants for the type of job you seek. Use the correct name and title of your addressee. In your résumé avoid using personal pronouns referring to yourself.

8. *Use good judgment in mailing your message.* Generally, be prompt. Sometimes it may be advisable to use special delivery to reach an executive at the best time, usually in the middle of a week. (However, some surveys show that letters answering a popular ad get better results if they arrive on about the eighth day rather than among the hundreds mailed the first seven days after the ad appears.) The only enclosure with your letter is the résumé. You might *offer* to send samples of work, transcripts, or recommendations, but don't send them with the initial application.

Résumé

After you have evaluated your assets and researched job opportunities and employers' requirements, you are ready to prepare your written "sales promotion." This job presentation consists of the résumé (also spelled "resume" or "resumé") and the application letter. Though the prospective employer will read the letter first, you should prepare the résumé first; for it includes facts on which the letter will be based.

Résumé contents and layouts vary widely; there is no one best type. This section discusses the possible contents and ways of presenting a résumé. From the following checklist you can select the parts that best fit your background and the job you seek. Then arrange them in any desirable order. "Accentuate the positive" honestly.

CHECKLIST FOR A RESUME

1. **Opening section:**
   Your name, address, telephone number, picture (?)
   Job or career goal
   Summary of basic qualifications

2. **Education:**
   Advanced schooling and training—school names, locations; dates attended, degrees and certificates
   Major, significant pertinent courses (required or elective), academic honors, grade point averages; special skills

3. **Work experience:**
   Employer names, locations; dates (month year to month year); titles and positions held; duties; supervisors (or number supervised)
   Volunteer work, research, tutoring, publications, etc.

4. **Activities, achievements, awards:**
   School, community, etc.; travel, languages, self-support, other facts

5. **Personal data:**
   Birthdate, birthplace, health, height, weight, marital status, dependents, military service, hobbies

6. **References**

Opening Section

The information in the opening section (or upper part of the résumé) gives the reader a general picture of the applicant.

Title. The title can range in content from your name alone, to your name and the title of the job you are applying for; to your name, address, and telephone number and/or the name of the firm receiving the job presentation. For example:

1. Résumé of Robert A. Fitchitt for Public Accounting

2. Data Sheet of Deanna D. Bowman
   4504 18th Avenue NE
   Akron, Ohio 44304
      Phone: 543-1072

3. Qualifications of Betty Jo Anderson
   for a Position as Business Teacher
   in the North Shore School District

4. RESUME
    LAURENCE H. FLINN
    13605 S. E. 171th Place
    Renton, Washington 98055
    Telephone: (206) 926-6031

Whatever title you choose, try to include your address and telephone number near the top of your résumé where your prospective employer can see and use them easily. A single person might have two addresses listed on the résumé—permanent (parents') address and temporary school address. You can include both if they serve a good purpose.

Picture. Although including a picture on a résumé was formerly considered almost "standard procedure," this practice has been rare during the 1970s. Under Title VII of the Civil Rights Act (amended in March 1972), an employer must extend exactly the same treatment to all applicants regardless of race, color, religion, sex, or national origin. The personnel officer may like a photograph (and even require one) for every employee as a record in each personnel file, but pictures cannot be used for *discriminatory* purposes in hiring applicants.

However, an applicant may include a picture if it might be helpful. The reader can better visualize the applicant if a photograph is included, and an interviewer on campus can better remember the applicant when the hiring decision is made. Nevertheless, especially in mass mailings of "prospecting" letters and résumés, it is usually better to *omit* the picture. But you can have a photograph ready if needed. For a favorable impression of you, the picture should be your best head-and-shoulders view (about 1¾ to 2 inches wide by 2 to 2 ¼ inches long) taken by a professional photographer.

Job or Career Objective. One entry that interests every employer is the job (or professional) objective. This statement is sometimes in the heading (see examples 1 and 3 on page 386) or it is under a separate title. If you can do two quite different kinds of work—for instance, accounting and teaching—you should prepare two separate résumés, each with a specific objective and then feature different phases of your background in each.

Be careful to avoid inflexible titles or too narrow statements of objectives, because they decrease the scope of your availability. If a firm is seeking a sales representative, for example, the reader will discard a résumé with a sales manager job objective (even though, unknown to the employer, the applicant would accept a sales job as a start). When your immediate goal is different from the ultimate goal, you should state both in your job objective, as in the following:

1. An accounting position with a reputable public accounting firm which is a leader in its field. The position should eventually lead to management advisory services. (Notice the implied compliment to the firm.)
2. To begin work in the comptroller's office of a small wholesale organization located in the Northeast, preferably in or near New York City, with goal of qualifying eventually for general management responsibilities. (Mention your preferred locality only if you have strong geographical preferences.)

3. A position in your management training program with the goal of participating in some management phase of your overseas operations.
4. To work in your firm as an expeditor or coordinator with the eventual aim of a position in construction management.

Summary of Basic Qualifications. Immediately after—*or before*—stating your objectives (what you *want*), you can sometimes favorably impress the employer by emphasizing what you *offer*. Such a summary statement is effective if you have two or more *outstanding* qualifications that are basic or especially important for the job, like those below:

1. Offering six years of progressively more responsible experience in office management and business administration, in addition to a master's degree in policy and organization.
2. Bachelor of Arts degree with a major in personnel management and with emphasis in psychology, sociology, and business.
   Four years of part-time experience working with people.
   Student counselor in Alaska, summer of (year).
3. M.A. and B.A. degrees in Engineering.
   Six years' work in electronics.
4. Bachelor of Arts in Business Administration—major in transportation.
   3½ years of full-time experience—specialization in in-bound cargo movement with steamship agency; and shipping department, order desk, and inside sales with manufacturing firm.

Education

The first major section following the résumé opening should state the most important qualification you can offer for the job (or the job area). If you are a recent graduate and education is your strongest selling point, cover this area first—in detail. The more years you are away from school, the less educational detail is required. But even applicants who have been away from school for a while should include (usually later in the résumé) names and locations of schools as well as dates attended and degrees earned.

If education is your main qualification, you may want to include all the items shown on the Résumé Checklist (page 386), provided this material strengthens your presentation. Include the name, location, dates attended, and degrees or certificates earned at all post-secondary schools you attended. (Even high school may be mentioned if its reputation or location somehow ties in with the job qualifications.) The number and kinds of courses to list vary with the type of work requested. Show that you have an acceptable background in the area of the requested work and also a broad understanding of the arts and sciences (if true). Also list useful elective courses related to your interest and the job. Good examples are courses in written communication, speech, and human relations; also others that helped you to reason objectively to a conclusion or to perform any skills needed for the job.

Grades are a controversial subject. To many employers, grades indicate how well the graduate has mastered program studies and met numerous requirements. As a result, applicants for some areas—such as accounting, teaching, and research—need high grades before they can be considered by the more desirable organizations. For other applicants, grades are weighed together with various factors: for example, a graduate who has had to work while in college, has dependents, and has participated in extracurricular activities isn't expected to have as high grades as a person who has not had to use time for such nonclass endeavors.

For positions that require the individual to work closely with customers and employers, personality is more important than grades; examples of such areas include selling, management training, and secretarial work. Furthermore, a graduate with a straight A cumulative grade point needs to prove he or she possesses more than intelligence, because the average employer is wary of an applicant who has little or nothing but high scholarship to offer.

Illustrated below are various ways to show pertinent facts about academic background. Rearrange your own educational material so it best presents *your* preparation for the job you seek.

1. Emphasis on degrees and grades:

Master of Business Administration in Quantitative Methods, University of Michigan; Autumn 1974 through Winter 1976; Grade point, 3.7 (possible, 4.0)

Bachelor of Arts in Mathematics, University of Ohio; Autumn 1971 through Spring 1974; Grade point, 3.8 (possible, 4.0)

2. Concise listing of schools; then degrees, standing, major:

EDUCATION

University of Kansas	Lawrence, KS[2]	Business Administration	1974-76
Everett Junior College	Everett, WA	Liberal Arts 1972-74	1972-74
U.S. Air Force School	Denver, CO	Electronics	1969-71
Martin High School	Martin, WV	College Preparatory	1965-69

Degrees:	Bachelor of Arts in Business Administration, U.K., 1976
	Associate of Arts and Sciences, E.J.C., 1974
Standing:	Top 5 percent of class at both E.J.C. and U.K.
	Valedictorian, high school
Majors:	Operations Management and Finance

3. Off-campus technical training sponsored by a firm or branch of government or taken independently. List it as a subdivision under EDUCATION (centered heading)—after listing schools:

Technical Training

In addition to the academic education shown above, I have more than 800 hours of management and technical training:

Harbridge House, Inc.	Boston, Management Seminar	3/75-5/76
IBM Education Center	Chicago, Computer Programming	6/74-1/75
Military Service Schools	Radar theory, antisubmarine warfare	'56-62

[2] Abbreviations, if clear, are permissible on résumés.

4. Listing of relevant courses as a subdivision (under EDUCATION, center heading, and schools) when your strongest qualification is education:

Special Relevant Courses

In Major	In Nonmajor
International Business Principles	Written Business
Economics of Underdeveloped	Communications
Countries	Speech Principles
International Marketing Research	(Group Discussion)
Overseas Operations Management	Principles of Operations
International Marketing	Management
Multinational Sales Forecasting	Scheduling and Inventory
Models	Control

5. Inclusion of course information with the schools instead of in a special subdivision (as in 4):

Education
  University of Illinois, Urbana--Sept. '72-June '76
    Major: Accounting (42 quarter hours)
    Grades: Overall--3.01 (out of a possible 4.00)
             Accounting--3.51

    Accounting courses:[3]
      Federal Income Tax
      Special Tax Problems
      Auditing Standards and Principles
      Case Studies in Auditing
      Basic Accounting Principles
    Other relevant courses:
      Personnel management, human relations,
      finance, marketing, economics

  Shoreline High School, Seattle--Sept. '67-June '72
    Grades: 3.56 (out of a possible 4.00); top 5 percent of class

6. Listing of grade point averages if not all were good. Put your best foot forward—and still be honest. If your overall average is just so-so because of poor grades during your freshman and/or sophomore years, give the average for your major, for all business courses, or for your junior and senior years combined.

Work Experience

Any kind of work experience—related or unrelated—reveals information that helps the employer to evaluate the graduate. Work experience similar to that which you are applying for indicates you like the type of work in question and may shorten the training period. However, all types of work experience disclose pertinent facts about the applicant's work habits and personality, give a source for references, and perhaps show job preferences.

---

[3] You might also list to the right of each course the number of credits earned or (if grades are especially high) the grade for the quarter or semester.

You need to be thorough in describing your work experience. If you are a recent graduate still in your twenties, you should account for all your jobs that are worth mentioning back to a certain age—perhaps 16 or earlier. If you are an older applicant with extensive experience, you will probably place Work Experience *before* Education. Also, you may prefer to include only the more recent jobs that best relate to the position you seek; the employer will appreciate conciseness, instead of a long list of irrelevant material.

Usually, for the standard "general" résumé, list your jobs in chronological order with the present or most recent first. Try to include at least:

1. Type of work performed and your title[4] (supervisor, bookkeeper, and so forth)
2. Name and location of company[5]
3. Time worked (month year to month year)
4. Whether job was part-time (otherwise employer will interpret statement as full-time employment)

In addition, you should add the following if they strengthen your presentation:

1. Duties—work involving responsibilities, adaptability, similarity to what you're applying for, integrity, supervisory or budgetary functions, knowledge of products.
2. Name of immediate superior—if this person is still there and will be a good reference.
3. Accomplishments—if they're important; unique or innovative projects

Arrange the facts for each job in the most "selling" order. You can begin with your job title,[6] or employer's name, or dates you held each job, or the functions you performed on each job.

1. Job title first:

<u>Office Manager</u> Fifth Investors Corporation, Norfolk, VA.; full
    time from September 1973 to August 1975. Duties included super-
    vising 10 typists, checking typed material before printing, writing
    letters to publishers, and assisting with purchase orders.

<u>Service Representative</u> Pacific Northwest Bell, Seattle, WA.; full
    time from February 1972 to September 1973. Duties included giving

---

[4] Be honest. If you were a laborer, say "laborer." Don't try to put on airs by camouflaging the title. For example, don't say "sanitary engineer" if you were a garbage collector; say "garbage collector."

[5] If you are currently employed and do not wish to disclose your employer on your résumé, you can merely identify the firm by industry; for example, you might say "a medium-sized manufacturer of electronic equipment." That will give the reader some indication of your company without divulging its name and perhaps jeopardizing your job. If a firm's name is now different from what it was when you were employed there, state the present name and "(formerly . . .)."

[6] Be sure to follow rules of parallelism—making two or more elements in a series similar in grammatical word structure. "Manager," "Representative," and "Bookkeeper" are all parallel to each other because each is a job title. "Managing"—which is a kind of work, not a title—would not be parallel to the other three titles.

service to telephone customers regarding telephone installations, questions on bills, complaints, and selection of additional telephones.

Assistant to Manager of Accounts Payable, Associated Hardware, Tacoma, WA.; full time from June 1970 to February 1972. Duties included figuring discounts on statements, filing, typing, posting accounts, writing checks.

2. Employer first:

California State Highway Department 931 Ridgeway, Sacramento
Draftsman, March 1974 to December 1975**
   Duties: drawing roadway profiles and burrow sites
Bookkeeper, May 1973 to March 1974**
   Duties: keeping time and equipment records for division and
      preparing vouchers
Driller's Helper, January 1972 to May 1973*
   Duties: drilling test holes for proposed highway routes

Washington State Highway Department 1219 Capitol Way, Olympia,
Engineering Technician, November 1968 to December 1971**
   Duties: processing traffic data and interviewing on truck
      surveys
Saw Crewman, July 15, 1968, to November 1968*
   Duties: sawing wood supports in highway construction

*Full time.
**Part-time during school, full-time summers.

3. Dates first:

June 1975 to October 1975	Position:	Legal Secretary Taking dictation, transcribing, typing, filing, receiving clients
	Reference:	Mr. William McGee, McGee, Strom, Burner, Attorneys 9988 Hightower Building Dearborn, Michigan 48121
School Year September 1974 to June 1975	Position:	Legal Stenographer Weekday mornings--writing shorthand, typing, filing
	Reference:	Ms. Louise Jackson, Attorney Barnes, Jayne, Jackson, Associates Ridley Tower Cincinnati, Ohio 45221
Other jobs before 1974[7]		Worked as cashier in a restaurant Fridays and Saturdays two months, typed business letters for high-school principal, picked strawberries, helped with gardens.

[7]To indicate industriousness previous to the earliest full job entry, "Other jobs before (year)" is acceptable for applicants in their early twenties but may be regarded as inappropriate for older (30 or more) applicants.

4. Functions first:
   The following example is from a general-purpose résumé of a high-level executive who chose to omit dates of employment and names of employers. Usually these are included.

<u>FUNCTIONAL REVIEW OF WORK EXPERIENCE</u>

<u>General Management</u>:	As Vice President and General Manager of a highly diversified million-dollar company, was responsible for six operating divisions. Reduced personnel turnover and increased profits by over 40%. Instituted methods and techniques of modern creative management.
<u>International Management</u>:	As Manager of International Operations of a company whose sales exceeded six million dollars annually, was responsible for the overseas sales and distribution of four producing divisions. Products included plastics, pipeline coatings, and treated wood products.
<u>Management Consulting</u>:	Conducted seminars on a worldwide basis for . . .

If you have had little or no paid employment but have done volunteer work, tutoring, or research (perhaps even published a report) without pay, you may list such responsibilities under Work Experience or under Activities.

Activities, Achievements, Awards

Participation in extracurricular and cocurricular activities is usually a good indication of an applicant's personality—ability to work with others, leadership, and emotional stability. When listing your activities, mention any offices you held as well as projects on which cooperation, teamwork, and sincere interest in other people (or projects) were needed. Include athletics, writing (such as journalism), speaking (such as debate), professional fraternities, and student organizations that involve working with people. A leader or active participant in any worthy activity is far more valuable to an employer than a nonparticipant who is merely a "joiner" with numerous affiliations. Awards may be listed in this section or under Miscellaneous Relevant Facts.

You may want to list your activities in two or more divisions:

College and high school

College and (military) service

Community and other

Always identify (in parentheses) any activity the employer might not know the significance of:

Delta Sigma (national business fraternity)

Alpha Sigma Phi (social fraternity)

Beta Alpha Psi (accounting honorary)

Purple Shield (underclassmen's activities honorary)

Pilgrim Club (Congregational youth group)

Statements like the following indicate recognition, achievements, awards, and services:

1. Recognition, achievement, awards

   a. "High school salutatorian."
   b. "Most valuable student—Elks Club Award."
   c. "Mistress of ceremonies at Olympic College Spring Awards Assembly."
   d. "My name appears in the second annual edition of *Who's Who among Students in American Junior Colleges.*"
   e. "Eagle Scout."
   f. "4-year scholarship at Whitworth College."
   g. "Dean's list for high scholarship" (dates involved).
   h. "Two-year varsity basketball letterman."
   i. "Outstanding senior male at (university)."

2. Service

   a. "Assistant coach—Little League Football—Ballard Team (city, state)."
   b. "Member of (year) World Deputation Team from University Presbyterian Church, (city). Sent to Yukon Presbytery of Alaska. Worked with high school, junior high, and primary age children—teaching and counseling."
   c. "Volunteer hospital work."

Personal Data

Various personal details about an applicant may be placed in the opening section or later in the résumé—after the more important Education and Work Experience (or Activities) sections. As the Résumé Checklist (page 386) shows, included under Personal Data are birthdate (and/or age), birthplace, health, height, weight, marital status, and number of dependents. Sometimes military service and hobbies are listed in this section, but if information for either of these is extensive and important for the job, it may be in a separate section (with specific title).

Although laws forbid an employer to *ask* you about religion or ancestry, you can include this information—if lawful[8] and you think it will help you get an interview. Some employers don't care whether or not they know this type of information, yet most won't react negatively if you include it. If you're in doubt, leave it out.

Good health is a prime requirement on most jobs because it determines both the physical and mental performance of the individual. You can indicate physical fitness in the Personal Data section or elsewhere by listing:

A statement that you have excellent health with no physical defects, if true.

The sports you participate in. An active swimmer, football or basketball player, or a contestant in intramural activities must be in good condition.

[8]See discussion under "Picture," page 387, regarding Civil Rights laws.

Your hobbies that require activity, endurance, strength, and stamina. Examples include hiking, fishing, mountain climbing, boating, and bowling.

If your health is unsatisfactory, or if you have a physical handicap or a disfiguring burn or birthmark, you need to weigh carefully what you include in your job presentation. If you feel the interview will probably eliminate you from further consideration because of your defect, perhaps you should not apply or you should state your disadvantage on the résumé or in the application letter. But if you think you can sell the employer—once in the personal interview—on your overall qualifications, omit any statement about health or defects that could keep you from getting the interview.

The same advice applies to age. If you think the employer may consider your age negatively (assuming that you are too inexperienced or overexperienced for the job you seek), but you feel you can sell him on your qualifications during an interview, you might omit age on the résumé. Or (usually better) you can indicate your age *after* listing your other excellent qualifications, so the employer reads them before seeing your age. (A federal law protects applicants ages forty through sixty-four against age discrimination.)

Here are two of many ways to list personal data:

1.
Birthdate:	June 22, 1952	Marital status:	Single
Birthplace:	Richmond, VA	Military	U.S. Army
Height:	5'11"	service:	(dates)
Weight:	175	Hobbies:	Reading
Health:	Excellent		Hiking

2. Age: 25   Weight: 125 pounds   Height: 5'4"   Married (1 child)

Military experience, if significant for the job, may be in a separate section or listed under Personal Data with more details than in example 1 above. Here are suggestions:

1. Received Air Force commission on (month day, year). Air Force pilot from (month day, year, to month day, year). Received honorable discharge as Captain on (month day, year).
2. Serving eight years (year to year) in the Coast Guard Reserve with meetings every Thursday night and two weeks' summer training each year. Satisfactorily completed five years of service. Six months of basic training: (month day, year, to month day, year).
3. Six years in the Army Reserve (month year to month year). Active duty: (month day, year, to month day, year). Honorable Discharge.

Hobbies may also be listed in detail (under Personal Data or elsewhere) if they relate to job qualifications; for example:

1. Requested work:
   a. "Study the stock market."
   b. "Tutored first-year accounting students during junior and senior years of college."
   c. "Editor of school paper."

    d. An especially important report (oral or written) or article relating to your field of interest.

    e. Ability to write and/or speak foreign language(s).

2. Creativity—designing clothes, photography
3. Mental activity—playing chess, reading
4. Fine arts—music, painting, drama
5. Household tasks—cooking, sewing, knitting

Other Relevant Facts

If there are other relevant facts that you should include on your résumé, but they don't fit comfortably in one of the sections described above, put them in this separate "catchall" section. Also, if you have a single entry for work experience or extra-curricular activities—not enough to justify placing elsewhere—include it in this section. But beware of mentioning anything that might cause a negative reaction, for example, hobbies relating to gambling. Also a salesperson should have hobbies that reveal physical fitness and ability to deal with people—not stamp or coin collecting. But for an accountant these last two hobbies are good—they show patience and attention to detail.

    Given below are suggested entries that reveal some aspects of the desired qualifications discussed earlier in the chapter.

1. Expenses earned while you attended college

    a. "Completed college working full time."

    b. "Worked full time and supported family while attending college part time from (month, year, to month, year) and full time from (month, year, to month, year)."

    c. "Earned 100 percent of my college expenses by working summers since (year)."

2. Indication of integrity

    a. "Secret classification security clearance—The Boeing Company—(year to year)."

    b. "I have taught Sunday School at the First Lutheran Church of (town)."

    c. Bonded

3. Personal data

    a. Parents' occupations (if work is closely related to the job you're applying for).

    b. Your engagement to be married.

    c. Spouse's education (if he or she has college education).

    d. Results of personality test or interest test.

4. Preferred location (for example "Prefer Pacific Northwest—will relocate")
5. Publications/Patents—any papers that have been presented at society meetings or published in trade journals; also patents awarded or under application
6. Skills—typing speed, shorthand speed, calculator use, use of office machines
7. Travel (to indicate knowledge of conditions and customs elsewhere)
8. Willingness to relocate (for example, "I will relocate in any city within the United States")
9. Willingness to travel (for sales work)

References

Various pros and cons about whether to include references on the résumé are discussed here. In general, if you are writing to one employer (or a few) for a position you know is available, to play it safe include references. You usually have nothing to lose and sometimes much to gain. However, if you are mailing your résumé to a long list of employers, you'll be safer to merely state, "References will be sent upon request." (Then you won't risk having your references bothered by too many inquiries or being tired recommending you over and over again. Also, when you receive a request for references, you will know the specific kind the employer wants.)

Many employers don't want references until the interview. In fact, many employers question the use of references at all—especially the ones the applicant offers. The most worthless is the "to whom it may concern" message you carry with you, and next in line are the references of friends. You know the references you choose will say only nice things about you; otherwise you wouldn't give their names. The best references are those employers dig out for themselves.

On the other hand, some employers expect to find references in the initial written job presentation and consider the résumé incomplete if the names are missing. Some employers like to see—even if they don't check—what references the applicant uses. If they see a name they know and have confidence in, or one in a particular field, they might check on the applicant even before the interview.

If and when you give references, list about three to five. The most appropriate names include present or former employers and professors. Also acceptable is a character reference whose name or occupation is respected. State each individual's full name, title, organization (if any), complete business address and telephone number. Since you obviously should get permission to use the names you're listing in this section, you need not say "with permission."

Examples

In summary, the résumé should contain selling facts about yourself in an easy-to-read, well-organized format. Figures 11-1, 11-2, 11-3, and 11-4 illustrate a variety of résumé contents and layouts.

Figure 11-1 is a personalized one-page, résumé containing both the job objective and the employer's name in the heading. It is especially useful when you know there is a job opening for the work you can and would like to do, and you want to type an individual résumé to that employer. Notice it also lists references (though including them is a matter of personal choice).

Figure 11-2 is a general purpose résumé typical of those that college graduates with limited working experience can send. Education—the strongest selling point—is listed first, in detail; and pertinent activities as well as other relevant facts are detailed to strengthen qualifications. (An applicant with much work experience can, of course, also use the general-purpose résumé; but work experience would come before education.) This type of résumé is easily processed for mass mailing to many prospective employers. References are omitted and "will be furnished upon request." If desirable

```
                    QUALIFICATIONS OF ALICE G. O'BRIEN as
              STAFF ACCOUNTANT WITH BURTISE, HARTMAN, AND ASSOCIATES
            Home:  3241 Lakeside Drive, Seattle, WA  98102; Phone:  354-9876

EDUCATION      University of Washington, Seattle, January 1974-August 1975;
                  Bachelor of Arts degree in Business Administration
               Chico State College, Chico, California, October 1969-June 1972

                  College courses developing a thorough understanding of
                  corporation, partnership, and proprietorship accounting
                  and financial analysis:

                  Accounting (40 quarter hours): Auditing (Public and Internal),
                  Consolidations, Cost, Equity, Federal Income Tax, Fiduciary

                  Related Courses (60 quarter hours): Business Communications,
                  Business Law, Corporate Finance, Computer Programming, Data
                  Processing, Economics, Money and Banking, Statistics

EMPLOYMENT     June 1974-   Assistant Accountant, Purchasing and Personnel
               Present      Depts.** Doctors Hospital, Seattle, WA

               Dec. 1972-   Full-charge bookkeeper*
               Dec. 1973    Central Medical Clinic, San Francisco, CA

               June 1972-   Billing Clerk*
               Dec. 1972    Cole Transfer and Storage, Seattle, WA

               July 1968-   Bookkeeper and assistant to Secretary-Treasurer**
               Sept. 1969   Hillside Hospital, Seattle, WA

                 *Full time
                **Part time during school; rest, full time

ACTIVITIES,    Member and Treasurer, Beta Alpha Psi, Accounting Honorary, UW
HONORS         Chairperson, Student Asscoiation's Scholarship Fund Drive, UW
               Chairperson, University Church, Youth Activities Campaign
               Award winner, Junior Scholarship Cup, Alpha Alpha Sorority
               Dean's Honor Roll, UW School of Business Admin., 3 quarters

PERSONAL       Birthdate and place: March 26, 1950, Pasadena, CA
               Height:  5'7"   Weight:  132 lbs.    Health: excellent
               Earned 80% of college expenses.  Hobbies:  tennis, swimming, golf

REFERENCES     Ms. Nancy Green       Mr. James Black        Dr. Fletcher Myran
               Personnel Director    Manager                Prof. of Accounting
               Doctors Hospital      Central Medical Clinic School of Bus. Admin.
               909 University St.    944 Jackson St.        University of Wash.
               Seattle, WA 98104     San Francisco, CA 64003 Seattle, WA 98195
               Phone 423-9017        (415) 222-3333         543-9999
```

Figure 11-1. *Personalized, one-page résumé.* Job objective and employer name are included in the heading.

Resume of Jeanette D. Murdocks - page 2

Experience (continued)
Assistant Claims Adjuster--Central Administrators, 559 John Street,
Akron, Ohio, summer 1973
Supervisor: Mr. Mike Owen
Duties: Processing claims for health insurance
Part-time jobs before 1972--Waitress in Jolly Roger Restaurant, drugstore
sales clerk, and library assistant.

Honoraries, Clubs, Activities

College
Phi Beta Kappa, academic scholastic honorary
Alpha Lambda Delta, freshman women's honorary
Vice President, Alpha Alpha Sorority
Representative for Women's Commission
Three academic scholarships: Austin James, Faculty Wives, Panhellenic

High School
National Honor Society and Torch Club--three years; secretary one year
President, Business Education Club
Editor, Annual
Outstanding Graduate 1972 (chosen by Ohio State University Alumni
Association)

Other Relevant Information

Write and speak the French language.
Office skills include: Typing (60 wpm); operating adding machine
(10 key), electric calculator, mimeograph, ditto machine; taking
shorthand (125 wpm).
Hobbies and interests include: bowling, gardening, stamp collecting

References

Will be furnished upon request.

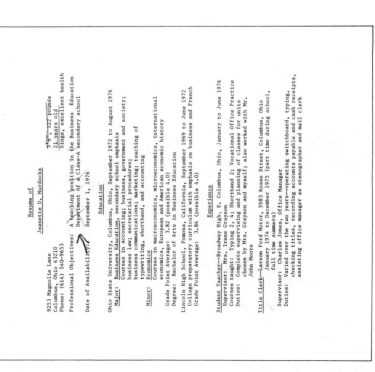

Resume of
Jeanette D. Murdocks

9253 Magnolia Lane   5'6", 122 pounds
Columbus, Ohio 43210   21 years old
Phone: (614) 540-9653   Singe, excellent health

Professional Objectives: A teaching position in the Business Education
Department of a Class-A secondary school
Date of Availability: September 1, 1976

Education

Ohio State University, Columbus, Ohio, September 1972 to August 1976
Major: Business Education, secondary school emphasis
Courses in accounting; business, government and society;
business law; secretarial procedures;
business communications; marketing; teaching of
typewriting, shorthand, and accounting
Minor: Economics
Courses in macroeconomics, microeconomics, international
economics, European and American economic history
Grade Point Average: 3.82 (possible 4.0)
Degree: Bachelor of Arts in Business Education

Lincoln High School, Pomona, California, September 1969 to June 1972
College preparatory curriculum with emphasis on business and French
Grade Point Average: 3.84 (possible 4.0)

Experience

Student Teacher--Broadway High, E. Columbus, Ohio, January to June 1976
Supervisor: Mrs. Irene Grayson
Courses taught: Typing 2, 4; Shorthand 2; Vocational Office Practice
Duties: Complete supervising and planning of classes for units
chosen by Mrs. Grayson and myself; also worked with Mr.
John Moore

Title Clerk--Larson Ford Motor, 5983 Rosse Street, Columbus, Ohio
January 1974 to December 1975 (part time during school,
full time summers)
Supervisor: Charles Jones, Office Manager
Duties: Varied over the two years--operating switchboard, typing,
checking titles, recording accounts payable and cash receipts,
assisting office manager as stenographer and mail clerk

Figure 11-2. *A general-purpose résumé.*(on two pages)

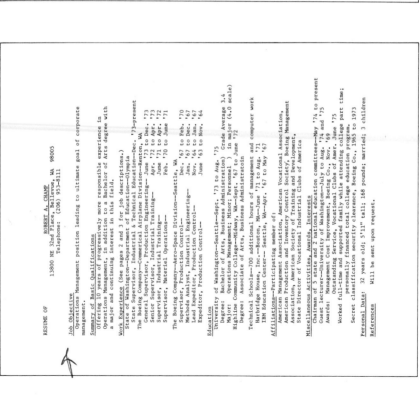

Figure 11-3. *General-purpose résumé on three pages*—for an "older" applicant (over 30). Concise summary on first page (left, above) is attached to a functional summary on page 2 (right, above) and page 3 (see page 401).

RESUME OF ROBERT A. CHAMP--page 3

Functional Summary of Job Responsibilities (Continued)

Supervisor, Materiel Operations (February 1970 to June 1971)	Supervised 42 employees and high-rate production operation, manufacturing aircraft parts to production standards and precision tolerances for research and development, production and spares programs, working on both military and commercial contracts. Developed production controls, flows, methods, and "work-arounds."
	THE BOEING COMPANY - Aero-Space Division (1963-1970)
Supervisor, Production Control (September 1968 to February 1970)	Performed administrative functions and developed management controls for Production Control Manager with staffing of over 700 employees. Performed data processing system evaluations and special studies and projects to resolve operational problems.
Supervisor, Production Control (December 1967 to September 1968)	Supervised 35 employees and production support expediting and shipping operations for research and development, production and spares programs, working on both military and commercial contracts.
Methods Analyst, Industrial Engineering (January 1967 to December 1967)	Performed computer programming and related systems evaluations. Developed production and inventory control programs to control over 10,000 different part numbers. Developed division systems and operating procedures and coordinated their implementation with department managers.
Lead Expeditor, Production Control (November 1964 to January 1967)	Worked directly with Company quality control and the U.S. Air Force in effecting final customer acceptance and delivery of end products. Directed work of 15 production expeditors to facilitate manufacturing and supply of all parts to support production requirements and schedules for assigned airplane and missile sections and support equipment.
Expeditor, Production Control (June 1963 to November 1964)	Expedited the supply of parts for assigned airplane sections based on production requirements and schedules. Controlled critical production "line stoppage items" such as: Landing gears, wing installation components, and associated equipment.

Figure 11-3. (Continued) *Third page of general-purpose résumé with two-page functional summary*

```
                                          ✓

     Thomas R. Muchley          ********* OBJECTIVE **********
     951 Compson Road
     (city, state, zip)         A line management position with respon-
     (telephone)                sibility for corporate or divisional
                                profits.  Alternatively, responsibility
                                for top level contract negotiations or
                                client development.

                         EMPLOYMENT

     Dates:
       Oct. 1966-Present     Standard Industrial Supplies, Inc.
       July 1956-Sept. 1966  ABC Products, International

     Functional Review of Work Experience:

     General          As Vice-President and General Manager, am responsible
     Management       for six operating divisions.  Reduced personnel turn-
                      over and increased profits by over 40%.

     Profit           Directed development of a successful analysis and
     Planning         profit planning system to help with management
                      decisions on profit lines and areas.

     International    As Manager of International Operations, was responsi-
     Management       ble for overseas sales and distribution of four
                      producing divisions.  Products ranged from inter-
                      mediate chemicals and pipeline coatings to treated
                      wood.

     Financial        Maintained financial relations with investment
     Communications   bankers, security analysts, and clients through face-
                      to-face and written communications.

     Report Edit-     Edited monthly Management Reports (printed for
     ing and          distribution to 950 company managers).  Wrote and
     Writing          compiled award-winning annual reports.

     Staff            As Assistant Manager of Personnel, supervised a staff
     Management       of eight interviewers and testers for hiring both
                      office and warehouse personnel.  Devised policies for
                      training, rating, and disciplining staff employees.

                          EDUCATION

     M.B.A. in Management, University of Illinois, 1972.
     B. A. in Business Administration (Management and Organization),
         University of Kansas, 1956, cum laude.

                       PERSONAL DATA

     Birthdate:  January 27, 1935  Health:  Excellent  Married:  3 children
     Foreign Languages:  Fluent Spanish; academic studies in German and
                         French

         FURTHER DETAILS AND REFERENCES UPON REQUEST
```

Figure 11-4. *Functional résumé* (one-page)

to have only one page, this résumé could be condensed by rearranging facts and omitting some details.

The third example, Figure 11-3, is useful for applicants with extensive work experience (listed before education). Though this example shows a three-page résumé, the applicant could mail only the first page, if necessary. However, pages 2 and 3 give a detailed "functional summary" of job duties.

Figure 11-4 illustrates a one-page functional résumé especially adaptable for the person who has had impressive work responsibilities related to the job sought. It is also useful for the applicant with long job stability and few employers. Notice that Mr. Muchley had only two employers in 20 years.

Letter of Application

The application letter is just as much a sales letter as any message selling a product or service[9]—and the résumé is an enclosure. In your letter you tell the prospective employer *what you can do for him and why you feel you are qualified.* You interpret only the important points in your résumé as they *relate to the specific job requirements.* Try to focus on what you can contribute to the employer (your "buyer"), not how much he or she can offer you. In just a few paragraphs—probably five—you must "sell" readers to the point where they want to know more about you. The checklist on page 404 may be a helpful guide when you plan the content of your persuasive "sales" application letter. Subsequent pages discuss ways to develop each item listed.

Opening for Favorable Attention

The beginning of the letter should catch the reader's attention in a "businesslike" manner. It should also state definitely that you are applying for a job—not inquiring about one or studying this phase of personnel for a school project. Furthermore you should identify the job (or job area) you're interested in.

Given below are examples of different kinds of first paragraphs for an application letter. You can adapt these suggestions to your needs whether you write a "prospecting" (unsolicited) letter to firms that have not announced an opening or a "solicited" letter about a known available position. Also, if appropriate, you may combine two of the kinds of openings into your one first paragraph, as shown in some of the examples.

Summary Opening. One of the most effective openings includes a summary of your two or three outstanding qualifications. Like the first paragraph of an article in a newspaper, the summary gives in capsule form the important points you'll expand in the message.

1. Retailing experience in a department store similar to yours, business knowledge gained academically, plus a sincere interest in these areas have helped me learn the basic requirements for running a department efficiently. I would like to contribute the practical skills I have acquired by becoming a part of your management training program.

[9]The application letter should, however, always be individually typewritten, although other sales letters may be processed for mass distribution.

CHECKLIST FOR APPLICATION LETTER

A. Attention (1 paragraph)

1. Businesslike beginning. Usually choose one or two:

   a. Summary—perhaps two or three outstanding qualifications
   b. Name—an individual or office the reader is familiar with
   c. Question—for reader benefit
   d. News item—related to employer
   e. Other relevant reader-oriented statement

2. Mention of specific job or field of interest

B. Interest, Desire, Conviction (2 to 4 paragraphs)

1. Discussion of your qualifications from a reader-benefit or reader-interest viewpoint. Include your:

   a. Education and training—related to job requirements
   b. Work experience—related to job requirements
   c. Significant personal attitudes, interests, and/or qualities—related to job requirements

2. Reference to résumé (once)

C. Action (1 paragraph)

1. Request for interview . . . at reader's convenience, with suggestions

2. Easy action

   a. Phone number
   b. Hours you can be reached
   c. Reply envelope or card enclosed only rarely. Consider reader!

---

2. If hundreds of effective retail calls, thorough knowledge of point-of-sale, and imaginative merchandising help make a brewery representative, then I've begun to learn the business. I would like to put this practical field experience to work for (name) Brewing Company.

3. It is my understanding that a continuity writer for your station must have an interest in and knowledge of classical music. She must have ambition and a desire to achieve. Above all, she must be able to write. I have these qualifications and should like to be considered for the job.

Name Opening. If someone has suggested you apply to a particular firm for a job, you can use that person's name in the opening—unless he or she has asked you to keep it confidential. Whether you identify this individual by title depends on how well the reader knows him or her.

1. Dr. James Hermann, Professor of Accounting and Chairman of the Accounting Department at (university), has informed me that your firm is looking for an accounting major who is interested in managerial accounting. I should like to be considered for the opening in your training program.
2. While I was visiting in Chicago last week, Miss Wilma Hutton introduced me to your sales manager, Mr. Webster. At that time I expressed my desire for a position with your sales organization. Mr. Webster referred me to you.

Question Opening. A properly phrased question at the beginning is another way to catch the employer's attention.

1. Can you use a salesperson with mechanical aptitude, a university education, four years of selling experience, and a strong desire to succeed? I will graduate from the University of (state) in December.
2. Do you need a reliable office manager with a broad background of business training and experience who can speak Spanish or Portuguese? If you do, I should like to be considered for that position.
3. Will you need a marketing employee six months from now who believes she can help increase (name company)'s profits? If you will, please consider me for a position as a marketing management trainee. My qualifications include . . . .

News-Item Opening. Sometimes you can mention a news event if it ties in with your desire to work for a certain firm.

1. In a recent (Name) Journal article I read with interest that your firm is planning to open a branch office in Mexico. Because my college background and work experience, plus facility with Spanish, fit your basic requirements for a Research Assistant, I would like to apply for that job in your branch office.
2. Your firm's consulting activities, and especially its work in "information systems," may attract you to an individual with my qualifications and aspirations. My academic concentration on "open systems theory," coupled with practical experience, would enable me to perform well as a member of your management consulting staff.

Other Beginnings. You should of course, design your own opening—the one most appropriate for you and for the particular person to whom you are writing. As the following examples illustrate, you can state an interest, previous experience with the same organization, a belief, or your present situation.

1. Swimming pool operation and maintenance have been of interest to me for the last few years. At the same time I have been studying business at the University (name). I would like to combine these two interests by working for Pools as a salesperson and pool maintenance consultant.
2. We both know that American Can Company prefers to pick its management trainees from the qualified employees in its lower echelons. After working six and one-half years in the various departments of Canco and attaining my college degree this June, I will be qualified to be of further benefit to our Company as a future manager.

Middle Paragraphs for Interest, Desire, Conviction

After you have caught the reader's attention, you proceed to present your basic qualifications for the job you're applying for. In the short space you have (perhaps no more than three paragraphs) you can't afford to repeat *unnecessarily* what is on the résumé. You need to select and emphasize key points, considering carefully every word in every idea you include. The emphasis is on how you can be helpful to the employer!

As with most sales letters, *facts and figures* are more convincing than the writer's opinions. But these facts must relate to the buyer's needs. When you write each paragraph, ask yourself "So what?" How do these facts relate to the requirements for *this* job and *this* employer? In a solicited letter answering an ad, be sure to cover in a positive way every qualification the ad specifies. If you have a shortcoming (maybe you're too young or have no work experience), emphasize other positive qualifications to strengthen the reader's confidence in your capabilities.

The order in which you present these paragraphs is also important. If you use a summary opening, you'll organize the paragraphs in the same order as the qualifications are listed in the opening—with the most important qualification first. If you don't have a summary opening, you'll still organize by discussing the most important qualification first. So that the reader doesn't divert attention to the résumé before finishing the letter, don't refer to the enclosure until the next-to-last or last paragraph.

Usually you'll devote one middle paragraph to selling your qualifications on education, one on work experience, and another on significant personal qualities— *pertinent to the job requirements.*

Education. Most recent college graduates consider education their most important qualification; if so, they should discuss it first—in the letter as well as in the résumé. However, an applicant must be careful not to imply that a college degree—even a Master's Degree—is the only qualification for the job. Employers who hire college graduates look beyond the degree, to determine what the applicant can do or what the degree indicates about personality. They appreciate such signs of intelligence as ability to think logically, sound judgment, mental alertness, and good grades. In the paragraph on education you can:

1. Show that you have both a broad background in business (or arts and sciences) and also depth in a major or at least a certain area.
2. Highlight your overall education by showing how your college studies prepared you for the work (or area) you seek. Talk in terms of work and duties, *not* merely course titles.
3. Explain how and why you supplemented your major with important electives outside your major. Report writing, marketing research, and case courses should prepare you to gather facts. Sound judgment might be reflected in the reports you had to write for case courses, or perhaps in the results of a team project—especially if you headed your division or group. An important oral or written presentation in or outside of class shows ability to think clearly. Or perhaps you can mention the satisfactory outcome of a knotty problem you faced.

Examples

1. The program I followed at the University of (state) included 40 credit hours of accounting courses—up-to-date procedures, principles, and theory—that afford a firm basis with which to grow in the auditing profession. Courses in data processing, in addition to my work experience at a computer installation, have led me to be especially interested in the auditing of such systems.
2. Training I received in production control and planning at (name) college, enables me to analyze, study, and recommend methods of work simplification in factory projects. Concepts learned about time and motion studies will help me conduct a thorough investigation in any work area. Additional studies on person and machine output rates, personnel relations, and business communications provided knowledge to make job analyses and to write clear, concise reports.

Work Experience. The jobs you've held—full- or part-time, related or unrelated to the position you're applying for—help strengthen your qualifications. Try to tell concisely how you performed some functions and what you accomplished. Through discussing responsibilities you had in one or more previous jobs, you can show:

1. You gained experience that will help you understand (or learn faster) the special techniques required for the new job.
2. You can adapt to people and to various assignments.
3. You like to work with people and help them.
4. You've supplemented your academic training with related work experience.
5. You can handle responsibilities.
6. You are familiar with and aware of the business world.
7. You can adjust to the new job with only a minimum of training.
8. You're a hard worker.

Examples

1. For the past four summers while working in your office as a shipping clerk and assisting in the accounting department, I have gained considerable knowledge of the techniques and terminology unique to the accountant in this industry. This previous work experience with your company will enable me to adjust to your program with only minimum training.
2. During my employment at (name) Food Centers, I have ordered merchandise for a store operating at a volume of $40,000 a week, formulated pricing policies, supervised merchandise allocation of the shelves as well as the activities of about 25 employees. This background has helped me develop a working knowledge of the food industry and also the capacity to help make policy decisions on retail food-store operations.

Personal Attitudes, Interests, Qualities. In another paragraph or two you can highlight a few personal attitudes, interests, or qualities that relate specifically to the job requirements. You might discuss (1) your ability to work with people; or (2) your attitude toward employment—your interest in the field, company, or geographic area; or (3) your personal qualities.

Ability to work with people—to genuinely like them and want to help them—is a priceless commodity to sell.

Examples

1. My past work has given me the experience of handling people in the customer service relationship, as well as the employee relationship. As an assistant manager of a Household Finance Corporation office and as a collection department supervisor for the National Bank of Commerce, I found out fast that the ability to get along with people is essential. The exercise of good judgment based on often incomplete information, in varying situations, and sometimes difficult circumstances gave me the opportunity to develop confidence in my abilities. Opportunities to work constructively with many types of people is something I enjoy very much.

2. I have been able to further develop my interest in communicating and working with people in several capacities. Being the daughter of an Air Force officer, I have lived throughout the United States and in foreign countries and have spent most of my summers traveling. Furthermore, as hospitality chairman of my sorority, I organized all affairs held at the house and acted as hostess for guests. As a result, I have learned to make friends quickly and to feel at ease with many types of people—attributes which will help me be beneficial in a retailing position.

Attitude toward employment—interest in the field, company, or area—should be substantiated by proof.

Examples

1. My interest in construction developed in high school, working summers and part-time in residential home building. Upon graduation, I decided on a career in construction management, and consequently realized that a college background in business, combined with on-the-job experience, was essential preparation. As my interest and work experience show, I am very enthusiastic about a career in this field. Employment in construction completely financed my college education. Even in my spare time I am building a chalet, as the enclosed data sheet shows.

2. To supplement my marketing major, I sold men's clothing for three years part-time or full-time during school; this sales experience should give me a head start in your training program. Undoubtedly the most important possession a stockbroker must have is sales ability. I can sell, I enjoy selling, and I want to continue to sell. What's more, I proved my sales potential by winning the Arrow Shirt contest which I have mentioned on the enclosed data sheet. Selling stocks appears to be a challenge and I welcome that challenge.

3. Last summer I had the privilege of going to Alaska and working with high school, junior high, and primary age children. My work was in teaching and counselling. I traveled throughout the interior of Alaska and visited the University of Alaska. After meeting the people, seeing their problems and understanding the transition that Alaska is going through, I decided I want to return and work with the students at the Univeristy there.

Desirable personal qualities can be shown by citing various parts of your background—schooling, jobs, and/or extracurricular activities. You may want to give evidence of adaptability, versatility, responsibility, ability to apportion time, recognition by peers, and/or industriousness.

Examples

1. As the enclosed data sheet shows, I found it necessary to work while completing my formal education. In fulfilling the roles of student, spouse, mother, and provider at the same time I learned to be punctual and to apportion my time—requirements also confronted by an "audit team" in completing an audit within a time and fee limitation.

2. While attending the University and before being married in the summer of (year), I held many responsible positions in my fraternity including vice president and treasurer. In recognition of my efforts, my fraternity brothers elected me to Pi Omicron Sigma—a national fraternity service honorary. A record of my fraternity affairs (as well as my work experience) is included on the data sheet enclosed in this letter.

3. While attending the University, I worked part-time or full-time during the school year and up to 80 hours a week (on two or more jobs) each summer. I was entirely self-supporting throughout my college career, and feel I can offer your company qualities of adaptability, perseverance, and patience developed from working hard on many jobs with many kinds of people.

Toward the end of the message—usually in the next to the last paragraph but sometimes in the last paragraph—refer the reader to your résumé. The best way to make this reference is by directing the reader's attention to some data on the résumé (see examples 1 and 2 above and the sample letters at the end of the chapter).

Last Paragraph

The last paragraph of your message usually asks for action—just as a sales letter does. Without begging or commanding, you ask for an interview and (if appropriate) say you will come to the employer's office when he or she suggests. Make action easy by giving your telephone number and hours to call if someone can't answer the phone throughout the day or evening.

Examples

1. May I have an interview to discuss my qualifications with you in greater detail? I can come to your office whenever you suggest. My telephone number is 331-1123, where I can be reached any weekday after 4 p.m.

2. Early in April my husband and I will be moving to (town) where he will take up his new post with the Forestry Service. Will you please notify me of a time after April 6 when I may come in to discuss my qualifications with you?

3. My class schedule allows me to come to your office any afternoon except Tuesdays. May I have an interview to answer any questions about myself that you might have? You can reach me by telephoning 997-1234 before 10 a.m. or after 4 p.m.

4. Since I will be in (city) from March 22 to March 27, I will be grateful for the opportunity to see you during that time to discuss further my desire to serve as one of your investigators. After you have reviewed my qualifications and examined the enclosed data sheet, will you please name a convenient time in a letter to me at my Seattle address.

5. After you've had an opportunity to review some of the statements in this letter and on the enclosed data sheet, will you please call me at 896-6622 after 3 p.m. or write me about the possibility of beginning a career with (name of company). I'll appreciate the opportunity to discuss my qualifications with you.

Even if you're sending your job application hundreds of miles away, you might still ask for an interview if you think the company has a local representative who can screen you in person. Here you must ask the employer to tell you the local representative's name, or ask the company to arrange the interview for you with the local representative.

Although the résumé and this letter give you some idea of my qualifications, I am eager to have a personal interview with you. Or perhaps I could discuss my qualifications in greater detail with your regional personnel representative. Please let me know how I can get in touch with her or him.

If you know that it will be impossible for you to come to an interview at your own expense, offer to send the employer additional information upon request; between the lines you're hoping he will understand that you can come to his office if he pays your way.

If you wish additional information about my background, please let me know. I'll be glad to send it to you promptly.

Sample Letters of Application

The following application letters apply suggestions discussed in this chapter. Letter 1 illustrates both content and layout of an effective application letter that can accompany the résumé shown in Figure 11-1. Notice how well this applicant relates highlights of each paragraph to the job she seeks—staff accountant in a CPA firm which, she knows, has an opening.

Letter 2 shows the content of an application from a 21-year-old college graduate seeking a teaching position in a high school business department. It is a prospecting letter, because the applicant does not know whether an opening exists. Although the résumé may be neatly processed for frequent use, the letter must be individually typewritten and addressed to the superintendent or whoever is in charge of hiring business teachers in each city. Layout may be similar to that in letter 1 or any other appropriate letter style (as discussed on pages 117–124).

Letter 1
Solicited application for a staff accountant position. This letter accompanies Figure 11-1, page 398, personalized, one-page résumé.

3241 Lakeside Drive
Seattle, WA 98102
March 7, 19--

Mr. John Q. Burtise, CPA
Burtise, Hartman, and Associates
834 Exchange Building
Bellevue, WA 98004

Name and summary opening (attention)

Dear Mr. Burtise:

Professor Fletcher Myran has informed me that your firm is looking for a competent staff accountant. With thorough college training in account- ing and related studies, varied bookkeeping experience, and proven ability to work efficiently, I feel I could be an asset to your staff.

Training (interest)

To prepare adequately for a public accounting career, I have completed 40 quarter hours of accounting at the University of Washington, with a grade point average of 3.5 (on a 4-point scale). Two electronic data processing courses I studied, in addition to the accounting, provided information that will be useful in working with your clients who use computers. My studies in speech and business communication enable me to present clearly the financial data and reports for superiors or clients.

Varied bookkeeping experience (desire and conviction)

Since your firm specializes in medical accounts, I believe I could be of special benefit to you because of my interest and work in this area. At age 18 I was preparing weekly payrolls for 60 hospital maintenance employees. This position included keeping time and equipment records, calculating payroll deductions, writing monthly labor union benefit reports, and handling accounts payable. Later, as full-charge bookkeeper for a medical clinic and as assistant accountant in a hospital, accuracy and speed were necessary to meet deadlines at these fast-paced offices. My responsibilities included billing accounts receivable; monthly closing of general ledger; preparing financial statements, cost control data, and quarterly government tax reports. This experience will be useful in audits and analyses for cost control.

Personal qualities (conviction)

Serving as treasurer of the accounting honorary and chairperson of two charity drives required honesty, tact, and initiative. These qualities will be an important part of my code of ethics as a public accountant. By referring to the enclosed resume and contacting former employers, you will be able to form a more complete idea of my personality.

Easy action

Will you call me at 354-9876 to name a time when I may come, at your convenience, to talk with you about being your staff accountant? I am usually home after 3 p.m. each weekday.

Sincerely,

Alice G. O'Brien

Alice G. O'Brien

Enclosure: Resume

Letter 2
Prospecting application to a school superintendent for a high school teaching position. This letter accompanies Figure 11-2, page 399, general-purpose résumé.

Dear Mrs. Roberts:

Question and summary opening (attention)
Next September will one of your high schools need a business teacher who can make learning realistic and interesting for the students? If so, please consider me for the position. My qualifications include a liberal business background, work experience, and enthusiasm for teaching.

Liberal business background and specific courses (interest)
In August this year I will graduate from Ohio State University in Business Education. Studies in business, education, and economics (my minor) have received special emphasis in my program. I am now prepared to teach any of these business courses that you offer on the secondary level: typing, shorthand (Gregg or Forkner), office machines, accounting, and business law or communications. If you are considering adding a course in economics to your curriculum, I will be happy to present to you my ideas about the advantages of teaching economics in high school.

Work experience (desire and conviction)
Two years of steady office employment and previous summer work have given me valuable insight into the growing needs of the business community for vocationally trained high school graduates. This practical experience expanded my knowledge of business education. I am better equipped to communicate to my students in an interesting manner the relationships between their goals and the requirements of the business community. The different positions I have held developed qualities of tact and adaptability, which I consider important when working with young people.

Personal attitudes and qualities (desire)
The past semester of student teaching--mentioned on the enclosed resume--convinced me that high school teaching is my chosen career. I will work with the same zeal that helped me earn an A minus overall grade average throughout college and high school.

Easy-action request
An opportunity to discuss further your requirements and my qualifications will be appreciated. To arrange a meeting, will you please contact me at the above address?

The next example illustrates a prospecting letter from the 32-year-old experienced supervisor who wrote the three-page résumé shown on pages 400–401.

Letter 3
Prospecting application to an airline executive for a position in operations management. This letter accompanies Figure 11-3, pages 400–401, general-purpose résumé with functional summary.

Dear Mr. Williams:

Summary opening (attention)
The extensive experience and academic background I have had in Operations Management would enable me to make a substantial contribution to your company. Please consider me for an assignment which will lead ultimately to corporate management.

*Extensive
experience
and
personal
qualities
(interest;
conviction)*

Previous jobs and a carefully selected education program have been pursued with this management goal in mind. Administering and supervising Operational projects and personnel, as well as chairing numerous committees developed my leadership qualities. The practical managing experience has given me a firm foundation for obtaining results with cost and schedule constraints under pressures of "produce or perish." My accomplishments in each job were acknowledged by substantial salary increases. In my present government position I have worked with senior and corporate executives in business, industrial, labor, education, and government organizations.

*Relevant
college
education
(desire and
conviction)*

A related college education has improved my ability to help develop the overall corporate objectives so important to your firm. The broad base provided through a business administration program increases one's scope to see the "big picture" and provides methods from which to proceed logically.

*Easy-action
request*

The enclosed resume includes additional information. Page 1 summarizes my work experience, and pages 2 and 3 further detail specific jobs performed. After you have reviewed this information, will you please call me at 953-8111 anytime between 9 and 5 to state a time when I may discuss my qualifications with you? If you wish further information, I will be glad to send it to you promptly.

Exercises

1. Assume that you must write an application letter with résumé. You are applying for a job of your choice at the time you'll actually be mailing your written job presentation.

    In preparation for this assignment, find out what the personnel director (or other interviewer) will be looking for in you when you apply for a particular job (or job area) at a particular type of company, agency, or organization (department store, insurance company, brokerage firm, pharmaceutical house, school).

    Use the library and placement offices for information about an organization of your choice. If sufficient existing publications are not available locally, you might write to an organization of your choice (but not the firm to which you plan to send your application letter and résumé), asking for answers to your questions or arranging for an interview with the appropriate officer.

    The purpose of this assignment is to find out what qualifications the prospective employer looks for when screening you for your career job. Although you're not getting answers from the prospective employer, you will from sources that should reveal comparable information on the qualifications considered most important.

    Prepare a list of 10 (or more) questions you must know the answers to before you can write your application. All your questions must relate to a particular job or job area. (You may use the answers later for a report-writing assignment.)

    Listed below are several questions that you should consider. At least, they're possible springboards for the questions you must find answers to.

    a. What are the basic qualifications that you look for when you screen a recent college graduate for a job in (your career area)?
    b. For this type of work what major do you think is best?
    c. Outside the major what courses (business or nonbusiness) do you think will be helpful on the job?
    d. What kind of previous experience do you look for in the applicant?

     e.   How do you evaluate personality from a written job presentation?

     f.   How important are grades?

     g.   To get into this type of work, what initial job should I apply for?

     h.   Do you prefer references in the initial written job presentation?

2. Prepare a letter of application with an accompanying résumé for the career job you plan to get into after completion of your college education. Address it to the firm of your choice and to the individual who should receive it. [Instead of sending your presentation to a particular person, you might want to direct it to a particular department within the firm or to the title the receiver possesses (such as personnel manager).]

    To make this material as useful to you as possible, date the letter the month and year you actually plan to send it. For example, if you're graduating this year, the date of the letter should precede that of graduation by enough time (4 to 9 months) to have the job sewed up when you're ready to go to work. But if you're a sophomore, and have at least two more years of college and then two years of graduate school, use the date you'll actually be sending the letter.

    Use only facts, as far as possible, in both your letter and résumé. If you are dating the letter in the future, assume the activities (especially schooling, work experience, government service) that will most likely take place between now and then. This timing permits you to update the written job presentation when you're ready to revise, type, and actually send it.

    Try to make your message and data sheet so convincing and selling that they will stand out from many others that may be received the same day. Both should be neatly and accurately typed—100 percent correct in spelling and accurate in facts and figures.

3. On the day your application letter and résumé (Exercise 2) are due to be handed in, bring them to class and exchange them (or copies) with a classmate—perferably one you do not know very well. Each of you will then evaluate the other's written job presentation. Assume you are the addressee of the letter, a stranger to the applicant. Would the letter and résumé convince you to invite the writer to your office for an interview? Why or why not? On a separate sheet write your answer to these questions. Also list (a) specific good qualities of the letter and résumé and (b) specific suggestions for improvements. Sign the sheet and return it to the writer, together with the letter and résumé. If your instructor wishes, each student will hand in these comments along with the letter and résumé. (No changes should, however, be made on these messages before the instructor reads them.)

4. Below are six application letters. Explain orally in class which ones will most likely result in an interview. Which are totally unacceptable? Why?

Letter A
Application to a large department store for a position in management trainee program.

Please consider me for a position in your management trainee program. My qualifications include four years of college training with a major in marketing, experience in the retailing field, and a sincere interest in working with people.

Because I was interested in the business field from the time I entered the University of (state), I geared my four-year program toward a degree in this area. Majoring in marketing and taking courses specifically oriented to retailing, such as Retail Profit Planning and Business Control and Retail Sales Promotion, have given me a basic foundation in understanding retailing fundamentals.

Working in a retailing establishment over vacations for the past two years, I have had the opportunity to apply these concepts. The practical experience of taking charge of several departments during regular employees' vacations has given me a more complete understanding of the importance of good merchandising and of providing customer satisfaction. It also helped me to better realize the necessity for coordination between departments and personnel in making the organization successful. With the large amount of tourist trade, I was constantly dealing with people of varied interests and personalities in a business atmosphere.

I have been able to further develop my interest in communicating and working with people in several capacities. Being the daughter of an Air Force officer, I have lived throughout the United States and in foreign countries and have spent most of my summers traveling. Furthermore, as hospitality chairperson of my sorority, I organized all affairs held at the house and acted as hostess for guests. As a result, I have learned to make friends quickly and to feel at ease with many types of people--attributes which will help me be beneficial in a retailing position.

My excellent health is reflected in my enjoyment and year-round participation in the outdoor activities you will find listed on my data sheet.

May I have an interview to discuss my qualifications with you in greater detail? Please telephone me at 543-2024 and suggest a time which will be convenient.

Letter B
Application to CPA firm for a position as staff assistant.

Please consider me for the position of staff assistant, for which my degree in accounting, plus a varied practical experience, provides a background.

The program I followed at the University of (state) included 40 credit-hours of accounting courses--up-to-date procedures, principles, and theory--that afford a firm basis with which to grow in the auditing profession. Courses in data processing, in addition to my work experience at a computer installation, have led me to be especially interested in the auditing of such systems.

My practical training includes an internship with Arthur Young and Company, which gave me an appreciation of an auditor's responsibilities to his clients and the public. Several of my prior jobs have contributed to my awareness of other business problems--for example, the delicacy of customer (client) relations in a "service" profession. Having dealt with dissatisfied customers as well as delinquent debtors, I feel that I can display the tact implicit in an auditor's duties.

As the enclosed data sheet shows, I found it necessary to work while completing my formal education. In fulfilling the roles of student, spouse, father, and provider at the same time, I learned to apportion my time--a requirement also confronted by an "audit team" in completing an audit within a time and fee limitation.

May I discuss further with you my qualifications for the position of staff assistant in your firm? Please call me at 632-5583 or write to arrange a time when I may come in.

Letter C
Application to grocery chain for accounting position.

With my vast and diversified working experience in a (town name) Safeway store and my 5 years' college training in accounting and economics, I am well qualified to apply for an accounting position with Safeway Stores, Inc.

Having successfully completed studies in managerial and financial accounting while earning my degree at the University of (state), you will find that I can handle any accounting situation with ease and confidence.

While working in the many departments in Safeway in order to finance my college education, I became thoroughly familiar with every phase of operation of one of your stores. Because of my pleasing personality, my ability to get along well with others, and my excellent work record, I was chosen to supervise the night stock crew during the summers of (year) and (year).

My work experience with Safeway has been both valuable and enjoyable for me; therefore, I wish to continue working for your firm in my chosen field.

After you've had a chance to verify some of the things I've said about myself in this letter and on the enclosed data sheet, will you write me about the possibilities of working in one of your West Coast offices?

Letter D
Application to a firm for sales position.

Please consider my application for a position in your sales department. My qualifications are a Bachelor of Arts in General Business, a thorough and working knowledge of accounting and finance, and a sincere interest in selling.

I am seeking a position in your company in selling because I feel that I have the necessary qualifications to do a good job for the company, while learning the basic components of your needs. I selected your firm because it is the most rapidly expanding company in this industry and a leader in research and development, which I recognize as essential to maintain your present status. I feel that I can contribute toward these goals. I have studied the basic background of the transportation industry, and am deeply interested in furthering my knowledge, to the benefit of the company. I have enclosed a resume of my personal background, complete with a transcript of my grades.

After you've had time to review my application and data sheet, will you please call me or write. My address and telephone numbers are on the enclosed data sheet. Thank you for your consideration.

Letter E
Application to brewery to be sales representative.

If hundreds of effective retail calls, thorough knowledge of point-of-sale and imaginative merchandising help make a brewery representative, then I've begun to learn the business. I would like to put this practical field experience to work for Sick's Rainer Brewing Company.

Field work as an Assistant District Sales Manager for the Joseph Schlitz Brewing Company gave me an opportunity to plan and execute sales promotions that sold beer. I have proven ability to open non-buying accounts, secure floor displays, sell additional packages and achieve point-of-sale dominance.

In addition, I have conducted route analyses, set up key account systems and conducted sales training meetings for wholesaler personnel.

Frequent contact with retailers and consumers enabled me to handle consumer complaints and utilize a good layman's knowledge of the brewing process.

After you've had an opportunity to review some of the things I've said in this letter and on the enclosed data sheet, will you write me frankly about the possibility of beginning a career with Sick's Rainier Brewing Company?

I would appreciate an opportunity to discuss my qualifications.

Letter F
Application to a newspaper for position as assistant music and drama editor.

In reference to your advertisement in Editor & Publisher (3/14) for an assistant music and drama editor, the offer is worth an inquiry because of my deep interest in theater. But, very frankly, I'm afraid it would have to be an exceptional salary offer to lure me so far from the East Coast and what I'm convinced are its greater professional opportunities.

However, you will find samples of my reviews and a brief resume attached. Should you desire to continue this correspondence further, I will send you references and other material customary to a job application.

My experience in motion picture-theater reviewing with the Sun has been limited to "filling-in" for the regular critic during his vacations or illnesses. Prior to that, I wrote a theater column in a weekly newspaper in Bath, Pa., a sideline to my daily reporting. I have engaged in all phases of amateur theater as an outside interest. I am not well versed in music—though I am confident in my critical capacities. Again, I have filled-in at times for the Sun's music critic and, if need be, can also submit samples. I have handled general assignments and beats.

Your advertisement mentions "opportunity for advancement," without further elaboration. Your offer of the position of assistant music-drama editor would be considerably more attractive if coupled with a commitment to go to your Washington, D.C., bureau in two, or three, years or to whatever overseas bureaus the Daily Blat may sponsor, subject only to your complete dissatisfaction with the work produced for you.

The tendency, of course, of most newspapers is to fill the opening with the run-of-the-mill newsperson who is panting at the door and willing to accept chicken-feed. Consequently, I have little reason to expect a favorable reaction to this letter. If I am mistaken, I hope you will advise me of the maximum salary you can pay for this position, the set-up at the Blat and any arrangements that you would consider feasible. I hope we can discuss this matter further, but only with your understanding that I expect to drive a hard bargain.

My home address appears below and on the resume. Please address your reply accordingly.

12 Other Job Application Messages

The time you'll spend—and the number of messages you'll write—in getting your career job depends on economic conditions, need for graduates in your area, and your own qualifications and standards. If you're sending your job presentation when it's a seller's market and you have unusually good qualifications, you might land the job you want right away. But if the conditions are reversed, you can spend many weeks—even months—finding the right niche for yourself.

To be on the safe side, begin your job hunting at least four to nine months before graduation, and send your written job presentation with résumé to more than one firm. But don't send out too many—say 50 or 100—at one time. Limit the number to 10 or fewer and then wait for replies before you mail more.

This chapter discusses the job interview, follow-up messages from applicant to employer, and follow-up messages from employer to applicant.

The Job Interview

As you know, the goal of your application letter and résumé is to get an interview. Assume now that you achieved your purpose with your written "sales" presentation. The desired telephone call, letter, or telegram from the employer asks you to come for an interview on a certain day and time. That interview may be the most important step toward your getting the desired job. This section presents suggestions regarding preparation for the interview, conduct during the interview, questions frequently asked, and negative factors to avoid. (For *interviewer's* responsibilities see pages 652-658.)

Preparation for the Interview

Always prepare for an interview before you go to it. Remember that the interview is a two-way street. Your primary purpose is to get the best job suitable to your capabilities. The employer's goal is to get the best person available for the job. Take a look at yourself from the employer's point of view. In hiring you, the employer is making an investment that over a few years will mount to thousands of dollars considering salary, fringes, and taxes. Naturally the employer wants a quality product.

As the New York Life Insurance Company says so well in its booklet, *Making the Most of Your Job Interview:*

> The employment interview is one of the most important events in the average person's experience, for the obvious reason that the 20 or 30 minutes spent with the interviewer may determine the entire future course of one's life. Yet interviewers are constantly amazed at the number of applicants who drift into job interviews without any apparent preparation and only the vaguest idea of what they are going to say. Their manner says, "Well, here I am." And that's often the end of it, in more ways than one.

> Others, although they undoubtedly do not intend to do so, create an impression of indifference by acting too casually. At the other extreme, a few applicants work themselves into such a state of mind that when they arrive they seem to be in the last stages of nervous fright and are only able to answer in monosyllables.

These marks of inexperience can be avoided by knowing a little of what actually is expected of you and by making a few simple preparations before the interview.[1]

Adequate preparation includes knowing yourself, familiarizing yourself with the company, listing questions you want to ask as well as answers to questions you'll probably encounter, paying attention to your appearance, and checking details about the meeting place for the interview.

The most important preparation relates to knowing yourself. But, then, you have already looked critically at yourself before you wrote your résumé and application letter. You should know the job or the job area you want to apply for, the requirements for the job, and how your qualifications (both your strengths and weaknesses) compare with the requirements.

In addition to knowing yourself, you should bone up on the company. You can find excellent references in your library or school placement office and from employees of the company itself. Among other facts you should know are the age of the company, location of its plants, types of products and services, its growth over the years (especially the last few years), and its prospects for the future. You'll make a favorable impression on the interviewer if you sincerely show interest in the company and show knowledge about it gained through your own initiative.

Another important step in preparing for the interview is to jot down questions you want to ask the interviewer if he or she doesn't first give you the answers. The questions you might ask relate to possible formal or informal training the company offers after employment, company policy about moving your family to a new location, what type of management system the firm uses, the average age of the executives, whether they are promoted from within, why the person you're replacing left the firm, and perhaps also the company's profit picture (if you didn't find it in your research). The *last* questions may relate to fringe benefits and salary.

Also you want to anticipate questions the interviewer will ask you. You can definitely expect to encounter revealing questions relating to what you have done; what you think about what you have done; your interests and hobbies; relationship to friends, school and work; your colleagues and family. Shown on pages 423–425 are questions frequently asked during the employment interview.

Once you know yourself, have studied the company, and have prepared your questions and answers, you still need to consider your appearance and details about the meeting place. Appearance includes both your overall neatness and the clothes you wear. Be sure your hair and fingernails are clean and your hairstyle is appropriate. Wear conservative clothes appropriate for the office, clean your shoes, and use lotions or perfumes sparingly. Also see that accessories complement the suit or dress. Then there are details about the interview itself. Definitely know when and where the interview will be held—and be there 10 to 15 minutes early. Being late is inexcusable. Also

---

[1]*Making the Most of Your Job Interview,* New York Life Insurance Company. Copies of this 12-page booklet may be obtained in reasonable quantity without cost or obligation from your New York Life Agent or the New York Life Office in your community.

know the full name and address of the company, the interviewer's name and current title, and how to pronounce his or her name. Put a working pen or pencil along with a small notebook in your coat pocket or purse. If the job requires creativity or high grades, you might take along samples of your work or your transcript of grades.

Before you go into the room where the interviewer is, try to relax, If possible, sit quietly in the waiting room, and convince yourself that the interviewer is an individual who merely wants to find out whether you're the person for the job. In turn, you *want* to show the interviewer that you appreciate the opportunity you're being given and furthermore that you're eager to tell about yourself.

Conduct during the Interview

From the time the interviewer first sees you until you leave, he or she will be observing you carefully and listening to everything you say and do. To make the best impression, you need to:

1. Show interest. You can do so by the way you sit and look alert, by eye contact, and by questions you ask.
2. Be courteous. Don't chew gum, and don't smoke unless the interviewer invites you to do so.
3. Be honest and sincere at all times. If you begin to exaggerate or fabricate details— and you're caught—the interviewer will be less likely to consider you as a favorable candidate for the job.
4. Be yourself. Don't try to put on airs. By being yourself, you'll be on more familiar ground, seem more comfortable, and be more at ease.
5. Be a good listener. By doing so, you will be ready to reply to a question the interviewer asks, seem interested, and also receive valuable clues from the interviewer's statements.
6. Avoid the negative attitudes or actions listed on pages 425 and 426.

When you first see the interviewer, smile and greet him or her by name (if you know the name). From then to the end of the interview you should take your cues from the interviewer. If he or she offers to shake hands, do so. Be sure your grip is firm, not a bone-crusher or limp fish. Also remain standing until invited to sit down; the only exception is when you're in a small room and the interviewer remains seated or sits down immediately. Look at the interviewer and keep the proper eye contact throughout the interview. But don't stare!

Be on guard at all times for nervousness. If your hands want to wander or play with objects, put these hands in your lap.

After the warm-up period (exchange of pleasantries to develop rapport) be ready for the interviewer's first questions about your qualifications or interest. You might be asked, "Why are you interested in this company?" If so, merely give the answer you previously thought out. Or the interviewer might say, "I see from the company (or placement office) form that you're interested in making marketing research your career. Tell me how you prepared yourself for this area." Your answer may include excerpts from your education, work, and/or activities. Throughout the questioning, the interviewer tries to get information needed to evaluate you and what you can do for the company. Keep your replies positive and concise (but generally more than "yes" or "no").

Shown below are other suggestions to consider:

1. If you are strong in extracurricular organizations and the interviewer hasn't mentioned that area, watch for an opportunity to ask, "Are you interested in my extracurricular activities?" The interviewer is not likely to say "no." Highlight those that relate to the job requirements.
2. When desirable, explain why you could help the company in this job and why you like doing this kind of work. (If useful, pull out of your briefcase some examples of your past work.)
3. Be prepared to ask sincere questions about the company because doing so shows interest.
4. Never make a slighting reference about a former professor or employer. Assume part of the blame yourself. If you can't say something nice about a person, don't say anything.
5. Know the current beginning salary range for your type of work.
6. Throughout the interview, smile at appropriate times—but don't maintain an artificial, plastered smile at any time; it's unnatural and insincere.
7. Be alert for signs from the interviewer that the interview is about to end. And when you depart, be sure to thank the interviewer for seeing you.
8. Tactfully ask for some kind of commitment as to when the interviewer will let you know the decision.
9. If you are offered the job, you can accept immediately or ask for time to think it over.

Questions Frequently Asked during the Interview

Shown below are 80 questions frequently asked during the employment interview. Mr. Frank S. Endicott, Director of Placement, Northwestern Univeristy, made the compilation from 92 companies he surveyed.[2] Try to answer these questions orally or in writing *before* you go to an interview.

1. What are your future vocational plans?
2. In what school activities have you participated? Why? Which did you enjoy the most?
3. How do you spend your spare time? What are your hobbies?
4. In what type of position are you most interested?
5. Why do you think you might like to work for our company?
6. What jobs have you held? How were they obtained and why did you leave?
7. What courses did you like best? Least? Why?
8. Why did you choose your particular field of work?
9. What percentage of your college expenses did you earn? How?
10. How did you spend your vacations while in school?

[2]You'll find these questions in the New York Life Insurance Company's booklet, *Making the Most of Your Job Interview.*

11. What do you think about our company?
12. Do you feel that you have received a good general training?
13. What qualifications do you have that make you feel you will be successful in your field?
14. What extracurricular offices have you held?
15. What are your ideas on salary?
16. How do you feel about your family?
17. How interested are you in sports?
18. If you were starting college all over again, what courses you would take?
19. Do you prefer any specific geographic location? Why?
20. Do you date anyone regularly? Is it serious?
21. How much money do you hope to earn at age 30? 35?
22. Why did you decide to go to this particular school?
23. Do you think that your extracurricular activities were worth the time you devoted to them? Why?
24. What do you think determines a person's progress in a good company?
25. What personal characteristics are necessary for success in your chosen field?
26. Why do you think you would like this particular type of job?
27. What are your parents' occupations?
28. Tell me about your home life during the time you were growing up.
29. Do you prefer working with others or by yourself?
30. What kind of boss do you prefer?
31. Are you primarily interested in making money or do you feel that service to humanity is your prime concern?
32. Can you take instructions without feeling upset?
33. Tell me a story!
34. Do you live with your parents? Which of your parents has had the most profound influence on you?
35. How did previous employers treat you?
36. What have you learned from some of the jobs you have held?
37. Can you get recommendations from previous employers?
38. What interests you about our product or service?
39. What was your record in military service?
40. Have you ever changed your major field of interest while in college? Why?
41. When did you choose your college major?
42. Do you feel you have done the best scholastic work of which you are capable?
43. How did you happen to go to college?
44. What do you know about opportunities in the field in which you are trained?
45. Have you ever had any difficulty getting along with fellow students and faculty?
46. Which of your college years was the most difficult?
47. What is the source of your spending money?
48. Do you own any life insurance?
49. Have you saved any money?
50. Do you have any debts?
51. How old were you when you became self-supporting?
52. Did you enjoy your four years at this university?
53. Do you like routine work?
54. Do you like regular hours?
55. What size city do you prefer?
56. What is your major weakness?
57. Define cooperation!
58. Do you demand attention?
59. Do you have an analytical mind?

60. Are you eager to please?
61. What do you do to keep in good physical condition?
62. Have you had any serious illness or injury?
63. Are you willing to go where the company sends you?
64. What job in our company would you choose if you were entirely free to do so?
65. What types of books have you read?
66. Have you plans for graduate work?
67. What types of people seem to "rub you the wrong way"?
68. Do you enjoy sports as a participant? As an observer?
69. Have you ever tutored an underclassman?
70. What jobs have you enjoyed the most? The least? Why?
71. What are your own special abilities?
72. What job in our company do you want to work toward?
73. Would you prefer a large or a small company? Why?
74. Do you like to travel?
75. How about overtime work?
76. What kind of work interests you?
77. What are the disadvantages of your chosen field?
78. Are you interested in research?
79. If married, how often do you entertain at home?
80. What have you done which shows initiative and willingness to work?

Negative Factors to Avoid

Mr. Endicott, who compiled the 80 questions most frequently asked in interviews, also surveyed for negative factors evaluated during the employment interview which frequently lead to rejection of the applicant. Shown below are 50 of these factors as reported by 153 companies.[3]

1. Poor personal appearance
2. Overbearing—overaggressive—conceited "superiority complex"—"know-it-all"
3. Inability to communicate clearly—poor voice, diction, grammar
4. Lack of planning for career—no purpose and goals
5. Lack of interest and enthusiasm—passive, indifferent
6. Lack of confidence and poise—nervous—ill-at-ease
7. Failure to participate in activities
8. Overemphasis on money—interest only in best dollar offer
9. Poor scholastic record—just got by
10. Unwillingness to start at the bottom—expects too much too soon
11. Excuses—evasiveness—hedges on unfavorable factors in record
12. Lack of tact
13. Lack of maturity
14. Lack of courtesy—ill mannered
15. Condemnation of past employers
16. Lack of social understanding
17. Marked dislike for school work
18. Lack of vitality
19. Failure to look interviewer in the eye
20. Limp, fishy hand-shake

[3] *Making the Most of Your Job Interview.*

21. Indecision
22. Loafing during vacations—lakeside pleasures
23. Unhappy married life
24. Friction with parents
25. Sloppy application blank
26. Merely shopping around
27. Wants job only for short time
28. Little sense of humor
29. Lack of knowledge of field of specialization
30. Parents run applicant's life
31. No interest in company or in industry
32. Emphasis on personal friends
33. Unwillingness to relocate
34. Cynical
35. Low moral standards
36. Lazy
37. Intolerant—strong prejudices
38. Narrow interests
39. Spends much time in movies or watching television
40. Poor handling of personal finances
41. No interest in community activities
42. Inability to take criticism
43. Lack of appreciation of the value of experience
44. Radical ideas
45. Late to interview without good reason
46. Never heard of company
47. Failure to express appreciation for interviewer's time
48. Asks no questions about the job
49. High-pressure type
50. Indefinite response to questions

In summary, the interview involves at least two people—the interviewer and the interviewee. To find out if the applicant (interviewee) is the individual for the job, the interviewer will consider the interviewee's background, qualifications, personality, and attitudes. Then the interviewer will evaluate this information, along with facts from other sources (references, tests, and so forth), and decide whether or not to invite the applicant to join the company or to invite him/her to the home plant for further interviews with other officials. As the interviewee, you need to prepare well for the interview and then sell yourself (during the interview) by showing interest, being sincere and natural, stating your qualifications, and behaving like a person the company would want on its working force.

Follow-up Messages from Applicant to Employer

You strengthen your chances for the job you have applied for when you follow up your application letter and résumé. Of the three ways to follow up—in person, by letter, or by phone—the written message is one of the most effective because employers can analyze the applicant's qualifications at their convenience. They can also more easily compare a large number of applicants at one time—either on the job or at home in the evening.

A written follow-up is effective for several good reasons:

1. Only a few applicants use a follow-up—probably fewer than 10 percent. Thus, the employer is favorably impressed by one.
2. A follow-up shows the applicant is genuinely interested in the job or the company.
3. This message indicates determination. Some firms won't reply to an applicant for a sales job until a follow-up arrives. Other firms intentionally mail the sales applicant a negative reply. The employer reasons that the applicant who follows up when applying for a sales job will follow up on prospects—even those who say no—when on the job in a sales territory.
4. A follow-up indicates courtesy (if it follows an interview), serves as a reminder to the employer, permits better understanding of the applicant (through submission of additional information), and shows sincerity.

This section covers first the two all-important and most frequently used types of initial follow-up messages and then presents other types involved in getting a job.

The Initial Follow-up

The first follow-up you'll use is either (1) a follow-up to the interview or (2) an inquiry about the application letter and résumé when the employer doesn't reply.

Follow-up to the Interview. After you have had your interview, you should send the interviewer (or the appropriate company official) a written thank-you.[4] Remember, the interviewer spent some valuable time to talk with you; and for reasons of courtesy alone, you need to acknowledge this time, attention, and consideration. Only when you are told during the interview not to write will you refrain from sending this message.

In most instances this message is short—less than one page—and its organizational pattern is that of a good news or neutral letter:

1. In the opening paragraph, state the main idea—express thanks for the interview or say you're returning a completed form. (If you don't thank in the opening do so in the last paragraph.) Also identify the job and perhaps mention the time and place of the interview.
2. In the middle paragraph(s) you discuss one or more of the following ideas:
   a. Mention how you *now* feel about the firm or a job with the firm—now that you have visited the plant, listened to the interviewer talk, and toured the facility. Of course, you write only favorable responses.
   b. Add new material that might be helpful in determining your qualifications. For example, assume you've been considering continuing your education in the evenings after graduation. Then in the interview the employer says the company favors junior employees improving themselves by attending college at night. You go home, think over this idea, and decide to begin night classes. That's new material you can mention in the message. Other new material is reporting that you completed an assignment the interviewer gave you at the time of the interview (such as to read a brochure, see someone, or take a test).

---

[4]A Cincinnati executive, reviewing 35 different jobs in his company for which hundreds of applications were received, gives this tip: "In each instance the job went to the thoughtful applicant who followed up the interview with a sincere thank-you note." Numerous other executives as well as applicants have confirmed the effectiveness of these follow-up messages.

   c. If you think the interviewer questioned one of your qualifications or you think you might have made a negative impression concerning one statement during the interview, include honest, positive facts to rebuild confidence. For example, if the interviewer seemed to want an older person, convince him or her that you are mature because you've dealt successfully with all types of people on your various jobs; or you have assumed responsibilities; or you have had to allocate your time as student, spouse, and breadwinner. Or if you think you "muffed" it on one or more areas, try to reestablish your credentials.

   d. Other ideas which can occasionally strengthen your presentation are: (1) your favorable reaction to points covered by the interviewer and (2) highlights of qualifications discussed during the interview. (These two suggestions aren't as important as (a), (b), and (c) because they're a rehash of what the interviewer already knows.)

3. In the last paragraph you can use one or more of the following:

   a. Offer to send additional information upon request.

   b. Thank for the interview (if not done in first paragraph).

   c. Say you can come in for another interview.

   d. Indicate hope (or confidence) that your qualifications fit the firm's requirements.

   e. Mention you're looking forward to a favorable decision.

   f. Ask for an opportunity to prove you can help the firm's sales, growth, and so on.

The best time to send the follow-up to an interview is a day or two after the meeting—at least within a week.

With this organizational plan in mind, study the following two examples of effective follow-up messages. Both applicants were successful in getting the job they sought. In each case the employer stated that the follow-up letter helped greatly.

Message 1 is from a 22-year-old applicant seeking his first career job as a sales representative after college graduation. Notice how convincingly he surmounts what appeared to be a shortcoming by showing that his responsibilities *during* college were equivalent to two years' business experience *after* college.

Message 1
A successful after-interview follow-up to a national industrial firm.

Dear Mr. Simonson:

Your interview with me yesterday was both enjoyable and informative. Thank you for your courtesies and the interest you took in my qualifications as a sales representative for your firm.

During the conversation you mentioned that you were particularly looking for a person who had at least two years' business experience since finishing college. I agree with you that the knack of working with people and the mature outlook gained from practical experience are valuable for a prospective sales representative. These qualities were firmly developed in me <u>during</u> my college years.

As my resume shows, to obtain an Industrial Engineering degree I added an extra year of engineering and business courses to my studies. In various college activities my responsibilities were mainly with

people. As Publicity Manager for <u>The College Engineer</u> magazine--
after careful planning plus enthusiasm and drive--I increased sales
25% over the previous year. As president of our fraternity, I
worked harmoniously with our 80 members and sold the alumni on the
support we needed. My part-time and summer jobs during college
ranged from clerking in a grocery store to tutoring first-year students. I believe these activities, jobs, and additional studies have
given me a background of experience and judgment equivalent to the
two years' business training your firm would like its sales representatives to have.

You will find, I believe, that I can develop into one of your top
industrial sales representatives, Mr. Simonson. Will you give me the
opportunity to prove this statement?

Message 2 is from a 27-year-old recent accounting graduate applying for an accounting job in a community college. During the interview the college official was concerned
whether the applicant—a quiet, soft-spoken individual—had adequate qualifications
for leadership; she would have to supervise the work of six bookkeepers in the college
office. This letter helped her get the job:

Message 2
A successful after-interview follow-up to a college vice president and finance officer.

Dear Dr. Millard:

Thank you for taking time on April 4 to talk with me regarding my
application for the accounting position in your office. As you requested, I am enclosing the transcript of my grades from the University
of (name).

During my five years at the (name) Company I worked in a lead capacity
with many people. The experience I gained would be useful for the job
you outlined. For the first two of the five years I was responsible
for quality control in the Pensar Division. As one of my duties I
supervised ten employees and trained new people to visually and
dimensionally inspect vendor-made parts purchased for use on the program. When I requested night-shift duty so I could carry 10 to 15
credit hours at Mason Junior College, I was given full responsibilities for the inspection duties on that shift, a position I held three
years.

Four years of college studies (with no financial help) while holding
full- and part-time jobs and raising a family indicate my perseverance. My school and work record of continuous four-year attendance
(except for a three-day virus illness last summer) will assure you of
my regularity and dependability on the job. We are buying a home in
Blanktown and will enter our daughter in the school system here next
fall; so my family is well established here.

I believe my education and 10 years of work experience will qualify
me to assume the accounting and office responsibilities you pointed
out to me. Please let me know your decision. You could depend on
me to be a hard-working, mature staff member.

Inquiry about Application Letter and Résumé. If you haven't received a response to your written job application within three weeks, you are justified in sending an inquiry. Although it is unlikely your material was lost in the mail, it is possible the receiver misplaced or forgot about it. Anyway, a well-run organization should acknowledge—and if it does not, you certainly should inquire.

This type of follow-up is usually shorter than the one written after the interview. Since many firms keep the written job presentation for six months or longer, all you really need do is give enough identification so the employer can locate your material. The inquiry should include: identification of job sought, date of application letter previously sent, and (if appropriate) a request for an interview. In addition, some employers suggest you also include one or more of the following:

1. Interest in job
2. Date of availability
3. Offer to send additional information upon request
4. Telephone number
5. New material about qualifications
6. Reasons for wanting to work for the company
7. Status of application
8. Highlights of major qualifications already given in the application letter

Don't repeat information the employer already possesses. Included in this category is the same résumé because it takes up valuable file space. No personnel manager likes to receive an application letter—and then one or two follow-ups—each with another copy of the same résumé. Given below are two examples of acceptable inquiries.

Message 1
Emphasizes identification of applicant's file.

Dear Ms. Lindsell

On January 15, (year), I sent you my application letter and resume for an opening in your management training program. Because I'm very much interested in your firm and its future, I'm inquiring whether you received this material.

Please let me know what information you wish about my background. And, of course, I can come for an interview whenever you suggest.

Message 2
Includes highlights of the applicant.

Dear Mr. Huget:

Perhaps you will remember I sent you my application for a position in your grain department on February 8. I am primarily interested in cash grain purchasing and the use of the futures market as related to the operations of your company.

You may recall that the principal points in my letter were that:

1. I have conducted a research project into the use of the commodity exchanges by members of the Iowa grain industry, and am now finishing the writing of the results for my Master's thesis.
2. I have a college degree in Business Administration and plan to receive a Master of Arts degree in June, (year), in marketing.
3. During 18 years on an Iowa farm, I became familiar with most of the grains in the grain industry.

I hope that you can use a person with my background. If you wish any further information, I will be glad to send it to you.

Other Follow-up Messages from Applicant to Employer

In addition to the follow-up messages just discussed, a job-hunting campaign can include quite a few other types. The following pages discuss and give examples of some of these.

Answer to a Noncommittal Letter. Assume that you have sent your application letter with résumé—maybe even had the interview. Then you receive the following:

Dear Miss Randolph

We were pleased to receive your excellent application for employment.

We are very much interested in your capabilities but regret that at the present time, we cannot make use of them; with your permission, however, we will keep your name on file and if anything should develop in the future, get in touch with you.

Thank you for your interest in our organization.

What should you do? At first you might interpret this message as a routine refusal. However, the employer has said, "with your permission ... keep on file," and you should assume that the message is sincere and you will definitely be considered when an opening occurs. A short message like the following is quite a satisfactory reply:

Dear Mr. Lewis

Thank you for your reviewing my qualifications for (type of job).

Will you please keep my name in your files so that you can consider me when a future opening in that field takes place. You can count on me to do a thorough, accurate job if I may join your staff.

I like what I read and hear about your organization--and hope some-day to be part of such an organization.

If you receive a message that says essentially what Mr. Lewis wrote to Miss Randolph but does not ask your permission, a reply is optional.

Reply to Request for Additional Information. Occasionally an employer, interviewer, or school will request additional information about your background. If such a situation arises, think carefully about the topic(s) that have been asked about. As with the initial presentation, analyze your background thoroughly, so that you will include all the important details to back up and strengthen your presentation; then organize and write. You'll probably use an outline like the following:

First paragraph:	Thank for interview and express eagerness to tell about whatever is asked for. Also identify the topic(s) you are discussing.
Middle paragraphs:	If asked about two qualifications (say interest in field and interest in company), write separate paragraphs for each. The discussion will be persuasive—quite similar to the middle paragraphs that create desire in the application letter.
Last paragraph:	In your last paragraph you might express: 1. Availability for another interview 2. Any other idea that rounds out and strengthens the message.

Given below is such a presentation. The admissions office of a law school asked the applicant to fill out the necessary form and separately to talk about her interest in law and give highlights of her background.

```
Admissions Council
University of (state) Law School
(city, state zip)

Gentlemen

As you requested, I am returning the completed Form A and a brief
discussion of two questions you asked for:  my interest in law and
highlights of my background.
```

Interest in Law
```
Before going into my background, I want to explain why I want a
degree in law.  The need has been there since childhood.  Unlike most
childhood fixations--teacher, doctor, and dancer--the desire to be a
lawyer has stuck with me since the age of twelve.  More than a child-
hood dream is involved though.  I feel that a law degree and the
ability to use it embodies one of the most valuable assets a person
can own.

To me law pervades every aspect of our society.  Law is where the
action is.  It is one of the few professions that enable a person to
be actively involved in forming her culture while at the same time
enabling her to find a highly satisfactory role in life.

Specifically I plan to concentrate on corporate law with a later
concentration on international legal business relationships.  This
area needs good lawyers, and I want to prepare myself to fill that
need.
```

Background
```
Following is a brief sketch of my background that will help you in
assessing my ability to study law.  As the enclosed form shows, I
was born in Germany.  Though still a German citizen, I plan to go
```

through naturalization during (year) to become a citizen of the
United States. I was reared in South Africa from the age of three
and as such am bilingual, speaking and writing both German and English
without any accent or faults in composition.

I used my undergraduate years to gain as wide a knowledge of as many
disciplines as I could. My program emphasized political science,
social sciences, some humanties with a later concentration on general
business courses. This was, in my mind, the most useful road toward
my eventual goal.

My transcript that you should have received by now shows I spent five
years on my bachelor's degree. The extra year was necessitated by
a scarcity of funds in my family. Part- and full-time jobs have put
me through school and have allowed me to save enough money to attend
law school. Although outside work has detracted from study time, I
feel that the work discipline and the ability to communicate and work
with all types of people more than offset any loss in academic learning.

If you should need any additional information to aid you in your
decision, please let me know.

Even if admissions had asked the applicant to send in only the completed form, she
might voluntarily include a letter like the one above to bolster her presentation. If so,
the same format could be followed, the only change being in the first paragraph:

Thank you for sending me the requested application to Law School.
Enclosed are the completed Form A and a brief discussion of my
interest in law and of my background.

Acceptance of Invitation for Interview. This type of good-news message has as its
main purpose acceptance, which should appear in the first paragraph. Usually the
employer leaves it up to you—at least within a limited time span—to decide when to
make the trip. In turn, you must be considerate of the working days and hours of the
employer. Give a choice of several times within a certain week so that the employer can
choose the most convenient date and hour. The last paragraph should express sincere
interest in the forthcoming interview. Message 2 on page 441 is a good example of an
applicant's acceptance of an invitation for a plant interview.

Follow-up after Interview. If you receive no reply by the promised date, remember
that it takes time for the employer to interview all applicants, route the qualifications
to interested officers in the organization, and make a final choice. However, if you
have waited what you consider ample time and also *beyond* the promised date of
notification—especially if another firm is waiting for your reply—you might want to
write a nonpersuasive inquiry similar to the one below.

Dear Mrs. Johnson
Four weeks have passed since I had the opportunity to talk with you
about an opening in (field). At that time you said you'd notify me
of your decision by (date).

Meanwhile, another firm has offered me a position and has requested a
reply within the next 10 days. Before answering them, I would like
to know whether you have reached a favorable decision as to my working
for your company.

I sincerely prefer your firm, and will very much appreciate your
reply before (date).

Request for More Time to Decide. Sometimes the situation arises in which you receive an offer while you still have several interviews to complete, and you need more time before making a decision. Although you're taking a chance by asking the offering firm to give you more time to decide, usually the employer understands and wants you to be satisfied in your final selection. You usually preface the request with a buffer paragraph; then you explain and add a paragraph on your particular interest in the firm. The last paragraph should keep the door open for you to make a hurried decision if the employer decides not to grant the extension. Also ask for a confirmation of the extension if the employer decides in your favor. Message 5 on page 442 is a good example of a request for more time for the final decision.

Acceptance of Offer. When you receive an offer you want to accept, reply soon— perhaps within a week. Begin with the good news—that you accept with pleasure. In this first paragraph identify the job you're accepting; the next paragraph might give details about moving (if distance is involved) and reporting for work. Naturally what you say in this explanation depends on what the employer has already told you during the interview or in the job-offer letter. End with a rounding-out paragraph indicating you're looking forward to working for the firm. (See message 7, page 443, which is a good example of an applicant's acceptance.)

Rejection of Offer. Occasionally an applicant will need to turn down a job offer. When you refuse an offer, you're writing a bad-news message. The organizational pattern is: buffer, explanation, refusal (implied or expressed), and a friendly, positive closing. Even more important than the outline, however, is the attitude you have toward the company. Remember this firm seriously considered your qualifications and spent its time and money to bring you to the plant for an interview. If your refusal is discourteous and abrupt, you leave a bad impression and perhaps cause an unfavorable attitude toward *all* college applicants.

Shown below are two examples of well-written job refusals. Notice the outline, tone, sincerity, and positive approach.

Message 1
By a business administration graduate to a personnel director.

Dear Mrs. Adamsen

Thank you for offering me a position in your management training
program.

During my job hunting these last six months, I've sent applications
to several firms that I regard highly--only those I could be happy

working for. Fortunately for me, both you and another firm offered
me a job. Because my qualifications, interest, and background fit
in more closely with the other job, I have already mailed in my
acceptance.

I do thank you for your consideration of my qualifications, the
thorough one-day interview at the plant, and the opportunity to meet
all department heads in production. I'll always think of your
organization as one in which management treats the employees as a
highly prized commodity.

Again, thank you for your consideration. I will always remember it.

This refusal is effective because it is simple and sincere from beginning to end. In a
tactful way it explains first, then refuses the offer, and finally follows up with a paragraph that genuinely compliments the firm.

Message 2
By a graduate in education to a superintendent of a school district.

Dear Mr. Selby

I appreciate your offer to teach business education in one of
Winchester's high schools.

As I explained in our interview on April 21, my wife and I must find
jobs in the same locality. Since the interview, we have received an
offer for both of us from Mrs. Jackson of the Logan school system.

I hesitate to decline your offer since the experience in the
Winchester system would be both profitable and enjoyable. However,
under the present certification requirements, my wife must teach one
year before completing her education. Since it is unlikely that
she will be able to teach in this area, we find it necessary to
accept the Logan positions.

Please keep my qualifications as a business education teacher in
mind when openings develop in the future.

This message, like the previous one, is straightforward, sincere, and positive. Furthermore, the applicant doesn't burn his bridges behind him; the reader will probably consider him when an opening occurs.

Follow-up Messages Written by Employer to Applicant

Not only should you be able to write messages the applicant must send, but also—
since you will be in business someday—you need to dictate effective messages that will
go to the applicant.

Invitation to Interview

As the employer writing this letter, you must realize that this message is second in
importance only to the offer itself. Thus you must make the reader feel that you

genuinely want a personal interview. Also clearly get across that you'll help in every way possible—for example, you'll send a round-trip ticket, reserve a hotel room during the stay if necessary, and reimburse all incidental expenses. In addition ask which dates will be convenient for a visit. Maybe you will make responding easier by enclosing a card (see message 1, page 440.)

After you receive the applicant's acceptance of the invitation you'll send a reply similar to message 3 on page 441. You not only enclose a check for travel expenses, but give all necessary details and indicate interest in the forthcoming visit.

Notification of Impending Visit on Campus

Instead of asking applicants to come to the plant, you might notify them that you will come (or return) to the campus (or elsewhere) to interview. You're writing to the applicant because he or she is one of the graduates you particularly want to talk to. Qualifications on the application letter and résumé interest you. Messages 1 and 2 below are notifications of an impending visit. In addition to giving the details about the visit, you have the opportunity to "sell" the applicant on something ("selling" in message 1 and "your interest" in the applicant in message 2).

Message 1
Sells the applicant on being a sales representative.

Dear Mr. McTaggart:

Last fall I wrote you concerning job opportunities with (name of firm). I will again be on campus this winter and would like very much to see you.

As I told you earlier, we have many openings for graduates—openings which include the functions of development, design, headquarters marketing, technical sales, manufacturing, and others.

Before our get-together I want to describe briefly now (firm's) position of sales engineer. The word "salesman" in this country is tainted. Many people picture him as a used car dealer—public beware; door-to-door salesman; loud-mouthed extrovert; or an order taker with catalog, order blank, and poised pencil.[5]

The industrial sales engineer is anything but these. He (or she) is technically competent. He solves engineering problems for his customers. He is an innovator. He thoroughly enjoys being with many types of people. He possesses empathy, which is the capacity to understand another person's feelings or ideas. He is principally interested in the large conceptional problems of engineering. And, with experience and further study he becomes competent in several engineering disciplines, because in industry the several branches of engineering cannot be separated.

One other thought. In American industry today you'll find most of the jobs for engineers in technical sales. Also, here's where the money is, and this job is the route to higher management.

---

[5]The third paragraph might seem negative, but it is directed to an applicant who exhibited an unfavorable attitude toward selling, and who needs to be convinced of the true picture.

I will be at the University of (state) on February 16, (year), for interviews. Please arrange to see me by contacting your Placement Director.

Message 2
Sincerely compliments the applicant on her qualifications.

Dear Miss Webster

Thank you very much for coming to the Placement Office at the University of (state) for an interview with (name of firm). Since you and I had our visit, I have interviewed on approximately twenty other college campuses and talked to approximately 200 students.

This has been my first opportunity to review the resumes of these students from which I have selected approximately 15% suggesting further interviews. Mary, you are included in this group of students whose scholastic ability, personality, grooming, motivation, and overall personality place you in the upper 15% of those I have talked to.

Our spring interview date at the university has not been definitely established at this time, but as soon as it has been, I will drop you a note; if you are interested, arrange to be placed on our spring interview schedule in the Placement Office. You may recall that we select somewhere between ten and fifteen young men and women each year to go through our Management and Underwriter Training Program which runs from the third week in June until the middle or end of September.

Again we commend you for your fine scholastic record you have been able to maintain and at the same time be responsible for 100% of your college expenses. We look forward to visiting with you again in the spring for I feel certain we both have much to offer each other by way of ability and opportunity for growth.

Request for Further Information

During the interview you may have questions about the applicant's enthusiasm or sincerity toward the company or toward his or her chosen field. To check on your hunch you might ask for a written statement of why the applicant wants to work for your firm or get into this type of occupation. Or you might ask the applicant to show why he or she is the individual you should hire for the opening. Or you might simply need additional information, as the letter below illustrates:

Dear Mr. Juntwait:

Recently we had the pleasure of talking with you in connection with our college recruiting activity. Thank you for the time you gave us.

Our staff has had the opportunity to review your qualifications and we are interested in learning more about you. Accordingly, will you please complete the enclosed application and return it to me by (date). Also explain in an attached letter your interest in (name of field). After this information reaches us, we will get in touch with you on a more specific basis.

```
Thank you for your interest in (name of firm); we look forward to
hearing from you in the near future.
```

Another type of "request for information" is the letter that asks the applicant to do something—perhaps to read a brochure, have an interview with a local representative of the firm, or take a test. The purpose of such requests is make sure applicant is getting into the right field, as the letter below illustrates:

```
Dear Steve:

Thank you for taking the time to learn more about (firm).  You have
the attitude and appearance that make a good sales representative.

During the next few months I suggest that you find out all you can
about the practical area of industrial sales.

Since you do not graduate until June of (year), if you still feel
that this is the type of career you would like to pursue, please
contact our local (city) District Manager for a more detailed inter-
view.  Her name is Mrs. A. I. Theriot, and can be reached at:

                         (name of firm)
                         6536 - 6th Avenue, South
                         (city, state zip)
                         Phone:  (number)

It was a pleasure talking with you.  And the best of success in your
studies.
```

Offer of a Job

When you send a job offer, begin by telling the good news in a friendly manner. In the first paragraph also identify the job and state the salary (usually on a monthly basis). In the following paragraph(s), try to anticipate any questions the applicant might have—such as what moving expenses the firm will pay—and answer them. (Naturally you won't go into detail about expenses until he accepts.) Also leave the door open for applicant to ask questions before making a decision. Be sure your tone is appropriate—convey that you're interested in the applicant and sincerely want him or her to join your organization (see message 4, page 442.)

Grant of a Time Extension

If you believe an applicant has a sound reason for requesting more time to consider an offer, you may decide to grant the extension. Grant the request in the first paragraph, explain (and in general terms set the cutoff date), express interest in the applicant, and end on a friendly and positive note. (See message 6, pages 442–443.)

Reply to Applicant's Acceptance

Even when the applicant has accepted your job offer, you still need to remember the value of public relations. The applicant doesn't expect a long letter, but abrupt messages can be disappointing. For example after receiving message 8 (see page 443), the applicant felt let down because the employer didn't show any interest—"enthusiasm" is perhaps a better word. The you attitude of this message could be improved by a few small changes. For example, the second paragraph could begin with "You will receive . . ." instead of "We will forward . . ." And, *if true*, a sentence like the following could be inserted before the last paragraph:

> With your potential and our company's expected growth you will, I am certain, become a likely candidate for broader responsibilities.

Refusal of Job

A refusal—even a tactful one—is a blow to the applicant, and the tone of your refusal is very important. At all costs you want to avoid leaving the applicant with a lasting negative reaction to your firm.

The individuals being turned down don't want limp excuses or outright false statements. They want honesty—but not discourteous bluntness or crudeness of expression. They will appreciate sincere, complimentary remarks about qualifications; proper consideration of background; and proper personal attitude. Give applicants the feeling you realize that you're talking to intelligent human beings.

In the first paragraph, give a buffer—appreciate their interest in the firm or the opportunity to talk with them, or thank them for coming in for interviews. In the second paragraph, explain. You should first say something neutral (for example, you have reviewed the qualifications) and then refuse in as positive a way as possible. One of the best explanations seems to be "there are several other candidates whose overall qualifications are more in line with our requirements."

Be sure your last paragraph is positive and friendly. Wish the applicants success, tell them you enjoyed the opportunity to talk with them, thank them for the interest in the firm. Obviously you won't repeat in this paragraph what you said in the first.

Below is an unusually effective refusal, which follows the outline just discussed.

```
Dear Mr. Cotter:

Thank you very much for taking your time to be interviewed and
tested for the position of Systems Engineering Representative with
(firm).

We have reviewed your educational background, work experience, and
aptitude tests, along with others we are considering for employ-
ment. Our analysis indicates that there are several other candidates
whose overall qualifications are more in line with our requirements.

We enjoyed having the opportunity to interview you and sincerely
appreciate your interest in (firm). Please accept our best wishes
for success in your chosen career.
```

Some taboos to be avoided in writing your refusal are given here.

1. Refusal in opening

```
We have considered your qualifications; however, we do not have a
position available for you.
```

2. Abrupt refusal in the first sentence of the second paragraph

Unfortunately we have no opening for you.

3. No reason for refusal

A review of your qualifications indicates that you have a background which is commendable in many respects; however, we are not in a position to further pursue the matter of employment with (firm) at'this time.

4. Negative attitude ("sorry," "unable," "regret," "cannot," "not suited," "do not feel," "do not have," "delay")

In view of our needs, however, we do not feel additional interviews would be mutually beneficial or advisable.

We realize this is disappointing news, and. . . .

5. Vagueness

I hope that we shall have an opportunity to review our mutual interests again at some future date.

Based on your recent interview and your qualifications, we cannot encourage you about employment with (firm) at the present time. (Which was significant, the interview or the qualifications?)

6. Abrupt ending

Should an opening develop, I will be in touch with you.

Situation

Now that you have studied separately different types of messages that the employer and applicant use in securing a job, study the letters below, which were written over a period of time by an applicant for an operations management position with a national firm and the representatives of the firm.

Message 1
Mr. Hanson, Supervisor of Employment Personnel Services, invites applicant for plant interview. The plant is about 1,000 miles from the campus.

October 28, (year)

Dear Mr. Webb:

Following our recent interview on campus, we wish to invite you to visit (name of firm) for plant interviews; you will receive the necessary expenses for air travel to (city), and return, as well as incidental expenses.

If a plant visit is agreeable to you, please let us know when you can make the visit and we will confirm a mutually agreeable date. A card is enclosed so that you can notify us of your plant visit decision. If possible, plan to spend one full day at the plant.

Thank you for the interest you have expressed in (name of firm). Upon confirming an interview date, we will forward a check covering your travel expenses, details for getting to the plant, and we will also reserve hotel accommodations in (city) if you so desire.

Message 2
Applicant's reply to message 1; acceptance of invitation.

November 4, (year)

Dear Mr. Hanson

Thank you for inviting me to visit your plant. I very much want to study your organization and operation.

Because of class schedules and previous commitments, the best dates are November 15-19 inclusive. Any one or more of these days permits ideal timing for the trip.

I'm looking forward to visiting your plant and talking with both management members and workers in production.

Message 3
Reply by certified mail to Message 2; Mrs. Benson, Assistant Supervisor of Employment Personnel Services, give details for visit and encloses check.

November 7, (year)

Dear Mr. Webb

Thank you for informing us of your intended visit to (firm) for interviews. We have set the date on November 18 and are enclosing a check to cover your plane fare, meals, and miscellaneous expenses. Please retain any receipts for air travel and lodging for our expense account purposes.

We have arranged prepaid hotel accommodations for you for Monday, November 17, at the Sheraton-Palace Hotel, (city). You can come to the plant Tuesday morning in a company car which leaves our (city) Office every morning at 6:45 a.m.

To get this car you should report by 6:30 a.m. to the Mail Room, Twelfth Floor, Equitable Life Building, 120 Berkeman Street, (city). Because of the early hour, you can plan on having breakfast when you reach the plant. You will be able to return to (city) from the plant in the same manner, leaving here at 4:40 p.m. and arriving in (city) at about 6:30 p.m.

The interest you have expressed in (name of firm) is appreciated, and we look forward to your visit on the 18th.

Message 4
Job offer by Mr. Dorman, General Superintendent, following plant interview.

November 22, (year)

Dear Mr. Webb:

We are pleased to offer you employment as a Management Trainee, assigned to our Industrial Engineering Department. Your starting salary on this position would be $--- a month.

Should you decide to join our organization, we will provide the cost of travel for you and your wife and move your household effects.

Thank you for the interest which you expressed when you visited the plant; I am sorry that circumstances did not permit me to meet you then. We hope that you will decide to make your·career with us. If you have any question concerning our offer or employment in general, please call Mrs. R. A. Benson in the Personnel Office. Her telephone number is 543-4889 (area code 123).

Message 5
Applicant requests more time for final decision.

December 2, (year)

Dear Ms. Benson:

Mr. Dorman just sent me a job offer as a Management Trainee in the Industrial Engineering Department and said for me to get in touch with you if I had any questions concerning the offer.

Before making a final decision concerning this offer, I will appreciate your allowing me until January (year) for my reply. My reason for requesting this extra time is to permit me to complete my interviews with several other companies--especially those that have already invited me to visit their plants. By doing so, I will have satisfied myself that I am selecting the organization of my choice.

At the moment, even with these other opportunities, I am more interested in (reader's firm) than all the others because there are many aspects of your company which appeal to me. I was particularly impressed by the speed, efficiency, and precision of the manufacturing plant.

If you need my decision before the end of this month, please let me know as soon as possible so that I will have the opportunity to make my final decision. Also, if you are giving me this extended time, please notify me to that effect.

Message 6
Mrs. Benson gives applicant extension of time to accept offer.

December 11, (year)

Dear Mr. Webb

As you requested, we will be glad to allow you additional time to decide whether you want to accept our previous offer to work for (firm).

We realize that you have many things to consider to reach a final decision regarding employment; therefore, we want to allow you as much time as possible for your evaluation of all opportunities. In order for us to establish the proper control on our recruiting activities and to make plans for the coming year, I will appreciate knowing your decision as soon as possible. However, inasmuch as you will not be available until June (year), your advising us a couple of months from now will be quite acceptable.

We feel that you are well qualified for the career employment opportunities available within (firm) and hope that you will decide to make your career with us.

I wish you and your wife the best of health and cheer during the coming holidays; and if I can be of any further assistance, please write or telephone me. My number is 543-4889 (area code 123).

Message 7
Applicant's acceptance.

January 5, (year)

Dear Ms. Benson:

I am glad to accept your offer of $--- a month as a Management Trainee in your Industrial Engineering Department.

Since graduation is Saturday, June 13, (year), my wife and I plan to leave (city) the following Monday, June 15. We should arrive in the (city) area the following day--Tuesday, June 16. Allowing a few days to locate living accommodations and to get settled, I should be ready to start work on Monday, June 22. Please let me know if this schedule is satisfactory with you.

I am very pleased in becoming a member of your organization; it is with great appreciation that I look forward to what I am sure will be a very profitable future with (name of organization).

Message 8
Benson's reply to applicant's acceptance.

January 13, (year)

Dear Mr. Webb:

We are very pleased that you are coming with us, and we look forward to seeing you on June 22.

We will forward travel expenses in May and will contact you at that time regarding moving arrangements.

Please contact us if we can be of any assistance before that time.

Exercises

1. Below are four refusals to applicants by outstanding national companies. Evaluate by telling what you like and dislike about each message. Be specific in your discussion. Which one does the most satisfactory job?

a.

Thank you for coming in to discuss employment possibilities during our recent visit to your campus.

As you can appreciate, there is considerable competition for our limited openings. It is always a difficult task to select a few people from the many fine candidates we are given the opportunity to consider. After careful consideration of your qualifications with regards to our specific job requirements, we will be unable to offer you further encouragement.

We do, however, appreciate your interest in (firm) and extend our best wishes for success in your business career.

b.

In reply to your letter of application dated January 5, (year), we do not have an opening on our staff. However, we shall be pleased to keep your application on file for future vacancies.

Thank you for writing us.

c.

The delay in advising you regarding employment possibilities with (firm), following your interview with our recruiter, has been due to your application and file being forwarded to departments dispersed over a wide geographic area.

Your background and qualifications have now been carefully reviewed by these various departments; but, we regret we are presently unable to offer you a position that would be of mutual advantage.

We appreciate your interest in (firm) and wish you every success in the future.

d.

Thank you for scheduling an interview with (firm), giving our recruiter, Mr. C. W. Lindenmeier, the opportunity to talk with you during our recent visit to your campus. He commented favorably about his conversation with you.

We have carefully reviewed all openings anticipated near your availability date which we believed might be of interest to you. I am sorry to inform you that we were unable to locate a position matching your background, training, and interests. We are, however, taking the liberty of holding your application on file should any appropriate openings develop in the near future.

I do regret that we cannot offer you more encouragement at this time. We appreciate your interest in our activities and wish you every success in beginning your professional career.

2. Evaluate the following message. Applicant sends application letter with résumé to a large department store but receives no reply after three weeks. This letter is his follow-up inquiry.

> After some puzzlement on my part as to why I had not heard from you regarding employment with your company one way or the other, I decided to check with the Student Placement Center about my credentials which you did not have at the time of the interview and still do not have.
>
> I found that two of my appraisal forms had not come back. After checking with the two individuals involved and finding that there was a mistake in not sending them in, I am certain that my credentials will be sent to you very soon. Please let me know if you are still interested in me.

3. Evaluate the three messages below. The applicant is a graduating senior who sent her application letter with résumé to a large department store chain in a large city 1,000 miles from the campus. In the letter she mentioned she'd be in the city between winter and spring quarters (usually the latter part of March) and requested an interview, which she received.

Message 1
Applicant receives this offer after she returns to the campus.

> As a result of our conversation with you, we are pleased to offer you the opportunity to join the (firm) Executive Training Program at a starting salary of $--- a month. Employment is contingent upon your passing a medical examination which will be given when you start work here in (city).
>
> Enclosed for your perusal is a copy of our Annual Report, which we trust you will find of interest.
>
> We look forward to receiving your favorable consideration of this offer, and I am sure you will find this a most stimulating opportunity.

Message 2
Applicant accepts job offer.

> April 17, (year)
>
> It is with pleasure and excitement that I accept your offer to join the (firm) Executive Training Program. I have been reading the Annual Report you enclosed and am looking forward to working for as fine a company as (firm's).
>
> Will you please tell me when you want me to report after graduation, where, to whom, and at what time? I can be in (city) within two weeks after University of (state) commencement exercises June 13.
>
> If you need any further information before giving me the details of my assignment, please write to me at my (city) address before June 9 and at my home address after that date.

Message 3
Reply to applicant's job acceptance and inquiry.

April 21, (year)

Thank you for your letter of April 17. We are pleased to know that you will be joining our Executive Training Squad this summer.

You may report for work any Monday convenient to you. You indicate that June 29 would be a convenient date. This is most acceptable, and we will look forward to your reporting at 8:55 a.m. to the Personnel Department, which is on the eighth floor. You may enter the building through the company entrance (on Westfall near Donson Street) and the guard at the door will direct you to the Personnel Department.

Enclosed is a booklet, which is given to all new Training Squad executives when they report for work, which may answer many of your questions. We are also enclosing a booklet which is given to every new employee which will give you information as to dress regulations, etc.

Congratulations on your coming graduation. We look forward to seeing you again on June 29.

4. Assume you sent your application letter and résumé to the personnel manager of a particular firm; shortly afterward you received an invitation to come to his office for an interview. He is located in your city. During the 30-minute interview, he asked you questions about your qualifications and explained company policy, beginning salary, and other pertinent information. Write a follow-up for one (or each) of the possible outcomes below:

   a. At the end of the interview he told you he'd notify you of his decision.
   b. At the end of the interview he asked you to write him why you want to get into the type of work you're applying for.
   c. At the end of the interview he asked you to visit the manager in one of the organization's several local retail stores; while there you should interview the manager and other employees to find out whether you want to make a career in this type of work. Then you're to write the personnel manager if you're still interested. Assume you are favorably impressed.

5. Assume you mailed your application letter three weeks ago but have received no reply. Send an inquiry to the firm.

6. Assume you received two offers for career jobs.

   a. Write the acceptance message.
   b. Write the refusal message.

7. As the employer, you must refuse a graduating senior the job she applied for because her qualifications aren't as good as those of the others you interviewed. Furthermore, one reference indicated this person is a troublemaker. Write the refusal message.

8. As a graduating senior, you received the following letter from Mrs. Alexander, Recruiting Coordinator. Unfortunately you can't see the representative on Janu-

ary 30. However, you're very much interested in working for this company. Write the appropriate message to the coordinator, assuming any facts you wish as long as you don't alter the assignment.

Dear (your name):

Please forgive my resorting to a form-letter to reach you--but time is getting short and I want to let you know that one of our executives plans to visit your campus soon.

His primary purpose will be to interview (year) graduates for career employment with our newly-merged organization. As you might imagine, we have an even greater horizon now to present to promising young people like yourself. Moreover, we have a number of good summer job opportunities for undergraduates this year.

In any case, I have been alerted to your fine summer employment record with us and assure you our interest in you continues strong. Accordingly, if you want to explore a position with us, I urge that you sign-up to see our Corporate Recruiting Representative when he visits your Placement Office on January 30.

If you cannot make that date, please drop me a line and let's try to arrange for you to visit some nearby branch office. I am enclosing a return envelope for that purpose, together with a copy of our Annual Report and some other literature for your reference.

Meanwhile, accept our sincere best wishes to your forthcoming graduation.

9. What kind of an impression do you think the following applicant made on the firm considering him for a management job? Given below are the details.

The applicant was invited in for an interview at company expense. He lived in Madison, Wisconsin, and the company was located at Rockford, Illinois. Although it was only normal to use plane, train, or bus for transportation, he felt he could get "in" with the company by saving them money—by hitchhiking.

Here's the expense account he submitted to the company for reimbursement:

Bus fare in Madison, Wisconsin	$ .25
Bus fare in Janesville, Wisconsin	.25
Dinner at Rockford, Illinois	2.95
Hotel room and tip, Rockford	6.50
Movie	2.00
3 cokes	.45
12 cigarettes (2 of the fellows I hitchhiked with borrowed these from me)	.30
Hamburger and coke for lunch at Peoria	.65
Hotel room and tip Peoria, Illinois	5.50
Shoe shine	.40
1 suit cleaned (1 of the fellows I caught a ride with had been drinking and spilled a bottle of beer on me)	1.95
	$21.20

Write

10. Assume that three weeks ago you had an interview on campus with a representative of a national company whose head offices are 1,000 miles from you. Before parting, the interviewer asked if you would be willing to come to the head offices some day for further interviews, and you had replied that you would be gald to. Today you receive the following letter, dated February 2, from the Personnel Manager:

Dear (your name):

It is with a great deal of pleasure that I confirm our invitation to visit us in (city) in order to pursue further the possibility of your joining (firm name). We have arranged a schedule for which we would like to have you arrive at our Executive Offices at (address) at 1:30 p.m. on Monday, April 10, and be prepared to stay with us through the following day.

As I pointed out during our brief meeting, at (firm name) we feel strongly that the matter of selection is a "two-way street," and we look forward to this chance of making you better acquainted with us and the opportunity we offer. Also, of course, we would like to review your qualifications more fully.

I know you have already accepted our invitation for further interviews, but we would appreciate a letter indicating that you still plan to come. It might be a good idea if you were to make airline reservations right away and let me know the flight numbers. I will then reciprocate by sending you an open ticket drawn on the airline you designate.

We will make a hotel reservation for you for the night of April 10, and for the night of the 9th too if schedules require you to come the night before. As a last point, please keep track of the incidental expenses incurred by your trip so that we may reimburse you for them.

That would seem to cover it, (your name), but please let me know if you have any questions. I'll be looking forward to seeing you again.

Write the complete, thoughtful, friendly letter this invitation calls for. Before you do so, however, consider the kind of airline passage you should reserve. Should it be first-class? Coach? Economy? Why? Why do you think the employer leaves the choice up to you? (You might also discuss in class the kinds of incidental expenses that will be appropriate for you to include in your later request for reimbursement—after this second interview. See, for example, the list in Exercise 9.)

11. If you and your classmates would like practice interviews, try this assignment. For one interview half the class members will volunteer to be job applicants and the other half will be employers' personnel representatives. For a second interview all students will switch roles.

Each interview will be based on an application letter and résumé the applicant has written (as, for example, Exercise 2, page 414) and, presumably, mailed. In class students will merely exchange these papers.

Each interview should preferably be about 20 to 30 minutes in length between students who do not know each other well. Both the applicant and the assumed personnel representative (or higher executive, if appropriate) should make all necessary preparations before the interviews. The applicant (interviewee) should review pages 420–426. The employer's representative (interviewer) will find helpful suggestions in Chapter 18, pages 652–657, regarding how to conduct an interview. He or she will, of course, also study the applicant's résumé before conducting the interview and know something about the company the interviewer represents.

13 Collection Messages— Written and Oral

After a borrower gets a loan or a customer purchases something on credit, payment should be made within a specified period—according to the terms of the agreement. When obligations are not paid on time, collection messages become necessary. Customer reasons for not paying are usually one or more of the following: they've overlooked the invoice or statement; they're dissatisfied with the merchandise, delivery, billing, or handling of a complaint; they're temporarily short of funds; they're chronic debtors.

Collection messages have an important twofold purpose: to *get the money* and to *keep customer goodwill.* These messages may be delivered by mail, phone, personal visit, or telegram. To carry out the twofold function requires an understanding attitude and effective messages appropriately planned and timed throughout the collection stages. Most collection procedures have similar basic characteristics whether the messages concern retail credit (to customers) or mercantile credit (to business firms), and whether they are for open account or installment credit. For various reasons, they also have differences. This chapter discusses:

1. Right attitude for effective collections
2. Collection stages
3. Variations in collection series
4. Telephone collection procedure

Right Attitude for Effective Collections

A debtor may be touchy about how and when the creditor asks for payment even though it is for a legitimate debt. The longer past-due the payment is, the more difficult the situation becomes. The right collection attitude for a creditor requires an understanding of human nature plus careful choice of collection appeals and knowledge of the debtor's past credit record as well as regulations affecting collection policies.

Understanding of Human Nature

When you send a collection message, remember you are communicating with a person, not with an account number. Each person has a different mental filter, with attitudes, prejudices, perceptions, and problems. All human beings have feelings and react negatively to offensive expressions, sarcasm, anger, and insults just as quickly as you do.

The fairest assumption to make is that your customer honestly wants to pay as agreed. The majority of customers will pay when reminded. However, conditions change and with them the customers' ability and willingness to pay may also change. Some debtors conscientiously promptly write or telephone their reasons for lateness and explain when they will make their next payments. Some remain silent, and a few are repeatedly uncooperative.

A tactful, courteous attitude coupled with firmness and patience always collects more money in the long run than impolitely worded demands. As a collection manager you are on a tightrope regarding messages to customers with past-due accounts. If you're too lenient, some individuals may pay other bills that seem more pressing, and you won't get the money coming to you. On the other hand, if you threaten or bully customers, they may not pay either.

How and *when* to probe for the reason a debtor hasn't paid is important. (Whenever possible, you want to avoid turning an account over to a collection agency because everyone loses except the agency.) Some people just don't know how to manage their financial affairs. Merely putting pressure upon them to pay is not enough. The understanding creditor may show them how to pay, perhaps help them plan their budgets (if appropriate) and arrange terms of payment so they can pay their debts and regain their self-respect. The unhappy person who has suffered temporary financial embarrassment because of family illness or business reverses appreciates collection messages that are considerate and helpful: that individual is more likely to do his best to cooperate.

In result-getting collection letters, expressions like "you are delinquent" should not be used; phrases such as "two payments are delinquent" or "the delinquency of this account" are less offensive because they are impersonal. "Past due" has a better connotation and is preferred.

All you have learned about courtesy, concreteness, and consideration for the customer is important for effective collection messages. Also the suggestions for proper attitude in bad-news letters (pages 242–243) apply to collections too.

Choice of Collection Appeals

As you will read later in the discussion on "Collection Stages," those collection messages which must be *persuasive* should include well-chosen appeals. These choices relate closely to the attitude you have toward the debtor. The following positive and negative appeals are effective in persuasive collection messages:

Positive appeals stress cooperation, fair play, pride.

Cooperation, the mildest appeal, caters to one's desire to be considerate of others—in this case, loyal to the creditor who has been courteous and friendly in asking for what is rightly due. (This should not, however, be a whining "poor me" appeal.)

The *fair-play* appeal is usually developed by reviewing the facts—how long a payment has been past-due—and showing that since the creditor has carried out his part of an agreement, the debtor (customer)—to be fair and honest—should keep his promise and pay.

The *pride appeal* should be subtle, not a high-pressure tactic. You can develop this appeal in various ways by referring to what you know the customer is proud of—a good credit record, sometimes the items bought, or the respect and good reputation enjoyed in the community.

Negative appeals stress the debtor's self-interest and arouse emotions of fear. The individual who cares little about cooperation or fair play may be motivated to pay when you show what he or she will gain by doing so, or will lose by further delay.

The *self-interest* appeal usually has two objectives—to show the value of the present advantages the customer has and to convince him that further delay may cause him to lose them.

Fear appeal, instead of stressing the value of keeping various benefits, stresses the loss of such benefits (good credit standing or possessions). It also emphasizes the extra expense of a lawsuit.

You can use effectively one or a combination of these appeals in a persuasive message. Your choice of appeals is influenced by your attitude regarding the type of debtor, knowledge of collection policies, and the place of the message in the collection stage.

Types of Debtors

Debtors can be classified—broadly—into three categories: good-pay, fair-pay, and poor-pay.

The good-pay customer pays on time and needs little or no reminding. For those few times when a reminder is necessary, you can usually collect payments after pleasant reminder messages using the direct-request pattern—without appeals. On the rare occasion when his account becomes past due, you will persuade him through a positive appeal to cooperation or fair play.

The fair-pay customer always pays but slowly, and often needs reminders and persuasion. Your attitude toward payment should be firmer and your reminders are more frequent. This customer may be a very respected, honest person in your community, but perhaps absentminded or just disorganized in his paying and business habits. Like the good-pay customer the fair-pay customer will respond to positive appeals; but instead of motivating by appeals to cooperation and fair play, you may have to use pride and self-interest appeals. Because of procrastination sometimes two or more payments are past due, and you may have to caution about the risks involved—and occasionally bring in a mild negative appeal.

The poor-pay customer is repeatedly late in payments. This customer has probably received numerous collection notices before, not only from your firm, but from other creditors. He ignores the pleasant, mild reminders because he knows there is still time to delay before his creditors get tough. Sermons and scolding bore him. For this type of individual you include a few surprises and shocks—and more negative than positive appeals. You must persuade him to pay because not doing so will be detrimental.

You will see how to use the various appeals in collection messages when you read about "Collection Stages," which are directly concerned with the debtor's past payment record.

Knowledge of Collection Policies

Besides understanding human nature and choosing collection appeals carefully after considering the debtor's past credit record, you and your assistants need also to know your firm's collection policies and government regulations. They may relate to various time limits on installment or mortgage late payments, foreclosures, and procedures regarding consumer credit and collections.

An effective collection policy necessitates bringing the debt to the debtor's attention *promptly* and *regularly,* with *increasing firmness* as the past-due period lengthens. Just how soon after payment due date the messages should be sent varies also according to the type of credit account, the particular debtor's situation, and your firm's collection policies. These factors also influence the time interval between collection messages and overall length of the collection process, as is discussed later in this chapter.

To summarize, the right attitude for collection messages requires tact, courtesy, consideration, fairness, firmness, and a positive viewpoint. It requires understanding of human nature, knowledge of collection appeals and the customer's past payment record, plus adherence to your firm's collection policies and government regulations.

Collection Stages

The first notification the customer receives after purchasing on credit or borrowing money on a loan is a statement (bill) or invoice showing the amount owed. This notification usually lists the transactions for the time period involved and states the terms and date of payment.

If the customer does not pay by the due date, you begin to send a series of messages called a *collection series.* Though the length, content, and collection methods of a collection series may vary according to circumstances, a well-planned series usually has three stages. The messages in each stage vary in number but usually follow a somewhat typical organizational plan and general assumption.

1.	**Reminder** Stage	Plan:	Routine request
		Assumption:	Oversight
		Number:	Varies from 1 to 6 or 7
2.	**Discussion** Stage	Plan:	Persuasive request (modified)
		Assumption:	Something unusual happened
		Number:	Varies from 1 to 5 or 6
3.	**Urgency** Stage	Plan:	Persuasive request (modified)
		Assumption:	Debtor may need to be scared into paying
		Number:	Usually 1 or 2

Regardless of stage in the collection procedure or other differences, all collection messages should make clear two facts—the amount due and the account number. Also, an easy-action reply envelope, perhaps postpaid, is appreciated and often speeds the reply.

Reminder Stage

Messages in the reminder stage are routine, direct requests. They range in number from one to several. In this stage, all you want to do is to jog the customer's memory. You first present the *main question or subject,* then *explain* (when necessary), and end the message by *requesting action.* You don't attempt to persuade by using any of the five appeals. Although some reminders—especially those sent to installment credit and slow-pay customers—might have a personalized inside address, generally they are obvious processed forms to avoid any suggestion that you are questioning the customer's integrity or ability to pay. They usually range from one or more standard statements (usually not itemized) to printed cards to an obvious form letter on company letterhead stationery.

The statement(s) following the first one might include rubber-stamped or hand-written messages that say "Please" or "Perhaps you have forgotten" or colorful stickers like the four shown here (which can be purchased in quantities from a printer).

Shown below are examples of a printed card and three short letter reminders which are obviously processed forms on the firms' letterheads:

Reminder 1
A printed form 3¾ by 6½ inches in size on green pastel paper. A large department store sends it to a customer along with a second statement (and sometimes a leaflet advertising new merchandise items—for sales promotion.

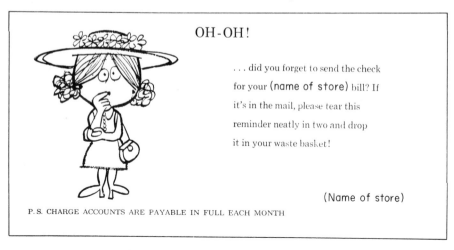

Reminder 2
A short form-letter request from an oil company to a credit-card customer who had previously received a statement and a form-notice reminder.

Dear Customer

Main idea and amount due

It's easy to misplace statements and overlook form notices. That's why we're sending this letter to remind you of your balance amounting to $___.

Action

The account is somewhat past due and we would appreciate your sending us a check in the next few days.

Reminder 3
A processed form-letter reminder on savings and loan association letterhead—for one overdue installment.

Dear Mrs. Grown:

Main question

Have you overlooked the first payment on your account?

Explanation with amount and date

As shown in your mortgage, your monthly installments of $___ are due on the ____ of each month. The first payment is now past due.

Action

Please send your remittance today and make future payments promptly so they will reach this office on time. If you have already mailed payment, please accept our thanks and disregard this notice.

Reminder 4
A lighthearted rhyme used as a processed form letter on stationery of a national wholesaler of formal wear—for reminders to apparel shops; signed by credit manager.

Dear Sir:

> HOW ABOUT--
> a little pen
> a little ink
> a little time
> a little think
> a little check
> short and snappy

> is all we need to make us happy.

This little reminder refers, of course, to the $----- balance on your account.

Humor, witty short poems, anecdotes, and pictures that relate to the creditor's business or products can be quite effective—if they are used in the reminder stage, but not later, Nevertheless, think seriously how the customer might react to humor. In the first place, there's nothing funny about owing money or trying to collect money. Furthermore, what is funny to you might not be funny to another person. Four devices that have proved ineffective (and annoying to some people) are:

1. The upside-down message saying the collection manager is so upset that he or she wrote the letter upside down
2. The letter with a completely blank body, the message appearing only in the postscript.
3. The message that begins "Maybe you've heard this one: Why are little birds so sad in the morning? Answer: Because their little bills are all 'over-dew.' It may remind you that we have a little bill that is overdue. If you feed it a check . . . ."
4. The "humorous" reminder based on an off-color, inappropriate "joke."

Discussion Stage

If you receive no response after the routine-request reminders you sent to the customer, you progress into discussion stage messages that are *persuasive* requests. In this stage you begin to personalize your messages by using an inside address and a salutation with the customer's name. You assume that something unusual has happened. For some reason unknown to you the customer cannot or doesn't want to pay. (Do *not* revert again to the "oversight" assumption used in the reminder stage.)

When you consider the situation from the customer's viewpoint, you realize that repeated requests for payment are unwelcome. To get the customer to read your messages, you will need to *attract attention* in the first paragraph. You try now to begin with a reader-interest theme—something beneficial, pleasant, interesting, and/or important to the reader. Your *desire-conviction-proof* paragraphs may include facts, figures, and reasons why the debtor will benefit by doing as requested. Well-chosen *appeals* (see pages 453–454) will help convince the customer and stimulate a desire to do what is right.

Depending upon the type of debtor and account, discussion messages range in number from one to five or more. Usually your first message is an inquiry, asking if something is wrong and inviting the customer to send either an explanation or a check; the positive "cooperation" appeal may be effective. Successive messages become progressively stronger, ending with a hint of negative appeal in the last discussion message. You may also include more than one appeal in any message. Regardless of the number sent, your discussion-stage messages aim to *get the payment or an explanation*—if there is a reason for not paying. Then you may be able to make mutually satisfactory alternate payment arrangements.

Some small business and professional firms that have no collection department continue their collection efforts by merely attaching colorful discussion-stage stickers on their monthly statements. These, of course, require no typing. They do attract attention by both their appearance and their opening question or comment. However, they are impersonal and may be weak in appeals; sometimes also, in the request. Notice, for example, that neither sticker 1 or 2 below include any appeal. Sticker 1 asks for a reason but fails to request payment. Sticker 2 rightly asks for either a reason or prompt payment. Stickers 3 and 4 mildly appeal to fair play and self-interest respectively; and they omit asking for an explanation. Nevertheless, in some businesses any of these stickers can be useful in the early part of the discussion stage, when they are attached to statements showing the amount due, the account number, and, of course, the customer's name and address.

For more persuasive requests it is better to write personalized letters. If necessary, they can be essentially form messages—individually typed by automatic or magnetic card typewriters—identical for many customers but personalized by insertions of variable information, as in letter 1. Notice how skillfully this letter avoids suggesting a negative idea about the reason for nonpayment. It does *not* ask if something is wrong with the store's merchandise or service or billing; yet if any of these should happen to be problems, the customer is free to mention them and thus help "to expedite any possible adjustment." Easy action is provided by lines at the bottom for the customer's reply and by an enclosed envelope.

Letter 1
A tactful, persuasive, personalized form letter from a department store to a good-pay customer.

Dear (Mr., Mrs., Miss, Ms. name):

Attention (compliment)	The privilege of serving you is certainly our pleasure. For this, we extend our sincere thanks.
Appeal (cooperation)	You have always been cooperative in the past by keeping your account paid on time according to your credit agreement. As we have received no remittance from you for over three months, we wonder if you have a question concerning the balance.
Request for reason or check	Whatever information you request will receive our prompt attention, as we want to expedite any possible adjustment.
Easy action	A note at the bottom of this letter will do. Then just mail it—or your check for $— in the enclosed envelope.
Goodwill	Your cooperation will be greatly appreciated.

Another popular way to attract attention and also make action easy is by a message that begins with this statement: "There Are Two Sides to Every Story." The rest of the message may be in the shape of an open book. The left side is marked

"This Is Ours"; the right side, "This Is Yours." The creditor's "story" may end with sentences like these: "Won't you give us *your* side of the story? If there is no question, how about sending your remittance right away . . . for the amount shown on the attached statement. YOU NOW HAVE THE FLOOR!"

In letter 2 a wholesaler includes several appeals to the mercantile customer. By reviewing the facts about the overdue account and mentioning the high-quality merchandise plus a willingness to help, the writer makes a fair-play appeal. In addition, the compliments on the dealer's good-pay record and the reiteration of the value of a favorable credit rating develop both pride and self-interest appeals.

Letter 2
An effective personalized letter from a wholesaler to a mercantile customer.

Attention (agreeable comment)	It would be nice if we could get together in person to talk over your overdue account with us, but the demands of our businesses and the distance make this impossible.
Facts and compliment	Your account is 80 days past the final due date on our terms of 2/10 net/30. This is exceptional, considering your past prompt payment record with us; and we would like to know what is wrong.
Pride and self-interest appeals	You have worked many years to establish your favorable credit rating, Mr. Jones. It allows you to stock high quality furniture such as the Allwood chairs when you need them and even take advantage of a discount if payment is made within 10 days. You can have an adequate supply of merchandise on hand at all times without maintaining a large amount of cash for working capital. Your credit rating not only makes conducting of your business easier but also allows you to establish yourself with new suppliers quickly and easily.
Fairness appeal	Is there anything we can do to help you overcome a difficulty? We want to be fair with you. I'm sure we can work some kind of a plan for payment that will be compatible with your situation. Of course, the most satisfactory solution would be a full payment of the $629.57 in the return mail. If you cannot manage this, then send us a frank explanation of the problem you are facing and we will see what plan we can come up with to clear your account.
Easy action, with suggested time	The enclosed envelope is addressed to come directly to my desk unopened, Mr. Jones. I hope to see it again next week with your check for the full $629.57 inside. If this is not possible, then use the envelope to send me a full explanation of your situation so that we can help you find a solution.

The writer of the next letter uses the positive pride and self-interest appeals plus the negative loss-of-comforts-and-advantages appeal. Even though this borrower owes three payments, the letter (from a bank's lending officer) avoids a scolding tone and tries to keep the customer sold on the values of home ownership.

Letter 3
A bank lending officer's helpful persuasive request to a borrower for a home loan.

Attention (pride appeal)	You have probably often heard the statement, "There's no place like home."
Appeals to self- and family interests	You and your spouse made a wise decision when you invested in your present four-bedroom home. Close to schools, your church, and stores, it has the ideal location for your growing family. Your loan department personnel here at (name bank) were glad to help you with financing by extending you the loan you needed three years ago.
Comfort, security	So that you can continue to enjoy the comfort and security of owning this home, it is important that you keep up your payments on your loan. Four messages have been mailed to you about the three payments that are now past due:

Easy-to-read facts	May 10	$152.00
	June 10	152.00
	July 10	152.00
	Late charge	15.00
	Total	$471.00

Economic self-interest and risk-of-loss appeals	It is easy to become so accustomed to a privilege that we take it for granted. You were fortunate to buy when you did, for today the same kind of home--even without the playroom and patio you have--would cost you at least $5,000 more and at a higher interest rate. You'll agree you can't afford to risk losing the comforts and advantages you now enjoy.
Action	So please send your check for $471.00 today!

In any business you may find some customers who are repeatedly late in paying their bills. To such persons—who have in previous delinquencies received a variety of detailed letters from you (with inquiries and positive appeals), you may wish to concentrate on a negative appeal. The following letter emphasizes what the customer with a poor credit rating will experience.

Letter 4
A persuasive request with a strong fear appeal to the repeatedly late payer.

Attention	Just how valuable is your credit rating to you?
Self-interest appeal— positive	If you possess a good rating, you are able to buy on a charge basis whenever necessary. You can buy expensive items without paying the entire cost in cash at time of purchase. Also, if an emergency arises, your credit will be helpful.
Self-interest —negative appeal	However, if your record in various places shows you are a poor credit risk, this valuable possession of credit will be lost. You are likely to be subjected to the unpleasantness of drastic collection measures. In addition, your credit reputation will follow you wherever you go. It

will take years to restore a good rating. You may be deprived of items you would like to purchase, because of the necessity for paying cash.

These are facts. We mention them only so that you will not take lightly the possible loss of your credit which may follow unless your account with us is paid.

Action

It is still possible to salvage your credit reputation. Please use the enclosed envelope to mail your check for $ (amount) today in payment of this account which has' been overdue since (date). If you cannot pay it all immediately, you will find us willing to discuss a definite arrangement to take care of it. Please call me at (number).

For chronic "delinquents" you might omit the offer (in the last paragraph) to discuss a payment arrangement and simply ask for full payment.

Urgency Stage

During the reminder and discussion stages most messages may have been signed by someone in the credit or collection department. In the urgency stage—for greater impact on the past-due customer—messages may be signed by a higher executive, such as a vice president or even the president, in some firms.

Even in this last stage the messages still aim to keep the customer's goodwill. (Even when credit is no longer available, the customer may still purchase with cash.) These messages follow the persuasive request plan and use the strongest appeal—fear. They mention the unfortunate consequences of collection enforcement if you must resort to drastic action such as turning the account over to a collection agency or lawyer or repossessing the merchandise. You will usually tell the customer that you don't *want* to take this drastic action, but (because of your obligations to credit reporting agencies and company procedures) you must do so unless the debtor pays or explains.

Although you might feel exasperated and annoyed with the individual, you won't help your cause by showing anger, preaching, or using insulting, cutting remarks. In fact, you could get into a libel suit (see Appendix A). To protect yourself from legal problems, be sure to get your facts correct, make no malicious or defamatory accusations, and see that your messages are in sealed envelopes addressed to the debtor personally.

To offset the negativeness of the appeal to fear, it is often desirable to include at least one positive appeal—to give the debtor a chance to avoid the drastic action. The action request is firm and definite about the amount the borrower must send and the office to which it should be sent.

As the following examples illustrate, you can use one or two messages in the urgency stage. If two, the first one doesn't set a date for the drastic action, but the final message *always* sets the date.

Example 1
First of two messages in the urgency stage.

The time has come when we must write the kind of letter we dislike very much. In our previous letters we said about everything we could think of in urging you to pay your long overdue bill, which is now $355.70.

But you have made no replies to any of our requests.

The only thing left for us to do is to turn your account over to our attorney for collection. A lawsuit would require you to pay not only the bill but also the court costs. We don't want to do this without giving you one last chance to write and let us know your side of the story.

We have been good business friends for many years, (name). Please don't make it necessary for us to terminate our friendship in such an unpleasant way. Write us immediately--or better still, send us your check for at least a part of your bill. But do it today, please!

If you are using only one letter in this collection stage, you can still use example 1, adding the following paragraph before the final one:

For that reason we will delay action for five days--until July 22-- before turning your account over to Smith, Smythe, and Smothers.

If you feel that in the discussion stage messages you have given the debtor sufficient time to "discuss or pay" (especially when dealing with chronic late-payers), you might use a telegram or Mailgram as the first message in the urgency stage. According to Western Union, companies using Mailgrams report collection efficiency improvement of up to 70 percent.[1] You can, of course, send any length of message you wish. Here are two short messages that have shock value:

Example 2
Mailgrams as the first of two messages in the urgency stage—especially for chronic late-payers.

a. YOUR ACCOUNT #____ WILL BE REFERRED TO AN OUTSIDE COLLECTION AGENCY. ONLY YOUR REMITTANCE FOR $___ WILL STOP FORMAL CREDIT ACTION. SEND IT TODAY.

b. IMPORTANT YOU CALL COLLECT IMMEDIATELY (TEL. NUMBER) BETWEEN 8AM AND 4PM CENTRAL STANDARD TIME CONCERNING YOUR CREDIT CARD ACCOUNT NUMBER (____). PLEASE TELL THE OPERATOR YOU RECEIVED THIS MESSAGE.

---

[1] *How to Excel in the Art of Friendly Persuasion,* The Western Union Telegraph Company, April 1973.

Example 3
Final letter that sets a date.

Your account has just been referred to me, marked for "final action."

Because it is the policy of this company that every contact with our customers shall be one of courteous interest in their behalf, I am writing you this letter as a last appeal that you mail us your check for $623.02, or call personally to see us. I have withheld any action on your account and feel sure we can work out some mutually satisfactory arrangement for settlement.

I shall hold your account on my desk for 10 days hoping that you will attend to it at once. Unless I hear from you by June 25, I shall have no alternative but to assign your account for collection. I anticipate you will not force me to take a step that would have such a serious effect upon your credit reputation.

Example 4
Final message that sets a date. This printed form goes to customers who live within the city which is within the jurisdiction of the specific credit bureau.

No. 1982

Please Read This Carefully

_____ 19 _____

To: _____

_____
    Address   *City*   *State*

It is the purpose of this notice to inform you, as a matter of courtesy, of our intention to assign your account to the **COLLECTION DEPT.,**   **(CITY) CREDIT BUREAU**

for collection unless your remittance is in our hands on or before _____ 19____

This can be avoided if **PAYMENT IN FULL** is made on or before the above date, but you must **ACT WITHOUT DELAY.**

The amount is $_____

_____ (CREDITOR)

_____ (ADDRESS)

By _____

Pay your bills in full TODAY So that your Credit will be good TOMORROW

Variations in Collection Series

As previously stated, the basic psychology and characteristics of collections are similar for all types of business. However, the number and frequency of messages and the degree of insistence within each collection series vary because of debtor's paying habits, type of account, and creditor's business situation. This section discusses variations and describes collection practices in three businesses.

Debtor's Paying Habits

All competent credit and collection departments adapt their procedures to the quality of the risk (even though they may not all classify their customers into the absolute categories of good, fair, and poor risks). In general, the poorer the risk, the more frequent and forceful the message and the shorter the overall collection period.

Suppose, for example, that a firm has a standard collection policy of sending 10 messages for a good risk (over an eight-month period) before resorting to a collection agency or court. The same firm might send only seven messages to a fair risk (over a five-month period) and only five to a poor risk (in from six weeks to three months). The following table summarizes the kinds and number of messages this firm might send to each type of debtor.

Stage	Message	Appeals	*Number of messages to debtors*		
			Good risk	*Fair risk*	*Poor risk*
Reminder	Statements (monthly) One itemized, rest unitemized; with or without stickers	None	3	2	1
	Reminders	None	2	1	1
Discussion	Letters Ask what's wrong; offer help; ask for payment	One or more: a. Cooperation b. Fair play c. Pride d. Self-interest	3	2	2
Urgency	Letter(s) 1. Sets no date 2. Sets date	Fear (plus one or more of **a–d**) Fear	2	2	2
Totals			10	7	5

The collection procedure must be flexible to take care of unusual circumstances relating to the debtor. The time intervals between messages are usually longer in the beginning of a series (reminder stage) than near the end (urgency stage). Whenever the customer explains the reason for lateness (and perhaps agrees to a new payment plan), your collection department should of course cease sending the usual messages at the former time intervals. Customers become justifiably irked if they continually receive duns after they have paid or made special arrangements for payment. Also, whenever the firm adjusts an account balance because of a customer's complaint about goods or service, *some* department (adjustment, credit, or collection) should inform the customer of the new balance and see that the "late-payment charge" is removed from future messages.

Debtors also affect the number of collection series a firm has. Because some customers are late with payments several times a year, the firm needs more than one collection series. It is desirable that debtors do not get the same messages twice.

Types of Accounts and Creditor's Business Situation

The collection policy for *installment* accounts is basically similar to that of *open credit* accounts, but there are differences. In general, with monthly installments creditors tend to be somewhat stricter, because installments pile up quickly. As you know, some stores have installment accounts for large purchases which go over the customer's established charge account limits or for customers who do not have charge accounts.

If the goods are sold on a conditional sales contract, the seller retains title to installment-purchased goods until the last payment has been made and may repossess if the debtor defaults. This fact can be an effective fear appeal. However, if market conditions are unfavorable for disposing of used merchandise, the creditor will prefer not to repossess, but rather to give the debtor a time extension that will ensure full payment on the purchased item. This arrangement will of course affect the collection procedure and messages sent.

In *mortgage lending,* because of various laws requiring foreclosure within certain periods of nonpayment (perhaps three months), the collection procedure is stricter than for charge account selling.

For *utility companies*—those providing telephone, gas, water, electricity services—the collection policies are likely to be stricter because each month's usage adds new charges. The fear appeal in these firms' urgency-stage collection messages is that the service will be disconnected after a certain late period.

Different business situations also affect collection procedures. The department store's relation to its thousands of retail consumer customers is different from the manufacturer's or wholesaler's relation to the retailer. Because the manufacturer or wholesaler typically has a relatively large volume of business with a relatively small number of customers, each credit situation is investigated individually and collection messages are likely to be individually geared to each dealer's problem. Letters may be fewer—and perhaps longer—than those of the department store collection department. For the latter, the volume of business with each customer is relatively small, but the total is important. Large department stores have elaborate series of collection notices, letters, and telephone messages. Some have 50 or more form letters to choose from. Yet, for the more important or complex situation the credit or collection manager will compose original, personalized letters.

Collection Practices of Three Diverse Businesses

To illustrate differences and similarities among collection series, brief descriptions of the actual collection practices of three diverse businesses—a large department store, a savings and loan association, and a large utility company—are given below.

Department Store[2] This organization for the first four months uses only computerized statements and duns. A statement is prepared once each month for every account as of its billing date as long as a balance exists. All financial transactions which have occurred since the last billing date through the current closing date are identified.

The computer not only analyzes and evaluates many different conditions for each customer's account; with the information digested, the computer also automatically chooses the appropriate text from a selection of messages and automatically prints the customer's name, address, account number, and the chosen letter, incorporating into the body of the letter the exact amount owed (so current that it reflects payment received the day before). This entire procedure takes about two seconds.

After the first four months, the department store switches to manual communications (telephone, letter, and wire) to break the cycle of "no pays" that have built up; and a particular collector in the office becomes responsible to certain delinquent accounts. The telephone call is used throughout the collection effort that follows. After the initial telephone call, the collection effort follows no definite sequence. The collector uses extensively the telephone with personal letters and wires sandwiched in throughout the discussion and urgency stages.

The collector also uses personal, dictated letters either to confirm in writing what the customer agreed to over the telephone or to remind the customer that he (the customer) agreed to a payment plan and to ask why he has broken his promise. If the collector cannot reach the customer by phone, he uses one or more of five form letters. Form letter 4 is sent on the store's attorney's stationery. Form letter 5 informs the customer that he can still deal with the store; but if he does not, the next collection effort will come from the store's collection agency. (The average delinquency of accounts turned over for collection is eight months.)

In summary, the collection series for this department store consists of:

1. Computerized statements and duns that include the first statement, plus four monthly statements, three reminders, and two letters in the discussion stage.
2. Manual communications that complete the discussion and urgency stages. The store covers the urgency stage by telephone unless the past-due customer doesn't have a telephone; then it uses two form letters or wires.

Savings and Loan Association[3] The collection procedures of this particular savings and loan association are notable for the lack of any firm policy. Even though the association services over 4,500 loans, it doesn't have a formal collection

[2]The facts for the department store come from a 1970 master's thesis by Richard Craig Anderson, for the Graduate School of Business Administration, University of Washington, Seattle, Washington, entitled *Collection of Past-due Accounts: A Study of the System Used by a Large Retail Store in a City of 500,000.* Mr. Anderson has given permission to quote liberally from his material.
The schedule here refers only to the regular account—not to the flexible account, deferred account, or the 90-day account, each of which differs in length of the series but all of which follow the same format in the dunning sequence schedules. The collection department for this department store maintains twelve in-state and out-of-state offices. The number of credit or charge accounts at any one time varies somewhere between 250,000 and 305,000 accounts. In addition, there are another 100,000 to 125,000 dormant accounts. About 3.5 percent of the accounts that are opened at any given time are written off as bad debts. The number of accounts that are three or more months delinquent at any one time varies from 4,000 to 6,500.
[3]This association has assets of $72 million, one home office, and five branches (it is planning a sixth branch).

department. The responsibility for collections is shared between the accounting and the loan departments.

The first step toward the collection of a delinquent account is taken by the accounting department. Within 10 to 15 days after the due date of a loan, a first reminder is sent. A second, more strongly worded notice is sent if the account is still delinquent after 20 to 25 days.

When an account becomes one month delinquent, it is turned over to the loan department. An attempt at telephone contact is made by one of the two members of the loan department. If the individual involved cannot be reached by telephone, a brief letter is written. Both the telephone call and the letter are in the form of reminders, with emphasis on the importance of keeping the account current.

Each delinquent account two or more months past due is handled on an individual basis by the loan department. The action taken is generally determined by the association's past experience with an account.

The majority of delinquent accounts two months past due are notified that, in accordance with the terms of the mortgage note, the interest rate is increased to 10 percent per annum until such time as the account is again current.

Accounts three or more months past due are generally given a specific date by which the account must be current. Notice is given that if the account is not current by the specified date, it will be turned over to the association's attorney for foreclosure action.

As mentioned earlier, each of the more serious delinquent accounts is handled on an individual basis. As long as the association is able to maintain communication with the persons involved, it attempts to help them create a workable solution to the problems causing their delinquency. The association is very lenient and flexible in working with these accounts and will go to great lengths to avoid taking foreclosure action.

Utility Company (in a city with population over 1 million) Practically all gas meters in this city are read on a bimonthly basis. The customer is billed within 10 days, and a 10-day net payment period is shown on the bill.

Fourteen days after the net payment period has expired, the credit and collection department is notified of all unpaid accounts totaling $10 or more by receiving gas collection statements together with two notices. The first or reminder notice is mailed immediately.

In most cases the second or final notice follows seven days later. The final notice bears a seven-day expiration date after which a collector may call and discontinue the service. If an account shows a good payment record, the final notice may be preceded by a special reminder letter. Or the final notice may be followed by a letter. These exceptions are made at the discretion of the collection reviewer who directs the general collection activity.

Telephone Collection Procedure

As the preceding discussions indicated, both written and oral messages can be effective for collecting past-due payments. Basically, the goals, attitudes, and procedures are similar whether you collect by written communication or through oral contacts—face to face or by telephone.

The following quotation expresses some advantages of the telephone method:[4]

[4] Theodore N. Beckman and Ronald S. Foster, *Credits and Collections,* 8th ed., McGraw-Hill Book Company, New York, 1969, p. 533.

Increasing use is being made of the telephone in collecting, both in early and late stages of the collection process, for this method, because of its directness, often succeeds where other methods fail. One of the chief advantages of this method is that it is somewhat surprising to the debtor and may, therefore, catch him unguarded with small alibis and grievances with which to excuse his delinquency. It furnishes the collector a good opportunity to impress him emphatically with the urgency of payment, varying the appeals as the need arises. Frequently, when the reason for nonpayment is understandable, although the failure of the debtor to communicate it is not, a plan of payment may be worked out, usually with a partial payment to be made immediately. Thus, by telephoning nearly all can be accomplished that could be gained by a personal solicitation. Telephoning, however, is often the speedier method, the more flexible, particularly in tracing skips, the less costly, even in the use of long-distance service, as long as it is used with efficiency and discretion.

Because of the growing importance of the telephone in all three collection stages, this section focuses briefly on two special phases of telephone collection techniques: precall planning and the actual collection conversation.

Precall Planning

The steps a collector takes before an important telephone call—or a personal conversation—are similar to the first five planning steps before writing (see pages 28-33).

    1. Determine Your Purpose. Besides the general goal of collecting the money and keeping goodwill, you probably have a specific purpose too. Be sure to check all previous letters, calls, and any response to them. Is your purpose now to work out a special payment arrangement? Or to remind the debtor of a promise made recently but not kept? Or to urge the debtor to pay by a certain date? Or to present an important decision?

    2. Visualize Your Customer. First determine the right person to talk to. He (or she) should be the *only* one who is responsible for paying the bills. Try to judge whether the customer would respond better to a hard or a soft line. If the customer has just received the first overdue notice, your approach should of course be different from the approach to the customer who has ignored several previous contacts. Is the customer likely to be angry? Friendly? Cooperative? Hostile? The payment history is a good clue as to the way the customer will respond to your call.

    3. Collect All Necessary Facts. *(a) Determine if your own company is at fault.* Were shipments and billings correct? Were all payments recorded? If you find errors, take time to have them corrected before calling the customer to bring the account up to date. *(b) Check the past payment record.* How often were the customer's payments delinquent in the past? How long past due is the account now? If the customer has been late only once in the last year, he or she will probably more readily accept a payment plan than the customer who has been delinquent most of the year.

4. Consider the Ideas to Cover. *(a) Prepare the questions* you'll ask the debtor to determine reasons for not paying bills on time. You'll want to make the customer feel that you are both on the same side. Plan open-ended questions that allow the customer to do the talking rather than merely answering "yes" or "no." Good questions begin with the five W's—who, what, when, where, why, and the H—how.

(b) Be ready to present a payment plan. This is the heart of precall planning. The payment plan must account for all the overdue payments, not just one or two; and it must include a *specific* schedule that will bring the overdue account to current status. Prepare to sell the plan to the customer in a positive way, without insulting or harassing statements.

5. Plan and Organize. Prepare an opening statement and—at least in general— the order in which you'll present the material you want to cover.

Analysis of the Collection Call[5]

Like the well-written collection letter, the collection call should likewise be tactfully persuasive. The conversation contains the following parts:

1. Opening Statement. After identifying yourself and your firm, state the reason for calling. Then use a strategic pause—about six seconds. It is important that the pause be used in every call. Experience shows that if the customer is sincere in the desire to pay overdue bills, he or she will offer to pay or give a reason for not paying as soon as the reason for the phone call is given. Many collection calls are completed successfully immediately after this strategic pause.

2. Fact-finding Questions. As you hear the customer's answers to your preplanned questions, try to determine whether the payment plan you designed is realistic. Be ready to adapt it to meet the customer's situation. When you can say to yourself— using either your original plan or a newly devised one—"This payment plan will get the account current, and it meets my company policy," go on to the next step.

3. Presentation of Payment Plan. You might begin to focus the customer's attention on your plan by statements like these: "Well, I've been thinking seriously about your account, (name), and have come up with a plan of action that will get your account right back on a steady course. . . ." Or "(name), I'm glad you mentioned that you wish there were a way you could get your account back up there without having to do it today. I believe there is. How does this plan sound to you?" At this point you have focused the customer's attention on the payment plan. Regardless of who proposes the plan or how it is altered, if the final plan is a schedule of payments that will result in an up-to-date account, it is a satisfactory arrangement.

If the customer agrees to a plan, you have been successful and can move directly

---

[5]This section on telephone collection procedure is based on findings from the previously cited 1970 master's thesis by Richard Craig Anderson.

to closing the call. However, if the customer does not agree to all or part of the payment plan, you must take further action—namely, overcoming objections.

4. Overcoming of Objections. Almost always objections are postponements—reasons for not agreeing to the payment plan now. Three basic steps you can take in overcoming objections are:

a. Determine specifically what the customer is objecting to. You can't overcome an objection until you know what it is.
b. Get agreement on those parts the customer is not objecting to. It may be that the customer's objection only concerns one of the payment dates in the plan. If so, get agreement on all the rest.
c. Work out the parts the customer objects to. If the objections are minor, you can compromise as long as the plan is specific and it gets the account current. However, if the customer's objections are serious, you should be sure that the reasons are valid. Then stress the benefits to the customer of paying and keep-the account current.

5. Closing Statement. Summarize the payment plan and thank the customer. The following is an example of a good close. "Fine, Mr. Dawes. Now let me summarize to make sure that I have everything straight. You are going to send me a payment of $41.20 on Friday, the 16th. I should have that on the following Monday. Then you will send another payment of $41.20 on Friday, the 23d, which I should receive on the 26th. That will bring your account right up to date. Thank you very much, Mr. Dawes. Good-bye now."

After the call is finished, write down for future reference everything that was said. Note the pertinent information on a card and file it with any other information on the account. (Of course, if the customer does not abide by the terms of the agreement, you or another collector must take further action.)

Summary

A customer does not settle an account for one or more of the following reasons: overlooked paying, temporarily short of funds, forgot to pay, dissatisfied with something, or customer is a chronic debtor. When an account becomes past due, the creditor begins a collection series. Its goal is to collect the money and maintain goodwill.

A good collector must treat the customer with consideration, remembering the customer is also a human being and should be treated like one always. Furthermore, the collector must realize there are bound to be some customers who will not always pay when they should. And finally, the collector should try in every way possible to help a defaulting customer arrange to pay an account. The creditor does not want to sue, because everyone but the collection agency or attorney loses.

The collection series is a preplanned but still flexible procedure to collect from the past-due customer. It consists of three stages and five appeals. As the series progresses, each message makes greater pressure on the customer to pay. The length of the series and the insistence to pay depend on the credit reputation of the individual—

whether he or she is a good risk, a fair risk, or a poor risk. Contacts with the customer can be by mail, telephone, wires, or personal visits. Messages by mail consist of statements, reminders, letters, and wires. A collector who uses the telephone or makes a personal visit, should be versed in the proper procedure, which includes precall planning and detailed analysis of the call (or visit).

Exercises

1. Below are six collection messages that a dentist sent to patients with past-due installment accounts. Each letter has a typed personalized inside address and salutation above an obvious form message.
   a. Evaluate the effectiveness of each message. Pay particular attention to tone, presentation of facts, appropriateness of the obvious form letter, request for payment, helpfulness toward the patient, and proper use of the collection appeals.
   b. Attempt to describe the dentist's attitude toward patients who don't pay accounts promptly.

Message 1
First letter (accompanies second statement) from the credit department.

Please take note that your account is still in arrears to the amount of $____. We sent you a notice a short time ago, which was evidently ignored.

Inasmuch as we have received no payment for some time, you will readily understand our anxiety. Will you please let us have your check or money order by return mail.

Message 2
Second letter from the credit department.

We are sorry to be forced to call your attention to your account again. It certainly is not our intention to annoy you or cause you any inconvenience. You must realize, however, that it is all-important that these installment accounts be paid as agreed. Your failure to adhere to the terms we arranged causes a breach in the contract that can be overcome only by paying the account up to date.

We dislike using other methods than persuasion in order to collect, and we feel that you will readily acknowledge the fairness of our request to remit by return mail.

Message 3
Third letter from the credit department.

Please do not force us to call your attention too often to the past due balance of $____.

I am trying my best to avoid taking any action that might be disagreeable to both of us. This is our third letter, and you can make it our last by paying up.

Message 4
Fourth letter from the credit department.

Your failure again to pay as you have promised has caused us to seek some other method whereby we can collect the money due us. Since nothing can be done by writing letters, there is only one thing left to do--give the account to our agents and let them force collection.

Forced collections are poor substitutes for prompt and willing payment. For a person to accept services on a promise to pay, and leave it at that, calls for methods which are obnoxious to both creditor and debtor. You will find, however, if you care to investigate, that most of the time it is the debtor's fault. Attachments, levies, and garnishments can always be avoided if the proper interest is taken in the fact that you owe money. If you make a promise--keep it.

After all, you expect to get paid for work you do, and it is no more than right that you follow the same rule with respect to others.

Message 5
Fifth letter—this time from the manager of the business office.

The whole world frowns on those who refuse to pay their legitimate bills. Why? Because they are the type who live off the honesty of others. If there were no honest people, the credit business would not exist. But it so happens that the majority of people believe that a promise is a sacred thing. There are still some people left who regard honor before everything else.

When you buy on credit, the service or the merchandise is given to you merely on your word. If you are able to pay but refuse, you are breaking that chain of confidence that extends between the merchant and the consumer . . . you are living off the honesty of others.

Fortunately, there are only a few people who have no regard for their own promises.

Message 6
Sixth letter—this time bearing the signature of the dentist.

You know that we have addressed many letters to you requesting payment of your account. We have withheld giving the account to our outside agent because we have been hopeful that you would soon find your way clear to settle.

I don't think you have really placed this bill in its rightful position of importance. To you, perhaps, it is just a bill that some day you hope to pay. But to us it represents time, labor, and material invested, on which no return has been received.

I can't do a single thing now except to advise (name), our attorney, to file suit and hold judgment, if such be rendered, until some tangible asset appears that can be attached. Sometimes, after the thing has been almost forgotten, this means a sudden and severe embarrassment when you least expect it. Believe me, I would much rather see you try to pay a dollar every week.

2. Below are unusual collection messages. Which do you consider appropriate to send as reminders? Which would you not send? Give reason(s) for your decision.

Message 1
Below the personalized salutation appears the picture of a man in old, patched clothes.

You have received some of my letters in the past which were epitomes of that stateliness befitting the true nobility of executive correspondence. That was when I was a dignified Credit Manager.

Time, circumstance, and necessity force me to be candid and tactless. Yes—I am the miserable wretch whose portrait appears upon this page.

I was reduced to this plebian state by being a virtuous paragon standing high on a pinnacle of patience, turning a kind ear and an open heart to all who owed past due accounts. Then, one day not so long ago, those hounds of the Apocalypse, my creditors, began gnashing and clawing until finally the pinnacle was torn asunder and I came crashing down into an ignoble flight.

I stand before you in my darkest hour. In this, my most perilous moment, I beseech you . . .

PAY YOUR COTTONPICKIN ACCOUNT AND GET ME OUT OF THIS MESS! ! ! !

Message 2
Obvious form letter with no inside address. Attached is a real paper clip.

No! That little paper clip in the upper left-hand corner hasn't been left there by a careless stenographer. That's Elmer, our pet paper clip.

His sole purpose in life, as you know, is to hold two pieces of paper together. But our Elmer has enlarged his scope of usefulness and has accepted two very definite tasks which we have asked him to do:

1. To securely hold your check for $4,286.61 to this note, which will clear up that little account we've talked about, and . . .

2. . . . by doing so, to bind the amicable relationship which exists between our two companies.

Let's get this little matter under the bridge. What do you say?

Message 3
Obvious form letter.

Dear Customer

                                    Cordially yours,
                                    (signature, etc)

P.S. I'm practically speechless, but could whisper a hearty "thank you" for your check for $131.32 to clean up that balance on your June purchases.

3. Evaluate the effectiveness of the following early reminders that follow the statement(s). Which ones do you consider appropriate? Which ones do you consider inappropriate? Why?

Reminder 1
Obvious form letter on letterhead stationery from an oil company (added are the personalized inside address and salutation.

We know it is easy to lose a statement or forget to pay a bill, particularly if it is a small one.

In case one or the other happened in connection with your account for $___, will you consider this as a reminder to drop a check in the mail today?

Reminder 2
Personalized inside address and salutation with a typewritten body on letterhead stationery from a book store.

We want you to know that we appreciate your patronage and we hope therefore that we will not offend you when we mention that we haven't received anything on your account since we sent you your statement.

We would appreciate it if you could send us something this month.

Reminder 3
Printed message on a 3¾- by 7-inch piece of paper from a department store. There is no salutation and the inside address below the message also serves as the address for a window envelope.

It's such a small amount that you probably haven't bothered with it--only $___; nevertheless, we would appreciate receiving payment so we may balance our books.

Reminder 4
Obvious printed message on a 5½- by 7-inch paper from a weekly newsmagazine. There is no inside address or salutation.

Just a brief note to repeat our thanks to you for your interest in (name of magazine) and for your order that will bring you its quick, complete, and competent news briefing in the many eventful weeks ahead. I feel sure you'll find both pleasure and profit in its pages!

And may I add another thanks--in advance--to you for taking care of the enclosed bill promptly. I've sent this copy in case our previous invoice was mislaid or overlooked.

And from all of us at (name of magazine)--sincere wishes that your (name of magazine) subscription will mean the best of good news to you!

4. The following letters are from different firms to customers who have either monthly installment accounts or who receive utility services monthly. Compare and evaluate them regarding: considerate tone, appeals, and strictness in collection policies. Which one(s) do you prefer? Why? Can you find any serious errors?

Letter 1
Personalized form letter signed by the manager of a credit corporation to a borrower when the first monthly payment was six weeks overdue.

Your account was referred to me this morning as SERIOUSLY DELINQUENT. Upon reviewing it, I am indeed surprised that it is not up to date in payments. You have been extended every courtesy both by notice and letter, but there has been no response.

We go through the above-mentioned courtesies when an account becomes delinquent for a few days. Almost 100 percent of our customers APPRECIATE A COURTEOUS NOTICE AND MAKE PAYMENT PROMPTLY. Your FAILURE to do so, therefore, AMAZES us.

Your account is seriously past due. IS IT NECESSARY FOR US TO TAKE ANY FURTHER ACTION OTHER THAN WRITE THIS LETTER IN ORDER TO HAVE YOU SEND THIS AMOUNT BY RETURN MAIL?

Letter 2
Personalized inside address and salutation added to an obvious printed message on letterhead stationery from an electric power company.

Since you are one of our new customers and we have been unable to reach you by telephone, we are taking this opportunity to write to you to discuss your electric light account.

We would like to explain briefly our billing practices so that you will have a better understanding as to how our bills are rendered and when they are considered due. Bills are mailed to you five or six days after the date appearing on the bill and are due and payable upon receipt and become delinquent in fifteen days. However, if there is some particular time during the current month which is more convenient for you to pay your bill, will you please notify us so that we can note our records and in this way eliminate any unnecessary treatment in the handling of your account.

According to our records the statement recently mailed has not been paid. If there is some question regarding your bill, please call our Business Office at (telephone number) or come to our office at (address). Unless you wish to make other arrangements, we will appreciate receiving your payment within the next five days.

We welcome the opportunity of furnishing you with the electricity service and hope that we may continue to be of service to you.

Amount due: $____.

Letter 3
Personalized letter (dated February 28) from a real estate loan department to a borrower for a home loan.

Re: Loan No. 8-888888

Dear Mr. and Mrs. Green:

It has come to our attention that your account is presently delinquent for your February 1 payment plus late fee of $5.90 for a total
of $171.90. In addition, your March installment of $167.00 will be
due and payable tomorrow, at which time your full arrearage will
amount to $338.90.

This is to advise you that unless the full sum of $338.90 is received
in this office on or before March 6, your account will be placed before our Board of Directors for review, with a recommendation of
immediate referral to counsel for legal action.

Sincerely yours,

5. Evaluate the following two collection messages. In which stage do you think it
   would be appropriate to use each?

Message 1
Personalized letter throughout.

Dear Mrs. Kuper

This is not a dunning letter.

Neither is it an attempt to gloss over a serious situation with
fancy language concealing a strong-arm attempt to pry money out
of you.

Time and distance make it impossible for me to come to you for a
friendly chat, so I must ask you to accept this letter as the next
best thing. You owe us $64.25, long past-due. You have always
paid your commitments promptly. Therefore, there must be some
special reason for your delay in this case.

I am not so much interested in the cause of this delay as I am in
how we can help you over the rough spot. If one can't look to
friends for help in times of stress, who on earth can one look to--
and I hope our past relationship entitles us to be classed among
your friends.

We want our money, of course. But we also want to keep your
friendship. I am sure we can accomplish both ends by being
entirely frank with each other.

What is wrong? What can we do to help you?

I suggest you write me in full, in confidence. Perhaps between us
we can work out some plan whereby you can take care of the past-due
balance without crowding yourself too much and, at the same time,
we can continue to make shipments to take care of your immediate
needs.

Message 2
Obvious form letter with inside address and salutation typed in.

You must have a good reason for not having paid anything on your account after our recent letter--we are sure of that. But you do not tell us what the reason is.

If we only knew what the situation is, no doubt some arrangement could be made that would relieve your mind of the worry of an over-due debt, and satisfy us, too.

If you can, send in a part payment with your answer. Whether you can do that or not, at least tell us just what is wrong. Give us a chance to help. What do you say?

6. The following collection messages fall within the urgency stage. Your job is to determine whether each message is effective. In your evaluation, ask yourself whether the wording is too strong or not strong enough, whether the writer is still trying to help the individual, and whether the message accomplishes the twofold job of collecting the money and retaining the goodwill of the customer.

Message 1
Personalized inside address and salutation and typewritten body. Dated March 8.

It seldom becomes necessary for us to turn an account over to an attorney for collection. And on those few occasions when circum-stances leave us no other alternative, we consider it only fair to tell the customer exactly what we intend to do.

Certainly, you must realize that we have made every effort to be fair and patient in requesting that you settle your January account of $205.40. We have written to you several times, asking that you let us know how we could cooperate with you in getting this indebt-edness straightened out.

Your continued silence leaves us no other alternative than to refer your account to our attorney for collection--a step that we sincerely regret. So won't you respond to this final appeal for your coopera-tion and thereby avoid a procedure that can only mean embarrassment, inconvenience, and additional expense to you.

Unless we hear from you by March 22, we shall be compelled to transfer your account to the office of our attorney. Please use the enclosed reply envelope to let us hear from you.

Message 2
Personalized inside address and salutation and typewritten body. Dated October 16.

A short time ago you and Ed Taylor registered in our hotel on September 18 and stayed two days, checking out the 20th. The rate on this room is $20 per day. Our clerk, Mr. Newcomer, was on duty (his first day) when you checked out and he made an error and collected for only one day. You still owe us for that, and while Mr. Newcomer wrote you he would have to stand good for the $20 we thot you would send it to us. However you probably didn't give it much thot and perhaps have forgotten it. So we will appreciate your sending this to us at once.

For we are sure you would not intentially dismiss the subject and refuse to pay.

However, if this is not paid by November 1st, we are forced to turn the account over to the American Hotel Association and they would print your name in all the hotel magazines as one not paying hotel bill which would go to every hotel in the U.S.

I know you are a fine fellow and will take care of this. For we do appreciate the visit you made us and we want you to come back next time you are in (city). American (name) Show is now on. It's a wonderful show. Why don't you come see it.

Message 3
Personalized inside address and salutation and typewritten body. Dated May 31.

Over a hundred fifty years ago Sir Walter Scott said, "Credit is like a looking glass, which, when once sullied by a breath, may be wiped clear again; but if once cracked can never by repaired." The importnace of a good credit rating has not changed today.

The barbecue you bought at Wardman's in January will continue to give many hours of enjoyment as you use it in your backyard this summer. We, however, have become concerned about your account listing that purchase. It is past-due almost four months. Because of our satisfactory past dealings with you, we feel there must be something wrong, but you have not indicated this by a response to the other letters sent to you.

Because of your very active participation in community affairs, you can realize the importance of having a high credit rating in order to keep in good standing with the other merchants about town. Your good rating was given to us originally by the Lakeview Merchants' Credit Association of which we are a member. Our agreement with these people requires that we report all those accounts that are seriously past due. Because this is such a serious action, we always wait with our better customers like you hoping for an explanation or, preferably, payment of the past-due account. In keeping with the Credit Association's requirements, we, however, will have to refer your name to them by June 5.

To keep your credit "glass" from being broken, just mail your check for $71.60 to us in the enclosed prepaid envelope. Then come to the store and see the new attachments and utensils for outdoor cooking, which you will continue to enjoy this summer.

Message 4
Obvious form message without an inside address. This message appears printed on the inside of an envelope that the customer puts together and uses to send in the money owed.

You have disregarded the several reminders sent to you regarding the amount overdue on your account and I am wondering whether you realize the importance of making payments as agreed. You have even ignored my requests to call at the office so that this matter might be discussed. Now, two payments are past due.

The agreement that you signed provides that the merchandise is our property until fully paid for. I have not made any attempt to exercise our rights because I believed it unnecessary in your case. However, if you continue to disregard my letters, I shall be forced to proceed with more drastic measures.

I am, therefore, giving you seven days to pay the amount shown below. Our future action depends entirely upon you.

7. Your job is to rewrite the collection series that the dentist used. Instead of the selfish, insulting messages in Exercise 1 you will write messages that will include the twofold purpose of collecting—get the money and still keep the goodwill of the patient.

In the series, remember the patient is a human being with feelings. Include the amount due in each message and try to help the individual out of the dilemma. Don't threaten or preach. Also incorporate the following suggestions:

Message 1: Obvious form reminder on letterhead stationery.

Message 2: Personalized inside address and salutation with typewritten body. The message (in the discussion stage) will include a combination of the first 2 appeals—cooperation and fair play.

Message 3: Personalized letter, but you'll use the pride appeal.

Message 4: Personalized letter, but you'll use the self-interest appeal.

Message 5: Personalized letter (in the urgency stage): you'll use the fear appeal without setting a date on which you'll turn the account over to an outside agent.

Message 6: Personalized letter (in the urgency stage) using the fear appeal and setting the date you'll turn account over to an outside agent.

8. As owner of a small-town hardware store, you receive a letter this morning from Larry Moss, a long-time customer who owns and operates a 160-acre farm. He tells you his wife has been in the hospital for the last 10 days and he cannot pay you for $300 worth of supplies that will be due on July 1. Furthermore, he doesn't have insurance to cover any of the hospital expenses.

He promises to pay something on account in two weeks, and hopes to be able to pay up completely within a month. Answer the letter. Today is the last day of June. Moss is poorly financed, but you know that he is a hard worker and that his word is good. You will expect to hear from him by July 15.

9. You are the manager of a swimming school that offers swim lessons as its main service. Nine sessions cost $27. Each class is small, no more than five children. Your office requires parents who sign their children up for lessons to pay a $5 registration fee and the balance—$22—on the first day of the lessons.

Just recently Mrs. Richwitch signed three of her youngsters up for lessons. You had a terrible time getting her to pay the registration fee. Although you tell your customers that if they don't pay a registration fee, you cannot hold a space for them, you do not often follow through with the threat, since people usually pay the fee. Mrs. Richwitch finally did come through with the registration fee, but when the lessons began, she asked if she could wait to pay the $66 balance.

It is now the third lesson and she still hasn't paid. Furthermore, you learn that she placed a fourth child in a class on the second lesson without paying the registration fee or balance. You checked with the instructor to find out how this happened, and he explained Mrs. Richwitch said that the office had told the child to be in the class. The instructor was new and didn't realize that such an action was highly irregular.

You must explain to Mrs. Richwitch that if she wants her fourth child in class, she will have to register and pay the balance. Also, you want to remind her of the outstanding balance. You have tried to telephone her, but no one ever answers. She didn't accompany the children for their last lesson, either. She owes you $93, including the fees for the fourth child, and you want to collect. Write a letter that will get the money and at the same time keep the goodwill of Mrs. Richwitch. You feel she has plenty of money because she lives in a very exclusive residential area and you notice her name often on the society page of the local newspaper.

10. As controller for Apex Corporation, manufacturers of plastic toys and specialties, you need today to write a personalized collection letter. You have just received today (July 25), from the U&I Distributors, a check for $182.37 in payment of your May 5 invoice of $213.16. You note they have deducted $4.26 cash discount which you can't allow because of late payment. With terms of 2-10 E.O.M., this invoice should have been paid by June 10, but this customer's check was dated and mailed more than a month later. Also you need to know why they deducted the $26.53; so far as your records show, there is no such amount anywhere. Write them an appropriate inquiry and request for their payment in full.

11. You are Credit and Collection Manager of the Midtown TV and Electronics Sales Company. Yours is one of the three major such stores in the city. Mr. James Johnson, a resident of your city, has been a credit customer of yours for six years, and his record is "good."

On February 10 this year Mr. Johnson bought a portable tape recorder for $72.90 and charged it to his account. March 1 you sent him a bill for this amount, due March 10. April 1, since you had not heard from him, you sent a second bill. May 1 you sent a third bill, with a sticker at the bottom saying, "You Forgot, Didn't You? Please mail us a check now—while you have it in mind." On June 10 the account is considered 90 days overdue. Address a discussion letter to Mr. Johnson, offering to help any way you can. Make the basic purpose of your letter a reply from him—either a remittance, a letter, a phone call, or a personal visit. Prepare the letter as a form message with a personal inside address and salutation. Make it sound personal, but write it so that the body is applicable to any "good" customer with an account 90 days overdue.

12. Assume you are assistant manager of Quality Hardware, a neighborhood store carrying a complete line of hardware and electrical supplies. The store is located in a fast-growing, attractive residential section of your city; and there is only one other, but very small, hardware and variety store in the same shopping district. Most of your credit customers are homeowners, living within two miles of the store, and you are at least casually acquainted with most of them. Being active participants in the social life of the community, they are mentioned frequently in the society columns of the local newspapers.

You have made a list of those customers whose accounts are more than three months overdue—with balances of between $30 and $150—and who have not used their accounts since they became past due. Assume you are including on this list only those customers who have never before been seriously delinquent on payments to you, though they have all been trading with your store for two to five years. You are not worried about their eventual payment, but you would like to collect these accounts now to reinvest the money tied up in them. The following reminders have already been mailed to these customers:

An itemized statement

A second, unitemized statement with a sticker, "Your prompt attention to this account will be appreciated."

A mild letter of reminder, suggesting that payment of the account has been overlooked

A stronger reminder, appealing to cooperation in paying up

A third letter based on the fair-play appeal, indicating that you have supplied quality merchandise at moderate prices, have waited patiently for payment, and feel sure the customer will show fairness by paying the amount due.

Today is November 20. You decide to write a friendly, informal "discussion" letter with a definite request for an answer or preferably a check. It is to be essentially a form letter, but as it will be personally typed for each customer, you may have some variable paragraphs. (Indicate the variables by parentheses.) Probably the most effective appeals will be to pride, self-interest, or loyalty to your store. Each of these customers will naturally wish to protect his or her credit standing in the community and maintain a record of reliability as your charge customer. As you are a member of the local Retail Hardware Merchants Credit Association, your collection department automatically reports to the association the names of customers whose payments are seriously past due. If you mention this, do so not as a threat, which might offend the customer, but as an indication of your honest desire to protect the customer's credit reputation. Try to induce each customer to pay the past-due account immediately, or at least to make definite arrangements for payment. Be so courteous and tactful that you will retain the customer's goodwill and patronage.

14 Goodwill Messages

So far, the messages you have studied are necessary in the usual course of business. Their chief purpose is to take care of day-to-day problems through requests, replies, and announcements. In contrast, the letters and memos covered in this chapter are not absolutely essential or required for the operation of a business. Their main purpose is to convey a friendly, usually unexpected, message that builds goodwill.

Besides being friendly, unexpected, and outside the usual course of business, goodwill messages have several other characteristics in common. Their organizational plan resembles *a good-news or neutral message*—most important idea first, then brief comments and details (if any), and a final cordial ending (if needed). Like all letters, goodwill messages should be honest and sincere and avoid gushiness or wordiness. They can be sent to the reader's home or office. Depending upon their content, destination, and quantity, goodwill messages may be typewritten, handwritten (for an extra, personal touch), or printed, perhaps on special paper appropriate for the occasion or season. Unlike most business letters, however, genuine goodwill messages should not contain statements that try to sell the reader on buying additional products or services. Most people dislike messages that pose as "goodwill only" letters but that actually have strings attached.

A genuine goodwill letter is almost always favorably received, for at least two reasons:

1. The writer presumably is not sending the message because of some business scheme.
2. The message comes as a pleasant surprise, for the recipient doesn't expect it. Bills will come if money is owed, but a thank-you from the seller for paying promptly or congratulations for winning an honor or celebrating a special anniversary isn't expected.

An important value of goodwill messages is that their effects sometimes develop months, even years, later. Because these messages reach out in a pleasant, friendly way to readers, they are remembered when the recipients want to buy products or services. Especially when competing firms sell goods of almost identical quality and prices, customers tend to buy where they get that extra ingredient—service with friendly, personal consideration and appreciation. Thus, although goodwill messages omit sales talk, they are actually an excellent way to promote business, as the following discussion and examples illustrate.

Thoughtful persons—especially executives—often write messages designed to foster friendly relations with customers, suppliers, and others by:

1. Congratulating or giving deserved praise
2. Expressing appreciation
3. Extending seasonal greetings
4. Conveying sympathy
5. Welcoming and/or offering favors
6. Showing continuing special concern

Congratulating or Giving Deserved Praise

A sincere, enthusiastic note of congratulations or deserved praise—sent promptly—can have an unforgettable impact on the recipient, especially because not many people take the initiative to send such messages.

Congratulatory Messages

The opportunities for congratulating are numerous, for congratulations may relate to any significant news about an individual's business, family, or personal achievements. For instance, you might congratulate a business executive when his firm has opened a new branch, reached its twenty-fifth or fiftieth anniversary, moved to larger quarters, attained a publicized milestone in total volume of sales, received a well-known award for distinguished service to the industry or community, or achieved special favorable publicity. You might congratulate an individual when she or someone in her family has made a significant achievement or won an honor. Among the events and activities that merit congratulations to an individual are: election to an office; promotion; graduation; birth of a child; winning a competitive contest, scholarship, prize; making an outstanding speech; writing a good magazine article or book; performing well in a theater, debate, or other public gathering.

When you write a congratulation, "talk" informally and enthusiastically—without flattery—as you would in a personal contact with the recipient. Focus on your reader instead of on yourself. And write promptly—as soon as possible after you first learn the good news. The letters below are examples of various congratulatory messages. Letters 2 through 7 are well written.

Letter 1
A stilted, writer-centered congratulatory note about a promotion.

I have just read that you have been promoted to Vice President of your company.

I am sure your attainment unequivocally substantiates the exemplary service you are giving your employer. I believe you can be justifiably proud of your outstanding performance in the industry.

I forward my heartiest congratulations and wishes for your continued success in your endeavors.

Letter 2
A revision of letter 1, with improved tone and word choice.

Your promotion to Vice President of General Construction Company was great news. I was happy to read about you in this week's Trade Press.

If ever a man deserved the recognition your company has given you, you do. Your courage and hard work in developing new ways to promote the services of your firm have won the admiration of many, including your competitors.

Congratulations to you--and best wishes for your continued success!

Letter 3

A banker congratulates a businessperson on an election. (A similar note brought the banker who wrote it millions of dollars of business in installment loans.)

Congratulations, (name)

. . . upon being elected president of the Westside Lumber Dealers Association, as announced in yesterday's Times.

Under your capable leadership, this organization will reach a new high in activity and service.

Letter 4

A manager congratulates a customer for favorable publicity about the customer's business.

Heartiest congratulations to you on the splendid progress you have made with your poultry plant! It was a real pleasure for me to see your picture and read the feature article about your new cage house in the May issue of American Poultry Journal.

Verna Barns has spoken enthusiastically of your model operation and the excellent job you are doing. This article and its labor-saving suggestions have already been filed for future reference in our "idea" folder.

On my next field trip to Minnesota I want to meet you personally and visit your place. My very best wishes to you for your continued outstanding results with Erving's Chicks.

Letter 5

A vice president congratulates a scholarship winner.

Dear (first name):

We extend to you hearty congratulations upon your selection as the winner of the Beakins & Worth Foundation's scholastic award for excellence in accounting for 197_ at the University of (state).

Your achievement should be a source of pride to you, to your professors, and to your University. It is to young people like yourself that the accounting profession and the business and civic community look with confidence for their leaders of the future.

The best of success to you!

Sometimes, in addition to congratulating a person, you may want to send along a clipping of a picture or article published concerning the event. Some firms have specially designed folders to which such clippings may be attached with scotch tape or clips. Printed on the outside cover may be a message like "CONGRATULATIONS," or "YOU'RE IN THE NEWS," together with the company's trademark. For instance, the Carnation Company (dairy products) used a folder that pictured on the outside three carnations under the words, "CARNATIONS to You!" On the inside is an attractive design and this message:

```
We Read With Interest . . . The attached clipping about you and
                             thought you would be interested in
                             receiving our copy.
```

At Carnation we are always pleased to read about those people who
help make the Northwest such a wonderful place in which to live.

Sending an invitation or an inexpensive gift along with the congratulations, as in
Letter 6, can be an effective way to build goodwill. However, many other letters that
begin with congratulations are actually not true goodwill messages, but disguised or
obvious sales messages, like Letter 7.

Letter 6
*A retail store sends layettes with congratulations to parents of twins. (Letterhead
states: "Headquarters for clothes from crib to college.") Salutation is "Dear Mr.
and Mrs. (name)."*

May Barons add their congratulations to the many you have already
received. It is a pleasure to send two layettes for your twin
arrivals on April 23, 197_.

Your babies will no doubt model all garments beautifully. We are
happy to send you these "double congratulations" for your doubly
happy event--with compliments of Barons.

You can expect the layettes by mail within a few days. May you have
many happy days and years ahead.

Letter 7
*An obvious processed form message on a special letterhead picturing a baby and
many toys. (This is a sales letter.) Salutation is "Dear Parents."*

Congratulations! . . . for this is a proud time for you. And
your new baby is going to give you reason for pride for many years
to come!

To help you during this period of extra expenses . . . WE EXTEND
THIS SPECIAL INVITATION TO YOU TO SEE US FOR THE CASH YOU NEED.

You are invited to come in with the enclosed MANAGER'S INVITATION
at your earliest convenience. You can get a Cash Loan, up to the
amount shown, to pay doctor and hospital bills, buy things for the
new baby, pay old bills, or for any other purpose.

Come in today. Bring the special INVITATION with you. Choose
from our several popular plans. Receive the MONEY promptly!

Messages with Deserved Praise

In addition to congratulating people for various achievements that are in the news,
you may also find reason to give deserved praise for good service that has not been
publicized.

For instance, you might compliment your employee(s) on exceptionally fine work.
Also, as a customer, you might write to a company executive to tell him about unusu-

ally good service you received from his employee(s). Such sincere praise, judiciously given, is appreciated by both the executive and the employees; often the sincere compliments stimulate recipients to do even higher-quality work.

Sometimes your praise of employee service must be general, as in letter 8, because you do not know who performed the work for you.

Letter 8
A bank director praises a laundry's service by writing to its general manager.

You may be glad to know how much I like your Troy Laundry service on my shirts. Every morning I have a pleased grin as I pull one of your immaculately laundered shirts out of the smooth plastic case. Exactly the way I like it!

For the past dozen years or so I've tried several different laundries. But so far Troy has topped them all. I like the way your employees and machines roll my shirt collars neatly, press the shoulders without a wrinkle, AND sew on buttons whenever they're missing.

Your TV commercials first attracted Troy to me. I'm glad to tell you that I found everything those commercials say is true. Congratulations--and thanks!

Whenever possible, mention the person to be praised by name or identifying number. From time to time you will encounter employees—salespeople, bus drivers, police officers, teachers, clerks, and many others—whose service to you is far beyond the call of duty. A sincere note of praise written to the employee's superior has sometimes brought unexpected benefits to an otherwise unnoticed employee. One of many true stories with a happy ending began when an airline passenger wrote a letter to the company president praising an employee (Paul) who had traveled 26 miles in his own car and at his own expense to get medical care for a traveler sick in a Hawaiian town. The president showed the letter to the vice president, who wrote the employee a message of praise (Letter 9); and less than four months later Paul received a long-hoped-for promotion. Though his advancement was no doubt earned through years of good work, Paul felt that a letter such as the one the passenger wrote first brought him to the attention of management.

Letter 9
Letter of praise from an airline executive vice president to an employee.

Attached is a copy of a letter President Jack Doe has just received which is indicative of the unusually fine job you are doing for us in (name of town). There is no question but that you made a lifelong friend for Hawaiian Airlines.

Congratulations on a job well done!

I am requesting Bob Cann to make this letter a part of your permanent personnel file.

Expressing Appreciation

Everyone likes to know that his or her efforts are appreciated. Throughout your life you will have numerous occasions to express appreciation and thanks. As a business executive, you can express appreciation to customers, suppliers, employees, stockholders, and to many others whose activities relate to your business. Likewise, away from the office, you will also have many opportunities to send such personal goodwill messages. Some of these messages will pertain to favors extended repeatedly over a period of time; others will thank for one-time kindnesses.

Appreciation for Favors Extended over a Period of Time

When you write to established customers, you can express appreciation for their patronage, for prompt payment of bills, for recommending your firm to friends, or for other courtesies. Some of these messages may become part of your regular company policy; others will be written individually as the occasions arise. Often these thank-you letters contain words of praise, as in letter 1 below; sometimes they also include a small gift or a special privilege, as in letter 2.

Letter 1
A personalized form letter, individually typed, expressing appreciation for a prompt-pay record (sent once to each customer after a three-year good record).

Thank you, Miss Albrecht,

for the fine manner in which you have paid your bills year after year.

Such a customer as you, because of your spotless paying record, seldom hears from our credit department. But the manner in which you have handled your MacDougall account has often been noticed and appreciated. It has also established for you a credit record of which you may be justly proud.

We are pleased to have you as a MacDougall customer, and thank you sincerely for your splendid cooperation.

Letter 2
A computerized, personalized form letter sending appreciation and a lifetime privilege to a preferred credit customer.

We sincerely appreciate how promptly you have paid your (company name) account each month. Most certainly you can be proud of the excellent credit record you have established, Mr. Juntwait.

In appreciation to a preferred customer, your new credit card is now good for life!! Your card no longer carries an expiration date and is your companion for any purchases you make at (store) for the rest of your life.

Your card will be replaced about every two years. This will enable
us to update the number of years shown on your card. Also, it will
assure that your card remains clean, fresh, and attractive.

I hope you like your new card and that we may have the privilege of
serving you for a lifetime.

Though messages such as letters 1 and 2 are usually personalized form letters—with
matching insertion of the customer's name and address—some large companies have
found it desirable to send printed thanks, as in letter 3. Customers usually appreciate
even a printed message—unless the same message arrives every month for six months,
tucked in with the monthly statement (as it did for customers of one firm).

Letter 3
*A manufacturer's thanks for patronage—printed on special letterhead showing two
hands clasped and the word "THANKS" at the top in red.*

Too often in the rush of business life, we forget to say "THANK YOU"
so that you can hear it, but you can be sure we always appreciate
your patronage. It is our constant aim to please and satisfy you
more each time.

Serving you is a real privilege and we are grateful for your confidence in us. Anytime we can be of service to you in any way, just
pick up the phone and call us collect at (209) 887-6499.

Some favors require special notes planned for the situation, as letter 4 illustrates:

Letter 4
*A shop owner's personal thank-you to a customer who has recommended the shop
to friends.*

Yesterday, when Mrs. A. R. Wright visited us upon your recommendation,
I was very much pleased--both because she had come in and because you
like our shop well enough to recommend it to your friends.

You will be interested in knowing that so far nine members of your
Art Guild have become our steady customers. All of them mentioned
that you had recommended us and they respect your judgment.

Thank you, Mrs. Gunnerson, for your confidence in The Boutique and
its services. We will always try to do our best to give you the
service you expect.

Also, it is good for every successful person to express gratitude to the individuals—
perhaps a relative, coach, scout leader, teacher, or former employer—who have contributed something memorable to his or her life—especially if (as in letter 5) years have
passed since they met.

Letter 5
A professional person thanks a former Army officer.

Eight years ago, a young 1st lieutenant at Fort Ord, California,
went out of his way to arrange transportation for a young staff

sergeant who worked in his Section. The transportation was for a
unique purpose--not for a pleasure trip or for official duty, but
for an education.

Mr. Watters, I want you to know that the favors you did for me have
had a great influence on my life. At the time you arranged for a
jeep for my use in attending high school classes at Palo Alto, I
thought it just another ordinary event in my life. Never did I
dream that those twice weekly rides would become my first route on
the road to higher education. The diploma I received was the ticket
I needed for admission to college. However, I needed more than that.
I needed someone to encourage me and show me the benefits that a
college education would give to me. You were persistently trying to
convince me of this value during my last days of duty. And though
your work was filled with pressure and tension, you always managed
to remain calm and ready to cheer me on.

You helped me in so many ways; I'm deeply grateful to you. You'll
be glad to know that your wise words didn't go unheeded. I graduated
from the University of (state) last June and am now in my last year
of Medical School. Thank you for starting me on the road to a better
education. I hope some day to help other youngsters the way you
helped me.

Such thank-you messages are an appreciated surprise to their recipients, as the follow-ing typically sentimental excerpts from replies indicate:

(From the president of a publishing company) . . . I am most grateful to you for your delightful, thoroughly human letter. . . . It really brightened a rainy and over-cast day!

(From a retired teacher) . . . I can't tell you how much your letter meant to me. I'm in my 80s now, lonely, living alone in a small apartment, cooking my own meals. Though I taught school for 47 years, yours is the first note of appreciation I ever re-ceived. It came on a blue cold morning and it cheered me as nothing has in many years.

(From a former employer) . . . Your letter was so touching that as I read it tears of gratitude fell from my eyes. . . . You could not guess how much your words have warmed my spirit. I have been walking around in the glow of them all day long.

Letters of appreciation are also due to people who have spent many hours on a worthy cause—like serving on committees, soliciting funds, or helping with an election campaign. To save expenses, a form letter similar to letter 6 is acceptable.

Letter 6
A successful candidate thanks volunteer assistants.

Dear Mrs. Tomkins:[1]

During the city campaign just closed several hundred public spirited
citizens gave of their time and personal service to do the necessary

---

[1] Instead of a personalized salutation, as in letter 6, a general salutation such as "Dear (commit-tee name) Member" could be used to further save time and expense.

mailing, telephoning, and campaigning which played so vital a part in the election. It is to you, one of these loyal workers, I want to express my sincere appreciation.

The fine work accomplished and the effort which no money can buy, come only from those who feel, as I do, a sense of responsibility for decent city government. I honestly believe that without the many tasks carried out by your committee the result would have been different.

Again I thank you for your part in the campaign and give you my sincere promise that I will do everything in my power to carry on in this city the kind of government for which you worked so diligently.

Thanks for One-Time Favors and Kindnesses

Thanking people promptly for any significant one-time courtesy is desirable for a successful business or professional person, as well as for everyone else with good manners. Whenever possible, a thank-you message should go to the person who: gives a speech without honorarium; writes a letter of recommendation for you; helps you win an honor or award; grants an informative lengthy interview; sends you a letter of praise or criticism about you, your business, employees, or others in whom you are interested; donates money, gifts, or awards. Some firms even thank new customers for a first purchase or first use of a new charge account.

Of course, circumstances will govern the length and content of these thank-you notes, which may range from a few sentences to several paragraphs. Letters 7 through 11 are thank-you messages which thoughtful, courteous businessmen and women have written on various occasions.

Letter 7
A program chairman thanks a popular speaker—in an unusual, but gracious and sincere, letter.

At the risk of contradicting the general theme of your talk on "The Freedom of Movement" at the Uptown Business Luncheon meeting last Thursday, may I say that you made captives of all of us.

Believe me, I did not--after noting what was a record attendance for our meeting--speak lightly when I told you that your reputation as a speaker, a scholar, and, above all, a charming guest of honor had preceded you.

I cannot resist adding, with all due apologies to Shaw--"What really flatters a man is that you think him worth flattering." On this point, certainly--and I speak with confidence for the club members and and our guests--there is not the shadow of a doubt.

We hope that your future will provide some respite from hard work and that you will be free to join us again. Thank you so very much.

When a customer compliments your firm or employees by letter, you should acknowledge the praise by writing a note similar to letter 8. Also acknowledge criticisms, as letter 9 does. A short message is usually sufficient (unless some explanation is necessary), and even a postcard acknowledgment is better than silence. A large, nationally known publishing firm, for instance, sends a card labeled "Post-o-gram" with this mimeographed message: "We appreciate your comments on (name of book) and the interest which prompted you to write. If we may serve you any time in the future, please let us know."

Letter 8
A company president thanks a customer for her complimentary letter about an employee.

Thank you very much for your warm and cordial letter of August 29. It is really a pleasure, upon opening the morning mail, to find a letter like yours.

Nothing gratifies me more than to learn that the efforts of our employees are so thoroughly appreciated. Many people are quick to write criticisms, but seldom does anyone take the time to say something nice. So it is always pleasing to hear from the many, many people who are satisfied.

We will do our best to continue to provide you with the service you like.

Letter 9
A passenger traffic manager thanks a passenger for a criticism.

Thank you for taking a few moments of your valuable time to fill out the comment card while a recent coach passenger on our (name of carrier) December 18.

We are sorry to learn of your disappointment in your recent trip. In this connection, we have referred your comments to the Supervisory Officer for his information, investigation, and correction.

Giving you prompt, courteous service on every trip is our constant aim. We look forward to serving you many times in the future.

For thank-you messages that acknowledge money donations, the explanation section usually should include a few details telling the success of the campaign or how the funds are being used, so that the donors will feel good about having contributed. If you are an officer in an organization that must solicit donations year after year, appreciative messages similar to Letters 10 and 11 may well serve as incentives for future donations.

Letter (memo) 10
A plant manager thanks employees for generous contributions.

```
TO:       All employees
FROM:     John Mains, Manager, Plant 2
SUBJECT:  Plant 2 UGN Contributions 197_
```

On behalf of the United Good Neighbor Fund I thank all of you who so generously contributed to our UGN campaign.

This year, our Plant had approximately the same number of contributors

as last year, but a <u>21%</u> increase in contributions! Our Company goal
was a 9% increase. Obviously we have substantially exceeded that
amount.

Thanks again for your strong support at a time when it is needed more
than ever.

Letter 11
The president of a civic charity board thanks donors.

THANK YOU!   THANK YOU!   THANK YOU!

Words cannot adequately express our deep appreciation for the gift
you sent in response to our Christmas letter for the poor. Because
of kindhearted friends like you . . .

>   Many hungry fathers, mothers, little children have
>   enjoyed a special Christmas dinner. Surely they
>   are thinking "THANK YOU."

>   And the shabbily dressed--as they left with a "change
>   of clothing" bundle under arm. Surely they are
>   thinking "THANK YOU."

>   And the children--if you could have heard their cheers
>   of joy as they opened their packages. Surely they
>   are thinking "THANK YOU."

They are all grateful there are "people who care." Thank you for
your generosity and thoughtfulness. You can take satisfaction in
knowing that your contributions have helped bring happiness to these
deserving people.

Extending Seasonal Greetings

If appropriate, you can send a seasonal message to customers (or others) near any special holiday—New Year, Valentine's Day, St. Patrick's Day, Easter, Memorial Day,
Independence Day, Thanksgiving, Christmas—or any other season that may be meaningful to your recipients. The main purpose of these messages is to extend season's
greetings and good wishes, although they often also express appreciation. Sometimes a
small gift—calendar, ornament, picture—accompanies them. In any case, the message
should preferably be unique for your type of business as well as the season, and appropriately different from others the reader may receive during that season.

Because most companies choose the Christmas and New Year holidays for their
seasonal greetings, this section focuses on these messages. Of course, if the type of
product or service your firm sells can be appropriately linked with any other special
day, greetings sent then will have less competition and probably receive more attention.

Often, originality in special letterhead designs—symbolic of both the firm's business
and the season—adds to the effectiveness of the message. For example, the president of
a popular firm that sells heating products has his firm's greetings multilithed on a folding card which pictures on the front an attractive etching of a historical fireplace (different each year and suitable for framing). The greetings also include a brief story
about that particular fireplace; his complimentary closing is "Warmly."

If a firm operates internationally, a different nation's Christmas custom could be featured each year in the season's greetings. Or if a firm's customers are concentrated in a geographic area where a certain nationality predominates, the greeting might be tied in with an appropriate national tradition. For instance, a bank's public relations manager sent the following message (individually typewritten in green) on a Christmas letterhead picturing a lighted candle in a holder.

Message 1
A Christmas greeting and gift linked to a pleasant custom.

Lighting candles on Christmas Eve is another of those old Scandinavian customs like smorgasbord dinners. The legend says that these candles must not be made or purchased for the occasion, but that they must be a gift from friends--or the flame will not burn brightly.

In tomorrow's mail you will receive a candle from us--to carry on that friendly tradition. Along with it go our best wishes.

All of us here--your staff and directors in the (name) bank--say "thank you" for your continued patronage. It adds to our Christmas cheer to know that we have loyal friends like you.

We all wish you a warm and happy Christmas and an interesting New Year in 197_.

Though individually addressed and personally signed messages are ideal, most business firms find it necessary—because of volume and expense—to send undisguised form messages. Many send conventional Christmas or New Year greeting cards signed by a facsimile of an officer's handwriting. Some have the entire message written (and processed) in an executive's handwriting on specially designed colorful Christmas letterheads. If space allows, you can have all officers—sometimes even all employees—personally sign your organization's greetings, as in message 2. Another interesting alternative is to include individual pictures of all employees, as in message 3, which can help customers become acquainted with the employees.

Message 2
A form-letter Christmas greeting signed by all 21 employees (message is typewritten on green and gold paper bordered with colorful holly, bells, and ornaments).

TO OUR FRIENDS:

SEASON'S GREETINGS

There are days for sending merchandise
        And days to send a bill
But this one day of all the year
        We send you just GOODWILL!

Yes, it is Christmas-time again. We want to take this opportunity to say "Thank You" for all the favors you have shown us . . . and wish you a Very Merry Christmas and a Prosperous New Year.

We've sincerely appreciated the business you have given us in the past, and we'll try mighty hard to merit your continued goodwill in the future.

May you and your family have a wonderful Holiday Season and may the coming year be the happiest of your life. That is our Christmas wish for you.

Message 3

A Christmas form letter surrounded by 1-inch facial pictures and names of 40 employees (message is printed on white paper edged with a star and sketches of the three wise men bearing gifts; at the bottom are the words, "Serving (city name) since 1919.")

One of the real joys of the Holiday Season is the opportunity for the expression of goodwill and the exchange of friendly greetings.

In this spirit of friendship and with sincere appreciation for the pleasant relations we have enjoyed with you, we extend the Season's Greetings and wish you Health and Happiness every day of the New Year . .

Conveying Sympathy

When people suffer a serious misfortune, they may be encouraged by messages of sympathy from business associates as well as from personal friends. Because they pertain to sad or unpleasant circumstances, goodwill letters of this type are much harder to write than those already discussed. However, in times of distress, the recipient may value these messages even more highly than expressions of congratulation or thanks.

You can express condolence to a customer, competitor, colleague, business friend, or employee. The occasion may involve a death, accident, loss of material possessions (such as a business wiped out by fire or flood), sickness, major operation, or other misfortunes that can happen to an individual. Expressions of sympathy can be shown by cards, flowers, attendance at a funeral, offers of tangible help, visits, written messages, or a combination of several. This section concentrates on the individual messages you can write expressing sympathy.

If you are writing for your company and the relationship is purely a business one, your secretary can type the message on letterhead stationery. Otherwise, use your own stationery and write (preferably not type) what you want to convey.

Although you cannot mechanically follow a set outline for expression of sympathy, here are suggestions to consider:

1. Begin with the main idea—sympathy and identification of the problem (such as accident, death, or loss of business).
2. Add only those details, if any, that are desirable for the circumstances. (For example, when writing to a survivor, you might express how much the survivor meant to the deceased.) Make all statements restrained and sincere.
3. Stress the positive—the good characteristics and best contributions of the deceased or ill person (if you knew him)—rather than the negative (pain, suffering, distress).
4. Offer assistance, if appropriate, but don't dwell on details. Perhaps you will offer to lighten a customer's monthly payments, or move a due date forward, or make your warehouse available to a friend whose factory burned down.

Omit such business matters as the amount the customer owes you, how long a debt is past due, or similar subjects which can and should be taken care of in another letter.

5. End on a pleasant, positive reassuring idea, perhaps looking to the future. Below are acceptable messages of condolence.

Message 1
Memo telling employees about the sudden death of a coworker.

```
TO ALL EMPLOYEES:

We are saddened by the death of Thor Bjornsen.  Thor was killed in
a private-plane accident last Friday enroute to a conference.  Funeral
services will be held tomorrow at (name) funeral home, 1111 Broadway
Avenue, at 1:00 p.m.

Thor was one of the finest chaps in the company--always helping
others, especially newcomers.  He was tops in his field and was
generous and kind.  We will all miss him.

Thor's family does not want flowers for him; so arrangements have
been made with the Children's Orthopedic Hospital of (city name)
to receive sums for a memorial fund.  Address contributions to
Thor Bjornsen Memorial, 333 Ridgeway Road, attention of Mrs. Jackson.
Checks are to be made payable to the Children's Orthopedic Hospital.
```

Message 2
A personnel director's condolence to a widowed customer (whose wife he had never met personally).

```
With profound sorrow we have just learned of the death of your wife.

Though there is little one can say or do to lessen the grief that
must be yours, we want you to know the heartfelt sympathy of all
your friends at Boardson's is with you.

We hope that the cherished memories you have of your many years
together will comfort you in the months ahead.
```

Message 3
Sympathy letter to a business friend whose store burned to the ground.

```
Dear Joan

The announcement on television yesterday about the widespread fire
in your buildings distressed us greatly.  I want to convey our
sympathy to you and your employees.

If there's anything that I as an individual can do to help you at
this time, please call me (here at the office:  894-6666, Ext. 562,
or at home:  445-2323 evenings).  Also you're welcome to use (at no
charge, of course), our company's Lander Street warehouse (about
500 sq. feet) to store any materials during your reconstruction
period, and our conference rooms for offices and meeting places as
long as you need them.

All the employees at the (name) Company join me in wishing you a fast
recovery.
```

If Joan were an out-of-town customer with an outstanding balance on her account, the sympathy message might have included an offer like the following to replace part of the second paragraph:

> If we can help you by extending your credit terms and the payment date on your account, just let me know. I'll consider it a privilege to come to your aid to show--even in a small way--how much we appreciate your friendship and business through the years.

Welcoming and/or Offering Favors

Some of the good-news messages discussed in Chapter 7—for instance, those granting credit or acknowledging first orders—include a welcome to the customer; and some grant favors that the customer asked for.[2] Also, many sales letters offer a favor or gift. All those messages are necessary in the daily course of business operations.

In contrast, the welcome and favor-offering letters discussed in this chapter are those "extra" messages that are not absolutely essential but are written mainly to build goodwill. The favors are freely offered, not written in answer to a request or to sell.

Sometimes these welcome messages go to persons who have not yet dealt directly with your firm or perhaps not with your department. Among them are messages you may send to newcomers in a city or state, to new employees in your firm, or to new employees in your firm, or to new "customers" of an organization whose work is related to that of your firm. Notice how letters 1 and 2 focus on the welcome and service, and do not try to sell the reader anything. Letter 3, however, though it welcomes and offers services, is quite obviously an "account catcher"; it is more of a low-pressure sales letter than a strictly goodwill message.

Letter 1
A secretary of state welcomes a new incorporator in the state.

> Your name has been listed as one of the incorporators in a filing just made in my office, and I am pleased to extend a warm welcome to you.
>
> It is a real pleasure to have been of service to you and your fellow incorporators in a matter which reflects your confidence in the continued growth and prosperity of our state.
>
> You have our sincere good wishes that you will find this confidence amply rewarded in the success of your venture.

Letter 2
A hospital pharmacist welcomes each newly admitted patient. (This letter or card could bear the pharmacist's picture. Salutation is personalized.)

> Welcome to (name) Hospital. Although you probably will not see me while you are here, I will be working for you. My function is to

---

[2] For favorable credit and order acknowledgments, see pages 208–215, for favor grants, page 216.

cooperate with your physician and nurses to assure you the best in
drugs and pharmaceutical service. Here at (name) Hospital we take
a personal interest in every patient. We want you to know that we
are here to help ensure your speedy recovery.

Letter 3

*A bank vice president welcomes a Navy officer to the area and offers assistance. (A
low-pressure sales message—quite useful for business, but not strictly a goodwill
message.)*

We understand that you are soon being transferred to the Washington,
D.C., area. It is indeed a pleasure to bid you a warm welcome to
your new duty station, and we should like to help you make the change
as trouble free as possible.

If you contemplate securing quarters before your arrival, let us
know and we will send you a list of Real Estate Agents compiled by
the Chamber of Commerce of Arlington County, Virginia.

Convenient banking facilities established before or immediately on
your arrival help in the transition period. The enclosed map of
Arlington County shows you how close we are to a number of service
installations. The booklet "At Your Service" lists the many ways we
can assist you. The enclosed card of introduction and the reply
envelope are for your use either on your arrival in Arlington—or
before that time, if you wish to establish convenient banking services
before you come.

We look forward to extending you a personal welcome here at (name)
Bank.

To welcome a new customer or to let a once "lost" customer know that renewed
patronage is appreciated, letters 4 and 5, respectively, are acceptable.

Letter 4

*A savings and loan officer welcomes a new savings account customer. (Though para-
graph 2 contains resale material, it does not try to sell the reader on additional
services.)*

It is a pleasure to welcome you to membership in our association.
Many thanks for opening a savings account with First Federal.

Here your savings are safeguarded by careful management, investment
in sound home loans, and insurance of accounts by the Federal
Savings and Loan Insurance Corporation, an agency of the United States
Government. At the same time we maintain ample reserves for the
purpose of meeting withdrawals, should you need all or any part of
your savings; and in addition you earn an above-average dividend on
your savings, compounded semi-annually at the regular rate.

You receive the same personalized services at either of our offices—
the Mountview Savings in the Southside Shopping Center or the downtown office.

Please call on me or any member of our staff when we can be of service
to you. Our telephone number is 543-4444.

Letter 5
A credit manager welcomes back a long-absent customer.

```
The return of a good friend is as happy an occasion in the business
world as it is in one's private life.  Your recent purchase here at
Baylor's was the first to be charged to your account for a consider-
able time . . .
```

```
and we take this opportunity to welcome you again to the Baylor Store.
Thank you for your patronage.
```

```
You can be sure that it is our sincere wish to serve you to your
complete satisfaction.
```

The last example, letter 6, is an offer of a favor at "no charge or obligation" to non-customers and customers. This message, unlike letter 3, contains no direct sales plug for the writer's organization and does not ask the reader to buy or sell stock through the writer's firm. Thus, although the reason for the letter is probably to promote sales eventually, here it is mainly a goodwill message.

Letter 6
A stock brokerage firm's vice president offers a free current report. (A small, printed fill-in form is at the top of the letter; salutation is personalized.)

```
I'd like to offer you a Thompson Fynch service that many of the
investors in (city name) have come to value highly:  the opinion
of our Research Department about any stock listed on the New York
Stock Exchange.  If you'll just write the name of the stock on
the form above and mail it to our Central Information Bureau,
I'll get an up-to-date report from our Research Department back
to you just as promptly as I can.
```

```
Then, if you have any questions about the report, please call me
at (206) 549-2222.  I'll be glad to make an appointment at your
convenience.
```

```
We are pleased to do this, (name), whether you have an account
with us or not.  There is no charge or obligation for this service.
In fact, the only charge you ever pay at Thompson Fynch is the
minimum commission when you buy or sell securities.
```

Showing Continuing Special Concern

Another type of goodwill message shows that you are sincerely interested in maintaining confidence in your firm's goods and services. To demonstrate your concern, you can write various follow-up requests and announcements to customers, stockholders, suppliers, or employees. The purpose of these goodwill messages is to get feedback on products used or returned, to maintain the firm's good image, or to help the customer get the best use from your products which he has already bought.

For example, some firms systematically send messages similar to letter 1 to solicit comments from their product users and maintain quality control.

Letter 1

A manufacturer of outboard motors strengthens goodwill by inviting purchasers' comments. [3]

HOW DO YOU LIKE YOUR EVINRUDE?

A good part of the boating season has slipped past since you bought your motor.

We hope you've had the opportunity to log a lot of pleasant hours with it. We're going to ask a favor of you--a report from you on the "good conduct" of your motor. (Or your frank criticism, if you have any you wish to make.)

For over 60 years our steady aim has been to make the most perfect outboard motors that can be built. We've spent millions on engineering, fine production facilities, and the most rigorous testing any manufacturer can give his products.

But there is one test that really tells how successful we have been. And that is your complete satisfaction, as the owner and user of our product.

Will you please send us your comments? For your convenience, a blue "stamped" envelope is enclosed--and if you like, simply jot your reply on the back of this letter.

Thank you--here's wishing you many seasons of happy boating.

Besides getting comments from present owners of a product, some firms seek to find out—through messages like letter 2—why former owners returned various items.

Letter 2

A department store shows concern for customer desires by inviting comments and reasons for return of merchandise.

Recently you had occasion to return, for a $48.30 refund, an item purchased from (store name). Your opinions regarding that item and our service are valued highly.

We desire to provide an adequate selection of quality merchandise and to see that our sales force is courteous at all times. In this instance we are sorry the product did not fulfill your desires, and we want to be sure that in returning the item you received the same courtesy as when it was purchased.

Will you please jot your comments and suggestions for improvement on the back of this sheet and mail it to us in the enclosed stamped envelope? We will very much appreciate your assistance, for it will enable us to provide the kind of service you like.

If your corporation has a widely dispersed management group and a large number of stockholders, many of whom cannot attend the annual meetings, and you want to exchange viewpoints with these stockholders, you might consider writing a goodwill-building message similar to letter 3. (Each has a personalized salutation.)

[3]Courtesy of Evinrude Motors, Milwaukee, Wisconsin.

Letter 3

The senior officer of a nationwide public utility invites stockholders to have an individual visit with a management representative.[4]

Across the nation in recent years, Bell System management men and women have met with over half a million AT&T share owners like you in their homes and offices for face-to-face discussions of the telephone business. Viewpoints have been exchanged, questions cleared up and in many instances assistance provided on matters of mutual interest.

These informal discussions have benefited our owners and your Company to such an extent that visits with share owners have been made a part of management's responsibility in Bell System Companies.

With over three million share owners we cannot hope to visit them all at once or in a short period of time. So, from month to month and on a random basis, we select a number of share owners to be visited.

We would like very much to visit you. I am arranging, therefore, to have one of our Bell System management representatives in your area get in touch with you in the near future for this purpose.

If your company is planning to expand, a letter similar to letter 4 builds goodwill by letting your customers know you have a continuing concern for their needs and preferences.

Letter 4

A department store invites customers to send suggestions before a planned expansion. (Letter is dated January 2; salutation is "Dear Customer.")

This letter has a double significance. First, of course, we wish to send you and your family our very best wishes for a happy and prosperous New Year. We also want to tell you that we appreciate having you as a customer of (name of store) and we thank you for your patronage.

The second reason for our writing you has to do with our planned expansion of five floors on the present building. Inasmuch as our whole aim in this expansion will be to improve our service and our merchandise, we thought we might ask your advice.

If you have any thoughts regarding the improvement of our business, we would be very grateful if you would pass those thoughts along to us. For instance, there may be some new departments that you would like to see us have or there may be some new types of merchandise that you would like to have us carry. Or again, you may have some thoughts on the improvements of our physical layout, lighting, or customer facilities of any kind.

We are sure that you do have some ideas in this respect; so if you would jot down anything you might think of on the back of this letter and return it at your convenience (in the enclosed envelope), we would appreciate it. After all, we want the new (name) to be your store from top to bottom.

Any comments you send will be welcome and appreciated.

[4]Courtesy of Mr. Charles E. Wampler, formerly vice president and secretary of American Telephone and Telegraph Company, New York, N.Y.

Still another excellent way to show concern for your customers (and others) is by anticipating (hopefully forestalling) complaints. If you discover that your company (or a supplier) has made an error which directly affects customers, you have the opportunity to admit the mistake to everyone who may be affected by it—before any customer finds it necessary to ask for an adjustment. Those who have done this (rather than staying silent hoping only a few people will discover the error) have usually been pleasantly surprised at the loyalty, appreciation, and fairness of their customers.

Among the many examples of the goodwill-building power of announcements made to forestall complaints, two are mentioned below:

1. Following a serious storm a subsidiary of Bell Telephone Company sent an inquiry to customers asking them to name, on an enclosed reply card, the period for which they had no service and to state how many days they wanted the company to deduct from their phone bill. Most customers complimented the firm for its forthright message (and its "excellent emergency action"), and they appreciated but rejected the firm's offer to reduce the phone bill.
2. A candy department manager, upon discovering after Christmas that about 50 out of 200 charge-customer orders for a certain quality gift-box candy had been incorrectly filled with slightly lower-quality candy than ordered and sent to the customers' friends, wrote to all 200 customers offering to send a free replacement. As the store did not know which of the 200 customers had been incorrectly served, the manager invited everyone whose friend had received a gift box with a certain code number at the bottom to ask, on an enclosed reply card, for a free box of the ordered candy; he need not return the original. Although obviously at least 25 percent of the customers could have honestly asked for a replacement, less than 5 percent did so. All others who replied—including those whose friends had received the "wrong" candy—thanked the store, commented on the good quality candy their friend enjoyed, and declined the free offer.

The managers who sent these messages were sure that the small cost of their letter was far outweighed by the resulting goodwill.

In the first paragraph of this type of announcement you frankly admit the mistake and sometimes announce the "good news" adjustment that you will make. The explanation section contains an apology (if it isn't in the opening) plus whatever details are desirable for showing how the error occurred. Like other adjustment-granting letters, this announcement should emphasize positive aspects, and convey a sincere desire to serve the customer correctly, as in letter 5.[5]

Letter 5
The customer service manager of a national oil company announces credit to customers' accounts for an error made by a supplier (completely processed form).

```
Dear (firm name) Credit Card Customer:

We owe you an apology . . . and have credited your account for
$7.83.

The Hot Tray that was shipped to you in response to your recent
order was not the model pictured in the advertising brochure.
This error on the part of the supplier of the hot tray has just
recently been called to our attention.
```

[5] See also the example in Chapter 5, page 100.

Since you did not receive the correct merchandise, we are crediting your account with the total cost of the tray you purchased as
a meaningful way of correcting this error. Please keep your hot
tray as a small gift from (firm name).

If you would still like to receive the advertised hot tray, simply
check the box and sign and mail the enclosed order card.

We will be glad to send the tray to you as soon as possible and
bill you accordingly.

You can always depend on (firm name) for top quality.

In summary, a goodwill letter is one that you don't *have* to send and that doesn't
include a sales pitch or have strings attached. These messages congratulate, thank,
greet, sympathize, welcome, offer favors, or show special concern for the reader—without including any obvious sales material. The message plan is direct—main idea, details,
courteous close.

Exercises

1. Below are two messages about free gifts the companies offer. Is each one truly a
    goodwill message? If not, why not? What do you like or dislike about each one?

    a.

    The Next Issue of (name of free booklet)

    will be mailed on Monday, October 25. The (name of booklet) is sent
    free each month to business firms employing three or more department
    heads.

    Before we address the envelopes for this issue, we want to make sure
    that our mailing list is complete and accurate. On the sheet that
    comes with this letter, you will find reproductions of <u>all</u> the Add-
    ressograph plates we have for members of your staff.

    Please take just a minute to go over the list. Make any corrections
    called for. Cross out the names of people who are no longer there.
    Add the names of members of your staff for whom we don't have plates.

    The (name of booklet) is "different." Each issue is of direct
    interest to supervisors and managers working with people daily.

    Please correct and mail the sheet today--in the enclosed envelope.
    No stamp is needed. You and your associates will then be sure of
    getting (booklet) free throughout the year.

    b.

    We know you will enjoy having this special edition of Pan American's
    197_ color calendar, compliments of (name) Travel Service. We hope
    that it proves to be both useful and convenient in your office.

    This affords us the opportunity to let you know that we appreciate
    the privilege of serving as your travel agent. We thank you for
    your past business and we look forward to hearing from you whenever
    we can assist you with future travel plans in connection with busi-
    ness or pleasure.

We handle all forms of transportation - air, rail, steamship, bus, as well as reservations for hotels, motels and U-drive service. Our daily delivery service to any downtown business office is a time-saver for you and your staff and we want you to feel free to make use of it.

ONE CALL DOES IT ALL! - 333-0020

2. As assistant customer service manager of a national airline, you need to write a letter to accompany a lost sorority pin which you are returning to its owner. The pin had fallen under one of the coach seats on Flight #742 to Chicago, June 29. No one wrote to report this lost pin; thus there has been considerable delay in establishing ownership. You first had to identify the sorority and then the chapter and where it was located, all of which was time-consuming. However, you were eventually successful in learning this traveler's identity through Joanne Jones, President, Alpha Chapter at Texas State College.

Ask the recipient of your letter to sign an attached lost property card and return it to you. Will your reply be a goodwill letter with no strings attached? Or will you include some sales talk and look forward to future business?

3. The following message was sent by the general manager of a hotel to all business executives who had attended a national convention there seven months before. Is this letter a goodwill builder? Why or why not? What improvements can you suggest? (Each letter has a personalized salutation.)

May I take this opportunity to thank you for your patronage to (name) Hotel and all of us here sincerely hope that you enjoyed your visit to (city).

Have you any friends or business associates that might be coming to (state name)? I would appreciate it very much if you would give me their names and addresses on the enclosed card so that I may send them a brochure of our hotel and invite them to stay with us while they are in (state).

The staff of the (hotel name) joins me in looking forward to your future visits with us.

4. A letter similar to the following was mailed by one firm to new parents. In this case the father was a bookkeeper. Comment on the tone and appropriateness of this message. Do you think the parents will like it? Why or why not? What improvements, if any, do you suggest? (Salutation is "Dear Mr. and Mrs. _____."

We're pretty proud, as you know, of the fine service we offer here at the (name) Products Corporation. And we always keep a keen eye out for new people who will contribute to the service our customers have learned to rely on us for, through the years.

That's why we were greatly pleased to hear about a potential book-keeper who might be interested in joining us, say around the year 1998 . . . name of James Ron Doe, Jr.

He's a bit small to be interviewed as yet, but tell him to drop in at his earliest convenience, won't you? We'll be delighted to make his acquaintance.

In the meantime, please accept our heartiest congratulations on the new arrival! We know that he'll grow up to be as fine a man--and bookkeeper!--as his father.

5. Evaluate the following letter; is it candid, sincere, and businesslike, yet also a goodwill builder? Assume the firm is a national manufacturer of calculating machines. Salutation is "Good morning, Mrs. Mardon:"

> We got to thinking about you the other day, and we realized, though it hardly seems believable, that a whole year has whizzed by since we shipped you the two Model XX Comptometers! But the calendar says so, all right, and we are impressed with how time flies.
>
> Now, on this first anniversary of your ownership of the two comptometers, let's just check to make sure they are giving you the service you had expected and paid for. We want you to know we think of you.
>
> Are these machines doing their job, Mrs. Mardon? Do your operators like them? Have any problems with them? Any questions you want answered? Do the machines need a year's checkup?
>
> Just jot down any remarks from your operators or yourself on the enclosed, self-addressed card and shoot it right back to us. We'll gladly help you promptly. And you'll be helping us to maintain the quality you expected when you decided to buy your two Model XX's.

6. Assume that one day six years from now you happen to read, in a professional or business journal, about a former college classmate of yours. She has been chosen to deliver the main address at the next regional convention of a national organization you belong to. You're pleased that she has gained a distinguished reputation as a technical expert in the field—all in the few years since her graduation. Write her an appropriate note of congratulation.

7. As manager of a wholesale hardware firm with customers in three states, you have just heard that Mr. Archie Oltimer will retire next month, after being in business for 45 years and your customer for 15. Mr. Oltimer's store is over 500 miles from your office—in a town not served by an airline—and you have never met him personally. However, his orders have come regularly through the years and his payments have been prompt. Now he has sold his store to a younger man. Write him a sincere message of appreciation.

8. This assignment can be a message you will actually mail. (If your instructor approves, you can hand in your carbon copy and mail the original.) Write a sincere letter of appreciation to one person who has had a profound and lasting good effect on your life. Perhaps he or she encouraged you to stick with a job when you almost quit, helped pay your college expenses, or contributed in any other special way(s) to your well being and achievements.

9. As manager of the foreign department of Your City Bank, write a congratulatory letter to Mr. Paul Mifford, who has just been elected president of Pan Xenia, international business honorary at his college chapter. Assume any other pertinent facts.

10. In the evening paper you read that Miss Adelle Adamson of the Harbor Products Company has been promoted to public relations director of the company. During the past 10 years you have had many business transactions with Harbor Products and most have been through the excellent, courteous service Miss Adamson gave your firm. You consider her one of those career women who has all the qualities needed for management, as well as personal charm. Yet she has been held back;

this is the first time Harbor Products has appointed a woman to an executive position. You personally know of several situations involving thousands of dollars, necessitating delicate yet efficient human relations, that Miss Adamson handled entirely herself, but in each case her "superiors" got the credit and praise. Write your sincere letter of congratulations to her now.

11. You are business manager of the Friedman Jewelry firm, registered jewelers in the American Gem Society. The largest bank in your city has just bought from you 35 of your $150 watches, which the bank will present to its employees who become members of the Quarter Century Club (25-year employees of the bank). The watches will be presented at a banquet two weeks from today. Your jewelry store has agreed to take care of all the service on these watches for one year free of charge. Write a letter of congratulation to be addressed individually to each new Quarter Century Club member, and include whatever goodwill-building material about your store is desirable. Make these people feel welcome to use your services.

12. Assume that you are customer service director for Prescott, Inc., a large manufacturer of silver holloware and flatware. Four times a year the major department stores send your company the names of all the brides who have registered your silver patterns in the stores' bridal registries. The stores also send a copy of the purchases made for each bride. You would now like to send to each bride who has received some of your silver a goodwill letter giving her helpful hints on caring for her silver. You sincerely hope she will get maximum satisfaction from your silver. Go to a nearby jewelry firm or department store and collect the data necessary for giving her helpful hints on cleaning and caring for silver. Remember, your goal is not to sell any more silver. You are just writing a goodwill letter to young brides.

13. You are the public relations officer for the light company in your city. Every four months you receive the names and addresses of people moving into your community. This list specifies whether they are building a house, buying, or renting. In any case you would like them to know that if they have any electrical equipment in their home, you have repairers who will come to service these appliances free of charge for labor. The only charge is for parts. You also want to tell them about your home economist who will make house calls to help the homemaker learn to use electrical applicances in the most efficient manner. This home economist comes equipped with recipes and helpful hints for household management and will answer any questions the homemaker may have. Write a letter explaining your services and the fact that they are complimentary. If you need more information for this letter, check with your city light company for additional details to include.

14. You are manager of a large sporting goods store located in a wealthy suburb of a large city. Many avid weekend hunters come into your shop. Every year you compile a record of names and addresses of customers who purchased shells and hunting equipment during that year. In the past the state game department has published annually a brochure listing the hunting season dates for the coming year. This year, to cut down on expenses, the state has eliminated these brochures, but has sent a complete brochure to all sporting goods stores explaining the regulations and the season dates. You would like to write a letter telling your customers the season dates and explaining to them that you have a complete listing of the regulations posted in your shop if they would like more information.

15. Write (or revise) a goodwill message that relates to one of the following situations.

   a. A Christmas or other seasonal greeting for your company. (Choose a line of business you are familiar with.)
   b. Condolence to the wife or husband of a long-time employee who died.
   c. Message to someone in the hospital because of an automobile accident.
   d. Thanks to a customer for being prompt in making loan payments the last three years. (Assume a bank or savings and loan association.)
   e. A message accompanying a clipping you're sending to a business friend.

16. As customer relations manager of the National Products Company, write a checkup letter to all business executives who have bought one of your machines to be used in their offices. (Assume any machine with which you are familiar.) Your letter is to be mailed one month after a machine is sold—to check on performance and to catch minor annoyances before they become major grievances. You want to make sure the machine is doing a good job for the reader, or you might want to know if the operators have any questions you can help answer. Will you enclose something for easy answering? Make sure your readers understand that your purpose is to help maintain the high standards for which your products have been famous, not to sell more machines.

17. The following letter from an auditor to the office manager of business firms he visited uses a play on words. Do you think the tone is appropriate and the message pleasingly unique? What do you like or dislike about the letter? It is dated December 18 and addressed individually, "Dear Mr. (name)."

   I enjoyed the friendly atmosphere of your office during the brief time I was with you this year. Then your financial statements were done and I was on my way--to another office and another short story.

   With 197_ almost gone it's time again for a statement--this time a personal one in which friendship and goodwill rank high.

   As I look back over my own accounts I know that many things have been left undone. With the end of the calendar period coming near, it's time to stop and credit them to your account.

   I wish to enter my appreciation for the courtesies you and your staff showed me, the pleasure I felt in working with all of you, and the "Thank you" I thought of but might have left unsaid.

   Let me record all these, so my thoughts will be clear, while I send you BEST WISHES for a HAPPY NEW YEAR.

18. You are the public relations director for a company that sells electric food choppers and blenders for home use. Each person who buys one of your blenders is asked to fill out a card telling the serial number of the machine purchased and other pertinent information—address, date, and place of purchase. The computer that you put these cards into sends you back a complete list of people who have taken the time to fill out the card and send it in. You would like to send these people a letter thanking them for registering their blenders. In addition you want to give them a free booklet that includes 10 prize-winning recipes for use with the blender. (The recipes were submitted by other customers to a national contest your firm sponsored recently.) They are not in the booklet each owner receives with the blender.

19. As credit manager of a city department store, write a goodwill form letter that can be sent to customers who are moving out of the city. Among the ideas to include in this letter are: your appreciation of the customer's past patronage, good wishes for happiness in a new home, and a suggestion that your credit card be retained for identification when opening accounts in the new location. You will be glad to answer any credit inquiries. Also, though the customer is no longer in the city, merchandise through your mail-order service is available, even a phone call to your "Personal Shopper" can be used to order goods. Offer to send your store's monthly news sheet about seasonal offerings. Though one of the ideas mentioned here is sales promotion, rather than a strictly goodwill idea, you may want to include it anyway because it is part of your continuing service to the customer.

20. You are public relations manager of a firm that manufactures lighting fixtures. Yesterday you read in *Illuminating News*, a trade journal, that one of your good customers—Patrice O'Leary—has just opened her fifth lighting goods store in Florida this month. The article states that the store is considered the largest and most modern store of its kind in the Southeast, in keeping with the tremendous growth of the area. You recall that eight years ago, when you were credit manager, you first opened Ms. O'Leary's charge account with your factory; she then had only one store. Through the years she has placed increasingly larger orders with your firm and has paid them all promptly. Though your lighting fixtures have had a part in her success, resist the temptation to claim credit yourself or to dwell on the merits of your products. Write Ms. O'Leary a letter of congratulations.

PART 4

REPORTS

15 The What and How of Business Reports

I. MEANING AND CLASSIFICATION OF BUSINESS REPORTS
   A. What Is a Business Report?
   B. How Are Business Reports Classified?
II. PREPARATION BEFORE WRITING REPORTS
   A. Define the Problem and Purpose
   B. Consider Who Will Receive the Report
   C. Determine Ideas to Include
   D. Collect Needed Material
   E. Sort and Interpret Data
   F. Prepare the Final Outline
III. PARTS OF THE REPORT BODY
   A. Introduction—Eleven Elements
   B. Text—All Necessary Explanation
   C. Terminal Section—Summary, Conclusions, Recommendations
IV. ORGANIZATION AND OUTLINE OF REPORT BODY
   A. Plans for Organizing Report Body
   B. Ways to Organize Report Text Section
   C. Methods of Outlining
V. VISUAL AIDS
   A. Headings as Directional Signs
   B. Graphic Materials for Quantitative Data
VI. QUALITIES OF WELL-WRITTEN REPORTS
   A. Completeness and Conciseness
   B. Concreteness, Conviction, Objectivity
   C. Clarity
   D. Consideration and Courtesy
   E. Correctness
VII. EXERCISES

Thousands of modern businesses need various reports to carry on efficient operations. In almost any kind of responsible business job—whether you are a management trainee, a salesperson, an accountant, a junior executive, or a vice president, you may have to write reports. Your communication effectiveness, and often your promotions, is affected by the quality of reports you write.

Three chapters in this text are devoted exclusively to written reports. In addition, as you proceed in your study of reports, you will see how some parts of Chapters 1 through 6 and Appendix B also apply to reports. You may occasionally find a brief review of them helpful, because a sound understanding of the communication process, planning steps, business writing principles, and formats of related business messages is desirable for effective report writing.

This chapter provides a general overview of business reports and suggestions to help you prepare and write the report body. It includes: meaning and classification of business reports; preparation before writing reports; parts of the report body; organization and outline of the report body; visual aids; plus qualities of well-written reports.

Chapter 16 illustrates short, informal reports; and Chapter 17, long, "formal" reports. Chapter 18 includes suggestions for oral reporting.

Meaning and Classification of Business Reports

Because of the wide variety of reports, they can be and have been defined and classified in a variety of ways. This section introduces you to two aspects of business reports—what they are and how they are usually classified in business.

What Is a Business Report?

Although the following statement is only one of many good ways to define a report, it covers adequately the types of reports presented in this book: A business report is an impartial, objective, planned presentation of facts to one or more persons for a specific, significant business purpose. Usually a report pertains to a more complex topic than is covered by the typical one-page factual business letter or memorandum. It requires more attention to organization, visual aids, and other techniques for improving readability. Also, to be impartial and objective a report presents accurate, reliable information logically, without emotional appeals.

Reports travel upward to supervisors and management policymakers; downward and horizontally to those who carry out the work and policies; and outward (outside the firm) to stockholders, customers, the general public, and perhaps to government officials. A report may be written or oral, but most significant reports are written. The report facts may pertain to events, conditions, qualities, progress, results, investigations, or interpretations. They may help the receiver(s) understand a significant business situation; carry out operational or technical assignments; and/or plan procedures, solve problems, and make executive decisions.

How Are Business Reports Classified?

You can classify business reports in at least six different ways—according to:

1. *Frequency of Issue:* . . . whether periodic or special. The periodic report comes out at regular intervals, such as daily, weekly, monthly, or yearly. The special report involves a single occasion or unique situation.
2. *Origin:* . . . whether authorized or voluntary; also whether private or public. You write authorized reports when requested or authorized to do so by another person. The voluntary report you write on your own initiative. The "private" report originates in a private business firm; the "public" report originates in a government, school, or other publicly financed office.
3. *Function:* . . . whether to inform or to analyze. The informational report merely presents the facts and a summary—without analyzing, interpreting, or drawing conclusions or making recommendations. Among the informational reports that have special names are "progress reports."

   The analytical report presents facts, analyzes and interprets them, and makes conclusions as well as recommendations if needed. Some analytical reports have special labels—such as "recommendation report," "proposal," and "justification report."
4. *Subject Matter:* . . . usually in keeping with the department from which the report originates. Examples include: accounting, advertising, collection, credit, engineering, finance, insurance, marketing, operations, personnel, production, and statistical reports.
5. *Formality:* . . . whether formal or informal. Formal reports are generally long[1] and about complex problems. They always include—in addition to the body— some or all of these prefatory and supplemental parts:

   Prefatory parts—cover; title fly; title page; letters of authorization, acceptance, approval, transmittal; acknowledgments; table of contents; table of tables; synopsis, abstract, or summary
   Body—introduction, text, terminal section
   Supplemental parts—appendix, bibliography, index

   Informal reports are generally short,[1] and usually include only the body. Some informal reports, however, may have a title page, transmittal, and appendix.
6. *Type or Appearance:*[2] . . . mainly influenced by report length and formality. Reports **a, b, c,** below are popular types of informal, short reports; **d** is the formal, long report.
   a. *Memorandum report* uses memo format with TO, FROM, SUBJECT, DATE heading; is usually single-spaced, and used within the organization.
   b. *Letter report* uses letter format with letterhead, inside address, salutation, complimentary close, signature area, and reference section; is usually single-spaced; and goes outside the organization.
   c. *Printed report* has printed blank lines and spaces left for the writer to fill in pertinent specific facts and figures. It is used both inside and outside the firm.

---

[1] Meanings of the terms "long" and "short" vary depending upon circumstances, as illustrated in Chapters 16 and 17.

[2] In addition to these types, there is one called the *standardized form report.* It is called "standardized" because the department or company dictates the wording and order of the headings for the purpose of uniformity. Actually this report isn't a type because policy can decree standardization of headings in all types of reports.

    d.   *Formal report* is usually longer than the **a, b, c,** reports above and includes parts other reports don't have. It is used both inside and outside the organization.

You have probably noticed that the various classifications do not place reports into mutually exclusive categories. In fact, one report may be part of all the categories—as, for example: a monthly authorized analytical memo report from the marketing department.

Preparation before Writing Reports

As with letters and memos, you want to consider the planning steps (first discussed in Chapter 3) before you begin to write a report. This planning process is, of course, much more detailed for long, formal reports than for shorter presentations. Nevertheless, for all reports adequate preparation *before* writing involves *six important steps* regarding purpose, reader, ideas to include, facts to collect, interpretation, and organization.

Define the Problem and Purpose

The first planning step is to analyze the problem involved and know the purpose of your report. Ask questions like "WHAT is wanted?" "HOW MUCH?" "WHY?" "WHEN?" The answers will help you determine your problem, purpose, scope, and limitations (in time and perhaps funds).

The central purpose of many business reports often is to help the receiver solve a problem and/or make a decision. For example, if your firm is experiencing too great a turnover of employees, that's a problem. The purpose of the report may be to find out what causes the high turnover and—better yet—how to keep the employees after they have been hired. Your scope might include surveying all employees or a random sample; you might also need to find out how other firms have solved similar problems. Or, in other reports, your problem may be concerned with an investment and a choice between two or more methods, machines, or policies. Your questions might be: "Which proposal is better?" "Should we buy, rent, or lease?" "Should we choose X, Y, or Z machines?" and so on.

Consider Who Will Receive the Report

Visualizing your reader and his or her needs is an extremely important step in business report writing. Who wants (or needs) this report? Who will read it? How much detail do they prefer? What is the reader's point of view? Experience? Knowledge? Prejudice? Responsibility? Is the recipient an officer of your firm? Stockholder? Customer? Government official? Will the report be sent to several—or perhaps hundreds—of persons at the same time? Will it be passed on from the primary reader(s) to secondary readers? What are their needs and interests?

If your report goes to, say, your department supervisor, you can use technical terms and abbreviations used in your area. But if it is routed to other departments within your firm—or if it goes to someone outside the firm, your language may have to be nontechnical, with intricate explanations. Also, department heads may want and need a substantial number of facts, figures, and details. On the other hand, top management members may prefer few details and perhaps a one-page summary.

Determine Ideas to Include

In short reports this third step may involve merely writing down the general ideas and topics you'll need to develop in order to accomplish the report's purpose. For some reports, formulating hypotheses is desirable (even essential) as a basis for determining what information you'll need; and then you will jot down the tentative topic headings in a preliminary, tentative outline. In long reports you should formulate a working plan—as discussed in Chapter 17.

Collect Needed Material[3]

From what sources will you get the needed facts and figures? For some reports you may have all the data in your head or nearby records.

For other reports—those requiring a thorough investigation on an enormous problem—collecting material may involve much "leg work" and perhaps both secondary and primary research. A good start may be in company and city libraries. Any publications already in print—books, magazines, newspapers, pamphlets, or government documents—are known as *secondary data*. Some researchers have saved for their company hundreds of hours—and dollars—by avoiding unnecessary duplication of research and reporting because they first consulted already printed materials. *Caution:* Check your sources' reliability carefully; not everything is true just because it is in print! Are the facts unbiased and accurate? Slanted, prejudiced, or incorrect?

To collect *primary data* (that which you "dig up" firsthand from unpublished information), you may use—with permission:

1. Records from your organization's files
2. Original letters, diaries, minutes
3. Questionnaires[4]—mailed, telephone, or taken in person
4. Interviews
5. Personal observations—such as counting cars in a parking lot at different hours of the day or observing mannerisms of individuals as they approach a cashier to pay their bills
6. Experiments—such as comparing two groups in which all factors are the same except your "experimenting" with one variable factor. This method is common in measuring effectiveness of advertising and communication media.

[3] If you need additional details on research methods, see books such as the following which specialize on report writing: Leland Brown, *Effective Business Report Writing*, Prentice-Hall, Inc., Englewood Cliffs, N.J., 1973; Raymond V. Lesikar, *Report Writing for Business*, Richard D. Irwin, Inc., Homewood, Ill., 1969. Both also include bibliographies for further study on business reports and communication. Another extensive bibliography on business and technical writing is in *The Journal of Business Communication*, published by the American Business Communication Association, University of Illinois, Urbana, Ill., Winter 1975, pp. 33–67.

[4] For suggestions on wording questionnaires, see pages 149–150.

Words of advice from experienced researchers and report writers are: Collect all possible data that might be needed. Record your notes on cards or sheets of paper any size you prefer, usually with only one fact or idea on each.

Perhaps you already have your own good system of preparing note cards; that's fine! If you need suggestions, you might find these helpful:

1. At the top of the sheet (or card) place the heading under which the information will be filed. (See your preliminary outline, made in step 3.)
2. Next, write the data source—author, book name, or title of article and magazine name; edition, publisher, city, state, date, page numbers. (In long reports you'll need this information for your bibliography.)
3. Record (with any of your own abbreviations) the facts you need. Decide whether you should quote verbatim, paraphrase, or merely record the gist in your own summary words. When in doubt, write a little more than you'll need— rather than statements so inadequate or vague that you must discard them later.

Sort and Interpret Data

The amount of brain work in this fifth step depends of course on the complexity of your research as determined by purpose and reader needs. In a short, informational report this step may take only a few minutes. In a long, analytical report based on masses of detailed data from many sources, this step may require weeks of study, re-arranging, and analysis between the first sorting and the final interpreting of data. Your analysis and interpretations should of course be objective, free from your own personal bias (if you have any).

If some (or all) of your facts came from questionnaires, you will need to rearrange and analyze the data after you have tabulated the answers. Column after column of figures, perhaps on computer printouts, are meaningful only after they are carefully analyzed so they can be grouped under appropriate headings. *Always* consider what information is most important to the reader and what is not applicable.

Prepare any desirable charts, graphs, and tables (in rough draft) before beginning to write the report (see pages 526–532 for suggestions on graphic aids.)

Now is also the time the reconsider the logic of your hypotheses and whether any main ideas in your original, tentative outline should be revised. Occasionally, after in-vestigating your primary and secondary sources, you may find that some points in your tentative outline are not logical or possible to complete. Conversely, some areas which should have been included in the outline were omitted. And so you now revise, add, and delete topics where necessary.

Prepare the Final Outline

After careful analysis and interpretation, you will make the final outline. But before preparing this important outline, you will need to know what constitutes the report body and consider methods of organizing and outlining. These areas are discussed in the next two sections of this chapter.

Parts of the Report Body

One part that every report has is the body. This part includes (or implies) three sections—introduction, text, and terminal section.

Introduction—Eleven Elements

The purpose of the introduction is to orient the reader toward better understanding the rest of the report. You can include in the introduction any of the following elements if they are helpful to the reader(s) and apply to your report:

Authorization
Problem
Purpose
Scope
Limitations
Methodology
Sources
Background
Definition of terms
Brief statement of the results
Plan of presentation

A brief explanation of the 11 elements follows:

1. *Authorization* tells the name of the person (if any) who asked the writer to tackle the report. If no one did (as in a voluntary report), then this introductory element doesn't appear. But when you do include the authorization, present it in conversational language—such as "as you requested" or "as (name), (title) authorized" rather than stiff language—such as "pursuant to your request."
2. *Problem* is usually defined in the early portion of the introduction. In fact, many introductions begin with the problem and then proceed with the purpose—which is often determined by the problem (see step 1, page 516).
3. *Purpose* is the one element that must appear in every introduction. Furthermore, it is the most important single element because it determines what the writer includes in the report. You must clearly get across to the reader what the purpose is, by a statement like "The purpose of this report is. . . ." Among other names for purpose are: objective, aim, goal, mission, object.
4. *Scope* relates to the boundary of the investigation and hence of the report. If you are finding out by questionnaire what married women customers between 19 and 30 years of age with three or more children think about something— that's your scope or boundary. You don't consider anyone else.
5. *Limitations* refers to limitations such as time, money, research assistance, or available data. Without sounding negative, the writer should mention those factors that precluded further investigation.
6. *Methodology* means the method(s) of collecting information. You might get data by reading library materials, by interviews, by survey, by observation, or by experiment. In production reports, you may need to describe apparatus and materials used for experiments.

7. *Sources*—primary and/or secondary—are all those that furnished information for your report. You may include publications, company records, letters, minutes, documents, interviewees, employees, homeowners, and so forth.

If you are writing an informational report of your own experience, you are your own source you relied on for the statements made in the report. But if you leaned on other sources, you state them. You well know that a fact, figure, or statement is only as good as its source. For this year's population of your city, you don't rely on 1950 or 1960 census when more recent figures are available. Mrs. X, an authority in the field, is much more reliable a source than Mr. Y, who is a novice in the field.

8. *Background* (or history) of the situation being investigated is sometimes included if the reader needs the information to grasp the overall picture. But include only enough of the past so the reader clearly understands the present discussion; emphasis throughout the report should be on the findings or results.

9. *Definition of terms* is sometimes vital. If you use any term that has several possible interpretations, you need to tell the reader the exact meaning you have in mind.

Actually you can define terms three different places within a report—in the introduction, in a glossary at the end of the report, or within the text of the report. The introduction is the best place when you have only a few (say one to three) terms to define and the meaning dominates throughout the entire report. If you have many definitions, a glossary is the best. Defining each word as you develop the text is also quite acceptable—especially when the words don't carry the impact of those defined in the introduction—when the discussion of each word being defined doesn't prevail throughout the whole report.

10. *Statement of the results* in the introduction tells the reader at the beginning the decision—whether or not to buy, which machine is the best, who is your choice of applicant. Then as the reader reads the details in the text, he or she knows how the ideas fit together. This element is appropriate only when the terminal section comes at the end of the body and when revealing the decision before the discussion is psychologically sound.

11. *Plan of presentation* tells the reader in what broad areas (major divisions) the text is developed and the order the topics will be presented. This preview is usually at the end of the introduction; in a one-page report it may be omitted because the reader can see at a glance what the report covers.

Try to include in your introduction all elements that are desirable for giving your reader the orientation needed, but omit all unnecessary elements. If one or more lengthy elements tend to make the introduction disproportionately long, you can take them out of the introduction and place them separately under specific headings or as part of the appendix.

In short reports the few needed elements may be combined into one or two paragraphs with or without the title "Introduction." In some short, periodic reports (especially those covering the same topics every period), you might even omit the introduction if its contents are the same each period and your reader knows them.

For long formal reports the introduction may occupy a full page or several pages, but usually less than one-tenth of the entire report. In these long reports the title "Introduction"—or a meaningful substitute—always precedes this section. Also, subheadings (for example: Purpose, Scope and Need, Background, Methodology, or Plan of Organization) should always be used whenever such guides would be helpful to the reader.

Text—All Necessary Explanation

The longest portion of any report body is the text. In fact, sometimes (in short, routine, periodic reports) the text may be the whole report—if introduction and terminal section are omitted. In this section you discuss and develop the necessary details that help you fulfill the report's purpose. As with all good business writing, include pertinent facts and trim away unessentials. Anything you think your reader will want to see immediately while reading the text should be in this section. Other materials—such as copies of questionnaires, supporting documents, long lists of figures (except for statistical reports), should be in the appendix.

The text is never labeled "Text." Its title may be "Discussion," "Findings," "Data," or other meaningful words. Or, instead of one main title for this section, you may use a series of headings throughout the text, corresponding to the main topics discussed in it. Both Chapters 16 and 17 illustrate various headings for the text portion.

The content, organization, language style, and visual aids of every report should be adapted to the reader's needs. The longer and more complex the content, the greater the need for careful organization, headings, transitional devices, and other qualities that aid in readability. Because these aspects are so important for the entire report as well as for its longest section, the text, they are discussed separately later in this chapter and illustrated in Chapters 16 and 17.

Terminal Section—Summary, Conclusions, Recommendations

Whether the terminal section appears before or after the text, it should be an integral part of the entire report and definitely add to its value. Its functions are to point up the whole report and make its final meaning clear and distinct. This terminal section should be based on the text and should not include new information. This closing merely summarizes, concludes, or recommends.

The terminal section for an informational report is usually called "Summary." For an analytical report, it is usually called "Conclusions" or "Recommendations" (or a combination—such as "Conclusions and Recommendations"). The terminal section is never labeled merely "Terminal Section."

1. *A summary* condenses the text discussion. But it doesn't have to condense the entire text—perhaps only the main points, or strong and weak points, or benefits and disadvantages.
2. *The conclusions* section evaluates facts discussed without including the writer's personal opinion. (Actually it's impossible to completely filter out personal opinion,[5] but you should be careful to make your evaluation only from data in the text. Disregard your own biases or desire for a particular outcome.) A variation of this type could be a forecast, such as an economist might make.
3. *Recommendations* go further and suggest a program of action based on the conclusions. If you make recommendations throughout the report, you will probably summarize them here. (The same is true for conclusions.)

---

[5] Regarding the influence of attitudes, opinions, and emotions, see pages 21-23.

Sometimes an unusual title such as "Benefits" or "Suggested Course of Action" is appropriate for the terminal section. Among other possible titles are: "Probable Developments," "Pertinent Suggestions," "Merits of the Plan," "Final Decision," "Forecast," and "Important Precautions."

Organization and Outline of Report Body

The way a report is organized has a distinct bearing on the manner in which it will be received and acted upon. The report's reader(s), purpose, and subject matter must be considered when you choose the organizational plans for the entire report body and the text section. Then you will need to outline the topics correctly.

Plans for Organizing Report Body

Inductive

The two main ways to organize the three sections of the report body are: logical and psychological. —*deductive*

Logical Arrangement. The words "inductive," "indirect," and "known-to-unknown" highlight the logical organizational plan. It is basically the same indirect plan you have used for bad-news and persuasive-request messages.[6] You present explanation *before* the main idea(s). For reports, the three sections are arranged in this order:

1 Introduction
2 Text (discussion)
3 Terminal Section

When should you choose logical arrangement for a report? In general, you may use this plan if you estimate that your reader:

1. Must have a detailed explanation in order to understand the conclusions and/or recommendations; for example, in scientific and technical reports
2. Is the type who will fight your decision unless he or she is first given complete details and becomes convinced by logical development of facts
3. Will consider your conclusions bad news, because they are contrary to the expected outcome of the study
4. Might feel less bias toward conclusions and be more likely to accept them if first given an analysis of important factors
5. Needs to be encouraged to read the entire report, not just the terminal section . . . and/or
6. Prefers that this report (or all reports) be organized in this order

Psychological Arrangement. The words "deductive" and "direct" briefly describe the psychological organizational plan. It is comparable to the direct plan you used for direct requests and good-news messages.[7] You state the main idea(s) *before* presenting explanation. For reports, the three sections may be arranged in one of these two ways:

[6]See Chapter 3, pages 35–36.
[7]See Chapter 3, page 34.

3 Terminal Section   *1* Introduction
1 Introduction   or   *3* Terminal Section
2 Text (discussion)   *2* Text (discussion)

In a lengthy report readers usually prefer the psychological arrangement because it gives them an overall picture before they delve into the mass of details. If the terminal section *isn't* at the beginning, some readers skip to the end of the report, read the terminal section, and then return to the beginning. Even in the one- or two-page memo report, many business executives prefer the psychological to the logical order. In general, you may (or should) use this plan if your reader:

1. Is a busy executive who wishes to know only what the conclusions are or what action is to be taken, where, and who has the responsibility
2. Prefers to determine quickly whether to scan the text for confirmation of conclusions or recommendations and whether the rest of the report is worth reading
3. Will consider your conclusions good news or neutral information
4. Can better analyze data if conclusions or recommendations are given first
5. Wants the writer's point of view promptly
6. Dislikes suspense and prefers to see the recommended action first so that the discussion then substantiates it . . . and/or
7. Prefers that this report (or all reports) be organized in this order

Ways to Organize Report Text Section

One of the most challenging tasks in report writing is to decide upon the best way to organize the mass of details in the text section. You must make this decision before you prepare the final outline (step 6, page 518) and, of course, before you begin writing the report. You can develop the text in one of the following ways:

1. *By Criteria.* Your topic headings will be the standards, factors, or characteristics—criteria—on which a decision rests. For example, if your report's purpose is to determine whether the firm should buy, rent, or lease trucks; or whether to open a new branch in City X or Y; or which applicant to hire for a management job, and so on, you first decide which criteria are important for the decision. You use them as headings; also you try to determine subtopics (subheads) under them.
2. *By Order of Time.* Programs, agenda, minutes of a meeting or convention, and progress reports or write-ups of an event or a procedure may follow this chronological arrangement.
3. *By Order of Location.* Real estate description of a house, for example, follows this plan. The realtor first describes the outside, then the inside; for the interior first the living room, then the dining room, and so on. This organization is useful for any orderly description focusing on space locations of units—whether they are in a house, factory, office building, shopping center, or international firm with branches widely distributed geographically.
4. *By Order of Importance.* First you present the most important ideas, events, or topics and proceed to the less important points. If all items are of almost equal importance, arrange them by some reasonable plan.
5. *By Order of Familiarity.* Always go from the simple or familiar to the complex

or unfamiliar because the reader can comprehend better what is known than what is not known. Going from the present situation to the proposed also fits into this category.

6. *By Sources.* This method is less desirable unless you are sure your reader is most interested in what each source revealed rather than in the criteria or other important ideas. You can use this way if, for example, you are reporting on prominent experts who spoke at the convention your firm asked you to attend (at company expense). (See for example, pages 559–560, Chapter 16.)

Methods of Outlining

After you have decided how to organize the body and the text, you will arrange the headings and subheads in an outline. A good outline, especially for reports two or more pages long, is an essential tool and a real time-saver. It will become your guide for writing the report. In a long formal report, it also becomes your table of contents.

The outline helps you—before you write the report—to see the relationship between topics, compare proportions and headings, check for loopholes in logical order, and eliminate overlapping. Before you word and set up the headings in your outline, you need to consider types of headings, formats of outlines, and parallelism.

Types of Headings. You can choose from three heading types: topic, sentences, or a variant. Topic headings are the most common. They consist of single words, a few words, or short phrases. Sentence outlines use complete sentences for the headings. A variant of the complete sentence drops the subject and begins with a verb form. Compare these examples of different ways to write one heading:[8]

Topic Headings
  Preparation   *or*   Preparation before Writing

Sentence Headings
  Preparation Is Essential   *or*   A Writer Should Prepare before
  before Writing Reports   Writing Reports

Variant Headings
  Prepare before Writing   *or*   Preparing before Writing

Formats of Outlines. Having chosen your organizational plan and the outline type, you next choose a way to show levels (degrees) for the various items in your outline. For short outlines (of only three or four headings and subheads), you may prefer a format of simple indentations. Longer outlines will be clearer if you use either the traditional popular numeral-letter combination or a decimal system (favored in scientific and some business reports). Compare the formats in the following table for numbering up to five degrees of headings. The numeral-letter system shows five heading degrees by alternating a specific style of numeral and letter: I, A, 1, a, (1). The decimal system shows five heading degrees entirely by numerals—1, 1.1, 1.11, 1.111, 1.1111; an additional digit to the right of the decimal indicates a degree subdivision.

[8]When you have chosen the wording for a particular heading, it should remain the same throughout the report.

Degree of heading	Numeral-letter combination				Decimal system		
1st	I.				1.		
2d		A.			1.1		
3d			1.		1.11		
3d			2.		1.12		
3d			3.		1.13		
2d		B.			1.2		
3d			1.		1.21		
3d			2.		1.22		
4th				a.		1.221	
4th				b.		1.222	
5th				(1)			1.2221
5th				(2)			1.2222
1st	II. etc.				2. etc.		

When arranging your headings and subheads in the report outline, remember these five *important cautions*:

1. Place most important ideas (for instance, your criteria) in the highest degrees of headings possible, considering report length, subject matter, and reader.
2. Try to balance the sections as well as possible. For example, if section I-A, illustrated above, had twelve subheads and section I-B had no subheads, the proportion would be lopsided. You might then try to narrow the scope of heading I-A (by rewording it and by rearranging facts) and broaden I-B.
3. Have at least two subheads if you divide any topic; for example, A-1 and A-2; *never* merely A-1.
4. Use good judgment in the number of headings for readability—neither too many (which could be annoying) nor too few.
5. Never use the report title as a heading or subheading.

Parallelism in Headings. For parallel construction, all headings of the same degree within any part of an outline should be parallel to each other. This means they should have the same grammatical form—all nouns, all phrases, or all clauses (or sentences). For example, in the numeral-letter outline above, the following headings should be parallel to each other: I and II; A and B; 1, 2, and 3 under I-A; 1 and 2 under I-B, and so on. However, note that subheads 1, 2, 3 under I-A need not necessarily be parallel with subheads 1 and 2 under I-B, even though they are all the same (3d) degree. Compare these headings for parallelism:

Not Parallel	Parallel	Parallel
Types of Headings	Types of Headings	Select Heading Types
Choosing Outline Format	Formats of Outlines	Choose Outline Formats
Make Headings Parallel	Parallelism of Headings	Make Headings Parallel

Visual Aids

To help improve both readability and appearance of a report, good writers use headings and—when desirable—also graphic materials. Because of their importance, these visual aids deserve special attention both before and during the actual writing of the report.

Headings as Directional Signs

The headings you have selected for your final outline will be directional signs for the reader of the finished report. Use headings within any report if they will help direct the reader(s) through the entire presentation. Whenever a heading has subheads, always first tell your reader what subheads are included under that heading *before* you discuss them. See, for example, the various transitional introductory sentences and paragraphs used in this chapter (and throughout the text) after all headings that have subheads. Notice the transitions come before the subheads are introduced.

The boxed material on page 527 shows one popular system of placing and typewriting the five degrees of headings you may need for various lengths of reports.[9]

Graphic Materials for Quantitative Data

Whenever you must present numerous figures (quantitative data) or describe a technical process or a procedure, well-planned graphic materials can help give your reader the picture more quickly—and interestingly. Graphic aids (also called visual aids) include tables, charts, graphs, pictograms, maps, pictures, and other display materials. They help you avoid cluttering your paragraphs with masses of figures. They also improve the physical appearance of the report, making it more interesting and inviting. This section suggests ways to correctly present visual aids for quantitative data and then illustrates several popular types.

Essentials for Correct Presentation. The following brief suggestions give you a general overview of essentials for correct presentation of graphic materials in your reports:

1. Usually the best place for each illustration is within the text discussion if it is directly relevant and the reader will need to refer to it while reading the report. Place it as close to the discussion as possible—preferably in the same paragraph or page (or, if it is long, on the immediately following page).

   Two other possible placements are: (a) in the appendix—if the information is only supplemental to the discussion and/or extremely lengthy (as, for instance, a five-page table); (b) in a footnote—if the illustration is small and concerned with the discussion but is not vital to it. This placement is generally not recommended, but it is useful if you feel your reader would rather refer to a small visual aid on the same page than turn to the appendix.

[9]Other styles of placement and typing (or printing) of headings may be acceptable too, but the chosen style must be used consistently throughout the report. If your typewriter has variable type, you may of course choose different type sizes and styles (including italics—with or without underscoring) as printers do.

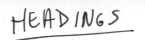

FIRST-DEGREE HEADING

You can use the first-degree heading for a report that requires
three or more degrees of headings. Choose it for the title of a
long report or an article, or for long-report headings of main
sections--introduction, each main division of the text, and
terminal section. It is centered, typed in all capitals, with
or without underscoring. Usually it is preceded and followed by
two blank lines (triple spacing).

Second-degree Heading

If the report requires two or three degrees of headings, you may
choose the second-degree for headings of main sections--introduction,
text (main divisions), terminal section--or for subheads under first-
degree heads. It is centered, with the first letter of each important word capitalized; it may be typed with or without underscoring.[1] Even when a report requires only one or two degrees of
headings, you can use this second-degree heading. Double spacing
before and after it is desirable.

Third-Degree Headings

If you prefer, you can use third-degree headings for a report
that has only one degree of headings. This heading is typewritten just like the second-degree heading except that it is
flush with the left margin. Preferably, underscore this
heading (whenever it is in regular size and style of type).
If a report requires only two degrees of headings, you can use
the second and third degrees or--for a more compact appear-
ance--third and fourth degrees. Double-space before third-
degree headings and either double or single space after them.

   Fourth-Degree Heading. When you need two or more degrees
of heading, you can use the fourth-degree heading. This level
is typewritten just like the second- and third-degree headings
except that it is indented, usually five spaces, from the left
margin and is followed by a period. It is always underscored
if regular type is used. The paragraph begins on the same
line as the heading.

   Fifth-Degree headings consist of merely the underscored
(or italicized) first key word or words of the first sentence
in the paragraph. You use this degree of heading when the
report requires all five degrees or when you started with
third-degree and are using third, fourth, and fifth-degree
headings.

2. Always introduce the reader to the illustration *before* you show it. Emphasize
    the highlights, averages, extremes, or other significant aspects of the illustra-
    tion—whatever is most important for the report you are developing. But don't
    detail all the minute data, for such unnecessary repetition will be boring and
    wasteful of space and reading time.

3. The sentence just before the visual aid may end with words like "as the following table (chart, picture, graph) shows (or illustrates)." If the visual aid is in the appendix, refer to it in the introduction and/or in the text.
4. Normally, do not number small spot tables, charts, graphs, and so forth when they are placed within a paragraph. However, in longer reports if you have several formal illustrations with a large amount of data, these should be numbered —Figure 1, Chart 3, and so forth—and they should have meaningful titles. They can then be included in separate lists of tables and/or charts after the table of contents, for easy reference.
5. Express important figures as simply and meaningfully as possible—perhaps in percentages, ranks, or rounded-off numbers. For example, your reader can more easily compare 3% with 75% (or $8,000 with $200,000) than $8,243.21 with $206,080.25. (If you are multiplying figures, do *not* round off *before* multiplying, for the results may be distorted.)

Following are illustrations and brief explanations of these popular graphic aids: tables, bar graphs, pie charts, line graphs, and pictograms.[10]

Tables. When you need to present quantitative information systematically in rows and columns, use a table. Titles of the rows are usually called "stubs" and titles of the columns are "captions," as marked in the following illustration of a numbered table:

	Captions			
MORTGAGOR'S	1974		1975	
NET EFFECTIVE	PROPERTIES	TOTAL	PROPERTIES	TOTAL
MONTHLY INCOME	ACQUIRED	INSURED	ACQUIRED	INSURED
LESS THAN $300	2.7	2.4	1.3	1.8
$300 TO 399	25.8	19.2	23.7	16.9
400 TO 499	33.3	28.8	34.5	21.9
500 TO 599	20.5	21.8	21.4	25.3
600 TO 699	10.5	13.5	10.8	16.2
700 TO 799	2.5	7.4	4.3	9.4
800 TO 899	3.7	3.6	2.0	4.5
900 TO 999	.2	1.5	1.5	1.9
1,000 TO 1,199	.4	1.2	.5	1.4
1,200 OR MORE	.4	.6	--	.7
TOTAL	100.0	100.0	100.0	100.0

Stubs

Table 3.   BORROWER'S NET EFFECTIVE INCOME

Bar Graphs. Easy to construct and understand, the bar chart is one of the most common and adaptable types of graphic presentation. Though there are several other variations of bar charts, three types you will probably use most often in your reports are the vertical, horizontal, and component bar charts—illustrated here.

Vertical bars are especially useful when a time factor is considered.

[10] The emphasis in this book is on presentation. If you need help in constructing tables, charts, and graphs, you can find detailed chapters in texts devoted entirely to statistics or report writing.

Cash generated by operations
(millions of dollars)

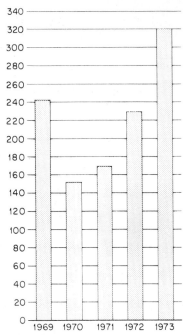

Figure 15-1 Example of a vertical bar graph. Dates are across the bottom scale. Millions of dollars—beginning on zero at the bottom—are up the left column, which helps to determine the height of each bar.

Horizontal bars are adaptable for many uses and several variations, two of which are shown here. Notice that though both graphs have word headings in the left-hand column, they differ in the ways their bar lengths are marked. Figure 15-2 has a bottom scale showing millions of dollars. In contrast, Figure 15-3 has no bottom scale but uses graph paper and shows a figure within or near each bar.

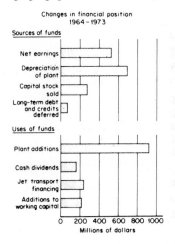

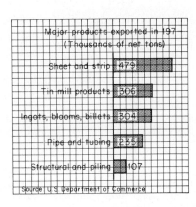

Figure 15-2 Example of a horizontal bar graph.

Figure 15-3 Example of a horizontal bar graph.

For extra clarity, you can have both a bottom scale and figures within the bars. With or without a bottom scale, every bar must be in exact, correct proportion according to a specific scale. Among other variations are showing totals and/or percentages at bar ends or listing these figures in nearby columns.

Component bar graphs, instead of having "solid" bars, have shading or hatching to indicate different data (clearly labeled). Usually the shading is darkest at the bottom (for the vertical bar) or left side (for the horizontal bar).

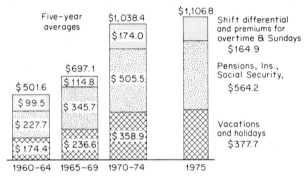

Figure 15-4 Example of a component bar graph. Notice that in this example the dates are across the bottom. The three bars at the left contain figures within the segments (components). The bar at the far right has the figures outside, immediately under the descriptive words. Either way is acceptable.

Pie Charts. When you want to show relative sizes of parts in a whole or group, pie charts are effective.

arranged clockwise w/ largest piece starting at 12 o-clock

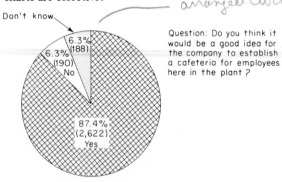

Figure 15-5 Example of a pie chart. To make comparison of facts easier, the pie segments (pieces) should be shown in percentages—and perhaps also raw figures, if useful. Notice that in the pie chart illustrated here the pieces are correctly arranged according to size—clockwise—with the largest piece starting at 12 o'clock; and each is clearly labeled.

Line Graphs. When you want to portray a trend or series of figures covering a large number of time periods, the line graph (page 531) is useful and fairly easy to construct.

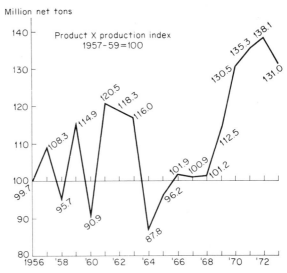

Figure 15-6 Example of a line graph. In a line graph, the time scale is usually across the bottom and the magnitudes are placed near a left-hand vertical line, as in the example shown here. One extra feature of this graph is that the peaks are clearly marked with figures.

Pictograms. You can present the same types of data in pictograms as in horizontal or vertical bar graphs. The main difference is that in the pictogram—instead of using lines to outline the bar rectangles, you insert simple small pictures that represent the data. Depending upon your subject matter, the pictures might be people 🧍 🧍 or moneybags 💰 💰 or houses 🏠 🏠 or any other simple pertinent sketches.

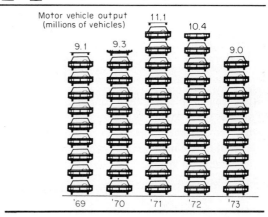

Figure 15-7 Example of a pictogram. As in the pictogram shown here, all units should be identical. Notice that each car represents the same number of units, 1 million vehicles. Pictograms are often used in reports to the general public, annual reports to stockholders, company advertising booklets, and magazine articles because they are interesting and attractive.

Maps and Other Visual Aids. Maps help reveal geographic facts and comparisons. They can show locations of natural resources (as in the map here), company offices, transportation routes, environmental or weather patterns, quantities of products sold in certain areas, and various other data.

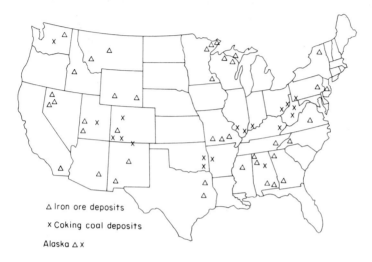

Δ Iron ore deposits

x Coking coal deposits

Alaska Δ x

Figure 15-8 Example of a map showing deposits of two natural resources. This map uses crosses and triangles to mark locations of two products. Other ways to show facts on a map are by use of different colors, shading lines, crosshatching, dots, numbers, or various sketches or pictures.

Among other visual aids that help enliven a report are cut-away drawings (like those showing parts of a machine), organizational charts, flowcharts, and photographs.

Qualities of Well-Written Reports

After you have completed your outline and any needed visual aids (in rough draft), you are ready to write the report. And then—before you transmit it—you'll revise wherever necessary. The way you write the report often determines whether it will be accepted by the management people involved.

Actually, all the business writing principles you studied in Chapters 4 and 5 also apply to reports. Because reports must be objective as well as interesting and because they are generally longer and more complex than letters or memorandums, they require special attention to all areas.

The following checklist summarizes ways to achieve the seven C qualities for good report writing. In addition, you will benefit by reviewing the writing principles (at least the "Checklist of Business Writing Principles" in Chapter 5 and reading "Check Points When You Edit Writing for Business" in Appendix B.

CHECKLIST OF C QUALITIES IN WELL-WRITTEN REPORTS

Completeness and Conciseness

1. *Include—in the body (introduction, text, terminal section) <u>all facts</u> needed to answer both primary and secondary readers' questions rele-vant to report's purpose.*
2. *Cover the <u>what, why, when, where, who, and how</u> whenever appropriate for purpose <u>and reader(s)</u>.*
3. *Give the person who requested the report <u>what he or she wants</u>*—detailed descriptions and figures or mainly highlights with minimum supporting data. (If this person didn't specify, use your good judgment and creative ability to design an effective, complete report.)
4. *Trim the body to essentials that fit purpose and reader requirements. Omit all irrelevant material* even if you devoted many hours (perhaps days) to gathering and preparing it. The busy executive needs a concise story on which to act.
5. *Avoid wordy, trite expressions, unnecessary repetitions, and <u>overuse of prepositional phrases</u>.* Instead of "Analysis <u>of the</u> data shows," write "Data analysis shows." Good business writing averages <u>only one preposi-tional phrase to every 11 words</u>.
6. *Include whatever prefatory and supplemental parts are desirable*, de-pending upon the report's complexity, length, and "formality." <u>Avoid unnecessary overlapping with the report body</u> (as, for instance, in the transmittal letter and the introduction.)

Concreteness, Conviction, Objectivity

1. *Use <u>specific words and figures</u>* ("52%" or "8,100 employees" instead of "many" employees) because they are essential for fair and convincing reports.
2. *Identify information <u>sources</u>* within the introduction, text, and/or ap-pendix. For long, formal reports include documentation. (See pages 612–616.)
3. *To <u>substantiate a source's reliability (if necessary for reader conviction)</u>,* state truthfully (briefly) whether the source is a recognized authority; where, when, how, and under what conditions the person made the quoted statements; and whether they are likely to be biased.
4. *Be sure you yourself are <u>objective in your quotations</u>, paraphrasing, and abstracting.* Do not quote a source out of context nor slant statements with your own intentional bias or opinion. Try to make the abstracted material a fair representation of the whole situation or area from which you abstracted; (See also Chapter 2, pages 17–21 on "Comprehension of Reality.")
5. *Consider carefully <u>the bases for your inferences</u>.* Inform your readers as to what portions of your statements are mere assumptions. Distinguish <u>between verifiable facts, inferences based on facts</u>, and your own assump-tions. (See also Chapter 2, pages 17–21 on "Comprehension of Reality.")
6. *<u>Avoid emotional writing</u>*, with glowing adjectives and adverbs based on your opinions.
7. *Present facts impartially, <u>showing both sides whenever necessary</u>. Don't discolor facts with your personal feelings and prejudices.*
8. *Use concrete nouns <u>as subjects of sentences</u>.* Whenever possible, avoid beginning sentences with abstract, intangible nouns or with expletives (*it* is, *there* are, etc.).

9. *Use mostly active—not passive—verbs.* (Read again the examples on pages 82–84.) Instead of the passive verbs in "An observer was sent around the plant to . . . , and it *was found* that . . . ," use active verbs: "Management *dispatched* an impartial observer to officially record incidents of . . . . He *discovered* that . . . ."

10. *Avoid the subjunctive as much as possible*, because it conveys contrary-to-fact ideas in the reader's mind. Instead of *would, could*, and *might* (all subjunctive), use *will* (future) or *can* and *may* (present tense). For example, instead of "For better product distribution your firm *would need* three branch stores; each *would have* a manager who *would . . . ,*" write: "For better . . . , your firm *needs* three branch stores; each *will* (or *can*) *have* a manager who *can . . . .*"

11. *Write in present tense whenever possible.* Besides using present tense when you refer to the present, use it also when stating a fact that was true in the past and is still true: "The manager informed the trainee that promptness *is* (not *was*) expected." Furthermore, use present—not future—tense when referring to something that seems to be happening in the future but actually exists now:

    a. In the introduction write, "This report *shows* . . ." (not *will show*) because the reader has the completed report before him and whatever you're referring to is present now.

    b. Instead of future tense: "Two years of challenging work *will be* ahead for those who *will enter* this program. They *will spend* six months in each area . . . ." write in the present tense: "Two years of challenging work *are* ahead for those who *enter* the program. They *spend* six months in . . . ."

12. *Base your conclusions (if any) or your summary statements on adequate facts and be sure your written presentation is logical.* Avoid unwarranted, hasty generalizations.

Clarity

1. *Phrase all statements so the reader can easily understand them.* Keep sentences within 17-20 words; paragraphs, 15 typewritten lines maximum. Include a topic sentence for each paragraph.

2. *Include definitions of any technical terms*—in the introduction, text, and/or appendix.

3. *In comparing figures, use percentages, ranks, ratios, or rounded-off figures for easier reader comprehension.* But show exact figures somewhere in the report, perhaps in a table right in the text or the appendix.

4. *Use graphic aids*—charts, graphs, pictures, etc.—whenever they help clarify your presentation of quantitative data.

5. *Discuss a graphic aid briefly (highlights) before you present it.*

6. *Use headings to guide the reader, but be sure your writing is clear and coherent without them.* In the sentence immediately following a heading, do *not* refer to the heading by the word "this" or another pronoun.

7. *Use transitional words and phrases* (such as also, on the other hand, similarly, for example) *to link sentences* and tie ideas together. For a list of transitional words and phrases see page 688.

8. *Use transitional sentences with forward or backward references to link paragraphs or sections.*

    a. A *forward* reference is placed at the end of a paragraph. For example, the last sentence in a paragraph about "Education" might lead to the next paragraph this way: "Thus education of the recent college graduate is important, but so is attitude toward employment."

    b. A *backward* reference sentence can effectively begin a paragraph and serve as both a transition and a topic sentence of that paragraph. In the previous situation, the attitude-toward-employment paragraph could begin with a topic sentence that ties the two paragraphs together like this: "Not only is education an important job qualification for a recent college graduate, but so is his attitude. . . ."

9. *Use introductory, summary or concluding, and transitional paragraphs to tie together sections of a report.*

    a. The *introductory* paragraph of a section serves a section the same way a topic sentence serves a paragraph. If a section has two or more subdivisions, always introduce them to the reader before you discuss them.

    b. A *summary or concluding* paragraph can be effective if a section is quite long—say three or more typewritten pages—but this final paragraph must definitely be helpful to the reader.

    c. A *transitional* paragraph is especially helpful in a very long report—perhaps with 30 or more typewritten pages. You add this paragraph somewhere in the middle of the report body to tell the reader where he is; it tells him what has been covered and what is yet to come.

10. *List and number conclusions or recommendations* if you have more than one.

Consideration and Courtesy

1. *Apply integrity in your research, analysis, interpretation, organization, and presentation of all facts, figures, comments.*

2. *Choose your organizational plan (inductive or deductive) for the most effective reader reaction.*

3. *Organize text topics after considering what will be most meaningful for the reader.* If possible, place favorable aspects before the unfavorable and the simpler ideas before the complex.

4. *Adapt writing style and formality to the reader* by using one of these choices:

    a. *In all memo and letter reports and* in other *informal* reports use the same informal style as in letters and memos—personal pronouns (I, we, you).

    b. *In longer, "formal" reports*—for instance to top company, public, or government officials or to the general public (and sometimes also in reports with controversial subject matter) you can use impersonal style in which you never refer to yourself at all. (But try to avoid overuse of passive verbs and expletives with this style.)

    c. *In a more formal report style*—seldom necessary or desirable in business reports—you might refer to yourself as "the author" and your assistants as "the research staff" or "committee" or a similar title.

5. *Handle disagreeable material tactfully and courteously.* If you know your findings are contrary to the reader's opinions or expectations, you might precede your unfavorable statements by a tactful statement like "Although one might have expected a different outcome, nevertheless . . . ." or "Considering your previous experience, a study of these data leads to an unexpected conclusion. . . ."

6. *Watch your tone and logic,* to establish or reinforce the reader's confidence in you, the writer.
7. *Base your recommendations, if any, on logical conclusions* resulting from the facts presented—and not on emotional appeals. *Omit "sales talk"; depend upon objective presentation* of facts.
8. *Omit your own opinions unless the reader asked for them and you clearly label them.*
9. *Make your report interesting as well as readable* by using topic sentences; headings; and tables, graphs, charts, pictures, or other graphic aids if they will be helpful. Also, occasional questions, pertinent stories, and examples spark interest.
10. *When a decision is close, present in the terminal section both the pros and cons;* list favorable aspects (advantages) before the unfavorable (disadvantages), usually in the same order as in the text discussion.

Correctness

1. *Double check accuracy of all facts, grammar, spelling, parallelism of headings;* relationship of prefatory and supplemental parts (if any) to the text; sentence structures; typing; and mechanics.
2. *Distinguish clearly between facts, opinion, inferences* throughout the text and in the terminal section.
3. *Word your conclusions accurately,* with conservative, unexaggerated statements. If they are based on an estimate, clarify the basis.
4. *Check to see that your report has all the other good qualities* of report language, readability, and objectivity already mentioned in this checklist.
5. *See that report layout is attractive and uncrowded,* with pleasing margins and white space.
6. *In a long report, check for accuracy of all prefatory and supplemental parts* (Chapter 17) as well as of the body.
7. *Include no new material in the terminal section.* It must be based on facts in the discussion section.

Exercises

1. Below is a message with a TO, FROM, SUBJECT, DATE heading. Is it a memo or a memo report? Why? Which organizational plan does this message follow? Evaluate the message as to its organization, tone, and probable effectiveness.

                                          DATE: May 10, 19__

```
TO:        All departments, Aloha Street Office
FROM:      Sally Rand
SUBJECT:   New Procedures for Checking Out Collection Folders
```

A check of the collection file shows that many folders are missing and aren't checked out to anyone; neither are they in the closed file. As a result, we ask your cooperation in solving this problem by following the new procedure outlined below.

Effective this date, all collection folders at the Aloha Street Office will be filed on the first floor in the Safe Deposit Area. Patricia Wallace will assume the responsibility for checking the folders in and out. You can reach her at Extension 222. If you receive no answer on this extension, call any New Accounts person to check out a folder.

Under no circumstances, is any folder to be removed from the file unless Patricia or someone in New Accounts checks it out. If you check out a file and then give it to someone else, it is your responsibility to notify the file clerk that you no longer have the folder. Otherwise, you will be held responsible for returning it to the file.

Please check your department and return any collection folders you are not using. We will appreciate your assistance.

2. Revise the following sentences and paragraphs to make them conform with the suggestions in this text. What principles does each violate?

    a. To have proper accounting control, your organization would need a central receiving department under the direct supervision of the chief accountant. His assistant, a receiving clerk would be responsible for all incoming and outgoing merchandise. At the time of purchase or withdrawal, all purchase orders and warehouse withdrawals would go to the receiving department, so that the clerk could make the proper entry in his ledger. In turn, the clerk would count all incoming and outgoing merchandise and would record it on proper sheets. Only then would he permit delivery to the department intended. By doing so, you would have an up-to-date record of your inventory.

    b. According to Mr. Metz, "two years of interesting work will be ahead for those who will enter the program." Six months will be spent in each of the four areas—plant, traffic, administration, and accounting. In each area, the trainee will become acquainted with the operations by working with an experienced craftsman. Sometime before the six months will be up, the trainee will take over the responsibilities of a line supervisor in that department.

    c. An observer was sent around the plant to investigate possibilities of employee carelessness as the cause for rising utilities. It was observed that many of the drinking fountains were left running continuously. It was also noted that lights were left on by many of the supervisors in offices while they were in the shop. And although not as prevalent, many of the lights are left burning throughout the noon hour. Finally it was observed that even on cold days many of the outside windows in the various departments were left open. Since most of the rooms have thermostats, the heating system is overloaded in trying to maintain constant temperatures.

    d. This corporation adheres to a policy of nonacceptance of gratuities from firms or their representatives with which the company has, has had, or may have business agreements, contractual or otherwise.

    e. The calculation of savings accomplished through absorption of volume is based on converting the increase in realization since the reference period to equivalent personnel.

    f. Production increased during the last quarter because there was less absenteeism, improved working conditions in the laboratory, metal shop, and factory, and equipment was maintained better; also we had more effective quality control procedures.

g. It was found that greater tensile strength was developed under high temperatures.

h. Following the approach outlined in your memo of April 5, the warehouse was surveyed for the availability of space for storage.

i. If you paint the shop in light colors, you can expect the following advantages: (1) reduced lighting costs, (2) increase the productivity, (3) the shop will appear larger. *nonparallel*

3. Assume the paragraph just before the one below discusses the firm's tax difficulties. In each blank space insert a transitional word or phrase from the list on page 688 (or any other source). The words in parentheses guide you toward the intended meanings.

> *Wages.* Labor relations present an even more pressing problem. The cost-of-living index is rising; (result) the company's wage policy may have to be reexamined. It is true that the ABC Amendment permits wage raises to be passed on to the consumer. (contrast) , many branches of the company will not recover the increased costs. The appliance division (instances) would encounter heavy sales resistance. (addition) , management will have to consider the effects of price increases or labor difficulties in an election year. (summary) , negotiations with labor will have to be taken with extreme caution.

4. Evaluate the following report by answering these questions:

a. What improvement can you make in the subject line?

b. Does the introduction orient the reader to the material that follows? Why or why not? What elements do you find in the introduction? Should it have a heading?

c. What is the purpose of the introductory paragraph immediately following the "Discussion" heading? Can you suggest a way to improve it?

d. If the writer had chosen to omit the heading "Discussion" and instead had placed the titles of the three reports as second-degree headings, what change would this choice have required in the introduction? Which setup do you prefer?

e. What degrees of headings does this report have? What degrees would it have if the change suggested in **d** were made?

f. Is the text organized logically or psychologically?

g. Underline all passive verbs. How many do you find?

h. Circle the active verbs. Does the report have more active than passive verbs?

i. Does each paragraph have a topic sentence?

j. Is the terminal section correctly labeled? Does it satisfactorily carry out its function? Why or why not?

k. Can you suggest any other corrections or improvements?

```
TO:        Malcolm Greene                    November 10, 19--

FROM:      Thomas Jones

SUBJECT:   Installment Credit Department Reports

Here is the report you requested concerning reports written by one
commercial bank here in (city).  I interviewed Diana Anderson,
assistant cashier at State National Bank, concerning business reports
used in her organization.  Since you are especially interested in
installment credit, I have limited my discussion to reports prepared
and used by the Installment Credit Department.
```

Discussion

The three types of reports used in this department and discussed in this report are the Inter-office Memorandum Report, Statistical Report, and Memorandum Report for the Credit File.

Statistical Report

The statistical report is compiled monthly by employees of the Installment Credit Department under Miss Anderson's supervision. The report is a statistical presentation of the total loan balance of each of the department's individual accounts. These individual accounts are then divided between punctual and delinquent accounts.

The purpose of a statistical report is to inform the department manager and the branch manager of the quantitative and qualitative aspects of the department's operations. The branch manager consolidates this report into a branch report which she then sends to the divisional manager and ultimately the executive vice-president in charge of operations.

The report is presented in table form to provide quick evaluation of the department's performance. This presentation points up delinquent accounts, which are given closer examination in the inter-office type discussed next. Since statistics are emphasized, little or no discussion is included.

Inter-office Memorandum Report

Miss Anderson or employees in her department write the inter-office memorandum to supply credit information to upper management and any other bank officer concerning any of their installment credit accounts. The upper management reports are the most important and are concerned with delinquent accounts.

Report writing training that all bank officers receive provides standard guidelines for credit appraising. Upper management evaluates the delinquent account credit reports on the basis of the thorough application of these guidelines and the validity of corrective action taken. The standard length is usually one page or less.

Credit File Memorandum Report

The credit file memorandum report is written by any bank officer. Each time a bank officer comes in contact with an installment credit account, he or she makes a report of any new information that has been learned. This report is then included in the account credit file and provides the bank with a more detailed picture of the account. This procedure guards against the possibility of one officer being the sole contact with an account and also enables any other officer to become familiar with that account quickly and easily by reading the credit file.

Although the credit file memorandum becomes part of an account's file, copies of these reports are sometimes sent to other interested bank officers; an example is a person who mentions over lunch that he wishes to organize an employee trust fund. The officer, upon learning this information, then makes a comment on a memorandum-for-credit-file form. A subject line is provided for the account name, and a colume is provided for the date and origin of the report. In the column the bank officer places the date and his or her name, and any persons to recieve copies, in this case the Trust Department.

The comment is entered opposite the date and is usually no longer than one or two lines.

Summary

The three types of reports used in the Installment Credit Department of State National Bank are statistical report, inter-office memorandum report, and memorandum report for the credit file. The statistical report is an operating report to upper management for the department with little or no discussion, while the other two are written reports concerned with individual accounts. The inter-office memorandum is used mostly for delinquent account evaluation for upper management, while the credit file memorandum contains any pertinent information about an account. All three go outside the department, but a copy of the credit file memorandum is retained in the account credit file to build a more complete file.

5. When you evaluate the report below, answer the following questions:

   a. Does the subject line clearly identify the subject of this memo report? If not, how can you improve it?
   b. Why should a writer initial the report?
   c. Does the introduction orient the reader to the material that follows? Why or why not? What elements do you find in this introduction? What improvements can you suggest?
   d. Do you like the three major divisions of the text or would you prefer only two? If two, and they were "Skills Needed" and "Training Needed"–what would be the two subdivisions under "Skills Needed"?
   e. What improvements can you suggest for the format and spacing of the numbered items?
   f. Is the terminal section correctly labeled? If not, what better heading can you suggest?

Date: October 19, 19--

TO: Superintendent, Frances Lasson
FROM: Robert Cummins, High School Placement Counselor
SUBJECT: Communication Skills Audio-Visual Center Needs

On October 10, as you requested, I asked Mrs. Ethyl Holmes, Management Representative of the Audio-Visual Center in (city), what communication skills high school people need to work for her company. This report will give the results.

According to Mrs. Holmes, students need training in both oral and written communication. Even though new workers may not be responsible immediately for writing, their writing skills are considered at the time of employment and during their early days on the job. This is because the Audio-Visual Center generally advances personnel from within the company.

Oral Skills Needed

Since the Audio-Visual Center hires most beginning workers in clerical positions, they must be able to communicate orally in the following ways.

1. Talking and listening on the telephone.

2. Receiving and introducing callers.

3. Working well with many other people.

Even though these are beginning jobs, the employee is responsible for the image of the company and must be able to communicate clearly and tactfully with customers and other employees.

Written Skills Needed

As the beginning worker advances, he or she needs to write more and more. However, even a beginner's duties could include the following.

1. Taking telephone messages.

2. Filling in office forms.

3. Writing routine letters.

4. Addressing envelopes.

If a worker advances to a supervisory position, he or she needs to write periodic evaluation reports on the people in the unit.

Training Needed

The Audio-Visual Center does not have any in-service training or company manual. Therefore, applicants must get their training in school. There are several specific areas that Mrs. Holmes thinks the schools should be teaching.

1. Students should learn correct telephone techniques.

2. Everyone, including young men, should learn to type.

3. Students must learn to write legibly.

4. All future employees should learn to spell correctly and use a dictionary.

5. Schools must teach correct business attitudes.

The last item is perhaps most important. Students must know that regular attendance, punctuality, appropriate dress, and getting along with others are every bit as necessary as their skills.

Conclusions

Teachers cannot assume that students can communicate well; they must teach them to speak, listen, and write. The Audio-Visual Center feels that these are qualifications for even the most basic job.

16 Short Reports

What business executives look for in a report is concise, accurate, unbiased material with appropriate supporting evidence to help them make needed decisions. The preceding chapter can serve as your general guide for good work in planning, organizing, and writing the body of any report, regardless of its length. However, short, informal reports require fewer elements in their introductions, fewer transitional devices for continuity, fewer headings, and a more personal writing style than do long, formal reports.

This chapter begins with a checklist of suggestions for writing short business reports, and then it illustrates those which are most frequently written in business—memorandum reports, printed and standardized reports, letter reports, and other short reports.

CHECKLIST FOR SHORT REPORTS

1. **Subject line.** In a memo report or letter report, identify the subject on the subject line.

2. **Introduction.** Explain the problem (if there is a problem), and clearly state the purpose. Also include other introductory elements that are necessary to orient the reader to the material that follows.

3. **Text.**
   a. Be especially careful to show both sides. Be impartial, eliminate personal feelings and prejudices, and emphasize facts. If you express an opinion, be sure the reader knows it's an opinion and not a fact.
   b. Organize your facts by the logical or psychological plan so that you have logical flow of topics with proper emphasis distributed throughout. You can emphasize an idea by showing more details; placing it in a prominent position; and using mechanical means such as amount of white space, capitalization, underscoring, visual aids, and repetition.
   c. Use headings to guide the reader through the report, but write your sentences and paragraphs so they can stand alone—as if the headings didn't exist.
   d. Use topic sentences for all your paragraphs, and use an introductory paragraph at the beginning of a major section that contains two or more subdivisions.
   e. Apply the seven C writing principles. (For details, see pages 532–536.) Throughout, make your writing easy to read; use understandable words, sentences averaging 17 to 20 words, concrete nouns, few adverbs, few adjectives, and paragraphs whose maximum length doesn't exceed 15 typewritten lines.
      Support your conclusions or recommendations with ample appropriate facts that are up-to-date and accurate.

4. **Terminal section.**
   a. If you have more than one conclusion or recommendation, list and number them. Also you might do the same in a summary, if desirable.
   b. Make certain that your terminal section is an integral part of the report and results logically from the facts already presented in the text. Usually list points in the same order as topics are discussed in the text.
   c. Don't include any new material in this section of the report.
   d. Remember that a summary condenses the text, conclusions evaluate the text, and recommendations offer specific courses of action.

Summary — condenses
conclusion — reevaluates text.
Recommendations — offer specific courses of action.

5. **Appendix.** Put material in the appendix that would clutter up the text. Use material that belongs in the report but isn't vital to the development or presentation of the text.

Memorandum Reports

In a broad sense any memorandum that answers a question with a factual explanation might be called a "report." Yet most of these memos are not the reports with which this chapter is concerned. Those memos that answer questions or inform with good or neutral news or bad news (usually on one page) are included in Chapters 8 and 9. They are organized in the same ways as good- and bad-news letters. Also, most of the directives that pass from business executives to their subordinates are actually various kinds of requests—which can be organized according to either the direct- or the persuasive-request plans (Chapters 7 and 10 respectively).

The memorandum reports covered in this section pertain to somewhat more complex day-to-day business problems. Although memorandum reports and memorandums use the same interoffice stationery (with TO, FROM, SUBJECT, DATE at the top) and although they may all use the logical (indirect) or the psychological (direct) plans, they differ in content and appearance of the message body. True, the borderline between a memo report and a memo is sometimes indistinct; the writer must decide which it is to be. Usually the memo report contains an introduction—stated or implied; a text; and a terminal section, sometimes omitted. Usually it has headings ranging from second- to fifth-degree headings, but not more than two (sometimes three) degrees of headings in any one report.

The examples in this section include both analytical and informational memorandum reports.

Analytical Memorandum Reports

To show you one way of planning, organizing, and writing an analytical memo report, the following discussion begins with a step-by-step analysis of a specific situation. Thereafter other examples illustrate a variety of analytical reports.

Analysis of a Specific Situation. Assume that Gene Mohr, manager of your bank's head office savings department has asked you (assistant manager of the personnel department) to help find a replacement for a teller who is quitting work and moving to another city. You advertised and 15 people applied for the job. After carefully checking their application forms, test scores, and your own interview notes, you narrowed your choice to the five best candidates. Then you wrote to their references for recommendations. After receiving the replies, you have chosen the three best candidates. Your task now is to evaluate each of the three in a memo report to Mr. Mohr. He likes you to analyze the facts for him—even rank the applicants—but he wants to make his own recommendations and decision.

Here are facts about the three applicants:

Helen True:
1 year business college; high school graduate with a 2.9 (out of a possible 4.0) grade-point average; completed in high school an office machines course with a grade of B; typing, 60 words per minute; arithmetic aptitude, excellent; neatly groomed for business appearance; excellent references—"highly dependable, courteous, and honest"; excellent health; 11 years of business experience—all with one company.

Thomas Mace:
High school graduate with a 2.5 GPA; completed in high school an office machines course with a grade of C; typing, 50 wpm; arithmetic aptitude, good; fairly neat and well groomed; good references—"Dependable, tactful"; good health; 6 years of business experience with two different firms; 2 years' military service.

Beth Astor:
1 year at the local 4-year university, with a 3.0 GPA; high school graduate with a 3.3 GPA; completed in high school an office machines course with grade of A; typing, 65 wpm; arithmetic aptitude, excellent; very neat, well groomed; references—"good worker but has difficulty getting along with others"; fair health; three years' business experience with three different firms; attendance irregular in two.

With all these figures facing you, where do you begin? One way is to group these facts under headings representing *criteria* (see item 1, p. 523) you will be using to measure the three people's qualifications. Notice that if you merely group them by their names as in the above list, comparisons are difficult. After some juggling, you decide that all the data fall under the headings of "Education and Skills," "Personal Qualifications,"[1] or "Probable Permanency with Firm." You can now arrange the backgrounds of the three applicants in working tables like the following:

Education and Skills

	True	Mace	Astor
Education	H.S. graduate 1 year business col.	H.S. graduate	H.S. graduate 1 year at university
Grade point	2.9	2.5	3.3 in H.S. 3.0 at university
Arithmetic aptitude	Excellent	Good	Excellent
Typing	60 wpm	50 wpm	65 wpm
High school grade in machines	Grade B	Grade C	Grade A

Personal Qualifications

	True	Mace	Astor
Appearance	Neat and well groomed	Fairly neat; well groomed	Very neat and well groomed
Dependability	Excellent	Good	Fair; but good worker
Compatibility	Excellent	Good	Fair; difficulty working with others

[1]Many times when organizing you have material that doesn't fit exactly anywhere. "Health" is an example of such material. So you organize such material as best you can; in this report it can fit under "Personal Qualifications" or "Permanency with Firm."

Probable Permanency with Firm

Number of jobs	1	2	3
Years of work	11	6 plus 2 military	3
Health	Excellent	Good	Fair
Attendance record	Excellent	Good	Fair (irregular in two firms)

Now you can begin to analyze and interpret the material. Suppose your interpretation results in the following ranks and points for these candidates (assuming you decide to assign 6 points for first place, 4 points for second place, and 2 points for third place):

Criteria	True Rank	Points	Mace Rank	Points	Astor Rank	Points
Education and skills	2d	4	3d	2	1st	6
Personal Qualifications	1st	6	2d	4	3d	2
Probable Permanency	1st	6	2d	4	3d	2
Total scores		16		10		10

From this analysis Helen True wins first place; and although Mace and Astor are tied for second palce in scores, it is obvious that Mace is ahead of Astor in two of three criteria. Thus he wins second place; and Astor, third.

Your next step is to write the report, in rough draft. You know you'll be sending a memo report because that's the form you use between individuals within an organization. And you'll use the logical organizational plan because Mr. Mohr told you once he preferred that plan for all memo reports.

The following discussion assumes you have already studied and interpreted the data in the tables shown above. You decide to leave the first table as it is and to place "Appearance" as the third item in the second table. In the "Probable Permanency" table you decide on these new criteria titles and arrangement order: "Experience" (instead of "Years of work"); "Previous jobs" (instead of "Number of jobs"). You have omitted such items as marital status and ages because the hiring decision is based on other criteria.[2] With that ground work completed, you begin to write—first the subject line, then the introduction, next the major divisions in the text, and finally the terminal section.

The subject line should contain no more than five to seven words, preferably. You decide on "Evaluation of three teller applicants."

For the introduction, the following list shows which of the 11 introductory elements (pages 519–520) you should include in this particular report. (The others are irrelevant.)

[2]Although Title VII of the Civil Rights Act does not specifically mention marital status, this topic is closely related to and often interpreted under sex discrimination. Furthermore, many states have laws that employers may not discriminate against applicants on the basis of marital status, age, or sex preferences.

Element	Comment
Authorization	Mr. Mohr asked you to assume the assignment.
Purpose	To evaluate the three applicants' qualifications for one opening as teller.
Background	You narrowed the applicants from 15 to 3.
Methodology/sources	You used application blanks, test scores, your own interview notes, and recommendations from references.
Plan of presentation	You will develop the text according to the three criteria for a teller.
Brief statement of your decision	Optional. You may tell Mr. Mohr that Mrs. True ranks highest of the three candidates; or wait to tell this only in the terminal sections.

When you put these six or seven elements into words and sentences, you might have an introductory paragraph like one of the following:

```
Here is the report you requested concerning evaluation of candidates
for a suitable replacement for your retiring teller.  On the basis
of company test scores, screening initial applications, my personal
interview with each applicant, and recommendations from references,
3 final candidates have been chosen from 15 who applied.  In evalu-
ating the candidates, primary importance has been placed on (1)
education and skills, (2) personal qualifications, (3) probable
permanency.  On the basis of these considerations, Mrs. True rates the
the highest of the 3 candidates.
```

or (for the reader who fights your decision before reading the text)

```
As you requested, here is the report concerning the evaluation of
candidates for a teller as a replacement for the employee who is
resigning.  Through careful screening of application forms, test
scores, my own interview notes and recommendations from references,
I have selected 3 out of 15 applicants for final consideration.
Mrs. Helen True, Mr. Thomas Mace, and Miss Beth Astor were chosen
on the basis of their teller proficiency, personal qualifications,
and probable permanency of their employment with our bank.
```

For the text you will use three main sections—one for each criterion. You will study each table (which you prepared in rough draft) and analyze the facts. If your reader wants all the details, you will include each exact table or a variation of it within the text. The discussion which follows concentrates on the section labeled "Probable Permanency...." Your procedure for the other two sections will, of course, be similar. What are the most important facts you can pull from the table? Avoid saying in sentence form before or after a table everything that's in the table; that wastes time and is monotonous. After careful thought you might write a paragraph like this to place before the table:

Mrs. Helen True's experience and her previous job responsibilities show a background and future potential for a greater degree of permanence with our organization than either Mr. Mace or Miss Astor. The following table shows that both Mr. Mace and Miss Astor might have a greater tendency to leave since they have less stable past employment records and they do not possess the excellent health that is preferable for the teller work.

After the table you might include comments like these:

Mr. Mace rates as a second choice. His two jobs in 6^3 years and good health are a better record than that for Miss Astor. Also in his favor is the fact that he plans to make a career of working with people.

For the terminal section you have the choice of a summary or conclusions, because Mr. Mohr doesn't want recommendations. Which would he prefer? If you decide on conclusions, you should state an overall evaluation of your preference and number the conclusions. Here, now, is the completed report:

Memo Report 1
A personnel department officer's analytical report to a savings department director

```
              M E M O R A N D U M   (Company name)
                              4
   TO:      Mr. Gene Mohr                DATE:  March 15, 19--

   FROM:    (your name)

   SUBJECT: Evaluation of Three Teller Applicants
   Here is the report you requested concerning the choice of a
   replacement for your teller who is resigning.  On the basis of
   information obtained from applications, test scores, personal
   interviews, and recommendations from references, I feel that
   of the 3 top applicants, Mrs. Helen True best meets the job
   requirements of permanency, education and skills, and basic
   personal qualifications, as discussed below.5
```

[3]Previous chapters in this text have adhered to the Rule of 10 regarding numbers. As discussed in the Appendix, pages 678 to 680, you should write out (with exceptions) numbers one through nine; but beginning with 10 you use the figure. Departing from the Rule of 10, this chapter uses figures in all examples for all numbers—except one. Because of a trend in business toward writing figures for all numbers (unless the number begins the sentence), you can decide for yourself what you prefer and act accordingly—in *in*formal reports and messages.
[4]Usually memos and memo reports don't include the title of the individuals because the people involved know one another and don't need any identification other than the name itself. But you will include titles if company policy so dictates or when the organization is large enough to justify a title for clarification. Also, when you're writing to a superior, it might be wise to include the title.
[5]The introduction for this memo report doesn't require a heading, but the main sections within the text and the terminal section have headings—parallel grammatically. Also all headings and the subject line should be underlined for emphasis.

Mr. Gene Mohr   2   March 15, 19--

Probable Permanency

Mrs. Helen True's experience and her previous job responsibilities show a background and future potential for a greater
degree of permanence with our organization than either Mr.
Mace or Miss Astor. The following table shows that both Mr.
Mace and Miss Astor might have a greater tendency to leave
since they have less stable past employment records and they
do not possess the excellent health that is preferable for
the teller work.

Criteria	Mrs. True	Mrs. Mace	Miss Astor
Experience	11 years	6 years	3 years
Previous jobs	1 firm	2 firms	3 firms
Health	Excellent	Good	Fair
Attendance record	Excellent	Good	Fair (irregular in 2 firms)

Mr. Mace rates as second choice. His 2 jobs in 6 years and
good health are a much better record than that for Miss
Astor. Also in his favor is the fact that he plans to make
a career of working with people.

Education and Skills

On the basis of education and skills, Miss Astor is an outstanding applicant. The table below provides facts in which
Miss Astor ranks consistently higher than the other 2 in
everything--education, aptitude, grades, and skills.

Criteria	Mrs. True	Mr. Mace	Miss Astor
Education	H.S. graduate 1 year busi-ness col.	H.S. graduate	H.S. graduate 1 year at uni-versity 3.3 in H.S.
Grade point	2.9	2.5	3.0 at uni-versity
Arithmetic aptitude	Excellent	Good	Excellent
Typing	60 wpm	50 wpm	65 wpm
H.S. grade in machines	Grade B	Grade C	Grade A

Although Mrs. True's results are not as high as those of
Miss Astor, she shows a more than adequate proficiency in her
skills. She should prove just as efficient and capable as
Miss Astor in a teller's position.

Personal Qualifications

Primarily on the basis of references from past employers,
Mrs. True possesses the personality that best fits the performance and image of the position. As the following table
shows, she is the only applicant of the 3 who has excellent
references with no additional qualifying statements by those
references.

Mr. Gene Mohr   3   March 15, 19--

Criteria	Mrs. True	Mr. Mace	Miss Astor
Dependability	Excellent	Good	Fair; but good worker
Compatibility	Excellent	Good	Fair; difficulty working with others
Appearance	Neat and well groomed	Fairly neat; well groomed	Very neat and well groomed

I am concerned about the references of Miss Astor because of comments of former employers about her ability to get along with her fellow workers.

Conclusions

1. Mrs. Helen True is the best suited to fill your teller vacancy. She rates highest in degree of expected permanence and in personal qualifications for the job. Although her professional ability does not rate highest of the 3 applicants, she ranks second and shows a more than adequate proficiency.

2. Mr. Thomas Mace rates as a good second choice, mainly on the basis of his expected permanence. He also rates second on compatibility. Although he does not rank as high on skills and grades as either of the other 2 applicants, his education and scores indicate he can can perform the job adequately.

3. Because of the questions raised in her references, I feel Miss Beth Astor is definitely in third place among these 3 candidates for this position. Another less desirable factor is her fair health and the uncertainty of her permanency with our organization. Her outstanding professional ability is too greatly outweighed by these 2 factors.

With this memorandum report, Mr. Mohr can quickly glance through the facts and decide whom he should hire.

Two Periodic Reports with Figures. Reports with many figures in the text require special attention for clarity, as the next two examples illustrate.

Memo Report 2
Hard-to-read report with many figures.

TO: Sarah Spade, Vice-president   DATE: November 3, 197_

FROM: Loren Monee, Treasurer

SUBJECT: Treasurer's Savings Analysis Report

The following schedules provide an analysis of the number and balances of the association's savings accounts in groupings of $1,000 for the month of October, 197_. These schedules were obtained

as a supplement report of our regular monthly trial balancing of
savings accounts. The accounts were processed October 23 and 24 and
reflect balances at those dates.

Total savings accounts were 5,098 with balances of approximately
$20,900,000. The average account balance for all classes of savings
accounts is $4,100.

A gain of 504 accounts has been registered since the October 197_
analysis for an increase of 10.97%. Account holders with balances
of $5,000 or more make up 35.79% of our savers. These savers hold
81.58% of the association's total savings dollars. Savers with
balances of $10,000 and over make up 17.65% of our total account
holders and they hold 52.21% of the total dollar value. This compares to 48.78% of one year ago for an increase of 3.43%.

Savings balances have increased $2,341,334 (including the crediting
of $568,850 in dividends) for the 12-month period October 197_
through September 197_. This represents an actual gain of $1,772,484
or 9.55%. Accounts with balances of $1 through $4,999 increased
$53,110 while accounts with balances of $5,000 or more increased
$2,288,224. Accounts in the $5,000 to $5,999 grouping showed an
increase of approximately $500,000 and in the $15,000 to $15,999
category gained $620,679. Savings certificates which have been issued
since January 2, 197_, totaled $4,005,000 or 19.16% of total savings.
New money invested in savings certificates was $1,347,572 (gross
$1,414,572 less withdrawals of $67,000) while transfers from existing
accounts equaled $2,657,428.

As a welcome contrast to Report 2, the following revision not only organizes the
many figures in table format but shows two comparisons—first by number of accounts
and percentages, then by dollar balances. This revision permits the reader to grasp the
data more quickly and more thoroughly. Notice that this monthly analytical report
omits a terminal section, which is actually unnecessary because of the various totals
shown.

Memo Report 3
Revision of Report 2 illustrates effective organization of many figures.

TO: Sarah Spade, Vice-president   DATE: November 3, 197_

FROM: Loren Monee, Treasurer

SUBJECT: Treasurer's Savings Analysis Report--October 197_

The following schedules provide an analysis of the number, percentages, and balances of the association's savings accounts in groupings
of $1,000 for October 197_. These schedules were obtained as a sup-
plement report of our regular monthly trial balancing of savings
accounts. The accounts reflect balances on October 23 and 24.

Comparisons by number of accounts and percentages

Total number of savings accounts	5,098
Gain of accounts since October 197_ (previous year). . . .	504
% of increase in number of accounts	10.97%
% of savers with account balance $5,000 or more	35.79%

```
% of our association's total savings dollars that
   these savers hold. . . . . . . . . . . . . . . . .    81.58%
% of savers with account balances $10,000 or more . . . . .   17.65%
% of our association's total savings dollars that
   these savers hold . . . . . . . . . . . . . . . . .   52.21%
% of increase over last year . . . . . . . . . . . . . .    3.43%
% that savings certificates are of total savings . . . . .   19.16%
% that savings balances increased (actual gain) . . . . .    9.55%
```

Comparisons by dollar balances

```
Total balances of all 5,098 savings accounts . . . . . $20,900,000
Average account balance for all classes of savings
   accounts  . . . . . . . . . . . . . . . . . . . . .   $4,100
Increase in savings balances Oct. 197_
   through Sept. 197_)  . . . . . . . . .   $2,341,334
Dividends included . . . . . . . . . .    $568,850

Actual gain (9.55% minus
   dividends). . . . . . . . . . . . . .   $1,772,484
```

Increase for savings account holders with balance of:
```
$1 - $4,999 . . . . . . . . . . . . . . . . . . . . .  $    53,110
$5,000 or more . . . . . . . . . . . . . . . . . . . .    2,288,224
$5,000 - $5,999 . . . . . . . . . . . . (approximately)    500,000
$15,000 - $15,999 . . . . . . . . . . . . . . . . . .      620,679
Total of savings certificates issued since
Jan. 2, 197_ . . . . . . . . . . . . . . . . . . . . .  $4,005,000
```

New money invested in savings
```
   certificates (gross) . . . . . . . $1,414,572
   Less withdrawals . . . . . . . . .      67,000

Net new money invested in savings
   certificates  . . . . . . . . . $1,347,572

Transfers from existing accounts . . . . . . . . . . .  $2,657,428
```

If you wish to discuss any part of this report with me, please let me know. I'll come to your office at your convenience.

Numerous other analytical periodic reports are written in business. They of course vary widely—in periods covered (daily, weekly, monthly, yearly) as well as in subject matter and purpose.

Justification Reports. Many analytical memorandum reports in business have a special purpose—to justify an expenditure of a change in procedures. Among various reasons for such reports are specific suggestions to help the organization increase profits, save time and money, reduce accidents, reduce employee turnover, and improve customer goodwill. Often these reports are voluntary—written by the suggestion-maker; but sometimes they are authorized (requested) after a thorough study has been made of a suggestion an employee left in a company suggestion box.

Reports 4*a, b,* and *c* show three ways to organize such a report, plans a and b are preferred because they give the busy executive the main ideas (conclusions) first.

a. *Psychological plan:*
   Conclusions before or after the introduction but always before the discussion
b. *Variation of psychological plan–*
   Commonly called "Justification Report"–for top management: Purpose, cost and savings, (sometimes also method of installation–if an intricate system), conclusions, discussion
c. *Logical plan:*
   Introduction, discussion, conclusions

The discussion section in any of these reports usually is 50 percent to 75 percent of the entire body.

Memo Report 4a
Organized by psychological plan

DATE: May 3, 197_

TO: William David, Director, Purchasing

FROM: Joan Swanson, Assistant Manager, Electrical

SUBJECT: Justifying Purchase of Wire-measuring Machine

Conclusions

1. A capital outlay of $200 for a wire-measuring machine will save us $452 gross or $252 net the first year and $2,060 net for the 5-year guarantee period.
2. The machine will save the clerk the cumbersome job of coiling up the wire and also free the customer's time by 10 minutes for each wire purchase.

Introduction[6]

Recently I became aware of a costly procedure in the electrical department--a procedure of hand-measuring wire which we should change because it is costing us about $450 of unnecessary expense each year. In addition to possible dollar savings, this report shows a convenience to both the clerks and the customers with the purchase of a wire-measuring machine manufactured by the Pacific Tool Company.

Possible Savings[7]

In our downtown hardware store we can expect savings in wages and in elimination of losses due to measurement errors after we change from the present hand measurement system to machine measurement of wire. (Similar benefits may be expected for our branch stores, but this report covers only the downtown store.)

Possible Savings on Wages

Presently we are hand-measuring the electrical (copper) wire on a yardstick that is permanently affixed to the counter. I made a random check of 100 purchases and found it takes an average of 15 minutes for one clerk to measure, coil, and price 50 yards of wire. The measuring machine can perform the same job in 5 minutes--a savings of 10 minutes or 1/6 of an hour for every 50 yards of wire.

---

[6]Introduction could also come before the Conclusions. The heading "Introduction" may then be omitted if the introduction is only a paragraph or two."
[7]This section could also be organized without the subheads.

Since business is booming so much that we always have to hire extra
help throughout the year, time saved in measuring means money saved
in wages. We sell an average of 2,000 yards of wire a month or
24,000 yards yearly and clerks' rate of pay is $4 an hour. With
a measuring machine there is a possible savings of $320 in wages,
as shown below:

Estimated time saved: $\frac{24,000}{50} \times \frac{1}{6}$ 80 hours

Estimated savings in wages: 80 x $4 $320 yearly

Possible Savings on Measurements
During the past six months, in my quarterly inventory checkups, I
have found that an average of 50 yards had left the store but was
not accounted for over each 3-month period. This 50-yard loss was
attributed to errors in measurement, although we have had no complaints of short measurement nor reports of excessive measurements.

At 22 cents a foot (or 66 cents a yard) for the wire, we can save
an additional $132, as the following figures show:

50 x 4 (quarters) x .66 = $132 savings realized if we
eliminate shortage loss
by hand measuring

We can realize a total gross savings of $452 ($320 and $132) yearly
with the measuring machine. And because the machine sells for $200
and carries a 5-year guarantee, we can save $252 net the first year
or $2,060 within 5 years ($452 x 5 - $200).

Convenience Factor

In addition to the dollar savings, both the clerks and the customers
will appreciate the convenience factor of the machine. Because the
wire comes in spools of 1,000 yards, the clerks now have difficulty
in hand-measuring less than a whole spool but a large quantity--say
150 yards--of wire. They must measure off 150 yards and then coil
it in some fashion so that it won't tangle and will be easy to carry.

As a contrast, the machine measures wire of all diameters, meters up
to 1,000 yards, and includes 3 parts:

1. A spindle to hold the spool of wire to be measured
2. A meter that measures and prices the wire
3. A spindle to receive and coil the wire that has been
   measured

Thus, this machine will not only eliminate mistakes in measurement
and pricing. It will save the clerk the cumbersome job of coiling
up the wire and also free the customer's time by 10 minutes for each
wire purchase.

Memo Report 4b
Variation of psychological plan

TO: Same as 4a   May 3, 197_

FROM: Same as 4a

SUBJECT: Same as 4a

Purpose

To show the dollar savings and convenience factor with the purchase
of a wire-measuring machine for the electrical department.

<u>Cost and Savings</u>

For a capital outlay of $200 for a wire-measuring machine, we can save an estimated $2,060 in 5 years.

<u>Conclusions</u>

1. Possible savings: $2,060 net for the 5-year guarantee period.
2. Convenience factor: For both clerks and customers.

<u>Discussion</u>

Recently I became aware of a costly procedure in the electrical department. By purchasing a wire-measuring machine manufactured by the Pacific Tool Company, we can save money and at the same time assure convenience to both the clerks and customers.

<u>Possible Savings</u>
(Same as that section in the psychological plan. If two subheads are used, they will be 4th-degree headings.)

<u>Convenience Factor</u>
(Same as that section in the psychological plan.)

Memo Report 4c
Organized by logical plan

TO: Same as 4a   May 3, 197_

FROM: Same as 4a

SUBJECT: Same as 4a <u>or</u> change to noncommittal
                    (See number 1 below)

Recently I became aware of a . . . (same introduction as for psychological plan, but the title "Introduction" is omitted because this section is the first part of the report body.)

<u>Possible Savings</u>

(Same as that section in psychological plan.)

<u>Convenience Factor</u>
(Same as that section in psychological plan.)

<u>Conclusions</u>
(Same as those shown in psychological plan.)

In the introduction for report 4a you let the president know your results—that a wire-measuring machine will save both money and convenience. But suppose you are a management trainee and you're writing to a 65-year-old penny-pinching owner whose usual reply when someone suggests a change that costs money is "We've been doing all right so far; why should I spend more money to buy something new?" When you write to this person (or to any one else who will begin to fight you if the decision given is before the facts), you'll need to change the report in the following ways.

1. You'll need a *noncommittal* subject line:

<u>Cost Comparison of Hand and Machine Wire-measuring Methods</u>

2. You'll need a noncommittal introduction:

```
Recently I became aware of a costly procedure in the Electrical
Department--a procedure of hand-measuring wire.  This report
compares cost and convenience factors of two alternatives--continuing
with the present hand method or buying a wire-measuring machine
manufactured by the Pacific Tool Company.
```

3. Text (same as above)
4. Conclusions (same as above)

With this presentation, you don't indicate the conclusions until the terminal section —until you have given all the facts to the reader.

Informational Memorandum Reports

In contrast to analytical reports, which give conclusions and/or recommendations, informational reports merely present and summarize facts. Obviously, information reports vary widely in content, depending upon the type of business, purpose, topics discussed, and readers' needs. The following examples illustrate three kinds of often-used informational reports; conference reports, progress reports, and monthly reports.

Conference Reports. The subject matter of conference reports ranges from summaries of personal conferences to write-ups of meetings attended by hundreds of persons.

For example, an advertising account executive may write a conference report after every meeting between the agency and a client. Its purpose is to record all decisions made concerning a campaign. A credit or collection manager may make similar reports after conferences with customers. Likewise, many other employees as well as executives may be responsible for writing reports after any significant conferences with individuals or committees. Organizing the text of such reports is usually by topics discussed. Some firms have standardized headings for the often-written reports to assure that the same information or main topics are recorded in all of them.

In a different situation, a company's delegate to an important convention may be asked to present a report to superiors. Its purpose is to inform other management personnel of significant happenings, decisions, or topics discussed. How would you organize the text of such a report? According to the list on pages 523–524, you might choose to organize by order of time, criteria, importance, or sources. In Report 5 the sales manager (who attended the firm's regional conference of sales managers) used a combination of the first three choices. The three main topics and their subtopics serve as guides (or criteria) for planning this particular sales campaign. Items a, b, and c under "Open Houses" are arranged by order of time; and the longest (and probably the most important) topics—"Open Houses" and "Promotional Programs"—come before the "Signing and Identification" heading.

Memo Report 5
A sales manager's report on a regional conference.

TO: Martha Gerbman   DATE: June 5, 197_

FROM: Matt Deaning   SUBJECT: Open Houses and Promotion

cc: Frieda Dinson   Lana Jarvis
       Terry Moran   Erick Brown
       June Donaldson   Pete Mallon
       Bill Campbell   Tyna Green

The following is a report on the items we discussed during our recent meeting in (city) regarding our XL product. The right-hand column lists names of those who were asked to be responsible for the items.

1. Open Houses
   Here is the tentative schedule that was established, subject primarily to availability of dignitaries at the ribbon-cutting ceremony.

   a. Employees' Meeting – Thursday, July 20   Terry Moran
      (1) Families will be invited, and sandwiches and refreshments provided.
      (2) This will provide an opportunity to dry run the tours being conducted on successive days.

   b. Ribbon-cutting Ceremony – Friday, July 31   June Donaldson
      (1) Dignitaries to be invited need to be agreed upon. We generally agreed that, as this occasion presents and exceptional opportunity to publicize the growth of new and nonpolluting industry in our state, as well as an opportunity to gain state and regional publicity for the expanding capabilities of our company in the XL product business, an effort should be made to include those state officials most capable of gaining this type of publicity.
      (2) Additionally, press invitations need to be extended to press releases developed.

   c. Distributor Event – Saturday, August 1   Martha Gerbman
      (1) Begin tour at 10 a.m. followed by lunch at Ritz Plaza Hotel.
      (2) Develop a program to impress upon the distributors our program for XL Product Division.

2. Promotional Programs

   a. The XL product brochure was reviewed and   Frieda Dinson
      relatively minor changes agreed upon. Another draft will be sent to Bill Campbell for approval prior to setting type. Bill Campbell will prepare and forward guarantee

copy to agency. This project is to proceed
as rapidly as possible. The agency will
prepare a list of names for the prefinished
RM product line.

   b. Introduction Brochure
     (1) We agreed that a brochure to familiarize Frieda Dinson
         our customers with the operation of the
         XL will be desirable.
     (2) We agreed that the procedure used for-
         merly in materials showing photographs
         of the various personnel will be a good
         approach. Agency will develop layout.
     (3) Those to be included in this brochure
         will be Tyna Green, Martha Gerbman, Bill
         Campbell, Lana Jarvis, Pete Mallon, Erick
         Brown, and John Raney, the sales secretary.

   c. Advertising and Direct Mail
     (1) A direct mail program directed to   Frieda Dinson
         builders needs to be developed, per-   and
         haps in conjunction with local   Matt Deaning
         distributors.
     (2) We agreed that advertising regions
         should be expanded to cover the entire
         region. This project will be further
         developed.

2. Signing and Identification   Matt Deaning

   a. Unit Signs
        White cardboard unit signs which will
        fold over the top edges of XL products
        displayed will be printed at the Print
        Shop. Design approved was forwarded to
        the Print Shop for production and
        delivery to the plant by June 23.

   b. Property Signs
        Building and property signs were agreed
        on and covered in a separate memo.

In Report 6 the assistant manager organized the conference report by sources, because the division manager was mainly interested in the presentations of the three national experts in the field.

Memo Report 6
An assistant manager's conference report (organized by sources, logically)

TO: Anthony Bloome   DATE: October 2, 197_

FROM: Verna Bennett

SUBJECT: Summary of St. Louis Regional Conference

Here is a brief summary of the St. Louis meeting that I attended
September 30 on coin service at military installations. Because
you are mainly interested in the presentations of John Klinest,

Wardman Jones, and Kathy Cummings, I am focusing this report on
their contributions to this conference.

John Klinest's Presentation

John Klinest conducted our meeting and introduced the subject.
Because of the current situation at military posts, coin service
at these posts will be a problem for years to come. It's important
to improve our service because:

1. The need is there. The present military situation requires
    more coin service.
2. Many of the young men and women on these posts are making
    their first real acquaintance with public telephone service.
    Their opinions of our service now are likely to be lasting.

A series of slides shown by Klinest pointed out that coin conditions
around the country vary from very bad (standing in mud puddles to
use coin kiosks) to very good. The coin center at (name) is so
plush it is used as a reception center for guests.

Wardman Jones' Presentation

Wardman Jones talked about some of the revenue characteristics of
military coin service . . .

(Three paragraphs follow, including itemized facts and figures.)

Kathy Cummings' Presentation

Regarding the traffic considerations, these were enumerated by Kathy
Cummings. She emphasized that . . .

(Two paragraphs follow, highlighting her suggestions.)

Plan of Action

John Klinest recommends the formation of an interdepartmental
district team to evaluate our coin service at (names) and report
their findings to higher management. They will use the attached
checklist.

Progress Reports.[8] As the name implies, progress reports show "progress," accomplishments, or activity for a certain period or stage of a major assignment. The
organizational plan is usually the logical, including topics similar to these:

Introduction (purpose, nature of project)
Description of accomplishments during the reporting period
Unanticipated problems (if any)
Plans for the next reporting period
Summary (overall appraisal of progress to date)

The example below is a general chairperson's progress report to the executive vice
president of the company, which is hosting the first purchasing managers' regional
convention in that city. It uses the logical organization plan.

[8]Progress reports may also be in letter-report format; see pages 568–573.

Memo Report 7
A general chairperson's progress report on convention plans (logical)

TO: Bruce Boyne, Vice President   DATE: November 9, 197_

FROM: Vivian Porte, Convention Chairperson

SUBJECT: Progress report on Purchasing Managers' Convention
January 26, 197_

To keep you informed about the activities of our planning committee
for the first regional purchasing managers' convention to be held in
our city, here is a brief summary of our progress so far. Because
some plans from now on will depend upon funds available and your
preferences, you will also find a few questions on which we will
appreciate your suggestions and approval.

<u>Date, Time, and Place</u>

The Tower Oaks Hotel offices are holding the following reservations
for us:

Date:	Tuesday, January 26, 197_
Informal luncheon:	12:15 - 1:30 Regency Room--for up to 100 persons
Conference rooms:	9:00 - 4:30 Mezzanine rooms 202, 203, 204 each accommodating up to 40 persons plus exhibit tables.

<u>Tentative Program</u>

So that the convention will have an appropriate official opening,
the committee members are delighted that you have agreed to express
the opening welcome--as Executive Vice President of the company
that is sponsoring the convention.

    <u>Keynote Speaker</u>.--You will probably be glad to hear that for
keynoter we can count on having Jonathan Harrison, Vice President
and General Manager of National Products Company. The topic he
has chosen is "The Challenge Ahead for Purchasing Shortage Items."

    <u>Other Participants</u>.--As the attached tentative program (Exhibit
A) shows, we will have ten outstanding business leaders on panel
discussions in the morning and afternoon sessions. A 15-minute
coffee break is planned for 10:30 a.m. and 3 p.m.

<u>Publicity</u>

Our first announcement in newspapers (local and in three states)
will be early in December. One or two other news stories should
appear during January.

If funds allow, we would like to mail two letters to all purchasing
managers in this region, along with a colorful brochure of the
conference program, exhibits, film specials, and evening entertainment for those staying in the city overnight. Exhibit B shows the
planned layout. The ABC Printer has quoted a price of $ for
200 copies and $ for 150 copies.

Estimated Financial Requirements

Exhibit C, attached, is a suggested tentative budget. The estimated total of $ excludes the cost of stationery, typing master copies, and mailing services. Norma Haney has assured me that these expenses can be taken care of through our company's usual supplies and postage budget and need not be itemized here.

We will appreciate any suggestions you may have about our estimated expenses and your approval of the needed funds. Then we can proceed to make the necessary arrangements.

Summary

To date many persons have already assisted our committee with their expressions of preferences and suggestions. We have hotel reservations firm, acceptances from keynote speaker and ten panelists, price quotations on a brochure for mailing, and tentative publicity plans.

You will receive from us a definite program soon after plans are completed and another progress report on December 10. We expect to devote many more hours to planning and writing. After that we can all look forward to an interesting and successful convention.

In the meantime, your preferences regarding publicity brochure, estimated financial needs, and any other suggestions you may have will be sinerely appreciated.

VP:wh
Attachments: Exhibits A, B, C

cc: Susan Rader
     Timothy Blythe

The next progress report example is organized psychologically—with summary first. Notice its unusual typing and placement of headings.

Memo Report 8
A manager's progress report on storage space improvements (psychological)

                                           DATE: April 19, 197_
TO: Annette Smith, Chicago Factory Representative
FROM: Nicolas Lamonter
SUBJECT: Progress report--First Floor Drug Produce Capacity
           Increased by 30% since January 1.

SUMMARY: During the past three months the first floor storage
             space for drug products at South Warehouse has been
             reorganized to provide storage space for 14,000 (Full
             Box value) additional cases of drug products. This ad-
             dition provides maximum storage with a minimum of
             brand blocking.

ACTION   1) The average daily shipment of each brand and size
TAKEN: of drug products was determined.
             2) First floor storage areas were rearranged to con-
                 form with the average daily shipments.

3) All drug product pallet patterns were reviewed and increased in size where possible.

DISCUSSION: A thirty days' supply of drug products is consigned to the Chicago Factory and is stored at South Warehouse. It is desirable to maintain a maximum inventory on the first floor to eliminate the double-handling of stock to the upper floors. In the past, no definite formula was used to determine the amount of each brand which should be stored on the first floor. Unnecessary movement of stock was taking place. Brand blocking made inventory control difficult and sacrificed storage space.

By means of storing a 25-day supply of each brand in designated areas on the first floor, maximum storage has now been obtained with a minimum of "brand blocking." First floor capacity has been increased from 48,000 to 62,000 (Full Box value) cases. Less stock movement is necessary. Inventory control has been simplified. Maximum warehouse height has been utilized.

Monthly Reports. Included in this section are only those informational reports that are written monthly in memorandum report format. (As you know, there are numerous other monthly reports; many are analytical—mentioned in the preceding section; many others are presented on special printed forms—discussed later in this chapter.) When a memorandum report is written each month about the same department and to the same reader(s), an introduction and terminal section are unnecessary. Report 9 keeps the home office informed about certain activities at the branches. The text headings help the reader grasp the main topics quickly and easily. Instead of the signature and typewritten title after the report's last paragraph, Mr. Kay could have initialed or signed his name near his typewritten name after FROM.

Memo Report 9
This monthly memo report—from the branch manager to an official at the home office—does not include an introduction or terminal section.

TO: A. B. Sea   DATE: November 2, 19__

FROM: U. R. Kay

SUBJECT: Branch Activities - October 197_

Personnel Training
1. October 31 marked the midway point of the second phase of the National Bank Offices' training program. Training is progressing satisfactorily and on schedule. With the termination of Pat Harris (Smith), we need to make a slight alteration in the program, but don't expect any delay or postponement of any training. In fact, this termination will advance the training of Mary Jackson and Jean Miller.

Business Development Activity

1. I again contacted Ann Kast, dentist, regarding transfer of funds from National Association of Orthodontists, of which she is national treasurer. She says she has received permission to transfer about $40,000 more to National Bank after January 1. This additional amount brings the total to about $75,000.

2. Although 3 employee vacations and one prolonged illness have disrupted my outside business call activity, I have made it a habit to attempt to converse with every broker, real estate agent, insurance agent, and attorney that comes into the office. Although it is difficult to assess results from the little additional time and effort spent on this form of intra-office business development, numerous phone calls for loan information and a couple of loan commitments were a direct result of this activity.

Customer Comments and Action Taken

1. An unusually high number of customers in October complimented us on the friendly and courteous service of our personnel.

2. I had one serious disagreement with a large savings account customer regarding his reluctance to reimburse National Bank for a check on which payment was stopped, a duplicate issued, both checks cashed by the customer, and both paid by the bank. He blamed National Bank for allowing this situation to happen and condemned our system for not catching this before we received our bank statement. He quizzed Helen Hunt unmercifully until I interfered and put a halt to it. When he started swearing, I invited him to leave the office. He finally calmed down and left. A check was mailed to us a few days later, and his accounts are still intact.

Building, Equipment, and Parking Lot Comments

1. We encountered the usual winter heating problem at Riverview Office--hot in the morning and cold in the afternoon. Blower fans are turned off at noon each day. We have told Lewis Company of this situation many times, but they cannot rectify the situation.

2. Interior clock does not keep correct time. Maintenance department knows about the trouble with this clock and will take care of it.

(signature and title of branch manager)

In summary, although one of the distinguishing features of memo reports is the three-part body (introduction, text, and terminal section), sometimes the introduction and/or terminal section may be omitted. When you understand the three basic plans for memo reports, however, you can adapt to the special formats and headings you'll encounter on the job.

Printed Form and Standardized Reports

To save time in writing often-used reports, business firms develop printed forms and/or standardized headings for reports.

Printed Form Reports

The printed form report should be used when a company follows or uses the same format often enough to justify the "jelling" of the report body, headings, and instructions into a printed form. The individual filling out the form merely adds the necessary figures, sentences, and identifications.

Although filling out this form is quick and easy, preparing it is more difficult. It should be clear and simple, to provide the needed information in the quickest and easiest manner. Those who will be filling out the form and using the information should be consulted. They can make suggestions before the form is drawn up and later they can evaluate the form in rough draft.

Shown in Figures 16-1 and 16-2 are printed form reports that business firms use. Among others are the company job application form, police officer's graphic location of a collision of cars at an intersection, Internal Revenue Form 1040 for reporting year's income, automobile accident report, claim for damages suffered, and the form the personnel worker fills out after interviewing an applicant.) In all examples, the form consists mainly of the text portion of the body. No introduction, terminal section, or even TO, FROM, SUBJECT are included because the reader is sufficiently oriented by frequent usage, report title, columnar headings, date and/or other information.

Standardized Reports

Though printed forms are adaptable for a tremendous variety of uses, there are situations that require another method of saving time. When the reader needs the same type of information in every report but the requested facts under each heading are likely to vary significantly in length depending upon the situation, standardized headings may be desirable. Such reports are called "standardized reports." The same headings are used repeatedly for any one type of report, but the report writer begins with a blank sheet of paper *not* with a printed form on which facts are filled in (either in handwriting on lined forms, or in typewriting).

Standardized headings for a company's reports assure uniformity and completeness of coverage and permit the receiving officer to know what to expect so he or she can compare it by periods. Also, the suggested format makes it easy for the report writer to include the data the receiver wants. The writer merely adds the needed information under each heading, without worrying about what headings should be used.

Among well-known examples of reports with standardized headings are the Balance Sheet and the Statement of Earnings and Expenses. Within any one firm the headings used for these reports are usually the same month after month. Here are three other examples:

Example 1
Standardized headings used by report writers for the Federal Aviation Agency

a. Problem	e. Alternative courses of action
b. Facts bearing on the problem	f. Recommendations
c. Discussion	g. Coordination
d. Conclusions	h. Attachments

SALESMAN'S EXPENSE VOUCHER

IMPORTANT ENTER ALL EXPENSES OF THE TRIP. ATTACH ALL HOTEL BILLS, ALSO RECEIPTED BILLS FOR OTHER EXPENDITURES OF $25.00 OR MORE EACH. ENTER COMPANY CREDIT CARD ITEMS IF ANY, INDICATE SUCH BY *; DO NOT INCLUDE IN TOTAL. SEE REVERSE SIDE FOR INSTRUCTIONS

NAME ______________________ FOR WEEK ENDED ______________________

DAY DATE	CITY	HOTEL	MEALS	ENTERTAIN-MENT (SEE BELOW)	FARE	TIPS	PARKING & TOLLS	STAMPS TEL. & TEL.	OTHER (SEE BELOW)	TOTAL	MILEAGE
SUNDAY											
MONDAY											
TUESDAY											
WEDNESDAY											
THURSDAY											
FRIDAY											
SATURDAY											
	TOTAL										

MAIL CHECK TO:

AUTO AT 8¢ PER MILE	
TOTAL EXPENSE	

SIGNED ______________________

CHECK NO. ____________

APPROVED ______________________

I. EXPLANATION OF ENTERTAINMENT:

AMOUNT, DATE, PLACE, TYPE (LUNCH, DINNER, THEATRE, ETC.) BUSINESS PURPOSE; LIST NAMES, TITLES AND BUSINESS AFFILIATION OF EACH INDIVIDUAL PRESENT (IF THE ENTERTAINMENT DIRECTLY PRECEDES OR FOLLOWS A SUBSTANTIAL BUSINESS DISCUSSION, IN ADDITION TO THE FOREGOING, SHOW DATE, DURATION, NATURE AND PLACE OF BUSINESS DISCUSSION)

(ATTACH ANOTHER SHEET, IF NECESSARY)

II. OTHER (EXPLAIN EACH ITEM)

Figure 16-1 Weekly expense voucher. When filled out, this report reveals each day's expenses and entertainment. It is approved by the district sales manager and reported to the regional office for reimbursement. Detailed instructions on the reverse side of the voucher explain what the sales personnel should include under each heading.

EMPLOYEE APPRAISAL REPORT

BRANCH _____ DEPARTMENT _____ DATE _____

EMPLOYEE _____ DATE EMPLOYED _____

JOB TITLE _____ RATED BY: 1. _____ 2. _____ 3. _____

Each factor has been subdivided into a number of degrees of application. Consider each factor separately and check only one degree for each factor. Indicate point value in right-hand column and Total.

PERFORMANCE FACTORS	DEGREE OF APPLICATION					Point Value
1. QUANTITY OF WORK Rate on basis of volume of work accomplished in relation to volume of work required.	1 __ 3 __5 __ Production inadequate	6 __8 __ 10 __ Substandard production - output below average.	11 __ 13 __ 15 __ Production satisfactory - maintains required output.	16 __ 18 __20 __ Production usually above average - works rapidly.	21 __ 23 __25 __ Production exceptional - consistently rapid worker.	
2. QUALITY OF WORK Rate on employee's performance in meeting established job requirements, accuracy and neatness.	1 __ 3 __ 5 __ Inaccurate and careless, work of poor quality.	6 __ 8 __ 10 __ Not thorough - frequent errors, or untidy work.	11 __ 13 __ 15 __ Average judgment, accuracy, thoroughness and neatness. Occasional errors.	16 __ 18 __ 20 __ Consistently accurate, neat and thorough - good judgment - few errors.	21 __ 23 __ 25 __ Exceptional judgment, accuracy and neatness - rarely makes errors.	
3. DEPENDABILITY Rate on the degree to which employee can be consistently depended upon to perform duties within the limits of his experience and training - consider work habits, attendance, and application - does he require prompting?	1 __3 __ 5 __ Undependable poor work habits or attendance - cannot work without prodding.	6 __ 8 __ 10 __ Requires considerable prompting to insure completion of assignments - irregular attendance.	11 __ 13 __ 15 __ Generally reliable - usually prompt in attending to duties.	16 __ 18 __ 20 __ Prompt and industrious - good work habits.	21 __ 23 __ 25 __ Can always be relied upon - exceptionally industrious.	
4. COOPERATION Rate on basis of general attitude toward his work and ability to work effectively with his supervisor and fellow employees.	1 __3 __ 5 __ Does not work well with others, antagonistic, does not willingly conform to established policies and procedures.	6 __ 8 __ 10 __ Occasionally difficult to handle - lacks enthusiasm.	11 __ 13 __ 15 __ Generally cooperative and helpful - usually displays satisfactory attitude toward his work.	16 __ 18 __ 20 __ Cooperates willingly - well accepted by fellow employees - adaptable and courteous.	21 __ 23 __ 25 __ Exceptionally cooperative - goes out of way to be helpful - very well liked.	

Form 795 Pers. K1 Rev. 6/54   TOTAL POINTS

Figure 16-2 Example of an evaluation form that a supervisor fills out for each employee twice a year and files in the employee's personnel folder.

Example 2
Standardized headings used by a real estate appraisal firm

a. Location and legal description
b. Description of improvements
   Roof   Interior walls   Electrical
   Exterior walls   Millwork   Plumbing
   Floors   Appliances   Heating
c. Valuation (with physical value table and comments)

Example 3
Standardized headings used by Dun & Bradstreet credit reporting service.

a. Data Universal Numbering System (DUNS)—a 9-digit code that identifies a specific business name and location. It is also the "address" of the detailed marketing and credit facts for each business listed in the Reference Book and in the Dun & Bradstreet Data Bank, or files.
b. Summary—overall highlights: buying name, ownership, line of business, date started, D&B rating, salient credit data facts.
c. Payments—how the business pays its bills.
d. Finance—financial condition and business trend, etc.
e. Banking—relations with principal depositories.
f. History—background and experience of principals and the business.
g. Operation—What the business does, how, under what conditions, etc.

Figure 16-3 illustrates a sample Dun & Bradstreet report. The initials CD near the top indicate the report is a complete revision or "condensation" of all previous reports on the same name.

Letter Reports

As the title indicates, a letter report uses the format of a letter—with date, inside address, salutation, body (different from a letter), complimentary close, signature, reference sections. Often it has a subject line typewritten a line or two below the salutation. Since this report goes outside the company, it is typed on the firm's letterhead. Its length may range from two to five (seldom more) pages. Pages beyond the first have the same heading (reader's name, page number, date) as for a letter.

Because this report goes to someone not part of your firm, you need an appropriate opening and closing. A "typical" report introduction is usually out of place, as is a "typical" terminal section—summary, conclusions, or recommendations.

The first paragraph of a letter report resembles the opening of a letter; yet you usually include the following elements found in an introduction:

Authorization (if one exists)
Purpose (always)
Problem (if one exists)
Statement of the results (optional)
Plan of presentation (depends on length of report)

Examples:

1. As you requested, I am glad to tell you our experience with the XYZ machine. Overall, we're quite pleased with its performance and dependability.
2. It is a pleasure to report to you our progress in the year just completed and look ahead with you for this year just started.
3. I have made an investigation of the Delivery Service Department, as requested in your January 7 letter, with regard to reducing the operating cost of the department.

The "CD" Report

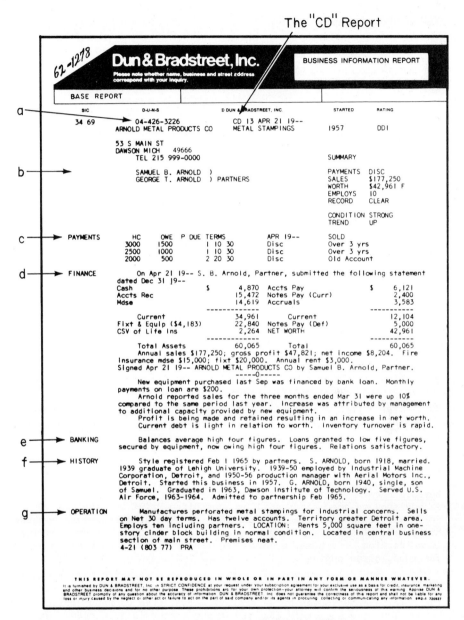

Figure 16-3   Dun & Bradstreet report using standardized headings.

4. While auditing your books last month, I noticed your firm does not have a centralized receiving department. The purpose of this report is to explain the present set-up and then show how a receiving department will benefit your organization.

The middle paragraphs comprise the text—and are identical to those used in any other type of report. Usually the emphasis is on the findings or results. This section can use headings if they help guide the reader in reading.

The last paragraph offers to discuss further or to come to the reader's office at his convenience. If you need to conclude or recommend, do so just before the last paragraph.

In letter report 1, Mr. Jones, a business manager in New Orleans informs an inquirer (Mrs. Davis, manager of another company in Tennessee) about his firm's one-year experience with a Ditto-Print Machine. Mrs. Davis wrote that the Ditto-Print Company gave her Mr. Jones' name as an example of a new (one-year) customer. She said she is especially interested in hearing Mr. Jones' comments on performance and dependability of the machine.

Letter Report 1
A manager's report on his firm's use of a machine.

Dear Mrs. Davis

I am glad to answer your request concerning our experience with the Ditto-Print machine. On the basis of our use and plans for this machine, I can assure you that we have been pleased with its dependability and performance.

Our present and expected use of this machine

As you know, we have had a Ditto-Print machine for about a year. Because of our success with the machine, we plan to install another one in another department in 6 months. Also, future plans include supplying eventually each of our 9 departments with a machine.

Dependability

The machine worked up to expectations during the first 2 months and needed only one minor repair; the repairman was prompt and completed his work in one day. Since then, the machine required no major repair except for the scheduled 6-month checkup.

Performance

In addition to good dependability, our Ditto-Print machine has performed well. We have realized considerable dollar savings because the secretaries can copy and distribute correspondence from suppliers in a fraction of a time formerly required. Also the machine turns out good, clean copies.

Although we have noticed poor copies when more than 100 were run off the same master, this is no problem for us because we seldom need to run more than 50 copies off a master. Also, when we need copies beyond 100, the secretary can make a new master in 5 seconds. We have also noticed that high-rag-content paper results in poor copies; but once again there is no real problem since we seldom use this type of paper for masters.

It has been a pleasure to help you, Mrs. Davis. Please let me know when I can be of future assistance.

Like all other unbiased reports, this one shows both the good and bad features of the machine. Mr. Jones' report also states (in the first paragraph) his overall favorable impression.

Perhaps you have already noticed that a letter report like the one above about a machine is organized the same way as a letter of recommendation you might write about a person—his or her work for you or credit record with your firm. In fact, as mentioned in Chapter 8 (page 195), basically "a recommendation is a confidential report."[9] If the inquirer asks you several (say five or more) questions about broad areas and doesn't furnish a printed report form for your answers, you will need to write a long, factual, objective message that is really a letter report. If your answers require more than one paragraph under each question, you should of course number the questions and/or use headings to help improve readability. Your own good judgment should guide you in choice of headings and format.

Besides writing letter reports to answer inquiries about persons or about products you don't sell, you may also need to write letter reports about the products (or services) your firm does sell. In general, the same care and techniques you use for planning and writing any other objective report should be used for these letter reports, whether they go to a government agency or a customer.

Another popular use of letter reports is the annual message the company president sends to stockholders. In many firms—especially the larger ones—this letter report is part of the printed annual report. However, in other firms the president's letter report is mailed on company letterhead stationery along with enclosed financial statements, as in the following example. Headings for this letter report are unique in placement and color (light blue).

Letter Report 2
A savings association president's annual letter report to shareholders

January 30, 19__

Dear Shareholder:

The year 19__ was one of change and adjustment for our state and, to a lesser extent, for your Association. In reviewing our activities it is a pleasure to report to you that the year was one of our most productive. Here are highlights of our accomplishments.

Growth
    Assets reached $9½ million by December 31, an increase of 10% during the year, as the enclosed comparative statements show.

    Deposits increased 9% to a new high of $7 million. Both branches contributed to this growth.

    Loans rose by $1/2 million, or 8.4%.

[9] Recommendation letters were included with good-news replies because they are important good-news or neutral replies to nonsales inquiries. See pages 194-198. For examples of answers to nonsales inquiries when information is unfavorable, see pages 248-250.

Capital structure by the year's end had increased over 25%
(from $ to $). Also that growth was reflected in
the increased book value of the permanent reserve shares from
$1.95 to $2.25 a share during the year.

Operations

During the year, your Association implemented the recommendations
for improving operation procedures proposed by management consultants late in (year). This action has resulted in visible
direct savings in excess of $2,000 on an annualized basis, and
it is expected that considerable additional amounts will be
saved as the program continues.

Your Association's electronic data processing, communications,
and record-keeping system was expanded during the year. A
savings customer now may make deposits or withdrawals at either
branch tied in with the computer, and the transaction is promptly
recorded in the customer's deposit book.

Personnel changes

Trustees. With a deep sense of loss and regret we report the
passing of our esteemed trustee (name - and two sentences about
that person).

Fortunately, the Association has elected an outstanding business
leader (name) to the Board to fill the vacancy. (Two sentences
about the new trustee.)

Officers. The growth of your Association and the retirement of
two officers provided openings for advancement of qualified
people. Three officers were advanced in rank and four employees
were elevated to official positions. (Names and titles)

Staff. Two college graduates were hired as management trainees.
These young people and others of the staff are being prepared
for positions of responsibility and leadership.

A look at what lies ahead

The present year will be another year of adjustment and change.
We anticipate some pickup in the economy on the national scene
and in this area the last half of the year. Thus, insofar as
your Association is concerned, we would expect that savings for
the year will perhaps equal or possibly exceed the splendid
results of last year, with a fairly even growth over the twelve-
month period.

Perhaps the greatest challenge (and this we expect to meet
successfully) will be that of investing the inflow of funds
promptly and safely at a satisfactory rate in a period when
the local mortgage demand will not be as great as in recent
years.

We at First Federal continue to be optimistic with regard to
the future of our great nation, our state, and your Association.
Our long-range plans call for expanded activities, to continue
providing more and better service to an ever increasing number
of our citizens.

(signature)
Typed name, President

In addition to the various kinds of letter reports already discussed or shown, one more deserves special mention here. It is the *progress report*. If you are a management consultant, or an independent researcher, or a representative of a firm doing work under contract on a long-term (perhaps yearly) project for another company, you should report your progress periodically—in letter-report form. Under some agreements such reports must be made monthly, or quarterly, or semi-annually, or annually.

Basically, the general topics discussed in a progress report in letter form are similar to those outlined for a progress report in memorandum format. (See page 560.) Instead of having memo format, however, these reports will be typed on your firm's letterhead stationery and have the usual letter parts plus your signature and title at the end. Often they have attachments too. And of course if you have a staff of assistants and expenses that the contracting firm is to pay, you will need to attach an adequate accounting sheet of your payments and budget.

Other Short Reports

You will also see—and write—in business other short reports besides the memo report, letter report, and printed or standardized reports. The three most significant are annual reports, "dressed-up" short reports, and proposals.

Annual Reports

Every organization—business, government, religious, athletic, and so forth—has annual reports that summarize activities and financial affairs. For some small concerns the report is exceptionally "short"—consisting of perhaps a brief transmittal letter with one or two pages of financial statements. For other organizations—especially corporations which must report to their stockholders—the annual report may begin with a top official's summary similar to letter report 2 illustrated on pages 571-572. Sometimes the letter is the entire report (perhaps eight or more pages). If not, then the report body discusses operations and activities; and of course every annual report should have a balance sheet and statement of earnings and expenses.

Some reports also include pictures of officers, employees, products, machines, operations—plus charts or graphs and easy-to-understand explanations in nontechnical terms.[10] Financial statements also may have simplified discussions understandable by any stockholder with little knowledge of accounting. To see examples of various annual reports, you might write to selected corporations or consult your business or general library—or your campus placement office.

---

[10] For some large national and international corporations annual reports are often elaborate colorful brochures printed on glossy paper with 40 or more pages. As such, they are outside the scope of this chapter, for they are not "short." Actually, they are impressive advertising brochures for the public as well as stockholders. They also are informative for college graduates and others seeking jobs with reputable firms.

"Dressed-up" Short Reports

In some situations a comprehensive, important memo report or letter report would be more impressive if it had some of the "dress-up" features of a long report. If your report is, for example, four or five single-space typewritten pages long and has several attachments, you might consider using: a title page, transmittal letter or memo, the report body (typed in single- or double-space), plus an appendix for the attachments. For discussion and illustrations of these prefatory and supplemental parts, see Chapter 17.

To give you an idea of how one of the "short" reports already discussed in this chapter might be "dressed-up," let's look again at memo report 1 on pages 549-551. Suppose you were also required to attach to this report confidential copies of recommendation letters and test scores for each of the three tellers. Your report would then have 10 pages of attachments plus three single-spaced or five double-spaced pages of body (tables would remain single-spaced). If you decide to add a title page,[11] it will include the TO, FROM, SUBJECT, DATE information attractively set up in these three parts: (1) EVALUATION OF THREE TELLER APPLICANTS, (2) Prepared for Mr. Gene Mohr, Manager, Savings Department; and (3) By (your name), Assistant Manager, Personnel Department, March 15, 19___. You will then omit this information from the first page of the report. If you use a transmittal memo, you'll also make a few changes in the first paragraph of the report introduction, (as discussed on pages 606-607, in Chapter 17). Your 10 pages of attachments can become the appendix; pages will be numbered consecutively after the last page of your report. For example, if your report body (double-spaced) ends on page 5, the appendix first page will be page 6, and so on through page 15.

Short Reports for Proposals

A special type of report that has become increasingly important in business and industry as well as in government and education is the proposal. In a survey of the chief executives for 50 randomly selected manufacturing firms with $1 million minimum annual sales volume, 65 percent reported that proposals play an important part in the operations of their firms. Of these, over 50 percent said the part is "great" or "crucial."[12]

Like other reports, some proposals are short and informal; others are long and formal. In Chapter 17 you will read about "formal" proposals. The present section discusses an informal short report proposal. Usually it is in letter-report form, with attachments. Its purpose is (a) to get a project accepted and/or (b) to get your company—or you—accepted for work on a project. The proposal illustrated here is a sales presentation a firm makes to a prospective buyer. (Do not consider it a model of

---

[11] For an example of a title page, see page 622.
[12] Bill G. Rainey, "Proposal Writing—A Neglected Area of Instruction," *The Journal of Business Communication*, Vol. 11, Number 4, Summer 1974.

perfection; it is, however, an example of a fairly typical informal proposal to sell an installation product. You can probably suggest ways to improve it.) Before sending the proposal, the seller has visited the company's place of business, studied its present setup, and discussed its needs.

The proposal consists of:

Covering letter
Attached report on: Explanation of Spacefinder Filing System
Advantages of Spacefinder System
Present system now in operation
Proposed system
Cost of proposed equipment

Attention
Interest
Desire
Action

This letter and the attachment are comparable to the application letter and résumé; the letter sells, while the enclosure or attachment presents pertinent facts effectively. Notice that the letter follows the AIDA formula for sales letters. The first paragraph catches the reader's attention; the second and third paragraphs create desire by referring to facts and figures in the attached report (about present system and benefits of the Spacefinder System); the last paragraph asks for action.

The attached report permits the writer to streamline the letter without cluttering it with details. As with any good sales pitch, the report leads the reader through explanation and advantages of Spacefinder, details of the present system, and proposed system before it mentions cost. The letter and the report together constitute the proposal which is to convince the reader to convert to the new system.

```
Dear Mr. Jaysen

We are pleased to present the attached proposal to (name of receiver's
firm) for a conversion from drawer files to TAB PRODUCTS' Spacefinder
Filing System.

In addition to quoting facts and figures, we have laid out on quarter-
inch grid paper the present system you now use in the vault on the
third floor.  The vault is drawn to exact scale and the drawer files
now being used are placed in their present position.  Using an over-
lay we are able to illustrate how much space you can save in this
vault and yet increase efficiency in locating records and returning
them to the file.  Also you can use this floor plan in the future to
expand storage in the same area.

It is a proven fact that the Unit Spacefinder Filing System does
increase filing efficiency by 50%.  We have time studies made by
firms other than TAB PRODUCTS which indicate this increase.

On the attached pages I have indicated floor space savings and
efficiency factors using the Unit Spacefinder System.  If you need
further information, please call upon me for assistance.  My tele-
phone number is 111-2222.  Thank you for this opportunity to quote
on TAB PRODUCTS Unit Spacefinder Filing System.
```

PROPOSAL
to (name of receiver's firm)
for conversion to TAB PRODUCTS' Spacefinder
Filing System

Explanation of Spacefinder Filing System

The Unit Spacefinder Filing System differs from shelf filing
in many respects. We have proven in many filing areas, both
large and small, that the Unit Spacefinder is at least 20%
more efficient than steel shelf filing and 50% more efficient
than drawer files. Any addition of personnel to the "Records
Staff," because of expansion or increased work load, is a
costly annual expenditure. Efficiency means person-hours,
which in turn, means dollars.

What creates this added efficiency? I have listed below the
efficiency factors of Unit Spacefinder.

1.   First,of all, you don't file in a drawer, on a shelf, or
     in a cabinet - you file in a container. The Unit Box is
     4" wide. This means that the documents have support
     every 4". This need is one of the most important required
     in lateral filing. The more support, the easier it is
     to "in-file" and pull records.

2.   The unique "stair-step" effect, caused by the angle in
     which Unit Boxes are hung, gives you easier accessibility
     never before possible. This accessibility is an exclusive
     feature of Unit Spacefinder. Every folder is perfectly
     accessible, easy to reach, and easy to see.

3.   You get flexibility. You can rearrange and expand without
     a lot of time-consuming bother, such as in the case of
     drawer files or shelf files. You create space where you
     need it simply by sliding boxes easily along rails. There
     is no need to transfer records handful by handful.

2

Advantages of Unit Spacefinder Lateral Filing System

The Unit Spacefinder concept of filing provides the following advantages:

1. A stair-step effect allows the folders to be readily identified and removed and replaced with the least amount of effort.
2. The unit boxes can be removed from the racks, a feature which allows:
   a. Work with the records at a desk for purging or for checking, etc.
   b. For fast fleeting of records by rearrangement of the unit boxes.
3. Visibility is a definite advantage. All folders are exposed to the file clerks and with proper indexing can be located at least 50% faster than when the folders are used in drawer files.
4. Flexibility of the Unit enables us to assure you we can tailor the Unit Spacefinder framework to fit your needs. It is free standing and does not have to be anchored to the walls or floor; therefore, if you need a different configuration to fit a particular location, we can easily meet your desires.

3

Present System Now in Operation

12 ea. 5-Drawer Legal Size Files

8 ea. 4-Drawer Legal Size Files

Total Filing Inches   2,300"

Total Floor Space   122.11 Sq. Ft.
  (including drawer pull)

Folders used are 3rd cut, top position right-hand side, legal. Filed in numerical sequence.
  a. Conversion factor - use same folders
  b. Use Colorvue Guide Cards which reveal inserted number on both sides.

Proposed System

Use combination of 42" and 30" Single Face Sections of Unit Spacefinder against wall and double-face Unit Spacefinder spaced 42" to provide ample aisle space.

Total Filing Inches   2,380"
Total Floor Space   47.02 Sq. Ft.

```
Conversion:                                                          4
   Present folders can be used.  Right hand tab allows easy
   identification of numbers.
   Guide cards should be inserted in file every two to three
   feet.

Summary
   1.  Increase in filing inches - 80"
   2.  Floor space released for expansion or other purposes--
       75.09 square feet
   3.  Efficiency increase - Minimum 35%

Cost of Proposed Equipment

1 ea. 5422   Initial 45" Legal Size Single  $172.90      $172.90
2 ea. 5334   Additional 42" Legal Size with
             workshelf, Single                 148.45      296.90
3 ea. 5404   Additional 30" Legal Size Single   93.50      280.50
1 ea. 5430   Initial 45" Legal Size Double
             with two workshelves              363.80      363.80
1 ea. 5408   Additional 30" Legal Size
             Double                             170.50      170.50
                                                          $1,284.60
100 ea.   C4345-2  Colorvue Short Guides                  $   32.00

Trim Color Standard -
   Desert Tan - Mist Green - Tab Gray
Colors on Color-sheet 3%

Delivery Schedule:  21 Days
   Terms:   Net 30 Days
     FOB:   Factory
```

The preceding illustrations and discussions have indicated the wide variety of subject matter, uses, and formats for memorandum reports, printed and standardized reports, letter reports, and other special reports. Yet, basically, all short reports have various characteristics in common. If you think logically and objectively, consider your reader(s), use good judgment with facts, plan and organize carefully, and achieve the qualities of well-written reports as suggested in both Chapters 15 and 16, you will turn out commendable short reports on the job.

Exercises

Situations That Require Discussion but No Writing
1. Evaluate the memo report below by discussing:
   a. Clarity of the subject line
   b. Reason for omission of an introduction
   c. Appropriateness of headings
   d. Reasons for omission of a terminal section
   e. Quality of content and wording
   f. Consistency of paragraph openings

TO: H. H. Helium   DATE: May 2, 197_

FROM: R. R. Ralston

REGARDING: Office Activities Report for September, 197_

PERSONNEL

The employees are all taking A.S.L.I. courses. The manager signed up for Insurance; but since there were insufficient registrants, the course was not offered.

Miss Lee was on vacation for 2 weeks and one day. During this time, Mrs. Santa Marie attended Orientation at our Main Office.

I hope to begin training Mrs. Mueller on insurance within 4 weeks. This is later than I had originally planned, but I ordinarily have taxes paid by this time.

BUSINESS DEVELOPMENT SITUATION

I made 8 completed calls on Realtors to discuss our restricted sale clause. I was invited to attend a sales meeting. This resulted in my addressing 8 sales people and answering their questions.

UNUSUAL OCCURRENCES

I was subpoenaed to appear in court on September 17 as a witness on one of our escrows.

POLICY OR PROCEDURAL PROBLEMS

We were notified on 3 separate occasions, by the U.S. Postal Service, that our metered mail was being deposited with wrong dates or illegible dates. This led to our inquiring about the postal service and what is expected of us and why. As a result, we have a better understanding of the system and what we can do to give our customers better mail service.

Also the time for last mail pick-up on various mail boxes throughout the city were obtained.

One of our Series 05 SAC customers came into the office to change the name on his account. We discovered that we had sent all 05 SACs to the Main Office shortly after July 10, 197_, and did not keep any on hand. This has now been rectified and we have a couple on hand to serve our customers without inconveniencing them.

2. You are director of personnel training for a large industrial organization. Among your many duties is the operation of a particular 2-week "School for Executive Development" seminar for middle management every fall. Although the firm pays for teaching salaries and books, you must account for certain expenses such as supplies and transportation.

In previous years you used the services of an outside agency called Short Courses and Conferences to perform the typing, coordination, and other services connected with preparing notebooks and overall operation of the seminar. But you've been unhappy with the services of this agency because they seem quite expensive for the quality fo work turned out. Therefore for the last seminar, you assumed many of the services previously performed by the agency.

You saved the firm money, as the attached two financial statements submitted to you from Short Courses and Conferences show. Now you want to pass along the knowledge of this saving to your superior with the hope you'll get a raise for the additional responsibility you assumed.

Evaluate the following material you're sending to your superior, Mr. Daniel G. Myers, Staff Vice President. It consists of a covering memo report, analysis sheet, and the financial statements for the last two years. Myers is a person who expects all details even though he may not read everything. Furthermore, he wants to read just as little as possible.

   a. What is the purpose of the covering memo?
   b. What main ideas does the memo include?
   c. Should the memo have included a statement about getting a raise? Why or why not?
   d. Paragraph 2 of the memo mentions two figures. Can you easily find them in the attachments? Does the memo make clear which attachment the writer is referring to?
     What improvement(s) can you suggest to help Mr. Myers know where to find proof of these figures?
   e. How would numbering the attachments improve the presentation?
   f. What other improvements can you suggest in the memo and/or the statements attached?

December 10, 1975

TO: Daniel G. Myers, Staff Vice-President

FROM: (your name), Director of Personnel Training

SUBJECT: Comparison of Short Courses and Conferences
           Financial Statements: 1974 vs. 1975

Attached is an analysis of the entries in the financial statements that Short Courses and Conferences sent us for 1974 and 1975. Overall I am well pleased with the substantially smaller amount we're paying for 1975.

You'll notice that the greatest decreases relate to duplicating: secretarial, clerical, and coordinating services; and indirect expense--a decrease of $1,841.53. Even in spite of inflation and the increases shown in the lower half of the attachment, the total bill is still $1,382.66 less than that for 1974.

In general the increases resulted from additional services rendered-- as explained briefly in parentheses below each entry.

Attachments

Analysis of 1974 and 1975 Financial Statements
from
Short Courses and Conferences

Decrease in Costs	1974	1975	Difference
Duplicating	822.04	146.12	675.92
Secretarial, Clerical, and			
Coordinating Services	963.35	69.85	893.50
Indirect Expenses	530.36	288.25	272.11
Postage	87.31	15.44	71.87
Supplies	42.07	4.00	38.07
Total	2801.80	1419.14	1382.66
Cartage	11.87	00.00	11.87
Photographs	43.20	00.00	43.20

Increase in Costs

Audio-visual	18.15	109.93	91.78
(more professors used these services)			
Room Rental	40.00	250.00	210.00
(more and higher-priced rooms)			
Telephone	31.95	125.00	93.05*

(*including $62.75 racked up by students. You received reimburse-ments for most of this amount)

Bus Tours	240.00	339.25	99.25
(Additional buses and higher fee)			
Parking Permits	13.50	33.50	20.00
(all professors received permits without charge)			
Copy Work	00.00	36.90	36.90
(special work requested by Rosen)			

School for Executive Development Seminar
September 1 - 13, 1974
FINANCIAL STATEMENT

INCOME:

Postage fees from participants		$ 72.00

DIRECT EXPENSES:

Classrooms		$ 40.00	
Supplies:			
Student Supplies	$ 42.07		
Postage	87.31		
Duplicating of Instructional Material (including typing)	822.04	951.42	
Secretarial, Clerical & Coordinating Services		963.35	
Bus Transportation		240.00	
Miscellaneous:			
Audiovisual	18.15		
Cartage	11.87		
Long Distance Calls	31.95		
Parking Permits	13.50		
Photographs	43.20	118.67	
Total Direct Expenses:			2,313.44
Balance of Direct Expenses Less Income			$2,241.44
INDIRECT EXPENSES:			560.36
BALANCE:			$2,801.80

School for Executive Development Seminar
September 7 - 19, 1975
FINANCIAL STATEMENT

EXPENSES:

Audiovisual	$	109.93
SC&C clerical services		69.85
Copy work		36.90
Duplicating		146.12
Indirect expenses		288.25
Postage		15.44

Room rental	250.00
Supplies	4.00
Telephone tolls	125.90
Gray Line tours	339.25
Parking permits	33.50
BALANCE:	$1,419.14

cc: C. Raleigh
     S. Burks (2)
MP:1m
Conference #450

Rewrites

1. The following letter report (also an acknowledgment to an inquiry) is quite good. Your job is to make it even better. Assume the customer asked about all the topics mentioned; thus, keep all the ideas but improve the letter report in these ways:

   a. Insert headings—second- and third-degree or third- and fourth-degree headings.
   b. Show more you attitude.
   c. Change at least five passive verbs to active voice (and of course make whatever subject changes are necessary).
   d. Tabulate some listed details—for easier reading.
   e. Make any other minor changes desirable for good business writing.

Thank you for your request for information relating to INSURED savings accounts in this Association. This reply includes facts concerning types of savings plans, security of savings, withdrawal of funds, and necessary forms for opening an account. I am also enclosing a copy of our latest financial statement and several pamphlets of general information which give you essential facts you desire about us and the savings accounts we issue.

We have two types of savings plans available--a passbook savings account and a six-month savings certificate.

Briefly an insured passbook savings account may be opened for any amount at any time. Upon receipt of your remittance, we issue to you our savings passbook with the amount credited inside. Additional sums may be added in any amount and at any time you desire. Savings received on or before the fifteenth of any month are credited with earnings as if received on the first of the month. Savings received after the fifteenth receive earnings from the beginning of the next following month. When the fifteenth falls on a Saturday or Sunday, on which days we are closed, the time for receiving earnings from the first of the month is extended to the 16th or 17th as the case may be. Dividends (earnings) are credited to passbook savings accounts on March 31, June 30, September 30, and December 31 of each year. This is done automatically on these dates whether you send in your passbook or not. Gold Bond stamps are given as an extra bonus to passbook savers as outlined on the enclosed card. The current rate of dividend on passbook savings is 5½% per year, compounded quarterly.

In addition to our savings passbooks, we also issue insured six-month savings certificates. Designed to offer larger, longer term investors the maximum rate for insured savings, these certificates are issued for a minimum of $1,000, with larger amounts in multiples of $100. They differ from passbook accounts in several respects. Earnings on certificates begin on the day of purchase and are paid at the end of each six months on maturity dates. The certificates are in certificate form, and dividend checks are mailed to the certificate holders every six months from the date of issue, instead of being automatically credited to the account as is done on passbook accounts. Of course, if you have a passbook savings account with State Federal, the dividends on your savings certificate may be automatically credited to your passbook account upon your request. For your convenience, savings certificates are automatically renewed on the maturity dates for an additional six months unless you are notified at least thirty days prior to a maturity date. The current rate of dividend on six-month savings certificates is $6\frac{1}{4}\%$ per year.

Savings in this Association are INSURED up to $40,000 by the Federal Savings and Loan Insurance Corporation, Washington, D.C. We are also members of the Federal Home Loan Bank System, a reserve credit system for associations. We lend our funds upon the security of selected monthly reducing first mortgages on homes. So, you will see, there is really exceptional security for savings placed with us.

You will probably wish some information concerning withdrawal of your funds. It has always been the policy of this Association to pay withdrawals in PART OR IN FULL without notice. We have followed this policy ever since organization in 1926. However, a savings and loan association may require notice of withdrawal if necessary. If the country should again experience an economic emergency such as prevailed in 1932-33, it is possible that we would require notice. Under such circumstances it is quite likely that every financial institution would necessarily restrict withdrawals. This provision in the savings and loan laws is a wise one for the protection of the customers.

For your convenience I am enclosing a signature card which may be used either for an individual or a joint account. If you desire to open an account in your own name alone, you should use Form 100. If, however, you wish to open an account in your name jointly with some other person, probably another member of your family, you should use Form 200 on the reverse side of the card. If you desire a six-month savings certificate, the same signature card may be used.

We also have trust accounts, frequently used by parents in carrying savings accounts for children, or by persons who desire to hold funds in trusts for another. Signature card forms for this type of account will be mailed to you upon request.

I thank you kindly for your inquiry and extend to you a cordial invitation to use the facilities of this Association.

2. Given below is a report to shareholders. Assume this message appears on one side of an 8½- by 11-inch sheet and the annual statement of condition appears on the opposite side. Rewrite so that the information is easier to read. For example, can you put in table form some or all the figures and dates given in the first three paragraphs? And can you list the names and titles in the last two paragraphs? Also add an appropriate rounding-out last paragraph.

Report to the Shareholders
We ended our 61st year May 3, 19___, which proved to be a very good year. Our assets totaled almost $12,000,000 being $11,997,728.90, representing an increase of $430,315.75 which was due principally to the increase in home loans of $538,622.30.

Savings accounts reflected a total of $11,013,074.26, representing a gain for the year of $385,321.70, which was substantially greater than the gain in the previous year. During the year the Association repaid $265,000 to the Federal Home Loan Bank and had no notes payable May 3, 197__. Net operating income, after expenses, amounted to $558,293.40, reflecting an increase of $32,423.01 over the prior year. The operating ratio of the Association for the fiscal year was 17.87% of gross operating income which was substantially lower than the national average which is in excess of 27%.

During the year, $42,000 was added to reserves, $495,810.52 was distributed as earning on savings accounts and $20,482.88 was added to undivided profit. Total reserves were $514,000 and undivided profit $87,505.03, making a total of $601,505.03 representing over 5% of total liabilities. Our reserves and undivided profit places us in a rather enviable position and leaves no question, in my opinion, of our ability to continue at our present rate of return to our savings accounts.

At our Shareholders Meeting held Monday, April 5, the following were elected to serve as directors for the ensuing year: William E. Brady, Robert E. Becker, Stephen G. Mills, Mary A. Aitken, Daniel A. Roberts, Lisa L. Gifford, and Louise G. Hulett.

At the Directors Reorganization Meeting, immediately following the Shareholders Meeting, the following officers were elected: Chairman of the Board of Directors and President, Judy E. Brady; Vice Chairman, Robert E. Becker; Executive Vice President, Secretary and Treasurer, Stephen G. Mills; Vice President and Assistant Secretary and Treasurer, Louise G. Hulett; and Asisstant Secretary, William A. Dugger. Sylvia Reddie was reappointed Savings Officer and Bonnie Whittemore was appointed Head Bookkeeper. Fred L. Sharp was re-appointed attorney.

3. The head of the Tab Department wrote the following memo report to two management members because telephone activity was disrupting other work routines in his department. As you read this report, try to find out what its purpose is. Notice how frustrating it is to read the details without knowing how they fit into the overall picture. Then rewrite the report to make it clear. In the first paragraph state the problem, purpose, metholodology, and plan of presentation. Use appropriate headings and apply all other good writing principles you have learned to make your memo report as good as possible.

```
TO:     Tom Burkhard, Nancy Blair          DATE:  May 3, 19__

FROM:   Ray Durkey
```

During the week of August 19-23, 197_, a survey of telephone inquiries to the main office was conducted. The incoming calls to the Tab Department totaled 470. The source of these calls was as follows: Approximately 67% from main office tellers and branch office personnel; approximately 33% from all other main office personnel.

Due to the fact that the survey was conducted during a period of reduced activity, the findings are not representative of the peak periods throughout the year. Based on an analysis of weekly activity for the first half of 197_, the volume of telephone inquiries is projected at approximately 750–800 per week during the peak periods which occur during the first part of each quarter.

During the period of the survey an average of 90–100 calls per day were serviced by Tab. Even at this level, the telephone activity is becoming sufficient enough to be disruptive of the other work routines in the department.

It is recommended that another employee be hired and assigned to the Tab Department primarily for the purpose of servicing telephone inquiries.

Problems

1. Assume you have received a letter from the Assistant Dean of Students, Dr. Jean Inquirer, Administration Building, your college or university, stating that you have been selected in a random sample to take part in a survey. The information gathered will be included—without student names—in an orientation booklet for entering students. She asks you to answer these questions regarding your course costs for this quarter:[13]

    a. What is your year in college and major?
    b. How much did your textbooks cost you? Please mention course names and book titles, too.
    c. What other required course materials did you have to pay for and how much did they cost? (Include lab fees, if any, but exclude tuition fees.) Figure only prices of new texts and materials (but you may mention any savings you gained if you bought used items).
    d. What relation, if any, do you find between these total course costs and the number of credit hours your courses carry?
    e. What relation, if any, do you find between these total course costs and the college (Arts & Sciences, Engineering, etc.) or department (Business, Education, Art) in which they are offered? (Answer this question if you are taking courses in more than one department or college of this institution.)

    The only data you need are the prices of *new* books and materials plus lab fees, if any—for each course you are carrying *and* the credit hours of each course.
    In case you feel that this quarter is exceptional for you (perhaps because you are taking only one or two courses), you may, if you wish, include information for both last quarter and this one. Indicate clearly the costs and credits in each.
    Suggestions: Write your report in good business letter-report form[13]—with heading, inside address, subject line, salutation, and closing. Use well-chosen headings to mark the main divisions of your report. Keep your report factual, objective, and well-organized.

2. You are the new assistant to Mr. James Rohn, Regional Manager of Employee Relations and Education, (name company). Two days ago you received the following memo from him:

---

[13]Actually, for a survey of this type the inquirer should send a questionnaire form on which each respondent merely fills in answers. However, for purpose of this assignment, let's assume she sent merely a stamped envelope and that she is also interested in seeing how well college students express themselves in written reports. Make yours one of the best!

Will you please look into the film "(name)," review it, and report to me what you think of it? Specifically, I'd like (in a concise written report) to know:

1. What are the main ideas of the film?
2. What are its technical (and other) aspects--length, photography, method of presentation, quality, cost?
3. How useful would it be to our company and our branches?
4. What do you recommend we do--purchase, rent, or forget it?

Your office selects, from time to time, various instructional materials, visual aids, and other teaching materials for use in your management training program at the main office (your city). In addition, they are also available to the four branches whenever requested and when not used at the headquarters office. Each branch has its own trainees. Your company has 2,000 employees, of whom 900 are working within your home office area. The rest work in and out of the branches, located within a radius of 300 miles from the home office. About 30 percent of your employees are in some kind of supervisory or management capacity. They communicate not only orally, but also through letters, memos, and reports.

The one communication film that the company now owns is a sound filmstrip, in black and white, shown for the past 10 years, regarding essentially letter writing, Most of the older executives think it is still adequate. It's *Dear Mrs. Somebody.* Mr. Rohn (age 59) is always on the lookout, however, for the newest and best materials regardless of cost, as long as they can be justified as to their usefulness for the firm.

Assume that yesterday you reviewed this color film about which he asked you to report. If your instructor can show a film to the entire class—or if you have seen a film in another course—use the facts and title from that film for this report. If no film is available for class showing, assume you previewed *Management Communications* at the Audiovisual Services Center in your city.

This morning Mr. Rohn, in passing your desk, casually remarked he had heard of this film (the one you previewed) through a manager who sat next to him at a luncheon recently. Mr. Rohn's comments indicated, indirectly, what his hopes and preferences are about the use of this film in your company. After seeing the film, you now realize that your own honest conclusions and recommendations are contrary to Mr. Rohn's expectations. (This realization guides you in selection of an organizations plan for your report.) Regardless of whether you report on *Management Communications* or another film you saw yourself in a class, you are free to recommend whatever you wish, provided you objectively consider all facts.

Facts about the film *Management Communications:*

25 minutes long; produced and sold by BNA Incorporated, Bureau of National Affairs, 1231 24th St., N.W., Washington, D.C. Assume it costs $350. You've also discovered that the local Audiovisual Services Center rents it for a three-day period at $10 plus postage. They require at least 24 hours' advance notice, and they will ship films anywhere across the country, except to Hawaii and Canada.

Your rough draft notes on main ideas of the film are these:

Shows a series of modern office scenes with a manager and one, two, or three employees who are under her management. Scenes show good and bad techniques of communication by the manager. A narrator helpfully explains the differences in techniques. Color, excellent; acting, amateur.

Major viewpoints are empathy and credibility on part of management toward subordinates and customers. Empathy is crucial. The manager must be able to put herself in other person's place. To change a person's viewpoint, the manager must show that the person will benefit through the change. The manager must find out what the customer's or fellow employee's beliefs are, how he will change or resist the information he is giving, and what are his interests.

To be credible the manager must be competent, dependable, and enthusiastic. Competence is attained from a communication aspect. The manager must keep well informed and communicate necessary facts to subordinates so they in turn can transfer information to their subordinates. When possible, he or she should let them make suggestions before decisions are made; let them participate.

Being dependable requires that the manager not shirk managerial duties. The manager must not pass-the-buck by assuming no responsibility for actions or blaming them on another person. If he or she has an unfavorable management decision to pass on to the subordinates, it must be done in a way that assures them they can depend on the manager to help in every possible manner.

The manager must be enthusiastic and have enough energy to see things carried through to the end without complaining when work demands are heavy. The last four letters of "enthusiasm" may stand for "I am sold myself" (on whatever topic the manager is discussing), but the manager must be sincere.

Make any other necessary assumptions for your memo report and indicate them in a separate note clipped to the top of your report which you hand to your instructor.

This is the first report you've been asked to write for Mr. Rohn. Write it in memo report format; be sure it is well organized, with appropriate headings and subheadings. Mr. Rohn likes concise and complete reports. Try to keep this one within two typed pages (elite type), single-spaced, and trimmed to basic but important essentials. Show facts and figures regarding relative costs for renting or buying; consider home office and branch needs.

3. You are a management trainee for Central Advertising Agency, in which the ability to write good reports is an important qualification. Two days ago Mr. James Sorgens, Training Director, asked you to find out what types of reports are written by account executives in this firm. He suggested you interview Ms. May Emerson, Vice President/Account Executive at Central and then write him the best report you can about your findings. Yesterday during your interview with Ms. Emerson you jotted down the following notes (with her permission). Ms. Emerson also gave you a sample of each of the four reports most often written in the company and she added general comments on agency reports.

Account executive writes reports when directly involved in the situation. Otherwise, person involved and a/c exec. decide together who writes report. In all cases concerning the client, however, a/c exec. is ultimately responsible for reports concerning the client's campaign.

Bulk of reports written by a/c exec: job memo, memo report, conference (or meeting) report, and recommendation report.

Job memo report—most important in the office. An intraoffice report written to all depts. of the agency. Written by a/c exec as often as necessary whenever any action on client's campaign is called for. They give authorization and instruction concerning client's campaign. Generally, a/c exec writes these daily.

Memo report is written as often as necessary—usually daily. Short (usually one page)—to communicate information to a specific person within agency. This report concerns information dealing with many facets of client's advertising campaign needed by the a/c exec in performing his job or her job.

Recommendation reports—most extensive and comprehensive report by a/c exec. Written perhaps once or twice a year; gives client agency's recommendations, marketing plan, budget analysis, and advertising approach for campaign. Agency and client both have copy of this report; many are 20–30 pages long. Not only does a/c exec receive a copy, but so does head of agency and heads of all depts. involved with the a/c.

Important that a/c exec and the client understand always where campaign stands and how it is progressing. So that each one has a record of all the decisions made concerning the campaign, the conference report is used. Written immediately following a conference or meeting between agency and client. Purpose: clarify discussion and the decisions made at the meeting.

General comments:
General purpose of report—no matter what type—is to ensure and expedite communication between agency and its client or between depts. of agency. Emerson pointed out several items she thought this agency's reports could be improved upon. Also those items she thought made for good reports. Also provided information on format this agency uses for reports and what they have done to improve quality of their reports.

Too many reports are not concise. Tend to be wordy and too long; lack clarity; and negative. Ms. E. thought that if reports were more objective and emphasized positive rather than neg., they would help communication more. Also desirable factors: brevity and conciseness. In general, reports should communicate entire message in fewest words possible without sounding abrupt.

Format—no particular order or format is strictly adhered to. Whether text or terminal section comes first is not a written policy, but main points of discussion should ideally precede the discussion to expedite reading of report.

Company does not use any printed forms for reports, EXCEPT for the job memo report. Nature of a/c in question dictates form used for recommendation or conference reports. Headings are used to assist reader of report.

Because of volatile nature of the advertising business, no formal school in better report writing techniques is conducted. However, the American Assoc. of Advertising Agencies does provide some bulletins on better writing techniques. These help improve agency reports. Also, the acct. exec attempts to stress the qualities of conciseness, clarity, and other desirable points of report writing in informal discussions with other executives and with their subordinates.

Organize these rough draft notes into a complete, well-written, concise memorandum report, using logical plan and two degrees of headings. Assume you are attaching the four exhibits; be sure to refer to them appropriately within your report text. Remember to use topic sentences for paragraphs and to introduce subheads properly.

4. One of your duties as manager of Wilson's Manufacturing is to check the plant's suggestion box. Recently there have appeared a number of complaints about the unsightly, unsanitary mess in the washroom. Some employees have been careless about using and disposing of paper towels. Each dispenser has a built-in trash basket and even a sticker to remind employees to place used towels in the basket, However, the problem still persists.

    As a solution, you have decided to replace paper towels with a hot air hand dryer. At your request, Haworth Inc., makers of the Jetaire Hand Dryer, sent a salesperson to evaluate your needs. The salesperson made a cost analysis of your situation and also presented an estimate of the cost for changing to the Jetaire Hand Dryer. Wilson's has 200 employees and each employee visits the washroom an average of 4 times a day. The average number of paper towels used each visit is 2½ towels at a cost of $0.002 a towel. Assuming 22 working days a month, a 3-year cost figure for towels alone was derived. Haworth's salesperson also pointed out that there are "intangible" costs involved with paper towels. These include time spent in filling out purchase orders and the cost of mailing the order; cost per square foot of storage of the paper towels; costs in distributing, collecting, and carting away paper towels; and plumbing expenses for toilets and sinks clogged with paper towels. These intangible costs usually amount to 50 percent of the 3-year total cost of paper towels for any business.

    According to the salesperson, each of the 4 washrooms in your plant should have 3 Jetaire units. The units cost $120 apiece and together use about $4 in electricity per month. There is also an installation fee of $84 (for all machines).

    Because the estimated acquisition cost of the Jetaire Hand Dryers is over $500, it is necessary to receive authorization from Mr. Steve Wilson, the plant superintendent. He is a very busy person and often does not have the time to sort through a lengthy cost analysis report. He likes to know immediately what the cost and savings are in the company. Write a memo report bringing to Mr. Wilson's attention these points as well as other facts such as employee benefits. Include one or two concise, easy-to-read tables in your discussion section. For your organizational plan will you use 4a, b, or c (pages 553–557)?

5. As office manager of the Zelectron Company, you have been considering purchasing a Thermofax Copier-Duplicator to replace the standard ditto machine you now use. The Thermofax C-D, guaranteed for five years, consists of two parts—a ditto master and a ditto machine. It dittos copies like any other ditto machine, but it has the unique feature of a ditto master maker which in one step—through a thermal heat process—produces a ditto master identical to those usually typed on a typewriter. Thus the Thermofax C-D keeps hands, clothes, typewriters, and desks clean. Also, it eliminates costly time spent typing ditto masters. Masters can be used over and over even with revisions and additions. The Thermofax C-D also recharges worn out masters, duplicates 1, 2, 3, 4, or 5 colors in one operation, and prints on paper sizes from 3- by 5-inch to 9- by 14-inch on any weight paper. It needs no special typing or preparation, no plates, mats, or ink. It is always ready to use.

    Paula Fullbright, the area sales representative for Thermofax Inc., recently made a study of your company and presented you with a proposal for purchasing a Thermofax C-D. From the proposal you learned the following facts: Your company types an average of 12 ditto masters a week—each one taking about 15 minutes for a secretary to type. Twenty copies are then run off for each master. The average amount of time it takes a secretary to leave her desk, run off the copies, and return to her desk is 4 minutes. With a Thermofax C-D a secretary can make a ditto in 30 seconds. If the Thermofax C-D is located in the same position as the standard ditto machine was, 4 minutes is still the time needed to run off 20 copies. Total time spent for making a master and 20 copies with the Thermofax C-D is 4.5 minutes.

Included in the proposal was the following table:

Item:	Cost/copy	Cost/minute
Masters	$0.035000	
Fluid	0.000450	
Paper	0.003680	
Labor		0.070000

Basis of Cost

Masters — C–6 @ $35.00/set*	one master for 100 copies
Fluid — $3.60 per gallon	one gallon for 8,000 copies
Paper — $3.68/set*	8½" x 11" white
Maintenance — $109.00 per year	
Machine — $625	
*Set equals 1,000 units	

The data in the above table hold true for both your standard ditto machine and the Thermofax C-D, with the exception of the maintenance cost, which is $36.00 per year for your standard ditto machine.

Your assignment is to write a memo report to Mr. James Davis, Purchasing manager of Zelectron, recommending the purchase of a Thermofax C-D. Just as important as the actual costs are other factors, such as the ease with which a secretary can make copies, and the machine's versatility as a copier. Use good headings, and an appropriate table. Will you organize by the logical or psychological plan? Include one or two well-planned tables in your discussion section.

6. You are the supervisor of Chemco Distributors, a chemical supply house in Denver, Colorado. In order to ease the daily work load of your secretaries, you have been considering purchasing several Mini-Pack tape recorders.

The Mini-Pack is a tape recorder about the size of a large transistor radio and has all the advantages of the traditional tape recorder, plus the advantages of a dictaphone. Mini-Packs should be very helpful in your firm since much of the secretaries' time is involved in taking and transcribing dictation from company officials and sales representatives. The Mini-Pack uses cartridge tapes that record for two hours, one hour on each side, and runs for 50 hours on one transistor radio battery. Cartridges are especially convenient since there is no confusion with threading tapes and rewinding. The Mini-Pack also has a volume control and a "view window" which shows the amount of recording time left on the side in use. Like a dictaphone, the Mini-Pack has a foot pedal (which starts the tape when pressed), a forward switch, reverse switch, and an earphone similar to those on a standard dictaphone.

At your request a representative from Sonat, makers of the Mini-Pack, came to Chemco Distributors and prepared a proposal (cost analysis) for the purchase of 10 Mini-Pack recorders. The findings, based on the operations at the Chemco Distributors are as follows:

Present operations

Average number of min/letter secretary spends in taking dictation . . .	10
Average number of min/letter secretary spends in transcribing notes . .	7
Average pay/min for a secretary (base is $4.20 hourly).	$0.070
Average number of letters dictated by each executive and transcribed by a secretary weekly	60

Average number of min/letter executive spends dictating 10
Average pay/min for an executive (base is $6.60 hourly) 0.110

With Sonat "Mini-Pack"
Average number of min/letter secretary spends in transcribing the
    recording 4
Average number of min/letter executive spends recording 9
Pay scales and number of letters weekly remain the same
Costs of Mini-Pack per unit $80

Your assignment is to write a memo report to Wilma Schuman, purchasing manager of Chemco Distributors, recommending the purchase of 10 Mini-Pack tape recorders. Miss Schuman will be interested in not only the cost of the machines, but also their versatility and possible nonfinancial benefits to the company. Include 1 or 2 good tables.

7. You are the executive vice president of a wholesale house that supplies industrial chemicals to many manufacturers throughout your state. In the 10 years you have been in business you have used a standard dictating machine. Recently you purchased a new product on the market called a Mini-Pack. A Mini-Pack is a small tape recorder which has the advantages of both a tape recorder and a dictating machine. It is small (about the size of a transistor radio), costs only $80, and runs for 50 hours on one transistor radio battery. The Mini-Pack uses cartridge tapes that record for two hours, one hour per side. Cartridges are convenient because time is not wasted in fiddling with threading tapes and trying to remember which side you want to record on. The Mini-Pack is also equipped with a volume control and a "view window" which tells you the amount of recording time left on the side in use. It also has a foot pedal (which stops the tape when pressed), a forward speed, a reverse speed, and an earphone similar to those used on a standard dictating machine.

    You have been able to put the Mini-Pack to good use. Since it is portable, some of your sales staff take Mini-Packs to conferences and then later give the tapes to secretaries to be transcribed. (As a result, your sales people have accurate records of meetings well in advance of the published minutes). Your traveling sales representatives are also able to dictate letters while they are on the road, when facts are fresh in their minds, and have a secretary type messages out when they return. Recently you have been recording company meetings and having a secretary transcribe the tapes afterward, thereby providing valuable reference materials for all employees. Even the secretaries prefer the Mini-Packs to the standard dictating machines. They no longer have to take shorthand notes (they did before when all of the machines were being used), and it is much easier to handle the compact tapes.

    There have been some problems with the Mini-Packs, but none of them are serious. The Mini-Pack does not always pick up conversation that is farther than 5 or 6 feet from the microphones. Also, sometimes noise close to the speaker drowns out conversation in the background. However, you have compensated for this by putting the speaker in a central position when recording conferences. The Mini-Packs are not as durable as the standard dictating machines. The cases are made of plastic and will crack if dropped or squeezed into a briefcase. If they are properly handled you believe they will last one or two years more than the sales representative's estimate.

    Yesterday you received a letter from Mr. Jeff Green, Purchasing Manager of XL Distributors in Denver, Colorado. He has been considering buying several of the Mini-Packs to give to his executives for dictating letters and reports to secretaries. Since he is planning on buying a large number of Mini-Packs, Mr. Green has decided to ask you for your experience with them before making the investmant. The Mini-Pack people gave him your name as a new customer.

Your assignment is to write a letter report to Mr. Green telling him your comments on the Mini-Pack. Mr. Green is sure to know all the sales information; what he wants is your experience on such areas as dependability, performance, and versatility.

8. So far you have been reading the text's discussion of reports and listening to your professor's interpretation. You will now find out for yourself the types of reports you'll be writing on the job after graduation. Select an organization similar to the one you hope to be associated with after graduation and interview someone on the job who has a job similar to the one you want. If you can't interview this person consider her or his superior.

In preparation for this assignment, hand in to your professor the answers to the following in memo format. (The purpose of this screening is so your professor can make sure you ask appropriate questions and that no more than one student in class goes to the same firm.)

   a. The name of the company. If you plan to be an accountant in a C.P.A. firm, choose a C.P.A. firm; if you intend to get into personnel work, choose an organization that has a personnel department.
   b. Name of the individual you'll interview and/or that person's title. Be sure to choose someone who can tell you the types of reports you'll be writing on the job after graduation.
   c. Purpose of the interview. To be sure the questions you'll ask fulfill the purpose of the assignment, jot down in one sentence the purpose of the interview—"The purpose of the interview is to find out all I can about the types of reports I'll be writing on the job in my chosen career." Keep this purpose in mind as you select your questions. All questions should relate directly to this purpose.
   d. List at least 10 really pertinent questions you plan to ask the officer you will interview. Consider questions to which you want answers and arrange the questions in the order you'll be asking them. Given below are a few examples of questions you might want to ask.
      (1) What types of reports does your (firm) prepare? (Please specify whether memo report, letter report, formal report, or printed form report.)
      (2) Which of the above-mentioned types of reports are written most frequently? least frequently?
      (3) Who usually prepares the report? (Individual versus group, lower-echelon versus upper-echelon.)
      (4) What are some common weaknesses in these reports?
      (5) What make(s) a good report?
      (6) What is the most frequent arrangement of the body of the report? (Logical versus psychological.)
      (7) How long a time, on the average, is spent preparing each type of report?
      (8) Do employees work on the report more during working hours or more at home?
      (9) What is the difference between a report going upward to management and downward to the workers?
      (10) In what way do you feel your (firm's) reports may be improved?

Write a memo report to your professor about your findings. Be sure to include a subject line, body (all three parts), and necessary headings. The text should include more than one main division but perhaps no more than two or three. Also, you might need subheadings for one or more of the major divisions in the text.

9. You are a college student and member of the University Church. Through your efforts and the help of the college student-youth group, you designed and put into operation a special tutoring program to help foreign students—in your church and at the nearby university—get the help they needed in their conversational English.

   You decided to create this program as a result of conversations with foreign students in your congregation. The foreign students said that they would like to have someone get together with them individually so they could practice conversing in English. You assigned a volunteer student to each foreign student seeking help. These two were required to meet at least once a week for a quarter (a 10-week period). This, however, sometimes did not work out and you had to ask the volunteer to leave. It hurt the foreign student more if the sessions were not regular. Some volunteer-foreign student pairs have sessions that last longer than one hour a week. Other pairs meet for only the stipulated one hour a week.

   The tutors are volunteers, which has presented some problem. Due to the intrinsic appeal of this program, many people volunteer. So far you have been able to keep up with the foreign student demand. Some tutors are poor. Some say they will contribute and don't and others contribute a lot of time.

   Publicity is very important for getting the program going. Ads in the church bulletin and university papers are instrumental in recruiting volunteers and informing the foreign studetns.

   In addition to meeting with the foreign student one hour a week, each tutor is required to meet with the other tutors one Sunday every month to discuss problems. The tutors must remember that they are talking with a student, and must not take a condescending attitude. And at no time should the tutor ever question the foreign student's religious beliefs. The tutor must remember that although this is a religion-oriented program, the tutors' function is not to convert or judge other people.

   Yesterday you received a letter from Mr. Floyd Lowers at another church in a nearby city asking for information about your program because he is interested in setting up a similar program.

   You had some problems giving the tutors ideas for variety in meeting with their students. You created a list which was given to each tutor which had all sorts of ideas—like studying together, hiking and other sports, shopping together, and driving around in a car. There were also games suggested which would help the foreign student practice English.

   When the foreign students sign up for tutors they are given envelopes which tell them the do's and don't's according to the goals. You also give both the tutor and the student a way to end the relationship if they don't get along. The student is free at any time to terminate the meeting arrangements and ask for a new tutor. The tutor can also ask for a new student. Strict confidence is maintained in this regard, and a lot of juggling does occur.

   On the whole the program has been a great success. Many new and lasting friendships have resulted. The tutors also found that they learned a tremendous amount from the foreign students. There has been a cultural exchange which has helped both the student and the tutor.

   Reply to Mr. Lower's request and report your experience—both the good and the bad—with organizing and operating the program.

10. As a follow-up to the interview discussed in Exercise 1 in Chapter 11, report your findings to your professor. Use memo-report format and a logically organized body (first the introduction, then the text, and finally the terminal section). The text should consist of at least two major divisions—but not more than three or four. If you use subsections in one or more major divisions, remember you must

have at least two subsections for each division and the major division should begin with an introductory paragraph that introduces the reader to the overall division and its subsections. Single-space within paragraphs but double-space between paragraphs and before and after headings.

You should be able to say what you need to say adequately in a report between one and two pages in length. Unless your professor tells you otherwise, the purpose of the report is to inform the professor what qualifications the company (or the person you interviewed) wants to find in a graduating senior who is applying for a specific job or for a job in a specific field.

11. One month ago Henry Merry, manager of the clothing department of Walden's Department Store since 1955, announced his upcoming retirement. As the supervisor of all departments, you were asked by Lisa Walden (vice president in charge of personnel) to recommend a suitable replacement. For three weeks you have been interviewing applicants and compiling profiles on currently employed personnel that are qualified to handle the position. Walden's has no policy of seniority when it comes to hiring departmental managers. Emphasis is placed on individual qualities of leadership, ability to work with others, and a general knowledge of business operations. Previous management experience is not necessary, since most of the daily management routine can be quickly learned on the job.

Having carefully considered all 27 qualified employees and applicants, you have narrowed the field down to 3 main candidates, one of whom you must recommend to Ms. Walden. On the basis of your recommendation, she will make the final decision.

The following are the three candidates' qualifications to consider in your report:

Phil Bradshaw:

At age 45, Phil has earned a high school diploma, received an honorable discharge after serving 6 years in the Army (2 years as a master sergeant), worked 4 years in construction and then 6 years selling magazines on the road, and has worked in Walden's clothing department the last 11 years. Among the clerks he has the most seniority. Often when Mr. Merry was absent because of illness or for business reasons, Phil was asked to act as manager. Company policy requires that each departmental manager keep a personality and efficiency inventory on all employees in his department. In the inventory Mr. Merry praised Phil's ability to handle the managerial duties in his (Merry's) absence, but he also noted that Phil had trouble in getting along with some of the employees. At times Phil was "bossy" toward new employees, even when he was not acting as manager.

Kirk Bryde:

At age 25, Kirk will receive his master's degree in marketing at the end of the current quarter. From an interview with Kirk and a résumé he has given you, you know that he is a capable leader and has the type of personality that will get along well with employees in the department. In college he was captain of the track team. Most of Kirk's working experience has been part-time or full-time summer employment. For the last 2 years he has worked in a small clothing store in the university district. A reference from the manager of the store was quite complimentary and noted especially Kirk's ability to keep himself busy when there were no customers to wait on.

Claire Weaver:

At age 38, Claire has a B.A. degree in history and English, taught high school English 9 years, worked in the home furnishings department at Walden's for 3 years and in the present clothing department the last 4 years. The principal of the high school where Weaver taught told Mr. Merry by letter he has no unfavorable criticism of the job done at any time, but Weaver quit teaching because she had disciplinary problems. However, both faculty and students in high school liked her. In the personality and efficiency inventory, Mr. Merry wrote that Claire is one of the best workers he has ever managed. She never questions any request given her by Mr. Merry or by any of the other employees. Claire also gets along with all employees and seems to be the most popular among them. She has never been in a managerial position, but she does have a sound knowledge of the operations of the clothing department.

12. Write a job description of a job you are holding now or have held. Assume your employer needs the description for the new employees who are to succeed you. You are being promoted. If the work you do (or did) is the same day after day, describe one day's work in detail. If it differs each week or month, or there are certain special responsibilities on certain days, be sure to explain specifically. For example, on what days are various reports or activities due? Use appropriate headings to make reading easy. Your job description report will be filed permanently in both the personnel department files and in those of your department head.

17 The Formal Report

The formal (sometimes called "long") report is merely an expansion of the shorter one. The body of both a memo report and a formal report consists of an introduction, a text, and terminal section organized either logically or psychologically. Both have headings and other visual aids when desirable. "Formal" merely means the report includes certain prefatory and supplemental parts; it does not mean the level of language is formal. You should continue to use easily understood words and apply the same good writing principles as you do in an informal communication.

The formal report, however, generally covers a more complex problem than the memo report. Consequently, the needed preliminary investigation plus gathering, sorting, and interpreting data, as well as the writing and editing, are often far more time-consuming and costly than for memo reports. This chapter presents additional information you will need regarding the following aspects of formal report writing: proposals; working plans; prefatory parts; supplemental parts; documentation and explanatory notations; plus writing, revising, and typing.

Proposals

Before undertaking a costly, time-consuming project for which financial assistance is required before proceeding with the long, formal report, the researcher needs to write a proposal.[1] Also, a business or industrial firm that seeks the award of a large contract from a government agency or another firm must submit a proposal (bid) before being considered.

As you know, the first three planning steps before writing any report—authorized or voluntary—pertain to the problem and purpose, readers' needs, and ideas to be included. (See pages 516–517.) When you have completed the third step—and you know you must seek approval and/or funds, you can begin planning your proposal.

If you seek funds, you must determine which firm or agency may be interested in granting funds for your type of project. In general, the best advice for writing a proposal to a specific funding agency is to be sure your objectives match the philosophy and program of the funding source. This may require an interview with an agency official or at least research on your part about the agency's (or company's) philosophy. Follow meticulously the proposal requirements of the funding source. It may require for all proposals certain headings, details, format, number of copies, deadlines, and so forth. Adhering honestly and accurately to all requirements will work to your advantage. Whenever possible, use the outline and same words the agency has in its literature or guidelines. Don't use jargon that only you and your assistants can understand.

Outline

The following suggestions include various topics you may be asked to discuss in a written proposal. Only very long and comprehensive proposals, of course, include all (or almost all) these topics. Obviously some situations will require only a few headings. For some, a four- or five-page proposal discussing three or four topics may be suffi-

[1] For an example of an informal proposal, see pages 574–578.

cient. For others, the total presentation covering perhaps fifteen specific topics might run to fifty or more pages. Obviously, the information required for a $1 million grant will be much more comprehensive than for a $200 allowance.

Problem

Clearly define the problem. If it's a community problem, is it specific for the local area or a general one? If it's a company problem, does it concern a certain branch or area—such as shipping delays, shoplifting, inventory control, poor customer relations, excessive purchase returns, or what?

Background . . . what led up to the problem. Be concise.

Need for solution. Is it urgent? critical? why?

Purpose (Objectives)

State objectives concisely and clearly. Are they measurable? achievable?

Avoid including too many objectives or too broad a purpose.

Scope

Define the boundaries of your project. Will you study one area of a community? or a company? or a department? or of a severe problem? What boundaries are you setting to accomplish your objectives?

Procedures

What specific methods will you use? Are they scientifically sound?

What are you going to do? how?

Who is involved?

What is your plan of attack? Can your methods solve the problem?

Identify specific activities and state your time schedule for each; for example, initial planning and organizing, search of literature, interviews, correspondence, questionnaires, experiments.

Include estimated calendar dates if possible.

Consider and identify variables, if any, in the project.

Make clear your sequence of steps in the project.

Allow sufficient time for data collection and for unexpected problems.

Equipment and Facilities Available

Show you have thought deeply enough to realize what facilities will be needed.

State what equipment and facilities you already have for use and assure that you can get the rest. Depending upon type of project, you might, for example, need a movie camera, computer, programmer, 10 desk calculators, a nearby library, typewriter(s), duplicating machines and services (for questionnaires, etc.), even a car, truck, boat, or small plane!

Personnel Qualifications

Include an organization chart; perhaps a flow chart.

Show job descriptions, names, and one-page resumes for top personnel (with their permission) who will assist on your project.

State your own experience and past successes with similar projects. Include dates and references (with permission) so that the prospective funder can verify your statements.

Evaluation

State how data generated in your project will be handled and stored.

If you are planning a community or a company project, state what factors will determine whether your project can be done again in another community or company branch.

Show how you will evaluate how well the project is working while it is underway and how you'll determine whether to continue it, change directions, or terminate it.

State the likelihood of success. Do not promise more than you can do.

Can you guarantee a solution within stated boundaries?

Some problems (crime, cancer, drug abuse, etc.) may be so complex that no one expects any one researcher to solve them. In your proposal, protect yourself from charges of misrepresentation by honestly estimating (conservatively) what probable outcome can be expected. Even a partial solution of an adequately limited problem may be a step in the right direction.

Budget

Do *not* overbudget; funding sources quickly reject a padded budget. Be realistic.

List: Salaries and fringe benefits for all staff assistants and yourself

Equipment and consumable supplies needed to reach objectives

Travel requirements (estimate miles, type of transportation, number of persons who will be traveling)

Miscellaneous expenses and indirect costs

Allowance for the unexpected

Provide justification for each budget item.

In general, before you agree to work on a lengthy project for any firm or agency, see that a suitable written agreement covers your costs, hours of work, time schedule; and make sure you understand what penalties, if any, apply for delayed performance or nonperformance. Sometimes consulting a qualified financial counselor is advisable.

Format

After you have written, in rough draft, your answers to all pertinent topics, arrange them in a coherent order. If your discussion under one topic is too brief, you may need to expand on it, or perhaps group the information under another, broader heading—unless of course the agency's guidelines prescribe exact headings and order of arrangement.

The format of the proposal includes many of the parts found in formal reports. Here is one possible suggested format:

1. *Prefatory parts*
   Title page
   Table of Contents
   List of Tables (if any)
   List of Figures (if any)
2. *Body of proposal*
   Introduction
      Problem
      Need
      Background

Objectives/Purpose
Procedures
  Methods and sources
  Plan of attack
  Sequence of activities
  Equipment and facilities available
  Personnel qualifications
Evaluation
Budget
  3. *Supplementary parts*
Agency forms
  Budget justification
  References
Tables or figures (if any)

Writing Style

You will be wise to apply all the business writing principles and report writing techniques when writing the proposal. In its digest on proposal writing, the Washington State Office of Economic Opportunity includes the following excellent advice:[2]

> First impressions are very critical. None is more so than that first impression your proposal gives to the reader when submitted to an agency or foundation for consideration. Many proposals are lost at the first look by the reader. He appraises the proposal immediately in terms of:
>
> 1. General appearance
> 2. Neatness
> 3. Specific appearance of:
>   a. Table of Contents
>   b. List of Figures
>   c. Title Page
>   d. Maps
>   e. Graphs
>   f. Charts
> 4. Consistency of Style
> 5. Title—is it grandiose or does it properly describe the project?
> 6. Completeness
> 7. Professionalism
>
> Therefore, you cannot afford to skimp on the time you spend in "polishing" your proposal. Each item must be checked and re-checked. Since you have spent many hours developing the proposal idea, and further hours researching and writing before your first draft, why risk your investment over poor typing, proofing, graphics, etc. Some of the most important time spent working on the proposal will be that spent on the final draft.
>
> If you are not an artist it might be advisable to employ one to prepare the cover, charts, graphs, etc. The cost is minimal when you consider the potential return.
>
> Be sure you and your typist are familiar with an appropriate typing style. Learn it well and be sure to follow it consistently . . . Select one which best fits your needs and adopt it for all your proposals.

[2]Lon F. Backman, Program Development, *A Digest on the Elements of Proposal Writing,* Washington State Office of Economic Opportunity, Olympia, Wash., December 1971.

Don't accept or be satisfied with sloppy typing or art work. Make sure it is re-worked until satisfactory. You want all the final copy to be neat and clean prior to submission.

The preceding suggestions on proposal outline, format, and writing style can be adapted to all kinds of proposals. If, instead of seeking funds for a comprehensive research study, you are writing a proposal which is your company's bid on a $3 million sales or construction contract, the basic characteristics of the formal proposal are similar. You will of course need to know the capabilities of your firm's products and services and be scrupulously accurate.

Working Plans

When someone—inside or outside of your company—requests that you investigate a problem and write a report, you first make sure you know what the person wants or needs. Be sure you are told, orally or in writing, clearly what is expected of you.[3] You should know the problem, purpose, scope, procedure to follow in collecting data, and deadline for completion. If your employer (or whoever has requested the report) doesn't give you complete information, you need to ask questions until you understand the assignment thoroughly.

After you receive the assignment, you use the given facts for informal talks with people associated with the problem and with authorities on the subject, preliminary review of materials existing in libraries, study of company records, and so on. Use whatever sources will give you the necessary background and understanding to proceed further with the investigation—through the first three planning steps (discussed on pages 516-517). Given here are a suggested outline and a sample working plan.

Outline

The culmination of preliminary investigation is a working plan that you'll present to the person who asked you to make the report.[4] If no one authorized you to take the assignment, you still should make out a working plan for your own benefit. In this working plan—perhaps a memo to the employer in your own organization or a letter to someone outside the firm—you'll include:

1. Problem
2. Purpose

---

[3] In a formal report of a public nature, the one authorizing or commissioning the report notifies the report writer in a letter called a *letter of authorization*. The message will be bound with the formal report's prefatory pages, usually just before the transmittal letter.

[4] In addition to the two contacts already mentioned—at the very beginning during the authorization and at the completion of the preliminary investigation—the authorizer and the report writer might have further consultations if warranted and appropriate. These additional contacts might occur: (1) at the completion of the investigation—after the writer has collected and studied the material and determined the results; (2) after the writer has made the final report outline; and (3) after the writer has written the report but before he or she officially submits the finished report to the receiver.

3. Scope
4. Limitations
5. Use of the report
6. Type of reader(s)
7. Tentative outline (your main text and terminal section headings)
8. Method(s) of collecting data
9. Work-progress schedule

The whole idea of the working plan is to tell the one who authorized the report (or yourself) the way you understand the problem, the purpose, the use of the report, and so on, and to make sure you see eye to eye. Be sure you understand who your readers will be. Do you have both primary and secondary readers? Are they familiar with the subject or will they need background material? Are they biased, antagonistic, or favorably inclined toward the subject?

In the outline you want to show the areas you'll investigate and discuss in the report—and, if possible, subdivisions for each major area. Also indicate the type of terminal section you'll have—summary, conclusions, and/or recommendations—and whether you are arranging the parts logically or psychologically.

Example

The following working plan is from a researcher in a management consulting firm to a department head. It is typewritten on the firm's intraoffice memo stationery, in memo form.

TO: Nina Vandeline   Date: April 12, 197_

FROM: Tom Browne

SUBJECT: Working Plan for Study on Treelane Homeowners Association

Confirming our conversation of April 8, here is my working plan for the study you requested concerning Treelane Homeowners Association, a development in south XY County.

<u>Problem:</u>
The Association's programs are not meeting the needs of its members. The benefits the Association affords are rarely taken advantage of my homeowners. They share assets consisting of a clubhouse, park, swimming pool, and fishing pond. In addition, the Association has a charter which outlines rules and guidelines all homeowners are supposed to follow for (1) making changes in their property, (2) general regulation of pets, and (3) use of the common area.

However, rules are often ignored. Social activities are rarely attended by many homeowners. Business meetings have a very poor attendance record. Communication is poor. Some owners are hostile.

<u>Purpose and Objective</u>
I will determine the causes for the above stated problems and make recommendations to help Treelane become a more effective organization.

My plan is to find the attitudes and interests of individual homeowners and apply my findings to aid officers in modifying the organi-

zation. My findings and proposals will hopefully lead to an organization which involves homeowners and helps them to receive benefits
they are paying for.

Limitations
My evaluations must be limited to programs which are useful and
stimulate interest and modifications of property within the budget.
The study is limited in time, in that the recommendations are needed
one month from today.

Scope
I will evaluate only those changes which are practical and feasible
and which have apparent potential for bettering Treelane.

Procedures for Gathering Data
A questionnaire will be sent to all homeowners. In addition to the
replies received from homeowners, I plan to interview all officers
and to examine--with your permission--the records of the Association.

Division of Problem and Tentative General Outline
The problem will be divided into three parts: (1) social activities,
(2) physical property, and (3) rules.

First a questionnaire must be prepared to find out what preferences,
dislikes, and ideas property owners have. The data will be analyzed,
and selected recommendations will be evaluated by talking with
officers and looking at the budget.

Tentative Conclusion
The homeowners association needs social activities which will involve
more property owners. This change will stimulate interest in the
organization and decrease the hostilities now present.

Work-progress Schedule
Data will be collected by Friday, April 22; organized and interpreted
by Monday May 6. Report outline will be ready by May 9. The final
report will be submitted by May 12.

Prefatory Parts

One of the distinguishing features of a formal (or long) report is that it has some or all
of the following prefatory parts: cover, title fly, title page, letter of authorization,
letter of transmittal, table of contents (contents), table of tables, abstract.[5]

Cover (Design and Wording of Title)

Many reports combine the cover and title page for the top page. But you can dress up
a formal report by using both. Obviously, you need a cover to which the reader will re-

[5] In the left-hand column below are the prefatory and supplemental parts of the formal report.
To the right of each entry is the location in the memo report where you find similar information:

Cover/title page	to, from, subject, date
Title fly	not needed
Letter of transmittal	introduction
Table of contents	plan of presentation (in introduction)
Table of tables	table(s) in text
Abstract	introduction and terminal section
Appendix	appendix
Bibliography	sources used (in introduction)

act favorably. Sometimes a simple hard cover (both for the front and back), with a properly placed title, will suffice. You can type the title on a gummed label, or type or print it directly on the cover itself. However, with a little imagination and a subject that allows you the possibility, you can design a more complex cover—one that ties in with the material being discussed. For example, assume you're writing a report in which you're suggesting that the firm switch from its present printed personnel form to a more effectively worded and comprehensive form. The cover can consist of parts of both forms with a title superimposed. Or, if you're discussing foreign compact cars, a picture of one of the cars and an attractively arranged title could make an effective cover. But beware of overdoing—of making your cover gaudy or ludicrous.

Your title must exactly and specifically identify the overall subject of the report. As you ponder the wording of the title, here are a few suggestions to consider.

1. Keep the title short (usually about eight words maximum); omit "the," "a," and "an" whenever possible. Also wordy are "A Report on . . . ," "A Survey on . . . ," "Constructive Criticism . . . ," "Recommendations for Improvement for . . ." A long title kills interest and can cause filing errors. If you must use many words, use a short main title and a longer subtitle, as shown below:

   MARKETING POLICIES OF OREGON'S HAZELNUT GROWERS ASSO-CIATION

   Appraisal of methods to increase demand for hazelnuts, with emphasis on value and effectiveness of advertising, sales promotion, price policies, and distribution channels.

2. Use your imagination to create a title that catches the eye.
3. Whenever possible, stress results rather than procedure or the way you collected your material.
4. Avoid an air of mystery—such as a title in the form of a question.
5. Pay particular attention to the scope of the report. For example, "Agricultural Products in (State)" is misleading if you're discussing only grains, vegetables, or fruits.
6. Include whichever of the five W's (and How) seem pertinent.

Title Fly

Only when you have both a cover and title page can you use this blank sheet of paper which is located between the two parts. As in books, it acts as a buffer or relief when the reader opens the book.

Title Page

Whether or not your report has a cover, the title page usually contains the title, as well as names of the recipient and sender, and the completion date—each of which should have a separate focal point on the page. As illustrated on page 622, the title page should be attractively arranged. It may be in four sections or in three sections; if the latter, you combine date with author's identification. If appropriate, you add pertinent facts about the individuals involved, such as title, department, and organization. Date of completion must agree with the date on the letter of transmittal.

With a cover, the title page uses the same weight paper as the text sheets do; as a combination cover-title page this part might have a heavier weight—similar to that for the cover.

Letter of Authorization

The person authorizing or commissioning the formal report notifies the report writer in a letter called a letter of authorization. In a formal report of a public nature, this message becomes one of the bound prefatory pages. Although it is often omitted from the business formal report, it may of course be included.

When you are in the position of authorizing a report, organize your message by the direct-request or good-news plan. And be sure to make clear just what you are authorizing. Take care of the items that you know a researcher needs to know.

Letter of Transmittal

The letter of transmittal officially conveys or transmits the finished report. When you're writing to a large group of people, you label it as a preface and set it up as one. The receiver is the individual who authorized the report or who needs the information. In the transmittal you tell the reader what you'd say to him or her if you were handing the report to him or her. Regardless of whether the body of the report talks in the third person, you can use first and second persons in the transmittal. You want to adhere to all the rules of letter writing for a transmittal. Use the good-news organizational plan. Basically, this letter includes transmittal, authorization, and purpose plus any other ideas listed below:

Main idea
Transmittal
Authorization
Purpose
Need or use of report

Explanation and/or highlights
Perhaps a brief indication of outcome—in general only. Indicate conclusions and/or recommendations *if* you think the reader will consider them good (or neutral) news and *if* an abstract or terminal section with the same information doesn't appear at the beginning of the report—just a few pages after the transmittal.
Perhaps a comment or two on an interesting matter closely related to the report but not discussed in it; or writer's comment outside the limits of the report.
Background and methodology are sometimes stated briefly.

Courteous ending
Acknowledgments to people who assisted[6]
Indication that later reports may be necessary or forthcoming
Willingness to discuss
Offer to assist with future projects

---

[6] In some formal reports acknowledgments are in a separate section instead of in the transmittal or preface.

You need to be careful not to include the same elements in both the transmittal and the introduction or the transmittal and the abstract or synopsis, if any, for the needless repetition would be annoying.

For an example of a brief transmittal see the airline informational report on page 623. Notice it contains authorization, purpose, use of report, a little background, and willingness to discuss.

The example that follows is a transmittal for an analytical formal report. Notice it briefly indicates the outcome and the writer's recommendation. (The 33-page report itself discusses both in detail; its terminal section is on page 32.)

```
(Name and inside address)

Dear Mrs. Larson:

Here is the report you authorized October 18 regarding a survey of
market potential on Bigg Island.  The purpose of this report is to
present an analysis of data collected about the possible implementa-
tion of home-care service at Bigg View Convalescent Center.

You will be pleased to learn that our survey indicates a generally
favorable reaction to the project.  The report includes survey results
in five areas:

      Social structure
      Age range
      Percent over age 65
      Financial structure of persons over age 65
      Preferences for convalescent care

On the basis of the survey made, I recommend that Bigg View Convales-
cent Center initiate a home-care service and a program of extensive
informal education of the Island's population.

I have enjoyed making this study and appreciate the opportunity to
help you reach a reliable decision concerning the home-care service.
Please call me if you have questions or I may assist you in any
further analysis.

                              Sincerely yours,

                              (signature, typed name, title)
```

Table of Contents

The table of contents shows the major and minor divisions of the report and their respective locations within the report. On page 624 is the contents for the airline report. Notice that the writer sets apart the body of the report from the letter of transmittal and bibliography by indenting the introduction, major divisions of the text, and the summary. If you wish, you can separate the body even more by putting all its major parts in capitals (also shown on page 624). If you preface the introduction, major divisions of the text, and terminal section with Roman numerals (I, II, III, etc.), you should preface their subdivisions with capital letters (A, B, C, etc.). For further subdivisions, you use Arabic numerals (1, 2, 3, etc.) and then lowercase letters (a, b, c, etc.).

Naturally you must prepare the table of contents after typing the rest of the report —or at least after making a typewritten draft—so you'll know the correct page numbers. Use leaders (dot space dot space dot) to lead the eye from the name of each entry to the page column on the right. Every entry shown in the table of contents must appear exactly as it does in the body. But not every heading in the body has to appear in the contents. Usually you show no more than three degrees (first, second, and third) of headings.

If the appendix includes several different entries (questionnaire, reprint of a statute or regulation, various tables, or other visual aids) you can show them in one of two locations: (1) if you have only a few entries, as subdivisions of the appendix on the contents page; or (2) if you have a rather extensive appendix, as subdivisions of the appendix on the appendix title page. You may then show the page number for the first page of each entry.

Table of Tables

Label this prefatory page according to the type of formal visual aids shown throughout the text. If the illustrations are all tables, you'll label the page "table of tables" or "list of tables." Follow the same procedure for charts, pictures, and so forth. If you have a mixture of tables, charts, and other visual aids, consider a title that encompasses them all; perhaps a "table of illustrations" will suffice.

This prefatory page serves the same function for the visual aids as the contents page does for the coverage of the report. If space permits, you can include both the table of contents and table of tables on the same page. Whether the latter is combined with the table of contents or by itself on the page, the layout begins as shown below:

Table of Tables

Table		Page
1	(title)	6
2	(title)	9
3	(title)	11
4	(title)	13

Abstract

As a prefatory part, an abstract[7] can definitely perform a vital service for the reader. An abstract is an abbreviated, concise, accurate representation of a report, document, or publication. Usually it is placed at the bottom of the title page or on a separate page immediately preceding the report body. Abstracts may be "descriptive" (also called "indicative") or "informative."

Descriptive Abstract. This type of abstract merely states what the report contains. It includes purpose, methods, and scope, but omits the results. The reader must read

[7]This prefatory part carries various labels—"abstract," "synopsis," "introductory summary," "precis"—but they all are prefatory summaries that come before the report body.

the report to find the results, conclusions, and/or recommendations. A descriptive abstract can cover in fewer than 100 words any report, whether it is ten or a thousand pages long. Its length does not depend on the report length. For example, a descriptive abstract of the airline report (pages 622–631) might be:

> This report shows the development of the present reservation system of United Airlines. Based on interviews with four United Airlines executives of the Regional Sales and Service Division, and the firm's Publicity Fact Book, the report shows three systems used from 1930 through 1970 and beyond.

Informative Abstract. Not only does the informative abstract include purpose, methods, and scope; it also has statements of results, conclusions, and/or recommendations. Because it contains more helpful information—the report's highlights all on one page—it is preferred by most readers. The busy manager after scanning the abstract, can determine whether he wants to read further.

Besides being a useful prefatory part of a long, formal report, informative abstracts also serve other important functions. Some firms circulate to all their management personnel only the abstract *without* the report. (The person who originally authorized the report of course gets the complete, original report.) Those who receive only the abstract can decide whether they need the original report, which is then sent to them upon their request. This practice saves much time and expense, especially when reports are 50 or more pages long.

Another important use of abstracts is for reports, articles, documents, and such that are published. A well-written abstract can communicate contents to many more business associates. In brief reading time colleagues can scan abstracts in their professional and business journals, thus keeping up to date on literature in their special field. The quality of an abstract may determine who and how many ever see the full document. Those who find interest in the abstract may send for the original write-up.

If you are working in a certain professional area or industry, your long report informative abstract may be widely circulated within the area or industry. For example:

> Reports from companies working on government contracts may have an initial distribution of less than 100. Yet, on NASA-sponsored company information for the space program, 9,000 copies of abstracts are circulated to potential users of these company reports (and this within two to four weeks after the report is released).[8]

Though the informative abstract length varies somewhat in proportion to the report length, it should be confined to fewer than 500 words (preferably on one page). To show you how abstracts vary, here are three examples:

Example 1
An informative abstract of the airline report might begin with the same two sentences shown for the descriptive abstract above and then continue with a summary similar to the four paragraphs shown on page 13 of the report.

[8]David L. Staiger, Manager of Publications, Society of Automotive Engineers, Inc., "What Today's Students Need to Know about Writing Abstracts," in *The Journal of Business Communication*, 3(1):30, 1965.

Example 2
Informative abstract on a 7-page published report[9]
The authors undertook a survey of the attitudes of personnel officers of 250 large organizations concerning the need for communication courses at the graduate level. The survey found that communication skills were rated of extreme importance by executives of large organizations, some believing it to be the single most important function of management personnel.

Example 3
Informative abstract on a 32-page published manual[10]
Because of the vast increase in the scientific literature, technical writers must help the reader grasp ideas quickly. For this purpose, headings and introductions are two of the most useful devices.

Headings give the reader immediate insight into large blocks of information and help him digest them rapidly. Accordingly, they are an exceedingly valuable aid to speed reading.

Although headings are greatly helpful, they are not sufficient. They sometimes are ambiguous, they do not give reasons, and they look neither backward nor forward in the article—they are concerned only with the present. They therefore need supplementation by introductions, which supply this information that headings, because of their brevity, cannot give.

Introductions, in contrast to headings, are complex devices. They have five transitional functions; therefore, a complete introduction is made up of five parts. This manual defines the functions, names the parts, and shows how to use them.

The manual thus is concerned with the heading-introduction technique, and its aim is to show how we can use this technique to help the reader grasp our idea fast.

One more, popular use of abstracts should be mentioned here. If you are invited to present a report at a business meeting (planned perhaps eight months in advance), the chairperson may ask you to send an abstract for distribution before the conference. The abstract may be requested even before you have started writing your report or talk. The well-planned abstract you write for the chairperson can contain the topic sentences you will use later to develop your report and talk. In this situation the abstract is written before, not after, the complete report.

Supplemental Parts

The special parts that are added after the body of a long, formal report are called supplemental or appended parts, or addenda. They include the appendix, bibliography, and index.

Appendix

You put materials into the appendix when you need to include them somewhere in the report, but they aren't essential in developing any part of the text. The appendix per-

[9] James A. Belohlov, Paul O. Popp, Michael S. Porte, "Communication: A View from the Inside of Business," *Journal of Business Communication*, 11(4):54, 1974.

[10] F. Bruce Sanford, "Heading-Introduction Technique," *United States Department of the Interior*, Fish and Wildlife Service, Washington, D.C., Circular 283, page 1, 1968.

mits you to avoid cluttering the discussion (text) with exhibits, copy of a questionnaire, and pamphlets that are unnecessary to read for the right understanding of the report but which may be useful as reference or as supporting information.

With short reports, you merely add the appendix sheets directly to the report. But for a formal report, you place a sheet of paper (the appendix title page) between the last page of the body and the first page of the appendix. If you have enough material in the appendix to justify a separate table of contents, show the contents below the title on the appendix dividing sheet, in order of the page arrangement. (See, for example the appendix dividing sheet in this text, page 663.)

Each separate entry (sample forms, detailed data for reference, table, picture, questionnaire, chart, map, graphic representation, blueprint) in the appendix naturally requires an identifying title. As a rule you should refer the reader to every entry in the appendix in the report body (within the discussion itself or in a footnote).

The last page of the appendix is the ideal place for any table or illustration the reader will need to refer to throughout the report. You can set up this table on a pull-out sheet and tell the reader about the sheet in the letter of transmittal or introduction. Such an arrangement permits the reader to keep this master table—or whatever is on the sheet—in full view at all times.

Bibliography[11]

The items listed in a bibliography are the sources referred to in the report. This supplemental part usually follows the appendix. Among the published sources included in a bibliography are books, government publications, yearbooks, public documents, encyclopedias, pamphlets, bulletins, magazines, and newspapers. In addition, a business report bibliography may also include unpublished sources such as manuscripts, interviews, responses to surveys, and organization letters or documents.

You can present bibliographic entries in a single orderly list under the one heading "Bibliography" or under various pertinent subheads. For example, if your list is long and varied, you might arrange sources within broad groups such as books, periodicals, and government publications. Furthermore, if you include unpublished sources, you might choose a broader main title like "Sources Consulted" instead of "Bibliography" (which literally refers to a list of books).

A popular way to arrange bibliographic entries is in alphabetic order by authors' surnames. For each published source include information about the:

1. *Composition*—author's full name (surname first) and title of the book, article, report, or pamphlet. For coauthors, reverse only the surname of the first au-

[11] Space in this book allows only highlights about bibliographies and footnotes. For additional details on numerous variations in content and setup, you will find these publications helpful: William Giles Campbell and Stephen V. Ballou, *Form and Style: Theses, Reports, Term Papers*, 4th ed., Houghton Mifflin Company, Boston, 1974; Erwin M. Keithley and Philip J. Schreiner, *A Manual of Style for the Preparation of Papers and Reports*, South-Western Publishing Company, Cincinnati, 1971; Kate L. Turabian, *A Manual for Writers of Term Papers, Theses, and Dissertations*, 4th ed., University of Chicago Press, Chicago, 1973; *United States Government Printing Office Style Manual* (Abridged, Revised Edition), U.S. Government Printing Office, Washington, D.C., 1973.

thor: Thompson, Robert, John Jones, and Mary Smith. If more than three authors are involved, reverse the first author's surname but don't list the other names: Thompson, Robert, and others.

2. *Publication*—publisher's name, location, edition, date, total pages in the publication.

For examples of two (among several) ways to set up a bibliography, see Figure 17-1 and the airline report bibliography, page 631.

Some bibliographies are *annotated*. They contain, just below the composition and publication information about each entry, also a brief statement about its content and value. For example:

Concentrates on basic principles and techniques of writing technical reports. Focuses on data gathering, data analysis, and the scientific method. Contains good examples.

Index

The index lists topics alphabetically and guides the reader to various places that discuss certain subject matter in the report. Only in very long reports will you need an index if it is necessary to help the reader find specific subjects and items alphabetically.

Documentation and Explanatory Notations[12]

As you know, when your report contains quotations and/or specific facts from various sources, you need to acknowledge those sources. By documenting your report you not only give credit where credit is due, but also help convince your reader that your data are trustworthy and you are willing to let him examine the references. Your introduction states methodology and mentions sources at least in general; your text discussion refers to them when it is desirable to clarify the origin of specific facts or figures. In addition, the bibliography—especially in long reports—lists sources, usually alphabetically, as a supplemental part after the report body.

This section discusses three methods of presenting sources and additional explanatory or incidental comments within the text portion of the report. You can use (1) footnotes, (2) numbers referring to a list of references, or (3) citations within the text.

Footnotes

Of the three methods, footnotes are the most versatile and usually they are convenient for both the report reader and writer. Place a raised superscript number in the text immediately after the word or sentence to which a footnote refers; and place the footnote at the bottom (foot) of the same page. You can number each footnote consecutively according to page, section, or report. Include footnotes when you want to:

[12] For further readings on these topics, see publications listed in footnote 11.

1. Give credit to a source you used. Naturally you don't give credit to anyone or anything if the information is common knowledge or if you are relying on your experience. But you are plagiarizing if you make a statement belonging to someone else and you don't credit that source.
2. Explain or give additional information that relates to an idea in the text but isn't important enough to include in the discussion or shouldn't interrupt the discussion.
3. Show a cross reference—to direct the reader to another place in the report—such as to a particular page in the appendix.

If your report includes more than five documented sources, you can identify them both in footnotes within the text and in a bibliography. If the report has fewer sources, you can use footnotes without a bibliography.

When the Report Includes a Bibliography. Your footnotes citing sources will be shorter if your report has a bibliography than if it does not include one. Since each bibliography entry contains all pertinent information about the source, you can limit the footnote details to:

Last name(s) of author(s) and title of book, report, or article; page on which the information appears in each publication.

Figure 17-2 illustrates one long report page listing four footnotes. Notice how much shorter these footnotes are than the corresponding bibliography entries in Figure 17-1. The footnotes in Figure 17-2 differ from the corresponding entries in Figure 17-1 (bibliography) in these ways:

1. Only the author's last name (surname) is listed, along with title of the composition. If two or three authors are involved, only the surname of each is included; and if more than three authors, you can write the first author's surname plus "and others."
2. Only the page number of the citation is listed, *not total* pages in the book.
3. Each footnote is numbered, to correspond with the superscript appearing in the text discussion on the same page. Bibliography entries are not numbered; they are arranged alphabetically.

You can also use these shortened footnotes when you need to credit the same source more than once throughout the report. Most readers will find such footnotes easier to understand than the Latin expressions "ibid." (meaning "in the same place"), "op. cit." ("in the work cited"), and "loc. cit." ("in the place cited.")

When the Report Does Not Include a Bibliography. If your entire report (or a chapter of a book) cites fewer than five sources, you will usually not include a bibliography. Your footnotes citing sources must then contain information as complete as that in the bibliography. But instead of stating total pages of a book, each footnote states only the page on which the reference appeared.

For examples of how the sources listed in Figure 17-1 would be written in foot-

Figure 17-2 A long-report page. Four shortened footnotes are listed; the report has a bibliography (shown in Figure 17-1).

and better communication helps all employees to know whether they are entitled to receive straight pay.[1]

For management, these increased hourly wages would amount to a substantial increase in the restaurant's operating costs.[2] This straight holiday wage must be paid on holidays even when the restaurant is closed.

Problems Regarding Vacation Pay

Another high wage expense that would have to be paid to employees is vacation pay. The union's newly adopted rules[3] demand that each employee receive a full week's paid vacation if he has worked for the company one full year. Employees who have worked from two to ten years will receive two weeks' paid vacation and those working ten or more years will get three full weeks.

Our management believes vacations are necessary for its employees. But they—and the City Restaurant Managers' Association—feel the union demands are too high for a restaurant like ours where over 90% of the help is only part-time (3-4 days a week).[4] Our vacation pay is as

[1]Rogers and Roethlisberger, "Barriers and Gateways to Communication," p. 29.
[2]Shore, Operations Management, p. 242.
[3]Restaurant Employees Adopt New Rules," Seattle Times, p. C-4.
[4]Statement by Helen Smith, President, City Restaurant Managers.

Figure 17-1 A bibliography. Sources are listed in alphabetical order. (Footnotes are on text pages as in Figure 17-2.)

BIBLIOGRAPHY[13]

A. Books[14]

Campbell, James H., and Hal W. Hepler, Dimensions in Communication: Readings, Wadsworth Publishing Company, Inc.., Belmont, Calif., 1970, 218 pages.

Perrin, Porter G., Writer's Guide and Index to English, 5th ed., Scott, Foresman and Company, Chicago, 1968, 818 pages.

Shore, Barry, Operations Management, McGraw-Hill Book Company, New York, 1973, 544 pages.

B. Periodicals[14]

Belohov, James, Paul Popp, Michael Porte, "Communication: A View from the Inside of Business," The Journal of Business Communication, Volume 11 (4): (Summer 1974), pages 53-59.

Bernstein, Lesley, "How to Right a Report," Business Management, September 1968, pages 46-48.

Rogers, Carl R. and F. J. Roethlisberger, "Barriers and Gateways to Communication," Harvard Business Review, July-August 1968, page 29.

C. Newspapers[14]

"Restaurant Employees Adopt New Rules," The Seattle Times, December 3, 1975, page C-4.

D. Interview

Smith, Helen, President of City Restaurant Managers, December 10, 1975.

13This list could also be titled "Sources Consulted."
14In correct typewriting, underscore any publication that represents the entire issue—such as a book, bulletin, periodical, newspaper, or pamphlet. Use quotes for part of a whole—such as an article in a magazine or a chapter in a book.

notes if the report had no bibliography, see the items included in Figure 17-3. Whenever your report has no bibliography, each footnote typed on a text discussion page should be as complete as those in Figure 17-3. The only exceptions are when you need to credit the same source more than once throughout the report. Then write the footnote for the repeat listings as if the report had a bibliography.

Other Uses of Footnotes. Besides naming sources, footnotes have two other uses (see items 2 and 3, page 613). When you need to offer the reader additional explanation and facts or refer him or her to other pages within the report, you may do so in a footnote. Word these statements conversationally, as has been done throughout this text.

Numbers Referring to a List of References

A method of documentation used by some professional journals and academic writers is to place the footnotes at the end of the report or article, *not* at the bottom of each page. As with the "footnote method" discussed above, the raised superscript number in the text is placed immediately after the word or sentence to which a footnote refers. But the numbers always progress consecutively throughout the report, chapter, or article. Each number refers to a certain numbered footnote in a list at the *end of the paper.*

The list may be titled "Notes and References" or "List of References" or, sometimes, merely "Footnotes." Entries appear on the list in the same numerical order that the citations occur in the paper—*not* in alphabetical order (as in a bibliography). Each entry about a source contains:

Facts about the composition—author's full name and title of the book, article, etc.

Facts about publication—publisher's name, location, date, and page number of the citation.

Figure 17-3 shows how 10 entries for sources and notations are listed numerically at the end of a paper. In contrast, notice that the bibliography—Figure 17-1—lists alphabetically 8 of these same 10 items. As you know, in the footnote-bibliography method all items—including number 5 (explanatory note) and number 10 (cross reference) are covered in footnotes within the text; the bibliography lists only sources.

This method of documentation, gathering all notes and references at the end, is not best for the reader. But it saves the writer time and space by not typing footnotes on the same pages as the referenced items. With this method the reader, however, must continually turn pages to the back of the report in order to read the referenced items immediately.

Citation within the Text

A third method of documentation is by placing a citation right within the text. Sometimes you can weave into a sentence the minimum essentials of a citation. For example:

```
                    Notes and References
      ¹Carl R. Rogers and F. J. Roethlisberger, "Barriers and
   Gateways to Communication," Harvard Business Review, July-
   August 1968, p. 29.
      ²Barry Shore, Operations Management, McGraw-Hill Book
   Company, New York, 1973, p. 242.
      ³Restaurant Employees Adopt New Rules," The Seattle Times,
   December 3, 1975, p. C-4.
      ⁴Helen Smith, President of City Restaurant Managers,
   comment in an interview, December 10, 1975.
      ⁵The total number of departmental supervisors was 75.
   Because of incomplete data, however, 9 supervisors were not
   included in the final analysis.
      ⁶Porter G. Perrin, Writer's Guide and Index to English,
   5th ed., Scott, Foresman and Company, Chicago, 1968, p. 418.
      ⁷James H. Campbell and Hal W. Hepler, Dimensions in
   Communication: Readings, Wadsworth Publishing Company, Inc.,
   Belmont, Calif., 1970, p. 119.
      ⁸Lesley Bernstein, "How to Right a Report," Business
   Management, September 1968, pp. 46-48.
      ⁹James Belohov, Paul Popp, Michael Porte, "Communication:
   A View from the Inside of Business," The Journal of Business
   Communication, Vol. 11, No. 4, 1974, pp. 53-59.
      ¹⁰See also Table 15, p. 35, of this report.
```

Figure 17-3 List of notes and references. Items are in numerical order; superscript numbers refer to items in the same order as listed in the discussion. *No* footnotes appear on text pages.

According to Lewis Benton (*Supervision and Management*, McGraw-Hill Book Company, 1972, p. 54), absenteeism can be controlled by. . . .

or

Another writer—Leslie Bernstein (in "How to Right a Report," *Business Management*, September 1968, pp. 46-48)—states that. . . .

You can also use this method for backward or forward cross references to save the reader's time. For example, within a text paragraph you might insert a parenthetical sentence like: "(See Item 4, pages 52-53.)."

This placement of the citation within a sentence or paragraph is convenient for both reader and writer, but it has limitations. If the citation is long, the sentence also becomes undesirably long and the thought is interrupted by the citation. Furthermore, this method is not so easily adaptable for adding long, parenthetical explanations.

In summary, as with everything else for good report writing, use good judgment in your choice of documentation method and be consistent. All three methods have advantages in certain situations. Consider the type and length of note or reference and whether your reader would prefer reading it immediately, or as a footnote, or at the end of the report. If you are writing a report for publication in a journal, use whatever documentation method the journal editors require.

Writing, Revising, and Typing the Formal Report

Before you begin to write the first draft of your formal report body and other parts, you should have completed the following preliminary work—discussed in Chapter 15:

> Considered the problem and purpose, reader(s), and ideas to include (see steps 1–3, pages 516–517.)
>
> Collected all needed material—secondary and primary data (see step 4, pages 517–518)
>
> Sorted and interpreted data (step 5, page 518)
>
> Organized the data and prepared final outline for your introduction, text, and terminal section (step 6 and pages 518–525)
>
> Prepared all visual aids (pages 525–532)

Writing the First Draft

With your research materials close at hand—sorted in piles or in folders under your outline headings—you can now begin writing. Perhaps you'll start with a section you consider easiest for you. That's a good way to feel comfortable with the job. Try to complete a section—or at least a subsection—without stopping. Writing a long report will seem easier if you think of it as a series of short reports (your main report sections), linked coherently by your well-planned outline and appropriate transitional devices.

In the first draft pay no attention to spelling, punctuation, grammar, or form. Just get the ideas down on paper. If you allow your thoughts to flow freely, you're more likely to have a smooth overall presentation than if you stop frequently to check on spelling or to polish a sentence. While writing your rough draft, leave wide margins and plenty of space between lines for later revisions. Also, make your first draft as complete as possible. Later, when revising you'll find it is easier to delete material if necessary than to insert new material. Generally, it is better to allow several days to write a long report. Don't try to cram it all into one eight-hour session, for exhaustion and rushing will adversely affect the quality of the report.

Some writers begin with the introduction; others finish the text first. Either way is acceptable as long as you include those elements in the introduction that will best orient the reader to the rest of the report. If the length of your introduction to a 15- to 25-page double-spaced typewritten report is more than 1½ or 2 pages, you should find out what element causes this lengthiness. For example, if an introduction is four pages long because the problem or background material has required three of the pages, take the problem or background material out of the introduction and make it the first main section of the text.

In the text, beware of using too many major divisions; for a 15- to 25-page report you probably shouldn't have more than three or four major divisions. If you have more than that, look critically at your outline to see whether you can and should regroup or combine sections. Although the divisions don't all have to be the same length, every main division should include enough substance and length to justify its position of importance. Introduce ideas or figures at the best time in the development of the report—at the time the reader needs to know or use them. Of course, a report with a hundred or several hundred pages will have proportionately more main divisions; in fact, it may have "chapters" each with its own main divisions and subdivisions. Remember to insert footnotes where necessary, too.

The terminal section should be a logical outcome of the material in the text. As you know, you may label it summary, conclusions, or conclusions and recommendations; or you may want to consider one of the other possible titles, such as those listed on page 522.

Besides completing your first draft of the report body, you should also write a draft of the abstract, letter of transmittal, and bibliography, if you'll have one. (See discussions on prefatory and supplemental parts, pages 604–612.) You can also set up the table of contents and the table of tables (if any) in rough draft; but only after the final typing is finished can you know correct page numbers for these tables.

Revising the Rough Draft(s)

When you have finished the first draft, set it aside for at least one day. This "cooling off" step allows you to get away from the writing long enough to look objectively at the material and to see more clearly the weaknesses in the draft.

Editing the first draft requires cool objectivity. Searching self-criticism is a must; what seemed just right in the first writing may seem ridiculously out of place upon second reading. Remember too that the best writers revise and rewrite and revise and revise several times when necessary!

A few handy supplies are useful when you revise a long report. You'll need a pencil (perhaps a red pencil, too), a stapler, cellophane tape, extra paper, and a pair of scissors or a razor blade. As you read your draft critically, you can use your pencil(s) for small corrections in the margins and between lines, or to cross out unneeded sentences. However, if you find a section that needs major reorganizing, use your scissors (or razor). A paragraph out of place on one page may be cut out of that page and stapled or taped to another page after you have cut it apart at the place where the insertion belongs. (Use a backing sheet underneath each cut page if necessary.) Likewise, you may need to write an entirely new paragraph; it too you can insert into a section after you have cut the sheet at the right place.

Just rereading each word of the report isn't the best way to approach the all-important job of revising and editing. Instead you should:

1. Look critically at the title, abstract, introduction, and terminal section—these four areas your reader considers first. If these parts are weak or vague, the reader may reject the entire report—regardless of how good it might be. The title should tell the reader clearly and concisely exactly what the subject of the entire report is. The abstract should reveal the problem, purpose, sources used, and results. The introduction should adequately orient the reader to the material so that he or she will better understand what is covered in the text (discussion). And be sure that the terminal section doesn't contain new material, that

it produces what you promised or agreed to in the introduction, and that it stems logically from the information in the text.

2. Check the letter of transmittal, introduction, and terminal section (if it precedes the introduction and text) for repetition. The reader who has to read the same information two or three times right away, will react unfavorably.

3. Check the headings throughout the report to make sure they match the entries in the table of contents. All major and minor sections in the table of contents must have headings in the text; but not all headings in the text (such as fourth- or fifth-degree headings) need to appear in the table of contents. Also check to to see that you have indicated correctly the relation of major and minor parts and that headings of the same degree are parallel.

4. Examine the text for transitions. Have you tied your sentences together within a paragraph? Have you tied your paragraphs together within a section? Have you tied your sections together?

5. Now edit the entire report for the C qualities. Read again every one of the 43 items in the checklists on pages 532–536. Checking them will help you to see that your report is
   Complete and concise
   Concrete, convincing, objective
   Clear
   Considerate and courteous
   Correct

6. If desirable, read "Check Points When You Edit . . ." in Appendix B.

Typing the Formal Report

After you have revised the draft(s) to your satisfaction, the report is ready to be typed (by yourself or your secretary). Although various authorities have different rules for typing this material, the suggestions here are for one of the acceptable methods. Whatever method you use, be consistent. An appropriate, consistent typing style is extremely important for the overall appearance of the report. The report should make a favorable impression in its overall appearance, spacing, margins, footnote setup, and pagination, in addition to its well-written content.

Overall Appearance. Regardless of how well written your report is, if it is carelessly typewritten, it will create an unfavorable impression in the mind of the reader.

You can give the correct initial impression if you choose a quality bond white 16- or 20-pound typing paper. Next, be sure your ribbon produces a dark impression and be certain the keys are clean. If your secretary is using a manual typewriter, check to see that the typing is done evenly so that all the words make the same impression. If possible, the punctuation marks should be hit lightly enough so that they don't produce noticeably deep gougings in the paper. Erasing is okay if it is hardly noticeable. Be neat—avoid smudges, streaks, curled ends, wrinkled paper, and any other distractions that might divert your reader's attention from the message.

Double Spacing versus Single Spacing. As a rule, you double-space the body of the formal report and indent paragraphs (usually) five spaces). But you single-space for

1. Quotations and examples of two or more typewritten lines. (If this material consists of two or more paragraphs, double space between them. (Also indent margins of the quote five spaces to the right and left of the double-spaced material.)
2. Contrast—to set off or emphasize a list of items.
3. Footnotes.
4. Some tables and other visual aids.

If saving filing space and paper is important and if a long report is to be used entirely within the firm, single spacing may be preferred.

Margins. In addition to the following suggested margins, you need to add ¾ inch for binding on each page except the top sheet (cover). Although you usually bind the report on the left-hand side—like a book—you can bind at the top. Acceptable margins are as follows:

First page of prefatory parts (preface or letter of transmittal,[15] table of contents, table of tables, abstract), *body*, and *supplemental parts* (appendix, bibliography, index) has a top margin of 1½ inch. All other margins are the same as for other pages.

Other pages: Top, bottom, and side margins are 1 inch (plus the ¾ inch allowance for binding at either left side or top).

Footnote Setup. As Figure 17-2 illustrates, a footnote goes at the bottom of the same page on which it is cited (by the superscript number within the text). Separating the last line of the discussion and the first footnote on the page is a line (usually 18 strokes long) flush with the left margin, with double spacing before and after the line. Single-space within footnotes and single- or double-space between footnotes.

Pagination. Every page in the report—except the cover and title fly—should have a number. For the prefatory sheets use small Roman numerals; for the body and supplemental sheets use Arabic numbers, according to these guidelines:

1. *Prefatory parts page numbers* are centered and placed ½ inch from the bottom of each sheet. Count and number the prefatory pages as shown below.

Cover	don't count or number
Title fly	don't count or number
Title page	count (i) but don't number
Letter of transmittal	count and number; a one-page letter shows page ii at the bottom; a second page of the transmittal shows page iii.
Table of contents	count and number each page
Table of tables	count and number
Abstract	count and number

[15]The transmittal letter is typed on company letterhead (if you are writing it as an employee of the firm; and of course the letter is centered attractively on the page. If you need tips on letter layout, see pages 117–124).

2. *Body and supplemental parts page numbers*—for the report bound at the left— are usually placed ½ inch from the top of the page, aligned even with the right margin. The exception is that the numbers for first pages of parts are either omitted (though counted) or placed ½ inch from the bottom of the page. They are then either centered with the typing on the page (as for prefatory parts pages) or aligned with the right margin.

If your report is bound at the top, your page numbers are ½ inch from the bottom of the page as for the prefatory parts page numbers.

Example of an Informational Formal Report

The following airline report applies many of the suggestions given in this chapter and Chapter 15 for writing a formal report.[16] Although the illustration here is printed, to save space, bear in mind that when typewritten the body should be double-spaced and arranged according to the typing guidelines just presented. As you read this report, notice the following:

1. Page 622 could serve as a combination cover and title page, or a title page alone.
2. The letter of transmittal and the introduction function as useful entities without unnecessary overlapping of material.
3. The table of contents separates the body from the prefatory and supplemental parts by means of indentation and capitalization.
4. The introduction includes the introductory elements (purpose, sources used, definition of terms, and plan of presentation) necessary to orient the reader. In such a short introduction, subheadings aren't necessary. But when the introduction is longer and more complicated, subheads like the following help the reader scan quickly: "purpose," "scope and limitation," "methodology."
5. The italics used throughout the report illustrate how you can tie together sentences, paragraphs, and even sections of the report. (Naturally these italics did not appear in the actual report.)
6. The bibliography alphabetizes by groupings—books, magazines and pamphlets, and interviews (unpublished sources).
7. The author of the report bound the pages at the left-hand side, numbered the prefatory sections with small Roman numerals, and numbered the rest of the report and the supplemental part with Arabic figures.

---

[16]Although the information in this report is true, names of persons have been changed and some dates have been altered. Also the airline has probably introduced by now more up-to-date technical advances.

THE DEVELOPMENT OF UNITED AIRLINES'
PRESENT RESERVATION SYSTEM

Prepared for
Mr. Charles E. Betz, Manager
Public Relations Department
Association of Travel Agencies

by
Pamela F. Whatmore
Staff Assistant

April 22, 197—

(LETTERHEAD)

April 22, 197_

Mr. Charles E. Betz, Manager
Public Relations Department
Association of Travel Agencies
1412 S.W. Meridan Street
St. Louis, Missouri 43123

Dear Mr. Betz

As you requested, here is my report concerning the development of
the present reservation system of United Airlines.

I'm sure the managers of travel agencies throughout the United
States will appreciate learning how United has expanded. In the
beginning, the line boasted a fleet of 20 planes, each having a
capacity of four passengers. At that time, however, the company
was doing well when it averaged two passengers a plane. Today,
United has a fleet of 394 jet planes with a passenger capacity of
up to 342 a plane. United's service area has expanded from 20
cities to 114 cities in the United States.

If you have any questions concerning my report, I will be glad to
come in to discuss them with you.

Sincerely

(Signature)

Pamela F. Whatmore
Staff Assistant

CONTENTS

INTRODUCTION

Today the public takes the convenience of obtaining flight reservations for granted. *However*, at one time, flight reservations were impossible to get, because the airlines carried only mail. Not until the mid-1920s did anyone even consider carrying passengers.

This report shows the development of the present reservation system of United Airlines. Nearly all data came from several interviews with United's personnel. Mr. Cowper Middleton, special assistant to the regional vice president, explained from past experience both the methods of operation and problems of the separate station allocation, Central Control, and the Ramac systems. Information concerning the Instamatic and Unimatic systems came from interviews with Mr. Earl Brown, Mr. Jerome Gogulski, and Mr. W. C. Woodard, who are all executive members of the Regional Division of Sales and Service for United Airlines. The main source of secondary information was the United's Publicity Fact Book kept only by United offices and not available to the general public. This book supplied facts about the most recent computer system, Unimatic.

To increase the readability of this report, Input-Output devices (I/O) need defining. An Input device consists of a receiver that receives messages transmitted from some other location. An Output device is a transmitter which transmits information to another place. I/O devices refer to both of these machines.

This report discusses the refinement of United's reservation system in three stages. Discussion for each stage includes the dates and methods of operation and problems which arose in these operations.

*

ORIGINAL SYSTEM, CENTRAL CONTROL, AND RAMAC—1931-1961—

The period from 1931 to 1961 is divided into three sections: the original system from 1931 to 1948, Central Control from 1948 to 1956, and Ramac from 1956 to 1961.

Original System (1931-1948)

The original system consisted of separate station allocation of tickets with its own particular problems.

Operation

Originally, reservations or seats on a plane were doled out to individual stations located along a certain flight plan. A station master sold as many seats as he could and then gave the remaining tickets to the pilot, who took them to the next station. The next station master then received these tickets and tried to sell them at the last minute. In most cases it was impossible to do so. *Therefore*, the station master sent his unsold tickets, in addition to the extra tickets, to the next station.

Problems

The drawbacks of *this* original system can plainly be seen. A snowball effect arose which ended with the last station having many unsold seats. *These* seats might have been sold if the station master had received *these* tickets a week before.

---

*The horizontal line across the page and the page number permit you to realize you're progressing from one page to the next one.

3

To further complicate the system, station masters were extremely possessive over their allotment of tickets—whether or not they could sell them. If one station sold all its tickets and needed more, the normal procedure was to get in touch with one of the station masters along the line and buy some of his seats. *However*, station masters were very reluctant to give away any of their seats, since there was always that slim chance that they might be able to sell the seats. *As a result*, the station master wanting more tickets found it almost impossible to get extra tickets when needed. *To further aggravate the situation*, shortly before a flight was due to arrive, *this* same station master who had asked for the tickets received all the extra tickets from station managers who hadn't sold theirs. Because of the uncertainty involved, one station had no way to expect receiving the extra tickets. *This difficulty* in obtaining extra tickets caused much inconvenience to both the station master and his customers.

Another drawback to this system occurred in the booking of adjoining flights. For example, a person would call an agent and ask to make a reservation from Seattle to Denver. To take care of this transaction and confirm it was not a problem. *But* if the customer wanted to make a return flight reservation, the station master had to teletype

4

Denver and ask if and when room was available. Denver then checked and teletyped the information back. Often Denver did not reply promptly, and many customers ended up waiting over 24 hours for their reservations.

The adjoining flight problem *was further complicated* if the person wanted to make several connecting flights. The amount of time and paper work involved in contacting each station to confirm space was tremendous. *This method* also left a lot of room for human error.

Central Control (1948-1956)

In order to keep ahead of the competition, United had to employ a system to speed up the reservation system. Central Control was the answer.[1]

Central Control was instigated in 1948. *This arrangement* made it possible for the first time in the history of the company that every station had the same opportunity to sell any seat on any flight. The central control office was located in Denver and connected by direct phone lines or teletype to all cities served by United.

Operation

Central Control worked in the *following* manner. Each station was allowed to sell so many seats on every flight, without clearance from the Central Control office. After a flight was booked to a predetermined level, each sale had to be individually cleared to avoid overselling. The individual posting has to be done by a secretary who

[1] Taylor, *High Horizons*, p. 97.

5

transcribed the information off the teletype or telephone. Beginning with the customer placing the reservation, confirmation took 17 hours.

Problems

As passenger demands increased, Central Control was not fast or accurate enough to handle them. The telephone method of reporting became inadequate, because often stations called in and got a busy signal for long periods of time. The speed of the reservationist also limited the speed of Central Control. United could not afford to rent more telephone lines and hire enough people to cover the increase in passenger traffic.

Ramac (1956–1961)

To solve the problems of Central Control, United introduced Ramac. Introduced in 1956 and located in Denver, Ramac was the first system of its kind to be used in the airline industry. Input-Output devices (I/O) connected Ramac to all the major cities. The *smaller* cities were connected to Ramac by teletype.[2]

Operation

Ramac operated on an IBM punch card system. The I/O devices in the major cities consisted of a keypunch transmitter and a keypunch receiver. At the place of sales, a reservationist punched all the reservation information on a card and placed it in a transmitter which relayed the message to Denver. In *that* city, *another* machine processed the sale and kept track of the total sales on each flight. When a certain flight

---

[2] Roberts, "Univac Flies with United," p. 35.

6

reached the predetermined level, the computer signaled the keypunch transmitter to transmit the message "stop sales" to all the stations.

All the cities that did not have I/O devices transmitted the sales information to Denver by way of teletype. *This* sales information arrived in Denver on perforated ticker tape emitted by the teletype receiving unit. *This* perforated tape *then* entered another machine which translated the perforations into keypunched cards. To transmit the "stop sales" message to these cities, a punched card placed in Denver's teletype transmitter relayed the message to the stations. The station received the message on perforated tape and *then* had a decoding machine print out the message.

No matter where the messages came from, once they became punched cards in Denver they were all handled the same way. Denver had two processing computers working at the same time. The machines recorded the sales and kept track of the total number of passengers on each flight. By working two machines at one time, United protected itself against time lost because of mechanical malfunctions or breakdowns in one machine. *These* two machines served as a check on each other.

Ramac cut down and eliminated much of the time *lag present in Central Control.* It also cut down on the number of human handlings for a reservation and *in this way* reduced the possibility of human error. The total transaction time, *which under Central Control took 17 hours,* was now reduced to 45 minutes.

7

Problems

United was unable to expand Ramac to cover the increasing passenger traffic. The storage space in the main computer of the Ramac system was not large enough to store the flight information necessary for making reservations.

INSTAMATIC—1961-1970—

Since Ramac was no longer efficient, United installed a new system called Instamatic. It was centrally located in Denver and consisted of an immense computer connected by means of I/O devices to the 114 cities that it serviced. Reservation time was now eight seconds.

Operation

Operating Instamatic required a complex communication network. American Telephone and Telegraph rented to United 18,916 miles of communication wires connecting United to all its ticket agencies. *This* communication system made United the owner of the second largest communication network in the United States, surpassed only by our national defense early warning system. With *this* network and its 1,200 agents, United processed 550,000 eight-second reservations a day.[3]

Instamatic was a numeric IBM system that understood only numbers read into it. *Therefore,* the I/O devices looked like the keyboard of an adding machine, consisting

---

[3] *United Publicity Fact Book,* p. 13.

8

of numbers from 1 to 10. *In addition to the numbers,* it also had special numeric coded messages, similar to ZIP codes, indicating facts such as destination and place of departure.

The procedure for making a reservation under the Instamatic system was simple. For each reservation a reservationist wrote on a special card the vital information such as flight number, sales date, place of departure, and destination. *This* card and a special preprinted code card placed in a transmitter relayed the reservation information to Denver. The computer in Denver read the information, checked the flight to see if space was available, and within seconds sent the answer back. If space was available, a panel light flashed on confirming the reservation. If confirmed, the reservation transaction was complete at this stage. The computer *then* added one to the seats-sold list and was ready to accept more reservations on any flight.

Instamatic handled the same information *that Ramac did,* but it stored more information. The main computer in Denver stored all the information needed for flight reservations. It kept track of the number of spaces sold on each flight, *in addition to* the number of spaces available on the flights on all other airlines that connected to United.

Problems

Even though Instamatic's system of sales was relatively simple and speedy, it *too* began to show signs of obsolescence.

9

Masterfiling, once the most efficient way of recording and storing reservations, became too time consuming. In the masterfile, the special handwritten cards were arranged first by date, then by flight, and finally by the names of the passengers. To find the actual record of a reservation, it was necessary to know the flight, date, and name of the passenger. If any of *this* information was missing, the process for finding a masterfile card was long and involved. The cards had to be hand sorted one by one until the correct card was found.

In addition to being too time-consuming, masterfiling took up too much room. United kept masterfile cards for 90 days. As passenger traffic increased, 90 days worth of masterfiles used too much valuable space.

Another problem in the Instamatic system was that the Instamatic computer read only numbers. *Therefore*, a person's name could not be read into the computer. As a result, when a reservation office wanted a passenger list for a flight they had to wait for it to be teletyped from Denver. *This* procedure became too time-consuming and inaccurate.

Instamatic *also* faced a language barrier. Since different airlines used different computers, and *these* computers used different languages which were not interchangeable, direct communication with the computers of other airlines was impossible.

Instamatic served its purpose well; but the need for faster service, more accuracy and storage space contributed to the need for a *new* computer installation.

10

UNIMATIC—1970 AND BEYOND—

United purchased Unimatic in 1964 and put it into operation in 1970. Its headquarters became Chicago.

The delivery of a new Boeing plane greatly necessitated the installation of Unimatic. United realized it had no place to store the information connected with the flights of this plane. They had two choices for a reservations system: revert back to the station master situation or install a new, more expensive computer system. Since the former choice was not practical, the latter was the only alternative.

Present Operation

Unimatic, like Instamatic, has I/O devices in all major cities. *These* I/O devices consist of a set of headphones and a cathode ray tube which looks like a TV screen. All the *other* equipment—pencils, paper, and reference material—has been removed. Below the screen is a regular typewriter keyboard. A large panel of specially coded buttons to the right of this keyboard gives the computer prefabricated messages. As material is typed, it appears on the television screen. *This screen* allows the reservationist to see what is being recorded. When a transaction is written up correctly, a button is pushed and all the information is cleaned off the screen and sent to the computer in Chicago. Then, within seconds, the "message waiting" button lights up, and when the button is pushed, the confirmation appears on the screen just as the computer recorded it. *This* second viewing of the message on the screen is a means of double checking to

11

make sure there is no error in the reservation. At this point the entire transaction is complete.

This system can give information in any form desired. If one wants to know what the most popular flight is, he can ask the computer and it will print the most popular flight.

Unimatic can handle any kind of information. For example, if a reservationist needs to pick up some bread on the way home from work, she can remind herself by typing a note on the screen and asking the computer to store this message until five o'clock. At five o'clock the "message waiting" button lights up. She can then press the button, and on the screen will appear the message to pick up the bread.

Unimatic *also* gives flight information in any form required. *For example*, Unimatic can print all the flights that a Pamela F. Whatmore has reserved in the last year. Unimatic will not only give a list containing the reservations for Whatmore, but *also* for all other names with similar spelling, if the name had been misspelled at the time of the reservation.

Under Unimatic, masterfile cards are all stored in the memory banks of the computer instead of in filing cabinets. Any information in the memory banks can be printed out upon request. There is no need to know all the information required by Instamatic to recall a reservation. Now all that is needed is the name, and then the entire history of all the transactions carried on by that individual within the past year will be printed out.

12

Unimatic has *also* eliminated the need for the teletype machine. No longer is there a need to teletype the passenger lists to various stations because Unimatic automatically prints out passenger lists upon request at the station requesting the information.

Future Operations

One of the most important aspects of the Unimatic system is its future operations. All totaled, it will be able to do 17 separate jobs.[4] *For example*, Unimatic is expected to handle crew assignments, plane routing, keep track of weather conditions, and many other jobs associated with the airline industry. United knows that what is done today won't be good enough for tomorrow, but there are many plans for Unimatic. According to United's president, J. C. Watson, Unimatic's future chores will include everything that can be economically justified. It is hoped that Unimatic will be able to print tickets, record hotel and rent-a-car information, and handle all the information concerning flight patterns and crew assignments.

Right now Unimatic seems fairly comprehensive, but even now United is making plans for more complex uses for Unimatic. It is hard to say what will follow Unimatic. Future speculations include a fully automatic system in which vending machine tickets and computerized scanning units check tickets for confirmation. *This* system will eliminate many of the jobs that are now present. Vending machine tickets, along with

[4]Statement made by Jerome Gogulski, Executive of the Regional Division of Sales and Service.

13

computerized baggage handling and smooth coordination of all aspects of flying, will result in the lowest fares possible with the maximum customer satisfaction.

SUMMARY

The present reservation system is a product of successive introductions of time-saving devices to remedy problems that became too big to ignore. The separate allocations of seats—during the original reservation system—did its best to meet the customer demands in the early years of the airline industry. *This* system presented problems that Central Control—the *next* system—helped correct. Central Control's problems were *then* solved by the introduction of automated devices.

The introduction of automated devices started with the computer centers of Ramac. Ramac solved most of the Central Control problems and served United well for many years. Eventually, *however*, Ramac *too* became obsolete and had to be replaced.

The *next* installation was Instamatic, a more complex computer. Instamatic simplified the process for making reservations. With the increase in passenger traffic and fleet size, Instamatic lacked the potential for handling future reservation information.

Instamatic's obsolescence gave way to the installation of a *bigger* and *better* computer system—Unimatic. Unimatic provides the potential for handling future reservations and much more. It will depend on the technological advances in all fields and the applications of these advances to the problems that will develop in the future of United Airlines.

14

SOURCES CONSULTED

Books

Taylor, Frank J., *High Horizons*, McGraw-Hill Co., Inc., New York, 1968, 496 pp.

Magazines and Pamphlets

Roberts, Henry, "Univac Flies with United," *Business Week*, December 25, 1970, pp. 33–39.
United Publicity Fact Book, Publicity Department, UAL, Chicago, June 1970, 207 pp.

Interviews with United Personnel

Brown, Earl, Executive of the Regional Division of Sales and Service, February 11, 197–.
Gogulski, Jerome, Executive of the Regional Division of Sales and Service, March 1, 197–.
Middleton, Cowper, Special Assistant to the Regional Vice President, March 30, 197–.
Woodard, W. C., Executive of the Regional Division of Sales and Service, February 15, 197–.

In summary, the formal business report is "formal" because of its parts—not because it uses formal language. Each prefatory and supplemental part should serve a useful purpose for the reader; if it doesn't, it should not appear in the report. Writing a formal report becomes easier for the writer when the writer has performed carefully and thoroughly the research steps before writing. And he or she is certain to have a better piece of writing when he or she has properly revised the first draft and considered the importance to the reader of the report's overall presentation.

Exercises

1. Choose a problem which you can solve by experimentation, survey, and/or observation, and write your proposal to the organization that is concerned with the problem. Or (if more appropriate) assume your proposal goes to a funding agency whose philosophy is in keeping with the problem you propose to research. Here are suggestions for topics—but feel free to choose your own.

   a. Try to solve a problem related to a firm's product development; plant expansion; improvement of a sales, accounting, or purchasing system; or curtailment of shoplifting.
   b. Analyze a problem in your community—crime(s) in a certain area, a traffic snarl situation, poor citizen involvement in local issues, need for attracting new industry or keeping young, educated persons in the community.
   c. Undertake a project in one of your college classes—or survey a sample of the student body regarding an important campus problem.

   Follow thoughtfully the suggestions in this chapter regarding proposal writing. Organize your topics under appropriate headings and write a proposal that meets all requirements as to content, format, and writing style. Then submit your complete proposal to (a) your instructor and/or (b) your class in an oral presentation. If (b), distribute copies of your proposal to every class member 2 days before your presentation. Be prepared to defend your proposal and to have the class critique it.

2. If you need practice in organizing topics under meaningful headings, try this assignment. Assume the sales manager of ABC New Car Agency in your city has asked you, a management consultant, to review and evaluate the agency's sales system. The internal control seems to be weak and something is causing problems.

   The main purpose of your study is to determine the strength of the internal control and its effect on the financial papers for new-car sales.

   You have just finished both secondary research and primary research. Two new accounting books (assume names) substantiate your concept for internal control. In your primary research you interviewed four middle managers and 15 or 20 employees. You studied the personality of the sales staff and the viewpoints of other personnel. You observed the personnel performing their duties and their interactions. Up to now you have information under the following topics, jumbled and in no useful order.

   File clerks' job
   Keypunch operator's responsibility
   Dealership's environment
   Title clerk's functions
   Salesperson's personality
   Internal control by buyers' orders
   Personnel system's internal control

Dealership's history
Sequence of signatures in sale of a car
Accounting clerks' duties
Control system's procedure
Title clerk's work
Sales staff's functions
Flowchart of new vehicle sales system (You have drawn this on 7 pages)
Dealership's new vehicle sales system
Introduction
Conclusions
Sales manager's part
Bibliography

Choose the main headings for the text of this report (3 or 4 should be sufficient. Then organize these 19 topics under the main headings and wherever they belong in a complete outline of the well-planned formal report.

3. Your assignment is to write a formal report whose body is approximately 15 to 25 double-spaced pages. Choose a topic that is broad enough to justify the length. Yet beware of a topic so broad that it would require volumes. If possible, consider a subject that you know something about, or one that especially interests you.

Try to find a topic that involves a business problem. (For example, you might know there's too great a turnover of employees in a certain department.) From the problem, and with some thought on your part, you can determine the purpose of your report. Other ideas that you can use as a springboard for a topic are listed below, pertaining to problems involved in:

Accounting, Credits, Collections
The accountant's role in cost reduction and analysis
Computer programming and errors in monthly statements
Problems and progress of accounting in X Company
Accounting contributions to the effective management of X Company
Problems involved in a bank's converting to a computerized operation
Policy or procedure and degree of communications used by X Company in col-
    lecting retail accounts.

General Management and/or Labor
The functioning and problems of your campus student-body governing organi-
    zation; accomplishments and recommendations for greater effectiveness
A profit-sharing plan for X Company
Would hiring handicapped workers be charity or good business for X Company?
A program for achieving optimum discipline in X Company
Business outlook for Y industry or X Company
How X Company (or your campus) has met the energy crisis and what should
    still be done
A proposed program (or plan) for hiring and training of minority groups in X
    Company
Development of a profitable ski area on a certain mountain.
Suggestions for X Company's response to Z Union's attempt to organize
    workers
Recommendations for a formal salary scale for X Company

Personnel Administration
Development of a personnel testing program for X Company
Analysis of the merit rating system of X Company

A safety program for X Company

The performance of women in top executive positions

Survey, interpretation, and recommendation—after a study on attitudes toward certain recent troublesome problems:

a. Opinion of X Company's employees regarding wages, working hours, parking, food services, promotion plan

b. Opinion of students in your school regarding grading, credit hours for certain courses, student parking, housing

c. Opinion of X Organization's members regarding membership dues, requirements, privileges, new clubhouse

Marketing

A promotional program for introduction of X product

A new plan for X Company to offer incentives to sales personnel

Where should X Company locate its next supermarket?

How can X Company measure effectiveness of its advertising?

How downtown merchants can cope with suburban shopping centers.

After you have clearly determined the purpose of your report, state it in one sentence. Then begin your preliminary investigation (Steps 1, 2, and 3 on pages 516–517). At this point in your research submit to your professor (or anyone he or she suggests) a memo report of your working plan. Be sure to include in this memo at least the following: problem, purpose, methodology, readers (both primary and secondary), and suggested outline. In this outline show the order for the introduction, major divisions of the text, subheadings for each major division, and the type of terminal section.

After you have approval of your working plan, you can begin to collect your data; then organize this material and interpret it. With the completion of this last stage—interpretation—you can draw conclusions and make recommendations. Naturally if you're writing an informational report, you'll skip interpretation of material and merely summarize. Also at this time you should prepare (at least in rough-draft form) your tables and any other necessary visual aids. If your professor requests it, submit the final outline that you'll follow in writing your report—the one that will become your table of contents.

Now you should be ready to write. Choose the right time and place and follow the rules outlined in the chapter—both for the first draft and the revision. After your final revision, you can type (or have typed) the body of the report in final draft, or you can first write the necessary prefatory and supplemental parts. In this report assignment include at least the following: cover, title fly, title page, letter of transmittal (or preface), and table of contents. Also you'll need to include other parts—especially appendix and bibliography—if your report requires them. If the transmittal may affect part of what's included in the body, you should at least plan the transmittal before the final typing of the body.

Although the content and presentation of the material are most important, also remember the role that mechanics play. Be sure you have nothing that detracts your reader from concentrating on what you want to tell. Thus, be sure the spelling, grammar, punctuation, and appearance are acceptable.

PART 5

NONWRITTEN COMMUNICATIONS

CHAPTER 18:
Oral Communication within Groups

CHAPTER 19:
Interpersonal and Other Nonwritten Communications

18 Oral Communication within Groups

The ability to communicate effectively orally as well as in writing is, as you know, highly valued in business. Throughout each working day businessmen and business-women use words and gestures to convey ideas and impressions to customers, colleagues, and others.

Though this textbook has discussed mainly written messages—letters, memorandums, and reports—several chapters have also prepared you for oral communication. Important concepts useful for both oral and written communication are discussed in Chapter 2, The Process of Communication and Miscommunication; Chapter 3, Planning before Communicating; and Chapters 4 and 5, Business Writing Principles (the seven C's). In addition, Chapter 12 includes suggestions for the job applicant's interview and Chapter 13 discusses collection techniques using the telephone.

This chapter briefly covers various aspects of oral communications within groups: speaking and oral reporting, listening, and leading and participating in conferences.

Speaking and Oral Reporting

The preparation for writing letters, memos, and reports is similar to the preparation for giving a business talk. Yet oral and written communication also have their differences. This section first discusses similarities and differences in speaking and writing, then preparation for the oral presentation, and finally the presentation itself.

Similarities and Differences in Oral and Written Presentation

When you're reporting to someone on paper, you need first of all to remember the purpose and the reader. The same is true for business talks. The purpose determines what you say, and the audience dictates how you'll say it. In both a written report and an oral presentation you need to collect, classify, interpret, and organize your material. In both you need, many times, to use visual aids and indicate to the reader or audience the points of transition. In both you orient the reader (or audience) in the introductory remarks, give details in the discussion (text), and summarize or conclude at the end. Throughout you apply the writing principles (seven C's).

In many ways communicating orally is easier than writing a letter, memo, or report. In the first place, you have had more practice in expressing your ideas orally. Furthermore, you don't need to bother with troublesome mechanics such as spelling and punctuation. And you have the aid of facial expressions, tone of voice, and gestures to make meaning clear. Finally, you have immediate feedback from the audience. If you notice raised eyebrows, excessive coughing, blank expressions, or other signs that indicate boredom or lack of understanding, you can clarify your point by restating or using an illustration or you can simply ask if the listeners understand.

Although communicating orally may be easier for the reasons just mentioned, giving a speech or oral report to a group does deserve special attention for both the preparation and the presentation.

Preparation for the Oral Presentation

Preparing for a speech or oral report requires these steps, most of which—as you will recall—are similar to those for writing reports, letters, and memos.

1. Determine the purpose
2. Analyze the audience and the situation
3. Choose the ideas to include in the message
4. Collect and interpret data[1]
5. Organize the data
6. Plan visual aids
7. Rehearse the talk

Determine the Purpose. Just as in written communication, the purpose determines what you say. Are you merely informing? Are you trying to secure belief or action through persuasion? Or are you simply trying to entertain? In business you'll probably use either of the first two of these goals.

Whenever possible, choose a topic that interests you and that you know something about. Then you'll have more incentive to tackle the assignment, won't have to spend so much time in collecting your material, and will possibly even enjoy the challenge of giving the best presentation possible.

Analyze the Audience and the Situation. As with letters, memos, and reports, you need to consider the people you'll be talking to. In addition to deciding why you're talking to them, you need to consider the size of the group, age range, sex, and occupation. Whenever possible, also estimate their attitude toward your subject, their interests, capabilities, prejudices.

If you're talking to a small group, you can be relatively informal, omit using a microphone, and use small visual aids. If you're to speak at a regional or national meeting in a large auditorium, you'll have not only a microphone but also different visual aids that you can use with either a stationary or a mobile speaker system.

Ages, occupations, and capabilities of the group determine the educational level of your presentation and the choice of words and illustrations. For example, you will prepare a different talk to college students than to company management trainees or to retirees, even if the general subject is the same. Also, if you're talking only to accountants, you can use appropriate technical expressions and tie in your illustrations with their professional background. But if the audience consists of individuals from various occupations, you need to prepare your speech so that everyone will clearly understand what you're saying—in this case you'll avoid technical expressions and use general examples. If the composition of your audience makes it necessary for you to give them background so they will understand your main points, by all means give this background early in the presentation.

---

[1] It is unnecessary to dwell on steps 3 and 4 in this section because the speaker follows the same research procedure as the writer does when preparing a written report (See Chapter 15.)

Furthermore, you should find out the attitude as well as prejudices your listeners have toward your subject. If you're talking about a controversial topic, giving bad news, or persuading, you need to be careful not to say anything bluntly, crudely, or inappropriately—in a way that will irritate the audience or turn them off so they don't listen further.

Organize the Data. One of the most important planning steps is organizing your materials so that the audience can easily follow you throughout your talk. You organize your talk like a report—introduction, text (discussion of details), and conclusions. (For suggestions on logical or psychological arrangement see pages 522-523.) In the introduction you catch the listener's attention with the problem (if any), the purpose, and often with a promise of an answer to the problem. You orient the audience with the same introductory elements you use for a report. Near the end of the introduction, you state your plan of presentation—what you are going to say. Then you say it—by discussing the details of your text. And you end your talk with a terminal section in which you tell what you've said.

Plan Visual Aids. To help get your message across to the audience, you may also need to plan meaningful visual aids for display at appropriate times. First decide whether you will distribute handouts for each person in the audience or whether you will display all visual aids from one spot. The latter procedure is usually better, because your audience will focus attention on what you are displaying instead of shuffling papers and reading when you would rather have them listen. (However, if you think they would benefit from taking copies home, you can distribute them after your talk.)

The most common devices for "one spot" displays are chalkboards, flip sheets, cards or posters, and projectors. Each has some advantages, depending upon subject matter and audience size.

Chalkboards are useful when you wish to write brief, significant points or figures on it either before your talk begins or while you are talking. If you will have much material for the board, plan if possible to place it there before your talk session begins. The board can be covered until you wish to reveal your display. However, if you prefer to draw or write as you talk, do it without turning your back to the audience. The chalkboard visual aids are usable only, of course, when the audience will be seated near enough to see and easily read the notations on the board.

Flip sheets contain a variety of material on large separate pages, fastened at the top and attached to an easel or stand the right height for easy audience viewing. The size of sheets as well as the words, charts, tables, or drawings on them can be modified somewhat in keeping with expected audience and room size. One advantage of using flip sheets instead of a chalkboard is that you can prepare them before you come to the room where you'll be speaking. Another is that they can be larger and of better quality than when material is written with chalk. Furthermore, during your talk you need merely flip pages in any order you wish and more quickly focus your eyes again on your audience. Also you can skip pages or add facts on sheets whenever desirable.

Cards or posters can serve the same purpose as flip sheets. They can display the same kinds of drawings and materials, provided they are large enough to be easily read by the audience. An advantage is that you can arrange them easily in any sequence. They are not attached to any easel. Disadvantages are that when they are large and of heavy posterboard they are cumbersome both to carry and to hold up for display. Pointing to pertinent parts is also difficult unless the speaker has someone else to help hold the poster while he or she talks.

Projectors that are most adaptable for displaying business materials are the opaque and the overhead. Both project images on a screen or wall for clear viewing by any size audience. The opaque projector must be used in a darkened room. The overhead has the advantage of being usable in a daylight or lighted room.

With the *opaque* projector you can use any typewritten, handwritten, or printed materials or various specimens just as they come from your files. You can project the exact charts, tables, letters, graphs, or pictures from your written report. And you can point (with any pencil) to the parts of them as they are projected on the screen.

To use the *overhead* projector you must first convert your display materials into transparencies. These can be prepared quite inexpensively either on your company's spirit duplicating or Xerox machine, on one of the various other modern transparency makers, or by professional photographic methods. While projecting the transparencies to your audience you can write on them (usually with black grease pencil). You can also add overlays of more drawings when necessary—as, for example, when explaining the development of a certain manufacturing or marketing process.

Rehearse the Talk. After you have considered all the steps discussed above, you are ready to apply them by rehearsing your talk. This step is vital for a beginner and is also used occasionally by some experienced speakers. Here you want to simulate the forthcoming talk. Know your opening sentence word for word. Also be sure you can deliver the talk within the time limit allotted you on the program.

How can you practice in a physical and psychological atmosphere close to that of the actual performance? To begin with, find a room that approximates the one you'll be speaking in. And if possible practice aloud. Talk so that a friend (real or imaginary) in the back row can easily hear and observe you. Have thorough command of your subject; and use cards, an outline, or a list of points if you'll be using them before your audience. Know what to say and then determine how to say it. Use the bodily action you plan to use for the actual performance. Even include the actual visual aids you'll need to accomplish the purpose of your presentation.

Remember, your real audience will be judging you mainly on your attitude, bodily action, voice, speech content, and choice of words. Whether the main purpose of your oral presentation is to inform, to explain, and/or persuade, your own sincere interest in the subject, audience, and task has an important influence on your effectiveness. Be eager to share your thoughts with your audience. Have a friendly, confident, courteous attitude toward your listeners.

Bodily action—posture, movement, gestures, and facial expressions—and voice must be natural and contribute rather than detract from your message. Occasionally, while speaking you may need to change your position—to relax, to indicate a transition between one portion of the talk and the next, or to secure a desired reaction from your audience. Your voice should be loud enough so everyone can hear, but not so loud that a blast on the microphone irritates listeners. A pleasant variety in tone is appreciated by the audience. Also desirable is an occasional pause to give the audience an opportunity for your ideas to "sink in."

Presentation of the Talk or Report

When you reach the podium, place your notes in a usable position. Also pause to make eye contact with your audience, and show you're a friendly individual by having a sincere, pleasant expression before you begin to talk. If you have prepared yourself well, you should experience little or no stage fright. But if you are nervous, remember that you feel more nervous than you appear to others, and that after the first few moments you will feel more comfortable.

Introduction. Your audience will already know the title of your talk because it is on a printed program and/or stated by the person who introduces you. You may begin with a greeting like "ladies and gentlemen," "ladies," "gentlemen," "members of _____," "fellow_____," or whatever is appropriate to the group and the occasion.

Before making your planned introductory statements, acknowledge the comments of the person who introduced you and perhaps ad-lib a few brief appropriate good-natured remarks. Then proceed with your introduction. State the problem (if there is one) and your purpose—always. Also include other introductory elements that adequately orient the group to your talk. If you are reporting on a study, briefly describe your methodology. A natural transition to your text is stating your plan of presentation.

In addition to using an opening that begins with the problem and perhaps promises an answer, you have other ways to catch the attention of your audience.

Tell a story that is related to your subject or that establishes background for development of the purpose

Make a startling statement—perhaps indicating briefly a surprising outcome of your study

Ask a question that makes the audience start to think

Give a familiar quotation that leads into your subject

Tell a humorous story or joke related to the subject

Use an illustration that relates directly to the subject

Refer to the subject, its timeliness, its importance

Refer to the occasion, the audience, or reason for meeting

Naturally, the right opener depends upon the purpose of the talk and the audience.

Be especially aware that humor is effective only when it occurs naturally as the talk develops. Also remember—as you must for letters and memos—that what is humorous to one person may be offensive or boring to another.

Discussion (Text) When you have completed your introduction, you begin developing the text orally in the same way you develop the written formal report. (However, because of a specified time limit, you usually must omit most of the detailed data of a long written report and concentrate on perhaps one or two phases.) Remember to apply the following:

1. Lead your audience through the speech or report. Since you don't have headings, you must clearly indicate when you complete one section and begin with another. You can do so by:
   a. Changing your bodily position
   b. Using topic sentences or introductory paragraphs
   c. Checking off a major heading already on the chalkboard as you begin the discussion of that section.
2. Use visual aids when desirable to get across your point.
3. When you do present a visual aid, be sure you face your audience; at the same time don't obstruct the audience's view of the visual aid.
4. It's perfectly correct to use notes or an outline as a guide. But avoid leaning on such aids too much. Also, don't read long passages—especially the entire report—since you are sure to turn off your audience this way.
5. Pay attention to your audience. If you notice restlessness, excessive coughing, side conversations, excessive doodling, whispering, or dozing, you need to adjust your material and delivery. Other helpful clues on how the audience reacts to your talk are their facial expressions, shoulder shrugs, smiles, laughs, nods, and applause.
6. Your emphasis should be on your audience; use proper eye contact throughout your talk.
7. Avoid any unfavorable bodily actions that might distract the audience and keep them from concentrating on your message.
8. If you still feel nervous at this stage of your presentation:
   a. Introduce some physical object in your speech—talk about it, demonstrate it, or use the chalkboard. Once you're occupied and doing something with your hands, you'll calm down.
   b. Move about the platform—be active. Bodily actions help conceal nervousness.
9. Instead of sprinkling "uh's" in your talk, hesitate between sentences without uttering a sound.

Summary or Conclusions. When you have finished discussing the text portion of your talk, you begin the terminal section—a summary or conclusions. As for a written report, you'll list conclusions when you have more than one and, naturally, will not introduce new material.

In some talks you can end with a story that highlights or illustrates your main ideas. If your purpose was to persuade, urge the audience to take the recommended future action and include suggestions to make their action easier. When you begin this terminal section, let the audience know you have completed the last major section of the text and are now starting the conclusions. Keep them concise. Saying "In conclusion" is usually a welcome signal to listeners—who then expect the speaker to finish within a few minutes.

In summary, you need to prepare for your oral presentation by considering the purpose of the talk, your audience, the situation, the material and the way you organize it, and by rehearsing thoroughly. With the right attitude, knowledge of the content, and the right rehearsal you can give an interesting talk; also you can reduce or eliminate possible stage fright by

1. Choosing a topic that interests you and that you know something about.
2. Preparing well—thoroughly know your material, make notes, and rehearse in an atmosphere like the one for your actual speech.
3. Memorizing your opening sentence.
4. Introducing some material object in your discussion, talking about it, demonstrating it—or using visual aids.
5. Moving about the platform to help cover up nervousness, indicate transitions, and/or to secure audience reaction.
6. Having the right attitude toward yourself and your audience. Forget yourself and concentrate on your audience.

Listening

Because an individual in business spends most of the day listening and talking, listening plays a vital role. When someone speaks, he is attempting to inform, persuade, or entertain one or more other individuals. But most individuals hear—they don't listen. Just what is listening, then? It means to see the expressed idea and attitude from the speaker's point of view, to sense how it feels to him, to achieve his frame of reference in regard to the thing he is talking about. Good listening requires various responsibilities of the listener and brings valuable results.

Responsibilities of the Listener

The speaker has the responsibility to communicate as effectively as possible, but the listener also has responsibilities. He cannot sit back and contentedly assume he has nothing to do. Like a speaker, the listener needs to prepare himself (before he listens); then, as he listens, he must concentrate on both the verbal and nonverbal message of the speaker.

Prepare for Listening. As a listener in a group you are influenced by the speaker, the message, other listeners, physical conditions, and your own attitudes and opinions. The first three you cannot control, but the last two you can do something about before the talk.

To give complete attention to the speaker and the message, you must choose whenever possible a position that allows you to see his gestures and clearly hear the tone of his voice and the emphasis he gives to certain parts of his presentation. Also sit up straight and look directly at the speaker. Should you become too relaxed, you might not give your full attention to the message. If you find that you're sitting near disturbing individuals in the audience, or are distracted by bothersome noise, you should move to another location. Also consider other negative factors—such as a draft from a window or door, excessive heat from a register, and undue glare—that might distract your attention from the speaker and the message.

Concentrate on the Verbal Message. Because good listening is correctly decoding what the speaker says, you must concentrate on the verbal message. Once the talk begins, be attentive to everything the speaker does or says. Don't let your mind wander—although that's not an easy task because the mind thinks much faster than one can talk. You should use this "spare time" to think about what is being said. If the speaker hasn't organized the material well, try to figure out the purpose and understand how the major points and their subdivisions develop that purpose. Also check facts for soundness and accuracy, and separate facts from opinions.

Furthermore, exercise emotional control by withholding evaluation of the speaker's ideas until the end of the talk or until you understand his viewpoint. Decode his words as he meant them. Put aside your bias. Keep your mind open—don't turn him off because you disagree with a statement or his haircut or clothing. Don't allow yourself to make frozen evaluations. Try to keep your personal attitudes, opinions, and emotions from affecting your listening.[2] Naturally, there's a danger involved if you try too hard to understand the speaker's viewpoint, because you might accept the speaker's reasoning to the point when you abandon your beliefs—without sufficient reason.

Also Concentrate on the Nonverbal Message. In addition to the actual message, you want to observe the speaker's gestures, tone of voice, and physical movements. Do they seem to reinforce or contradict what he or she is saying? If trying to paint a portrait of a sincere, dedicated person, does the speaker show some dishonesty? Is this person actually timid when trying to play the role of an individual full of confidence? If the speaker tries to tell the audience one thing and at the same time uses gestures that betray his or her true feelings, the nonverbal message may be the one to believe.

Results of Good Listening

Good listening pays valuable dividends. It

1. Permits the speaker and listener(s) to improve communication because each side is more receptive to the other's viewpoint.
2. Leads to positive attitudes.
3. Shows the speaker that the listeners are interested; in turn, the speaker tries harder to give his or her best presentation.
4. Results in obtaining useful information so that the listener can make accurate decisions.

[2] For a discussion on frozen evaluations and the influence of attitudes, opinions, and emotions, see Chapter 2, pages 20–23.

5. Creates better understanding of others and thus helps the listener to work with others.
6. Helps the one speaking (especially in an interview) to talk out problems. Remember that a person needs to receive as well as give help.

Leading and Participating in Conferences

As a manager you may—for various reasons—call a conference of selected department heads, supervisors, and/or employees. Or you may be one of those invited to attend a conference. The number of participants may range from 5 or 6 to 15 or 20. An effective number may be 10 to 15. The purpose of such a meeting may be to inform, to suggest a solution to a problem, or to discuss ways to solve a problem.

The **informational conference** is called only when the conference leader wants to check to see that the conferees understand certain information he or she has for them. Generally, however, written memos—without a meeting—suffice to bring the needed information to those concerned.

In the **suggested solution conference** the executive presents at the beginning of the conference a solution which is definitely only a suggestion for solving a company problem. The conference discussion then centers about the suggestion. All those attending contribute their ideas.

The **problem-solving conference** is called when the executive has no adequate solution to suggest regarding a problem and seeks suggested solutions from the conferees. Because this type of conference requires the most careful planning and presiding by the leader, as well as challenging participation by the conferees, this section discusses the planning steps and procedures for the problem-solving conference. You can use most of the suggestions, of course, for all types of conferences.

Planning Steps for the Problem-solving Conference

The preliminary steps in planning a conference are basically similar to those used before writing a report:

1. Analyze the problem and determine your purpose
2. Decide who the participants (conferees) will be and notify them appropriately
3. Choose the topics (ideas?) to be considered and distribute information to participants sufficiently before the conference so they may prepare
4. Take care of the physical arrangements for the meeting place

Analyze the Problem and Determine Purpose. A good conference topic must be timely, genuine, really important, and meaningful for the conferees. It must present a difficulty or controversial question that is within the experience of the conference attendants. Also it should be limited adequately so that conferees are able to solve it—at least partially—within the conference time. It should be about a matter that can be acted upon after the group has arrived at a solution or conclusion.

Decide upon Participants and Notify Them. When you inform the conference participants about the meeting, try to stimulate their interest in the problem. State the importance of the topic before they come to the meeting. Your memo—or letter to those outside the firm—may include suggested reference materials and whatever brief background explanation may be desirable to motivate the conferees. If you think they should bring any materials from their department, your message should invite them to do so. Follow the *direct-* or *persuasive-request* plan in your message, depending upon the motivation you think the conferees need.

Choose Topics to be Considered and Distribute Information. Although this step is not always possible, it is desirable if you have useful information (perhaps background material for the problem) that the conferees should have before they come to the conference. Mail copies of the information to the conferees at least several days before the conference so they may have time to prepare their understanding and thoughts on the matter.

Take Care of Physical Arrangements. Regarding the meeting room, consider thoughtfully such physical arrangements as seating, materials, and atmosphere. Have someone arrange chairs in a circle—perhaps around a conference table—or in a diamond or "V" shape, so all conferees can easily see one another. Chairs should be sufficiently comfortable (but not too soft so that participants slouch while seated).

Among the possible needed materials to consider are: chalkboard(s), chalk, eraser, pencils, paper, charts, and perhaps a projector or visual aids such as charts, tables, graphs. Drinking water, glasses, and ash trays, if smoking is allowed, should be handy. Name cards may be desirable if the conferees come from different firms or widely separated departments and are not personally acquainted. The room itself should, of course, be adequately lighted, heated, ventilated, and quiet so it is conducive to free discussion.

Procedures during the Problem-solving Conference

Plan to start the conference on time and end it on time. The following steps which the conference leader should take during the problem-solving conference are also basically similar to those you take when writing the analytical report:

1. Introduce the problem and purpose of the conference
2. Stimulate discussion to gather facts
3. Sort, select, and interpret the data
4. Arrange facts in order of importance and make a decision
5. State the conclusion(s)

Introduce the Problem and Purpose. For the success of the conference, the right introductory statement is critically important. Obviously you should prepare your introductory statement before the conference, but don't memorize nor read it to the conferees. Present it in a natural, informal way.

As the leader, sell the topic to the conferees by showing why it is both interesting and significant for their serious consideration. If true, impress the conferees with the fact that they have a personal stake in the success of the conference. Show genuine enthusiasm yourself. Make clear the importance of the solution to the company and therefore to the conferees' own jobs.

State the problem clearly and concisely. Use as many of the five W's as are pertinent—what, when, who, why, when—and the how. Write the statement of the problem on the chalkboard. If desirable, give adequate background for the problem and state the scope and limitations of the conference. Define any unusual terms that will be used.

Stimulate Discussion to Gather Facts. In general, try to encourage all conferees to participate, and do keep the discussion "on the beam." Write subtopic headings on the chalkboard (or overhead projector) to help spark discussion on each topic in turn. List on another board the possible solutions of the problem as conferees suggest them. Ask questions and keep participants from wandering onto irrelevant paths or from chatting among themselves while someone else is expressing his or her views. Get conferees to analyze their own thinking as much as possible. Sometimes if the original contributor of an idea cannot add to it, another conferee may be able to carry it further. If a participant's statement is vague, rephrase it clearly before you write it on the board.

Maintain an atmosphere of goodwill and cooperation throughout the conference. If a situation becomes tense or some members are reluctant to speak or are annoying or antagonistic, apply the techniques you have learned for handling bad-news situations. Try to be tactful, considerate, understanding; and show a sense of humor. Sometimes an appropriate interesting or humorous short story can quickly revive flagging interest. Here are other tips for handling difficult conferees:

The reticent, nonparticipating member may respond if you first ask a question he or she can answer by a simple "yes" or "no." Then whenever possible, ask him to give the conferees some information which he is sure to know because of his job, training, or experience. Thank and praise him as much as you can; he may then be more likely to enter the discussion confidently.

The "know-it-all" may be forced to justify every statement he or she makes. Whenever possible, ask other conferees for their opinions of these statements. Sometimes, if necessary and you feel the majority are annoyed by this arrogance, you may tactfully quiet the person by asking for a show of hands from the group, which strongly outvotes these suggestions.

The long-winded conferee who talks on and on, you may thank when he or she is at the end of a sentence, and then recognize someone else. Or you might move the discussion to another highly important point, perhaps with a statement like, "Well, we have two more points to consider before we wind up this meeting, so let's move along to the next topic now."

The erroneous member whom the other members—out of respect—are reluctant to correct, may require an especially tactful comment by you, the leader. As with any bad-news message, avoid direct criticism, sarcasm, or ridicule. Shield the person's pride. "When praising people, single them out; when criticizing them, put them in a group." Perhaps analyze a similar case without referring to the speaker personally.

The conferee who shows personal animosity toward another member or members may be turned off by your directing a question to another conferee.

Sort, Select, and Interpret the Data. After you have listed conferees' suggestions on the board, encourage participants to consider advantages and disadvantages of each suggested course of action. List them separately on the board. As leader, be careful not to impose your own opinions on the group. Encourage each group member to feel a sense of responsibility for the success of the analysis. Good listening by everyone to what others offer is extremely important. (The Suggestions on pages 644–646 about good listening apply in a conference as well as in a large auditorium!)

Get members to feel they are working as a group toward the collective solution to the problem, rather than allowing each member to force his or her views upon the rest. Regroup suggestions, as desirable: get the group to select the important ones, to interpret them, to compare, and to evaluate.

Arrange Facts in Order of Importance and Make a Decision. This step is comparable to writing the final outline and arriving at conclusions before you write a report. But in a conference you invite the conferees to determine the order of importance of the facts. Some suggestions may belong together under a main heading; some may need to be eliminated entirely because of irrelevance or disadvantages. Depending upon the problem, conferees may have to consider various criteria—costs, safety, employee relations, union rules, and so forth.

State the Conclusion. As with any written analytical report, the terminal section is of crucial importance. Before you dismiss the conference, review what the group has accomplished. Summarize what part(s) of the problem conference members have solved or partially solved. Mention only the highlights. Don't merely repeat the details of the discussion or those on the chalkboard. State the decision (conclusion) clearly and definitely. You might begin your statement of the conclusion by saying "You have agreed . . ." or "You have suggested . . ." rather than "I think this is what should be done." If the group arrived at several conclusions, list them, preferably in order of importance.

Exercises

1. For a four-minute speech, select any topic you are familiar with—a sport, favorite food, event, place, gadget. Introduce yourself to the class, tell what your topic is, develop it (in any instructive or entertaining way you wish), and summarize your talk. After you have finished, your class members will make constructive suggestions.

2. Assume you have been asked to present your long-formal report[3] orally at an informal conference attended by 10 managers in your company. Their work is closely concerned with the subject matter of your report. Prepare your report presentation thoughtfully. Usually a mere "summary" of the report is not the best method, because it may be too general to be meaningful to your listeners. In addition, if appropriate, select specific highlights about the problem and its solution. Choose the ideas that are most likely to be of interest and importance to your audience. For example, you might introduce to them the three or four most important factors you considered in the report. Be well informed about the overall highlights of your report and be prepared to defend your findings in a question-and-answer session (by your class members) immediately after you have presented your report. (In your presentation, you will of course, *not* read many parts of the report to the audience. Make your talk businesslike with the right tone—neither lecturing nor "entertaining."

3. In this assignment you are a member of a five-person group, which is a panel on a conference program. The chairperson your group selects will coordinate your group's activities. Together the five of you will select a topic for your group's study. (Preferably select one related to business communication or an assumed company problem.) On the day of the conference, your group will have 25 minutes to report on its study. You, like every other member on the panel, have 5 minutes to present the one project area assigned to you. Your chairperson might (or will, if your instructor assigns it) prepare and hand to the instructor a one-page outline of your group's topic and show what phase each panel member will speak on. This summary may also show what research each group member did and the bibliography of his or her secondary research. The chairperson introduces the panel members to the class before they make their presentations. Afterward, your group will have a five-minute question-and-answer period with audience participation. By any method your instructor specifies (written or oral) the class members can then evaluate each panel member's presentation—perhaps on a 1–5 scale.

4. Prepare a 10-minute lecture on one of the chapters in this textbook. Or, if your instructor approves, choose a recent magazine article on business communication or in your major field of interest. Bring with you an appropriate aid which is large enough to be legible to every member of the class to see while you are speaking. Make it neat, clear, and as attractive as possible. Plan to refer to the aid during your talk. Be careful to keep your listeners' attention so they won't continue to look at the aid after you are through with it! Plan to speak from note cards; do not memorize your talk. Invite your audience members to interrupt you (by raising hands) if they have questions. Sometimes the questions may be antagonistic, just to give you the opportunity to handle such a challenging matter and to show how quickly you can gain composure.

[3]See Exercise 3, pages 633–634.

19 Interpersonal and Other Nonwritten Communications

As a business or professional person, you will communicate orally not only within groups (as discussed in Chapter 18) but also in an individual person-to-person basis. Your work will likely at some time include interviewing, dictating, and giving various instructions or demonstrations. This chapter includes suggestions for handling these communications more effectively.

Interviewing

Interviewing is a conversation with a purpose; it uses all the forms of communication already discussed in this text—speaking, listening, and writing (notes during or after the interview and the interview write-up).[1] Some of the different types of interview are:

Selection and placement interview—to hire the right person for the right job
Vocational guidance interview—to help an individual find his or her best vocation
Counseling interview—to help the emotionally disturbed
Survey interview—to help marketing persons find answers to their assignments and problems
Group interview—used for problem-solving
Diagnostic interview—used by clinical psychologists

The discussion here concentrates on interviewing candidates for employment in business. Although business men and women use various types of interviews,[2] the material in this section covers the patterned interview[3] because it is used most often and is considered most effective in getting truthful responses from the candidate. The interviewer guides and controls the conversation but encourages the interviewee to speak freely and at length about relevant topics.

This section focuses on interviewing from the *interviewer's* standpoint. Chapter 12 includes suggestions for the applicant who is the interviewee. (See pages 420–426.) The topics here include objectives of the patterned interview, interviewer's preparation for the interview, procedure during the interview, and the evaluation.

Objectives of the Patterned Interview

The fourfold objective of the patterned interview for a job applicant is to

1. Match the applicant and the job by judging qualifications and areas that other sources cannot assess.

---

[1] The interview write-up consists of a one- or two-page report with a paragraph on whatever areas are pertinent to the interview. It may cover items such as early home life, education and training, work experience, current off-the-job life, personal characteristics, and overall summary. The beginning of the body shows blank lines for interviewee's name, date, the topics considered and name of interviewer. At the end (you might call it "conclusion") is a scale where the interviewer checks his overall rating of the applicant or others interviewed.

[2] Interviewing candidates for employment in business encompasses the screening or preliminary interview, final interview, follow-up interview, direct interview, indirect interview (or nondirective interview), and the patterned interview.

[3] The patterned interview is a combination of both the direct and indirect interviews. In the direct interview the interviewer keeps very close control at all times by directing limited and specific questions. On the other hand, in the indirect interview the interviewer makes little or no attempt to direct the applicant's conversation.

2. Give the applicant essential facts about the job and the company—to help the candidate decide whether to accept the job if it is offered or to look further.
3. Instill a feeling of mutual understanding and confidence in the applicant who accepts the job. (If he or she begins work with the right attitude toward the firm, the employee will be happier.)
4. Promote goodwill toward the company—whether the applicant does or does not receive or accept the job. It is especially important to give the right impression to the candidate who is disappointed by a turndown.

Interviewer's Preparation for the Interivew

The interviewer must prepare for the interview—as thoughtfully as if he or she were going to give a talk.

As an interviewer, you need to have a clear picture of your company's organizational structure and detailed information about the job(s) for which you are interviewing. Knowing organizational structure permits you to talk with confidence and give the applicant necessary facts about your company. If possible, you should have a job analysis for each position so you know what to look for in the applicant.

> This job analysis is an orderly and systematic study of the characteristics, duties, and responsibilities of a specific job. Included also are job operations and working conditions; training needed; aptitudes; attainments; type of personality, character, or temperament required.

If a job analysis isn't available, at least be familiar with the work environment, requirements for the position (including personality) and salary.

Your next step is to decide the areas you must cover in the interview (and the necessary questions) so that you can determine what qualifications a successful candidate should have. These areas usually include the critical requirements for the job, character, personality, general make-up of the individual. Then think how each applicant can demonstrate the skills and qualities that the job requires. Usually you attain your goal by use of questions about what the applicant has done; what he or she thinks about what he or she has done; his or her interests and hobbies; relationship to friends, school, and work; his or her colleagues and family. Finally set the interview up so that you can gain the most information possible from the candidate.

In addition, you need to consider the physical setup of the interview. Choose a quiet room where there will be little or no interruption. Arrange the furniture so that a desk does not separate you from the applicant. The ideal arrangement is to have chairs for you and the applicant, on one side to break down the formal roles of questioner and questioned. Arrange your schedule so that no one has to wait very long. Furthermore, check the waiting facilities. If possible avoid having applicants stand in the hall—especially in long lines. A quiet waiting room with chairs and magazines gives a much more favorable impression and is more relaxing.

Procedure during the Interview

The interview itself consists of a warm-up period and a planned period of information seeking and giving.

Warm-up Period. You should react to the applicant at the beginning of the interview in the same way you would to a friend who visits you at your office or home; Especially important are a firm handshake, warm smile, and friendly tone of voice.

Because the applicant is probably nervous—or at least unfamiliar with the surroundings—you want to begin the conversation with small talk. You might refer to the weather (that it's cold, fair, rainy, or humid), to an event of the day, or to a topic relating to the applicant's outside interest (athletics, sailing, mountain climbing). This is the time to begin to develop rapport and to show you are friendly and sincerely interested in the applicant. With the proper warm-up, you gain the applicant's respect and (hopefully) confidence.

Outline and Content of the Interview. After the brief warm-up period, you start the interviewee talking on the subject you want to know about. A good outline to follow is a straight chronological sequence.

You begin with the applicant's early home background, and then move through education, work history, and off-the-job activities to self-evaluation. In this coverage you check technical qualifications (ability to do the job), drive and aspirations (willingness to do the job), social effectiveness and emotional balance (relations with others and self), character (trustworthiness), and other factors you need to measure for success on the job. They might relate to physical vigor and energy, spouse's attitude toward the job, financial stability, willingness to travel, willingness to make permanent moves.[4] Especially important are those aspects of the candidate's personality that relate to interest patterns, attitudes, character, and temperament.

When you have learned the necessary qualifications and behavior of the applicant, you can turn your attention to telling about your company—salary, fringe benefits, and other facts of interest.[5] Also give the applicant the opportunity to ask you questions relating to the job or company.

At all times you need to keep control of the interview and at the same time get the applicant to talk. The ideal interview should *seem* like an unstructured conversation, but you should not permit it to proceed aimlessly. As a critical listener, you must notice gaps and omissions in the applicant's discussion and observe reactions, comments, and gestures. Listed here are suggestions you need to follow to be an effective interviewer:

1. Let the applicant do most of the talking. If you talk more than 50 percent of the time, you are interviewing yourself—not conducting an interview.
2. Use brief verbal responses that will keep the applicant talking—prod with questions such as "Tell me more," "That's interesting," "What happened then?"
3. Give your entire attention to the interviewee and respond by encouraging facial expressions, movement and expression of the eyes, and nods of the head.
4. Allow pauses in the conversation if you think the applicant will reveal important information. But avoid lengthy pauses or a pause when the applicant has definitely finished a topic.

---

[4]Theodore Hariton, *Interview! The Executive's Guide to Selecting the Right Personnel*, Hastings House Publishers, New York, 1970, pp. 25–34.

[5]Some interviewers reverse this pattern by first discussing the firm.

5. Try to understand the applicant, who in turn may volunteer really useful information.
6. Make self-expression easy for the applicant.
7. Respect the feelings of the other person even though you consider the person wrong.
8. At all times accept what the applicant says. Never frown, show surprise, or show disapproval.
9. Avoid the impulse to cut the applicant off or change the subject abruptly.
10. Never argue.
11. Sit on the same side of the desk as the applicant and use informal, plain language.

Checklist for Effective Interviewing. Following is a checklist that should help you review whether you are carrying out the role of interviewer well.[6]

1. Try to make a favorable impression on the candidate during the first few minutes of the interview.
2. Refrain from making any judgment about the candidate during the first few minutes of the interview.
3. Put the candidate at ease.
4. Pause after the candidate has seemingly finished a remark to give him or her a chance to talk further.
5. Occasionally repeat parts of the key sentences of the candidate in a questioning tone to secure elaboration.
6. Ask one question at a time.[7]
7. Make your questions clear, tactful, and pertinent to information you need.
8. Avoid wording questions so as to suggest the answers wanted.
9. Appear interested in the candidate and give him or her full attention.
10. Avoid expressing approval or disapproval of the candidate.
11. Avoid indicating your own attitude.
12. Use language appropriate to the candidate.
13. Ask no personal questions until after rapport has been established.
14. Allow the candidate to digress briefly without abruptly returning him or her to the point.
15. Talk as little as possible.
16. Control the direction of the interview.
17. Obtain maximum information on all relevant points.
18. Follow up leads the candidate makes.
19. Spend most of the time exploring areas on which information could not be obtained as well from other sources (reference check, for instance).
20. Get a complete work history.
21. Take notes of important points.
22. Avoid taking notes when the candidate is under stress.
23. Hear and see the vocal and physical mannerisms of the applicant as well as listen carefully to all statements.
24. Give the candidate an opportunity to ask questions.
25. "Sell" the job if this is deemed desirable.
26. "Sell" at the right time.

[6]Milton M. Mandell, *The Selection Process: Choosing the Right Man for the Job*, American Management Association, Inc., New York, 1964, pp. 220–221.

[7]For a list of 80 questions frequently asked during interviews, see Chapter 12, pages 423–425.

27. Continue observing until the candidate leaves the room.
28. Give the applicant a good impression of the organization before leaving.
29. Allow the candidate ample opportunity to do himself or herself full justice.

A good interviewer asks questions that are revealing—questions concerned with attitudes. The interviewer might ask, for example:

What would you say was the most promising job you ever had?
What did you like least about that job?
What kind of people do you work with best?

Given below are other suggestions about the use of questions.

1. You can learn more about the applicant from the "why's" of actions than from "what's."
2. Broadly worded lead questions that introduce a new topic steer the applicant in the right direction and permit you to sit back, evaluate statements, and throw in only occasional probes or comments: Example: "What are some of the things you like to do off the job when you are not busy working—your outside interests and activities?"
3. Follow-up questions should also be broadly worded.
4. You need to phrase each question carefully to elicit the desired information.
5. Use of the implied question—silence—tells the applicant you feel he or she has more to say and places the burden on the applicant to take it from there.
6. An indirect question such as the following encourages further elaboration without asking a direct question: "Please explain that in a little more detail."

The nonverbal message can be as revealing as anything the applicant actually says. Blushing, stammering, casting eyes downward, or barking out an angry reply, tell far more than words. You can partially but reliably judge any statement from the tone and inflection of the person's voice, gestures, hesitations, and general conduct. Behavior tells much about personality and social skills.

Pitfalls to avoid relate mainly to the following biases, prejudices, and other weaknesses within the interviewer:

1. Halo effect—tendency of the interviewer to form an overall opinion about the applicant on the basis of a single aspect of his or her makeup.
2. Stereotype error trap—tendency to categorize the applicant on the basis of a few surface clues.
3. Expectancy error—tendency of the applicant to anticipate the needs and preferences of the interviewer and to respond accordingly.
4. Ideal image error—interviewer's mental picture of the ideal person may not necessarily coincide with the person who can actually be most effective on the job.
5. Personal bias of the interviewer—poor handshake, biting of fingernails, gum chewing, loud clothes, poor eye contact.
6. Pseudoscience and myth—judging the applicant's character, mental ability, attitudes by means of handwriting, outward features, date of birth, number of

letters in the name, lines or marks on the palm of the hand, and shape and bulges of the skull.

7. Stereotyped, mechanical interviewing—same questions in same order, no adaptation to the individual, no stimulating exchange of ideas, no interplay of attitudes. In turn, the interviewer receives stereotyped answers that don't appraise qualifications.
8. Illusion that previous experience, of itself, guarantees ability to do the job well.
9. Being swayed because the applicant needs a job—even though the necessary qualifications are lacking.
10. Talking too much by interviewer—not listening.
11. Poor preparing for interview.
12. Asking inappropriate questions.
13. Being discourteous and rude toward the applicant.
14. Jumping to conclusions.
15. Accepting facts without probing to determine meaning and accuracy.
16. Leaving unexplored gaps.
17. Allowing applicant to guide the interview.
18. Depending on memory to conduct interview and to evaluate the applicant's qualifications.
19. Asking another question when the applicant merely hesitates a moment.
20. Appearing to be critical and cold toward the applicant.
21. Not observing nonverbal clues (gestures, voice changes, hesitations).
22. Poor questions:
    a. Leading questions that invite a given response: "Would you agree that . . . ." "Are you in favor of . . . ."
    b. Loaded questions—use of language that reveals one's own biases and prejudices; in turn, the applicant will slant answers accordingly.
    c. Dead-end questions that elicit only "yes" or "no" answers.

Evaluation of the Information

When you have drawn the desired information from the candidate, you must form an overall opinion of what the applicant said during the time with you and supplement it with vital facts from other sources.

Here is a list of clues which often serve as indicators of the applicant's state of mind and general makeup.[8] They should prove useful to you as an interviewer in your evaluation.

1. *Behavioral and psychological symptoms*

Positive	*Negative*
a. Early arrival	a. Late arrival
b. Alert, responsive attitude	b. Inattentive, dull attitude
c. Emphatic attitude	c. Condescending or withdrawn attitude
d. Relaxed manner	d. Tenseness, fidgetiness, body tremors
e. Smiles	e. Frowns
f. Clear voice	f. Choked voice, mumbling

[8] Hariton, *Interview: The Executive's Guide to Selecting the Right Personnel*, p. 58.

2. *Verbal symptoms*

a. Sticking to the main point	a. Changing the subject
b. Incisiveness	b. Overgeneralizing or too much detail
c. Relevant responses	c. Irrelevant responses
d. Well-organized presentation	d. Disorganized presentation
e. Appropriate use of humor	e. Uncalled-for levity
f. Spontaneous replies	f. Long pauses before replying
g. Speaking well of people	g. Criticism of others
h. Candor	h. Rationalization, evasiveness

No one candidate will usually possess all the requirements you are measuring. One might not have all the work experience you'd like, but might compensate for this weakness with an abundance of drive and personality. You must select the right person for the job. But if you choose someone whose ability is far above or below the job level, you'll be doing a disservice in three ways—to the applicant, who will not remain on the job very long; to the company, which will lose money for the time the employee remains on the job; and to yourself, who will lose face with yourself, the applicant, and the company.

In summary, your job as interviewer is to find out if the applicant is the individual for the job. After the interview you consider the facts gained from the interview about the applicant's qualifications, attitudes, personality, mannerisms, appearance. You will then evaluate this information, along with facts from other sources (references, tests, and so on) and decide whether or not to invite this candidate to join the company or to invite him (her) to the home plant for further interviews with other officials.

Dictating

After you have planned a letter, memo, or report, you will probably type it yourself, dictate it to a secretary, or make a rough draft in longhand. Should you dictate, you are expressing your ideas orally. Here are suggestions that will help you be sure you'll be signing your name to the message you want to mail (or to use effectively as basis for a speech or report):

1. Enunciate clearly. Very few persons can speak clearly with candy, gum, or cigarettes in their mouths. Be especially careful with plurals, and words that sound alike, such as fifty and sixty. ("Five o" and "six o" are much more definite.)
2. Spell unusual words and names when using them for the first time. Transcription errors resulting from dictators' lack of care on suggestions 1 and 2 have ranged from embarrassing or comical to costly and disastrous. For various examples of such errors, see the discussion on Correctness in Chapter 4.

   Two examples are noteworthy here. A department supervisor, intending to write to the Dungeness Crab Company, began his dictation (to a new secretary) with this statement, "Send the following letter to Dungeness Crab Co." (He pronounced the last word as "ko.") The result? His letter—which he unfortunately signed and mailed without reading the inside address—was addressed to "Mr. Dunjen S. Crabco."

Another dictator's poor enunciation and omission of spelling on an unusual name resulted in a $4,000 damage suit. His firm's wrecking crew—instead of razing an empty house at 560 McDonough Street—had begun to tear down an empty house at 516 McDonald Street!

3. Dictate—at the beginning of the message—any special instructions such as extra carbon copies for certain persons, unusual tabulation of figures, or your desire for a rough draft only. For a complicated message—report, letter, memo, speech, etc.—you will surely want to edit and revise before it is mailed. Thus be sure to ask for a rough draft, double-spaced. Otherwise your assistant may unknowingly type the usual, say, five carbon copies. Your correct instruction can save precious time as well as paper and supplies.

If your office has a magnetic card or magnetic tape typewriter, you and your typist can save still more time. You can then make changes or additions easily without having an entire report draft retyped. (See Footnote 4, page 33.)

4. Always dictate as much punctuation as your transcriber needs to turn out an accurate, attractive message quickly. At least dictate "paragraph" to indicate each new paragraph; "quote" "unquote"; "parenthesis" "close parenthesis."

5. Dictate at a normal rate, just as you talk. Avoid long pauses followed by rapid dictation. It is thoughtful to slow down a little when reading, for instance, an inside address or a policy number.

6. Let your secretary use his or her initiative as to grammar corrections, additional punctuation, and arrangement of your letters, memos, and reports.

7. When dictating a reply to a letter received, you can save both your time and your stenographer's time if you dictate only the name of the addressee. Your stenographer can later copy the full address from the letter you return after you have dictated your reply.

8. Keep the mail you are answering in an orderly pile by turning each letter (or memo) upside down when you have finished answering it. After all your dictation is completed, your entire pile of answered incoming correspondence will be in order for your stenographer to obtain needed information, attach file copies, and so forth.

9. In addition to these dictation tips, you can save yourself and your company time and money by having definite dictation periods (for instance, a set time each morning and/or afternoon) with no interruptions by telephone or callers.

10. See also "Suggestions for Cutting Correspondence Costs" later in this chapter for pointers regarding dictation efficiency when you give instructions.

Giving Instructions and Demonstrations

Another important reason for oral communication in business and industry is to give instructions and/or to demonstrate. Whether you are a relatively new employee being moved to a different job in another department, or a supervisor in charge of many employees, you will need to give various, clear, person-to-person instructions. In some jobs (such as selling, computer programming, and numerous technical jobs—you will also need to demonstrate. Your oral communications can be crucial for efficient company operations.

Clear Instructions on Individual Jobs

Perhaps you have at some time started on a new job and been "trained" by an employee whose explanations were "as clear as mud." After hearing her or him race through incoherent comments, you were not only uninformed, but also confused. By asking numerous questions, you may have eventually learned enough to perform the job. Many needless and costly errors are made, however, because of faulty, vague instructions and because the listeners are reluctant to ask questions.

Whenever you have the responsibility of training someone in the duties for a job, be sure you have a clear understanding yourself of the job description. Preferably write it out clearly first and then present it orally step by step. Follow also the seven C principles (Chapters 4 and 5) to make your instructions complete, concise, concrete, considerate, clear, courteous, and correct. Demonstrate, whenever desirable, and help your listener to follow your instructions. Welcome questions by asking, "Now what questions have you?" Answer them tactfully.

Suggestions for Cutting Correspondence Costs

In an effort to help cut the ever increasing costs of written communication (see Chapter 1, pages 7-8), you can do your part within your own company. Briefly, here are suggestions to get you started.

1. To eliminate needless repetition of basic instructions, standardize them and put them in writing for your transcribers. Develop simple code words to indicate frequently used instructions—such as "CEPO" for "Send a carbon copy with enclosure to our Portland office."
2. Expand the efficiency of your secretarial help. As a guideline, a good stenographer using an electric typewriter and transcribing machine can turn out 30 to 35 one-page letters in a seven-hour day. See that these assistants receive helpful instructions.
3. So that typists can do other work while you dictate, and thus save time, use machine dictation and stenographic pools as much as possible (except for the top executives who have private secretaries). Dictation equipment operates about twice as fast as a secretary can write in shorthand.
4. To speed replies and save time and money—on correspondence between branches and departments, and sometimes to outside inquirers—use the short-note-reply technique. Merely jot down your answers to written inquiries on the bottom of incoming messages; then make copies of the sheets and send them out as the answers; file the originals. See that all concerned employees have proper instructions.
5. Dictate less and delegate more. Develop effective interchangeable form paragraphs and use them wisely to handle your repetitive situations. Dictate only the basic ideas and let your subordinate compose the routine letters. Be sure he or she has adequate information.
6. Increase your use of typing pools and automatic typewriters.
7. Use modern, high-speed metering devices.
8. To save on paper, carbons, and miscellaneous supplies, whenever possible and desirable use a smaller size paper—even postcards. For interdepartmental messages requiring a certain number of carbons, try using carbon sets instead of onion-skin and regular carbon paper to save the time usually required for handling and inserting the individual sheets.
9. Use form letters and memos whenever desirable. (See pages 137-139.)
10. Instruct employees to use the telephone to convey short messages. You can say a full 450 words in three minutes. The maximum charge for a daytime station-

to-station three-minute call dialed within the continental United States is under $2 and considerably less after 5 p.m. and weekends. If your firm has a WATS line (wide area telephone service) you can save still more on various long-distance calls.

11. Accurate postal addresses and ZIP codes save time and costs (caused by delays if mail is inadequately zipped.) See that your mail room employees have access to correct ZIP designations.

12. Instruct employees to be careful to place sufficient postage on mailed materials —based on weight and class of mail. (Collection of additional postage, either from the sender or from the addressee is costly to the Postal Service and offers a potential for delayed delivery.)

13. If your firm originates and receives large volumes of mail, instruct someone to periodically review mail-room activities, especially when mail-room employee turnover rates are high. Assure that there is continuity of understanding of company policies and postal mailing requirements. This is particularly true for bulk rate mailings which have presorting and sack labeling requirements.

Exercises

1. Using your one-page résumé (that you prepared for Exercise 2, page 414), make a transparency suitable for use with an overhead projector. Then prepare a 3-minute presentation to your class. Choose two questions from the list on pages 423–425 and assume your interviewer has asked you to answer them. Tell the class which questions you are answering. While you are delivering your three-minute talk, the class will view your résumé transparency on the screen behind you. Then your instructor and/or your class members will "interview" you on what you said, or on something in your résumé, or on any other pertinent question. The class (and your instructor) will offer constructive criticism on your persuasiveness in answering the two questions they asked you. They will comment also on the quality of your résumé and your verbal as well as nonverbal expressions. (If your instructor approves, your class might elect a chairperson who will convey to each speaker the suggestions from the class. Individual student suggestions will thus be made through the chairperson instead of directly.)

2. For practice in impromptu speaking, follow the assignment in Exercise 1, except that instead of preparing a three-minute presentation on two questions of your choice, you will be asked to speak three minutes on any of the 80 questions your instructor (or class members) select for you—without previous "warning."

3. To prepare for a "stress interview," bring your résumé to class on the day this assignment is due. Your instructor will ask one student (or several) to act as interviewer(s). If possible, they will be seated around a "conference" table. You, the job applicant will be asked questions about your résumé and your interest in or knowledge about the company with which you are seeking a job. At least one of the interviewers will be instructed (unknown to you) to react negatively toward you or toward some answer you give to a question. Try your best to keep your composure and to "sell" your interviewer(s) on your capability for the job.

4. For practice in handling an oral communication situation for which you have no opportunity to prepare in advance, try this assignment. It is comparable to the performance-appraisal interview you may have some time on a job, either as an employee being appraised or as a supervisor who does the appraising. Assume that in your company each supervisor fills out every six months a personnel appraisal

form similar to Figure 16-2, page 567. On the day this assignment is due your instructor will select two students at a time to come before the class. One of them will be asked to be the employee and the other, the supervisor. Your instructor will hand to the supervisor a rating form which he presumably filled out on the employee. It has some favorable and some unfavorable entries. It contains also a short paragraph of details on why he or she has rated the employee as he or she has— preferably with specific examples on each topic. The employee receives from the instructor a separate paragraph stating some reasons the employee may give as to why he or she performed as he or she did. Both the supervisor and the employee will have a few minutes to read these statements before the interview. Then the supervsior will open the interview. Both supervisor and employee will have a businesslike discussion for 10 (or more?) minutes. Some comments will be on touchy subjects. Prepare yourself well by reading the suggestions for interviewer on pages 652–658 and for interviewee on pages 420–426.

5. Present to the class a five-minute instructive explanation on how to perform the duties of a particular job you are familiar with. After you finish, call on a class member to tell as well as he can what he learned. (This procedure tests not only your instruction clarity but also the listener's attentiveness.)

6. Demonstrate (in five minutes) the use of a small appliance, hobby tool, or toy. If possible, have another class member stand behind you, back to back. He/she will follow your instructions as you state them orally. At the completion of your communication, see whether your listener's result is what you intended it to be.

Appendixes

Appendix A: Legal Aspects of Your Business Communications

When you apply integrity, honest consideration for your reader, and the Golden Rule in your business communications, you should be safe in the eyes of the law. Yet as a cautious, sensible businessperson—and as a consumer—you need to realize that there are legal dangers even in some true statements. On the other hand, not all untrue words that appear to be libelous will lead to a lawsuit.

Thousands of statute laws and decisions have been passed in the 50 states and federal government. Changing social and business conditions necessitate changing laws from time to time. Furthermore, the right to freedom of speech versus the individual right not to be libeled have led to various legal privileges under various conditions. No single chapter can begin to cover even partially any specific legal interpretations applied to business writing.

The purpose of this section is to call to your attention some of the legal risks and complications that may occur in business communications. An overview of pertinent legal concepts should be helpful to you both as the writer and the recipient of business messages. However, because ignorance of the law excuses no one, you may need a lawyer to advise you on specific details that apply to some complicated situations. The discussion here is necessarily a brief general introduction only; no liability is assumed for its completeness. Yet if you are aware of the risks discussed here, you can avoid harmful utterances and costly misunderstandings. This section briefs you on:

1. Defamation
2. Invasion of privacy
3. Fraud
4. Other areas of concern

Defamation[1]

The unconsented and unprivileged "publication" of a false idea which tends to injure reputation is defamation. Oral defamation is slander. Written defamation constitutes a libel. You can be sued for defamation if you intentionally "publish" the false idea that injures reputation and for which no legal "privilege" exists. Because the words "publication" and "privilege" have important legal significance, they are discussed first; then follows a sampling of defamatory terms.

Publication. In the legal sense, the unconsented intentional or negligent communication of defamatory matter to a third party is "publication." Any means of communication by which some third party (anyone other than the person attacked) actually receives the defamatory idea can effect a "publication."

If you tell Mr. X to his face privately that you consider him incompetent or a swindler, you are within your legal rights; only he has heard your statement. But if you intentionally communicate the defamatory statement to at least one other person who is not "privileged" (as defined later), you can be in serious trouble. The derogatory qualities that make a statement defamatory are the same for libel and slander.

---

[1] Unless otherwise footnoted, this discussion on defamation is based on Arthur B. Hanson, *Libel and Related Torts*, Vol. I, The American Newspaper Publishers Association Foundation, Inc., New York, 1969, pp. 21–195.

Because libelous statements are more permanent, laws pertaining to libel are more severe than those about slander. The writing (for libel) may be any permanent communication—such as a letter, circular, picture, photograph, cartoon, newspaper, recorded tape, or phonograph record.

Even a sealed letter addressed and mailed to the person you are accusing can result in actionable publication if you knew or should have known that it would be intercepted by or shown to a third person. For this reason, a letter containing unfavorable information about a person (or organization) and any collection message about past-due payments should be mailed only in a sealed envelope and addressed so that it will be read only by the addressee. Adding the words "Personal and Confidential" or "Personal" is a good precaution. Another precaution is to use an opaque envelope and to fold the message in such a way that it cannot be easily read when held up to a light.

A defamatory telegram also is actionable against the sender if its defamatory meaning is communicated to a third person. In an interstate transmission, governed by federal law, the telegraph company may also be held liable, but only if the message is obviously defamatory and the agents of the company who actually transmit it know the sender is not "privileged" to send it.

Accidental communications to third persons (by eavesdroppers or unauthorized letter readers) are not actionable unless you knew of or should have foreseen such possibilities. A mere possibility that someone may have seen or overheard the statement is not enough.

Dictation to a stenographer is considered by most authorities to be a publication which is conditionally privileged with respect to matters reasonably related to the ordinary conduct of the business.

Privilege. A legal right to communicate defamatory information in certain situations is "privilege." The privilege may be "absolute" or "conditional."

Absolute privilege is mainly limited to three general areas: judicial proceedings, legislative proceedings, and the acts of important government officials, usually executives. Thus judicial officers, attorneys, and all parties participating in a judicial proceeding are absolutely privileged to make defamatory statements during and as part of the trial, if they bear some relationship to the matter under consideration.[2] Letters between parties or attorneys relating to a controversy are also privileged. However, defamatory statements about a case made outside the ordinary course of a judicial proceeding, such as comments to reporters in the hallway, are not entitled to the absolute privilege for judicial proceedings.

Similarly, legislators and government officials are absolutely privileged to make defamatory statements in the performance of their official functions, but not if the statements are irrelevant to the public matter then under consideration. For example, a member of the highway commission in New Mexico made a defamatory statement about a highway contractor at a commission meeting with reporters present. A superintendent of banks in California made libelous statements concerning his former attorney. In each case the Supreme Court of the respective state held that these public officials were protected by an absolute privilege in the exercise of their executive function. In contrast, a public official would not be absolutely privileged to defame his subordinates when publicly explaining why he dismissed them.[2]

A conditional (qualified) privilege applies to several situations in which the interest of either the participants or society dictates that communication in good faith should not be hampered by fear of lawsuits. Thus defamatory statements made in the ordinary commercial activity are qualifiedly privileged, whether they are interoffice messages or sent to persons outside the company, when the recipient has a lawful interest in the topic of discussion. For example, the person who answers an inquiry about the performance of an employee or about the credit record of a customer is obligated to take reasonable precautions to see that the information sent is accurate. And he or she must avoid intentional deceit. If he or she intentionally or carelessly misleads the inquirer who seeks information about another person (for instance, a credit or job applicant), he or she may be sued for damages.

Thus whenever you send requested information to an inquirer (prospective employer or creditor, for instance, who might suffer a loss if he or she employs or lends to an unworthy applicant), make every effort to tell the truth and to reply in good faith without malice. When the truth about an individual or an organization is unfavorable and directly related to a question you are asked to answer, try as much as possible to protect the good name of the one involved. Also indicate in your reply that the information was requested and ask that it be kept confidential. Likewise, when you request someone to send you personal information about another person, show in your letter that you have an interest to protect and promise to keep the received information confidential. You will thus help the informer protect himself against a libel suit. (However, under some of the new public disclosure laws confidentiality may no longer be possible.)

Privilege does not apply to unreasonable disclosure and publication of particulars concerning a debtor to his or her employer, relatives, and to the public by such devices as "deadbeat lists" or obvious communications forms which may be read by others who have not requested the information and have no immediate need of it.

Privilege also does not apply to defamatory statements which are unrelated to the purpose of the particular privilege. If for instance a former employer is requested to recommend an applicant for a new employment, the privilege pertaining to his or her response does not extend to defamatory remarks not related to job qualifications. Also, the former employer may lose the privilege if the response uses such violent or abusive language that the real motive in the reply is evidence of malice or some other improper purpose. Furthermore, if the former employer knows the statement is false, clearly the privilege is defeated. If he or she is negligent or unreasonable in believing it to be true, jurisdictions differ as to whether the privilege is lost.

The risk of liability for criticism of public men has decreased significantly in the United States since the Supreme Court decided the *New York Times* case in 1964. Under the *Times* rule, criticism or comment about the public conduct or fitness for office of public officials, and statements about the public conduct of other voluntary public figures is privileged even if it is based on or includes erroneous material—unless

---

[2] Paul P. Ashley, *Say It Safely: Legal Limits in Publishing, Radio, and Television*, University of Washington Press, Seattle, 1966, pp. 43–47.

there was actual knowledge of falsity or reckless disregard for whether the material was true or false. Two prongs to the rule are: (1) the inclusion of both fact and opinion within the privilege of fair comment, and (2) the degree of "malice" (intent to injure) necessary to defeat the privilege, constituting knowledge of falsity or reckless disregard for truth. The Supreme Court has included within the public official designation: a city commissioner; a group of parish judges; a county attorney and chief of police; an elected court clerk; a deputy sheriff (and others). The "public figure" to which the rule applies is a person "intimately involved in the resolution of important public questions" or one who by reason of his or her fame shapes events in an area of concern to society at large, and as a result, already has as much access to the mass media "both to influence policy and to counter criticism" of his or her views and activities as does a "public official." The Supreme Court has found a university athletic director and a retired Army General who was actively involved in a federally enforced school integration to be within the class of public figures covered by the *Times* rule.

Defamatory Terms. Among the terms that have been judged libelous, the following are a representative (but incomplete) sampling of words to be avoided or used with caution when you refer to a person or an organization:[3]

bankrupt	drug addict	incompetent	quack
blackmailer	faker	inferior	racketeer
Communist	falsified	insolvent	shyster
corrupt	forger	kickbacks	swindler
crook	fraud (fraudulent)	misappropriation	thief
deadbeat	gouged money	misconduct	unchaste
dishonest	grafter	misrepresentation	unworthy of credit
disreputable	hypocrite	profiteer	worthless

In the collection of debts or in attempts to collect any claim alleged to be due or owing, the collector should not unreasonably oppress, harass, or abuse any person. Harassment and abuse includes abusive language, anonymous or repeated telephone calls at odd hours, and anonymous c.o.d. communications.

Some statements are defamatory because they malign a characteristic necessary in a person's work (provided the occupation is legal). Thus, in most jurisdictions it is defamatory to impugn the financial responsibility of a merchant, but not of a teacher, because ability to obtain credit is essential only to the merchant. Also it has been held defamatory to attribute Communist sympathies to a public official, but not to an engineer. And, as already discussed, it is defamatory to impugn the competence of an employee to perform duties required by his or her job. But such statements may be conditionally privileged if made in the ordinary course of business activity, as discussed above under "Privilege."

The truth is usually adequate defense in a libel suit, especially if there is no evi-

[3] Philip Wittenberg, *Dangerous Words—A Guide to the Law of Libel*, Columbia University Press, New York, 1947, pp. 282-308.

dence of malice. But if the writer cannot prove his or her statements to be true or prove that there was adequate reason for writing them, he or she may have to pay large money damages.

Invasion of Privacy[4]

The unconsented, unprivileged, and unreasonable intrusion into the private life of an individual is "invasion of privacy." Unlike defamation, privacy can be violated although no publication to third persons takes place and even though the matters delved into are true or not particularly harmful to reputation. The concept of right of privacy is analogous to that of trespass, which gives one the right to keep unwarranted intruders off one's land not because of any resulting emotional distress or loss of rents, but merely to ensure the solitude of landowners.

This section discusses two aspects of invasion of privacy: use of a person's name, photograph, or other identity without permission, and physical surveillance of records, reports, and letters by persons not entitled to examine them.

Use of a Person's Identity. If a person's name, photograph, or other identity is used without permission on a sales letter or advertisement (or other permanent publication—not word of mouth), that person may have cause for legal action because his or her right of privacy has been violated.

Recovery and monetary awards have also been granted for publication of x-rays and other medical pictures, for pictures of a deformed infant, and for undue publicity of a delinquent debt.

Yet, not every use of another's likeness or identity is actionable. In some states it must be unreasonable under the circumstances, as well as unprivileged. Using pictures of an All-American football team on a beer company's calendar which also contained advertising was held (in one case) not to be an invasion of team members' privacy because they were public figures and there was no false implication of endorsement. But using a person's picture to illustrate a story about dishonest tactics of cab drivers would shed false and unfavorable imputation on the person and would be an invasion of privacy.

Unreasonable publicity of private life may also result in legal action and costly money awards to the offended person. A classic case (cited in *Libel and Related Torts*, page 203) is one in which the plaintiff, a former prostitute and the acquitted defendant in a notorious murder trial had reformed, married, and pursued a respectable life in a new community which knew nothing about her former life until the defendant revealed the whole story in a movie, using her name. She was allowed a cause of action for publication of these true but embarrassing personal facts.

In the "pink letter case" (mentioned in *When You Need a Lawyer*)[5] a suggestive letter bearing a woman's signature was mailed to 1,000 men. Handwritten in a femi-

---

[4]Hanson, op. cit., pp. 197–206.

[5]Kenneth and Irene Donelson, *When You Need a Lawyer*, Doubleday & Company, Inc., Garden City, N.Y., 1964, pp. 245–249.

nine hand, the letter was mechanically reproduced on pink stationery and mailed by a mailing agency. The name signed to the letter was that of the principal character in a motion picture the letter was advertising. Unfortunately, it also turned out to be the name of a woman living in Los Angeles—the only person by that name listed in the City Directory or the telephone directory. When the letters began arriving (in hand-addressed, pink envelopes), many wives must have looked at their husbands with a quizzical eye. But it was worse for the plaintiff, who began getting telephone calls from the men. She also worried for fear that some irate wife might shoot her—for the letter invited the men to meet the signer in front of a certain theater on a certain day and to look for a girl "with a gleam in her eye, a smile on her lips and mischief on her mind." The court felt that the plaintiff should be compensated for invasion of right of privacy.

If you wish to use the picture or identity of an individual for your advertising or sales letters, for instance, be sure first to get previous consent and make clear just how the picture or identity is to be used. An individual may have indicated consent by willfully posing for a photograph, but alteration of the photograph or using it in a way to carry objectionable implications is an invasion of privacy.

Physical Surveillance of Records, Reports, and Letters.[6]   The right of privacy may also be violated if records, reports, and letters are read by persons not entitled to examine them.

Powerful binoculars, long-range telephoto cameras, and "zoomer"-type television cameras have been used effectively (and illegally) in recent years to look through windows at important papers lying face-up on desks, at models of new products and designs, and at charts displayed at conferences. These techniques have become so common in certain areas of industrial espionage that elaborate security precautions are taken to keep designs and models in windowless rooms and to keep blinds drawn at all times in certain offices.

Modern technology has added to these existing situations the possibility of passing visible light or reflected infrared energy through an envelope and taking pictures of the contents. These pictures can then be read (deciphered) by persons skilled in reading handwriting or typing where lines are inverted or superimposed. Also available is a needle-thin "flashlight" that can be inserted in a sealed envelope to "light it up" for quick reading by a trained investigator. You can help to greatly reduce or even prevent this type of surveillance by using—when desirable on certain very confidential material —envelopes with a random pattern printed on them to make them opaque and/or inserting more than one sheet of paper in them.

Fraud

The intentional misrepresentation by one party to a contract of a material fact which is relied upon by the other party to his injury is fraud.[7] Both as a seller and a buyer

---

[6] Alan F. Westin, *Privacy and Freedom*, pp. 78-79; copyright 1967 by The Association of the Bar of the City of New York. Reprinted by permission of Atheneum Publishers, USA.

[7] Michael P. Litka, *Business Law*, Harcourt Brace Jovanovitch, Inc., New York, 1970, pp. 152-153.

you need to be aware of the elements of fraud as well as the significance of warranties so that you can better detect and avoid fraudulent practices.

Elements. The elements of fraud are: (1) false representation of fact, not opinion, intentionally made; (2) intent that the deceived person act thereon; (3) knowledge that such statements would naturally deceive; and (4) that the deceived person acted to his injury.[8]

The misrepresentation need not be a direct falsehood for fraud to be present. In fact, failing to reveal defects or confirming false impressions by remaining silent can be sufficient. To constitute actionable fraud (for lawsuit), the misrepresentation must be of a *material fact*—a fact that induced the contract. Statements of the seller's opinions and "puffing" (boastful sales talk about the value of the goods) are permissible. The buyer is not justified in relying on such statements; they do not become part of the bargain and are not warranties. The main test for fraud is to ask, "Would the other party have entered into the contract had he known the truth?" Opinions may lead to fraud if they amount to deliberately false statements made by a recognized professional in the field, whose opinions may reasonably be relied upon in the contract. Opinions, however, must be in regard to an existing or past fact and not to forecasts or predictions.[9]

Warranties. In most sales contracts the seller undertakes certain obligations concerning the nature, title, and quality of the goods being sold. When these obligations are expressly stated or implied and when they actually induce the sale, the obligations are called "warranties." They are guarantees by the seller with respect to the goods sold. Warranties may be express or implied.

An express warranty affirms a fact or a promise the seller made to the buyer in bargaining concerning the nature of the goods—description, grade, or model. Such a promise becomes a basis for the contract even though the term "warranty" or "guaranty" is not used.

Implied warranties are considered part of the bargain even though the parties themselves say nothing about them. For instance, the seller warrants that he or she is conveying a good title to the goods. Also, under the Uniform Commercial Code (adopted by all 50 states) if the seller is a merchant with respect to goods of that kind, he or she warrants that the goods are salable and are fit for the ordinary purposes for which such goods are used. If the seller knows the buyer intends the goods for a particular purpose and that the buyer is relying on the seller's judgment as to their suitability, there is an implied warranty of fitness for that particular purpose.[10]

According to the U.S. Postmaster General, in the Post Office Department's informative booklet *Mail Fraud Laws*,[11] fraudulent schemes sent through the mail are cost-

---

[8]William J. Robert and Robert N. Corley, *Dillavou and Howard's Principles of Business Law*, 8th Edition, Prentice-Hall, Inc., Englewood Cliffs, N.J., 1967, p. 1027.

[9]Litka, loc. cit.

[10]Litka, op. cit, pp. 470–474.

[11]*Mail Fraud Laws—Protecting Consumers, Investors, Businessmen, Medical Patients, Students*; U.S. Post Office Department, Washington, D.C., 20260, June 1969.

ing the American consumers an estimated $500 million a year. Among the many dishonest rackets to trap the unsuspecting consumer are: fake contests, home improvement offers, auto insurance frauds, charity appeals, missing heir schemes, fake business opportunities, worthless medical cures, and fake correspondence-school programs promising "exciting, high-paying jobs."

The U.S. Chief Postal Inspector lists the following ways you can help enforce mail fraud laws:

> To stop a dishonest scheme, inspectors must find that you and others buying a product or service were cheated as a result of claims the seller made in an intentional effort to defraud. Mail fraud violations occur when a general scheme or pattern of fraud exists.
>
> When you believe mail fraud exists, hold all letters, including envelopes and other evidence related to the questionable scheme. See if your neighbors or business associates have also received similar material.
>
> Bring such information to the attention of a postal inspector in your area by contacting him directly or through your postmaster.
>
> Inspectors cannot investigate a case simply to force a supplier to speed up deliveries, obtain refunds, or to otherwise act as an intermediary in settling unsatisfactory transactions. In such instances the dissatisfied buyer should:
>
> > Seek an adjustment or settlement with the seller.
> > Bring his complaint to the attention of the Better Business Bureau, Chamber of Commerce, Trade Association, or publication which carried the ad.
> > Seek relief through civil suit if a breach of contract may be involved.

Most states now have consumer protection divisions in the Attorney General's office, and they can be very helpful too.

Other Areas of Caution in Business Writing

Among the many other unmailable materials that may violate United States Postal Laws are letters and printed matter concerning lotteries, obscene literature, extortion threats, and solicitation of illegal business. Space does not permit discussion of these items here. You can obtain booklets on most of these subjects through your local postmaster or the U.S. Government Printing Office, Washington D.C., 20402. And if you are in doubt about the mailability of any particular material, you may submit a request to the Office of the General Counsel, Mailability Division, Post Office Department, Washington, D.C., 20260. A ruling will be furnished as promptly as circumstances permit.

The sending of unordered merchandise through the mail does not violate postal laws unless it is sent c.o.d. However, persons receiving such unordered items can:

> If the package has not been opened, write "Return to Sender" and put it back into the mails.
>
> If the article is not wanted, set it aside for a reasonable period of time and if unclaimed, destroy.

Treat unordered merchandise as an unconditional gift if living in a state where the laws apply.[12]

The sending of unsolicited credit cards is illegal, as specified in the Consumer Credit Cost Disclosure Act.

Another caution pertains to the copying of certain documents. Congress, by statute, has forbidden the copying of the following documents and items under certain circumstances: United States government obligations or securities, such as Treasury and Federal Reserve Notes, National Bank Currency, Certificates of Indebtedness, silver and gold certificates, paper money, and others; also U.S. Savings Bonds (except for campaign publicity for their sale), Internal Revenue Stamps (except in copying for lawful purposes a legal document on which there is a cancelled revenue stamp), postage stamps cancelled or uncancelled (except for philatelic purposes provided the reproduction is in black and white and is less than ¾ or more than 1½ times the linear dimensions of the original); postal money orders; bills, checks or drafts for money drawn by or upon authorized officers of the United States; and other representatives of value issued under any act of congress.

Also forbidden is the copying of copyrighted material without permission of the copyright owner; certificates of citizenship or naturalization (except foreign naturalization certificates); passports (except foreign); immigration papers; obligations or securities of any foreign government, bank, or corporation; draft registration cards, selective service induction papers bearing certain information; badges, identification cards, passes or insignia carried by military, naval personnel, or members of the various federal departments and bureaus such as FBI, Treasury (except when ordered by head of such department or bureau). In some states copying auto licenses, automobile certificates of title, and drivers' licenses is also forbidden. For these items—and others not listed here—penalties of fine or imprisonment are imposed on those guilty of making illegal copies.

As a final caution, in general, remember to:

Be honest and fair in all your business transactions and correspondence.

Avoid any statements and acts that may be considered defamation, invasion of privacy, or fraud.

Keep yourself well informed on responsibilities in other legal areas of concern.

Consult an attorney when in doubt about the handling of any complicated situation that might involve legal risks.

[12]*Mail Fraud Laws*, 1969.

Appendix B: Mechanics and Style

Abbreviations

In business letters and reports, abbreviations are appropriate for the following titles: Mr., Mrs., Ms., Messrs. (as for a law firm of Messrs. White, Green, and Black). Other common abbreviations are: Jr., Sr., Mt. (Mount), St. (Saint), Inc. (Incorporated), Ltd. (Limited), D.C. (District of Columbia); compound directions, NW. or NW or N.W. (Northwest); and the professional degree symbols such as B.B.A., Ph.D., M.D., C.P.A. The title Dr. (Doctor) is usually abbreviated, especially when the first name or the initials are used with the surname.[1]

The following words should be spelled out whenever possible: president, superintendent, honorable, reverend, professor, building, association, department; as well as street, boulevard, avenue, east, west, north, south. City names, and generally state names, should also be spelled out. It is best to use abbreviations sparingly. A good rule is "When in doubt, spell it out." However, if you are using the new U.S. Post Office Department two-letter state abbreviations on envelopes, you may wish to abbreviate the state the same way in the inside address for consistency. (See footnote 13, page 126.)

Check Points When You Edit Writing for Business

For clarity and emphasis:

1. Use conversational words. If you have a choice, use the simpler word.

   Pompous words: utilize, comprehend.
   Simpler words: use, understand.

2. Guard against misplaced modifiers and drifting participles.

   Incorrect: Having been run through the computer, the clerk used the figures for his report.
   Correct: After running the figures through the computer, the clerk used them . . . .

   Incorrect: As one of our best customers, we invite you to open a charge account.
   Correct: As one of our best customers, you are invited to . . . .

3. Make verb tenses say what you mean.

   a. If a past finding continues to be held a fact, it is usually clearer and more forceful to employ the present tense.
   b. Use the present tense wherever you can logically. It applies to things that existed in the past, still exist, and apparently will continue to exist.

---

[1] Some authorities suggest abbreviating "doctor" when the first name or initials precede the surname (Dr. John Brown) but spelling it out in a salutation (Dear Doctor Brown). Business people, however, feel that applying two rules is impractical, and they abbreviate "doctor" in both situations.

4. Use punctuation to help the reader.

    Confusing: Ever since these people have been demanding justice.
    Clear: Ever since, these people have been demanding justice.

    Confusing: That that is is that that is not is not.
    Clear: That that is, is; that that is not, is not.

5. Avoid "this," usually, unless a noun follows.
    Mr. Lucas once lost $5,000 that he had invested in farm mortgages and this made him question all types of investments.

    Improve clarity by adding "experience" after "this."

6. Use strong, vigorous words—active verbs, concrete nouns, specific adjectives and adverbs.

7. See that a paragraph has a topic sentence. Also a section—especially with sub-divisions—should have an introductory paragraph.

8. Tie your writing together with transitional words, phrases, clauses, and paragraphs.

9. Keep the average sentence length 17 to 20 words. The maximum paragraph length in a formal report should not exceed 15 typewritten lines; maximum paragraph length for a letter, 10 typewritten lines.

10. Whenever possible, use the indicative mood—not the subjunctive. Many times you can change "would" to "will," "could" to "can," and "might" to "may."

11. Avoid Latin terms that many readers don't know. Instead, use the better understood Anglo-Saxon synonyms.

    Say: about   *Not:* circa
            following   sequents
            that is   i.e.
            for example   e.g.

For conciseness:

1. Rescue verbs that are smothered or hidden in nouns and infinitives.

Wordy	*Concise*
In nouns:	
a. take a look	look
b. held a meeting	met
c. had a discussion	discussed
d. The function of this department is the *collection* of accounts.	This department *collects* accounts.
In infinitives:	
The duty of a clerk is *to check* all incoming mail and *to record* it.	A clerk *checks* and *records* all incoming mail.

2. Limit "it . . . that" constructions.

    a. It is known that we must reduce pollution vs. We must reduce pollution.
    b. It is clear that . . . vs. Clearly . . . .

3. Avoid overusing "it is," "there is," and "there are" at the beginning of sentences.

    Wordy: There are four rules which should be observed.
    Concise: Four rules should be observed.

4. Remove needless repetitions.

    a. For example, substitute "it" or another appropriate pronoun for the noun.
    b. Use a shortened form for a very long noun, after using the complete noun once; for example, American Telephone and Telegraph becomes AT&T.

5. Shorten wordy phrases.

    a. Instead of *for the purpose of*, use *for.*
    b. Instead of *due to the fact that*, use *because.*
    c. Instead of *in the event that*, use *if.*

6. Omit repeated numerals (unless in a legal document or on a check).

    Wordy: Eleven (11)
    Concise: 11

7. Eliminate "which" clauses whenever possible.

    a. He ordered desks which are of the executive type.
    b. He ordered executive-type desks.

For correctness:

1. Avoid switching from third person to first, and/or second person. If you write in the third person (impersonal writing), don't use I, me, we, us, and you.

2. Vary your sentence structure. Instead of beginning most sentences with the subject followed by the verb, you should begin some sentences with a different sentence structure—such as a dependent clause. Also sandwich some short sentences among longer ones.

3. Be sure subject and verb agree.
    a. A *study* of these two reports *shows*—(not show)
    b. The *details* in this memo *confuse*—(not confuses)

4. Be sure you have parallel construction.

    Incorrect: We will be glad to answer any questions you may have if you *write* to the above address or by *calling* us at 679-6622.
    Correct: We will be glad to answer any questions you may have if you *write* to the above address or *call* us at 679-6622.

    Incorrect: clerk, manager, selling.
    Correct: clerk, manager, salesperson.

5. Be sure you spell every word correctly. Always use the dictionary when you are in doubt.

6. Avoid ending a sentence and beginning the next sentence with the same word(s).

    Not good: Your son will enjoy using a portable electric typewriter. A portable electric typewriter . . . .

    Better: Your son will enjoy using a portable electric typewriter while he is attending college. This machine . . . .

7. As a rule, most verbs of the senses—taste, feel, see, smell, hear—take an adjective, not an adverb.

    Not correct: The dinner tastes deliciously.
    Correct: The dinner tastes delicious.
    Also correct: I feel well. (In this sentence "well" is an adjective.)

8. Don't overuse a word in the same sentence or paragraph unless you do so intentionally to emphasize.

    Not good: The important subject on which I am going to write is the subject of inflation, a subject of great importance to ordinary citizens.
    Improved: I'm discussing inflation—a subject that is important to most people.

9. If a major division of a report has subdivisions, it must have two or more—never just one—subdivisions.

10. Have at least two or more lines of a paragraph on a page.

11. Syllabicate between syllables and limit your word division to no more than four words on one page. Also never syllabicate the last line on the page or on three consecutive lines.

12. In a double-spaced report you can show quoted material of three or more lines as single-spaced without quote marks. Also this single-spaced material has shorter lines than the double-spaced lines.

Dangling Participles

A participle is a word that ends in "ing" or "ed" and looks like a verb; yet it actually is an adjective that must modify a specific noun or pronoun. If it doesn't, it is called a dangling participle.

The three most common forms of dangling participles are caused by the writer not observing the following rules:

1. The participle should be placed close to the word to which it refers, and there should be no intervening noun to which the participle might seem to refer.

    Unclear: A complete *report* is submitted by our branch office, *giving* details about this transaction. ("Giving is the participle; it should modify "report," but it seems to modify the intervening noun "office.")

Clear: Our branch office submitted a complete *report, giving* details about this transaction. (Now the participle clearly modifies "report.")

2. A participle at the beginning of a sentence (or at the beginning of a second independent clause in a compound sentence) should refer to the subject of the sentence or independent clause.

Unclear: *Having* been boiled for the proper length of time, the *homemaker* took the shrimp off the stove. ("Having" modifies the subject "homemaker" when the participle should modify "shrimp.")

Clear: *Having* been boiled for the proper length of time, the *shrimp* were taken off the stove by the homemaker. (Now "having" modifies the right word—"shrimp," which is the subject of the sentence.)

or

After the shrimp had boiled for the proper length of time, the homemaker took them off the stove. (This sentence discards the participle.)

    Here's a simple way to see if the participle beginning the sentence properly modifies the subject: State the subject "shrimp" and follow it with the participial phrase, "having been boiled for the proper length of time." If the two parts give you the meaning you want "shrimp, having been boiled for the proper length of time," then the participle is modifying the right word. But if you are boiling the homemaker, something is wrong.

3. A participle following the main clause should refer to a definite noun, not to the general thought expressed by the clause.

Unclear: These accounts disappeared from the vault, thus *causing* us very much worry. (Instead of modifying a particular word, "causing" modifies the entire clause that appears before the comma.) Suggestion: Reword so that you don't have the participle in the sentence.

Clear: Because the accounts disappeared from the vault, we are very much worried.

Clear: These accounts disappeared from the vault, a fact which caused us much worry.

Exercises.   Identify all dangling participles in these sentences, tell whether each one violates form 1, 2, or 3 just discussed, and then correct all errors.

1. Being an old customer, we know that you are familiar with our Christmas displays.
2. The check arrived 6 days late, causing me to write a collection letter.
3. Realizing our mistake, a new check was immediately sent to replace the first one.
4. Being larger and more attractive, these offices should make your work more pleasant, thus enabling you to work better.
5. Being a savings association, our customers do not have checking accounts here.
6. Please go down to the main office, and lying on the manager's desk you will find a copy of the latest report.
7. Having been baked for 2 hours, the girl took the roast from the oven.
8. Changing your monthly loan payments, it will be necessary to get approval from the loan department.
9. Having been an outstanding keynote speaker, we can offer you this special award.
10. To enjoy 5% earning, a savings account should be opened.

Numbers as Figures or Words[2]

In general—use the figure instead of the word because the reader can more easily read the figure and grasp its meaning. In invoices, tabular materials, purchase orders and the like, always use figures. In letters and reports—use the rule of 10 (spell out numbers 1-9; use figures for numbers 10 or higher) except for amounts of money and for isolated cases, as shown below.

1. *If a sentence begins with a number, express the number in words:* This rule is used when the sentence cannot be effectively revised.
   Fifty applicants were interviewed for the position.

2. *When a number standing first in the sentence is followed by another number to form an approximation, express both in words:*
   Fifty or sixty will be enough.
   Note: Try not to begin a sentence with a number. Rewrite the sentence to place the number within or at the end of the sentence.
   The confirmation request was answered by 559 businesses.

3. *When a sentence contains one series of numbers, express all members of one series in figures.*
   We *had* 25 applicants from Arkansas, 15 applicants from Texas, and 6 applicants from Oklahoma.

4. *When a sentence contains two series of numbers, express the members of one series in words and those of the other series in figures:* If this rule is not followed, confusion results because of too many groups of numbers.
   a. Five students scored 95 points; seventeen students scored 30 points; and eleven scored 75 points.
   b. Three senior accountants made $50 a day; two semi-seniors made $40 a day; and five junior accountants made $35 a day.
   Note: For clarity, tabulate more than two series of numbers.

Name of Accountant	Daily Rate	Estimated Working Days	Total Estimated Earnings
Barlow, Helen	$50	3	$150
Dickinson, Al	35	2	70
Oman, Charles	40	1	40

5. *When an isolated number is below 10, express it in words.* This rule does not apply to exact dimensions or amounts of money.
   a. The new salesman sold eight refrigerators last month.
   b. She hit a 6-foot pole.
   c. This paper is 8½ inches wide.

6. *When numbers are expressed in words, as at the beginning of a sentence, use a hyphen to join the compound number, twenty-one through ninety-nine:* A compound number usually acts as a compound adjective.
   Fifty-six accounts; twenty-one women; ninety-three men.

[2]Most of these rules have been adopted by the Committee on Teaching Materials and Aids of the American Business Writing Association (now renamed the American Business Communication Association).

7. *When one number immediately precedes another number of different context, express one number in words; the other, in figures:*
   a. The specifications call for twenty-five 2 x 4's.
   b. The deposit slip listed four 5's as the only currency.
   c. You ordered 275 three-inch bolts.

8. *When a numerical quantity contains more than four digits, each group of three digits should be set off by a comma (starting at the right).* (Obviously, this rule does *not* apply to dates, street numbers, serial numbers, and page numbers.) 1,000; 1,021; 5,280,000; 60,000; 600,000

9. *Express amounts of money in figures.* The following practices are recommended.

   a. *When an amount of money consists of dollars and cents, always express the amount in figures:* The dollar sign should precede the amount (unless in a tabulated column). The invoice total was $5.51. The bonds were sold at $999.50.
   b. *When an amount of money consists only of dollars, omit the decimal point and the double zero:* The invoice is $150. The check is for $5. Exceptions: (1) When the amount is tabulated in a column which includes both dollars and cents, include the double zero.

$$
\begin{array}{r}
\$\ \ 250.80 \\
200.00 \\
312.70 \\
286.50 \\
\hline
\$1,505.00
\end{array}
$$

   (2) When a series of money amounts contains mixed figures, include the double zero for consistency on all even figures.
   The committee raised amounts of $15.00, $33.75, and $75.00 in the three rummage sales.
   c. *When an amount of money consists only of cents, write the amount in any of the following ways:*
   The piggy bank yielded $.57. The piggy bank yielded 57¢.
   The piggy bank yielded 57 cents. The piggy bank yielded 9 cents.
   d. *As a rule, do not write an amount in both figures and words. This procedure is necessary only in legal and financial documents.*
   The check is for $7   The total assets are $23,000.50.
   In financial papers write: Ninety-five dollars ($95.00)
                                  seven dollars ($7.00)
                                  twenty-three and 42/100 dollars ($23.42)
                                  twenty three dollars and forty-two cents ($23.42)

10. *Express the following numbers in figures, unless otherwise indicated:*

    a. Dates: October 3, 1972
                   3rd of October
                   Your letter of October 3 was most welcome.
    b. *House or room numbers:* (except number one)
    1503 Thomas Street
    One Lenox Drive
    c. *Numerical names of streets:*
         Over 10:   315 69th Street or 315 - 69th Street (Note two spaces or space hyphen space to separate house and street number.)

Under 10: 2930 Third Avenue or 2930 3rd* Avenue
*Many people prefer to use figures for all street numbers.
d. *Numbered items such as page numbers, chapter numbers, figure numbers, table numbers, chart numbers, serial numbers, and telephone numbers:*

page 10	Table X	Policy #V9109815
Chapter 10	Table 10	Policy V9109815
Chapter X	Chart 10	Claim No. 13189756
Figure 8	Chart X	Telephone 543-1111
Fig. 8	Service Serial No. 01845283	Telephone 333-1111

e. *Decimals:*

10.25	3.1414	.3535

f. *Dimensions:*

8½ x 11 inches	2 x 4 inches
8½ by 11 inches	2 by 4 inches

g. *Time:*

7 A.M. (reserved for headings)	7:35 P.M. (reserved for headings)
7 a.m. (more commonly used)	7:35 p.m. (more commonly used)
seven o'clock	seven in the morning

h. *Percentages:*

35%	6%
99.99%	6 percent
0.09%	

i. *Fractions:*

1/32	one-half	4¾
3/64	two-thirds	or
25/64	one-fourth	4.75
25/100	three-fourths	

Listed below are sentences that contain numbers in the form of figures and words. If any number is used incorrectly, cross out what's wrong and add the correct usage directly above the error. Don't mark any number that is used correctly.

1. 5 policies lie on my desk.
2. Two men and 8 women work in this office.
3. The insured's car hit a 10-foot pole.
4. 10 men scored 94 points; 17 men scored 110 points; and 3 men scored 143 points.
5. May I have 100 12-inch rulers.
6. This morning I answered 17 letters.
7. You'll find the answer on page 10.
8. Mary came home at 7 o'clock.
9. She works from 8 a.m. until 5 p.m.
10. Thanks for the $50.00 loan.
11. The car hit a ten-foot pole, rolled over, and then fell down a 20-foot embankment.
12. The gate is six feet, three inches tall.
13. Your lot is 45 feet wide and one hundred thirty-two feet deep.
14. Please send the policy to 1 South Fifteenth Street.
15. Thank you for your check for twenty dollars.
16. Please buy 17 3-cent stamps.
17. The 3 items are on sale for $15, $16.95, and $20.

Punctuation Makes Sense

Punctuation is important because it helps the reader understand what you are saying. That's the whole purpose of commas, periods, dashes, and all those other little marks— to make reading easier and clearer.

Comma

The study of the comma is especially worthwhile because this symbol gives more people trouble than any other kind of punctuation.

You use the comma:

1. When you address the reader directly.
   a. Please let me know, Mr. Jones, when you will be in Tucson.
   b. I'll certainly appreciate your taking care of this assignment, John.
   c. Mr. Smith, that was a fine speech you gave to our group last week.

2. When you mention a person's title after his name or his name after his title.
   a. This man is Mr. A. B. Jackson, President of Acme Company.
   b. Mr. Julius Roller, Jr., has done a splendid job.
   c. Our representative, Mr. Hall, will see you next week.

   Note: You omit commas in an expression like "my brother George" when a one-word name (George) follows the title (brother) and you have more than one brother. If you have only one brother: "my brother, George, . . ."

3. When the year follows the month and the day.
   On October 4, 1970, I started working for this company.
   but
   I was born in July 1951.

4. When the sentence contains a series or list of more than two things or persons:
   a. He raises turkeys, chickens, and geese.
   b. Mr. Smith, Mr. Snow, and Mrs. Hull appeared in court.
   but in the names of business firms, the last comma is usually omitted.
   In any event, follow the usage of the particular firm.
   Merrill Lynch, Pierce, Fenner & Smith Incorporated.

5. When you can add *and* between two words that describe something.
   You are an efficient, hard-working fellow. (You are an efficient *and* hard-working fellow.)
   but
   A right mental attitude makes for happiness. (It doesn't make sense to say "A right *and* mental attitude makes for happiness.")

6. When a sentence has two clauses separated by *but*. (A clause is a group of words that include a subject and verb; on the other hand, a phrase is a group of words that do not include a subject and verb.)
   I like this car, but it is too expensive for me.

7. When a sentence has two clauses separated by *and* and one clause or both clauses are long:

   a. You need a thorough knowledge of forestry, and you can get that knowledge from on-the-job training.
   b. His name is John, and he told me some of the most fascinating tales about the South Pacific.

   but

   I like you and you like me. (No comma is necessary when both clauses are short—say, usually no more than five words each.)

8. When a sentence begins with a long dependent clause (one that cannot stand alone and that starts with such words as although, since, because, as soon as, after, when):

   a. As soon as your letter reached me this morning, I called Mr. Doe.
   b. Although his plan was incomplete, he received general approval.

   but

   c. His plan received general approval when the president received favorable comments from all his department heads. (When the dependent clause comes after the main clause and is closely connected with it, no comma is used.)
   d. After Malcolm won he retired from professional sports. (When the beginning dependent clause is short, no comma is necessary).

9. When a word or clause that follows the name of a person or thing isn't necessary to identify that person or thing:

   a. This man, who went without sleep for two days, fell asleep at the wheel.
   b. Boston, the capital, is the largest city in Massachusetts.

   but

   c. A man who went without sleep for two days fell asleep at the wheel. (Here the who clause is necessary to identify "man.")
   d. Buy the book *Investments* the next time you go to the bookstore.

10. When a loosely connected word or phrase is included in the sentence (this form is called a parenthetical word or expression):

    a. You will agree with me, however, that he is a great risk.
    b. Yes, I agree with you.
    c. You did a fine job, to be sure.

11. When two verbs come together.
    Whatever is, is right.

12. When two figures come together in a sentence.
    In 1971, 432 employees took their vacations in July.

13. When two sentence elements may be misunderstood or look strange if read together:

    a. *Wrong:* Ever since we have enjoyed working with him.
       Right: Ever since, we have enjoyed working with him.
    b. *Wrong:* Inside business went on as usual.
       Right: Inside, business went on as usual.

14. When a sentence contains a quotation:
    a. "Rules," he said, "are made to be broken."
    b. He said, "Rules are made to be broken."

15. When the first word of a sentence ends in "ing" and modifies the subject.
    Looking further into this man's record, we find he was arrested twice.

16. When a sentence omits a word (usually a verb).
    One of the men involved in the accident is a mill operator; the other, a logger.

17. When the state follows the city.
    Denver, Colorado, is called the mile-high city.

Period is used:

1. To end a sentence:
   This firm has several branches throughout the state.
2. To show omission of words from a quoted sentence.
   "Fourscore and seven years ago our fathers brought forth on this continent a new nation, . . . dedicated to the proposition that all men are created equal . . . ." (The fourth period stands for the period that ends the sentence.)
3. To indicate abbreviation: Mr. Dr. Inc. a.m. p.m. N. E. NE. J. E. Doe *but* omit period after many organizations or government agencies: AFL, RCA, TVA, AT&T
4. For decimal sign: 13.5% .04 $374.22
5. In tabulation: 1.
                    2. (only one space after the period.)
                    3.

Semicolon

The semicolon serves a similar purpose as the period that ends a sentence but shows a closer relationship between sentences.

Semicolon is used:

1. Between clauses that can stand alone and the second clause begins with words such as *however, nevertheless, consequently, therefore, morever, hence, likewise, furthermore,* and *namely*:
   He has an excellent background in education and work experience; however, I cannot find much information concerning his extracurricular activities on or off campus.

2. Between closely related clauses that can stand alone and don't have any word between them:
   I prefer a man who has worked his way through school; he prefers an individual who has devoted his entire time to schooling and has a high grade-point average.
   but you may use a comma to separate very short main clauses not joined by words listed in number 1 above.
   I stopped, I aimed, I fired.

3. Before expressions such as *for example, that is, namely, for instance,* and *in fact* when they fall in the middle of the sentence.

> Three of our offices have been redecorated; namely, Everett, Longview, and Bellville.

4. When a comma is in at least one of two clauses, both of which can stand alone and a word such as *but, and,* or *or* lies between the clauses:

> On January 16, 1972, you mailed your report to us; but it didn't arrive until January 27.

5. When a sentence contains a series and at least one part of the series has a comma:

> The speakers included Mr. Robert Jule, Vice President of Sales; Mr. Dennis Greiner, Secretary; and Mr. Jack Blue, Comptroller.

Colon is used:

1. To show any formal statement or list that follows:

a. This is what he said: "Choose a job you'll enjoy living with for the rest of your life."
b. That house has four rooms: front room, dining room, kitchen, and bed-room.

Note: To show emotions or greater emphasis, you should use dashes instead of colons.

2. To separate hours and minutes: 4:50 a.m. 8:35 p.m.

3. After the salutation in a business letter: Dear Mr. Jones:

Dash is used:

1. To emphasize:

> When you don't know how to spell a word—use a dictionary.

2. To set off a series within the sentence:

> These men—Mr. Smith, Mr. Jones, and Mr. Peterson—asked me about this type of account.

Hyphen is used:

1. To break a word at the end of a line: sub-   knowl-
                                             stantial   edge

2. To tie together words thought of as a unit:

a. up-to-date information
b. letter-writing contest
c. secretary-treasurer
d. his take-it-or-leave-it attitude

    e. 40-foot pole

    f. short- and long-run objectives.

but don't hyphenate when the first word is an adverb ending in "ly."

    slowly moving object

3. In numbers 21 through 99 that are spelled out:

    a. fifty-five

    b. ninety-nine

    c. one hundred seventy-six

4. To separate ex, elect, and self from the next word:

    a. ex-president ex-President Johnson

    b. president-elect

    c. self-control

5. To avoid an ambiguous or awkward combination of letters:

    Examples: re-address, pre-election

Exclamation mark is used:

1. To indicate strong emotion:

    a. What a beautiful car!

    b. What a mess!

Question marks are used:

1. For direct question:

    a. What have you found out about this individual?

    but use a period or a question mark after a request:

    a. May we hear from you within the next 10 days.

    b. May we hear from you within 10 days?

2. To show doubt:

    In 1592 (?) Columbus discovered America.

Quotation marks

Here are three good suggestions to remember about punctuation before and after quotation marks:

1. All periods and commas go within the quotes.

2. Semicolons and colons always go outside the quotes.

3. Question marks, exclamation marks, and dashes:

    a. Go outside the quotes when they punctuate the entire sentence.

    b. Go inside the quotes when they punctuate only the quoted matter.

Quotation marks are used:

1. Around a direct quotation.
2. Around substandard words.
3. Around titles of magazine articles and book chapters (but not titles of magazines, books, and pamphlets).
4. Around typewritten words that would be italicized in print.

Apostrophe is used:

1. To show possession:
   woman's, women's, anybody's, Jones's, Moses', father-in-law's, someone else's

2. For omission of a letter or number:
   a. I'll, you'll, we've, don't, can't, hasn't, o'clock, isn't, it's
   b. the blizzard of '89

3. For plural of figures   7's look like 9's
   letters   p's and q's
   words used as words   You have five hope's in this letter.

Sentences to punctuate:

1. The price is high but the quality is low
2. Washington Lincoln and Franklin Roosevelt were well known presidents
3. Youll find up to date information in that book
4. My sister Mary now attends college
5. The person who finds my watch gets a $20 reward
6. The boys are smiling the girls are laughing
7. As we agreed on the telephone this policy will run until May 6 1979
8. What system of bridge do you play
9. The price is high and the quality is poor
10. You did a fine job John in handling this situation
11. When you come to the meeting you should see Mr. John Narver our personnel manager
12. It is wise therefore to trade with reputable merchants
13. A stitch in time saves nine says an old proverb
14. You can be certain Mr. Corbett that you'll have our answer within a week
15. In 1970 72 men from our office enrolled
16. Among those at the conference were Mr. A B Moe Superintendent Mr. Harris Lobe Sales Manager and Ms. Rollow Butts Educational Director
17. Having read the policy twice he was familiar with its contents
18. There was nobody there in fact when I arrived
19. His suggestion was this Think before you write
20. I always thought he was looney
21. This man who found my watch gets a $20 reward.
22. When she talks she lisps her ss and rolls her rs
23. Enclosed is a copy of our letter of February 12 1971 regarding the endorsement dated January 30 1971
24. Seattle Washington is the largest city in the Northwest

25. Please send the following Form A Form B and Form C
26. Be certain to read pages 4 15 17 22 and 30
27. This is your desk that one is mine
28. Nothing has been done according to Joe to change the picture
29. John said that he would do it
30. It takes guts to publish that report
31. As Pete ate John gave him an account of the accident
32. For the next two weeks send my mail to 441 South Estelle Wichita Kansas
33. I saw this man hit that pale blue four door automobile
34. In 1939 when World War II started you were only several months old
35. People who live in glass houses shouldn't throw stones
36. They asked me whether I had taken any courses in finance
37. My sister you will be pleased to hear is now an accountant
38. A man who is honest will succeed
39. Three students Henry Pete and Mary invariably have their assignments well prepared every day.
40. Its true that plenty of practice with proper guidance will improve your writing ability.

Syllabication

Syllabication is the division of words at the ends of lines to avoid a ragged right margin. In general, avoid this division of words because the material isn't as easy and as clear to read. The following rules will help you to syllabicate words correctly.

1. Divide words between syllables only. Examples: prod-uct, knowl-edge.
2. Do not divide at the ends of more than two consecutive lines of typing.
3. Limit the number of syllabicated words to no more than four to a full page of typewritten material.
4. Divide hyphenated words at the hyphen only. Examples: self-control, half-brother.
5. Never divide words of one syllable, nor words pronounced as one syllable. The addition of past tense does not necessarily add an extra syllable. For example, "guessed," "slammed," "learned," "backed," "seemed," and "glanced" cannot be divided because they are all one syllable.
6. Do not divide a four-letter word. If possible, avoid dividing words of five or six letters. Examples: upon, final, avoid.
7. In words having three syllables or more, a one-letter syllable should be typed on the preceding, rather than the succeeding, line. Example: sepa-rate, not sep-arate.
8. Avoid separating a one- or a two-letter syllable at the beginning of a word from the rest of the word. Example: apti-tude, not ap-titude; enough, not e-nough. Exception if necessary: Two-letter prefixes (ad, de, en, ex, im, in, re, un, up, etc.)
9. Never carry just two letters of a word to the next line. Example: newly, not new-ly.
10. When two vowels coming together are pronounced separately, divide between the two vowels. Example: cre-ated, gradu-ation.
11. As a rule, divide between a prefix and the rest of the word. Examples: trans-pose, con-sign.
12. As a rule, divide between suffix and the stem of the word. Examples: lov-able, announce-ment.

APPENDICES

688

a. Note that in such words as "ame-na-ble," "fea-si-ble," and "de-fen-si-ble," the termination is "ble"—and the vowel preceding it is considered a part of the preceding syllable.
b. When a root word ends with a double consonant, separate the suffix from the root word. Examples: guess-ing, tell-ing.
c. When a final consonant is doubled before a suffix, the additional consonant goes with the suffix. Examples: trip-ping, strag-gling, stop-ping.
d. Note that the endings "cian, cion, gion, sion, and tion" are kept as syllables, regardless of word derivation. Example: expres-sion.
13. When a consonant is doubled within a word, divide the word between consonants. Examples: fer-ret, tal-low, shut-ter.
14. Do not divide the last word on a page.
15. Do not divide abbreviations, contractions, figures, or proper names.

Transitional Words

Shown below are transitional words and phrases you can use in your writing as links to tie sentences together:

Addition:

again	equally important	in addition	next
also	finally	last	nor
and	first	lastly	secondly
and then	further	likewise	thirdly, etc.
besides	furthermore	moreover	too

Comparison:

| better yet | in like manner | similarly |
| here again | likewise | still worse |

Contrast:

although this may be true	but	nevertheless	on the contrary
and yet	however	notwithstanding	still
at the same time	in contrast	on the other hand	yet

Instances and Lists

in particular   for example   for instance   to illustrate

Place:

| adjacent to | here | on the opposite side |
| beyond | nearby | opposite to |

Result:

| accordingly | consequently | therefore | thus |
| as a result | hence | thereupon | |

Summary:

as has been stated	for instance	in short	to be sure
as I have said	in brief	in sum	to sum up
for example	in other words	on the whole	

Time:

| afterward | following | in the meantime | soon |
| at length | immediately | meanwhile | |

Trite Words

Below is a list of trite words and expressions that should be avoided in good business letters, memos, and reports.

above captioned (loan)
above numbered
acknowledge receipt of
advise (when you mean "tell" or "inform")
allow me to
and oblige
as a matter of fact
as of this date
as per (your account)
as per our (agreement, request, letter)
assuring you of our prompt attention
as the case may be
at an early date
at hand
at the present writing
at this writing
attached find, attached please find
attached hereto
avail yourself of this opportunity
awaiting your further orders (reply)
be that as it may
beg to (state, advise, inform, acknowledge, differ)
by return mail
come to hand
contents noted
date of July 1
Dear Madam, Dear Mesdames
Dear Sir, Dear Sirs
deem it advisable
dictated but not read
don't hesitate to (call, write)
due course
due to the fact that
duly (credited, entered, noted)
e.g. (avoid this Latin abbreviation)
enclosed herewith
enclosed please find
esteemed
even date
favor (meaning letter)
feel free to (write, call)
for your information
gone forward
has come to hand
henceforth
hitherto

(hoping to hear from you, I am) (remain)
i.e. (avoid this Latin abbreviation)
I have your letter of (date)
in accordance with (your request)
in answer to your letter (reply, response, reference)
in re
in reply wish to state
in the amount of
in this connection
it has come to my attention
kindly (when you mean please)
let me (may I) call your attention to
our Mr. Jones
party (when you mean an individual)
per (your request)
permit me to say
please be advised that
please be assured (informed)
please do not hesitate to
please find enclosed
prior to
pursuant to (your request, inquiry)
receipt is hereby acknowledged
re your letter of
recent date
reference loan number
referring to (your letter)
regret to advise
reply to yours of
replying to your letter of .
respectfully submitted (requested)
said (the said individual)
same (as a pronoun—thank you for the same)
subject loan
take pleasure
take the liberty
take this opportunity
thank you for your attention in this matter
thank you in advance
thanking you, we remain
the undersigned
the writer
this is to advise you
this will acknowledge receipt

under separate cover
undersigned
under the above subject
valued (letter, account
we are in receipt of

we regret to inform you that
we transmit herewith
wise (cost wise, product wise, personality wise)

Appendix C: Symbols Used in Marking
Letters, Memos, and Reports[1]

Ac	Check accuracy.	NNITS	Include nothing new in terminal section.
ACE	Avoid copying examples.		
ACP	Avoid copying problems.	NR	Avoid needless repetition.
AV	Use an active verb.	Om	Insert omitted word(s).
BC	Be consistent.	OS	Avoid obvious statements.
BMS	Be more sincere.	P	Use correct punctuation.
BNF	Give best news first.	Pos	Use positive language.
BP	Follow good business practice.	PC	Use parallel construction.
Cap	Capitalize.	PH	Place this letter higher on the page.
Cl	Make meaning clear.		
CSAD	Give clear statement of action desired (tell what and how, and encourage quick action).	PL	Place this letter lower on the page.
		PRI	Put reader into this.
DA	Date the action if desirable.	Psy	Use good psychology here.
DP	Avoid dangling participles.	PV	Keep the correct point of view.
DS	Double space.	RA	Recheck assignment.
EA	Remember "easy action."	RB	Show reader benefit.
Fig.	Use figure(s).	Refs	List references.
FW	Use fewer words; condense.	Reo	Reorganize.
GRF	Give reasons first.	RPF	Recheck problem facts.
HCA	Hyphenate compound adjectives.	Sal	Use appropriate salutation.
		SL	Avoid stereotyped language.
H&E	Is this honest and ethical?	SO	Spell out.
HHE	How can you help the employer?	Sp	Use correct spelling.
		Spec	Be specific.
ITI	Interpret this idea (give concrete evidence to illustrate the point).	SR	Strengthen resale material.
		SS	Improve sentence structure. (Watch unity, coherence, emphasis).
K	Eliminate the awkward expression.		
		STP	Subordinate this point.
LC	Lower case (don't capitalize).	TAP	Improve tone and/or psychology.
Log	Make this logical.		
M	Improve margins.	TNT	Include typed name too.
MII	Place most important idea first.	UA	Strengthen you attitude.
Na	Insert name or initials.	UAC	Use antecedents correctly.
Neg	Can you eliminate this negative?	UAW	Use appropriate word(s).
		V	Use correct verb.

[1] To help you recognize the symbols easily, note (a) in those that are composed of two or more capitals, each capital letter represents the first letter of an important word in the comment; for instance, BNF—best news first. (UA is an exception.) (b) the symbols with only one letter capitalized represent a part of one important word; for example, Log—logical.

#	Insert space.		down, across).
e	Delete.	/syl	Divide word correctly.
tr	Reverse order of letters or words; w*rods*	plan	See text for proper planning.
⌒	Close up (leave no space).	⁋	Make a new paragraph.
↑↓ ← →	Move copy this direction (up,	X	Serious error making paper un-mailable.

Index